FINANCIAL

ACCOUNTING

FINANCIAL ACCOUNTING

SECOND EDITION

John Arnold
Tony Hope
Alan Southworth
Linda Kirkham

Prentice Hall

New York   London   Toronto   Sydney   Tokyo   Singapore

This edition 1994 by
Prentice Hall International (UK) Limited
Campus 400, Maylands Avenue
Hemel Hempstead
Hertfordshire, HP2 7EZ
A division of
Simon & Schuster International Group

Typeset in 10/12 pt Palatino
by MHL Typesetting Ltd, Coventry

Printed and bound in Great Britain by
Redwood Books, Trowbridge, Wiltshire

Library of Congress Cataloging-in-Publication Data

Financial accounting / John Arnold ... [et al.]. — 2nd ed.
    p. cm.
  Includes index.
  ISBN 0-13-317868-4
    1. Accounting. I. Arnold, John, 1944–   .
  HF5635.F53   1994   93-37866
  657—dc20   CIP

British Library Cataloguing in Publication Data

A catalogue record for this book is available from
the British Library

ISBN: 0-13-317868-4

1 2 3 4 5 98 97 96 95 94

Contents

Preface

In the nine years since the first edition of this book was published, financial accounting has featured frequently, and often unfavourably, in the pages of the financial press. Much of the comment has focused on the use of 'creative accounting' by listed companies, on the inadequacies of current accounting practices, and on the apparent inability of the accountancy profession to 'get its house in order'. Whereas issues such as accounting for changing prices occupied accountants in the mid-1980s, the 1990s have been dominated (in financial accounting terms) by areas such as accounting for brand names and other intangibles, off-balance sheet financing and the general failure of accounting statements to reflect the real performance and position of organizations, particularly those like BCCI, Maxwell Communications and Polly Peck International which crashed with little advance warning. In many people's eyes, financial accounting is in a state of crisis.

In spite of the current turbulence, most of the principles and concepts introduced in the first edition of this book remain valid. Indeed they are helpful in explaining the current problems and in developing solutions. For that reason, we have not changed substantially the core material which underpinned the first edition. However, we have received many helpful comments on the presentation of that material and, in consequence, we have made numerous structural revisions. In addition we have added a substantial amount of new material which both clarifies and expands upon the first edition and which should help the reader to understand better the current state of financial reporting.

In an increasingly complex world, characterized by private sector and public sector organizations of all shapes and sizes, the importance of efficient systems of communication between organizations and those who participate in them is of vital importance. Financial accounting is one means by which an organization provides information to its participants (e.g. shareholders and other providers of funds, employees, customers, suppliers and government). Our aim in this book is to provide a foundation for understanding the principles upon which financial accounting systems are based, by explaining underlying concepts, existing practices, and possible alternatives to existing practices. We believe that the importance of such an understanding is not restricted to accountants; almost all of us come into regular contact with numerous organizations, whether as customers, employees, shareholders or in some other capacity. Our ability to get the most from such contacts will be enhanced by an ability to understand financial accounting systems.

This book should be of interest to those with little previous knowledge of financial accounting. Its contents should be of value to first and second year university students and others who wish to understand the bases upon which organizations prepare their accounts and who wish to appreciate the strengths and limitations of those accounts. It should also be of value to those who are familiar with accounting practice but who lack knowledge of its conceptual underpinnings. The book is divided into four parts.

Part 1 provides a basic framework by looking at the role and context of accounting, particularly financial accounting, at those who use accounting information for decisions and the sorts of decisions they make, and at the ways in which financial accounting is regulated. Much of the material on the regulation of accounting is new.

Part 2 explains the fundamentals of the conventional accounting model, introduces its three basic statements, the balance sheet, income statement and cash flow statement, and discusses how the information reported in these three statements might be interpreted by decision makers.

In Part 3 we address the problems of the conventional accounting model and consider alternative accounting methods which might be used to measure an organization's performance and position. Thus virtually all of the material from the first edition is included in Parts 1–3, although some of it has been pruned to make way for new and, we believe, more relevant material.

Part 4 of this edition contains three completely new chapters and Part 5 a summary and review of the book.

The three new chapters cover more advanced issues which are of topical interest and which are likely to remain so for some years: the development of 'conceptual frameworks' for financial reporting and the problems of harmonizing accounting practices internationally; accounting for groups of companies; and accounting for intangible assets such as goodwill and brand names. We believe that these new chapters add further relevance and interest to the book. They should be of particular interest to readers who hope to undertake a more detailed study of financial accounting in the future.

In addition to the changes detailed above, we have incorporated many suggestions made by reviewers and have included numerous new exercises and further reading references. In all, it is fair to say that this edition represents a major revision of the first edition. However, we have tried not to change the basic nature of the book because most of those who have used the first edition seem to have been happy with it.

For teaching purposes, the book should continue to fit neatly into an undergraduate course of twenty lectures and a teacher should be able to select suitable class problems from amongst the discussion topics and exercises provided at the end of each chapter. A Teacher's Manual is available from the publishers.

We remain indebted to all those who helped with the first edition and whom we acknowledged in our original preface. Others have helped with the second edition. Cathy Peck of Prentice-Hall International was patient but persistent in ensuring that we did eventually deliver the manuscript. We are also indebted to a number of anonymous reviewers who provided Prentice-Hall International with thoughtful and detailed suggestions of ways in which the first edition could be improved and brought up to date. We are grateful to Methuen London for permission to reproduce the extract from *Monty Python's Big Red Book* on page 3; to E.H. Booth and Co. Ltd for permission to use their annual report to illustrate the principles developed in Part 2; and to Professors Don Egginton, Richard Macve and Ken Peasnell for allowing us to plagiarize in Chapter 17 some of the material which appeared in the research monograph, co-authored with John Arnold and Linda Kirkham, *Goodwill and Other Intangibles*. We owe a very special debt to Hilary Garraway who, almost single-handed, word-processed a succession of drafts of the new manuscript cheerfully and encouragingly and frequently outside office hours! Finally, we thank the students at the University of Manchester and the Manchester Business School for refusing to accept our instruction without justification and explanation. Their often perceptive comments have forced us to clarify our own thinking, to question many accepted practices and to suffer some embarrassing moments. Such merit as this book has, owes much to them.

John Arnold
Tony Hope
Alan Southworth
Linda Kirkham

Introduction

The subject matter of this book, financial accounting, is concerned with the ways in which organizations communicate information about their performance to the 'outside world'. The book is aimed at readers who may have little previous experience or knowledge of accounting. For that reason, our primary intention is to provide a conceptual foundation and framework for financial accounting, i.e. we will attempt to provide the reader with a thorough understanding of the ideas which underlie the preparation of financial accounts, and the concepts which might be used to choose between alternative methods of financial accounting. Clearly such an understanding is incomplete without some knowledge of how accounting is practised. This we also attempt to provide. It is, however, a difficult task to write an introductory accounting book which balances well the (often conflicting) theories and practices of accounting. The balance must in the end be determined by what the authors believe to be the purposes of an introductory accounting text.

We believe that a detailed study of the practice of accounting, without a prior understanding of underlying concepts, is likely to be of relatively short-term benefit. The detailed conventions and rules of accounting can and do change quickly — largely as a result of changes in the environment in which organizations operate and as a result of developments in accounting theory and thought. Thus we have chosen to direct attention primarily to the conceptual foundations of financial accounting and to its broad practical basis. We do not intend to offer a detailed and extensive examination of current accounting practice, as embodied in company law and in the recommendations of the professional accountancy bodies and accounting standard setters.

Our emphasis means that, if the sum total of the reader's knowledge of financial accounting is limited to the contents of this book, he or she would almost certainly *not* be able to prepare the financial accounts of ICI, Marks and Spencer, Unilever, Ford, Sainsbury, or even the local newsagent or solicitor, in accordance with the current rules specified by company law and by the professional accountancy bodies and accounting standard setters. On the other hand, the reader should be able to understand the concepts upon which those organizations' financial accounts have been prepared and, perhaps more important, he or she should be equipped to evaluate both current accounting practices and the changes which will inevitably be made to those practices in the future. To summarize, our purpose is to provide the reader with a foundation in financial accounting which will be useful for decades, rather than with practical knowledge which may be out of date within a few years or even months.

The book contains four main parts and we now discuss each one in turn, both to explain its importance and to explore its interdependencies with the other parts.

Part I   Basic Framework

Part 1 provides an overview of the role and purposes of financial accounting. The financial accounts or reports of an organization are one source of information available to those who wish to evaluate its performance and prospects. It is important to recognize that the information in these reports comprises only one of a number of sources of information available about an organization. Thus, in order to assess the impact and usefulness of financial reports it is necessary to evaluate the additional or incremental information they contain, over and above that which is available from other sources. In order to identify the incremental effects of a particular piece of accounting information, the following questions must be asked (and answered). Who are the existing and potential users of the information? For what purposes will they use the information? How will the information influence the beliefs and, in consequence, the decisions and actions of users? How will the actions of users affect other members of the community? How much will it cost to produce the information? The answers to these questions are necessary in order to estimate the benefits and costs of providing the information.

In Chapters 1 and 2 we examine the role of accounting and organizations in society, and discuss the information requirements of different users of accounting reports. Of particular importance are the distinctions between different kinds of organizations (e.g. private and public sector organizations, large and small organizations, organizations which are guided largely by the profit motive and organizations, such as charities, which have other predominant objectives) and between different groups of users of accounting information (e.g. owners, employees, customers, government, suppliers). The existence of different types of organizations and of users with different information requirements means that there is no one system of financial accounting which is best for all organizations and users. Nevertheless there is, as we shall see, substantial common ground — for example, all interested users are concerned in one way or another with the survival of the organization.

In Chapter 3 we attempt to use this common ground to develop a set of criteria which might be used to assess the merits of alternative accounting methods. We also describe the role of company law and accounting standards in the regulation of accounting practice and introduce the statement of principles which is being developed by the accounting standards setting body in the UK. In subsequent chapters, we use the criteria we develop to evaluate alternative accounting treatments of an organization's transactions.

Part 2 The Conventional Accounting Model of the Organization

For many years, the financial accounts prepared by most organizations have consisted primarily of an *income statement* or *profit and loss account*, describing the results of the organization's performance during a past period, and a *position statement* or *balance sheet*, showing its position at the end of the period covered by the income statement. More recently, a third statement, the *cash flow statement*, has been added which describes movements in an organization's cash balances during a period. The approach which accountants have adopted (i.e. the basis for the figures appearing in each statement) emphasizes measurement of the transactions of the organization. The revenues arising from the transactions are matched with the costs incurred in earning the revenues. This matching of revenues and costs determines the organization's *net income* or *net profit*. Expenditures which have not been matched with revenues are shown in the balance sheet as assets. This *transactions-based* approach to the measurement of net income and financial position remains by far the most widely used approach in the Western world. Furthermore, the costs which are matched with revenues generally represent the original or *historical costs* of the resources utilized.

In Part 2 we describe the fundamental concepts underlying the preparation of historical cost transactions-based accounts. We begin in Chapters 4 and 5 by explaining how an organization's accounts reflect a real, physical process of transforming inputs (e.g. raw materials and labour time) into outputs (e.g. products for sale) and we explain the basic principles by which the results of the physical transformation process are expressed in financial terms in the form of a balance sheet and income statement, and introduce the accountant's recording technique — that of double-entry bookkeeping.

Expenditures which involve the acquisition of resources to be used by, and to provide benefits to, an organization over a number of periods are termed *assets*. Broadly speaking, assets are *fixed* if they represent part of the productive capacity of the organization and are expected to be owned by the organization for some years, or *current* if they are held for resale or for conversion to a form suitable for resale. Chapter 6 discusses the accounting treatment of fixed assets and the methods of charging to the income statement the periodic cost associated with their use. Such charges are known as *depreciation*. In Chapter 7 we discuss the accounting treatment of stock, the major current asset of most organizations, and explain the variety of methods available for charging the cost of stock used to the income statement. In Chapter 8 we turn to the organization's long-term obligations, both to its owners and to others who have provided long-term finance or capital. We describe the characteristics and accounting treatments of the sources of long-term capital available to the three main types of private sector, profit-orientated organizations — individuals, partnerships and limited liability companies. Although we concentrate primarily on such private sector, profit-orientated organizations to explain the basic framework of accounting in Part 2, most (but not all) of the principles discussed are applicable also to both public sector and not-for-profit organizations. The usefulness of such principles can, of course, be evaluated only in the context of the type of organization to which they are applied.

Chapter 9 provides a detailed example of double-entry bookkeeping and illustrates the historical cost transactions-based approach described in Part 2. After reading the first nine chapters the reader should have a sound understanding of the principles underlying the accounting model of the organization.

In the final two chapters of Part 2 we consider how the users of financial reports might interpret the information therein to evaluate the position and performance of an organization. In Chapter 10 we analyse a variety of ratios designed to measure liquidity, profitability and financial risk. Our primary emphasis is on the use of ratios calculated from historical cost accounts, but we also discuss the extent to which the use of ratios based on current values might be helpful.

A recurrent theme in the book is the relationship between an organization's net income and its net cash flow. The two amounts seldom correspond. In Chapter 11 we explain and evaluate the role of cash flow statements. It would be difficult to over-emphasize the importance of the role of cash in any detailed assessment of an organization's performance and prospects. Such an assessment requires an evaluation of the organization's ability to generate sufficient liquid funds (i.e. cash and near-cash assets) to meet its periodic obligations to pay employees, suppliers, lenders and so on.

Throughout Part 2, we illustrate the principles developed by applying them to a real company, E.H. Booth & Co. Ltd, a medium-sized food retailer. The Annual Report and Accounts of Booths for 1992 are provided in Appendix 1 at the end of the book.

Part 3   Limitations of the Conventional Model

In Chapter 12 we introduce several of the major problems associated with (conventional) historical cost accounting. One of the major weaknesses is its inadequacy as a means of measuring income and valuing assets when prices are increasing (or decreasing) at significant rates. It is important to recognize that even price changes of, say, 4% or 5% per annum may be 'significant' for this purpose. For example, an organization which purchased a piece of land for £500,000 fifteen years ago will, under historical cost accounting, continue to show it in its current balance sheet at its original cost of £500,000. And yet if land prices have risen by only 5% per annum since purchase, the current value of the land will be over £1 million. A further problem is that while some assets and liabilities are included in conventional balance sheets at outdated values, others are not included at all! A third weakness is that conventional accounting practice allows too many choices of accounting treatment. The range of income statement and balance sheet figures which may, in accordance with accepted conventions, be generated from a set of transactions is remarkably large. We discuss how and why the managers of organizations might use this flexibility to further their own self-interest.

In Chapter 13 we consider various accounting approaches which use measures other than unadjusted historical costs and which attempt to address the problems created by changing prices. The two main alternatives which we describe are *current purchasing power accounting* and *replacement cost accounting*. Both alternatives attempt to deal, in very different ways, with the problems within the transactions-based framework created by the use of historical costs when prices are changing. Under current purchasing power accounting, the historical cost numbers are adjusted by a general price index (such as the Retail Price Index), whereas under replacement cost accounting, the historical costs of resources are increased to their current replacement costs, often by the use of price indices which are specific to the resources concerned. The differences between the figures produced by the two methods tend to be small when relative price changes are low (i.e. when all prices tend to change at very similar rates) but may be very large when substantial relative price changes occur.

In Chapter 14 we return to the criteria developed in Part 1 and apply them to an evaluation of the various accounting methods described in Part 2 and in Chapter 13.

Part 4 Advanced Issues

In Part 4 we address some rather more advanced issues in financial reporting which are currently topical. Some of them will provide a useful foundation for those readers intending to go on to further study of accounting.

The development of statements of principles, or 'conceptual frameworks', has occupied and continues to occupy the attention of standard setters and academics around the world. In Chapter 15, we develop the material first introduced in Chapter 3 and devote particular attention to the development of a conceptual framework by the UK's accounting standards setting body, the Accounting Standards Board. We also identify some of the major reasons for variations in accounting practices between countries and consider the success of attempts to harmonize accounting practices internationally.

Chapter 16 introduces the many accounting problems created by the need to account for groups of companies which are linked together by common ownership or control. This is a particularly important topic for at least two reasons. First, there is an increasing number of often very large groups, many of which transcend national boundaries (the so-called multinational companies); these are of great significance to national economies. Second, group accounting provides one of the most fertile areas for the sort of creative accounting practices we introduced in Chapter 12. Unless the reader understands the fundamental principles of group accounting, he or she will not be able to interpret the accounts published by groups nor to appreciate the nature of many of the current controversies in financial reporting.

In Chapter 17, we consider one particular set of problems which are often associated with group accounting — the treatment of intangible assets such as goodwill and brand names. We devote an entire chapter to this topic, partly because it is of topical interest but primarily because the issues raised illustrate the myriad of conceptual and political problems faced by those responsible for recommending accounting practices and getting their recommendations accepted by those responsible for the preparation of accounting statements. In that context, the chapter serves as a useful means of revising many of the issues discussed earlier in the book and of pulling together some of the threads which run through it.

Part 5   Summary and Review

The final chapter — Chapter 18 — is a brief summary of the main themes of the book and of the conclusions we have reached.

We may thus summarize the main objectives we hope to achieve in the book.

1.   To provide a framework for the evaluation of alternative methods of financial accounting, based on the assumption that the primary purpose of financial accounting is to provide information which is useful for decision making.

2.   To explain the fundamental concepts and principles underlying historical cost accounting, so that the reader of financial reports may understand more clearly the basis upon which such reports are prepared, and appreciate both their strengths and their limitations.

3.   To describe and evaluate alternative approaches to the measurement of an organization's performance and position.

4.   Perhaps most important, to instil in readers a critical and analytical attitude to financial accounting, which will enable them to understand and evaluate the changes to financial accounting practices that will inevitably be made in the future, and perhaps even to make some contribution to those changes!

Basic Framework

CHAPTER 1

The Role and Context of Accounting

1.1   An introduction to accounting and accountants

This may be the first book on accounting that you have ever read. As authors, therefore, we have a great opportunity to influence your perceptions of accounting for many years to come. We have also a great responsibility to stimulate and maintain your interest in the subject. You may already have some preconceptions about accounting and accountants. These may be similar to those expressed by the chairman of the accounting department at the University of California[1] who commented, 'Suddenly students see accounting as a glamorous, sexy profession, thanks to the expanding role accountants play in business and government, and to the increasingly attractive salaries.' Or they may be closer to those expressed in the following extract from *Monty Python's Big Red Book*.[2]

> **Why Accountancy Is Not Boring by Mr A. Putey**
> First let me say how very pleased I was to be asked on the 14th inst. to write an article on why accountancy is not boring. I feel very strongly that there are many people who may think that accountancy *is* boring, but they would be wrong, for it is not at all boring, as I hope to show you in this article, which is, as I intimated earlier, a pleasure to write.
>   I think I can do little worse than begin this article by describing why accountancy is *not* boring as far as *I* am concerned, and then, perhaps, go on to a more general discussion of why accountancy as a whole is not boring. As soon as I awake in the morning it is not boring. I get up at 7:16, and my wife Irene, an ex-schoolteacher, gets

1.   See Lohr, S., 'Goodbye to the ink-stained wretch', *The Atlantic*, August 1980.
2.   *Monty Python's Big Red Book*, Methuen, 1971 (p.16).

up shortly afterwards at 7:22. Breakfast is far from boring, and soon I am ready to leave the house. Irene, a keen Rotarian, hands me my briefcase and rolled umbrella at 7:53, and I leave the house seconds later. It is a short walk to Sutton station, but by no means a boring one. There is so much to see, including Mr Edgeworth, who also works at Robinson Partners. Mr Edgeworth is an extremely interesting man, and was in Uxbridge during the war. Then there is a train journey of 22 minutes to London Bridge, one of British Rail's main London termini, where we accountants mingle for a moment with stockbrokers and other accountants from all walks of life. I think that many of the people to whom accountancy appears boring think that all accountants are the same. Nothing could be further from the truth. Some accountants are chartered, but very many others are certified. I am a certified accountant, as indeed is Mr Edgeworth, whom I told you about earlier. However, in the next office to mine is a Mr Manners, who is a chartered accountant, and, incidentally, a keen Rotarian. However, Mr Edgeworth and I get on extremely well with Mr Manners, despite the slight prestige superiority of his position. Mr Edgeworth, in fact, gets on with Mr Manners extremely well, and if there are two spaces at lunch it is more than likely he will sit with Mr Manners. So far, as you can see, accountancy is not boring. During the morning there are a hundred and one things to do. A secretary may pop in with details of an urgent audit. This happened in 1967 and again last year. On the other hand, the phone may ring, or there may be details of a new superannuation scheme to mull over. The time flies by in this not at all boring way, and it is soon 10:00, when there is only 1 hour to go before Mrs Jackson brings round the tea urn. Mrs Jackson is just one of the many people involved in accountancy who give the lie to those who say it is a boring profession. Even a solicitor or a surveyor would find Mrs Jackson a most interesting person. At 11:05, having drunk an interesting cup of tea, I put my cup on the tray and then . . . (18 pages deleted here--Ed.) . . . and once the light is turned out by Irene, a very keen Rotarian, I am left to think about how extremely un-boring my day has been being an accountant. Finally may I say how extremely grateful I am to your book for so generously allowing me so much space (Sorry, Putey!-Ed.)

Accountants and prospective accountants probably view themselves as 'glamorous and sexy' although they may view other accountants as 'Mr Putey' stereotypes. Your view will depend to some extent upon your understanding of what an accountant does. You may have heard that an accountant records financial events, and certainly his or her role includes that task. You may even be aware of certain financial statements which are the product of the accounting process, for example, the profit and loss account, or income statement, and the balance

Table 1.1   *Seaview Ltd — financial statements*

Income Statement for the year ended 31 December 19X0

		£
Sales		300,000
less: Expenses		
Cost of goods sold	120,000	
Depreciation	30,000	
Wages and salaries	70,000	
Administrative expenses	20,000	
		240,000
Income before tax		60,000
Taxation		25,000
Net income		£35,000

Balance Sheet at 31 December 19X0

Assets employed:	£
Property, plant and equipment	
(net of depreciation)	80,000
Stock	20,000
Debtors (amounts receivable)	50,000
Cash	15,000
Total assets	165,000
less: Creditors (amounts payable)	(40,000)
	£125,000
Financed by:	
Shareholders' funds	100,000
Long-term bank loan	25,000
	£125,000

sheet. An illustration of these two statements is provided in Table 1.1. The income statement reports the results of an organization's activities (its revenues less expenses) *over a period* of time, and the balance sheet reports the financial position of an organization *at a point* in time, i.e. what the organization owns (assets) and how those assets have been financed. We should point out here that the title of the organization, Seaview Ltd, refers to a limited company (hence Ltd). We discuss this type of organization in Section 1.5. At first glance these two financial statements may appear simply to be aggregations of various transactions recorded during the year, and even the smallest business has access to cheap computers and software which are capable of processing large amounts of financial data quickly and accurately. So if this is accounting, you may wonder why it merits being studied as an academic subject and why it is now taught in most British universities. You may also wonder why people appear to be willing to pay large sums of money for the services of an accountant. There has to be something else.

Fortunately there is.

Accounting should not be confused with bookkeeping. Whereas bookkeeping is the mechanical task of maintaining accounting records according to some pre-established rules and procedures, accounting is a much more complex process. It is concerned, among other things, with story-telling, bargaining and accountability. Above all accounting is concerned with *decision making*.

Every individual or group in society makes decisions about the future. For example, students make decisions about which courses to study, what clothes to buy and wear, how much to spend on books and how much on food, whether to apply for a bank loan, and so on; the management of the Ford Motor Company must make decisions about which models to produce, what prices to charge, which safety features to include, what wages to pay, which advertising media to choose, and which employees to promote; and the managers of a hospital must decide, among other things, how much to spend on drugs and how much on new equipment, which units to expand or contract, and how many nurses to employ. Some of these decisions are economic, some are social and some are a mixture of both, but in each case the decision maker requires information in order to make a rational decision. For example, in planning a new advertising campaign, the managers of Ford will need to know, *inter alia*, the level of success achieved by previous advertising campaigns, the cost of the proposed campaign and the changes, if any, in consumer tastes.

Accounting can contribute to these decisions. In general, accounting is concerned with economic decisions and the financial information required to make such decisions. Specifically, accounting is concerned with identifying which information will help the various decision makers, how it should be measured and how it should be communicated to them. This involves accountants in designing and implementing systems within which financial information can be processed, and in establishing the rules and procedures to be used in processing the information. One important reason, then, for studying accounting is to acquire the knowledge and skill to search through available economic and financial information for clues that will serve as guides to future action. In the remainder of this chapter we try to explain the role of accounting systems in present day organizations. We discover that there is no unique role, and that the use made of accounting information depends not only on the type of organization whose transactions are being reported, but also on the people involved in the organization, and the society within which the organization operates.

1.2   Accounting and organizations

Whilst accounting can contribute to the everyday decisions of individuals, for example a student, most accounting activity focuses upon organizations. These can vary from a simple campus snack bar with one owner to a multinational company (e.g. BP plc) or to a large public sector organization (e.g. the UK's

National Health Service — NHS). To progress further in our discussion of the role of accounting, we must identify the objectives (goals) of such reporting organizations, whatever their nature. Identifying the objectives of an organization is not an easy task. To begin with, organizations as such cannot have goals. Only the individuals who comprise the organization can have goals.[3] So where do we go from here?

At this stage you may feel like abandoning accounting as all we have given you are unanswered questions. Still, at least you should no longer believe that accounting is simply a matter of recording and aggregating and that the accountant is simply a bookkeeper. Instead, you may be thinking in terms of 'decision makers', 'information' and 'objectives'. What we must do now is construct a framework using these ideas, in order to facilitate our further study of the subject. In an attempt to identify the objectives of an organization, we shall begin by examining the relationship that exists between the people within an organization and the organization itself.

We stated above that organizations, as such, cannot have goals, and yet one aim of accounting is to report on how an organization is achieving its objectives. We must, therefore, identify which people are involved in a particular organization and ascertain whether their individual or group goals can be transformed into the objectives of the organization. This material is fundamental to an understanding of the remainder of the book and thus warrants particularly careful reading.

The correlation between the goals of the people involved, or participants, in an organization and those of the organization itself will differ from organization to organization. In some organizations there will be a wide area of agreement on, and commitment to, organizational goals. Professional bodies and charities fall into this group. One objective of the Institute of Chartered Accountants in England and Wales (of which all four authors are members) is 'to do all such things as may advance the profession of accountancy in relation to public practice, industry, commerce and the public service'.[4] This objective should correlate closely with the objectives of its 100,000 members. In other organizations the objectives of the participant groups may be in direct conflict. Consider, for example, two of the main objectives of the staff of a prison (and presumably those of society) which are to ensure that no prisoner escapes, and to restrict the availability of certain civil liberties. Presumably neither objective is shared by the prisoners. In such a case the goals of the organization are often taken to be the goals of the dominant group, i.e. the group which has the power, through force or influence, to impose its own goals.

Most business organizations lie between the two extremes of a professional body and a prison. Different groups of participants may have conflicting goals, but no

---

3. See, for example, Cohen, K.J. and Cyert, R.M., *Theory of the Firm: Resource Allocation in a Market Economy*, Prentice-Hall, 1965, p. 331.
4. *Supplemental Royal Charter of 1948*, Institute of Chartered Accountants in England and Wales, 1973.

one group has sufficient power to impose its goals upon the others although some groups may have more power than others. This raises the question of organizational survival. The survival of a charity or professional body is ensured as long as there is a sufficient number of people willing to work towards a common objective. A prison will continue to operate as long as the dominant group retains sufficient power to pursue its own goals to the exclusion of others. But how does a business organization survive if various groups have different, and maybe conflicting, objectives and no one group has the power to impose its own goals on the others?

To answer this difficult question we must develop the concept of an organization as a collection of individuals and groups. For a business organization or entity these individuals may be classified into several groups, the most obvious ones being employees, managers, owners (shareholders), creditors, customers, suppliers and government (Figure 1.1).[5] These groups come together to set up and perpetuate the particular organization. Each group contributes something to the organization and their participation is required to ensure the continuation of the organization — for instance Ford would not survive long without investment to finance its activities, a workforce to produce its vehicles or customers to buy them. However, if there are alternative opportunities for the participants — alternative investments for the shareholder, alternative suppliers for the customer, alternative employments for the worker — then the participants could choose to leave the organization. To survive, the organization must somehow ensure the continuing participation of all these groups.

In order to persuade participants to contribute to, and remain with, the organization, the organization must, in turn, offer some inducements — and these inducements must be linked to the objectives of the participants. Thus employees may seek employment for the purposes of earning a living and self-fulfilment. They may therefore be induced to join a particular organization because of monetary rewards in the form of high wages, and non-monetary rewards such as the status attached to their position, the friendship of colleagues and the proximity of the company to their home. Their contributions will include not only their work output, but also their ability to motivate those working with them. A customer's objective might be to obtain value for money and the inducements here might include competitive prices, a high quality product, and a convenient location.

Clearly, the inducements offered to participants will depend upon the objectives of those participants. However, not only do participants have different objectives, they may be in direct conflict with one another. For example, the desire by shareholders for a higher income from the organization (termed *dividends*) may conflict with an employee's objective of higher wages and a customer's goal of lower prices. The survival of an organization thus appears to depend upon its ability to manage a set of disparate and often conflicting objectives in such a way

---

5. Figure 1.1 is adapted from diagrams included in Chapter 2 of Laughlin, R. and Gray, R., *Financial Accounting Method and Meaning*, VNR International, 1988.

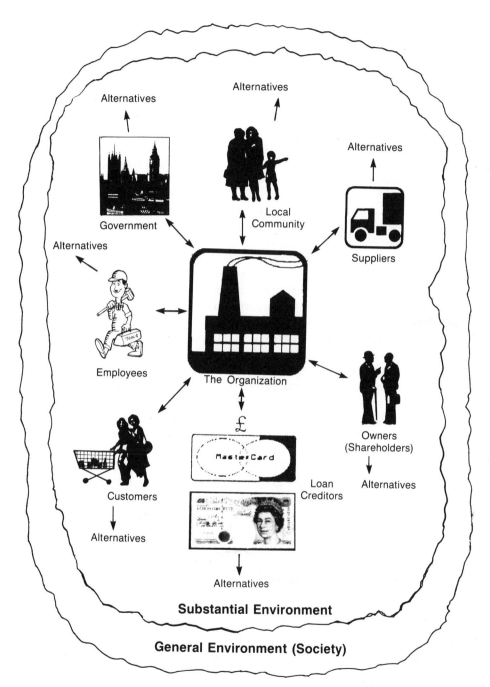

Figure 1.1 *Structure of an organization's environment*

as to ensure all participant groups are induced to stay with the organization. This is generally seen to be the role of one participating group — the managers. Like other employees, managers have goals and must be induced to participate in the organization in return for contributing to it. One of the functions (contributions) of managers is to coordinate the activities of other participants to ensure the survival of the organization. In particular, managers have the power to increase or decrease the inducements of different participating groups. Because the role of managers is necessary for the survival of an organization, the other participants may be willing to accept the manager's powers as long as they feel that organizational survival suits their own purposes. Ideally, managers would use their power to ensure that the inducements offered to each participant were greater than, and reflected, his or her contribution to the organization. Management's role, therefore, is that of attempting to satisfy the objectives of all participants, including themselves. The situation in practice, however, is more complex because participants' objectives are not static and because some more powerful participants may be able to exert a greater influence on management than can others.

The environment in which the organization exists is dynamic. For example, changes in the alternative opportunities available to participants will affect the inducements they require from the organization. Hence managers must ensure that an organization adapts to changes in its environment and pursues courses of action that will enable it to continue satisfying participants' needs. It is not surprising, therefore, that the lives of business organizations are characterized by periods of conflict between participants, during which attempts are made to renegotiate the distribution of inducements. Numerous examples are provided by the economic recession in the UK during the early 1990s.

During these years, new wage, productivity and staffing level agreements were negotiated with employees (e.g. British Airways and IBM), new rates of interest and terms of repayment were agreed with banks and other lenders, dividend levels were maintained for many shareholders despite falling profits (e.g. ICI), and some customers were able to negotiate lower prices and extended periods of credit. These changes might be viewed as a means of helping organizations to survive in the increasingly competitive environment created by the recession. For a variety of reasons many organizations failed to reach the compromises necessary to survive in the changed environment and, in consequence, ceased to exist. This period provides a rather dramatic illustration of the problems experienced by organizations in a dynamic environment.

We stated earlier that one of the functions of management was to coordinate the activities of participants to ensure the continuing survival of an organization. But the objective of most organizations is not simply to survive; it is to 'succeed'. The management function therefore extends to coordinating the contributions of the participants in the most efficient and effective way. Each participant could then share in the benefits of such efficiencies by being offered higher inducements (financial and non-financial) in the future. However, participating groups possess varying degrees of influence over management, and it is possible that, having extracted higher contributions from participant groups, managers might award themselves higher remuneration at the expense of shareholders' dividends, or pay higher dividends to shareholders at the expense of employees' wages.

To judge whether they are receiving satisfactory rewards for their contribution, relative to other participants, each participant group requires information specifying what was available for distribution and how it was distributed. For instance, before submitting a wage claim, employees might want information detailing the size of the organization's profits, the amount of the dividends paid to shareholders and the remuneration received by directors. An organization is comprised of, and accountable to, a disparate collection of participants. The provision of accounting information is one way that managers might discharge the organization's responsibility to its various groups of participants.

This is the organizational context within which accounting exists. From our view of an organization, accounting must have at least two functions. First, accounting represents one source of information which might be used by managers to help them coordinate the organization's activities in order both to ensure the survival of the organization and to make it as 'successful' as possible. It provides information for both planning and control purposes. *Planning* is the process of formulating a course of action. It involves the setting of goals, the identification of alternative ways of achieving these goals, and the choice of one of those alternatives. The role of accounting here is to provide clear statements of the *financial* consequences of each of the alternatives. Managers can then use this information, along with other non-financial information, to decide which course of action to pursue. *Control* is the process of monitoring the outcome of the chosen alternative — of checking whether the plans are in fact being carried out. The role of accounting is to provide financial information on the actual costs and revenues in a form which facilitates comparison with the planned costs and revenues. This branch of accounting is known as *management accounting*.

Secondly, accounting provides information for planning and control purposes to groups other than management. As noted above, these groups need to be reassured that management is not misusing or abusing its position of power in the organization. Accounting can provide information which enables participants to evaluate management's success in achieving organizational objectives, and to check the level of their own inducements relative to those offered to other groups. This is often referred to as the *stewardship* role of accounting. Groups other than management also need information to help them plan their future relationship with the organization (e.g. a shareholder may increase or decrease his participation in the organization). Therefore, in addition to providing information on the organization's past achievements, accounting should also provide some indication of any likely changes in organizational performance and the impact of those changes on the position of each group (other than management) relative to other groups, i.e. accounting has a role to play in *predicting* the future performance of organizations. This branch of accounting is known as *financial accounting* and is the subject matter of this book.[6] It should be clear that both branches of

6. Management accounting is explored in detail in Arnold, J. and Hope, T., *Accounting for Management Decisions*, 2nd edn, Prentice-Hall International, 1990.

accounting are concerned with providing accounting information to decision makers.

1.3   Financial accounting and the readers of financial statements

We now know that financial accounting is more than simply bookkeeping. It is concerned with providing information to decision makers (other than management) for stewardship and prediction purposes. Consider a shareholder who wishes to make an economic decision concerning an investment in Seaview Ltd, whose financial statements were presented in Table 1.1. The financial statements might comprise the only information the individual shareholder possesses about Seaview Ltd, as most readers of financial statements do not have access to the detailed information concerning an organization's transactions. Financial statements, therefore, provide *summarized information* about an organization's transactions for *external decision makers*. They are prepared by organizations of various sizes and types (e.g. profit and non-profit making) operating in both the private and the public sector. They are prepared by small organizations such as corner shops and local schools, and by large organizations such as Imperial Chemical Industries plc and British Rail; by private sector charities such as Oxfam, and public sector non-profit making organizations such as the National Health Service and the University of Manchester. The intention of each is to provide information to their readers; but who are 'their readers'? Do they differ from the participants?

Readers of financial statements differ from organization to organization. The readers of the financial statements, sometimes loosely termed the 'accounts', of ICI and the NHS may have similar characteristics, but they are not identical. Readers usually consist of individuals and institutions who are interested in the activities of the organization and who need information for some purpose of their own, for example in order to make a decision. The accounts of a campus snack bar, for example, should be of interest to the owner, to the manager of the local bank, if the bank has lent money to the business, and to the Inland Revenue (the tax authority). The readers of ICI's accounts might include the current and potential shareholders (owners), the managers, various financial institutions and individuals who have loaned money to the company, the Inland Revenue, the workforce, competitors, customers, suppliers, government and environmental groups concerned with monitoring corporate activities in the chemical industry. Oxfam's accounts will presumably be read by the administrators of the organization, together perhaps with those who have loaned or donated money to (or received money from) the organization, its employees and the Charity Commissioners. Thus the terms 'readers' and 'participants' may often be used synonymously although, of course, certain participants may not read the financial statements (e.g. a customer of the supermarket chain, Tesco plc), and certain interested readers (e.g. potential shareholders and creditors) may not (yet) be participants.

Some of the readers we have identified (e.g. a bank) are common to all three organizations, and some (e.g. the Charity Commissioners) are exclusive to only one type. But does it matter that different readers (often referred to as *user groups*) exist for different organizations? If all user groups require similar information then a standard set of accounts should suffice for all types of organization. For example, irrespective of the size difference between a corner shop and Tesco's, one might suppose that the readers of the accounts would be interested in the profits earned by those two organizations.[7] Whilst this may be a reasonable assumption, it is unlikely that the readers of Oxfam's accounts are interested primarily in its profitability. A charity does not view the generation of profit as its primary objective and a user of the accounts, such as a donor of funds, might instead require information on how effectively Oxfam has pursued its own particular objectives. In fact, as we have suggested earlier, it is unlikely that organizations such as ICI are concerned solely with making profit, and many readers of their accounts will also require information on how effectively ICI has been achieving its other objectives, for example the reduction of pollution levels and the raising of product quality. We shall examine the information needs of specific user groups in Chapter 2, but first we shall examine the impact of different types of society in influencing the role of financial accounting.

1.4   Financial accounting and society

So far we have described the general organizational context within which accounting functions and we have distinguished between management accounting and financial accounting. We now turn to a more detailed consideration of the role of financial accounting. In general, the role of financial accounting is to provide information to groups other than management so that they might assess how far their goals have been achieved, and to what extent and in what respects they might influence the behaviour of the organization in the future. In other words, financial accounting aims to provide important information to participants so that they might decide what action to take in respect of their involvement in the organization including, in the extreme, whether or not to continue or terminate their involvement. However, the specific role of financial accounting is determined largely by the society in which it operates. Different societies produce different types of organization and different participating groups with different objectives and different views about the value of contributions and inducements.

The types of organization referred to in the previous section are typical of those

---

7.   At this stage, we do not expect you to understand exactly what accountants mean by the word profit. Its calculation is a complex matter and we look at it in detail in later chapters.

which operate in a number of societies. However, large private companies such as ICI do not exist in some countries (e.g. Cuba), and in the USA there is no organization equivalent to the UK National Health Service. Moreover, you would have found neither private limited companies nor large public organizations in the UK at the beginning of the nineteenth century. Different cultures, different economic circumstances and different political philosophies give rise to organizations with different participants pursuing different objectives. Not surprisingly, the role of financial accounting differs from country to country and from time to time.

For example, in the first printed work on double-entry bookkeeping published in 1494, Luca Pacioli emphasized the importance of accounting records as follows:[8] '. . . it would be impossible to conduct business without due order of recording for without rest, merchants would always be in great mental trouble'. This may seem to us, 500 years later, to be quite a restricted viewpoint and yet, given the structure of society in fifteenth-century Italy, it would have seemed strange indeed had Pacioli recommended the disclosure of information about the merchant's business to, say, the employees. (Much of the merchant's trade required the hiring of ships and men to bring goods back from the Middle East. The men were hired for one 'venture' at a time — they had no continuing part to play in the merchant's business.) The function of accounting was to aid the merchant (owner *and* manager) himself.

Let us take another, more recent, example to illustrate the argument. A different society from that of Pacioli existed in Germany in the 1930s. A rapid rearmament programme and productivity drive was accompanied by the creation of new organizations designed for the complete control of specific industries. Companies and even industries were regrouped in order to attain self-sufficiency. The role of accounting was to provide statistics to serve as 'barometers' for the use of the public, or semi-public, organs of control. For this purpose uniformity was essential, and in 1937 some 200 uniform charts of accounts were made compulsory for the different branches of German industry and commerce. These compulsory charts were enforced in each occupied country during the Second World War and although they ceased to be compulsory in Germany in 1945, they were retained in France and are still used by the state in the planning and controlling of economic growth.

Accounting in the UK and the USA has concentrated more upon the micro-level rather than the macro-level, as suggested by the German and French examples. The emphasis in the UK and USA has been on disclosing to interested groups the details of the financial performance and position of individual business organizations. The number of such groups has increased as society, generally, has become more open and, as a consequence, demanded more accountability from business. In 1966, the American Accounting Association (AAA) defined accounting as:[9]

8. Pacioli, L., *Summa de Arithmetica, Geometrica, Proportioni et Proportionalita*, 1494.
9. American Accounting Association, *A Statement of Basic Accounting Theory*, American Accounting Association, 1966, p. 1.

the process of identifying, measuring and communicating economic information to permit informed judgements and decisions by the users of the information.

In 1991, the Accounting Standards Board (ASB), a body of accountants who are responsible for many of the rules governing UK financial reporting practice, stated that the role of financial statements is to:[10]

provide information about the financial position, performance and financial adaptability of an enterprise to a wide range of users in making economic decisions.

Although we shall develop our own view of accounting based upon these last two definitions, it should be clear that there is no single definition of the objective of accounting or of its role. Accounting does not exist independently of society. By providing information about the activities of an organization to interested parties, accounting must respond to the changing needs of society. Its role depends on, among other things, the type of reporting entity and the participants who need information. Hence, the individual merchant was the focus for the fifteenth-century Italian accounts; the state was the major influence upon accounting in Germany in the 1930s and remains so in several countries today; and, in the UK and the USA, the accounting process seeks to aid the decision processes of a variety of individual and institutional groups.

Taken at their face value, the definitions of the accounting process presented by the AAA and the ASB imply that accounting in the USA and the UK has adapted to changes in society by recognizing that financial information relating to business organizations is of interest to groups other than shareholders (owners). But does current practice reflect the thinking of the AAA or the ASB? In the nineteenth century, accounting was criticized by Marx as a tool of the capitalist. Marx saw it as serving an ideological role because it distorted the true nature of the social relationships which generate wealth through productive effort. He pointed out that financial statements emphasized the efforts of the labourer as 'bare material labour-power, a commodity',[11] and in so doing they confirmed the capitalist's view that wages are merely one more expense incurred in generating a profit for the owners. We have noted that, in the late twentieth century, accounting in both the UK and the USA is defined in terms of helping a variety of users, not simply the owners, make economic decisions, and we have emphasized how the efforts of a number of participants are needed to ensure an organization's success or survival. However, some indication of how far current accounting practice lags behind changes in society and developments in accounting thought, can be obtained from an examination of the income statement presented in Table 1.1. In its present form this statement would have attracted Marx's criticism because wages and salaries are classified as a *cost* or *expense* of

---

10. Accounting Standards Board, *The Objective of Financial Statements and the Qualitative Characteristics of Financial Information*, The ASB Ltd, 1991, para. 12.
11. Marx, K., *Capital*, Vol. III, Part 1, Progressive Publishers, 1966, p. 45.

generating profit for the owners, along with the cost of goods sold, depreciation and administrative expenses.[12] The focal point of this statement (the 'bottom line') is *net income*, which figure represents the amount available to the *owners* of the business after accounting for all costs.

A more recent example of how conventional financial accounting has failed to respond to changing conditions in society is provided by the growing criticism in the UK of its use in public sector organizations. Since 1980, public sector organizations in the UK have increasingly adopted financial accounting reporting practices similar to those developed for and used by the private sector. But critics have argued that such practices, focusing as they do on economic events and financial transactions, are inappropriate for organizations such as universities, prisons and hospitals where the objectives of the participants are largely non-financial.

Would you choose where to have your operation on the basis of which hospital had the lowest costs or the highest profit? Knowing a hospital has managed to reduce its costs to a minimum is of little help to a patient in deciding whether the quality of health care being provided is satisfactory. Reduced costs may be due to a more efficient use of resources or they may be due to the use of cheaper, less effective drugs, the employment of cheaper, less experienced medical staff or a reduction in the range of services on offer. The lowest cost hospital may also have the highest post-operative death rate! Thus, in order to evaluate how well a hospital is performing, decision makers will require additional (more important) information to that normally provided in conventional financial statements. If, however, such organizations provide users with predominantly accounting data, decision makers may have little choice but to base their economic, social and personal decisions primarily on financial criteria. This concern has led to the suggestion that financial accounting has a *political* role to play in the public sector by providing a rationale, for example, for closing down or cutting back on public services, or for investing in new sources of energy. This use of accounting information might be most effective when non-financial data are more difficult to identify and measure.

Much of this section has been concerned with examining the role of financial accounting in different societies. Not only does it have a different role in different societies, but it has more than one role in the same society. Clearly, we cannot examine all the roles of financial accounting in one introductory text. Hence, we will hereafter study financial accounting in the context, primarily, of private sector organizations in the United Kingdom, with references where appropriate to other sectors and other countries.

12. Note however that the form of Value-Added Statement advocated by *The Corporate Report*, Accounting Standards Committee, 1975, goes some way to counter this criticism. The wages paid to employees are shown as applications of value-added rather than as costs.

1.5   Financial accounting and UK organizations

In the previous section we considered how organizations and the role of accounting have been influenced by the societies in which they operate. In this section we introduce three types of business structure which dominate the UK private sector in the 1990s and which will be referred to frequently throughout this book. The three business structures are those of *individuals*, *partnerships* and *companies*. An important reason for focusing on these particular structures is that conventional financial accounting has developed primarily for these kinds of organization, rather than say, for public sector organizations or charities.

The first type of business structure — the *individual* — refers to a business owned by one person. Usually the owner is also the manager and such organizations tend to be rather small. Examples of individual businesses are found amongst farmers, window cleaners, plumbers, shopkeepers, accountants, solicitors and doctors.

A *partnership* structure is similar to that of an individual in many respects except that it has more than one owner. Once again this form of business structure is common amongst accountants, solicitors and doctors. Some accounting partnerships may have only two partners whereas the international accounting firm of Coopers & Lybrand has over 700 partners in the UK alone and over 5,000 partners worldwide.

The financial statements of both individuals and partnerships report upon the financial position and performance of the business entity, i.e. for reporting purposes, the business activities of the owners are separated from their personal activities. However, with a few exceptions, the business and the owner are not treated as separate entities for legal purposes. Thus, if an individual business or a partnership experiences financial difficulties, the personal assets of the owners (e.g. their house, car or television) are liable to be called upon to pay any outstanding business debts. The owners have what is known as *unlimited liability*.

Individual businesses and partnerships have existed in the UK for several hundred years. However the limitations of these business structures were exposed during the rapid industrialization of the UK in the nineteenth century. The Industrial Revolution led to the creation of large, highly-mechanized, manufacturing organizations. These organizations required funds to finance their large-scale operations and long production cycles, and few individuals or groups of individuals were sufficiently wealthy to supply them. The problem was how to encourage a large number of individuals and institutions to invest funds in an organization without giving them a voice in the day-to-day management of the business. A new business structure, the limited company, emerged which sought to encourage investment in private enterprise from individuals who would remain separate from the management of the organization by giving investors some protection from unscrupulous and/or incompetent managers.

A *company* is a business organization created by law. Individuals who wish to *incorporate* their business must register their company with the Registrar of Companies. Upon incorporation the company becomes a separate *legal entity* from those that own it and accounts must be prepared annually to report the financial position and performance of the company. The accounts are also filed with the Registrar of Companies and are open to public inspection by interested parties. Individuals and partnerships, in contrast, are not required to make their accounts public and few choose to do so voluntarily. A company must have at least two owners (called shareholders) and ownership is evidenced by the possession of share certificates.

Most companies enjoy *limited liability*, hence the term limited company. This means that if a limited company is experiencing financial difficulties, the creditors (e.g. banks which have lent money, customers who have paid deposits, and companies which have supplied goods) can look only to the company's assets for repayment of their outstanding claims. Unlike the owners of individual businesses and partnerships, shareholders cannot be asked to pay any cash into the company should the company's assets be insufficient to meet their claims. The shareholder's liability is limited to the amount they have paid or agreed to pay for their shares. Thus when Laker Airways went into liquidation in 1982, Sir Freddie Laker, as a major shareholder, lost all the money he had invested in the company. However, the creditors, including those customers who had paid for their flights and holidays in advance, did not have any claims upon Sir Freddie's personal wealth.

Limited companies may, since 1980, include either 'plc' (public limited company) or 'ltd' (private limited company) in their title. The difference lies in the restriction placed on the issue or transfer of their shares. Public limited companies offer their shares for public subscription, whereas private limited companies restrict their ownership. Most plcs issue shares which are traded on the International Stock Exchange and are thus known as *quoted* or *listed* companies. There are over 2,000 such companies in the UK. Most of the companies which are household names in the UK, e.g. ICI plc, British Telecom plc, Boots plc and Abbey National plc, are quoted companies. However, the vast majority of companies in the UK are private limited companies which are frequently owned and managed by the same people. The shares of these companies are *not* traded publicly.

Large quoted companies have so many shareholders that they cannot all be involved in the management of the company, even if they wanted to. For example, in 1991, Abbey National plc had issued 1,310 million shares which were owned by 3.7 million different individual and institutional shareholders. In such companies the shareholders appoint *directors* (i.e. managers) to exercise day-to-day control of the companies' activities, and it is the directors who are responsible (and accountable) for ensuring that the annual accounts are prepared and published. Thus in large companies, ownership is divorced from operational control and owners and creditors rely upon financial information supplied by the directors. However, because the accounts are prepared by the directors there is a need to ensure the accuracy of such statements. Hence, in order to protect

Table 1.2 *Auditors' report*

To the Members of Imperial Chemical Industries plc

We have audited the financial statements on pages 34 to 62 in accordance with approved auditing standards.

In our opinion the financial statements give a true and fair view of the state of affairs of the Company and the Group at 31 December 1992 and of the loss and cash flow of the Group for the year then ended and have been properly prepared in accordance with the Companies Act 1985.

KPMG Peat Marwick
Chartered Accountants
London
8 March 1993
Registered Auditors

shareholders and creditors there is a statutory obligation for the accounts of limited companies to be audited.

1.6 Auditors and accountants in the UK

Audits are undertaken by independent professional accountants (called auditors) who are appointed by the shareholders. The auditors examine the accounting system of the business, collect information about business activities, and verify the information to be included in the published accounts. They do not prepare the financial statements — that is the responsibility of the directors. After completing the audit, the auditor is in a position to express an independent opinion on the fairness and reliability of the company's financial statements and thus on the directors' stewardship of the owners' funds. More precisely, in the UK, the auditor expresses an opinion as to whether the financial statements comply with statutory requirements (embodied in the Companies Act 1985) and whether they give a 'true and fair view' of the company's position and performance. Deciding whether the accounts do give a 'true and fair view' is very much a matter of professional judgement for the auditor, but it involves, *inter alia*, checking whether the company has complied with a number of 'rules' which derive from accounting conventions, accounting standards and company law. These 'rules' will be examined in Chapter 3.

Table 1.2 reproduces the auditors' report to the shareholders (here termed 'members') of Imperial Chemical Industries plc. Independent audits are carried out not only on private sector companies, but also on nationalized industries, local authorities and charities, in which cases the auditors report to the appropriate minister, the members of council and the trustees respectively. Whatever the organization, all audits have a similar purpose, namely to provide some independent assurance that those entrusted with resources are made accountable to those who have provided the resources.

All auditors are professional accountants but not all professional accountants are auditors. So what else do accountants do? From our earlier discussions of the role of accounting in organizations and society and the different types of organization that exist, you will probably have already identified a number of roles for accountants. We will attempt to summarize some of these by categorizing accountants into three broad groups: those who work for companies in the private sector (accountants in industry and commerce); those who work for organizations in the public sector (public sector accountants); and those who work for accountancy firms (accountants in professional or 'public' practice).

Accountants working in industry and commerce are employed by companies in the manufacturing sector (e.g. Ford), the retailing sector (e.g. Sainsbury's), the banking sector (e.g. Lloyds), utilities (e.g. British Gas), the transport sector (e.g. British Airways) etc. Typically they will help to determine the cost of products, prepare budgets, prepare tax returns, and provide information for decision making by business management — for example, the opening and closing of factories and shops. These roles are usually attributed to the management accountant. The financial accountant will of course be involved with the preparation of the published accounts for external users but will also probably be involved in providing information for strategic decisions such as the acquisition of another company. Accountants in industry and commerce may also design and develop new accounting systems or revise the existing systems of a business.

Public sector accountants work for all types of public sector organizations including nationalized industries, local authorities, health authorities and government agencies. Many of their duties will coincide with those of an accountant in industry or commerce, e.g. involvement in budgeting and the provision of information for management decisions. However, because the profit objective has a lower priority in the public sector, the information required from and provided by the accountant will have a somewhat different emphasis.

Accountants in professional (or 'public') practice offer a variety of accounting services to companies, individuals, governments etc. As we have noted, they may carry out an audit of the records of a business organization. In addition they may provide a variety of tax services for their clients including tax planning and tax return preparation, and more general advice to management about running the business, i.e. management consultancy work. Accountancy firms range from individuals offering a bookkeeping service and tax and general advice to individuals and small businesses, to international partnerships offering a whole range of professional services.

The accountancy profession is dominated by six firms (the Big Six), each of which has offices throughout the world. The largest of these firms, KPMG has over 6,000 partners worldwide, and revenues in excess of $6 billion per year. Most of the largest business organizations and almost two-thirds of all quoted companies in the UK are clients of (i.e. are audited by) one of the Big Six (Table 1.3).

Table 1.3 *The ten largest UK companies and their auditors*

Public limited company	Market capitalization[1] (August 1992) £ billion	Auditors
Glaxo Holdings	21.7	Coopers & Lybrand
British Telecom	20.9	Coopers & Lybrand
Shell Transport	15.6	Ernst & Young/KPMG Klynveld*
British Petroleum	11.5	Ernst & Young
BAT Industries	11.0	Coopers & Lybrand
Guinness	10.7	Price Waterhouse
British Gas	10.3	Price Waterhouse
Hanson	9.8	Ernst & Young
Marks & Spencer	8.5	Coopers & Lybrand
Grand Metropolitan	8.4	KPMG Peat Marwick

* Joint auditors

[1] Market capitalization is the value of the company based on the number of shares multiplied by the market price per share.

Sources: *Financial Times, Accountancy*

Table 1.4 *Fee income split of the Big Six accountancy firms*

	Auditing %	Tax %	Consultancy %	Others %
Coopers & Lybrand	48	20	24	8
KPMG Peat Marwick	52	21	17	10
Price Waterhouse	39	27	25	9
Ernst & Young	43	29	19	9
Touche Ross	48	23	17	12
Arthur Andersen	24	18	53	5

Source: *Accountancy*

In recent years the large accountancy practices have developed the range of services offered to their clients. In 1992, auditing typically accounted for 50% or less of the total turnover of the thirty largest accountancy firms in the UK. The other services offered include: tax services, management consultancy, insolvency services (winding up a company which has gone into liquidation), advice on acquisitions and mergers, and even environmental audits (i.e. assisting companies in controlling their energy usage, pollution costs, etc.). Table 1.4 illustrates how fee income was earned by the UK offices of each of the Big Six accountancy firms.

1.7 Accounting as a social science

By illustrating the diversity of activities in which accountants become involved and by indicating their significance in UK society, we have attempted to demonstrate why accounting is such an important, complex and diverse discipline. Our argument so far has been to try to convince you that accounting is not simply a technique. It is something more than that. In fact, its different roles in different societies, and its ability to influence the behaviour of decision makers suggest that it might justifiably be seen as a social science.

The AAA's definition of accounting as 'the process of identifying, measuring and communicating economic information to permit informed judgements and decisions by users of the information'[13] links accounting to several other allied disciplines. For example, it is closely related to economics because it reports upon economic activities; to political science because the resolution of participants' conflicting goals is, in part, a political process; and to sociology because user needs are influenced by the beliefs and values of the society in which it is practised. Indeed, accounting could be described as a social science in its own right since it is concerned with the relationship between people and societies. It should come as no surprise therefore that many university departments of accounting are located in faculties of social studies or social sciences.

We can describe accounting as a social activity in the sense that it aims to influence human behaviour by providing information to decision makers. The actions of decision makers which result from using accounting information may have a number of potential consequences both for individuals and for society as a whole in terms of both the allocation of resources (e.g. between organizations), and the distribution of wealth (e.g. between different groups of participants). The importance of accounting as a social activity was reinforced as long ago as 1975 by the AAA[14] which stated that the purpose of the accounting process was to enhance 'social welfare' rather than the welfare of individual decision makers.

1.8 Financial statements and communication

Much of this book examines that part of the accounting process concerned with identifying and measuring economic information, i.e. determining which items should be selected for inclusion in the financial statements, and how they should be measured. However, appropriate identification and measurement of

13. American Accounting Association, *A Statement of Basic Accounting Theory*, American Accounting Association, 1966, p. 1.
14. American Accounting Association, 'Report of the Committee on Concepts and Standards for External Financial Reports', *Accounting Review Supplement*, 1975.

information are of little use unless the information is adequately communicated. At the beginning of this chapter we stated that accounting was concerned, among other things, with story-telling, bargaining and accountability. We have illustrated the bargaining and accountability aspects of accounting through the concept of an organization as a collection of individuals or groups. We close this introductory chapter by considering the communication aspect of the accounting process, i.e. what 'story' accounting aims to tell and how it aims to tell it.

The communication of information to permit informed judgements and decisions by the users of the information could describe a number of activities in society such as journalism, newscasting and even education. Indeed, stories or 'accounts' of events and people are part of everyday life. Suppose you read the following 'account' of a recent event in a newspaper:

> An elderly woman was injured yesterday as she was walking along a quiet street. The injuries occurred when a scruffily dressed youth charged towards her, pushed her to the ground and knocked her handbag from her grasp. The police are seeking the youth involved.

Consider for a moment your opinion of the events which took place, and of the youth involved. Now suppose you read the following account of the same event in another newspaper:

> An elderly woman was walking down Marple Avenue yesterday when a car driven at high speed by joyriders mounted the pavement. A young man, seeing what was happening, rushed towards her just in time to push her to safety. The police have asked the young man to come forward so that the woman can express her gratitude to him.

Has your opinion of the events and/or the youth changed? The first 'account' was not untrue but, by communicating the incident using certain words (e.g. 'scruffily dressed youth' instead of 'young man'), by selecting particular aspects of the event to be communicated (i.e. that the youth knocked the woman's handbag from her grasp) and by omitting others (i.e. that the woman was about to be hit by a speeding car), it gave a distorted and misleading impression of the incident.[15]

Whilst accounting is clearly different from journalism or news reporting in many ways, there are a number of similarities between them. Each is concerned with communicating information (i.e. giving an account of events). This information can be communicated in different ways and is capable of being distorted by the sender and misunderstood by the recipient. In accounting, as in journalism and education, the selection of information to be communicated and the method by

---

15. This example is based on an award-winning advertising campaign for a UK national newspaper, *The Guardian*.

which it is communicated (the choice of language) are important elements of the information-providing process.

Financial statements are prepared by individuals working within the organization — both accountants and other members of the management team. As managers have access to records of all the transactions and economic events which involve the organization during the year, one hopes that they will select the 'best' abstract of those events to communicate to the user groups. But what is meant by the 'best' abstract? If we were considering only the interests of the users of accounts, 'best' could mean that abstract which helped users to make the most informed judgements and decisions. However, from the viewpoint of management, who themselves comprise one participating group, 'best' may mean that abstract which best serves their own goals. We are aware that newspaper journalists often present abstracts of events which serve their own (or their proprietors') political and economic interests, rather than present abstracts which allow readers to make informed judgements and decisions. Similarly, managers may present an abstract which evokes decisions from user groups which best serve the needs of management, or best serve the needs of one user group at the expense of another.

The success, or effectiveness, of a 'neutral' communication might be judged by whether the recipient of the information makes the same response she would have made had she been given access to all the original information. A 'biased' communication might be deemed effective when the recipient responds in a manner intended by the originator. For example, consider the importance of including or excluding the information regarding the car driven by joyriders in the incident above. In accounting too, managers sometimes publish biased abstracts. This may be because they are unaware of the information needs of one or more user groups, or because they choose deliberately to ignore those needs, or because they wish to influence the behaviour of certain user groups. For example, when announcing the planned closure of a factory, or a coal mine, management in UK companies rarely provide employees and other user groups with the relevant disaggregated financial information for each factory or mine. We shall examine the specific information needs of several user groups in Chapter 2.

Having decided upon the appropriate abstract (the story to be told), a decision must be made about the way it is communicated, i.e. the language to be used. In accounting reports, this involves the use of accounting numbers and financial terminology. For example, although there are several ways in which an item of equipment can be described — size, weight, function, value — the basis of description in the financial accounts usually reflects the *cost* of the particular item, and only items which have an identifiable cost are generally reported. In addition, a language has developed in which everyday phrases may take on specific meanings, for example, 'depreciation', 'provision', 'reserve', 'current liability'.

It is important that the recipient of financial statements understands this language of accounting. Problems may arise if the reader and the preparer place different interpretations upon key terms or figures. A common misinterpretation concerns the figure attached to a company's assets. In Table 1.1, the stock of Seaview Ltd is disclosed in the balance sheet at £20,000. What does this figure mean? Does it mean that similar stock would now cost £20,000 (its replacement cost), or that the company would receive £20,000 if it sold the stock now (its resale value), or that the original cost of the stock was £20,000 (its historical cost)? Each of these alternatives can be used, in certain circumstances, in accounting reports.

It may seem that if the meaning was stated clearly, in 'plain English', problems of misunderstanding might be avoided. However, even 'plain English' is open to misinterpretation, as the following newspaper headlines illustrate:

> 'No water so firemen improvised'
>
> 'Injury forces Agassi to scratch'
>
> 'Save our trees — they break wind.'

It should now be clear that it is possible to manipulate or misinterpret accounting information. In Chapter 3 we shall examine various ways of reducing the risk of presenting 'biased' or misleading financial statements and ways in which the preparers of accounts are constrained in terms of what information they should communicate and how it should be communicated.

This chapter has described in broad terms, the role of financial accounting within organizations, and particularly within business organizations. Accounting is not concerned solely with the mechanical recording of business transactions, but with the much more complex process of economic decision making. All groups involved in an organization make decisions about the future and all require information to aid them in decision making. Accounting is concerned with identifying and measuring financial and other economic data which are then communicated to the various participant groups. The information required and communicated will be influenced by the society in which the organizations exist, because that society will influence both the objectives of the participants receiving the information and the type of reporting organization. As with other 'accounts' in society, the process by which accounting information is communicated will influence its usefulness to the recipients. In Chapter 2 we shall consider in more detail the information requirements of particular participants (users) and examine the implication of those requirements for the development of a financial reporting system.

Discussion topics

1. Discuss the relationship between accounting information and economic decisions. How can accounting help to resolve problems?

2. List the main participant groups interested in organizational survival and success. Do you believe that any of these groups dominate the others? What characteristics do the dominant group(s) (if any) possess?

3. Explain why the type of society influences the type of accounting information which organizations provide.

4. Suggest how accounting information might have a role to play in wage bargaining. Do you think there are any problems in using accounting information in this way?

5. List the main types of UK organization with which you are familiar. Contrast the purposes of producing accounting information for a UK public limited company such as ICI plc with a public sector non-commercial organization such as the National Health Service.

6. Discuss and explain each of the aspects of the AAA's 1966 definition of accounting, as outlined in Section 1.4. Give examples of economic decisions which may require non-financial information and non-economic decisions which may require financial information.

7. Explain the essential differences between the main types of private sector business structure which exist in the UK.

8. List the different kinds of services accountants provide. Why do you think there are so many accountants in the UK and worldwide? Do you think that their involvement in so many areas of business activity can be justified?

9. What do people mean when they describe accounting as a social activity? Do you believe that it is an appropriate description?

10. Why is the communication of accounting information so important? Do you believe that the communication process can ever be truly 'unbiased'?

Further reading

Freear, J., 'Historical background to accounting', in Carsberg, B. and Hope, A. (eds), *Current Issues in Accounting*, 2nd edn, Philip Allan, 1984.

Hopwood, A. G., 'Accounting and organisation change', *Accounting Auditing and Accountability Journal*, Vol. 3, No. 1, 1990.

Laughlin R. and Gray, R., Chapters 1 and 2, *Financial Accounting: Method and Meaning*, Van Nostrand Reinhold (International) Co. Ltd, 1989.

Renshall, M., 'A short survey of the accounting profession', in Carsberg, B. and Hope, A. (eds), *Current Issues in Accounting*, 2nd edn, Philip Allan, 1984.

Roslender, R. and Dyson, J.R., 'Accounting for the worth of employees: a new look at an old problem', *The British Accounting Review*, December 1992.

2

Accounting and

Decision Making

We suggested in the previous chapter that if the managers of an organization wished to act in the best interests of the other participant groups, they should select that summary of the organization's economic activities which best meets the participants' needs for information. In this chapter, we consider how the needs of particular participants (users) might be identified, and examine the implications of those needs for the development of a financial reporting system.

2.1   The users of financial statements

One approach to the identification of users' needs might be to ask them which information they would like to receive. However, this approach has many difficulties — in particular, users may be prejudiced by the type of information they receive currently and may be unaware of information which is at present unavailable to them. An alternative approach would be to first identify the types of decisions users might make, and then deduce the information they would need to make those decisions in as rational a manner as is possible. This is known as a *normative* approach. It is concerned with what people *ought* to do. This approach to the identification of the information requirements of user groups has played an important part in the development of accounting in recent years and we adopt it below. We identify some of the decisions taken by each of five participant groups (employees and trades unions, government, creditors and lenders, customers, and shareholders and investment analysts), and consider the sort of information which organizations might provide in order that these groups may make informed judgements and decisions. We do not consider here or elsewhere the decisions of managers.

Employees and trades unions

A discussion of the information requirements of employees is hampered by a lack of clearly defined models which describe employee and trades union decision processes. There are at least two reasons for this. First, many negotiations between employee and employer are conducted by trades union officials acting on behalf of the employees. (For example, the wage rates and conditions of employment for most railway workers are usually determined after negotiations between officials of the Rail, Maritime and Transport (RMT) union and members of the British Rail management team). For some decisions we need to identify the decision models of union officials, and for other decisions, the decision models of individual employees. Secondly, as we noted in Chapter 1, participants join an organization for a variety of reasons, not all of which are for monetary gain. Most of the research into loan creditors' and shareholders' needs has concentrated upon the monetary needs of these groups. However, a more complex relationship exists between the organization and the employee. For example, employees require not only a monetary reward for their contribution to the organization, but also respect from their peers, recognition from their superiors, a safe, clean workplace and stimulating tasks to perform.

Because this book concentrates upon the information contained in financial statements, we shall restrict ourselves to a brief review of some of the decisions which employees (or their representatives) must take, and which are likely to be based, at least in part, upon financial information.

If job opportunities are available, one decision facing all employees is whether to remain with their existing employers or to seek alternative employment. The factors influencing this decision will obviously vary from employee to employee. However, in almost all cases, financial reward will be an important consideration, although it will not always be the only one. Other (non-financial) factors such as job satisfaction, conditions of work, health and safety provisions and job security may affect decisions. In deciding whether to change jobs, an employee would presumably like estimates of future salary prospects, future job satisfaction, future working conditions and future job security, both from his/her existing employment and from other possible job opportunities.

Employees also make decisions concerning bargaining procedures with their existing employers; for example, regarding claims for wage increases and other conditions of employment. Employees, or their representatives, must decide what demands to make initially in the bargaining process and what financial and non-financial conditions to accept eventually. It is outside our scope to discuss such matters in detail. Indeed, as we noted earlier, the decision processes of trades unions and employees are not well understood at the present time. Nevertheless, it seems likely that, when bargaining, employees will need information about the likely amount of future cash available to their current employers both to pay wages and to create other conditions of employment that benefit employees. This will depend, in part, on the future operating profitability of the employer's business and on the ways in which resources generated from operations are to be divided between such various participants as shareholders and employees. The employee's bargaining position will also be influenced by the existence of, and opportunities offered by, alternative employment possibilities. In other words, decisions about bargaining procedures and decisions about changing jobs are not independent. In some cases, market forces will operate to ensure that similar rewards are offered for similar work by different employers.

Government

A government's need for information from public sector entities such as nationalized industries, is self-evident. A government generally bears the ultimate responsibility for the running of nationalized industries and its position may be thought of as similar to that of shareholders in private sector companies. A government's decision models may differ from those of shareholders, however, because its objectives differ from those of private individuals and organizations. For example, a government is likely to attach importance to such social factors as the level of unemployment, and the distribution of wealth. These factors will not generally concern shareholders. Also because the government spends taxpayers' money in providing funds to public sector entities, it will wish to scrutinize expenditure plans and to monitor the use made of cash invested. One might thus expect that the government would require, from each nationalized industry, the following types of information:

(a) forecasts of future cash flows;
(b) the amount of cash to be provided from government sources;
(c) the particular industry's expectations of the impact of its policies on the level of employment in that industry and on the environment; and
(d) reports of actual cash receipts and expenditure, and of the effect of past and current policies on employment and the environment.

Governments must also make various decisions which are directly affected by the behaviour and performance of private sector entities. A major decision facing any government concerns the determination of its future taxation policy. In making this decision, the government will consider factors such as the effects of different taxation policies on national economic performance, on national wealth distribution, on total taxation revenues likely to be raised from different policies, and on the ability to pay of those who are to be taxed. The information required from private sector entities will depend on the bases of taxation being considered. Thus, the effects of a tax on profits will depend on estimates of the future 'profitability' of private sector firms; the effect of a tax based on sales revenue or employee remuneration will depend on estimates of firms' expected sales revenues and wages costs, and so on. The effects of taxation policies will also depend on the ability of firms to pay the tax due under each policy, i.e. on the future cash they are likely to have available for this purpose.

Governments may also make decisions about other aspects of economic policy, for example relating to the control of prices, the granting of investment subsidies, and the regulation of wages and profits. Each of these decisions requires information from private sector entities, including estimates of their future performance in the areas to be covered by the relevant policies.

Government must also decide how much tax should be raised from each taxpayer, in the light of its taxation policy. In order to do this, each entity's taxable profit, taxable sales revenue, taxable employee remuneration, and so on, must be calculated according to the rules prescribed in the relevant legislation. As taxation assessments are rarely based on estimates of future performance, the calculations involved generally relate to some aspect of an entity's past performance. For the year ended 31 December 1991, ICI's tax bill amounted to £279 million, based on a reported pre-tax profit figure of £843 million.

Creditors and lenders

Creditors and lenders are individuals or organizations to whom an entity owes money. As the name suggests, lenders are those who have loaned money to the entity on the understanding that it will be repaid at some future time. The reward to the lenders is usually termed 'interest', and this is normally payable by the borrower for the period from incurrence to repayment of the loan. An entity's liability to its creditors normally arises because the creditors have supplied goods or services to the entity for which it has not yet paid. On 31 December 1991, ICI owed £2,304 million to those who had loaned money, and £1,000 million to those who had supplied goods and services to the company.

The two main decisions facing creditors and lenders, as far as their relationship with a particular entity is concerned, are first, whether to advance further credit (or make further loans) and second, whether to require accelerated or even immediate repayment of amounts due to them. Crucial questions in the minds of creditors and lenders when making such decisions presumably concern the security for their loans and also whether the entity will have sufficient cash available in the future to pay its debts, i.e. interest payments and loan repayments to lenders and payment of amounts owing to creditors. Such an estimate will depend *inter alia* on the cash the entity is expected to generate from its future operations, the other sources of funds available to it, the extent of its likely future expenditure on plant, machinery, property, fixtures, fittings and other assets, and the claims of other parties to whom it owes money.

Customers

Strictly speaking, all individuals need information from all the organizations of which they may become customers — both for goods or services for immediate consumption (e.g. food, drink, travel, entertainment) and for capital investment goods such as property, cars, washing machines, refrigerators and so on. Such information is concerned with the performance, quality and price of the goods and services to be acquired at the time they would likely be acquired, i.e. at some time in the future. The customer may also need information about the credit arrangements offered by the supplier, if the goods are not to be paid for at the time of purchase and, in the case of items which are not to be consumed immediately on purchase, the supplier's 'after-sales service'. An evaluation of after-sales service will include an assessment of its cost, quality and availability. The last of these will depend, in part, on the overall future prospects of the supplier. If the supplier is unable to generate sufficient resources to stay in business, it may be difficult for the customer to obtain satisfactory after-sales service!

It is unlikely that many individuals would go so far as to scrutinize a supplier's financial statements before buying a washing machine, or a personal computer, but consider, for example, the case of Rolls-Royce plc and one of its suppliers, Lucas Industries plc. The relationship between these two companies has existed for more than fifty years and Lucas Aerospace has supplied equipment for all Rolls-Royce aircraft engines including those currently being developed. Rolls-Royce's forecasts of its own future performance depend in part upon the continued survival of Lucas, and the price and quality of Lucas products as well as on the availability of alternative suppliers. Thus, in common with many other users of accounting reports, major customers will be interested in an entity's future prospects and profitability. (The interest in survival may be mutual. If a significant proportion of Lucas' output is sold to Rolls-Royce, then Lucas, as a supplier, has a vested interest in the continued existence of Rolls-Royce.)

In addition, the interest of customers in the price and quality of goods and services implies that they will require information which allows them to monitor price movements and changes in the quality of both goods and services. This monitoring role is often carried out by consumer organizations, for example the Consumers' Association, and their findings may be used to influence future policies of the organization. Since the privatization of several nationalized industries, industry watchdogs have monitored the activities of the newly-formed private sector companies. OFTEL, the telecommunications industry watchdog, has regularly restricted the level of price increases proposed by BT plc and has monitored BT's performance in improving its quality of service with respect to, for example, the speed with which faulty lines are repaired, the proportion of public payphones which are working at any one time, and the speed with which calls to directory enquiries are answered.

Shareholders and investment analysts

This last group of participants has been the subject of more research in accounting than that devoted to all the other groups together. This may be because the basic decision model assumed to be used by shareholders is relatively straightforward (i.e. often only one, quantifiable objective is assumed — to maximize shareholders' financial wealth) and because of the historical importance of owners' information needs (which were discussed in Chapter 1). This basic model has been the subject of several quantitative refinements and most of the research has focused upon shareholders of the larger listed companies, the shares of which are quoted on a Stock Exchange.

Under the heading 'shareholders and investment analysts', we include those who already own shares in a company (shareholders), potential shareholders, and those who advise shareholders and potential shareholders (investment analysts). A frequent decision facing these users is whether to buy, hold or sell shares in a particular company. To make such a decision, the shareholder (or his adviser) must estimate the value to himself of owning shares in the company and compare that value with the current market buying and selling price of the shares. As with many other goods, the buying price for the shareholder (customer) will normally be above the price at which he can sell, to allow for the costs and profit of the share 'dealer' (a person who trades in shares). A shareholder cannot buy shares directly from a company. He must use the services of an intermediary dealer, usually a stockbroker, although shares can also be bought and sold through other intermediaries, such as banks and share shops. If the value of the shares to the investor exceeds the buying price, he should buy shares. If the value is less than the selling price, he should sell shares, or refrain from buying if he does not own shares. If the value is between the buying and selling prices, he should simply maintain his existing holding. Thus the crucial part of this particular process is to estimate the value of a particular company's shares to an investor. Many ways of estimating share values are discussed in the accounting and finance literature. One of the most widely advocated share valuation models is known as the 'dividend valuation' model. This involves the discounting of expected receipts from a shareholding (dividends and capital distributions) to their present (i.e. today's) value using a rate of interest which is appropriate for the risk attached to the expected receipts. The model may be formally stated as follows:[1]

$$V_0 = \frac{d_1}{(1+i)} + \frac{d_2}{(1+i)^2} + \ldots + \frac{d_n}{(1+i)^n}$$

$$V_0 = \sum_{j=1}^{n} \frac{d_j}{(1+i)^j}$$

where V_0 is the current value of a shareholding to an investor, d_j is the receipt he expects from the shareholding at time j (i.e., the dividend or capital distribution), n is the last time at which a receipt is expected from the shareholding, and i is the appropriate discount rate.

1. Readers not familiar with the notions of discounted cash flows and the time value of money may find it helpful at this point to refer to the appendix at the end of this chapter.

In order to use the model for buy, hold or sell decisions, the investor needs information to enable him to estimate V_0, i.e. he requires estimates of future receipts from the shareholding and information about the risk associated with the expected receipts in order to select an appropriate discount rate. For this purpose, the notions of *portfolio analysis* which show how and why risk can be diversified, are of particular importance.[2]

A different decision facing existing shareholders is whether to intervene in the running of the company. In general, the running of a company is in the hands of its directors and managers. Shareholders generally intervene only if things go badly wrong. Nevertheless, the right of intervention is always available to shareholders — after all they *own* the company.

The impact of one shareholder's intervention depends very much on the size of his shareholding. The owner of 51% of the shares in a small company may intervene with great effect. The owner of 0.001% shares in ICI may find it extremely difficult to exert any influence, even though a 0.001% holding in ICI represents approximately 7,000 shares and an investment, at 1993 prices, of approximately £85,000.

In order to decide whether to intervene in the running of a company, a shareholder needs information that will enable him to assess the impact of his intervention on the value he attaches to the company's shares and on their market value. Such information will include the probability of intervention by other shareholders, the probable consequences of intervention, including the likelihood of its being effective, and the effect of each possible consequence on the future dividends expected from the company and on their associated risk.

2.2   Organizational size and financial statements

In Chapter 1 we pointed out that not all participant groups are common to all types of organization, and in Section 2.1 above we identified the information requirements of certain participant groups, e.g. trades unions, customers, shareholders and the government, which relate to the financial performance of organizations. In this section, we consider the means by which financial information is communicated to participants and, in particular, we consider why participants in large organizations are more interested in the *published financial statements* of the organizations than are participants in small organizations.

Consider again the snack bar which is owned and managed by an individual. Being involved in the daily management of the bar, the owner should be well aware of its financial position, and the annual accounts, which measure past performance and current position, will reveal little that is new. The employees

---

2.   For an introduction to portfolio analysis, see for example, Arnold, J. and Hope, T., *Accounting for Management Decisions*, 2nd edn, Prentice-Hall International, 1990, pp. 61–70.

of the bar work alongside the owner and, by observing the general level of custom, will normally be aware of the financial position. Negotiations over pay and conditions of employment will be held directly with the owner. The bank manager may have known the owner for a considerable period of time, and the business's overdraft may be secured by the deposit of deeds of the owner's house with the bank. In such circumstances, the bank manager is normally supplied with information upon request, e.g. monthly takings, breakdown of expenses, future plans, etc. Suppliers are paid either in cash or within the stated credit period, and customers pay cash. For such an organization, the annual financial statements might be viewed as providing confirmatory evidence of the financial performance and position of the business for the owner and the bank, and a basis upon which a tax charge will be levied. The importance of the annual accounts is diminished because more direct lines of communication exist between the various participants.

For larger organizations, these direct lines of communication do not exist and the importance of the published financial statements increases. The shareholders and potential investors in ICI are divorced from the daily activity of the company and the directors will rarely venture onto the 'shop floor'. The shareholders rely upon company reports, press comments and market data for information about ICI: the employees (approximately 128,000 in 1991) are not involved in company decision making and, as they are unable to assess the company's performance by simple observation, they require more information concerning their employment. In addition, the immense size of ICI implies that it will be the major customer for many of its suppliers (materials and services used totalled £8,285 million in 1991), and in turn will itself be the major supplier for many of its own customers (sales were £12,488 million in 1991, including over £9,000 million outside the UK). The survival of these suppliers and customers may depend upon ICI maintaining a specific output level.

As organizations become larger and more complex, not only do they involve more groups of participants, but they may also have a greater influence over the behaviour of those groups. At the same time, many informal channels of communication disappear and more emphasis is placed upon formal channels of communication. The published financial statements represent one such formal channel of communication.

2.3   Implications of users' information requirements

In the preceding sections we have considered briefly the sort of information which participants might require from financial statements. We have not attempted to develop detailed decision models in order to determine information requirements. Nevertheless, our *ad hoc* review provides a flavour of the sort of information users might be looking for if they are to make rational decisions.

Our analysis reveals an interesting phenomenon. In all but one of the decisions discussed in Section 2.1 (the assessment of entities' taxation liabilities by the government), the information required by users relates in part to some aspect or aspects of an entity's *future* performance. This revelation is hardly surprising. We have emphasized the role of accounting information in the decision processes of users. Decisions are concerned with choices between alternative future courses of action and thus information useful for decisions generally relates to the future. As part of the process of estimating aspects of future performance, users will require 'control' information. By control information we mean information about past performance which may be compared with the (past) estimates available to users. Such information should ideally include explanations of differences between previously estimated performance and the performance actually achieved. This helps users to evaluate the estimating procedures used, and make appropriate adjustments to existing forecasts. This sort of control information, involving the regular comparison of budgeted and actual performance, is a familiar part of management planning procedures. It should be an equally important part of the decision processes of other participant groups.

Our reasoning suggests that in general all users of accounting reports have two main, interdependent information requirements:

(a) forecasts of some aspects of the future performance of the reporting entity, and
(b) regular reports explaining both differences between forecast and actual performance, and changes in forecasts if expectations have changed.

The aspects of an entity's performance for which forecasts are required may, of course, differ from user to user. However, we noted in Chapter 1 that the survival of an organization depends upon its participants receiving regular inducements from the organization, and that many of these inducements are of a monetary nature. The review of user decisions and informational requirements in Section 2.1 suggested that many users are interested in the cash flows of the entity. These users include investors, creditors, employees, customers and the government.

It is significant that these user groups are concerned more with *cash flows* than with other measures of performance such as *accounting profit*, which we discuss at length in later chapters. There are two reasons for this. First, as we noted when describing the dividend valuation model, financial and economic theory suggests that all financial transactions be specified as cash flows to incorporate the impact of the time value of money, e.g. shareholders value their holdings on the basis of discounted *cash flows* rather than discounted *profits*. Interest is paid and received upon the amount of cash borrowed or loaned. Second, cash flows in and out of an organization are fundamental to business events. Business activity is normally on a 'cash to cash' basis in that most transactions involve some cash movement in either the short or the long term. 'Without cash the company could not survive in the economic world today, no matter how skilled its managers and workers. Cash at the end of the day determines its fate; indeed cash may be linked to the lifeblood of the company'.[3]

3. Lee, T.A., 'A case for cash flow reporting', *Journal of Business Finance*, Summer 1972.

If such a variety of users of financial statements desires information about forecasted and actual cash flows, and if cash is fundamental to the survival of the business, it would seem logical for entities to provide two types of financial statement:

(a) a statement of forecasts of the entity's expected future cash flows, and
(b) a statement of the entity's actual cash flows together with an explanation of the differences between the forecast and the actual cash flows.

However, published financial statements for participants other than management generally do not include forecasts of future cash flows. Typically these statements report on the *past* performance (the Income Statement and the Cash Flow Statement) and *current* financial position (the Balance Sheet) of an organization. In the next section we consider why entities have generally been reluctant to provide users with estimates of *future cash flows*, and in Sections 2.7 and 2.8 we examine the reasons why published financial statements have traditionally focused upon an entity's income for a period rather than on its *actual* cash flows.

2.4   Forecasts of future cash flows

In this section we are concerned specifically with forecasts of future cash flows. However, the arguments presented are equally applicable to forecasts of income or profit.

The provision of forecasted information would directly facilitate decision making by external users of financial statements. Many decisions of external users are based upon estimates of future events (see Section 2.1). In changing economic conditions, financial information about the past and present, as published in the annual financial statements, may be an unreliable guide to an organization's future activities and performance. Although it would be impractical to allow external users unrestricted access to an organization's internal records in order to obtain data on which to base their own forecasts, the provision of management-prepared forecasts offers an alternative solution. This may be a preferable alternative for two reasons. First, it would involve relatively few additional costs, as most responsible managements already prepare forecasts for internal planning. Second, management is in the best position to assess the demand for an entity's products, the corresponding input requirements for the production processes, and the various input and output prices in the industry in which it operates.

Such forecasts, however, would need to be treated with caution. Forecasts, by their very nature, are uncertain, and it is possible that shareholders, lenders, employees and others might not recognize management forecasts as merely the most probable outcome from a whole range of outcomes. Nor might they recognize that such forecasts may be based upon rather tenuous assumptions about future events. If users were to interpret the forecasts as precise estimates by management, they might, as a result, take poor decisions, and should the forecasts subsequently turn out to be inaccurate, they may lose confidence in both management and the financial reporting process. Given the central role of management in 'managing' the various participants in an organization, and the delicate balance that exists between the participants' inducements and contributions, such a loss of confidence in management could threaten the survival of the organization itself.

It is not easy to predict how users might react to the publication of management forecasts. 'Sophisticated' investors, such as financial institutions, stockbrokers and financial analysts will be aware of the uncertainty attached to forecasting and will recognize the limitations of management forecasts. Presumably, management's best estimate of the entity's prospects would be only one of many inputs to the sophisticated investor's forecasting model. On the other hand, a less sophisticated investor, or a trades union with insufficient resources to obtain proper financial advice, might not appreciate the limitations inherent in the forecasts.

Nevertheless, management-prepared forecasts should be more reliable as an aid to decision making than many other information sources. As we noted above, managers already produce detailed budgets internally for the purpose of planning and controlling the future operations of the company. Some of these budgets may be in physical terms — quantity of material used, number of hours worked, etc. — but most are translated into monetary amounts, i.e. cash flows. A lack of sophistication in financial matters by some users is not a valid reason for not publishing forecasts. Users will continue to make decisions about an entity whether or not the management provides them with forecasts, and a lack of sophistication could be lessened by increasing the level of financial education amongst users.

The publication of management's cash forecasts would provide the other participant groups with a yardstick against which to compare and evaluate management's future performance. Although this is likely to be seen as useful additional information by most participants it is less likely to appeal to managers. We suggested in Chapter 1 that, as a participant group itself, management has its own goals which, at any one time, may conflict with the goals of other groups. For example, it may not be in management's best interests to provide a warning to suppliers, customers or shareholders of a possible decline in future cash flows. In order to prevent management from issuing overly optimistic, or deliberately misleading, forecasts, it is important that they be held accountable for their forecasts. For example, it may be desirable for auditors to audit the assumptions underlying the forecasts, or for users to be allowed to take legal action against the managers should the users suffer losses as a result of acting upon misleading forecasts. However, the more stringent are the *ex post* controls, the more managers may be motivated to provide conservative and easily achievable forecasts, and the less willing they will be to undertake potentially profitable but risky ventures. The degree of control which should be exercised over management forecasts is thus difficult to determine. Too little control might encourage the managers of some companies to publish deliberately misleading forecasts, whereas too much accountability might cause them to become unduly conservative in both their forecasts and actions.

Further, the disclosure of assumptions regarding management's likely future actions might involve the disclosure of confidential information (e.g. the introduction of new products, the closing down of a factory, etc.) to competitors. The detrimental effects of such disclosures would at least be tempered if all companies were forced to comply with the requirement. However, if compliance was restricted to UK companies and UK subsidiaries of foreign companies it might still be possible for foreign companies to gain a competitive advantage in international markets from such disclosures.

Despite the possible detrimental effects of disclosing management forecasts, there is a growing body of opinion in favour of disclosure. In 1991, a working party set up by the Institutes of Chartered Accountants in England and Wales and of Scotland recommended that not only should companies provide a historical cash flow statement, but also that they should provide a statement of future prospects which would be a summary of the company's internal financial plan. It should contain projections in summary terms of the statement of assets and liabilities, the income statement and the cash flow statement for at least the next financial year, and possibly longer.[4]

2.5   Analysis and interpretation of financial information

Managers, who may have most to lose by the disclosure of forecasted information, comprise a powerful lobby opposing such disclosures. The uncertainty of the impact of published forecasts upon management policies and upon the behaviour of 'financially naive' user groups and 'financially sophisticated' competitor firms has added weight to this opposition. The implication for students of accounting is clear: we do not start with a clean slate. Estimates of future business performance might appear to be a natural candidate for disclosure in financial statements, but what appears beneficial to the interests of one group of participants may be detrimental to the interests of another.

As a result, some external users of financial statements are deprived of a basic input to their decision models, i.e. management-prepared forecasts of future cash flows. The information currently disclosed is concerned more with past performance and present position, which is, of course, determined by the results of past transactions. External users must analyse and interpret this historical

4. Arnold, J., Boyle, P., Carey, A., Cooper, M. and Wild, K., *The Future Shape of Financial Reports*, ICAEW and ICAS, 1991.

information in order to estimate an entity's future business performance and financial position. This state of affairs raises the following fundamental question:

> **How should users of financial statements analyse and interpret the (historical) data provided in order to obtain the (predictive) information required?**

This question has greatly influenced our approach in the writing of this book. It means that in the following chapters we will not always accept current accounting practices at face value, but, where necessary, will examine how easily they can be translated into information which might be useful for decision makers; and whenever a choice exists between alternative accounting methods we will stress the need to consider the extent to which each method translates into information useful to decision makers.

In the following sections we begin this process by considering why accounting practice has for so long focused upon the income of an entity rather than upon its actual cash flows.

2.6   Understanding the message

In Section 2.5 we pointed out that the users of financial statements do not receive directly (i.e. in published reports) the future-orientated information they require to make rational economic decisions. To make such decisions they must, therefore, analyse and interpret the historical information provided. It is important that this historical information is clear and unambiguous: only then will it provide a sound basis for further analysis. In Sections 2.7 and 2.8 we consider the reporting of actual (or historical) cash flows as a way of presenting clear and unambiguous information in published financial statements.

To achieve success in any form of communication, it is essential that the recipient understands the language used by the sender in constructing a message. Suppose an organization was not obliged to disclose its method of arriving at the figures appearing in its financial statements. It would be virtually impossible for a reader of those statements to evaluate the organization's business performance, or to compare its results with those of other organizations. And yet, such a situation existed in the UK until the 1930s. The directors of a company were not legally obliged to disclose separately the components of a company's balance sheet or profit and loss account. For example, the profit and loss account of Rylands and Sons Ltd for 1930 included an item: 'Dividends and Interest received, and Transfers from Contingency Accounts, and after charging Maintenance, Repairs, Depreciation, Income Tax, Salaries of Managing Directors, Bad Debts and other expenses, £106,752/16/9'.[5] The reporting of a profit figure down to the last nine pennies implies that the underlying calculations were very precise, and yet no information is provided on the relative size of the components of that figure. It is difficult to imagine any decisions for which such aggregated information would be useful.

This type of extreme problem could be eliminated by requiring entities to explain how each figure in the accounts has been calculated. However, this might entail the publication of long and tedious 'explanatory notes' (leading to information overload for the reader), and the comparison of the accounts of two or more entities would be an equally long and tedious process. An alternative would be to require all entities to report each item in the balance sheet and income statement in accordance with a predetermined set of detailed procedural rules. However, the activities of companies in different industries may be sufficiently diverse as to be incapable of being described satisfactorily by a single set of accounting policies — as we noted in Chapter 1, it is most unlikely that the activities of a charity could be reported adequately using accounting policies designed for reporting on the activities of profit-seeking companies. Complete uniformity, therefore, does not appear to be the answer. A compromise solution would be to require all entities to adhere to a set of *basic guidelines* (to ensure a certain degree of comparability) and, where choice exists between alternative accounting policies, to disclose which policy has been adopted. In fact, this describes current practice, and we shall examine this in some detail in Chapter 3.

However, it may seem that there is an obvious solution to the language problem in financial statements — all entities should report their activities in terms of actual cash flows paid and received. This proposal has several advantages. First, most of us understand the meaning of cash. It is not a nebulous concept like income or profit. Second, cash is a relatively objective measure. It is more difficult for an entity to manipulate a cash flow figure than to manipulate an income figure (for example, by changing an accounting policy). Hence published financial statements should be more comparable. Third, as we noted in Section 2.3, cash is fundamental to the survival of an entity and the reporting of past cash flows might provide some indication of the entity's future prospects. Yet, despite these advantages, the reporting of historical cash flows does not form the basis of conventional accounting practice. The reasons for this are examined in the next section.

2.7   Historical cash flows and accrual accounting

Cash has long been used as a medium of exchange. It is well understood and is suitable for a wide variety of transactions. Students often judge the state of

5.   Edwards, J.R., 'The accounting profession and disclosure in published reports, 1925–35', *Accounting and Business Research*, Autumn 1976.

Table 2.1 *Cash flow statements for Marcia Green*

	(a) Monday		(b) Tuesday	
	£	£	£	£
Cash receipts from sales		150		120
Cash payment:				
Purchases	100		—	
Barrow rental	2	102	2	2
Cash surplus		48		118

their well-being by reference to the balance in their bank account. At the beginning of each semester cash is paid into the bank account when the grant is received, and over the course of the semester cash is paid gradually, or rapidly, out of the account as expenditures are made. An assessment of a student's ability to manage his or her financial affairs might be carried out by examining the size of the cash balance (or overdraft) at the end of the year. In a sense, as we explain below, any surplus cash might be seen as profit. In addition, if prices were to remain stable and the student's spending pattern remained the same, the amount of surplus cash this year would give an indication of what might be saved next year also.

Cash balances fulfilled a similar role for Italian merchants in the fifteenth and sixteenth centuries. A 'trading venture' might have involved the exchanging of goods for silks and spices in the Eastern Mediterranean. Merchants would spend cash in purchasing the goods to be exchanged, in leasing or buying ships, in hiring crew and so on. Cash inflows arose only at the end of the voyage when the silks and spices were eventually sold in Italy. The success of the venture could be measured by counting the surplus cash after all expenses had been paid and the original investment recovered. This surplus cash represented profit from the venture, and *ceteris paribus* the size of the profit gave an indication of the likely profitability of similar ventures in the future.

A similar situation might exist today for a fruit and vegetable stallholder (see Table 2.1(a)). Consider Marcia Green, a stallholder who begins the day with £100 which she uses to purchase fruit and vegetables at the wholesale market on Monday morning. She pushes her (rented) barrow to a suitable pitch and sells all her produce for £150 by the evening. She pays her barrow rental of £2 and returns home with £148. The surplus cash of £48 represents her profit for the day and if trading conditions (including prices) are not expected to change, then Monday's cash surplus is a good indicator of the likely profit to be earned on Tuesday and on each subsequent day.

On first reading it might appear that the disclosure of cash receipts and cash payments and of the balance of cash held at the beginning and end of the period would provide the reader with information useful for decision making. We noted in Section 2.3 that users would like, ideally, an estimate of the entity's future cash flows and a report of actual cash flows together with explanations of any differences between forecast and actual results. In the examples above, actual cash flows have been disclosed and it is suggested that if conditions are stable, the amount of surplus cash at the end of the current period provides an indication of the likely cash surplus in future periods. In these cases, surplus cash reflects *maintainable profit*.

However, the position is not so clear-cut in practice. Each of the above illustrations is characterized by reference to a complete *trading cycle* — the student's 'profit' was calculated at the end of the academic year; the merchant's profit was calculated at the completion of the venture; and the stallholder's profit was calculated at the end of the day, at which time a full cycle of purchase and sale had been completed. In the real world such completeness is rare, at least over a fairly short period. The student's bank balance would have been less reliable as a measure of profit for the past year and an indicator of next year's surplus had he or she recently (i.e. near the end of the year) purchased food, books, etc. using a credit card, and had not yet settled the account. Similarly, Marcia Green might not trade solely on a cash basis. Hence, her trading cycle might not be completed at the end of each day. Suppose that on the following day: (i) the market allows her to settle her account at the end of the week, and (ii) although she sells all her produce for £150, she receives only £120 cash, as a regular customer had forgotten his wallet and the stallholder allowed him twenty-four hours to pay. Does the day's cash surplus of £118 (see Table 2.1(b)) measure the stallholder's business performance on Tuesday and can it be used to estimate her likely performance for the rest of the week?

This illustration suggests that a statement of cash payments and receipts might not reflect business performance or economic activity when transactions do not involve the immediate transfer of cash, for example when buying and selling on credit. Even so, credit transactions would not create reporting problems if we could wait until the cash was paid or received before preparing the financial statements, i.e. until the trading cycle was completed. However, most businesses buy and sell goods and services continuously, so that at any one point in time there will always be bills outstanding in relation to sales and purchases. Consequently, conventional accounting practice records transactions at the time of sale and purchase rather than at the time of cash receipt and cash payment.

A conventional financial statement for Marcia Green is illustrated in Table 2.2. On Tuesday, sales (as distinct from cash receipts) are £150, purchases (as distinct from cash payments) are £100, and as all the produce is sold, the *cost of goods sold* is £100 also. After deducting the barrow rental the profit for the day amounts to £48. This would seem to be a more realistic assessment of her performance on the day (i.e. compare this with the performance on Monday when the same economic activities generated an identical profit of £48) and it gives some indication of her future performance too. If she continues to sell £150 worth of goods each day then she should continue indefinitely to earn a profit of £48 each day. The cash surplus of £118 could not be so maintained even if conditions (prices) were

Table 2.2 *Income statements for Marcia Green*

| | (a) Monday | | (b) Tuesday | |
	£	£	£	£
Sales		150		150
Expenses:				
Cost of goods sold	100		100	
Barrow rental	2		2	
		102		102
Profit		48		48

stable because, for example, it ignores the amount which must be paid to the market at the end of the week.

The convention which distinguishes between the receipt of cash and the right to receive cash, and the payment of cash and the obligation to pay cash is known as the accrual convention. Conventional accounting is often termed *accrual accounting* to distinguish it from cash flow accounting.

At the end of the week when Marcia's trading cycle is complete, the cash surplus should be identical to the reported profit. Table 2.3 reconciles the two methods of reporting business performance. The results of the stallholder's operations on Monday and Tuesday are reproduced from Tables 2.1 and 2.2. On Wednesday Marcia again purchases goods for £100, on credit, from the market. Her account will be settled on Saturday. She sells all these goods for £150 cash and in addition collects £30 from the customer who had forgotten his wallet the previous day. On Thursday and Friday she again purchases £100 worth of goods on credit and sells them for £150 cash. On Saturday she sells £150 worth of goods and settles her account at the market. This amounts to £500 representing purchases of £100 each day from Tuesday to Saturday. For each of the first five days she has generated a (fluctuating) cash surplus, but on Saturday the settlement of her outstanding account produces a cash deficit, or net cash outflow, of £352. Totalling the daily figures we can produce a cash flow statement for the week. This is presented in the right-hand column of Table 2.3 and shows a cash surplus of £288.

The stallholder's income statement is identical for each day of operations, from Monday to Saturday. Irrespective of when the cash was actually paid and received, she has purchased goods costing £100 and sold them for £150 each day. For each of the six days a profit of £48 has been generated, which amounts to £288 by the end of the week. Thus the cash surplus and the profit generated at the end of the week are identical. This is an important point. It does not matter how large is the organization, nor how complex its transactions, all measures of profit will generally produce the same aggregate figure at the completion of the trading cycle and that profit figure will be identical to the cash surplus over the period.

This identity hides two major problems. First, as we shall see in the following

Table 2.3 Reconciliation of Marcia Green's cash flow and income statement

	Monday		Tuesday		Wednesday		Thursday		Friday		Saturday		Totals for week	
	£	£	£	£	£	£	£	£	£	£	£	£	£	£
Cash flow statements														
Cash receipts from sales		150		120		180		150		150		150		900
Cash payments:														
Purchases	100		–		–		–		–		500		600	
Barrow rental	2		2		2		2		2		2		12	
		102		2		2		2		2		502		612
Cash surplus/(deficit)		48		118		178		148		148		(352)		288
Income statements														
Sales		150		150		150		150		150		150		900
Expenses:														
Cost of goods sold	100		100		100		100		100		100		600	
Barrow rental	2		2		2		2		2		2		12	
		102		102		102		102		102		102		612
		48		48		48		48		48		48		288

section, many organizations do not complete their trading cycle until the business is wound up, which in most cases is many years after they have begun to trade. Secondly, although the aggregate profit figure over the life of the organization will be identical to the aggregate cash surplus, the pattern of cash and income figures reported within that period can differ significantly. We can see from Table 2.3 that a reader of the stallholder's accounts might make a different assessment of the stallholder's past performance and a different prediction of the future performance, depending upon whether he was provided, at the end of each day, with a cash flow statement or an income statement.

This is one dilemma facing all accountants. At the end of an organization's life, all methods of cash flow and income measurement will produce identical aggregate figures measuring the surplus/profit generated since the organization was created. Participants, however, require information on a more regular basis in order to make their decisions. The aggregate surplus/profit is therefore allocated over a series of reporting periods — usually of twelve months' duration.The choice of accounting method will determine the pattern of the surplus/profit figures reported in these periods, and this pattern may have a significant influence on participants' decisions.

2.8   The allocation of expenditure

Some cash outflows are used not to pay immediate running expenses, but to purchase assets, items which will produce benefits for the entity over a period of time, e.g. a student might use any excess of his grant over his living expenses to purchase stereo equipment, and the Italian merchant might purchase a ship which will be used on future ventures. If, after the first voyage, the merchant reports a cash deficit after taking into account the entire cost of purchasing the ship, does this mean the venture was unprofitable and that future ventures should not be undertaken? In this instance the trading cycle has not been completed because the ship has not been reconverted into cash.

Because users need regular information, most entities are currently required to produce financial statements every twelve months. However, as most organizations are going concerns (i.e. they are expected to continue to operate for the foreseeable future) they do not reconvert their assets into cash for the purpose of calculating a cash surplus. How, then, should an entity account for cash spent on assets which are still in existence at the end of the year?

Suppose our stallholder was successful. Having accumulated £20,000 she decides to open a shop. She purchases a truck for £10,000, signs a three year lease on a shop at a cost of £6,000 and purchases shop fittings for £3,000. Her bank balance is reduced to £1,000. She has spent cash of £19,000 on items which she hopes will last beyond the first twelve months and will contribute towards the generation of revenues and profits in future years. It would therefore seem inappropriate to charge the whole £19,000 as an expense in the first year of trading when the truck, the shop and the fittings are all available for use in the second year. On the other hand neither does it seem appropriate to ignore these items altogether in calculating how the business has performed in its first year. These items cost £19,000 and eventually they will be 'consumed', i.e. will wear out or expire.

This example illustrates another difficulty in relying on actual cash flows to measure past performance and provide an indication of future cash flows. Organizations often purchase assets which will last, and provide benefits, for several years. This may involve the payment of large amounts of cash in some years, but little or none in others. For example, if the truck for which the stallholder has paid £10,000 in year 1 lasts for five years, she will have no comparable expenditure in each of the next four years. To include the whole £10,000 as an expense in the first year would distort an evaluation of the year's business performance and could mislead users in estimating business performance in years 2, 3, 4 and 5. Major cash expenditures tend to be 'lumpy' and can distort year-by-year evaluations. Hence, conventional accrual accounting aims to smooth out the lumps by allocating the cost of assets to the years in which they are consumed. If the truck is expected to last for five years, the £10,000 would be allocated over the five year period by means of an annual *depreciation* charge. The £6,000 lease would be allocated over three years, and the £3,000 spent on fittings over their estimated useful life.

In Section 2.3 we suggested that most participant groups would benefit from some estimate of an organization's future business performance. We also suggested that when evaluating accounting alternatives we should consider how easily the information provided could be translated into information useful for decision makers. As direct forecasts are unavailable at present, it would seem helpful for users to receive an income figure representing maintainable profit, if such a figure could be used for estimating future performance, including that based on future cash flows. But does an income figure calculated according to conventional accrual accounting provide a sound basis for further analysis? Whereas cash flows are reasonably objective, easily understood and are comparable between organizations, the calculation of accounting income poses several difficulties for managers and accountants. For example, in spreading the cost of an asset over its useful life, they must consider various factors which may contribute to the determination of that useful life. Thus an asset's useful life may be affected by the intensity of its use, by its location or by economic and technological trends. Managers must also consider how best to allocate the cost over that useful life, for example should an equal amount be allocated each year, or should some weighting factor be applied so that most of the cost is allocated to the earlier years of the asset's life?

We saw above that the stallholder must answer these questions in determining how to account for a new truck. But similar problems arise in many areas of conventional accrual accounting. For example, how should a company treat expenditure of £10,000 on the research and development of a new product to be launched in two years' time? Should the whole amount be included as an expense this year, or should it be spread over the life cycle of the product? Should the treatment be any different if there exists some uncertainty over the viability of the new product? How should a company record £10,000 spent on an overhaul of factory machinery? Or £10,000 paid to production workers for producing goods, some of which remain unsold at the end of the year?

In all of these instances the cash outflow for the period is clear, but the expense to be charged in the current period is a matter of judgement. Managers and accountants can and do provide equally justifiable arguments to support alternative methods of calculating these expenses, and yet if other participants are to understand and have confidence in the figures reported by management there must be some consistency in the manner in which business organizations prepare their financial statements. If conventional, accrual accounting statements are to achieve satisfactory levels of objectivity, understandability and comparability they must be prepared according to specific, generally accepted guidelines and standards. In Chapter 3 we shall examine the role of such accounting standards in the UK, and their usefulness generally as a means of governing accounting practice.

By recording transactions at the time of sale and purchase rather than at the time of cash receipt and cash payment, and by allocating cash expenditure on long-lived assets over several periods, the accrual accounting method produces an income or profit figure which usually differs, often significantly, from the cash flow figure. Which is more useful to the users of financial statements — the smoother trend of the income figures or the more erratic cash flows? The answer is that neither the income statement nor the cash flow statement can provide a complete picture of a company's performance. The two statements (and the balance sheet) interrelate, but differ, because they reflect different aspects of a company's activities. Both statements provide the user with useful and complementary information.

First, the income figure is thought to be a good measure of *business* performance insofar as it reports on the *economic* activity of buying and selling goods and services. The cash flow figure reports on the *financial* activity of paying out and receiving cash. Second, in spreading capital expenditures over the useful life of the assets purchased, conventional accrual accounting adopts a longer-term view of the business. By looking beyond the current year the system produces an income figure which, it is argued, is an indicator of future business performance. The cash flow figure indicates, *inter alia*, whether the business is likely to survive into the long term. In the case of the stallholder's truck, conventional accrual accounting seeks to smooth out the lumpy cash expenditure to avoid distortions in the year-by-year evaluation. By recording the whole amount as an outflow, the cash flow statement might draw the reader's attention to the fact that in the short term the business has very little cash available and may be in a vulnerable position.

2.9   Summary

In this chapter we identified the information requirements of the major users of accounting reports. We noted that many of these users' requirements would be satisfied if entities provided two types of financial statements:

(a) a statement of forecasts of the entity's expected future cash flows, and
(b) a statement of the entity's actual cash flows together with an explanation of the differences between the forecast and the actual cash flows.

However, management has traditionally been reluctant to provide users with forecast information of any sort, and the business practices of buying and selling on credit and of purchasing long-lived assets lead to some ambiguities in the message given by a statement of actual cash flows. Hence, conventional accounting practice has long been based upon the accruals (matching) principle. Unfortunately, whereas cash flows are reasonably objective, easily understood and are comparable between organizations, the calculation of accounting income necessitates the use of judgement by managers and accountants. As a result, similar economic events can be reported in different ways because entities can choose to report those events on the basis of one of several, equally acceptable, accounting policies. Clearly, the users of published financial statements would benefit if all entities were required to adhere to a common set of guidelines when preparing these accounts. This describes current practice and in Chapter 3 we examine the regulatory framework for financial accounting in the UK.

Discussion topics

1. Discuss the information requirements of the following user groups:
   (a) employees
   (b) government
   (c) shareholders.

2. Which government departments might be particularly interested in the information contained in financial statements? For which purposes?

3. Are you aware of any instances in which trades unions have used published accounting information as a basis for wage demands? How were these negotiations resolved?

4. Why are managers so reluctant to publish forecasts? Can you think of any circumstances in which publication would be beneficial to managers?

5. Are there many decisions which are common to shareholders and lenders, and would thus require similar information?

6. Can you think of any circumstances in which participants other than managers might not like to see published forecasts? For what reasons?

7. Explain the relationship between organizational size and formal communication.

8. Explain why you think the reporting of past cash flows may be more understandable to users than the reporting of income figures.

9. Under what assumptions will the cash surplus from business activities reflect the business's maintainable profit? Is it likely that such assumptions are realistic representations of actual situations?

10. Distinguish between cash accounting and accrual accounting. Which expenses are likely to be measured in different ways if either of the two methods is chosen?

Exercises

2.1 Mr Alfonso is the owner of a small business, the Jago Co., which manufactures and sells footballs. Mr Alfonso expects that the business will earn net cash receipts of £5,000 after one year, £6,000 after two years, and £8,000 after three years. At the end of three years he expects to sell the business to Despina Ltd for £40,000. Assume that Mr Alfonso will withdraw all net cash receipts from the business for his personal use as they arise, that no cash flows are expected other than those described above, and that there is no uncertainty associated with the receipt of any cash flow. Mr Alfonso's discount rate is 20% per annum.

■ Calculate the discounted present value of the Jago Co., now and at the end of *each* of the next three years, immediately after the annual net cash receipts have been distributed to Mr Alfonso.

2.2 Mr Nabucco owns a 20% stake in a small, but prosperous, company which is considering investing £50,000 in a new process which will offer the following positive cash flows at the end of the following years:

Year 1   £30,000
Year 2   £25,000
Year 3   £10,000

Mr Nabucco is unhappy about the proposed investment because he would have liked an immediate distribution of cash so that he could have indulged himself and his wife in a Caribbean cruise at a cost of £10,000. Mr Nabucco can borrow and lend at the same annual rate as the company which is 10%.

■ Explain to Mr Nabucco what he should do to maximize his satisfaction. What would happen if the best rate of interest available to Mr Nabucco for borrowing was 20% per annum?

2.3 Once upon a time, many years ago, there lived a feudal landlord in a small province of Central Europe. The landlord, known as the Red-Bearded Baron, lived in a castle high on a hill, and this benevolent fellow was responsible for the well-being of many peasants who occupied the lands surrounding his castle. Each spring, as the snow began to melt and the thoughts of other, less influential, men turned to matters other than business, the Baron would decide how to provide for all his serf-dependents during the coming year.

One spring, the Baron was thinking about the wheat crop of the coming growing season. 'I believe that 30 acres of my land, being worth five bushels of wheat per acre, will produce enough wheat for next winter', he mused. 'But who should do the farming? I believe I'll give Idomeneo the Indefatigable and Idamante the Immutable the task of growing the wheat'. Whereupon Idomeneo and Idamante, two serfs noted for their hard work and not overly-active minds, were summoned for an audience with the Baron.

'Idomeneo, you will farm on the 20-acre plot of ground and Idamante will farm the 10-acre plot', the Baron began. 'I will give Idomeneo 20 bushels of wheat for seed and 20 pounds of fertilizer. (Twenty pounds of fertilizer are worth two bushels of wheat.) Idamante will get 10 bushels of wheat for seed and 10 pounds of fertilizer. I will give each of you an ox to pull a plough. The oxen, incidentally, are only three years old and have never been used for farming, so they should have a good ten years of farming ahead of them. Take good care of them, because an ox is worth 40 bushels of wheat. Come back next autumn and return the oxen and the ploughs along with your harvest.'

Idomeneo and Idamante genuflected and withdrew from the Great Hall, taking with them the things provided by the Baron.

The summer came and went and after the harvest Idomeneo and Idamante returned to the Great Hall to account to their master for the things given them in the spring. Idomeneo, pouring 223 bushels of wheat onto the floor, said 'My Lord, I present you with a slightly used ox, a plough broken beyond repair, and 223 bushels of wheat. I, unfortunately, owe Arbace the Ploughmaker three bushels of wheat for the plough I got from him last spring. And, as you might expect, I used all the fertilizer and seed you gave me last spring. You will also remember, my Lord, that you took 20 bushels of my harvest for your own personal use.' Idamante, who had been given 10 acres of land, 10 bushels of wheat and 10 pounds of fertilizer, spoke next. 'Here, my Lord, is a partially used-up ox, the plough for which I gave Arbace the Ploughmaker three bushels of wheat from my harvest, and 105 bushels of wheat. I, too, used all my seed and fertilizer last spring. Also, my Lord, you took 30 bushels of wheat several days ago for your own table. I believe the plough is good for two more seasons.'

'Knaves, you did well', said the Red-Bearded Baron. Blessed with this benediction and not wishing to press their luck further, the two serfs departed hastily. After the servants had taken their leave, the Red-Bearded Baron, watching the two hungry oxen slowly eating the wheat piled on the floor, began to contemplate what had happened. 'Yes,' he thought, 'they did well, but I wonder which one did better.'

- Prepare for each farmer (Idomeneo and Idamante) a statement of 'net income' for the period and a statement of 'financial position' at the end of the period. Provide full explanations of your calculations and note any reservations you have.

Further reading

Arnold, J., 'The information requirements of shareholders', in Carsberg, B. and Hope, A. (eds), *Current Issues in Accounting*, 2nd edn, Philip Allan, 1984.

Collins, W., Davie, E.S. and Weetman, P., 'Management discussion and analysis: an evaluation of practice in UK and US companies', *Accounting and Business Research*, Spring 1993.

Cooper, D., 'Information for labour', in Carsberg, B. and Hope, A. (eds), *Current Issues in Accounting*, 2nd edn, Philip Allan, 1984.

Cooper, D. and Essex, S., 'Accounting information and employee decision making', *Accounting, Organisations and Society*, Vol. 3, 1977.

Gray, R. and Perks, R., 'How desirable is social accounting?', *Accountancy*, April 1982.

Gray, R.H., Owen, D.J. and Maunders, K.T., *Corporate Social Reporting*, Prentice-Hall, 1987.

Pike, R., Sharp, J. and Kantor, J., 'The role of accounting information in valuing unlisted shares', *Accounting and Business Research*, Summer 1988.

Sherer, M. and Southworth, A., 'Accounting and accountability in the nationalised industries', in Carsberg, B. and Hope, A. (eds), *Current Issues in Accounting*, 2nd edn, Philip Allan, 1984.

Appendix 2A   The time value of money

The share valuation model introduced in Section 2.1 involves the discounting of expected receipts from a shareholding (dividends and capital distributions) to their present value using a rate of interest (or discount rate) which is appropriate for the risk attached to the expected receipts. The central feature of this model is that cash receipts expected at different times in the future are not simply added together to obtain a measure of the present values of those cash receipts. The model recognizes that £1 now is worth more than £1 at some time in the future, and the rationale for this is explained below.

The time value of money is the result of the existence of investment, lending and borrowing opportunities, of the preference that many individuals have for immediate rather than future consumption, and of expected inflation. These factors mean that those who wish to have cash for spending sooner rather than later incur a cost (pay a price) in so doing, and that those who are willing to defer having cash available for spending enjoy a benefit (receive a price). The prices paid or received are normally expressed in terms of interest rates which represent the costs or benefits of transferring money from one period to another, in much the same way as costs or benefits arise when other resources are acquired or disposed of.

In practice, a spectrum of interest rates exists at any time in the capital market (i.e. the market in which funds are borrowed and loaned). Rates of interest vary depending upon the amounts and risks involved, the status of the individual or entity concerned, and so on. To simplify our discussion of the role of interest rates in the measurement of wealth we make two rather unrealistic assumptions at this stage.[6]

First, we assume that there are perfect markets for borrowing and lending funds, i.e. perfect capital markets. Three conditions must be satisfied if this assumption is to hold:

(a) No lender or borrower is large enough for his or her transactions to affect the ruling market price for funds (the interest rate).
(b) All traders in the market have equal and costless access to information about the ruling price and all other relevant information.
(c) There are no transactions costs involved in using the market and no taxes that would alter economic decisions.

Second, we assume that the future is known with certainty. If these two assumptions hold, there will be a unique market rate of interest, which we shall call i, at which all users of the capital market are able to borrow or lend as much as they wish. Under the conditions assumed, competitive forces are likely to eliminate opportunities to lend or borrow at any interest rate other than i. The assumption of a unique market rate of interest leads to a useful simplification in the measurement of wealth; cash flows which arise at different points in time may be compared without any ambiguities which might arise if there existed a number of different possible interest rates.

Given the unique market rate of interest, i, an individual presently in possession of £C could lend it to yield £$C(1+i)$ after one year, i.e. return of capital, £C, plus interest £$C \times i$. (In these expressions and all relevant subsequent ones in this chapter, i should be interpreted as the rate of interest expressed as a decimal of 1. Thus, for example, an interest rate of 6% would be written as 0.06 and one of 20% as 0.20.) If capital and interest are loaned for a further year the total returns at the end of the second year will be £$C(1+i)(1+i)$, which equals £$C(1+i)^2$. In general, if an amount £C is invested for n years at an annual compound rate of interest, i, the amount to which it will have accumulated after n years will be £$C(1+i)^n$. This process is known as *compounding*, and enables us to re-express present values in terms of equivalent future values. A rational individual should be indifferent between £$C(1+i)^n$ after n years and £C immediately, because possession of the latter could be converted to the former by lending at the market rate of interest.

For purposes of measuring present wealth we are interested not so much in re-expressing present values in terms of equivalent future values as in the opposite process of re-expressing expected future cash flows in terms of equivalent present values. This process is known as *discounting*, and provides us with a common basis for measuring wealth, in terms of (discounted) present values.

6. Some of the implications of relaxing these assumptions are discussed in Arnold, J. and Hope, T., *Accounting for Management Decisions*, 2nd edn, Prentice-Hall International, 1990, Chapter 12.

Suppose an individual expects to receive £C after one year. What is the present value (PV) of the expected receipt? Let us think of PV as the immediate amount the investor would have to lend in order to accumulate £C after one year. Then:

$$PV(1+i) = £C,$$

and

$$PV = \frac{£C}{(1+i)}$$

(sometimes written as $£C(1+i)^{-1}$).

By similar reasoning, it may be shown that the present value of £C receivable or payable after two years is $£C/(1+i)^2$ and, in the general case, that the present value of £C receivable or payable after n years is $£C/(1+i)^n$. A rational investor should be indifferent between any expected future amount and its present value. For example, in the general case an individual expecting to receive £C after n years could convert it to $£C/(1+i)^n$ immediately by borrowing, and an individual with $£C/(1+i)^n$ could convert it to £C after n years by lending.

The equivalence between an expected cash receipt or payment and its discounted present value enables us to measure the impact of a future cash flow on an individual's or firm's present wealth. It also provides us with a means of calculating the total wealth of an individual or firm, and the present value of the shares of a company, provided we can estimate the amount and timing of all relevant future cash flows, i.e., the process is to estimate the future cash flows, discount them to present values and sum the present values.[7]

For example, a company expects to receive, and distribute to its shareholders as dividends, net cash inflows (i.e. cash receipts from sales, etc., less operating costs) of £50,000 after one year, £65,000 after two years and £100,000 after three years, and nothing thereafter. The relevant interest rate, i, is 15% (0.15) p.a. compound. Ms Windsor owns 10% of the company's shares. What is the present value of Ms Windsor's shareholding? Calculating the discounted present value of the expected dividends (net cash inflows) to Ms Windsor, and summing gives:

$$PV = \frac{5,000}{(1+i)} + \frac{6,500}{(1+i)^2} + \frac{10,000}{(1+i)^3}$$

$$PV = \frac{5,000}{(1.15)} + \frac{6,500}{(1.15)^2} + \frac{10,000}{(1.15)^3} = £15,837.90$$

The present value of Ms Windsor's shareholding is £15,837.90.

7. Although we have assumed the existence of a unique interest rate for discounting purposes, the procedure described is often valid in an environment where multiple interest rates exist. Of course, such environments create the additional problem of selecting a discount rate or rates which reflect the individual's or firm's particular borrowing and lending opportunities and the risk associated with expected cash flows.

We can now provide a symbolic representation of the model used above to calculate present value. The present value of a shareholding to an investor may be described by the expression:

$$V_0 = \frac{d_1}{(1+i)} + \frac{d_2}{(1+i)^2} + \frac{d_3}{(1+i)^3} + \ldots + \frac{d_n}{(1+i)^n}$$

where V_0 is the present value of a shareholding to an investor, d_1 is the dividend or other cash receipt expected at time 1 (i.e. after one year), d_2 is the dividend or other cash receipt expected at time 2 and so on, n is the last time at which a receipt is expected from the shareholding, and i is the appropriate interest rate.

This expression may be more conveniently written:

$$V_0 = \sum_{j=1}^{n} \frac{d_j}{(1+i)^j}$$

CHAPTER 3

The Regulation of Financial Reporting

3.1 The need for some accounting rules

In the previous chapter we considered the sort of information which participants might require from financial statements in order to make rational decisions. We also suggested that in larger organizations the published accounts are an important (sometimes the only) source of information about the organization's performance which is available to external user groups. Who then should decide what accounting information is to be provided in these accounts? Perhaps the management of the company should decide? After all, managers have access to information about all aspects of the organization's activities and so are in a good position to determine which information will be useful to the other participants.

However, there are at least two reasons why management should not be given complete freedom to determine what accounting information should be included in the published financial statements. The first is that of *information asymmetry*. Whereas managers have access to information about all aspects of the organization's activities, other participants do not. Managers, therefore, could exploit their position within the organization to further their own goals at the expense of others. For example, they might borrow in order to pay themselves a large increase in remuneration. Without some knowledge of the level of the managers' remuneration, the level of the organization's total borrowings, and the organization's operating performance, the lenders would be unable to make an informed decision about their continued participation in the organization.

The second reason is that of *comparability*. Let us suppose that managers could be relied upon to provide accounting information on items and transactions of interest to other participant groups. How should they report this information? We saw in the previous chapter that a simple financial transaction, such as the cash purchase of a truck, could be recorded in different ways, for example writing off the cost in the year of purchase, or allocating the cost over the life of the asset in a variety of ways. Valid arguments could be provided to support each alternative accounting treatment.

If the accounts were read by managers only, the choice of accounting treatment would be less important. One might expect managers to understand their own accounting policies, and of course, they could always obtain clarification and additional information as required. However, an external user group might be very confused and perhaps misled if, for example, the managers of Tesco chose to write off the cost of new lorries in the year of purchase, whilst the managers of Sainsbury's chose to depreciate them over a period of fifteen years, or not to depreciate them at all. It would be similarly confusing if the management of Sainsbury's chose to depreciate its lorries in some years, but not in others. Without some form of *standardized* accounting treatment of financial transactions, it would be very difficult for a user of accounts to *compare* the performance of an organization either through time or with the performance of other organizations.

It would appear, then, that if managers were given complete freedom to determine the content of published financial statements, the external users of accounts would be unlikely to receive the information necessary to make rational decisions. Consequently, over the years, regulators have acted on behalf of shareholders, creditors, employees and others, to develop a number of rules which govern financial reporting. Most of these rules seek to alleviate the problems of information asymmetry and the lack of comparability. They determine what information is to be included in published financial statements, and how it is to be presented. The greater the scope for misleading external participants, and the greater the need of those participants for comparable information, the more rules are required. Thus, in the UK, for example, the financial reports of a stallholder are subject to far fewer rules than are those of a public limited company.

But who are the regulators who determine the form and content of published accounts, and how do they arrive at their decisions? In the following section we outline the main sources of the regulations which govern the financial reporting of companies in the UK and we explain the form such rules take. In subsequent sections we examine some of the underlying accounting concepts or *conventions* which underpin these rules and which form the framework for traditional or conventional accounting.

3.2   The framework of accounting regulation in the UK

Looking through the published financial statements of a large UK company for the first time, you may be surprised by the amount, content and presentation of the accounting information. You would notice that they contain far more information than the simple income statements and balance sheets illustrated in previous chapters. You may wonder why certain information is reported in the way it is (e.g. in notes rather than in the profit or loss account or balance sheet), why some information is there at all and why some is not. The preparers of the published financial statements of UK companies must comply with specific rules governing the form and content of company accounts. These rules are laid down by a number of regulatory bodies. The principal sources of such regulation are the law and the accountancy profession (through its close involvement with the Accounting Standards Board). The process is illustrated in Figure 3.1.

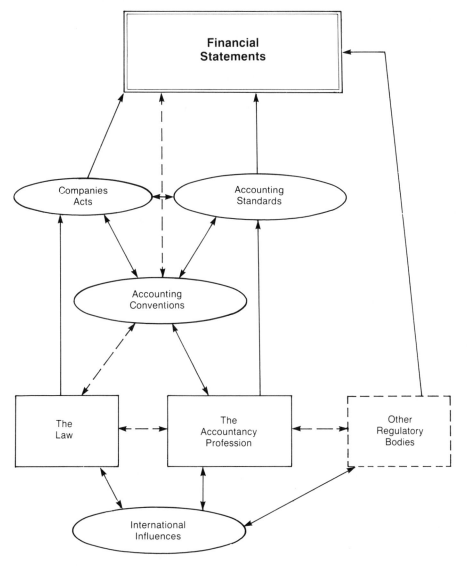

Figure 3.1 *Major sources and forms of UK accounting regulation*

The law

In the UK, much of the legislation governing the preparation and content of published accounts is embodied in the Companies Acts 1985 and 1989, which are concerned with the accounts of limited liability companies only. The Companies Act 1985 is essentially a consolidation of law which had previously been included in the Companies Acts 1948, 1967, 1976, 1980 and 1981. All the accounting provisions in the Companies Act 1989 are substitutions for, and amendments to, the Companies Act 1985.

Perhaps the most important accounting requirement of the Companies Act 1985, as amended by the Companies Act 1989 (hereafter referred to as the Act), is that all financial statements drawn up under the Act must present a *true and fair view*. This requirement is fundamental and overrides all the detailed rules on the content and format of financial statements.

The Act deals mainly with minimum disclosure requirements and is concerned primarily with the protection of shareholders and creditors. It provides a framework for *general disclosure* by requiring that certain financial statements (e.g. a profit and loss account and balance sheet) should be prepared and presented to the shareholders, and requires the *specific disclosure* of certain items (e.g. depreciation, directors' remuneration, auditors' remuneration and certain categories of loans and creditors).

These disclosure requirements resolve some of the problems associated with the asymmetry of information between the directors (the legal managers of the company) and some user groups. For example, the requirement to disclose directors' remuneration recognizes the potential for a director's personal interests to conflict with his or her duty to the company. They also enable user groups to compare the level of their inducements with those received by other groups. For example, the Act requires the disclosure of not only the directors' remuneration, but also the amount of dividends paid to shareholders and the amount of wages and salaries paid to employees. Finally, the Act requires that the directors not only present the financial statements to the shareholders each year at a general meeting, but also that independent auditors are appointed who will examine the financial statements and report their findings to the shareholders.

The accountancy profession

Information asymmetry and the lack of comparability between sets of accounts are two of the principal reasons why the publication of financial statements should be subject to regulation. We have seen above that the law addresses the problem of information asymmetry by requiring the disclosure of certain key items of interest to user groups. The accountancy profession also has published statements recommending the disclosure of specific data, for example, the amount spent on research and development during the year. However, in its role as regulator, the accountancy profession has been even more influential in achieving a significant increase in the comparability of financial statements. Many of the profession's regulations limit the number of alternative accounting treatments available to management. The result .has been an increased level of standardization in published accounts. Thus, whereas the law provides the general framework for *what* is to be accounted for in financial reports, the accountancy profession has traditionally provided detailed rules, in the form of *accounting standards*, about *how* items and transactions are to be accounted for.

The recommendations published by the accountancy profession have had an enormous influence on the form and content of financial statements over the past twenty or thirty years. During that time the process of issuing these recommendations, or standards, has changed in response to pressures from user groups, managers and the accountancy profession itself. Just as the form and content of published accounts are too important to be left to the management of companies, so they may be too important to be left to the accountancy profession, whose members are more involved in preparing and auditing the accounts than in using them. In order to better understand the strengths and limitations of accounting standards, we describe below the formal structure of the standard setting process in the UK.

Structure of the standard setting process

Between 1971 and 1990, recommendations from the professional accountancy bodies[1] in the UK and Ireland were in the form of Statements of Standard Accounting Practice (SSAPs). These standards were prepared by the Accounting Standards Committee (ASC), the membership of which was drawn largely from the major professional bodies. The standards covered a whole range of issues including disclosure of earnings per share information and the accounting treatment of stocks and long-term contracts. Over its life, the ASC issued new standards on issues for which there had been no previous regulation, and revised existing standards in the light of changing social and economic conditions. In November 1987 a major review of the standard setting process was undertaken and, as a result of the review committee's recommendations,[2] the ASC was replaced with a new structure.

Since August 1990, the professional accountancy bodies have no longer had direct responsibility for issuing accounting standards. However, although their

1. The Institute of Chartered Accountants in England and Wales, the Institute of Chartered Accountants of Scotland, the Institute of Chartered Accountants in Ireland, the Chartered Association of Certified Accountants, the Chartered Institute of Management Accountants, and the Chartered Institute of Public Finance and Accountancy.
2. Sir Ron Dearing (Chairman) (The Dearing Report), *The Making of Accounting Standards*, Report of the Committee, presented to the Consultative Committee of Accountancy Bodies, ICAEW, 1988.

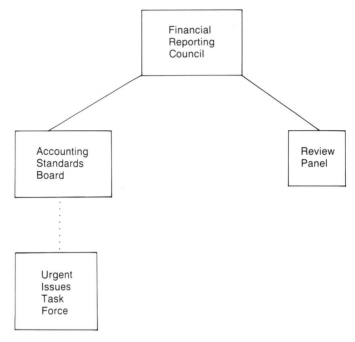

Figure 3.2   *The structure for setting and enforcing accounting standards*

specific role has changed, they continue to exert a major influence on the form and content of accounting standards. The responsibility for setting and issuing accounting standards now lies with the Accounting Standards Board (ASB). The ASB is part of a broader structure which includes the Financial Reporting Council, the Review Panel and the Urgent Issues Task Force (UITF) (see Figure 3.2).

The Financial Reporting Council (FRC) is the body charged with the broad overview of the standard setting system. Its functions include securing sufficient finance for the system, appointing the members of the ASB, the Review Panel and the UITF, 'and ensuring that their work is carried out efficiently and economically'.[3]

Although the FRC oversees the process of producing accounting standards, it has no input into the detailed rules. This is the sole responsibility of the members of the ASB, most of whom are professional accountants appointed for their technical accounting skills and expertise. The process of developing accounting standards involves the ASB in consulting with other groups before finalizing its recommendations. Normally, this can take many months, if not years, to complete (we explain this process further in Section 3.4). The ASB issues its

3. Sir Ron Dearing, 'Accounting standards: the new approach', *Accountancy*, June 1990, pp. 86–87.

recommendations in the form of Financial Reporting Standards (FRSs). At its inception in 1990, it inherited 22 extant SSAPs which continue to constitute recommended accounting practice until they are either replaced with FRSs or withdrawn by the ASB.

The UITF and the Review Panel have no predecessors in the UK. The UITF is an adjunct to the ASB. Its function is to tackle matters which require an urgent response and for which, therefore, the normal standard setting process would not be practicable. Generally, these matters are of a highly specialized nature (e.g. the first *consensus* of the UITF concerned 'supplemental interest on convertible bonds') and represent a small part of a more general issue. The more general issue might even be the subject of a current standard. Because of the highly specialized and detailed nature of these matters, we will not concern ourselves further with the activities of the UITF in this introductory accounting book.

The function of the Review Panel is essentially that of enforcing the rules laid down by the ASB and UITF. More specifically, it is concerned with monitoring departures from accounting standards by large companies. Prior to 1990, the recommendations of the ASC were not legally binding and the penalties for non-compliance were light. At worst, the relevant professional body would discipline the accountant responsible for preparing the financial statements. However, this was a rare occurrence in practice.

Since the implementation of the Companies Act 1989, all companies are legally required to state that their accounts have been prepared in accordance with applicable accounting standards and, if not, to give reasons for any material departures. This should make it easier for the Review Panel to identify companies which are not complying with the rules and, hence, to challenge their accounts. If an agreement cannot be reached with the company, the Review Panel, using powers delegated to them from the Secretary of State for Trade and Industry, may take the matter to a court of law. The courts have the power to order the company concerned to prepare revised accounts and may order that the costs be borne by the directors who were party to the defective accounts. Such action is, however, expected to be used only as a last resort.

Thus, whilst UK accounting standards remain the responsibility of the private sector (the FRC is actually a company which owns two other companies — the ASB and the Review Panel), and the new structure continues to be self-regulating (it makes and enforces its own rules), there now exists some statutory backing in the form of the Companies Act 1989.

One of the primary tasks of the FRC is to ensure that the work of developing and enforcing accounting standards is adequately funded. The annual financing requirements of the standard setting system are currently £2 million per annum plus any legal costs arising in connection with the Review Panel's work. This funding is raised from 'sponsors' who include the accountancy profession (via the CCAB), the Department of Trade and Industry, the London Stock Exchange and the banking community.

Each body within the regulatory structure — the FRC, ASB, UITF and Review Panel — is intended to contribute to the standard setting process. In Chapter 1 we drew attention to the different organizations which prepare financial statements and the wide variety of user groups which read them. Clearly, if accounting standards are to be useful to such a wide range of user groups, those groups should be represented on the bodies responsible for setting standards. A frequent criticism of the ASC was that its membership was comprised almost totally of preparers and auditors of accounting statements to the exclusion of those who use them.

In an effort to counter this criticism, the FRC draws its 25 or so members from a wider span of interests. Thus, whilst the professional accountancy bodies, industry and commerce (as preparers of accounts) are strongly represented on the FRC, some members do represent users of accounts, for example, stockbrokers and analysts, banks, trades unions and the Department of Trade and Industry. Although accountants still make the rules, through the ASB, the members of the FRC can influence the issues to be considered and the broad approach to be taken by the ASB. The success of the standard setting process depends, to a large extent, on the effectiveness with which the FRC carries out its duties.

Other sources of regulation in the UK

Accounting standards together with the Companies Acts 1985 and 1989 contain most of the regulations governing company financial reporting in the UK. However, some companies must also comply with regulations laid down in other legislation (e.g. the 1979 Banking Act), or by other institutions (e.g. the International Stock Exchange). Thus, for their shares to be listed on the International Stock Exchange of the UK and the Republic of Ireland, companies must comply with the accounting requirements set out in the International Stock Exchange's *Continuing Obligations*. The rules are mainly concerned with disclosure issues and constitute a slight extension to the disclosure requirements laid down in the Companies Act 1985. For example, listed companies must disclose additional information concerning directors' property and other transactions with the company. Essentially these requirements are intended to provide some additional protection to investors who risk their capital by further redressing the asymmetry of information which exists between directors (managers) and shareholders. As we noted earlier, in general, the larger the organization the more the participants rely upon the financial statements for their information, and the greater the need for accounting rules.

Whilst national bodies, such as the International Stock Exchange of the UK and the Republic of Ireland, are a direct source of accounting regulation, international bodies provide an increasingly important indirect source. We examine some of these international influences below.

International influences

Developments in telecommunications and transport have enabled companies to extend their business dealings to different countries and to seek the involvement of foreign investors, creditors, employees and customers. The shares of many large UK companies, for example ICI, Glaxo and British Telecom are traded on Stock Exchanges overseas, and even more companies obtain loans through an international syndicate of lenders. These developments have given rise to a need for a form of financial reporting that will satisfy the needs of users and potential users in more than one country. Hence, whilst the main sources of regulation in the UK are UK law and the UK accountancy profession, these sources respond to, and are influenced by, international developments and international bodies. For the most part, it is the second role of regulation — the standardization of financial statements to provide a higher level of comparability — which has been the subject of international pressures on UK financial reporting. Two international bodies which have influenced accounting regulation in the UK are the European Union (EU) and the International Accounting Standards Committee (IASC).

An important objective of the EU Commission, and other EU bodies, is to facilitate the flow of capital and people across the national borders of member states. It is generally accepted that this could be achieved more easily if the legal, tax and accounting systems of member states were harmonized. The EU hopes to accelerate the move towards harmonization by issuing *Directives* which must be incorporated into the laws of member states.

The Directives most relevant to financial accounting are the Fourth, Seventh and Eighth. In addition to setting out a number of disclosure requirements, the Fourth Directive lays down standard formats for the balance sheet and profit and loss account. It also adopts the principle of providing a 'true and fair view' as the overriding purpose of financial statements. The Seventh Directive is concerned with consolidated accounting (for groups of companies), and the Eighth Directive is concerned with the work and qualifications of auditors.

Some member countries had to implement major changes to their financial reporting practices as a result of the Directives. The impact was much less in the UK as many of the accounting requirements contained in the Directives were already enshrined in existing UK legislation or standards. Perhaps the biggest impact in the UK has been the conversion of flexible accounting rules previously included in accounting standards, into more rigid and binding legal requirements. We consider this issue further in Section 3.6, and again in Chapter 15.

The second major international influence on UK accounting regulations is the International Accounting Standards Committee, which issues recommendations in the form of International Accounting Standards (IASs). The IASC was founded in 1973 with the primary intention of increasing the international comparability of financial statements. Its members are drawn from professional accountancy bodies from about 80 countries. Although this body has no legal or professional authority, its standards influence the financial reporting practices of many countries, either by being adopted where no national standard setting body exists, or by being incorporated into domestic standards.

In the UK, whenever a domestic standard is produced, consideration is given to any IAS covering the same issue and an attempt is made to harmonize UK standards with those of the IASC. Consequently, when UK companies comply with SSAPs and FRSs, they are usually, although not always, complying with IASs. As the UK accountancy profession is an important influence on both the ASB and the IASC, it is perhaps not surprising that, so far, few conflicts have arisen between UK and international standards.

3.3   The context of regulation

We have noted above that both the EU and the IASC are committed to furthering the international harmonization of financial reporting. However, we must remember that the regulatory framework of the UK (and other countries) is very much a product of its own history and particular societal context.

In Chapter 1 we explained the need to understand the role and use of financial accounting in relation to the particular society in which it has developed. International differences in accounting practices result from underlying economic, legal, social and other environmental factors. Accounting has developed in response to the different needs of different users, and it is not obvious that accounting practices which have evolved naturally over many years should be discarded so readily in the search for international comparability. Just as accounting practices differ from country to country, so does the regulatory framework, the balance between public and private regulation, and the relative influence of the accountancy profession and the government on the standard setting process.

Thus, in the UK, a major part of the regulatory framework is dominated by the accountancy profession, acting through a network of self-regulatory bodies. In Germany most accounting rules are enshrined in law and it is the legal profession, rather than the accountancy profession, which is the more influential. Accounting practices and regulations similar to, but not identical to, those in the UK can be found in the USA, Canada, Australia, New Zealand and the Netherlands. In the UK, accounting regulation has developed primarily with the information needs of investors in mind. On the other hand in France, for example, the needs of government for information for taxation purposes are paramount and the accounting rules are, to a large extent, the tax rules. More legally oriented, or tax oriented accounting systems can be found in Germany, Japan, Switzerland, France, Italy and other Western European countries.

To appreciate the reasons for these differences it is necessary to explore such factors as the historical and current differences between legal systems, commercial practices and business structures; the power and influence of the accountancy profession; and government's attitude to, and control over, business organizations. We shall examine some of these factors in Chapter 15. However, a detailed study of the differences in international accounting practice and regulation is beyond the scope of this introductory text, and we refer the reader to a specialist textbook in this area.[4]

3.4   The role and usefulness of accounting standards

We turn now to a more detailed consideration of the role and usefulness of accounting standards. We saw in Section 3.2 that, in the UK at least, the accountancy profession has an enormous influence on the standard setting process and, through that, the regulatory framework. Our concern is whether accounting standards have been, or are likely to be, useful in improving accounting practice, and whether the regulation of accounts (and accountants?) is too important to be left to professional accountants. Although our discussion relates primarily to the UK, much of this section is applicable to the role and usefulness of accounting standards in many other countries.

Who should set accounting standards?

We have argued previously that management should not be given complete freedom to determine what accounting information should be included in published financial statements, and we have presented the case for some form of accounting regulation in the UK. But who should decide what information should be published? Who should make the rules? Should it be left to the accountancy profession, or are the economic consequences of accounting numbers too important for the regulation of financial statements to be left to accountants? Ideally, what characteristics and qualities should the standard setters possess?

First, they should be aware of the information needs of all users of accounts, and should appreciate the impact of different accounting methods on those needs. Second, they should be able to resolve the conflicts which exist between the needs of different users. Clearly the standard setters are in a position of power. Ideally they would exercise this power by choosing those accounting treatments which 'best' satisfy all user needs. This might be achieved by choosing between alternative accounting treatments on the basis of enhancing 'social welfare' rather

---

4. For example Nobes, C. and Parker, R., *Comparative International Accounting*, 3rd edn, Prentice-Hall International, 1991.

than the welfare of individual decision makers, i.e. standard setters might be expected to act 'in the public interest'. We might also add that they should have some knowledge of accounting!

We have explained in Section 3.2 that the major source of accounting regulation in the UK is in the form of accounting standards. Do those who currently have responsibility for setting standards possess these qualities? We have also explained that responsibility for setting accounting standards in the UK rests with the ASB, and that the ASB is comprised mainly of professionally qualified accountants. To understand whether it can fulfil its roles adequately we need to consider the process by which the ASB generates standards.

Currently, the procedure preceding the issue of a standard is broadly as follows. The ASB identifies an area of accounting practice on which it believes a recommendation is necessary. At this or later stages, the ASB may commission research into the issue from other parties or conduct its own investigations. Following this, it will prepare a draft standard in the form of a Financial Reporting Exposure Draft (FRED), containing recommendations for the measurement and disclosure of the relevant issue. If the topic is particularly controversial or difficult, or if the ASB wishes to stimulate discussion at an early stage of its deliberations, it may issue a preliminary draft of its proposals for comment in the form of a Discussion Draft (DD) or Discussion Paper. The DD would normally be circulated to selected interested parties, and their comments invited, before the ASB re-drafts the proposals in the form of a FRED.

FREDs are issued, and comments invited from the 'general public', for a period, typically, of three to six months. At the end of this period, the ASB reviews and, if appropriate, amends the FRED in the light of submissions it has received. The document is then issued as a Financial Reporting Standard (FRS) by the ASB.

We suggested above that standard setters should understand the various user needs for financial statements and be able to devise rules which, broadly speaking, are in the public interest. Does the present regulatory framework meet these requirements? Although the ASB is comprised mainly of professional accountants (from either practice or industry) and therefore unrepresentative of user needs, one could argue that users are given the opportunity to express their views during the consultative stages of draft standards thereby ensuring that the ASB is aware of different user needs. In addition, the Financial Reporting Council, which comprises representatives from various user groups, is expected to provide guidance to the ASB on its work programme and on broad policy issues. However, as it is unlikely that all views are represented equally in this process, accounting standards remain susceptible to the personal biases of ASB members and to political pressures from powerful interest groups. Whilst researchers can examine the public submissions of those organizations and individuals that comment on exposure drafts to ascertain whose views are influential, it is much more difficult to identify other (informal) sources of power, such as the influence exerted on auditor members of the ASB by their clients, or the extent to which the ASB considers the likely response of government to particular proposals. Formal power, however, is firmly in the hands of the members of the ASB. The central issue then is the extent to which the board members represent the interests of all groups who are affected by accounting standards.

We have now gained some understanding of the (essentially political) process by which accounting standards are prepared and issued. The recognition that standard setting is more of a political than a technical process leads us to the question — how useful are the accounting standards produced by this process?

The usefulness of accounting standards

We argued earlier that an important role of accounting standards is to increase the comparability of accounts by limiting the choice of alternative financial accounting treatments and by prescribing, where appropriate, a standardized accounting treatment. The aim of standardization is to ensure as far as possible that different entities apply similar accounting treatments to similar transactions. This aim could be achieved simply by prohibiting the use of all but one accounting treatment of each transaction, issue or event. This would be standardization based on *uniform* accounting practice, and could be achieved with little more than the random selection of one accounting treatment from the range available. Alternatively, standardization could be based on *best* accounting practice, which implies an evaluation of alternative treatments and the selection of that which best satisfies the relevant criteria.

This distinction reflects two of the many definitions given to the word 'standard' by the *Concise Oxford Dictionary*: ' . . . a measure to which others conform . . . ' and ' . . . a degree of excellence, etc. required for a particular purpose'.

Uniform standards of measurement are of great help in many spheres of life. For example, it is helpful for an interior designer to know that if she orders ten metres of fabric, the quantity she receives (based on the supplier's understanding of the length of a metre) should correspond to the quantity she expects to receive (based on her understanding of the length of a metre). The application of uniform standards to the preparation of accounting statements also has advantages. Perhaps the main one is that accounting numbers, both between organizations and through time, are comparable. In the extreme, if all accounting methods were standardized, two organizations which began the year with identical balance sheets, and which undertook identical transactions during the year, would report identical income numbers for the year and would have identical balance sheets at the end of the year. Under these circumstances, standardization would reduce the time and cost involved in preparing financial statements. There would be no need to include explanations of the bases upon which particular figures had been calculated because only one (uniform) basis would be acceptable.

The application of uniform accounting standards may, however, have some undesirable consequences. Such standards may limit the extent to which the preparer of accounts is able to tailor the financial statements both to meet the needs of user groups and to reflect environmental factors peculiar to the reporting entity. They may also restrict the development of accounting (towards best practice) by discouraging the preparers of accounts from experimenting with new ways of describing accounting transactions.

Similar benefits and costs would accrue to the users of the accounts. The financial statements of all reporting entities would be comparable, and there would be no need to spend time and money adjusting them to a common format and common accounting treatments before undertaking comparative analysis. However, there would be no guarantee that the uniform accounting treatment selected would provide the information required by user groups.

Although uniformity of accounting practice as described above has never existed in the UK, a high level of uniformity existed in the accounting systems of many of the former communist states of Eastern Europe. There, uniform accounts facilitated the aggregation of data for planning and control purposes, and the only user of the information was the state. Privatization and the move towards a market economy has revealed the inadequacy of such systems in providing useful information to a growing number of new and demanding user groups.

There is little doubt that, other things being equal, standardization based on best accounting practice is preferable to standardization based on uniform accounting practice. Unfortunately, this preferred form of standardization will remain unattainable unless, and until, there is agreement on what constitutes 'best' accounting practice. This problem arises because there is no conceptual framework underpinning the standard setting process — no comprehensive, coherent framework or criteria against which alternative accounting methods can be evaluated. Without such a framework, and despite the best intentions of all involved in the standard setting process, different accounting standards will continue to be based upon different (and often conflicting) criteria, and will be more likely to represent uniform practice rather than best practice. A discussion of the usefulness of a conceptual framework, and the difficulties in constructing one, is presented in Chapter 15. However, at this stage we consider it sufficiently important for our appreciation of current practice, which is described in some detail in Chapters 4 to 11, to introduce the topic.

3.5   A conceptual framework

In financial reporting, a conceptual framework is a comprehensive theoretical structure which provides a frame of reference for the development of new reporting practices and the evaluation of existing ones. In 1976, the Financial Accounting Standards Board (FASB),[5] which is the United States' equivalent of the ASB, described a conceptual framework as:

5. Financial Accounting Standards Board, *Scope and Implications of the Conceptual Framework Project*, FASB, 1976, p. 2.

> ... a constitution, a coherent system of interrelated objectives and fundamentals that can lead to consistent standards and that prescribes the nature, function, and limits of financial accounting and financial statements.

Since then, many alternative, but similar, definitions have been offered by both academics and practitioners, for example:[6]

> ... a set of basic principles that command general support and can be used to help with detailed decisions by increasing the likelihood of consistency and reducing the costs of analysis.

Whilst there is no one accepted definition, there is probably general agreement that a conceptual framework in financial reporting aims to provide a coherent set of principles or concepts which can be used as a theoretical basis for determining which events should be accounted for, how they should be measured and how they should be communicated to others. Thus, whilst a conceptual framework for financial reporting is theoretical in nature, it is intended to guide accounting practice.

In the light of the definitions reproduced above, we can identify a number of ways in which a conceptual framework might be useful in the regulation of financial reporting. It could:

- guide standard setters in establishing accounting standards;
- provide a frame of reference for resolving accounting problems which are not addressed currently in legislation or accounting standards;
- increase the level of comparability by reducing the number of acceptable, alternative accounting methods;
- help reduce the influence of personal biases and political pressures on accounting judgements;
- reduce the costs of analysis and the effort involved in resolving accounting problems;
- increase the level of user confidence in, and understanding of, financial reporting by clarifying the basis on which all accounts are prepared and presented.

Given these potential benefits, it is not surprising that standard setters around the world have, at various times, attempted to develop such a framework for financial reporting. Notable examples of conceptual framework projects are the FASB's *Statements of Financial Accounting Concepts*, the IASC's *Framework for the Preparation and Presentation of Financial Statements* and more recently, the ASB's *Statement of Principles*. We will consider the content and usefulness of these frameworks in more detail in Chapter 15.

---

6. Carsberg, B., 'The quest for a conceptual framework for financial reporting', in Carsberg, B. and Dev, S. (eds), *External Financial Reporting*, Prentice-Hall International, 1984, p. 25.

For now, it is important to note that, as yet, there is no single *agreed* conceptual framework for financial reporting to guide accounting regulators in the difficult task of standardizing accounting on the basis of best practice. This was acknowledged in 1991 by the Financial Reporting Council, which identified one of the fundamental problems of accounting standards as being 'the lack of a coherent body of thought on which individual standards can be based'.[7] However, at the time of writing, there are nineteen extant SSAPs and 4 FRSs. These standards underlie much of current practice and affect many of the computations and much of the analysis in the following chapters.

So what concepts and criteria did the ASC and the ASB use in recommending one accounting treatment at the expense of another? In the remainder of this chapter, we shall introduce the concepts, criteria and conventions underlying much of accounting practice in the UK, and shall consider whether they are consistent with our views of accounting set out in previous chapters. We shall conclude the chapter by identifying a set of criteria which will allow us, in the following chapters, to evaluate current accounting practice.

3.6 A practical framework

One of the earliest standards issued by the ASC, SSAP 2,[8] identifies four 'fundamental accounting concepts' (defined in the standard as 'broad basic assumptions which underlie the periodic financial accounts of business enterprises'), which are regarded as having general acceptability. These concepts are also included in the EU Fourth Directive and hence, since 1981, all UK companies must incorporate these four concepts into their reporting practices as a matter of law. Although it is acknowledged in the standard that the four concepts are 'practical rules' rather than 'theoretical ideals', they are recommended as 'working assumptions' to be adopted in the preparation of accounting reports. It is intended that these general rules or concepts are applied to all aspects of financial reports, even those matters not specifically covered by company law or accounting standards. The four concepts are as follows:

1. *The going concern* concept: It is assumed that the enterprise will continue to operate for the foreseeable future, and that no cessation of business or significant curtailment of operations will occur.

If a user was told that a company would soon cease trading, perhaps because it was facing bankruptcy, it is likely that she would require information different

---

7. Financial Reporting Council, *The State of Financial Reporting: a Review*, The Financial Reporting Council Ltd, November 1991, p. 7.
8. Statement of Standard Accounting Practice Number 2, *Disclosure of Accounting Policies*, The Institute of Chartered Accountants in England and Wales, November 1971.

from that which she would require if the company was expected to continue to trade profitably. She may, for example, wish to know the selling price of the company's fixed assets. This concept enables the preparers of accounts, under normal circumstances, to look beyond the immediate short-term, but it also requires them to inform users should there be any doubt over the company's ability to survive in its present form.

2.   The *accruals* (or *matching*) concept: Revenues and costs are recognized as they are earned or incurred, not necessarily when the cash flow relating to them is received or paid, and are matched with one another as far as possible. Hence the term 'matching concept' is often used instead of 'accruals concept'.

The significance of this concept in conventional accounting was introduced in Chapter 2. Its adoption means that the financial statements focus upon the economic activity of buying and selling goods and services, rather than the financial activity of paying out and receiving cash. Accrual accounting thus recognizes the business practices of buying and selling on credit, and of purchasing long-lived assets.

3.   The *consistency* concept: The accounting treatment of like items should be consistent both within each accounting period and from one period to the next.

If this concept did not apply, users of financial reports would be unable to assess whether changes observed in the measures of performance, e.g. the profit figure, were due to changes in the economic circumstances of the organization, or due to changes in the accounting treatment of certain items.

4.   The *prudence* concept: Revenues and profits should not be anticipated; they should be included in income only when realized in cash or in the form of other assets whose ultimate cash realization can be assessed with reasonable certainty. Provision should be made for all known liabilities, using the best estimate available of the size of the liabilities. In the event of conflict between this concept and any of the others, in particular the accruals concept, the prudence concept prevails.

That section of the prudence concept which refers to revenues and profits is intended to prevent the overstatement of profit. Although profit can be recorded before the cash is received, there must be a reasonable level of certainty that the cash will ultimately be received. In particular, it prohibits companies from revaluing an asset and recording the (unrealized) gain as a profit. The sections referring to the provision for liabilities and the possible conflict with other concepts, reflect the conservative nature of conventional accounting and emphasize an important objective of accounting regulation — that of protecting external participants, in particular shareholders and creditors, from unscrupulous managers.

The above concepts have been of great practical importance in the development of accounting standards in the UK. They were used by the ASC, when preparing a new standard, to aid its choice between alternative accounting methods. Although the ASC has been superseded by the ASB, many of the statements of standard accounting practice issued by the ASC are still operative, and, as we noted above, these four concepts are now enshrined in the EU Fourth Directive. They are, however, a disparate collection. Consistency and prudence are criteria for choosing between accounting methods. Going concern is an assumption about the economic position and prospects of the reporting enterprise. The accruals (or matching) concept defines a broad set of rules for measuring income. It implies that income should be based on transactions which have occurred and should represent the difference between revenues actually earned and appropriately matched costs.

The problem for standard setters has been how to apply these concepts to develop standardized accounting practices. We have noted that they might conflict with each other and yet there is little guidance on how to resolve such conflicts. Clearly, they fall far short of providing a comprehensive framework or set of criteria against which alternative accounting treatments can be evaluated. So what additional criteria should a financial reporting method strive to satisfy? What other criteria would provide useful guidelines for those responsible for developing accounting standards? Does the ASB operate within a more conceptual, comprehensive framework than its predecessor? In the following section we present what we consider to be the main criteria by which alternative accounting methods should be reported. We conclude the chapter by comparing our set of criteria with those adopted by the ASB.

3.7   Criteria for the choice of accounting method

It is the objectives of financial statements which determine the criteria by which financial reporting methods should be evaluated. We shall consider alternative objectives and criteria in Chapter 15, but at this stage we shall restrict our discussion to one objective. We believe that financial statements should provide information which is *useful* to users in making economic decisions. This is consistent with the objective of financial statements adopted by the ASB:[9]

> to provide information about the financial position, performance and financial adaptability of an enterprise that is useful to a wide range of users in making economic decisions.

We have referred repeatedly to the decision models of the users of financial statements. Hence, we believe that *relevance to user decision models* should be the

9. Accounting Standards Board, *The Objective of Financial Statements and the Qualitative Characteristics of Financial Information*, ASB Ltd, 1991.

primary criterion in choosing between alternative methods of reporting. Clearly, information which is relevant to a user's decision model is likely to be useful to that user.

Relevance

Relevance refers to the ability of information to influence the economic decisions of users. It may help them to make predictions about the outcomes of past, present or future events or it may assist them in confirming, or changing, their previous evaluations. The information may therefore be relevant by virtue of its *predictive* value or its *feedback* value. Predictive value would help users to increase the likelihood of correctly forecasting the outcome of past or present events. Feedback value would enable users to confirm or correct prior expectations.

The information must also be available to a decision maker before it loses its capacity to influence decisions. This criterion of *timeliness* suggests that the usefulness of accounting information is reduced, the longer is the time period between an event occurring and its being reported. Hence, a bank manager who is considering granting a loan to a company in the next few weeks will not be much assisted in his or her decision if he or she receives the information that the company generated a healthy cash flow in 1985. In general, one would expect the usefulness of published financial statements to diminish the longer the time lag between the reporting period and the publication date.

Reliability

Although we have selected relevance to users' decision models as the primary criterion for choosing between alternative accounting methods, it is not the only one. For example, accounting information could be highly relevant but so unreliable that to include it in financial statements may be potentially misleading. This explains, partly, why many regulators and preparers of accounts have resisted calls to include forecasts in financial statements. Ideally, we should prefer the information to be both relevant and reliable.

Reliable information should be free from error and bias. Users might therefore have more confidence in the reliability of the accounting information if they could verify the process by which the organization recorded the relevant events. However, it is not generally possible for the users of financial statements to verify the recording of each transaction undertaken by the organization. There are both too many users and too many transactions. In consequence, a limited checking of the transactions leading to items in the reports is generally carried out by an auditor.

Verifiability has two dimensions — it is concerned both with checking the documentary support for transactions, for example invoices and cash receipts, and also with their proper recording in the organization's books, i.e. that the event is recorded in the correct account. Verification thus ensures that the events took place and that they have been properly accounted for. It is not, however, concerned with whether or not the measurement methods used are appropriate, or relevant.

Sometimes, the existence of documentary support and the proper recording of the transaction are insufficient to ensure the reliability of the information. For example, an auditor could verify the purchase of a motor vehicle by examining the invoice, and could be satisfied that the transaction had been recorded correctly by checking that there had been a reduction in the cash account and a corresponding increase in the motor vehicle account. However, to verify the amount of depreciation charged during the year, the auditor would need to form an opinion as to the appropriateness of the asset life and the method of depreciation chosen by the managers.

At first, it might appear that managers' opinions are likely to be much less reliable information than 'factual' invoices. However, although they may be less verifiable, they may possess other attributes of reliability. For example, the criterion of objectivity is concerned primarily with the extent to which accounting information is free from bias. In many cases, this criterion is closely linked to the criterion of verifiability, for example, an accounting system that involves the reporting only of bank account transactions during a period would probably be more free from bias than one that involves the reporting of forecasts of future performance (although it may be less relevant). But the criterion of objectivity is broader than that of verifiability. Indeed it may be possible for information to be objective even if it cannot be verified by documentary evidence. In these circumstances the most helpful measure of the objectivity of an accounting method might be the extent to which the method reflects a consensus view. In other words, would several independent auditors arrive at the same conclusion when faced with the same set of data?

Using the idea of consensus can often reverse one's intuitive opinion as to what is, and is not, an objective measurement. For example, suppose that 1,000 spectators watch an exciting and high-scoring basketball match but receive no indication, apart from their own observations, of the score. On leaving the stadium they are asked two questions: What was the score? Was the game entertaining? One might expect intuitively that the answers to the first question would be more 'objective' than the answers to the second. Yet there may well be a greater consensus about the game's entertainment value than about its score. In this sense, the latter 'measure' is more objective than the former.

In addition to its being objective and verifiable, accounting information would be deemed reliable if users could depend upon it as a valid description of the underlying event or item. Hence, it should represent faithfully what it purports to represent and the financial statements should be truthful in that the 'financial picture' presented by accounting information should correspond to the economic events which underlie them.

For example, consider a UK company which reports sizeable cash and bank balances in its balance sheet. In the absence of any statement to the contrary, users might justifiably assume that these cash balances are freely available to the company. However, suppose now that the company conducts most of its operations overseas and that the cash and bank balances are held in a country which is subject to strict exchange control restrictions. In such a case, very few of the cash resources may be available for repatriation to the UK, and one could argue that, by reporting the foreign bank account balances as 'cash', the balance sheet does not 'represent faithfully' the underlying cash position of the company. In general, this criterion argues that the accounts should reflect the economic and financial substance of the situation, even if it conflicts with what is 'legally correct' (legally, the cash in the foreign bank is the property, or asset, of the company even though the company cannot obtain free access to the economic benefits which might result from the asset).

Comparability

It is possible that the information presented in the financial statements of a particular company is both relevant to user needs and reliable, but that its usefulness is limited because it is not comparable with information provided in previous years or by other organizations. Hence, comparability should be a criterion for choosing between alternative accounting methods.

The criterion of comparability has two dimensions: comparability through time (often referred to as consistency) and comparability between entities. As we shall see in later chapters, accountants are permitted sufficient flexibility in choosing methods of recording and reporting transactions to produce any one of a large number of figures as a measure of the outcome of a particular series of transactions. If accounting information is being used, for example, to monitor the profitability of a particular entity through time, it is important that the methods adopted to measure the components of profit are not varied from period to period. If the methods are varied, changes in reported profitability may result solely from changes in accounting methods. Similar considerations apply when aspects of the performance of two or more entities are being compared, i.e. similar underlying performances may result in very different reported measures if different accounting methods are used. Earlier in this chapter we noted that the potential lack of comparability between financial reports was an important argument in favour of regulation.

Understandability

The usefulness of accounting information depends in part on the extent to which those who use it understand the basis on which it has been prepared. Non-accountants might, for example, be surprised to learn that the reported income of an entity may bear little resemblance to the change in cash and bank balances during the period. Anyone who believes that reported income does represent the change in an enterprise's cash resources (i.e. who does not understand the basis on which income is measured) may make incorrect decisions in consequence.

Even relevant information would be wasted if it was provided in a form that could not be understood. This is not to say that the financial statements should explain every item in laborious detail. Rather, they should provide information which can be used by all, non-professionals as well as professionals, who have a reasonable knowledge of business and accounting and who are willing to study the information with reasonable diligence.

Measurability

Accounting is concerned primarily with the quantification of behaviour. It follows that, all other things being equal, a particular accounting system is to be preferred if it enables more events to be measured than other accounting systems. Thus an historical cost, transactions-based method of accounting would measure neither an increase in the value of an asset *after* it had been purchased, nor the benefit to the business of a skilled and loyal workforce.

Cost

A final criterion which clearly must be considered is the cost of providing the information. Ultimately, any accounting method must be evaluated according to the benefits it provides (i.e. the extent to which it satisfies some or all of the criteria we have discussed) and the cost involved in its implementation. Unfortunately, ascertaining the costs of providing information, like ascertaining the benefits, is substantially a judgmental process. Furthermore, the costs do not necessarily fall on those who receive the benefit — company managers and directors frequently complain that the users of accounts have benefitted greatly from the higher level of disclosure in published accounts, but that most, if not all, of the costs have been borne by the preparers of those accounts. Hence, it is often difficult to apply a cost—benefit analysis to individual accounting methods.

Choosing the best accounting method

The above descriptions of criteria that might be applied to the choice of alternative accounting methods are intentionally brief and somewhat imprecise. Our main aim at this stage is to highlight the wide range of criteria available. Ideally, we would expect accounting regulators to select that accounting method which best satisfied all of the above criteria. Unfortunately, conflicts exist which result in different methods scoring more highly under different criteria. For example, an accounting method based on the reporting of forecasts of future performance may go a long way to satisfying the criterion of relevance to user decisions but may fail to satisfy the criterion of verifiability, and hence reliability.

Conflicts between criteria complicate considerably the problem of choosing the most useful accounting method. But if a conceptual framework is to have practical relevance, some way must be found of resolving these conflicts. As a first step in resolving this difficulty we might attempt to rank the criteria, for example by gathering information from users about the criteria they think are most important to their decisions. However, such a ranking would not be a sufficient basis for establishing the most beneficial accounting method. Suppose that an agreed ranking of the four most important criteria was:

1. Relevance
2. Comparability
3. Reliability
4. Understandability

How could this ranking be used to choose between, say, method A (which is relevant and understandable) and method B (which is comparable and reliable)? In order to make this choice, we would need to quantify the importance of each criterion (perhaps by developing some form of weighting scheme). Such a quantification is unavailable at present. However, the ASB took a first step towards a ranking of criteria in its Exposure Draft, *The Objective of Financial Statements and the Qualitative Characteristics of Financial Information*, which will form the first two chapters of its Statement of Principles. The Board acknowledged the four principal qualitative characteristics of financial statements as identified by the IASC — understandability, relevance, reliability and comparability — but considered that a better insight could be gained by considering the interrelation between these characteristics and recognizing that relevance and reliability are the key characteristics that any piece of financial information must have in order to be useful.

Thus, once information has been identified as relevant and reliable, it should be presented to users in a way that enhances comparability and ensures that a reasonably diligent user will be able to understand it. The ASB presented its view of the interrelationship between these, and other characteristics, in the form of a chart, reproduced in Figure 3.3. Using the Board's terminology, qualitative characteristics are the attributes that make the information provided in financial statements useful to users. Materiality is presented as a 'threshold' quality, in that if the information is not material, it need not be considered further. The two primary characteristics are relevance and reliability. Comparability and understandability are also important, but secondary, characteristics. Information which is lacking in either comparability or understandability would be of limited usefulness, however relevant and reliable it was.

Thus the ASB is quite clear in its ranking of qualitative characteristics or criteria, and this ranking goes beyond the major characteristics. For example, the chart

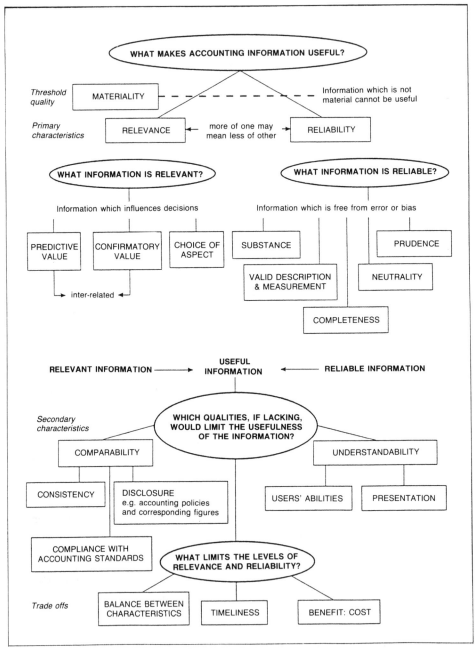

Figure 3.3 *The qualitative characteristics of accounting information*

implies that, *ceteris paribus*, if an accounting method possesses great predictive value, but at the expense of a low level of compliance with accounting standards, then it is satisfying a primary characteristic at the expense of a secondary characteristic. However, without some weighting of the criteria, it is still not possible to determine which method of accounting is 'better' when, say, method A possesses slightly more predictive value than does method B, but is much less understandable.

The ASB is aware of this problem and the chart refers to a set of 'trade-offs', situations in which more of one characteristic can be achieved only at the expense of a reduction in the level of another, or at a greatly increased financial cost. The Statement of Principles specifically refers to the need to 'achieve an appropriate balance among the characteristics', to 'balance the relative merits of timely reporting and the provision of reliable information', and to the constraint of the balance between benefit and cost. Such trade-offs are, and will remain, a matter of judgement. Consequently, it is important that those involved in preparing, using and regulating financial statements can at least agree upon the objectives of financial statements and on a ranking of the major criteria or characteristics. Such agreement will eliminate some of the more obvious conflicts and will provide a general framework within which individual preparers and auditors can exercise their judgement with increased confidence.

It would appear that the ASB has made a positive first step in developing a framework for the preparation and presentation of financial statements. In the following chapters we shall introduce many accounting methods currently practised in the UK. As we do, we shall evaluate them in the light of the objectives, criteria and characteristics referred to in this chapter. In particular, we shall assume that the objective of financial statements is to provide information about the financial position, performance and financial adaptability of an enterprise that is useful to a wide range of users in making economic decisions; and that accounting information is most likely to be useful if it is, primarily, relevant and reliable, and secondarily, comparable and understandable.

3.8 Generally Accepted Accounting Practice

In this chapter we have identified the need for some rules for financial reporting and outlined the sources and forms of such rules in the UK. Taken together, the accounting rules contained in legislation, accounting standards, stock exchange guidelines and the ASB's Statement of Principles constitute the current framework for financial reporting in the UK. Collectively these rules have come to be known as UK Generally Accepted Accounting Practice (UK GAAP).

However, as we noted in Section 3.3, the regulatory framework and the accounting practices found in the UK are very much a product of that country's underlying economic, legal, social and other environmental factors. Different factors have influenced the development of accounting practice and regulation in different countries. One might expect that regulators in the UK, where there exists a strong accountancy profession and a well established capital market, would focus upon different qualitative characteristics, and even different objectives, than would regulators in Germany, where there is a tradition of regulation through legislation and companies have traditionally raised finance from the banks rather than through the stock markets. Even societies which are considered to have many similarities with the UK have their own collection of accounting rules. For example, accounting practice in the United States is governed by US GAAP, which is not the same as UK GAAP, although the two frameworks have much in common. And yet, multinational companies operate, raise finance and publish financial statements in many different countries, and the EU issues accounting-related directives that have the force of law in several countries.

Clearly, there is a growing need to develop a (conceptual) framework that has international application. In Chapter 15, we shall examine the different objectives, accounting practices and regulatory frameworks that exist outside the UK, and review the search for an international conceptual framework. Nevertheless, despite the many different accounting methods which are used in practice, most Western financial accounting systems derive from the same basic model. It is to this model that we now turn. In the following chapters, we shall examine the traditional accounting model which underpins conventional accounting, and we shall begin to explain how one model can give rise to so many alternative accounting practices.

Discussion topics

1. Discuss the need to regulate the financial reporting practices of companies. Can you think of any arguments to support the case for no regulation?

2. Identify the different sources of accounting rules in the UK. Why do you think there is more than one source?

3. Explain the relationship between the Financial Reporting Council, the Accounting Standards Board, the Urgent Issues Task Force and the Financial Reporting Review Panel.

4. Do you believe the UK system of regulating accounting practice via both the law and the accountancy profession to be the best available? What alternative systems of regulation might be possible?

5. Distinguish between 'best' and 'uniform' accounting practice. Which characteristics do you associate with each of these two forms?

6. What is meant by a conceptual framework in financial reporting? How might it assist in regulating financial reporting?

7. Discuss the framework which has influenced the development of accounting practice in the UK. How is it different from a conceptual framework?

8. Discuss the main criteria applicable to the choice of reporting method. Can you think of any conflicts which would exist if such criteria were put into practice? Do you think that the ASB's ranking of the qualitative characteristics of accounting information will resolve these conflicts?

Further reading

Accounting Standards Board, 'Foreword to accounting standards', *Accountancy*, September 1991.

Accounting Standards Board, 'The objective of financial statements and the qualitative characteristics of financial information', *Accountancy*, September 1991.

Dearing, Sir R., 'Accounting standards: the new approach', *Accountancy*, June 1989.

Parker, R., 'Financial reporting in the United Kingdom and Australia', in Nobes, C. and Parker, R. (eds), *Comparative International Accounting*, 3rd edn, Prentice-Hall International, 1991.

Singleton-Green, B., 'The rise and fall of the ASC', *Accountancy*, August 1990.

Turley, S., 'Developments in the structure of financial reporting regulation in the United Kingdom', *European Accounting Review*, 1992, pp. 105–122.

Whittington, G., 'Accounting standard setting in the UK after 20 years: a critique of the Dearing and Solomons Reports', *Accounting and Business Research*, Summer 1989.

Woolf, E., 'That elusive conceptual framework', *Accountancy*, February 1990.

The Conventional Accounting Model of the Organization

The Transformation Process and Financial Statements

This chapter is the first of two which introduce and develop the traditional accounting model of an organization. A model can be defined as a simplified approximation of real-world conditions, constructed from a set of observed relationships. The real-world conditions which the accounting model seeks to simplify are the results of the economic and financial activities undertaken by the organization. There are three principal elements of the accounting model of the organization, representing the three main statements of financial accounting: namely the balance sheet (a statement of the financial position at a point in time), the income statement (a statement of the results of operations over a period of time), and the cash flow statement (a statement of the inflows and outflows of cash generated by the organization over a period of time).

As we saw in Chapters 1 and 2, whatever their size and complexity, most organizations — a parent—teachers' association, a cricket club, Marks and Spencer plc, the Post Office — produce some form of financial statements, although not all organizations are required to disclose the same type or the same amount of information. The structure of the organization in large measure determines the form and content of the three primary accounting statements — thus, for example, limited companies must meet the minimum disclosure requirements laid down by company law, whereas local associations and clubs are not subject to such constraints. Similarly, at present, smaller organizations are not required to produce a cash flow statement.

4.1 Accounting statements and the organization's operations

We begin this section with a statement of belief — a belief that has, in many ways, both provided the impetus for writing this book and also determined its content.

We believe that an understanding of the purpose of financial accounting, and its major financial statements, can best be achieved by placing the accounting function firmly within the context of the organization's business. To see most clearly how, and why, the accountant prepares the balance sheet, income statement and cash flow statement, it is necessary to understand the nature of the operations conducted by the organization.

To divorce the accounting figures from the operations to which they relate is to make the subject matter abstract and lifeless.

Because financial statements are prepared for a large variety of types of organizations — for example, for *public limited companies* such as ICI plc and Marks and Spencer plc; for *partnerships* such as KPMG Peat Marwick (one of the 'Big Six' firms of chartered accountants); for *individuals* or *sole traders*, such as the local butcher or greengrocer; and for *nationalized industries* such as the Post Office — we can best begin to appreciate the role of each of the elements of the accounting model by first considering the reasons *why* such organizations exist at all. In most cases the reasons are clear. In Western societies most limited companies, partnerships, sole traders and nationalized industries operate to provide goods and services to the public at a price sufficient to make profits large enough to reward their participant groups over an indefinite time period, and thus ensure their future existence. This objective, as we have seen in earlier chapters, is the prime — though by no means the only — reason for business activity in capitalist and mixed economies.

But how do such organizations generate profits? Every firm is a collection of activities that are performed to design, produce, market, deliver and support its products or services. They convert factors of production into the finished products and services which are sold to customers — the *transformation process*. For example, Nestlé uses labour, energy and machines to convert cacao, milk and sugar into chocolate bars. As we have intimated in Chapter 2, and we shall explain in detail later, the profit of the organization is not usually recognized until the finished goods or services have been sold or provided to the customer, and thus the total costs of the transformation process comprise all the costs necessary to place the goods in a saleable state (i.e. to the production costs must be added the costs of selling and marketing, administration and finance). The total of all such costs must then be deducted from the revenue to be received from the sale of goods to determine the organization's profit.

That the transformation process determines how profits are made is true of all organizations. For example, to determine how such financial institutions as banks or insurance companies make profits, we should examine and understand the *process* by which they provide financial services. National Westminster Bank plc does not manufacture finished goods in the same way as Nestlé but rather its process is to 'produce' and 'sell' such financial services as the lending of money and the providing of financial advice to customers. The costs of providing these services must be covered by the attendant revenues — in the form of interest charges, commission and fees — before a profit can be shown. Understanding the process by which an organization operates is the key to understanding the role of the financial accountant and the statements he or she must prepare.

Most organizations of any size and complexity employ a financial accountant (often with a responsibility for other accounting personnel) who records, measures and reports the results of the organization's transformation process, and its position at the reporting date. This role is, in many larger organizations, distinct and physically separate from that of the management accountant, whose primary concern as we saw in Chapter 1 is with the provision of information to managers, rather than to external parties. To illustrate the financial accountant's function we will, throughout this and subsequent chapters, devote most of our attention to the processes of manufacturing organizations. In the following section we will look at the physical process of the organization, i.e. at the method by which physical inputs are converted into physical outputs. This will provide an initial perspective of the need for, and the function of, two of the accountant's basic financial statements: the income statement and the balance sheet. In the later sections we shall see how the accountant places monetary values on these physical flows, such that all facets of the organization's operations which are recorded in the financial statements are expressed in financial terms. We shall see also how the use of cash as a medium of exchange in buying and selling physical resources provides the rationale for the preparation of a cash flow statement.

4.2   The transformation process

We shall use the term 'transformation process' to describe the process by which the organization links the markets in which it purchases its production factors, with the markets in which it sells its goods. As we have explained above, the costs of the transformation process include all costs necessary to place the goods in a saleable state, i.e. they include purchasing, production, selling, administration and financing costs. The process is illustrated in Figure 4.1 and is explained below.

Stage 1: Purchase of resources

The process begins when the organization (or more correctly, the manager responsible) purchases various factors of production. Some of these input factors might be easily guessed — for example, most manufacturing organizations require buildings, people, machines and materials to produce their goods. Others are somewhat less obvious, for example, light and heat and the supervision of labour, machines and material. The organization will normally purchase the production

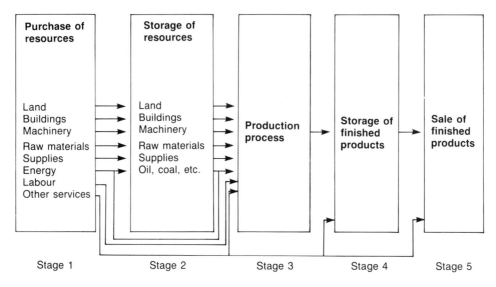

Figure 4.1 *Transformation process of a manufacturing organization*

factors in sufficient quantities to prevent shortages interrupting the flow of production. We will assume that the resources in Figure 4.1 have all been purchased and are owned by the organization. It is possible for assets such as land, buildings and machinery to be rented or leased. Labour, of course, cannot strictly be 'owned' in the way that other resources are. Rather the organization purchases the services which labour will provide.

Two types of resources may be distinguished. The first type we might term long-lived or 'fixed' resources, such as land, buildings and plant and machinery. These fixed resources constitute the organization's productive capacity, i.e. the organization can produce only up to the maximum capacity of its fixed plant and machinery (usually expressed in terms of machine hours) irrespective of the amount of raw material and labour it can acquire. Fixed resources are not expected to be consumed speedily and are intended to provide benefits or services over a long period of time. In fact, unless the organization is, say, a mining company, land is unlikely to be used up at all, and buildings only over a very long period. The useful life of plant and machinery depends upon a variety of factors such as the intensity of use, the degree of obsolescence, the amount of technological change, etc. Manufacturing plant and machinery may give services for any number of years in a range from, say, five to twenty-five. The second type of resource relates to other shorter-lived production factors such as raw materials, supplies, light and heat, etc. Raw materials, supplies and energy are used up continually and speedily in the production process.

We have, up until now, omitted any reference to the 'purchase' of labour from our categorization of fixed and current resources. At first sight, it may appear odd that the workforce is not treated as a fixed resource, even though it is likely that at least some of the workers (and managers) will remain with the organization for many years, providing services for much longer than some items of plant and machinery. However, in practice, accounts do not usually treat 'human' assets in the same way as plant and machinery, i.e. labour is not 'stored' awaiting entry to the production process, but rather it is treated as being 'used up' in production as and when weekly and monthly payments are made to the workforce.

Stage 2: Storage of resources

Once the production inputs have been purchased they must be physically 'stored' to await entry to the production process. Storage of production inputs is most easily imagined in the case of raw materials which are usually kept in a warehouse and, depending on the nature and perishability of the materials, stored in bins, shelves, vats, cartons, etc. prior to use. Production factors such as energy and lighting are not stored in bins and cartons, but rather they are drawn upon when needed (although, of course, if energy is produced by oil or coal, physical stores of such resources will exist).

The accountant describes stores of long-lived resources as *fixed assets* and stores of short-lived resources as *current assets*. The balance of production factors between those which are 'fixed' and those which are 'current' depends greatly upon the nature of the production process as well as upon the different prevailing market prices for the factors. For example, some processes are more capital intensive than others, and thus require a greater proportion of machine hours. Others are labour intensive and depend less on the use of machinery. The amounts of production factors in storage at any time represent those which have not yet entered the production process. They represent both fixed and current assets. As we noted above, labour hours are not physically stored in the same way as raw materials or machine hours — workers go home at the end of the day!

Stage 3: The production process

As and when demanded by the production manager, the raw materials are physically removed from the warehouse to the place of production (the manufacturing department), where they are 'combined' with the machinery (machine hours), the workers (labour hours), energy, consumables and other resources in predetermined proportions to produce the finished product. The length and form of the production cycle (the process of converting the raw input factors into finished goods) will depend upon the nature of the process. This is true both in terms of the number of units produced during the cycle (the production run), and also in terms of the time taken to operate the cycle. Some production cycles, for example shipbuilding and property construction, may take several months or even years; others, for example the baking of bread and the brewing of beer, take from a few hours to a few days. This helps to explain why heavy engineering companies and house builders have large amounts of work in progress (partly-completed products) whereas bakeries and breweries have very little. Whatever the method or speed of production the mechanics of the process are essentially the same — at one end, input factors enter the process in agreed proportions and, at the other end, finished products emerge.

Stage 4: The storage of finished products

On completion of the production run the finished products are transferred to the appropriate warehouse prior to their ultimate sale and delivery to customers. One major aim of the organization is to ensure that it strikes a balance between the number of finished units produced and the number which can be sold. Too much production may tie up scarce warehouse space which might be used more profitably, and also incur additional (and unnecessary) financing costs to support the high level of stocks. Too little production may entail lost orders and a deterioration in the relationship between the organization and its customers. The number of finished units in storage at any time represents the unsold amount of completed production. (In recent years many leading Western companies have adopted the Japanese practice of just-in-time (JIT) production, whereby goods are produced only when customers demand them. This reduces the amount of finished units in store but requires a very flexible and responsive production process. Some companies in the hi-tech electrical contactor industry operate on the basis of holding no work-in-progress or finished goods stock at the end of each day.)

Stage 5: The sale of finished products

The final stage of the transformation process is the sale of the completed product to the customer. A sale is usually deemed to take place when the finished goods are delivered to the customer. Thus the transformation process is complete on final delivery of the finished good, rather than on the date on which the cash is received from the customer. This final stage of the process will involve inputs from the sales, marketing and several administrative departments.

4.3   An illustration of the transformation process

We have argued strongly that an understanding of the mechanics of the transformation process is fundamental to an appreciation of the nature of the

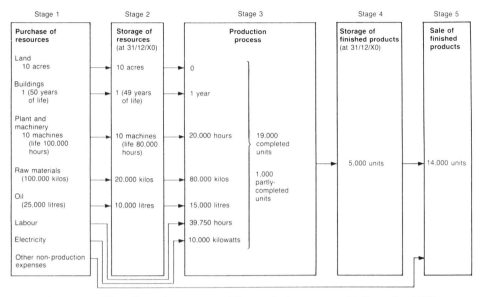

Figure 4.2 *Transformation process of Fratton Ltd — year to 31 December 19X0*

balance sheet and the income statement. We now provide a numerical illustration of the process to aid this appreciation. Figure 4.2 shows data relating to the activities of Fratton Ltd, a component producer, for the calendar year 19X0. To simplify the illustration we will assume that 19X0 is the first year of operation of Fratton Ltd, i.e. no resources are owned at 1 January 19X0.

During the year to 31 December 19X0 Fratton Ltd purchases all the resources shown in Stage 1 of Figure 4.2. Machinery, labour and materials are combined in a ratio of 1:2:4 (i.e. 1 machine hour : 2 labour hours : 4 kilos of raw material) to produce the finished component. Stage 3 shows that 19,000 completed units are produced during the year, and 1,000 units require a further 250 labour hours before they are completed, i.e. 1,000 units of work in progress are in hand at 31 December. Thus in producing the 20,000 completed and partly-completed units, Fratton Ltd has used up 20,000 machine hours, 80,000 kilos of raw materials, 39,750 labour hours, 15,000 litres of oil, and 10,000 kilowatts of electricity used to heat and light the factory. One fiftieth (i.e. one year) of the factory's useful life is deemed to have been 'used up' in production.

The information shown under Stage 2, the storage of resources, shows that, at the end of the year, there remain in storage the following physical means of production: 10 acres of land (no land having been used up in production); a factory with 49 years of useful life; 10 machines with a revised capacity of 80,000 hours (20,000 hours having been used in production); 20,000 kilos of unused raw material; and 10,000 litres of unused oil. During the year, 19,000 completed units were produced and passed into storage. Of these units, 5,000 remain in stock on 31 December (see Stage 4) and 14,000 have been sold and delivered to customers (see Stage 5). In selling these units, Fratton Ltd has incurred certain non-production expenses. In addition, 1,000 partly-completed units are in stock at the end of the year (Stage 3).

Remembering that we are, at this stage, dealing with physical quantities only, what can we glean from this simple example as to the nature of the balance sheet, the income statement and the cash flow statement?

4.4   The balance sheet — a statement of position

Suppose that the managers of Fratton Ltd wish to know the levels of physical resources owned by the company at 31 December 19X0, the last day of the first year of its operation. One way of doing this would be to stop the transformation process and take a 'mental' (or indeed an actual) photograph of the company at that date. What would the photograph of Fratton Ltd reveal? It would show the physical existence of three types of resources, corresponding with those listed under Stages 2, 3 and 4, as follows:

(a) *Stage 2: Storage of resources*
    10 acres of land
    1 factory (49 years of remaining life)
    10 machines (80,000 hours remaining life)
    20,000 kilos of raw material
    10,000 litres of oil

(b) *Stage 3: Production process*
    1,000 partly completed units

(c) *Stage 4: Storage of finished products*
    5,000 completed units

These photographs of an organization, taken at specific points in time, are equivalent to *balance sheets*, or position statements. They reflect the physical levels of resources owned by the organization, although as we shall see later in this chapter, the organization is likely to possess financial as well as physical resources. These financial resources will also appear in the balance sheet. Thus the physical balance sheet of Fratton Ltd would show a listing of the physical assets appearing under Stages 2, 3, and 4. We can now appreciate that a balance sheet includes assets in various degrees of transformation, and this can be emphasized by classifying those assets as either *fixed* or *current* (see Table 4.1).

Table 4.1 *Resources of Fratton Ltd as at 31 December 19X0*

Fixed assets	
Land	10 acres
Building	1 factory
Plant and machinery	10 machines
Current assets	
Stocks:	
Raw materials	20,000 kilos
Supplies	10,000 litres of oil
Work in progress	1,000 partly completed units
Finished goods	5,000 completed units

The categorization of assets

In practice, the listing of assets in the balance sheet is carried out in an ordered, systematic way so as to convey information in a readily understandable and comparable manner. What constitutes an appropriate ordering depends a great deal on the conventions used in particular countries. However, in most countries a distinction is normally made in an organization's balance sheet between fixed assets and current assets. The distinction is important because under historical cost accounting the rules for measuring fixed assets sometimes differ from those used to measure current assets.

Unfortunately, there is no unique rule for determining whether a particular asset should be classified as fixed or current. Even the Companies Act 'definition' which differentiates between fixed and current assets is not entirely clear. Fixed assets are defined as 'assets intended for use on a continuing basis in the company's activities' and current assets as 'assets not intended for such use'. However, broadly speaking, one or both of two tests are applied in practice: the *usage* test (in accordance with the Companies Act) and the *turnover period* test.

Under the usage test, the classification of an asset depends on its intended use. If the asset is to be held within an organization and used to generate revenue and there is no intention of immediate resale, it is classified as a fixed asset. If, on the other hand, the asset is to be used to generate revenue by being sold in its present or a modified form, or if it is to be converted into cash in some other way, then it should be classified as a current asset. According to the usage test, examples of fixed assets are plant and machinery, land and buildings, office equipment, fixtures and fittings, and motor vehicles. By the same test, current assets include items such as stocks of raw materials, work in progress and finished goods, amounts owing to the organization (debtors), and cash and bank balances.

The turnover period test, a favourite of economists, emphasizes the length of time an asset is to be retained by an organization, rather than its intended use. Thus assets which are expected to be retained for a relatively long period of time are classified as fixed assets, and those to be retained for only a relatively short time are classified as current assets. There is no precise rule for defining 'relatively long' and 'relatively short' periods of time: in many cases, however, a relatively short time is taken to be one year or less.

For most assets, the classifications given by the usage and turnover period tests coincide. Nevertheless, unusual situations can arise where the two tests lead to different classifications. For example, consider the case of a manufacturing organization that holds a stock of oil or coal to be used for heating its factories. The stock of fuel is used up, and replaced, every three months. According to the usage test the fuel is a fixed asset — it is a resource which contributes to revenue-earning activities and is not intended to be resold. Applying the turnover test, however, suggests that the fuel is a current asset — it is expected to be kept for only a relatively short period of time. This example illustrates the sort of dilemma that is sometimes faced when attempting to classify assets. In preparing accounts which must present a 'true and fair view', accountants must use their judgement to decide which classification is preferable in a particular case. Their decision should depend on the sort of information to be provided by the accounts; the task will be complicated if no clear criteria exist for making that decision. (The problem of conflicts between criteria for assessing different accounting methods was discussed in Chapter 3.)

Even if we ignore the possibility of conflict between the usage and turnover period tests, the classification of a particular asset should always be related to the nature of the firm's operations. Classification may depend on the nature of the organization owning the asset or on the purpose to which it is to be put. For example, a motor vehicle owned by a retail firm and used to make deliveries to customers is a fixed asset. The same vehicle, owned by a motor trader who intends to sell it as soon as possible, is a current asset. Similarly, a company which owns shares in another company could treat such an investment in either of two ways: on the one hand the shares should be classed as a fixed asset if the investor company owns the shares (and intends to continue owning them) so as to have some control over the decisions of the investee company. On the other hand, if the shares have been purchased as a means of investing a temporary surplus of funds, and are likely to be sold in the near future, the shares should be classified as a current asset.

4.5   The income statement — a statement of the result of operations

Suppose that, in addition to wishing to know the levels of physical resources owned by the company at 31 December 19X0, the managers wish to know also the *result* of the transformation process of Fratton Ltd for the year. Result is a tricky word. The result of a hockey match is the final score; the result of an examination is the mark awarded. Neither the match score nor the examination mark tell us anything about how the result has been achieved. We need to understand the nature of the process which produces the result. We might say that both hockey matches and examinations involve (or in some cases fail to involve) efforts on the parts of the players and students in order to produce accomplishments, i.e. that the result of an activity is the difference between what has been accomplished and what has been expended in effort. Thus to determine and understand the result of Fratton Ltd's transformation process, the managers must identify the accomplishment and effort involved in the process. We saw in Chapter 2 that the language of accounting contains certain basic principles which can help them do this.

Accomplishment is measured by the *realization* principle — which may be defined in physical terms as the quantity of finished goods sold to customers. Thus in accounting terms, accomplishment means sales and Fratton Ltd sold 14,000 components during the year. The *matching* principle identifies the amount of effort expended in producing that accomplishment. For manufacturing organizations in particular, the practicalities of this matching may be far from easy. The difficulty most frequently arises in cases where the manufacturing organization's level or volume of production does not equal its level or volume of sales, i.e. where the efforts associated with the production function do not correspond to those linked with sales.

If, for example, production exceeds sales in any period, it becomes necessary to determine how much of the effort incurred (i.e. resources consumed) in production is to be matched against the accomplishment (sales revenue) for the period and how much is to be carried forward to future periods to be matched against the accomplishments of those periods. Thus the result of Fratton Ltd's transformation process for the year ended 31 December 19X0 is represented by the difference between the accomplishment and effort in producing and selling 14,000 components. However, Fratton Ltd produced 19,000 completed units and 1,000 partly completed units during the year. Management must therefore identify which of the resources consumed during the year were consumed in producing and selling 14,000 components, and which were consumed in producing (but not selling) the remaining 5,000 completed units and 1,000 partly completed units.

Table 4.2 shows how the result of the transformation process (the income statement) of an organization such as Fratton Ltd can, in general terms, be represented.

4.6 Money as a measurement unit

In practice, the accountant does not report the organization's position and result (or performance) in purely physical terms. Perhaps the reasons are obvious. The physical resources, accomplishments and efforts listed in Tables 4.1 and 4.2 are expressed in different terms, or units of measurement, which makes it difficult

Table 4.2   *Result of Fratton Ltd for the year ended 31 December 19X0*

(Level of accomplishment — determined by the realization principle)		
Sales		14,000 units
Less:		
(Level of effort — determined by the matching principle)		
Resources consumed		
Materials	(4 kilos per unit)	56,000 kilos
Labour	(2 hours per unit)	28,000 hours
Machinery	(1 hour per unit)	14,000 hours
Buildings		1 year
Oil	(a proportion, say 14,000/20,000, of 15,000 litres)	10,500 litres
Electricity	(a proportion, say 14,000/20,000 of 10,000 kwatts)	7,000 kwatts

Result = (accomplishment less effort)

to appreciate their significance. Because such terms are not additive (e.g. 10 acres + 1 factory + 10 machines do not equal 21 units of anything!), it is not possible to form an overall view of the organization's position by adding up the total of these resources, nor of the organization's result by deducting the efforts from the accomplishments Thus in order to give some meaning to these non-comparable figures, accountants express *all* resources in terms of a common measuring unit. The measuring unit chosen is the monetary unit. As we shall see in later chapters, the use of money as a common measuring unit is not without its difficulties. This is particularly so if there is a lapse of time between the date at which the organization acquires its resources and the date at which it consumes them, and if in the intervening period inflation has affected the stability of the measuring unit.

There are several ways in which accountants can describe the resources, accomplishments and efforts of the organization in monetary terms. For example, they may use a measure of the current value or the historical cost of the resource, and we evaluate these different measures in Chapter 14. However, for the remainder of this chapter and for the immediately following chapters, we assume that assets in a balance sheet and expenses in an income statement are recorded at their historical costs. Table 4.3 illustrates how the assets of Fratton Ltd might appear in a conventional historical cost balance sheet.

4.7   Cash as a monetary resource and a medium of exchange

By expressing the organization's position in monetary terms we can build a much clearer picture of its different types of resources. Two types of resource are important — *physical* resources and *monetary* resources — and the difference between them is fundamental to an understanding of balance sheets. Most physical resources represent input factors to the production process (although

Table 4.3 *Fratton Ltd — physical assets shown on the balance sheet as at 31 December 19X0*

Fixed assets	£	£
Land	250,000	
Buildings	200,000	
Plant and machinery	100,000	550,000
Current assets		
Stocks		
Raw materials	20,000	
Supplies	3,000	
Work-in-progress	40,000	
Finished goods	240,000	303,000
		853,000

certain physical resources such as office equipment and cars do not affect the production process directly), whereas monetary resources represent the means of providing physical resources. Even though this chapter has focused on physical resources, it is obvious that many organizations would hold cash in hand, or in a bank account, and at any given date these cash balances should be recognized as part of the organization's resources.

Figure 4.3 shows the relationship between the generation of cash (the financial side of the organization's activities) and the transformation process (the physical side). Figure 4.3 is an important diagram which requires careful analysis. It shows that in order to purchase the resources required to undertake the transformation process, the organization needs *cash*; the physical activities of the organization depend for their existence upon the (prior) financial activities. Indeed, not only is cash a resource in its own right (a monetary resource), it may also be used as the medium of exchange to obtain physical resources at the beginning of the transformation process, and to sell finished goods at the end of the process. Clearly, knowledge of an organization's cash flows over a period, and its cash balances at various points in time, is crucial in evaluating both the financial performance and position of the organization. Cash generation and disbursement is the hub around which the organization revolves.

Four sources of cash are identified in Figure 4.3. In practice it is possible for the organization to draw on various sources but, for ease of exposition, we shall confine ourselves to four only: cash received from customers, who are termed 'debtors' if, as is usual in most manufacturing businesses, sales are made on credit rather than for cash; cash received from the owners of the organization; and cash received from both short-term and long-term lenders (we shall explain the difference between those two sources in the following section).

The two-way broken lines leading from the cash box to both owners and lenders require some explanation. As we noted in Chapter 1, in order to induce 'capital' contributions from both owners and lenders, the organization must usually offer some inducement, or reward, for the use of their cash in the form of annual, or semi-annual, payments. Thus lenders are rewarded by the payment of *interest*

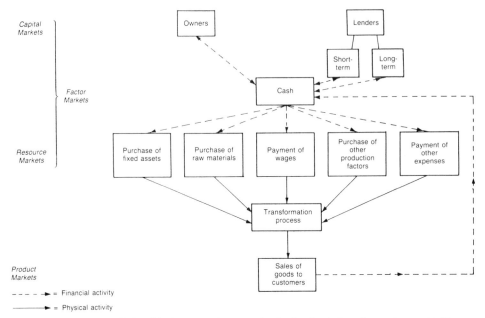

Capital
Markets

Factor
Markets

Resource
Markets

Product
Markets

---- ➤ = Financial activity

——— ➤ = Physical activity

Figure 4.3   *The relationship between the organization's physical and monetary activities*

on the funds they have loaned, and owners are rewarded by the payment of *dividends* if the organization is a limited company, or other agreed cash amounts which will depend upon the nature of the organization and its relationship with its owners. (We explore these areas further in the following section and in detail in Chapter 8.)

As well as showing the physical resources existing at the balance sheet date, Figure 4.3 suggests that the organization's photograph (balance sheet) may also reveal the existence of certain monetary resources — in particular that the organization may possess as yet unspent amounts of cash and have outstanding debts due from customers (debtors), to whom sales have already been made. Both unspent cash and amounts due from debtors are treated as current assets and

Table 4.4   *Fratton Ltd — assets shown on the balance sheet as at 31 December 19X0*

	£	£
Fixed assets		
Land	250,000	
Buildings	200,000	
Plant and machinery	100,000	550,000
Current assets		
Stocks	303,000	
Amount due from debtors	250,000	
Cash in hand	120,000	673,000
		1,223,000

thus a more complete listing of the organization's assets might appear as in Table 4.4, where the assets shown represent the total amount of resources available to Fratton Ltd with which to undertake future transformation processes.

4.8 Claims on the organization's assets

We have concentrated so far on the resources which an organization possesses at a point in time. However, we noted in the previous section that an organization requires a sufficient stock of monetary resources (cash) in order to purchase its physical resources, to pay the expenses of running the business, and to reward the providers of funds. In most cases this cash will come from the regular operations of the organization in the form of cash receipts from customers. In other cases the cash will be raised, at irregular intervals, from external sources, i.e. from 'capital' contributions from owners and lenders. (We will deal in Chapter 8 with the advantages and disadvantages of raising cash from different sources.) Hence, to obtain a complete picture of an organization's financial position at any point in time, the balance sheet should disclose not only the assets of an organization, but also the claims of interested parties on those assets, i.e. the sources of finance used to acquire those assets.

The total amount of the claims on an organization's assets are, for balance sheet purposes, categorized as being due to owners (the ownership interest in the organization) or to other claimants (lenders or debt holders) (see Figure 4.4). The difference is of great practical importance. Claims which belong to the owners (in a limited company these owners are called shareholders), comprising the subscribed capital and the undistributed or 'retained' profits, will generally be paid directly to them only if the organization ceases trading.[1] We should here distinguish between the capital subscribed by the shareholders and any dividends declared and payable by the company on such capital. Dividends represent claims

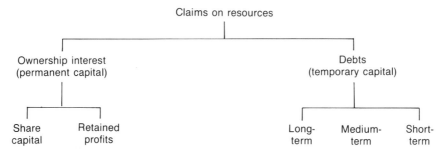

Figure 4.4 *Forms of claims upon the organization's resources*

1. Companies in the UK are permitted to purchase their own shares from shareholders if certain conditions are met.

due and are classified as current liabilities (see below) — whereas the subscribed capital will, in most cases, be repaid only on liquidation of the company. If, however, there is an active market in the organization's shares, which allows them to be traded freely, the owners may sell their shares on the (stock) market at a price determined by forces operating within the market (i.e. at the market price).

Claims belonging to debt holders are of a different order. These claims must be satisfied by particular dates, both as to the capital repayment of the debt and as to the interest on the debt. Repayment dates, and thus the very nature of debts themselves, may vary greatly. For example, an organization may borrow money which does not require repayment for ten or twenty years. This borrowing is classified for balance sheet purposes as a long-term debt. Alternatively, it may negotiate an overdraft with its bank, or an agreement of the time limit within which it must pay its suppliers of raw materials, both of which might be of the order of say three months. These debts are of a very short-term nature. Within these more extreme repayment dates exists a wide variety of other possibilities. The underlying point of importance is that the date of debt repayment determines its balance sheet classification. Thus, debts which are due for payment within one year are termed *current liabilities*; debts due for payment after more than one year are termed either medium-term or long-term capital, depending upon the time period involved. There is no hard and fast rule which differentiates the medium from the long term.

As all resources of the organization are, by definition, provided by some party, whether shareholders or debt holders, the total of the balance sheet assets must always equal the total of claims on such assets. (We will see shortly how this equality is preserved by means of the bookkeeping system.) We stress that this equality of assets and claims holds whatever method is used to 'value' the assets

Table 4.5 *Balance sheet in horizontal form — as at 31 December 19X0*

	£	£		£	£
Fixed assets			Ownership interest		
Land and buildings		100,000	Share capital		100,000
Plant and machinery		210,000	Retained profits		150,000
		310,000			250,000
Current assets			Long-term debt		
Stocks	100,000		10% loan (repayable in 19X8)		130,000
Debtors	50,000				
Cash in hand	10,000	160,000			
			Current liabilities		
			Bank overdraft	20,000	
			Trade creditors	40,000	
			Taxation due on profits	30,000	
					90,000
		£470,000			£470,000

Table 4.6 *Balance sheet in vertical form — as at 31 December 19X0*

	£	£	£
Fixed assets			
Land and buildings			100,000
Plant and machinery			210,000
			310,000
Current assets			
Stocks		100,000	
Debtors		50,000	
Cash in hand		10,000	
		160,000	
less: Current liabilities			
Bank overdraft	20,000		
Trade creditors	40,000		
Taxation due on profits	30,000		
		90,000	70,000
Total assets less current liabilities			380,000
Long-term debt			
10% loan (repayable in 19X8)			130,000
			£250,000
Represented by:			
Ownership interest			
Share capital			100,000
Retained profits			150,000
			£250,000

and liabilities. We can now present a more complete view of the organization's balance sheet, which shows not only the resources available, but also their means of financing, and thus the claims upon them.

Tables 4.5 and 4.6 offer two different balance sheet forms for a limited company. Table 4.5 shows a balance sheet in the more traditional 'horizontal' form, which shows assets on the left and claims on the right. This format is used extensively in many EU countries including Belgium, France, Germany, Italy and Spain. Table 4.6 shows exactly the same information in a vertical form. This lists the company's assets and then deducts the claims of creditors and lenders. The residual balance represents the net assets financed by the owners of the business. This vertical format is favoured by most companies in the UK.

Note that having been classified as fixed or current, the assets are listed within the two main headings in terms of their *liquidity*. In the UK and other EU countries, the list of balance sheet assets is as shown in Tables 4.5 and 4.6, beginning with the least liquid fixed asset (land) and ending with the most liquid current asset (cash). In the USA the reverse is true. The actual method of listing is unimportant in itself — it is simply the result of conventions adopted by the accounting and legal professions in previous years — but consistency of application is important. It aids understandability and facilitates the comparison of financial statements over time. For ease of understanding we will list balance sheet assets in the manner used in the UK and throughout the EU.

4.9   Revenue recognition in the income statement

Revenue recognition at the date of sale

We have defined a (manufacturing) organization's accomplishment for the period as relating to the number of units of finished goods which had been delivered and invoiced (or billed) to customers. Some justification for this definition is needed. It is by no means intuitively obvious that this is the only possible way of measuring accomplishment, and thus of determining revenue. Figure 4.5 suggests that at least two other alternative measures of accomplishment might be used; for example the total number of units produced (or even partly produced) during the period might be regarded as an appropriate measure of accomplishment, or, alternatively, the total amount of cash collected from customers might seem to be an appropriate measure. In order to decide how to measure accomplishment, and thus how to recognize revenue, certain criteria are needed. Two criteria in practice dominate all others and thus determine the recognition of revenue:

(a) all the work to be performed on the finished goods has been completed;
(b) the finished goods have been accepted by the customer, such that the organization has received an asset either in cash or as a promise to pay cash.

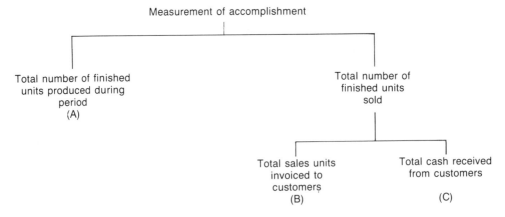

Figure 4.5 *Measures of accomplishment*

The application of these two criteria makes it easier to understand why revenue is recognized at the point of sale (point B in Figure 4.5) rather than at the time of production (point A) or the date of the receipt of cash (point C). In other words the physical act of invoicing (and in most cases delivering) goods to the customer indicates that all work on, and all services relating to, the finished goods have been performed and that the buyer has accepted the goods, either by a cash payment or by a promise to pay at some future date. Many business transactions are conducted on the latter basis, i.e. a certain period of credit is granted to the customer (say 30 days) at the end of which payment for the goods is required. It is at the point of sale that an objective measurement of the amount of revenue to be realized can first be made. This revenue constitutes the agreed price for the sale of the goods between the buyer and the seller. In Chapter 5 we will consider the problem which arises when the expected revenue is not in fact received, i.e. when customers do not pay in full for the goods they have bought.

Revenue recognition at the date of production

Based upon the arguments presented above, it would in most cases be inappropriate for the organization to measure its accomplishments in terms of units produced. This is because the organization cannot be certain that the work involved in production of the goods constitutes all the work or services necessary to place them into a saleable condition; nor can it be sure that the finished production will be accepted by customers, in terms of either quantity or agreed price.

Revenue recognition at the date of cash receipt

The third alternative method of recognizing revenue is to wait until the cash relating to the sale has been received from the customer. This method has some appeal. After all it is the receipt of cash from the sale of its products which largely determines the organization's ability to continue its operations. The reasons for its rejection within the income statement as the basis of recognizing revenue are probably two-fold.[2] In the first place the experience which the organization has gathered over previous years will provide a good basis for predicting the amount of cash to be received from customers, such that recognition of revenue at the point of sale constitutes a relatively objective basis for its inclusion in the income statement. Second, and more importantly, the accountant's income statement serves the function of identifying causes and effects. One such cause represents the sale of goods to customers, the effect of which is to generate in the same, or future, periods a receipt of cash from the same customers. If the organization

---

2. See Chapter 2 for a more general discussion of the relative merits of cash flow and accrual accounting.

recognized its sales revenue in cash terms such a relationship would be lost. For example, if cash received from customers during one period relates to sales made in the current and in preceding periods, then cash received from sales will not be 'matched' with the sales to which it relates. The following example of St James Ltd will help to make this clear.

Illustration

During the year to 31 December 19X2, St James Ltd sells 100,000 units of product X at £2 each, and 50,000 units of product Y at £3 each. Receipts during 19X2 were £325,000 which were made up as follows:

	£
Cash from sales of product X during 19X1 20,000 units × £1.50 (19X1 price)	30,000
Cash from sales of product Y during 19X1 10,000 units × £2.50 (19X1 price)	25,000
Cash from sales of product X during 19X2 75,000 units × £2	150,000
Cash from sales of product Y during 19X2 40,000 units × £3	120,000
Total cash received	£325,000

If the amount of £325,000 is shown as sales revenue in St James Ltd's income statement for 19X2 the effect would be to mismatch the sales with the cash received, by including in sales revenue cash received from the previous year's sales (£55,000) and excluding from sales revenue cash receivable from the current year's sales of £80,000 (i.e. 25,000 units of product X at £2 and 10,000 units of product Y at £3). Thus the correct matching of cause and effect in respect of sales would recognize for 19X2 sales revenue of £350,000, as follows:

	£
Revenue from product X (100,000 units at £2 per unit)	200,000
Revenue from product Y (50,000 units at £3 per unit)	150,000
Total revenue	£350,000

4.10   The cash flow statement

It should be clear from the arguments put forward in the last section why the cash received figure of £325,000 should *not* be reported as sales revenue in St

James Ltd's income statement for 19X2. This is not to suggest it is unimportant — far from it. In fact, the most fundamental point that can be made about the financial situation of any business organization is that it cannot survive without cash. Survival is conditional upon the receipt of cash sufficient to meet the cash payments due by the organization. However, the figures representing cash receipts and cash payments are disclosed, not in the income statement, but in the third major financial statement — the cash flow statement.

In previous sections we have seen that the balance sheet describes an organization's financial position at a point in time, and that the income statement describes what happened to the organization during the period between two balance sheets. However, the income statement reflects only operating activities, the matching of the organization's accomplishments (the amount of revenue recognized during the period) and its efforts (the expenses incurred in earning revenue for the period). It does not reflect the financing activities (e.g. the issue of shares), or the investing activities (e.g. the purchase of fixed assets) of the organization during the year.

The statement of cash inflows and outflows includes all of the financial activities shown in Figure 4.3. It differs from the income statement in that (i) it reports the cash paid during the period for fixed assets, raw materials, wages, etc., rather than matching the consumption of those resources to the sales generated; and (ii) it reports the cash received from customers rather than the sales made to customers. It also includes cash received from owners and lenders, neither of which would appear in any form in an income statement. Thus a cash flow statement for Fratton Ltd for 19X0 (its first year of operations) would include cash payments for the purchase of land, buildings, machinery, raw materials, supplies, energy and labour, and cash receipts from shareholders and lenders who provided the company's long-term capital, and from customers who bought the company's products. We provide an illustration of a cash flow statement in Chapter 5.

We have now reached a most important stage of our analysis. It has been our intention in this chapter to provide an intuitive 'feel' for the contents of the three main accounting statements — the balance sheet, the income statement and the cash flow statement — by understanding the processes undertaken by any particular organization. A few simple essentials of accounting should now be apparent. For example, when a customer buys a skirt at Marks and Spencer, she is reducing the level of finished goods in Marks and Spencer's *balance sheet*; the cash paid by the customer is a cash inflow in the *cash flow statement* and increases Marks and Spencer's cash resources in the *balance sheet*; and, provided that its costs of transformation are less than the price paid for the skirt, Marks and Spencer will show a profit on this transaction, which will appear in its *income statement*. In other words, an organization's financial statements are (financial) models of the results of the organization's activities and operations during a particular period. An understanding of the underlying activities and operations of the organization should greatly facilitate an appreciation of the nature and role of its financial statements.

In the following chapter we explain how the balance sheet, the income statement and the cash flow statement are generated from the accountant's recording technique of double-entry bookkeeping, and we develop further the links that exist between the three statements.

Discussion topics

1. Describe the transformation processes of the following types of organization:
   (a) a brewery
   (b) a bank
   (c) a food retailing company.

2. Describe the five main stages of the transformation process of a manufacturing organization. Discuss the relationship between the stages, and the relationship between the various stages and the contents of the financial statements.

3. Discuss the relationship between the various physical assets of an organization. What determines their balance sheet classification?

4. Discuss the production cycles of manufacturing organizations with which you are familiar. What determines the length of such cycles?

5. Explain the terms 'accomplishment' and 'effort'. Do you believe these terms are applicable to accounting? What types of revenue or expense would you expect to see under each heading?

6. Describe how assets are classified in a UK balance sheet. Can you think of any assets which do not fall easily into the 'fixed' and 'current' categories?

7. Why do particular organizations prepare their balance sheets on particular dates? What factors are likely to determine the choice of balance sheet date?

8. Why is it important to balance the amounts of physical and monetary assets owned by a manufacturing company? What are some of the possible effects of an imbalance?

9. Distinguish between the claims of owners and lenders. Why are the distinctions so important?

10. Explain the 'revenue recognition' principle and discuss the alternative ways in which revenue might be recognized.

11. What problems, if any, are inherent in the recognition of revenue at the time of sale? How might such problems be alleviated?

12. Explain the difference between the income statement and the cash flow statement.

CHAPTER

5

Financial Statements and the Accounting Equation

There are three principal statements of financial accounting: the balance sheet (a statement of the financial position at a point in time), the income statement (a statement of the results of operations over a period of time) and the cash flow statement (a statement of the inflows and outflows of cash generated by the organization over a period of time). In Chapter 4 we introduced these three financial statements and related them to the organization's transformation process. In this chapter we explain how each statement is generated from the accountant's recording technique of double-entry bookkeeping and we develop further the links that exist between the three statements.

The first part of this chapter describes a major element of the accounting model of an organization — its balance sheet. In many ways the balance sheet, which is sometimes referred to as 'the statement of financial position', is the most basic statement in all accounting. Some justification for this claim might be provided by the following observations:

(a) The balance sheet is the basis for the derivation of other important statements such as the income statement and the cash flow statement.

(b) The balance sheet, as we shall see later in this chapter, is the formal expression of the *accounting equation*, the bookkeeping equation which seeks to ensure that the assets of the organization are exactly equal to the claims on them.

(c) The balance sheet is the most 'intuitive' and easily understood document of accounting. Most of us, at some stage in our lives (for example, when negotiating a loan from a bank or a building society) will be required to compute a listing of our possessions. Such a listing of possessions is a major element in the construction of a balance sheet.

In the previous chapter we suggested that the purpose of a balance sheet was to present a photograph of an organization at a particular point in its life. We should stress that a balance sheet can be drawn up at any date in an organization's life. Thus the fact that ICI plc prepares its annual balance sheet on 31 December, and British Telecom plc (BT) prepares its annual balance sheet on 31 March does not mean that these large organizations could not produce balance sheets at dates other than 31 December or 31 March. The notion of a photograph of an organization holds at any time in its life, although of course, in practice, very frequent compilations of balance sheets would be costly and probably unnecessary.

5.1   The preparation of the balance sheet

The importance of historical costs

Having discussed the content, layout and purpose of the balance sheet in Chapter 4, we are now in a position to show how it might be constructed. Most balance sheets are, in practice, constructed on the basis of actual events which have occurred and which affect the organization — that is to say, they are constructed on the basis of *transactions* undertaken by the organization. Thus, the contents of balance sheets and, as we shall see later in this chapter, those of income statements too, are in most cases measured in terms of the transaction's actual or 'historical' cost. From the introduction of double-entry bookkeeping (in the fifteenth century), until the last twenty years or so, historical costs have been accepted, with little counter-argument, as the most appropriate basis for compiling balance sheets and income statements. The possible need to include the current costs of resources (i.e. today's costs) has been recognized only since the 1970s, as rates of inflation in many countries increased to levels far greater than had been experienced previously.

Thus, a conventional system of accounting has evolved, generally known as *historical cost accounting*, which is widely used throughout the Western world. However, it is important to recognize that historical cost accounting is not the only transactions-based approach to the measurement of income and value, nor is it the only system of accounting that can be implemented within a bookkeeping framework. Alternatives exist which involve the use of measures of the current, rather than the historical, costs of resources, and which continue to be the subject of much debate in accounting circles. However, both for the purpose of explaining and illustrating the bookkeeping framework and also to show how assets appear in balance sheets and expenses appear in income statements, we shall, in the following few chapters, remain with historical costs. We do this for two reasons. First, historical cost accounting remains the most widely used method of preparing accounting reports, and second, the adjustments required to convert historical cost figures to current costs are not very difficult — as we shall see in Chapter

13 — although they may have a significant impact on measures of income and position.

The basis of double-entry bookkeeping

Because the initial construction of a balance sheet represents our first sortie into the financial accountant's most traditional field — the field of bookkeeping — we will deal only with a very simple series of transactions. In later chapters we will increase the degree of complexity such that we will be able ultimately to prepare a full set of accounts (balance sheet, income statement and cash flow statement) from a more detailed set of transactions. Let us, however, begin our explanation of bookkeeping techniques by reiterating some basic relationships. We have suggested previously that each resource of the organization is the subject of a counter-claim, i.e. that it is owned by some third party. This in turn suggests that all transactions affecting the organization have two aspects, one recording the *acquisition* of a resource, the other recording the *source* used to finance the acquisition. This is fundamental to an understanding, not only of double-entry bookkeeping, but of the balance sheet too.

An organization begins with nothing. To operate, it must raise finance to buy resources such as equipment and raw materials. Suppose a company borrows £5,000 from a bank to buy a machine. The company now has an *asset*, a machine, with a cost of £5,000, and a *claim*, by the bank, on its resources, of £5,000. We can view the same situation in terms of sources and uses of funds. The bank loan of £5,000 is a *source* of funds, and the machine represents the *use* of those funds by the company. Thus each transaction comprises two elements and is represented by twin (or double) entries in the books of account — hence the term double-entry bookkeeping. The technique of double-entry bookkeeping bears a certain resemblance to the Newtonian law of physics, which states that for every action there is an opposite and equal reaction. One side of the entry is recorded on the left-hand side of the appropriate account and is termed a *debit* entry; the other side of the entry is recorded on the right-hand side of (usually) a different account and is termed a *credit* entry.

It is most important to realize that the terms debit and credit, when applied to the technique of bookkeeping, mean neither more nor less than left-hand side (debit) and right-hand side (credit) respectively. In no way does debit denote or imply anything 'bad' nor credit anything 'good'. What types of entry appear on the debit and credit sides we shall explain shortly. Of course, one major benefit of recognizing this duality of transactions, and using it as the basis of the recording system, is its provision of an automatic check on the arithmetical accuracy of the entries in the accounting books. This automatic check greatly helps any third party, for example the auditor, who wishes to verify the accuracy of the accounting records.

The accounting equation

It follows from the technique of double-entry bookkeeping that, at any point in time, after a number of transactions have occurred, total assets must equal total claims — in other words, all of the assets of the business, at any point in time, are subject to the claims of debt holders or owners. This relationship, which is commonly known as the *accounting equation*, may be expressed in the following form:

Assets = Liabilities + Ownership interest

The 'debits' and 'credits' previously referred to now come into play. The left-hand (or debit) side of the accounting equation is represented by the organization's assets, the right-hand (or credit) side by the ownership interest and liabilities. This leads us to a simple rule. Assets (or *uses* of funds) always appear on the debit side of the account; ownership interest and liabilities (or *sources* of funds) always appear on the credit side. This identity is expanded upon in Section 5.7 when we consider a wider variety of uses and sources of funds than that considered so far, but we cannot stress too strongly that the underlying principle remains exactly the same. We will repeat it once again, as follows:

Left-hand side = **Debit** = **Uses of funds**
Right-hand side = **Credit** = **Sources of funds**

The basic form of the accounting equation provides a first guide to the foundations of double-entry bookkeeping. The following example of Mr Elm shows how the accounting equation can be used to illustrate the effect of a particular type of transaction. These transactions do not involve any change in the wealth of the organization and have no impact on the income statement. In Section 5.7 the example is enlarged to accommodate transactions which affect the income statement and thus the wealth of the organization.

5.2   An illustration of double-entry bookkeeping

Mr Elm started business on 1 January 19X0. He undertook the following transactions during his first week of business.

1. 1 January: Paid £2,000 into the business bank account from his personal savings.
2. 3 January: Borrowed £1,000 at an interest rate of 12% p.a. repayable on 30 June and paid it into the business bank account.
3. 4 January: Bought a machine for £1,800, paying for it from the business bank account. The machine is expected to give service for 3 years, at the end of which it will be worthless.
4. 5 January: Bought 1,000 units of stock at £1 per unit, paying for them from the business bank account.

Table 5.1 *Mr Elm — accounting entries: transactions (1)–(4)*

Transaction	Bank	+	Other Assets		=	Ownership interest	+	Liabilities
	£		£			£		£
(1)	2,000					2,000		
(2)	1,000							1,000
(3)	(1,800)		1,800 (Machine)					
(4)	(1,000)		1,000 (Stock)					
	200	+	2,800		=	2,000	+	1,000
	Machine		1,800					
	Stock		1,000					

N.B. Numbers in brackets signify negative amounts (i.e. decreases in assets).

The accounting entries reflecting the above set of transactions are shown in Table 5.1.

Transaction (1) involves an introduction of £2,000 into the business bank account. Because the cash comes from Mr Elm's personal savings, and because Mr Elm is the owner of the business, the credit entry appears under Ownership interest. The term 'Capital account' is most commonly used in practice to describe an individual's 'Ownership interest'. Remember, we are recording the transactions of Mr Elm's business, which are separate from the personal transactions of Mr Elm. The business began with nothing. Mr Elm represents a source of funds to the business. The business now has an asset of £2,000 (cash) and a corresponding claim of £2,000 by Mr Elm. If we were to draw up a balance sheet on 2 January it would show the following:

> *Current assets*
> Cash   £2,000
>
> represented by:
> *Ownership interest* (Capital account)   £2,000

Succeeding adjustments to this balance sheet are provided by transactions (2) to (4). Transaction (2) increases further the cash balance, while correspondingly creating a liability in respect of the repayment of the loan. The entry for transaction (3) reflects a swap of assets, the purchase of the machine being financed from the business's own resources. Similarly, transaction (4) swaps cash of £1,000 for stock of £1,000. The final line of the accounting equation represents the position of Mr Elm's business (i.e. his updated balance sheet) after his first four transactions. The business has assets of £3,000 (bank balance £200, machine £1,800 and stock £1,000) represented by ownership interest of £2,000 and liabilities of £1,000. This is in accordance with the basic principle of the accounting equation, i.e. entries involving the uses of funds are recorded on the left-hand side, and entries involving the sources of funds are recorded on the right-hand side of the equation. The business has raised £3,000 and used it to buy a machine and some stock, and to invest the remainder in the bank. Equally, one could describe the situation in terms of assets and claims — the business has assets of £3,000, upon which both the bank and Mr Elm have claims.

The balances can now be taken directly from the accounting equation to construct a horizontal balance sheet or can be rearranged as a first step towards constructing a vertical balance sheet:

$$\text{Assets} - \text{Liabilities} = \text{Ownership interest}$$
$$£3,000 \qquad £1,000 \qquad\qquad £2,000$$

Thus, the interest of the owners in a business is equal to the assets of the business less the amounts owing to third parties. Adopting this approach, Mr Elm's balance sheet at 6 January would appear in vertical form as follows:

Mr Elm's balance sheet at 6 January

	£	£
Fixed assets		
Machine		1,800
Current assets		
Stock	1,000	
Cash	200	
	1,200	
less: Current liabilities		
Loan	1,000	200
Total assets less current liabilities		£2,000
represented by:		
Ownership interest (Capital account)		£2,000

5.3   General principles of double-entry bookkeeping

So far in this chapter we have seen how an organization's assets and the claims on its assets are affected by particular types of transactions. We have examined only transactions which do *not* affect the wealth of the organization, i.e. transactions which have no impact on the income statement. It is possible to identify four distinct sets of such transactions, each of which represents a flow of value from one account to another. These are as follows:

1. *Transactions involving an **increase in assets** accompanied by an identical **decrease in assets***
   Suppose that an organization buys raw materials for £1,000 for which it pays in cash. Two aspects of the transaction are relevant. The organization has both increased its assets (stock of raw materials) by £1,000, and

decreased its assets (fall in the cash balance) by £1,000. In effect a swap of assets has taken place.

2. *Transactions involving an **increase in assets** accompanied by an identical **increase in claims***

   Suppose that the organization finances the purchase of raw materials by obtaining a loan of £1,000. Once again the transaction has two aspects. As in the previous case, the organization has increased its assets (raw materials) by £1,000, but here no corresponding decrease in assets has ensued. The organization has not used its own funds to buy the materials but rather has contracted a liability of £1,000 due to be repaid to the lender at some agreed future date, i.e. it has increased the claims on its assets.

3. *Transactions involving a **decrease in assets** accompanied by an identical **decrease in claims***

   Suppose now that the organization repays the £1,000 loan originally granted to purchase the raw materials. This transaction constitutes the reverse of that in (2) above. Its dual aspects represent the reduction of £1,000 in the organization's cash balance, and an equivalent reduction in the amount due to the lender of £1,000.

4. *Transactions involving an **increase in claims** accompanied by an identical **decrease in claims***

   Suppose finally that the organization borrows £1,000 from its bank in order to repay the existing loan of £1,000. None of the organization's assets is involved in this particular transaction — it is simply exchanging one liability (the bank overdraft) for another liability (the loan) of an equal amount.

We can summarize the above four sets of transactions as follows:

1. An *increase in assets* accompanied by an identical *decrease in assets*
2. An *increase in assets* accompanied by an identical *increase in claims*
3. A *decrease in assets* accompanied by an identical *decrease in claims*
4. An *increase in claims* accompanied by an identical *decrease in claims*

Before we look at the preparation of a more detailed balance sheet we must understand more fully how wealth is created by the organization's activities. We thus turn our attention in the following section to the basis and compilation of the income statement.

5.4 The income statement

In this and the immediately following sections we will look at the second of the three major components of the accounting model of the organization — its income statement or profit and loss account. The two terms are synonymous but we prefer, and will continue to use, the former. It also seems to us a little incongruous that an account can apparently show both a profit *and* a loss at the same time! (However we should stress that the term 'profit and loss account' is used widely in practice. Indeed the Companies Acts 1985 and 1989 refer to Profit and Loss Accounts rather than Income Statements.) The purpose of the income statement is to provide information on the success (or failure) of the organization's operations for the period under review. The income statement occupies a position of great prominence with users of published accounts. For example, one of the statistics which is widely used to encapsulate a large company's performance for a period is its earnings (or income) per share; hence the primary emphasis given by users to the income statement, rather than to the balance sheet.

In Chapter 4 we suggested that the results of the organization's operations were determined by its *accomplishments* for the period less the *efforts expended*. We defined accomplishments in terms of sales revenue generated during the period and efforts in terms of expenses incurred during the period. The two guiding principles to be used in determining whether revenue or expense should enter the income statement we explained to be the *realization* principle and the *matching* principle respectively. A major purpose of the following sections will be to look in detail at some of the many different issues raised by the application of these two overriding principles to be used in determining income. However, before we examine these important issues we briefly turn our attention to an important underlying concept in the construction of an income statement — the relevant *accounting period*.

5.5   The accounting period

As we have noted previously, an income statement is a financial report of the result of an organization's operating activities over a specified period of time. We may, intuitively, think of such a period as comprising one year and indeed, most organizations do present *annual* reports of their performance and financial position. Yet there is no obvious reason why this should be so. The benefits to be derived from the use of such assets as buildings, machinery and, in some cases, stocks, last well beyond one year and in certain industries, for example heavy engineering and construction, the production process itself may last for over a year.

In former times accounts were not prepared annually, but rather at the end of a major activity or venture(s) undertaken by the organization. We explained this initially in Chapter 2. The organization of today cannot, however, wait until the completion of particular activities or ventures before accounts are prepared. Regular and timely information is required by owners and others to monitor the performance of the organization, to assess the efficiency of its management, to make decisions on the granting or withdrawal of funds and, in particular, to compare the performance of the organization over time and against other organizations. Thus an accounting period of uniform length (i.e. one year) is chosen. This uniformity does not, of course, extend to a common *date* for the determination of annual performance. Not all organizations report their performance on a calendar year basis (i.e. with a year-end of 31 December) and thus a variety of accounting year-ends exists. For example, the income statements of ICI plc and Nestlé SA (Switzerland) are prepared for the year to 31 December; those of British Telecom plc and Singapore Airlines Ltd (Singapore) for the year to 31 March and those of Bass plc and Siemens AG (Germany) for the year to 30 September. Very large organizations are also required to produce semi-annual information, so that their owners do not have to wait until after the end of the accounting year before they learn of the firm's progress. We should note here also that the published accounts of most organizations do not appear until some time after the end of their accounting year — a three-month time lapse is not unusual — to allow compilation and checking (by the auditors) of the accounting records.

5.6 The layout of the income statement

Income statements, which, unlike balance sheets, relate to periods of time rather than points in time, are usually constructed on a functional basis, i.e. the efforts involved in generating sales revenue are linked and classified according to their respective functions (for example, production, distribution, administration and finance). Thus a (summarized) income statement of a limited company might appear as follows:

Oval Ltd
Income Statement for the year to 31 December 19X0

	£000	£000
Sales revenue		400,000
less: Cost of goods sold (production costs)		250,000
Gross profit		150,000
less: Selling and Distribution costs	40,000	
Administrative costs	50,000	
Financing costs	30,000	120,000
Profit before taxation		30,000
Taxation		10,000
Profit for the year		20,000
Dividends		5,000
Profit retained for the year		£15,000

Conventionally, at least two income or profit figures are struck within the income statement. The first of these is the *gross profit* or 'gross margin' which reflects the difference between sales revenue and the cost of goods sold. The gross profit figure gives an indication of profit available to meet non-production expenses. The second figure is that of the *profit for the year* or 'net profit' or 'net income' which reflects the difference between sales revenue and all expenses incurred during the period. As we will see later in this chapter, the net income belongs to the owners of the organization and, if no dividend is paid (see below), is added to their ownership interest (i.e. it increases the value of their stake in the organization) in the closing (end of period) balance sheet.

Taxation and dividends

It is a feature of most economic structures that a tax is levied on the income of organizations, computed in a way determined by legislation. In France, Germany and several other European countries the 'profit before taxation' figure is usually the figure upon which the tax charge is based. The tax rules in these countries are virtually identical to the accounting rules. However, in the UK it is rarely the case that any organization's 'profit before taxation' represents its taxable profit. UK tax law prescribes a very detailed list of expenses and allowances which can be charged or claimed by organizations in computing the amount of tax payable to the government, and many of these differ from the accounting expenses charged in the income statement

Taxation appears in the income statement as a charge against income and, because taxes on organizations are not usually paid until after the period to which they relate, tax will also appear in the balance sheet as a current liability. Limited companies (both public and private) pay *corporation tax* on their profits; individuals and partnerships pay *income tax*. The tax rules and rates applicable to the different business structures change constantly. Yearly adjustments to the rules and rates appear in the Finance Acts passed by Parliament. The subject of business and personal taxation is a complex matter beyond the scope of an introductory text, and we discuss it no further in the main text of this book. However, we shall provide a brief explanation of the computation of the tax charge and tax liabilities of E.H. Booth and Co. Ltd in the sections 'An illustration from practice' at the end of the appropriate chapters.

In the case of a limited company it is usual practice to appropriate or distribute some of the income to the owners and to retain the balance within the company. Such a distribution is termed a *dividend*. If a dividend is to be paid, the profit for the year added to ownership interest — the profit retained for the year — will be reduced by the amount of the dividend.

To give a little more flesh to the rather bare income statement shown above, Figure 5.1 gives some indication of the types of expenses which might be included under each of the functional headings. The list is by no means exhaustive but

Production costs
  Raw materials used
  Wages of factory workers and supervisors
  Depreciation of factory equipment
  Insurance and rent of factory
  Factory heating and lighting

Selling and Distribution costs
  Advertising
  Salespersons' salaries and commissions
  Depreciation of vehicles
  Fuel costs

Administrative costs
  Salaries of Managing Director, accountant and office staff
  Computing facilities
  Office heating, lighting and telephone
  Depreciation of office machinery

Financing costs
  Interest payable on loans
  Bank overdraft charges
  Bad debt provisions

Figure 5.1 *Types of expense appearing in the income statement*

should give some clues to the different types of expense within the income statement.

5.7   The expanded accounting equation

In Section 5.1 we introduced the basic accounting equation as being:

  Assets = Liabilities + Ownership interest

and we showed, with a very simple set of transactions, how a new balance sheet is struck after each transaction. Because none of these transactions involved any change in the organization's wealth, we did not need to consider how the income statement (which measures changes in wealth) and the accounting equation are linked. This link will now be explored via the example of Mr Elm, introduced above. Before dealing with a further set of transactions, a more general analysis of the accounting equation is necessary.

  We have explained in Chapter 4 that the ownership interest of the organization comprises two elements: the amount of capital paid in by the owners and the amount of profit or income which has been retained in the business (i.e. which has not been distributed as dividends). Thus we can extend the basic equation as follows:

Ownership interest

$$\overbrace{\text{Assets} = \text{Liabilities} + \text{Paid-in capital} + \text{Retained income}}$$

The income statement for Oval Ltd presented in Section 5.6 shows that an organization's net income is simply the excess of revenues over expenses. Therefore the retained income portion of the ownership interest may be rephrased to represent the (retained) excess of revenues over expenses. This allows the basic equation to be further expanded to show:

Ownership interest

$$\overbrace{\text{Assets} = \text{Liabilities} + \text{Paid-in capital} + \text{Revenues} - \text{Expenses}}$$

This 'final' equation shows clearly that the changes in wealth of the organization, generated by the excess of revenues over expenses, belong to the owners and that, in consequence, the revenue and expense accounts are merely (important) subdivisions of the ownership interest account. Let us now return to the illustration of Mr Elm to see how a set of transactions involving changes in wealth is treated in the new, expanded accounting equation.

Section 5.2 showed that the balance sheet of Mr Elm, after four transactions, was as follows:

$$\begin{array}{ccc} Assets & = & Liabilities & + & Subscribed\ capital \\ \text{£3,000} & & \text{£1,000} & & \text{£2,000} \end{array}$$

Mr Elm now undertakes the following additional transactions, all conducted in January:

5. 10 January: Sells 100 units of stock for £2 per unit, paying the proceeds into the bank account.
6. 31 January: Uses the machine to customize the remaining 900 units of stock, which are sold for £5 per unit. Pays the proceeds into the bank.
7. 31 January: Pays the following expenses from the bank account:

Wages	£1,500
Advertising	£100
Insurance	£500
Interest	£10

The accounting entries reflecting the above transactions are shown in Table 5.2.

The first line of the equation comprises the closing balance sheet arising from transactions (1) to (4). Transaction (5), the sale of 100 units of non-customized stock on 10 January for £2 per unit, generates a profit to the business. Applying the accounting convention of matching, the historical cost of the stock is matched with the revenue realized from its sale, giving a profit of £100 (sales revenue of £200 less the historical cost of the stock sold of £100). How should transaction (5) be recorded? In fact the transaction comprises two identifiable components:

Table 5.2 *Mr Elm — accounting entries (5)–(7)*

Transaction	Bank £	+ Machine £	+ Stock £	= Liabilities £	+ Paid-in capital £	+ Revenues £	− Expenses £
Opening balances from entries (1)–(4)	200	1,800	1,000	1,000	2,000		
(5)	200		(100)			200	(100) Stock
(6)	4,500		(900)			4,500	(900) Stock (50) Depreciation
(7)	(1,500) (100) (500) (10)	(50)					(1,500) Wages (100) Advertising (500) Insurance (10) Interest
						4,700	(3,160)
Transfer of net income					1,540	(4,700)	3,160
	2,790	1,750	0	1,000	3,540	0	0
	+	+	=	+	+	−	

(a) Revenues are increased by £200 (the amount of the sale) and the receipt of the sale proceeds causes an increase in the asset 'bank balance' of £200.
(b) Disposal of the 100 units of stock, used up in generating sales, causes a reduction in the asset 'stock' of £100 — the historical cost of the stock sold — and this expense (cost of stock sold) is matched against sales in the expenses column.

The difference of £100 represents a profit to the business resulting from its trading activities and belongs to whoever is legally entitled to receive the profits of the business; in this case Mr Elm. Thus Mr Elm's ownership interest is increased by a net amount of £100, the profit on the transaction.

Transaction (6) involving the customization and sale of the remaining stock, has a number of aspects. The sale itself results in an increase of £4,500 both in the bank balance and in sales revenue. We must also recognize the cost of the customized stock that has been sold. The cost of the non-customized stock was £900 and this amount should be subtracted from stock and treated as an expense. The cost of using the machine to process the stock is less straightforward. The cost of acquiring the machine is £1,800. However, in return for this expenditure the business expects to receive productive services for three years. The nub of the problem is this. The business has paid £1,800 to acquire machine services which span more than one accounting period and, in order to calculate that part of the total cost to be matched with current revenues, some procedure is needed to allocate the total cost of the machine between all periods which are expected to benefit from its services. That part of the total cost which is treated as an expense of the period under consideration is called the *depreciation charge* for the period. Alternative methods of calculating depreciation were mentioned briefly in Chapter 2 and will be considered in more detail in Chapter 6. At this stage, we adopt the most common method of allocating the cost of a fixed asset, which is known as the 'straight-line' method. This method involves spreading the cost of the asset in equal parts over its estimated total life. In the case of Mr Elm's machine, the straight-line method gives an annual depreciation charge of £600 (£1,800 divided by 3), and thus a monthly charge of £600 divided by 12 = £50. This amount is deducted from the asset 'machine' and is also treated as an expense. Transaction (7) involves the payment of four items of expense: wages, advertising, insurance and interest for the month of January. In each case, the amount of the payment is subtracted from the bank balance and treated as an expense.

All transactions for the period have now been entered in the accounting equation. It remains to transfer net income (the difference between the revenue and expense columns) to ownership interest. Net income for the period is £1,540 (£4,700 − £3,160) and this amount is added to ownership interest. The totals of the columns in the accounting equation now represent the position of Mr Elm's business on 31 January. The business has assets of £4,540 (a bank balance of £2,790 and a machine with a depreciated cost of £1,750) represented by ownership interest of £3,540 and a loan of £1,000. The ownership interest balance comprises capital paid in of £2,000 and the net income for the period of £1,540.

Table 5.3 *Mr Elm — accounting statements for the month ended 31 January*

Income statement for the month to 31 January	£	£
Sales		4,700
less: Cost of stock used	1,000	
Depreciation of machine	50	
Wages	1,500	
Insurance	500	
Interest	10	
Advertising	100	3,160
Net income for the month		£1,540
Balance sheet at 31 January		
Assets		
Machine		1,750
Bank balance		2,790
		4,540
less: Liabilities		
Loan		1,000
		£3,540
Ownership interest		
Balance at 1 January		2,000
add: Net income for the month		1,540
		£3,540

Finally we can present the accounting statements for Mr Elm's business which portray its performance for the month of January and its position as at 31 January. The income statement for the month (a restatement of the revenues and expenses columns of the accounting equation) and the balance sheet at the end of the month (a restatement of the totals of each column of the accounting equation) are presented in Table 5.3.

Although Mr Elm's business generated a profit of only £1,540 during its first month of trading, the balance of cash at the bank on 31 January is £2,790. Clearly, there must be differences between the revenues and expenses recorded in the income statement and the cash receipts and payments recorded in the bank (cash) account. This is usually the case for most organizations and in the following sections we shall identify a variety of items which give rise to different figures in the income statement and the cash flow statement. Of course, as can be seen from Table 5.2, items which appear in the Bank account must have an identical corresponding entry in another account. If that corresponding entry is not in the Revenues or Expenses columns, it must be in another *balance sheet* column. The same is true for items which appear in the Revenues and Expenses columns.

Hence, some cash flows affect asset and liability accounts in the balance sheet but do not affect the income statement; and some revenues and expenses affect asset and liability accounts in the balance sheet, but do not affect the bank or cash account. It is because there are so many such items that users of financial statements need three financial statements — a balance sheet, an income statement and a cash flow statement — to even begin to understand the activities of an organization.

5.8   Income and cash flows

The income statement provides information on the results of an organization's operations for the relevant accounting period. We have seen that it is based upon two guiding principles — the *realization* principle and the *matching* principle. Revenues for a period are recognized at the point of sale, and expenses are matched to the revenues they create. This means that revenues are usually recognized before cash is received from the customer, and that many large cash expenditures, for example the purchase of a machine, are matched to revenues over a number of years. In addition some operating expenses may be incurred (and therefore charged to the income statement) in one period, but paid in a later (or earlier) period, e.g. electricity bills paid three months in arrears. Such expenses are *accrued* and charged to the income statement in the period in which they are incurred. In the remainder of this chapter we examine each of these potential differences between figures in the income statement and cash flow statement.

Revenue recognition

The recognition of revenue at the point of sale is not without its problems. We noted in Chapter 4 that revenue is recognized at the point of sale, rather than at the date of cash receipt. For most credit sales the cash is received by the organization within one or two months following the sale. Hence the difference between the revenue reported in the income statement and the cash receipt reported in the cash flow statement is simply one of timing. However, few organizations are lucky enough to transact all their business with customers who pay in full at the due date. Most organizations have experience of customers who fail to meet their debts, either in full or in part. It is therefore normal to anticipate the likelihood of some default in payment by customers, and to provide against the current year's revenue for such a possibility. If provision is not made against the current year's revenue, future periods may be charged with the effects of actions taken earlier — in this case actions concerning the granting of credit to unreliable customers. In other words there would be a mismatching of costs with revenues, such that the performance of the organization for the particular period would not mirror the results of actions taken in that period. Suppose, for example, a company made credit sales of £200,000 during 19X2. If it anticipates that 5% of this sales revenue recognized in 19X2 may prove to be uncollectable, it will reduce its net income for 19X2 by 5% of £200,000, or £10,000, and classify this amount in its income statement as a 'provision for doubtful debts'.

Revenue recognition is not a problem for Mr Elm. His business sells its stock for cash, as do Sainsbury plc, Tesco plc and many other retailers. There is no timing difference between the recognition of revenue and the receipt of cash, and no risk of bad debts. We must look elsewhere to explain the difference between the reported income and the net cash flow.

Matching expenses to revenues

Having looked, in both this and the previous chapter, at the problems of revenue recognition, we now turn to the other, more tricky, side of the income statement — the measurement and recognition of expenses. We should here draw a distinction between the often used but often misunderstood terms expenditure and expense. An item of *expenditure* is any cash payment made by the organization; an item of *expense* is any cost used up in earning revenue. Thus, not all items of expenditure are, as we shall see, treated as expenses, nor are all expenses necessarily represented by cash expenditure. For example, the purchase of shares in another company is an expenditure, though not an expense; depreciation of an asset is an expense though not an expenditure.

In principle, the recognition of periodic expenses is straightforward — just as efforts are matched with accomplishments, so are expenses matched with their associated revenues. However, for manufacturing organizations in particular, the practicalities of this matching may be far from easy. The difficulty most frequently arises in cases where the manufacturing organization's level or volume of production does not equal its level or volume of sales. If, for example, production exceeds sales in any period, it becomes necessary to determine how much of the expenditure incurred in production (e.g. how much labour, raw materials, use of machinery, etc.) is to be matched against the sales revenue for the period and how much is to be carried forward to future periods to be matched against the sales of those periods. The problem is thus one of determining the production or product costs for the period. Recognition of costs which do not attach to products is less difficult. Thus periodic costs such as general and administrative expenses are treated as expenses in the year in which they are incurred.

The determination of product costs represents one of the accountant's major problems. It is an important issue because it can significantly affect both the organization's income (via the charge for the cost of goods sold in the income statement) and also the value of stock shown in the balance sheet. We thus devote most of Chapter 7 to its consideration.

The matching of production expenses to sales is not a problem in the case of Mr Elm. All the stock produced during January is sold by the end of the month.

Table 5.4 *Mr Elm — cash flow statement for the month ended 31 January*

	£	£
Cash received from customers	4,700	
Cash payments to suppliers	(1,600)	
Cash paid to employees	(1,500)	
Cash inflow from operating activities		1,600
Interest paid	(10)	
Cash outflow from servicing finance		(10)
Purchase of fixed assets	(1,800)	
Cash outflow from investing activities		(1,800)
Owners' capital paid-in	2,000	
Loan	1,000	
Cash inflow from financing		3,000
Increase in cash		2,790

Therefore, all expenditure incurred in production is matched against the sales revenue for the period. In fact, by selling all of its stock for cash within the accounting period, Mr Elm's business has generated operating cash flows very similar to its operating profit. Hence, the principal reasons for the difference between the profit for the period and the increase in the cash balance must lie elsewhere. They are identifiable from an examination of Tables 5.1 and 5.2. The cash received from Mr Elm and the loan creditor is not revenue and has no impact on the income statement; the cash paid out to purchase the machine is not reflected in the income statement where only one month's depreciation of the machine is charged, i.e. the purchase is a cash *expenditure*, the depreciation is an *expense*.

These individual differences emphasize the fundamental difference between the income statement and the cash flow statement — the income statement reflects only *operating* activities over the accounting period; the cash flow statement reflects the consequences of *operating, investing* and *financing* decisions over the same period. Table 5.4 illustrates the comprehensive nature of the cash flow statement.

5.9   Accruals and prepayments

In the following final sections of this chapter we consider one further, common reason for the possible difference between reported income and cash flows — the importance of accruals and prepayments in determining income.

Table 5.5 *Ms Anfield's transactions*

During the year to 31 December 19X0, her first year of business, Ms Anfield engages in the following transactions:

1. Purchases 1,000 components at £12 per unit.
2. Pays suppliers £8,800 in respect of component purchases.
3. Pays lighting and heating costs of £2,000. An additional amount of £300, relating to the year to 31 December 19X0, is due but unpaid at the end of the year.
4. Pays six months loan interest to Mr Trafford. The loan of £10,000 was contracted on 1 January 19X0 and bears interest at 12% p.a.
5. Sells 800 finished units at £30 per unit.
6. Receives £21,000 from customers in respect of sales of finished goods.
7. Pays rent of £7,500 covering a period of fifteen months from 1 January 19X0.
8. Pays business rates of £1,250 covering a period of fifteen months from 1 January 19X0.

The meaning of accruals

The concept of accruals is central to the transactions-based approach to the measurement of net income and the determination of financial position. This approach, as we have explained, involves matching costs and revenues to determine net income. In consequence, it is necessary to understand how to incorporate the following types of adjustments into the measurement of performance:

1. Costs and expenses incurred which have not yet been paid (*creditors* or *accrued expenses*).
2. Revenues earned for which payment has not yet been received (*debtors*).
3. Costs or expenses paid, the benefits from which will not arise until a subsequent period (*prepayments* or *payments in advance*).

These different types of adjustments will now be illustrated by means of a numerical example, relating to the activities of Ms Anfield for the year to 31 December 19X0. These activities, which represent only a part of Ms Anfield's total activities for the year, are listed in Table 5.5.

Creditors and accrued expenses

Although very similar in principle, a distinction is sometimes drawn in practice between creditors and accrued expenses. The term 'creditors' is generally used to refer to amounts owing to, and billed by, suppliers of raw materials, components, etc., whereas 'accrued expenses' is used to indicate amounts owing in respect of other items of expenditure which may not yet have been billed. In the case of Ms Anfield, examples concerning creditors arise from transactions (1) and (2). Ms Anfield buys components during the year for £12,000 and pays her suppliers only £8,800 by the end of the year. Thus the amount she still owes at 31 December 19X0 (creditors in respect of component purchases) is £3,200. Transactions (3) and (4) provide examples of accrued expenses. Both the amount of £300 owing for lighting and heating and the £600 owing for interest are accrued expenses at 31 December.

Debtors

An example of the treatment of debtors is provided by transactions (5) and (6). Ms Anfield sells 800 components for a total of £24,000 and receives £21,000 from customers by 31 December. The balance still owing to her at that date (debtors in respect of sales) is therefore £3,000.

Prepayments

Transactions (7) and (8) provide examples of prepayments. The payments of both rent and business rates cover a period beyond the end of the year under consideration. For example, the rent payment of £7,500 covers the period of fifteen months from 1 January 19X0. Hence £6,000 (12/15 of £7,500) relates to the current year (19X0) and £1,500 (3/15 of £7,500) relates to the next year (19X1). The same consideration applies to the payment for rates. The three months' portions of rent and rates which relate to the next accounting period (£1,500 for rent, £250 for rates) are classed as prepayments.

5.10   The accounting treatment of accruals

In this section we describe the accounting treatment of each type of accrual. Note that we use only the appropriate headings within the accounting equation (i.e. Assets/Liabilities/Ownership interest/Revenues/Expenses) to explain each transaction. A complete set of the accounting entries is produced in Table 5.6.

1. Creditors

In order that the accounting records reflect accurately the cost of all the stock bought during the year, it is necessary to ensure that both purchases made and paid for, as well as purchases made and not yet paid for (at the end of the year) are included in the total cost. This is achieved in two stages:

(a) Increase stock of components (assets) and increase creditors (liabilities) by

Table 5.6 Ms Anfield — accounting entries (1)–(8)

	Assets				=	Liabilities			Income	
	Stock +	Debtors +	Prepayments +	Cash	=	Creditors +	Accruals + ...		Revenues −	Expenses
	£	£	£	£	=	£	£		£	£
Transaction										
(1)	12,000					12,000				
(2)				(8,800)		(8,800)				
(3)				(2,000)			300			(2,000)
										(300)
(4)				(600)			600			(600)
										(600)
(5)	(9,600)*	24,000							24,000	(9,600)
(6)		(21,000)		21,000						
(7)			7,500	(7,500)						(6,000)
			(6,000)							
(8)			1,250	(1,250)						(1,000)
			(1,000)							
	2,400 +	3,000 +	1,750 +	850	=	3,200 +	900 +		24,000 −	(20,100)

* Cost of 800 finished units sold = $\dfrac{800}{1000} \times £12,000 = £9,600$

the total amount of purchases for the year. Thus, taking the figures from transaction (1), we have:

Assets (stock) = Liabilities (creditors) + ... + Revenues − Expenses
   £12,000   £12,000

(b) Decrease cash (assets) and decrease creditors (liabilities) by the payments made to suppliers during the year. Thus, using the figures in transaction (2), we have:

Assets (cash) = Liabilities (creditors) + ... + Revenues − Expenses
   −£8,800   −£8,800

Note that these transactions have no impact on the income statement and that the amount appearing in Ms Anfield's balance sheet at 31 December 19X0 for creditors will be £12,000 − £8,800 = £3,200.

2. Accrued expenses

The matching of costs and revenues to arrive at a net income figure for the year dictates that the income statement should be charged with all expenses which relate to the particular year, irrespective of their date of payment. The treatment of accrued expenses *per se* is no different; it is simply necessary to increase the expense in the income statement by the amount due but as yet unpaid, and to create a liability for the same amount. Thus using the figures in transaction (3) which relate to the amount accrued we have:

Assets = Liabilities (accruals) + ... + Revenues − Expenses
            £300   − £300

The entry in respect of the costs actually paid of £2,000 is:

Assets (cash) = ... + Revenues − Expenses
   −£2,000   − £2,000

Thus the total charge in the income statement for lighting and heating costs is £2,300. The balance sheet at 31 December 19X0 will show £300 as accrued expenses, within the current liabilities section.

A similar procedure is adopted for the treatment of the six months' interest due on the loan from Mr Trafford as per transaction (4). Ms Anfield owes £600 for the period July−December 19X0. This gives:

Assets (cash) = Liabilities + ... + Revenues − Expenses
                   £600   − £600

The entry in respect of the loan interest already paid of £600 is:

Assets (cash) = ... + Revenue − Expenses
   −£600   − £600

Thus the total charge in the income statement for loan interest is what we would expect for a loan of £10,000 at an annual interest rate of 12%, i.e. £1,200. The balance sheet will show £600 as an accrued expense.

3. Debtors

To ensure that the income statement reflects the full amount of sales for the year it is necessary, as we explained in relation to the treatment of creditors, to make two entries in the accounting records, as follows:

(a) Increase debtors (assets) and increase sales revenue by the full amount of goods sold during the year. Taking the figures from transaction (5) gives:

Assets (debtors) = ... + Revenues − Expenses
£24,000   £24,000

(b) Increase cash (assets) and reduce debtors (assets) by the amount paid by debtors. Taking the figures from transaction (6) gives:

Assets
Debtors + Cash
−£21,000 + £21,000

Thus the amount appearing in Ms Anfield's balance sheet at 31 December 19X0 for debtors will be £24,000 − £21,000 = £3,000.

4. Prepayments

The requirements of the matching concept apply equally to prepayments as to accrued expenses. In this case it is necessary to exclude from the income statement any expenses which have been paid in advance of the period to which they relate. Thus the following entries would be made for the rental expenses (transaction (7)):

Assets   = ... + Revenue − Expenses
−£7,500 (Cash)
+£7,500 (Prepayment)
−£6,000 (Prepayment)   −£6,000 (Rent)

As prepayments are cash payments made in advance of the expense being incurred, the first entry represents the creation of a prepayment, which is treated for balance sheet purposes as a current asset. At the end of the year the prepayment is reduced by £6,000 (i.e. the yearly rental charge) and expenses increased by the same amount. The balance of the prepayment (£1,500) represents the prepayment of rent for the first three months of the following year.

Similar arguments hold for the payment of rates as per transaction (8). The entries are as follows:

$$
\begin{array}{lcl}
\text{Assets} & = \ldots + & \text{Revenues} - \text{Expenses} \\
-£1,250 \text{ (Cash)} \\
+£1,250 \text{ (Prepayment)} \\
-£1,000 \text{ (Prepayment)} & & -£1,000 \text{ (Rates)}
\end{array}
$$

5.11   Accruals: some further considerations

We now pursue further the question of accruals, and consider what happens in the next accounting period to the closing balances for creditors, accrued expenses, debtors and prepayments. Together with all the other balances on the bottom line of the accounting equation (arising from the other transactions undertaken by the organization) they form the basis for the balance sheet at the end of the current period. *Together with the other balances, they also provide the first line of the accounting equation entries for the next accounting period.* As far as accruals are concerned, their subsequent impact is as follows. In the next period, the amount of the cash paid to suppliers will not relate wholly to purchases made in that period, i.e. some of the cash paid will be used to reduce, or eliminate, the amount owing to suppliers (the opening creditor) at the beginning of the period. Similar considerations apply to accrued expenses, debtors and prepayments. The impact of one period's closing accruals on the costs and revenues of the next period is perhaps most clearly explained by considering the general relationships between costs and revenues, on the one hand, and cash payments and receipts on the other. A study of these relationships also serves to clarify further the nature of the accrued costs and revenues which are matched in conventional accounting income statements.

The relationship between the cost of raw materials acquired (purchases) and cash payments to suppliers is:

> Purchases = Cash paid to suppliers + Closing creditors
>   − Opening creditors

In Ms Anfield's case, purchases for 19X0 are:

> Purchases = £8,800 + £3,200 − £0 = £12,000

The same type of relationship holds with accrued expenses. Hence the charge for an expense in an accounting period is:

> Expense = Cash paid for + Closing accrued − Opening accrued
> charge   expense item   expense   expense

In other words, the charge against income for a period is the cash payment during the period plus amounts incurred but not yet paid at the end of the period, minus amounts paid during the period that were owing at the start of the period (i.e.

that relate to the previous period). For example, Ms Anfield's lighting and heating expense for 19X0 is:

Lighting and heating expense = £2,000 + £300 − £0 = £2,300

Suppose that, in 19X1, Ms Anfield pays lighting and heating costs of £2,700, and an additional amount of £100 relating to the year to 31 December 19X1 is due but unpaid at the end of the year. It is clear that £300 of the cash payment relates to the amount outstanding from the previous year and that £2,400 of the cash payment relates to the lighting and heating expense incurred in 19X1. Thus Ms Anfield's lighting and heating expense for 19X1 is:

Lighting and heating expense	= Cash paid	+ Closing accrued expense	− Opening accrued expense
£2,500	= £2,700	+ £100	− £300

Similar considerations apply to debtors and prepayments. Thus the sales revenue for a period is:

Sales revenue = Cash received + Closing debtors − Opening debtors

For Ms Anfield, sales revenue for her first year of business is:

Sales revenue = £21,000 + £3,000 − £0 = £24,000

Finally, the expense charge for an item subject to prepayments is:

Expense charge	= Cash paid for expense item	+ Opening prepayment	− Closing prepayment

Note in this final case that the opening (prepayment) balance increases the charge for the year while the closing balance decreases it. So, for example, Ms Anfield's rent cost (expense charge) for 19X0 is:

Rental expense = £7,500 + £0 − £1,500 = £6,000.

Of course it is possible that an expense is prepaid at the beginning of the year and accrued at the end of the year (or vice versa). However, by merging the prepayments and accruals equations we can identify a comprehensive relationship which will cover all eventualities. For example, suppose that in 19X1, Ms Anfield pays rent of £4,000, but that the rent for the month of December 19X1 (£500) is outstanding at the year end. Her rent cost (expense charge) for 19X1 is:

Expense charge	= Cash paid for expense item	+ Closing accrued expense	− Opening accrued expense	+ Opening prepayment	− Closing prepayment
£6,000	= £4,000	+ £500	− £0	+ £1,500	− £0

The above expressions are of great importance. As we have noted, they explain

Table 5.7 *Ms Anfield — accounting entries in the cash flow statement and income statement*

	Cash	Revenues − Expenses	Difference
	£	£	£
Payment to suppliers/cost of goods sold	(8,800)	(9,600)	(800)
Lighting and heating	(2,000)	(2,300)	(300)
Interest	(600)	(1,200)	(600)
Receipts from debtors/sales	21,000	24,000	3,000
Rent	(7,500)	(6,000)	1,500
Rates	(1,250)	(1,000)	250
Total Net Cash Inflow/Profit	£850	£3,900	£3,050

the relationship between figures representing cash receipts and payments in the cash flow statement and figures representing revenues and expenses in the income statement.

Table 5.7 presents the accounting entries which would appear in Ms Anfield's cash flow statement and income statement as a result of the eight transactions in Table 5.5. We can see that during the year to 31 December 19X0 the business generated a profit of £3,900, but a cash surplus of only £850, a difference of £3,050. Cash generated was only 22% of the profit generated. One reason for the difference is that Ms Anfield made sales of £24,000 but collected (by 31 December 19X0) only £21,000 from debtors. However, the time lag in receiving cash from debtors is only one of many reasons for the difference between net income and net cash flow. In fact, not one of the eight transactions generated a figure in the income statement which is identical to the related cash flow. This situation is not uncommon for most organizations. Indeed, as we noted earlier in this chapter, there may be far greater differences if we consider cash flows other than operating cash flows — for example, the cash expenditure on the purchase of a fixed asset and the obtaining of a loan from the bank.

We stated in Chapter 2 that no business organization can survive without cash. Survival is conditional upon the receipt of cash sufficient to meet the cash payments due by the organization. Yet the performance of an organization as measured by its income statement may, in certain circumstances, bear little resemblance to its performance as measured by its cash flows. The cash flow statement is important therefore not only in explaining the changes between two balance sheets, but also in providing an alternative view of the organization's performance.

Throughout this book the text includes frequent descriptions of the actual financial accounting practices of 'real-world' organizations. In addition, at the end of each of several chapters, we shall illustrate the various concepts and techniques introduced during that chapter by reference to the published accounts of E.H. Booth and Co. Ltd (Booths), an old, established company which owns and operates 21 supermarkets in the North-West of England. Booths' Annual Report and Accounts 1992 are reproduced in full in Appendix 1 following Chapter 18. In order to make sense of these sections it is essential that the reader refers to the relevant pages in the appendix.[1]

5.12 An illustration from practice — E.H. Booth & Co. Ltd

The balance sheet

The balance sheet of Booths (page 11 in Appendix 1) is presented in the vertical format. It contains the balances on the various accounts as at 4 April 1992, the company's year end. As is required by law, comparative figures for the previous year are also presented. This makes it easier for users to make comparisons between the two years and to identify major differences.

At first glance the balance sheet might seem rather sparse — there are fewer figures than appear in some of the illustrative balance sheets and balance sheet extracts referred to in previous sections of this book. Paradoxically, this is the result of the increased disclosure requirements which companies must now satisfy. Companies simply cannot fit onto one page all the information which is legally required. Consequently, key figures and sub-totals are presented on the face of the balance sheet, and the remainder is included in a series of notes to the accounts. Booths' accounts include twenty such notes (pages 14 to 19) and the user is referred to these notes by a number appearing alongside the relevant figure in the balance sheet (or profit and loss account or cash flow statement). The notes are as much a part of the accounts as are the figures appearing on the face of the three main statements. This is emphasized in the Report of the Auditors (page 9), in which the auditors state that they have 'audited the financial statements on pages 10 to 19'.

The vertical balance sheet is presented in such a way as to highlight key sub-totals which can be used to analyse the performance and position of business organizations. (We shall analyse Booths' financial statements in Chapter 11.) Assets are classified as fixed and current and, within each section, the separate assets are presented in order of increasing liquidity (Land and buildings appears before Fixtures, plant and vehicles in Note 8, and Stocks appears before Debtors in the balance sheet). Current liabilities are set off against current assets to provide a sub-total net current assets/(liabilities). This in turn is added to/(subtracted from)

---

1. Readers may find it helpful to photocopy the whole of Appendix 1 to have the relevant pages at hand whilst working through each section.

the fixed assets figure to produce another sub-total — total assets less current liabilities. Although quite a mouthful, this term is an important one — it represents the total amount of assets, net of current liabilities, which must be funded by long-term sources of finance.

Long-term liabilities in the form of medium-term and long-term loans (formally described as 'Creditors: Amounts falling due after more than one year' — see also Note 13, page 17), and 'Provision for liabilities and charges' together amount to £10,383,709 (9,795,942 + 587,767), which leaves £11,005,415 (21,389,124 − 10,383,709) of the assets to be financed by the owners. The Ownership interest in the company is represented by the 'Capital and Reserves' section.

The income statement

The income statement, or profit and loss account, of Booths (page 10) is clear and concise. As in the illustration of Oval Ltd in Section 5.6, Booths discloses a gross profit figure which reflects the difference between sales revenue (turnover) and the cost of goods sold (cost of sales). This profit is available to meet the 'non-production' administrative expenses. Booths generates some rental income from its properties and this is shown separately from the main business of retailing as 'Other operating income', in the profit and loss account.

Many key items of expense are missing from Booths' profit and loss account — items which are important inputs to the decision models of users. For example, there is no mention of the depreciation charge for the year, the wages bill or the directors' remuneration. However, as with the balance sheet, additional, legally-required information is included in the 'Notes to the accounts' (in particular Notes 2, 4 and 5) and some of these are referred to on the face of the profit and loss account.

The company's 'Operating profit' represents the total profit generated from operating activities. This sum is available to 'reward' the tax authorities and those participants who have provided finance for the company. Interest payable to lenders is treated as an expense and is deducted from the profit figure before the tax charge is calculated. The 'Profit on ordinary activities after taxation' (£815,394) represents the profit for the year which has been earned for the owners (shareholders) of the company. The directors of Booths have recommended that some of this profit (£132,306) be distributed to the owners as dividends, and the remainder (£683,088) be retained in the business. The dividends are *not* an expense of the business. The business has generated a profit of £815,394 for the owners. This profit 'belongs' to the owners, and the owners are appropriating some of that profit in the form of a dividend.

Most companies would transfer the profit retained for the year (£683,088) directly to the ownership interest section of the balance sheet. Booths complicates the issue somewhat by introducing a further adjustment — 'Transfer to general reserve'. This is merely a bookkeeping entry and will be explained in Chapter

8. However, the introduction of this entry does not affect the principles introduced earlier in this chapter. Thus, from the balance sheet and profit and loss account we can confirm that the profit retained after the payment of the dividends is added to the ownership interest, i.e. Capital and reserves:

Capital and reserves — 1991	£10,322,327
Retained profit for the year	683,088
Capital and reserves — 1992	£11,005,415

The cash flow statement

Booths' cash flow statement (page 12) is presented in several sections similar to those introduced in Table 5.4. The 'Net Cash Inflow from Operating Activities' (£4,252,948) includes the cash receipts from customers and the cash payments to suppliers and employees. Again, there is too much information to disclose on the face of the cash flow statement, and the breakdown of this figure is presented in Note 18. In fact, Note 18 calculates the cash flow from operating activities in a different manner from that adopted in this chapter. Both are equally acceptable and we shall reconcile the approaches in Chapter 11.

The section 'Returns on Investments and Servicing of Finance' discloses the amounts paid to lenders and shareholders. The 'Interest Paid' figure (£1,844,325) is higher than the 'Interest payable' figure (£1,774,026) in the profit and loss account suggesting that the accrued interest at the beginning of the year (subsequently paid in the current year) was £70,299 greater than the accrued interest at the end of the year. Although the dividends figure is identical in both statements the figure in the cash flow statement presumably represents, at least in part, the dividend recommended for the previous year which would have been paid during the current year.

As taxation is normally paid nine months after the year end, the 'Corporation Tax Paid' in the cash flow statement (£335,222) relates to the tax charge in the profit and loss account for 1991 (£320,300), rather than to the tax charge for 1992 (£588,939). In effect the whole of the current year's tax charge is an accrued expense which is paid the following year. The tax charge in the profit and loss account is an estimate of the tax liability (negotiations with the Inland Revenue can take several months, or even years!) and it is rarely identical to the ultimate tax paid figure. We examine further the tax charge and tax paid figures below and again in Chapter 8.

Booths invested £404,168 in purchasing new fixed assets and recouped £15,465 on the sale of some of its existing fixed assets. The net result of Booths' operating activities, its payments to lenders, shareholders and the Inland Revenue, and its net capital expenditure is a 'Net Cash Inflow Before Financing' of £1,552,392. It has generated a cash surplus, and has used it to repay some of the many loans outstanding (£969,250), and to boost its own cash balances or, more accurately, to reduce its bank overdraft (£583,142).

The major differences between the figures in the profit and loss account and the corresponding figures in the cash flow statement are as follows:

	Profit and loss account	Cash flow statement
Depreciation (Note 2)	£1,327,455	
Net capital expenditure		£388,703
Tax payable on ordinary activities	£588,939	
Corporation tax paid		£335,222

We shall explain and analyse the difference between depreciation and capital expenditure in Chapters 6 and 11. We examine the difference between tax payable and tax paid below.

Creditors, debtors, accruals and prepayments

In Sections 5.9 to 5.11 we examined a common reason for the possible difference between reported income and cash flows — the importance of the existence of accruals and prepayments in determining income. We know that for most organizations there are likely to exist costs and expenses which have not yet been paid (creditors and accrued expenses); revenues earned for which payment has not yet been received (debtors); and costs or expenses paid, the benefits from which will not arise until a subsequent period (prepayments). We can find some evidence of all of these in the accounts of Booths.

The balance sheet reveals that 'Debtors' amount to £311,946. However, this is unlikely to represent that part of credit sales for which payment has not yet been received. Outstanding credit sales are called 'trade debtors' in the UK (and 'accounts receivable' in the USA and elsewhere), and one would not expect to find many trade debtors in the accounts of a supermarket chain which sells almost exclusively on cash terms. Note 11 (page 17) confirms this view. Most of the Debtors' balance comprises 'Prepayments and accrued income'. Booths does not disclose the nature of these items, but Note 1 (page 14) reveals that, in addition to selling food and associated products through its shops, the company receives rental income from some of its properties. It is possible that some rents were due, but not yet received at the year end. Booths would have increased income (via 'Other operating income') and increased debtors to take account of this.

Similarly, we can see from the profit and loss account that Booths charged 'Interest payable' of £1,774,026 for the year. However, the cash flow statement reveals that 'Interest paid' was £1,844,325. Some of this cash payment must relate to interest accrued at the beginning of the year and we can deduce that 'Accrued interest' at the end of the year must be £70,299 lower (£1,844,325 − £1,774,026). Unfortunately, we cannot identify the opening and closing balances on the accrued interest account because Booths does not (and is not required to) disclose those figures. We do know, however, that accrued interest is a current liability and hence is included within the balance sheet figure for 'Creditors: Amounts falling due within one year' — £10,980,498. This figure is broken down in Note 12 and we can assume that the balance of accrued interest is included in the item 'Accruals' — £759,943.

The accounting treatment of accruals (and prepayments) involves entries in all three financial statements — an expense in the income statement, a cash payment in the cash flow statement (in the following year) and an outstanding balance in the balance sheet. One item which can be identified in each of the three statements of Booths is taxation.

We mentioned above that taxation is normally paid nine months after the year end so that in effect the whole of the tax charge in the profit and loss account is an accrued expense which is paid the following year. Consequently we should be able to apply to taxation the 'accrued expenses expression' introduced in Section 5.11:

$$\begin{array}{llll} \text{Expense} = & \text{Cash paid for} + & \text{Closing accrued} - & \text{Opening accrued} \\ \text{charge} & \text{expense item} & \text{expense} & \text{expense} \end{array}$$

We have stated in an earlier chapter that the complexities of the UK tax system are beyond the scope of this introductory text. So they are — and we should be grateful for that! A glance at Notes 6, 12 and 14 reveals references not only to corporation tax (CT), but also deferred taxation (DT) and Advance Corporation Tax (ACT) too. However, our basic accounting principles must hold. The terms 'deferred' and 'advance' suggest differences in timing only, between recognizing the (tax) expense and paying the bill. So, if we add together all three different types of tax (current, deferred and advanced) we might reveal the overall picture.

In the Profit and Loss Account (page 10), the total tax charge for the year is £588,939. In the Balance Sheet (page 11), the total accrued tax expense is included partly in 'Provisions for Liabilities and Charges: Deferred taxation' (£587,767) and partly in 'Creditors: Amounts falling due within one year'. Note 12 reveals the individual amounts for 'Advance corporation tax' (£44,032) and 'Current corporation tax' (£528,125) within creditors. In the Cash Flow Statement the total tax paid is shown to be £335,222 (see Table 5.8).

The use of a real example in this section has demonstrated the integrity of the principles introduced previously when more simple examples were used. You may well have found it difficult to follow at a first reading! If so, go through it again until you are able to identify where all the figures have come from. Having done so, you will find subsequent chapters much easier to understand.

Table 5.8

Expense charge	=	Cash paid for expense item	+	Closing accrued expense	−	Opening accrued expense
£		£		£		£
				587,767 DT		560,879 DT
				44,032 ACT		44,032 ACT
				528,125 CT		301,296 CT
588,939	=	335,222	+	1,159,924	−	906,207
Profit and loss account		Cash flow statement		Balance sheet		Balance sheet

Discussion topics

1. Suggest why historical cost accounting has remained for so long as the basis for preparing accounting statements.

2. Why is the term 'double-entry' used to describe the accountant's recording process? What is the likely derivation of the terms debit and credit? Why do you suppose they refer to the left-hand and right-hand sides respectively?

3. Explain the importance of the 'accounting period' concept.

4. Distinguish between product costs and period costs. Why does the proper determination of product costs present so many problems to the accountant?

5. Distinguish between expense and expenditure. Give examples, in addition to those discussed in the text, of particular items which do not fall into both categories.

6. Explain the difference between dividends, taxation and the major types of income statement expense.

7. What is the relationship between asset and expense? Explain the difference between the two terms by way of particular examples.

8. Distinguish between creditors and accrued expenses. What items would you expect to see classified under these two headings in the balance sheet?

9. Distinguish between debtors and prepayments. What items would you expect to see classified under these headings in the balance sheet?

10. Suggest two possible reasons why a company may show a surplus in its income statement and a cash outflow in its cash flow statement.

11. Examine the accounts of E.H. Booth and Co. Ltd (Appendix 1, pages 547–566)

and explain what, if anything, you have learned about the company from the information provided.

Exercises

5.1 Show how the following transactions would be recorded in an organization's accounting equation.

(a) A payment of £10,000 by the owner of the organization into its bank account.
(b) The purchase of 1,000 units of stock at a price of £5 per unit. Payment is made from the business bank account.
(c) The receipt of a loan of £20,000 from the organization's bank. The proceeds are paid into the business bank account.
(d) The purchase of a machine for £30,000 of which £5,000 is paid immediately from the business bank account. The balance is payable at a later date.
(e) The repayment from the business bank account of £5,000 of the bank loan.
(f) The exchange of 400 units of stock at £5 per unit for a second-hand motor van valued at £2,000.

5.2 The following balances appear at the foot of Maria Angelotti's accounting equation on 31 December 19X5:

Assets	£
Plant and machinery	72,300
Land and buildings	48,800
Cash at bank	4,100
Stock	26,600
Motor vehicles	18,900
Debtors (amounts owed by customers)	16,700
	£187,400

Ownership Interest and Liabilities	
Creditors (amounts owed to suppliers)	22,900
Long-term loan from Spoletta Finance Ltd	75,000
Maria Angelotti — ownership interest	43,800
Taxation due to the Inland Revenue	22,400
Bank overdraft	23,300
	£187,400

■ Prepare Maria Angelotti's balance sheet at 31 December 19X5.

5.3 Mr Daland commences business on 1 March 19X7. During March 19X7 he undertakes the following transactions.

1. Pays £20,000 into the business bank account from his own resources.

2. Borrows £25,000 from Ms Senta at an interest rate of 1% per month. Pays the proceeds into the business bank account.
3. Purchases machinery for £25,000. He pays £10,000 from the business bank account and agrees to pay the balance on 31 May 19X7.
4. Rents premises for an annual rent of £7,200, payable monthly.
5. Purchases 100 units of raw materials for £100 per unit. He pays for these units immediately from the business bank account.
6. Pays the following expenses from the business bank account:

Interest to Ms Senta	£250
Rent	£600
Wages	£1,000
Lighting and heating	£300
Other expenses	£350

7. Provides for a depreciation charge of £400 on the machinery.
8. Uses the labour and machinery to convert 50 units of raw materials into finished goods, which he sells for £200 each. Pays the proceeds into the business bank account.

- (a) Show Mr Daland's accounting equation entries for March 19X7.
- (b) Prepare Mr Daland's income statement for the month of March 19X7 and his balance sheet at 31 March 19X7.

5.4 Rosa Almaviva commenced business as a Basilio retailer on 1 January 19X9. During 19X9 she undertook the following transactions:

1 January 19X9
(a) Paid £45,000 into the business bank account, of which £30,000 was from personal savings and £15,000 was a loan from Don Curzio at 15% p.a. interest.
(b) Purchased a lease on a shop for £12,000 which she paid from the business bank account. The lease was for a period of 8 years and provided for an annual rent of £3,500, including rates.
(c) Purchased fixtures and fittings for £7,500, paid from the business bank account. The fixtures and fittings had an estimated life of 10 years, and an expected resale value of £1,000 at the end of that time.
(d) Bought from the business bank account 10,000 Basilios at a price of £2.00 per Basilio.

30 June 19X9
(e) Sold 4,000 Basilios at £4.50 each and paid the proceeds into the business bank account.
(f) Paid the following expenses from the business bank account:

Interest to Don Curzio	£1,125
Rent	£1,750
Assistant's salary	£2,100
Lighting and heating	£900
Telephone	£75
Other expenses	£1,200

31 December 19X9
(g) Sold 5,000 Basilios at £5.00 each and paid the proceeds into the business bank account.

(h) Paid the following expenses from the business bank account:

Interest to Don Curzio	£1,125
Rent	£1,750
Assistant's salary	£2,200
Lighting and heating	£1,250
Telephone	£85
Other expenses	£1,700

Rosa Almaviva wishes to provide for depreciation on the lease and on the fixtures and fittings by the straight-line method (i.e. by writing off, for each asset, an equal amount each year over the life of the asset).

■ Prepare an income statement for Rosa Almaviva for the year ended 31 December 19X9, and a balance sheet as at that date.

5.5 Sextus was a Roman entrepreneur who earned his living by sending ships to import spices and silks from the Far East. We shall use a little artistic licence in describing his activities. At the time that interests us, Sextus already has seven ships engaged in trade. He expects, however, that there will be a shortage of oriental goods in one year's time and he therefore resolves to buy an extra ship for one voyage. He expects to be able to buy a new ship for 10,000d, 7,500d payable immediately and the balance payable in six months' time. He would hire a team of oarsmen (since he disapproves of slavery) and they would be paid a wage of 1,000d on completion of the voyage. The voyage would take exactly one year, six months outwards to the oriental port and six months on the return. Sextus would have to spend 300d on provisions for the outward journey. He would also spend 4,000d on goods to be traded for silks and spices at the destination and 400d on goods to be traded at the destination for provisions for the return journey. On completion of the return journey, he would sell the silks and spices immediately for 8,500d but would have to spend 200d on selling expenses (transport and so on). He would also sell the ship at this time for an expected price of 8,000d. Sextus employs a clerk to keep the records and help with the administrative arrangements connected with the voyages of his seven ships already owned. This clerk, who receives a salary of 240d p.a., has enough idle time to be able to deal with the administration for the extra ship.

■ Prepare a calculation showing what gain Sextus would make from the extra ship.

Suppose that Sextus purchases the extra ship and that all the financial estimates given above prove exactly correct. He finds, however, that he has insufficient cash available to meet the second instalment of the price of the ship due six months after the start of the voyage. It is agreed that his friend Annius will provide the required amount and become a partner in the venture for the second six-month period. Sextus will repay Annius at the end of the voyage and also pay him one half of the gain from the voyage during the second period of six months. Unfortunately they neglect to agree how this gain should be calculated.

■ Prepare a calculation showing what you consider to be an equitable apportionment of the gain. You may assume (if you think it relevant) that the market price of six-month-old ships is 9,200d.

5.6 Nimmi Mundi commenced business as a retail chemist on 1 July 19X0. On that date she paid into the business bank account £20,000 from her personal savings, £20,000 which she had borrowed from her mother and £40,000 which was a loan from the bank. She had agreed to pay her mother an annual rate of interest of 10%, payable in arrears on 1 July each year. The loan from the bank carried a fixed rate of interest of 15% per annum, payable semi-annually and was secured against Nimmi's detached house in Didsbury.

On 1 July, Nimmi purchased some shop equipment for £7,500 which was expected to last 10 years, after which it would be worthless. She paid £25,000 for stock from another retail chemist who was taking early retirement. In order to service customers whilst she was dispensing drugs, she employed a sales assistant for £150 per week.

The following information relates to the first six months of trading:
- (i)   Nimmi paid a monthly rental of £600 on the 16th of each month.
- (ii) £2,700 was paid for business rates covering the period 1 July 19X0 to 31 March 19X1.
- (iii) The sales assistant was paid at the end of each week but, as the chemist was closed over the Christmas holiday period, he was paid for the first week in January in advance.
- (iv) Stock costing £30,000 and £40,000 was purchased on credit on 24 August 19X0 and 3 December 19X0 respectively. The supplier offered 30 days' credit to all customers and Nimmi took full advantage of the credit period before settling the account.
- (v)   Total cash receipts of £62,000 were paid into the bank account.
- (vi) Nimmi took £2,000 each month from the cash takings to cover her personal and household expenses.
- (vii) General expenses were paid out of the bank account amounting to £3,500.
- (viii) On 31 December 19X0 there was unsold stock which had cost £50,000.
- (ix) All interest on loans was paid on the due date.

- ■ (a) Prepare Nimmi's opening balance sheet as at 1 July 19X0.
  - (b) Construct the business bank account for the six months to 31 December 19X0 and calculate the change in cash balance over the six months.
  - (c) Discuss the limitations of using either the cash balance or the change in cash balance as an indicator of Nimmi's business performance for her first six months of trading.

5.7 The Balance Sheet of John Pogo who runs a photocopying business is shown below:

John Pogo
Balance Sheet as at 31 December 19X1

	£		£	£
Ownership Interest	18,000	Equipment		
		Cost	15,000	
Trade Creditors	2,500	*less:* Accumulated Depreciation	7,500	7,500
		Supplies and Paper		6,000
		Debtors		3,000
		Cash		4,000
	£20,500			£20,500

During 19X2 the following events occurred:
(1) Cash sales of £9,000 and credit sales of £20,000 were made.
(2) Paper and supplies costing £10,000 were bought on credit.
(3) Rent of £2,400 for the year to 31 December 19X2 was paid in cash.
(4) The equipment is estimated to last five years and to be worth £2,500 at the end of its life.
(5) Wages of £9,000 were all paid in cash.
(6) At 31 December 19X2 stock of paper was valued at £7,000, and £2,000 of the amount owing from customers had not been paid.
(7) The business paid all but £4,000 of the amount owing for purchases by the year-end.
(8) John Pogo withdrew cash equal to his historic cost net income for the year.

■ (a) Record entries (1) to (8) on the accounting equation worksheet.
(b) Prepare an Income Statement for the year.
(c) Prepare a Balance Sheet as at 31 December 19X2.

Further reading

Hendrikson, E.S., *Accounting Theory*, Irwin, 1982.
Nobes, C., *Introduction to Financial Accounting*, Routledge, 1992.

6

Fixed and

Intangible Assets

In this and the following chapter we consider the problems involved in defining and measuring assets (for inclusion in the balance sheet) and in determining the costs of using assets (for inclusion in the income statement). We begin, however, by reiterating the distinction between expenses and assets (first outlined in Chapter 5) since much of this chapter depends on an understanding of this distinction. We then consider the accounting treatment of *fixed* assets and the methods available for calculating that part of their cost which should be charged to each period's income statement. Finally we examine some of the problems inherent in the definition and measurement of *intangible* assets.

6.1 Distinction between expenses and assets — a review

We have seen in previous chapters how historical cost accounting involves the preparation of an income statement and a balance sheet, and we have explained that the organization's net income is measured by matching the revenues earned for the period with the costs incurred in earning them. The balance sheet includes costs incurred which have not, at the balance sheet date, been matched with revenues. This procedure gives rise to the problem of deciding which items of expenditure should be matched against revenue in the income statement (expenses) and which should be shown in the balance sheet (assets). Let us now remind ourselves of the principles.

Suppose that an organization purchases an item for cash or on credit (i.e. it incurs an item of expenditure). The item may be tangible, for example raw materials, fuel, computer equipment, stationery, machinery or property, or it may be a service, for example a person's labour, the use of a telephone, the expertise of a consultant, the use of accommodation or the hire of equipment. Whatever the nature of the purchase, one aspect of the transaction will be recorded by reducing the enterprise's cash balance (if purchase is by cash) or by increasing liabilities (if purchase is on credit). Because of the dual nature of all transactions, the second aspect will be either to increase assets by the amount of the transaction *or* to increase expenses (and hence reduce net income). The question is how to decide which items of expenditure are assets and which are expenses. The decision is of fundamental importance because it affects both the reported net income and the reported financial position of an organization, and thus the decisions of those who use its accounting reports, i.e. the decisions of the participant groups first discussed in Chapter 2.

Within the conventional transactions-based approach, the following guidelines indicate a general answer to the question:

- If the *full* benefits from the expenditure arise *during* the accounting period in which the expenditure is incurred, the *expenditure should be treated as an expense of that period*, e.g. the payment by Sainsbury plc of £849 million in respect of wages and salaries in 1992.
- If *some* benefits from the expenditure arise *after* the accounting period in which the expenditure is incurred, *that proportion of the expenditure relating to those future benefits should be treated as an asset*, e.g. the expenditure by Sainsbury plc of £538 million on new properties in 1992.

In the latter case, where the expenditure is treated as an asset, an appropriate part of the cost of the asset will be transferred to expense during each period in which benefits arise. Thus, under the historical cost approach, *the amount of assets in the balance sheet is represented by costs which have not yet been matched against revenues*. Most expenditures are matched against revenues eventually; the problem of the accruals-based approach is one of allocating the costs of assets between the accounting periods that benefit from their use. Different patterns of allocation lead to different patterns of net income through time, and it may be that different information will be conveyed to participants by one pattern of income than by another.

6.2 Fixed assets and depreciation

Under historical cost accounting, the cost of a fixed asset is charged to the income statement over a number of accounting periods, generally equal to the number of years of the asset's productive life. Thus the cost of most plant and machinery will be charged over fewer years than will the cost of buildings. Figure 6.1 reveals the range of lives assigned to fixed assets by Reckitt & Colman plc.

We can now look in greater detail at the calculation of the proportion of an asset's

---

Depreciation

Except for freehold land, the cost of properties, plant and equipment, after deduction of government grants, is written off on a straight line basis over the period of the expected useful life of the asset. For this purpose, expected lives are determined within the following limits:

Freehold buildings: not more than fifty years.

Leasehold land and buildings: the lesser of fifty years or the life of the lease.

Owned plant and equipment: not more than fifteen years. In general, production plant and equipment, and office equipment are written off over ten years; motor vehicles and computer equipment over five years.

Leased plant and equipment: on the same basis as owned plant and equipment or over the life of the lease, if shorter.

Figure 6.1 *Reckitt & Colman plc, extract from Annual Report*

cost (the periodic depreciation charge), and the consequent calculation of the written-down cost (or 'book value') of the asset for inclusion in the balance sheet. In other words, the depreciation charge and the asset's book value are simply two sides of the same coin — the charge determines the book value. It should be stressed from the outset that the terms 'depreciation' and 'book value' as conventionally used by accountants in preparing income statements and balance sheets have very specific meanings. These meanings may not accord with those used by non-accountants. A non-accountant asked to define depreciation might respond with a definition that referred in some way to *diminution of value*. For example, 'Which?', the magazine of the Consumers' Association, defines the depreciation of a car as 'the reduction in the value of your car over time'.[1] Similarly, a non-accountant if asked to provide a definition of value, might attempt to relate it to such concepts as 'worth', 'utility', or 'desirability'. Regrettably, such definitions do not coincide with those implied by the historical cost accounting treatment of depreciation. As we have seen, the purpose of the accountant's depreciation charge is one of cost allocation; depreciation is that part of the cost of an asset which has been or is being written off to the income statement, and the book value in the balance sheet is that part of the original cost of an asset that has not yet been charged against revenues. Under historical cost accounting the balance sheet asset amount does not necessarily bear any resemblance to such notions of 'current value' as current replacement cost or selling price, except by accident.

Other meanings of depreciation have been suggested. For example, depreciation is often referred to as a source of funds for the replacement of assets. Depreciation, however, does not generate any funds *per se*. It is *cash inflow*, in the form of sales revenue, which produces funds for the replacement of assets. A more charitable

1. 'Cut the cost of your motoring', *Which?*, February 1992.

Table 6.1 *Recording the purchase and depreciation of fixed assets*

	Assets			Net Income	
	... + Machinery +	Cash =	... +	Revenue −	Expenses
	£	£			£
19X1					
1 January Purchase	10,000	(10,000)			
31 December Depreciation	(1,000)				(1,000)
31 December Net book value	9,000				
19X2					
31 December Depreciation	(1,000)				(1,000)
31 December Net book value	8,000				

interpretation of the 'funds generation' view of depreciation might be that, by charging depreciation to the income statement, and thereby reducing income, the possible distribution of funds, equal to the depreciation charge, is prevented. (The relationship between depreciation and cash flow is explored further in Chapter 11.)

The accounting entries necessary to record fixed assets and associated depreciation are straightforward, and are illustrated in Table 6.1. When an organization buys a fixed asset, the amount of its total assets is increased by the acquisition cost and the amount of cash held is reduced by the same amount. If the asset purchase is on credit, the other side of the entry is to increase liabilities rather than to reduce cash. Subsequently in each future accounting period, the amount to be written off the cost of the asset (the depreciation charge) is calculated. (The method of calculating the depreciation charge is explained in Section 6.3.) This amount is then deducted from the previous written down value of the asset (appearing in the last balance sheet) and is added to expenses (i.e. deducted from current year net income). Thus the balance sheet will, at any time, show both the cost of the asset and the accumulated depreciation to date. This figure for accumulated depreciation represents the total of all the charges passed through the income statement. Hence on 31 December 19X2, the balance sheet of the company illustrated in Table 6.1 would show:

	£
Machinery:	
Cost	10,000
Accumulated depreciation	(2,000)
Net Book Value	8,000

All fixed assets are treated in this way, with one exception. The exception lies in the treatment of land. Land is not expected to be used up in production in the same way as other fixed assets and thus, under historical cost accounting, is normally recorded as an asset at cost, the amount of which is unchanged from period to period.

6.3   Methods of depreciation

A variety of methods may be used to calculate periodic depreciation charges. Under historical cost accounting, all are essentially methods of allocating the original cost of an asset, less its expected eventual residual value, between the accounting periods in which the asset is expected to be used. For example, the UK professional accountancy bodies commenting on depreciation, say that:[2]

> Provision for depreciation of fixed assets having a finite useful economic life should be made by allocating the cost ... less estimated residual value of the assets as fairly as possible to the periods expected to benefit from their use.

Most assets depreciate as a result of both *use* and the *passage of time*. *Ceteris paribus*, a machine which has never been used would still have a finite life — it may be the victim of technological advances, or it may simply deteriorate physically over time. Of those assets which are used, it is normally the case that the more intensively an asset is worked, the shorter is its productive life. Some methods of depreciation emphasize the passage of time in allocating the cost of an asset over its useful life; other methods emphasize the pattern of use.

In this section we describe the three most frequently used depreciation methods: the *straight line* method; the *reducing balance* (or declining balance or fixed percentage of declining balance) method; and the *sum-of-the-years-digits* method. The first of these three is by far the most widely used in practice. For example, the *European Survey of Published Accounts 1991*[3] which reports the accounting practices of 336 large European companies shows that 299 of these companies chose the straight line method of depreciation. The popularity of the straight line method rests largely on its simplicity of operation and its understandability.

Consider the case of an organization that purchases an asset, details of which are given in Table 6.2. The life expectation is based normally on the expected economic life of the asset rather than on its physical life, i.e. the expected life

2. Statement of Standard Accounting Practice No. 12, *Accounting for Depreciation*, The Institute of Chartered Accountants in England and Wales, revised January 1987, paragraph 15.
3. *FEE European Survey of Published Accounts 1991*, Fédération des Experts Comptables Européens, Routledge, 1991.

Table 6.2 *Details of an asset*

Cost	C = £15,000
Expected life	N = 3 years
Expected scrap (or resale) value at end of life	S = £3,000

is the number of years the organization expects to retain and use the asset. Such an estimate may be provided by the organization's engineers. The prediction of the expected economic life of the asset is of great practical importance. This figure, which represents the basis of the allocation of cost, determines both the periodic charge to the income statement and also the balance sheet book value. For example, if the depreciation charge is very high relative to the net income figure, as is the case in highly capital intensive organizations, the choice of asset life can greatly influence the organization's net income. In 1991, Blue Circle Industries plc charged depreciation of £78.6 million to its profit and loss account. This represented 63% of its profit before tax figure of £124.2 million.

The expected scrap or resale value represents the organization's best estimate of the amount it will receive for the asset at the end of its economic life. The difference between the cost of the asset and its expected residual value represents the total amount to be depreciated over the asset's economic life. We should, however, note that the original cost and expected residual value, although both expressed in money terms, are qualitatively different because of the dates at which they arise: the former is an observed payment whereas the latter is an uncertain estimate. The accounting problem is how to spread the depreciable cost of £12,000 (£15,000 − £3,000) between the three years of the asset's expected life.

The *straight line* method spreads the total depreciation cost evenly over the expected life of the asset. The income statement of each accounting period (assuming each is of equal length, say one year) is charged with the same depreciation amount, calculated from the following simple expression:

$$D = \frac{C - S}{N}$$

where D is the annual (or periodic) depreciation charge, and C, S and N are as defined in Table 6.2. Thus for the asset described in Table 6.2, the annual depreciation charge is:

$$D = \frac{15,000 - 3,000}{3} = £4,000$$

The *reducing balance* method charges as depreciation each period a constant percentage of the written down value (cost less accumulated depreciation) of the asset at the start of the period. The periodic depreciation *rate* may be calculated from the following expression:[4]

$$d = 1 - \sqrt[N]{\frac{S}{C}}$$

where d is the periodic rate of depreciation (expressed as a decimal of one) and N, S and C are as defined previously. For the asset described in Table 6.2, the annual depreciation rate is:

$$d = 1 - \sqrt[3]{\frac{3,000}{15,000}} = 0.415 \text{ or } 41.5\%$$

To calculate the depreciation *charge* for each year, the depreciation *rate* must be applied to the reducing book value of the asset as follows:

		£
Time 0	Cost	15,000
Time 1	First year's depreciation	
	(41.5% × 15,000)	6,225
Time 1	Written down value	8,775
Time 2	Second year's depreciation	
	(41.5% × 8,775)	3,640
Time 2	Written down value	5,135
Time 3	Third year's depreciation	
	(41.5% × 5,135)	2,135
Time 3	Written down value	3,000

The depreciation charges are £6,225 for the first year of the asset's life, £3,640 for the second, and £2,135 for the third.

Although the *sum-of-the-years-digits* (SYD) method is rarely found in the UK, it is used in the United States and elsewhere. It often gives results similar to those obtained from the reducing balance method and is easier to calculate. The depreciation charge for a particular year is found by multiplying the net cost of the asset (original cost minus expected residual value) by a fraction. The numerator

---

4. The depreciation rate, d, is calculated so as to reduce the original cost of the asset to its residual value over its expected life, i.e. a value for d must be found to satisfy the equation:

$$C(1-d)^N = S$$

Rearranging gives:

$$(1-d)^N = S/C$$
$$(1-d) = \sqrt[N]{(S/C)}$$
$$d = 1 - \sqrt[N]{(S/C)}$$

of the fraction is the number of years of the asset's life remaining at the beginning of the year under consideration. The denominator, which is the same each year, is the sum of an arithmetic progression, whose first term is the life of the asset and whose final term is one. Each intermediate term is equal to the previous term minus one. This rather cumbersome description masks an essentially simple process, which can be illustrated by the example of the asset in Table 6.2. Annual depreciation charges under the SYD method are as follows:

$$\text{Depreciation charge}$$
$$£$$

Year 1 $\dfrac{3}{(3+2+1)} \times (15{,}000 - 3{,}000) =$ 6,000

Year 2 $\dfrac{2}{(3+2+1)} \times (15{,}000 - 3{,}000) =$ 4,000

Year 3 $\dfrac{1}{(3+2+1)} \times (15{,}000 - 3{,}000) =$ 2,000

The numbers thrown up by the above examples illustrate some interesting characteristics of conventional depreciation calculations. The first concerns the objectivity and verifiability of the figures. These two criteria are frequently used in defence of historical cost accounting methods and we discussed their merits in Chapter 3. Yet in the above examples two of the three basic numbers used in calculating depreciation (expected life and expected residual value) are estimates and, in consequence, are not necessarily objective, nor can they be verified. We consider later in this section the adjustments that might be required if estimates of future life and residual value change during the asset's economic life.

The second interesting characteristic is that all three methods of depreciation provide the same total depreciation over the life of the asset and, consequently, if actual life and residual value are as estimated, all three have the effect of writing down the book value of the asset to its residual value by the end of its economic life. This is illustrated in Table 6.3 which shows the declining book value pattern of the asset under each depreciation method. The figures in Table 6.3 are expressed graphically in Figure 6.2.

Table 6.3 and Figure 6.2 also illustrate a third characteristic of the depreciation methods. Each method produces a different *pattern* of book value for the asset over its life and a different pattern of annual depreciation charges, even though the *total* depreciation charge is the same under each method. *These different patterns of depreciation charges contribute to different annual figures for net income.* If we assume that the organization acquiring the asset in our example has net income before depreciation of £7,000 p.a. for each of the three years of the asset's life, we can calculate its income under each method, net of depreciation, for each year. The figures are shown in Table 6.4 and Figure 6.3. If income before depreciation is

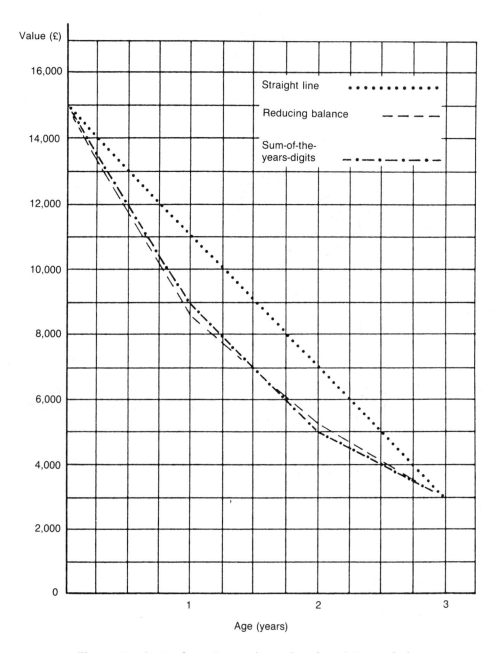

Figure 6.2 *Asset value patterns using various depreciation methods*

Table 6.3 *Asset 'book' value patterns using various depreciation methods*

		Straight line £	Reducing balance £	Sum-of-the-years-digits £
Time 0	Cost	15,000	15,000	15,000
Time 1	Depreciation (Income statement)	4,000	6,225	6,000
Time 1	Balance sheet 'Book value'	11,000	8,775	9,000
Time 2	Depreciation (Income statement)	4,000	3,640	4,000
Time 2	Balance sheet 'Book value'	7,000	5,135	5,000
Time 3	Depreciation (Income statement)	4,000	2,135	2,000
Time 3	Balance sheet 'Book value'	3,000	3,000	3,000
Total Depreciation		12,000	12,000	12,000

constant each year, the application of straight line depreciation results in a similarly constant stream of net income figures. Application of either of the other two methods results in a lower net income figure during the early years of the asset's life and increasing net income during the later years.

We noted earlier that the UK professional accountancy bodies recommend that the cost of fixed assets should be allocated 'as fairly as possible to the periods expected to benefit from their use'. This begs the question as to what is meant by 'as fairly as possible', but it appears that the straight line method of depreciation would be a suitable method for those assets which are expected to depreciate primarily on a *time* basis, and/or which produce benefits *evenly* over their useful life (e.g. buildings). The reducing balance and SYD methods might allocate more fairly the cost of assets which are expected to produce greater benefits (are used more intensively) in the earlier years of their life. Because these latter two methods charge a greater amount of depreciation in the earlier years of an asset's life, they are sometimes referred to as methods of 'accelerated depreciation'.

Which pattern of depreciation, book value and net income is preferable depends on the criteria selected for choosing between accounting methods. However, we should note at this stage that the differences between the patterns of depreciation and net income observed when one asset is owned, may be reduced or even eliminated if an enterprise owns a large number of assets and replaces some each year. Differences between book value patterns may also be reduced, though by a lesser amount. Suppose that the firm in our example owns three assets similar

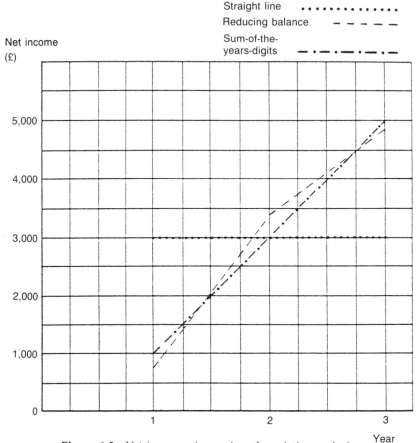

Figure 6.3 *Net income using various depreciation methods*

to the one described in Table 6.2 and replaces one of the assets each year. At the start of the year it will own one new asset, one one-year-old asset and one two-year-old asset. The depreciation figures in Table 6.3 show that whatever method of depreciation is used (provided the same method is applied to all three assets) the total depreciation charge each year will be £12,000:

	Straight line £	Reducing balance £	SYD £
Asset 1 (1 year old)	4,000	6,225	6,000
Asset 2 (2 years old)	4,000	3,640	4,000
Asset 3 (3 years old)	4,000	2,135	2,000
	£12,000	£12,000	£12,000

Table 6.4 *Net income using various depreciation methods*

		Straight line		Reducing balance		Sum-of-the-years-digits	
		£	£	£	£	£	£
Year 1	Income before depreciation	7,000		7,000		7,000	
	less: Depreciation	4,000		6,225		6,000	
	Net income		3,000		775		1,000
Year 2	Income before depreciation	7,000		7,000		7,000	
	less: Depreciation	4,000		3,640		4,000	
	Net income		3,000		3,360		3,000
Year 3	Income before depreciation	7,000		7,000		7,000	
	less: Depreciation	4,000		2,135		2,000	
	Net income		3,000		4,865		5,000
Total net income years 1–3			£9,000		£9,000		£9,000

This is because the total depreciation charge for one asset over its life is the same whichever depreciation method is used. The total written-down values of the three assets at the end of the year will be as follows (based on the figures in Table 6.3):

	Straight line	Reducing balance	SYD
	£	£	£
Asset 1 (1 year old)	11,000	8,775	9,000
Asset 2 (2 years old)	7,000	5,135	5,000
Asset 3 (3 years old)			
— prior to resale	3,000	3,000	3,000
Total written-down value	£21,000	£16,910	£17,000

Thus, for a company in a stable state replacing assets as they wear out, the total depreciation figure will be similar whichever method of depreciation is chosen but the total book value of the assets will differ. The methods will produce different total depreciation figures if the company is expanding quickly (a higher proportion of new assets) and/or asset prices are increasing (new assets have a higher historical cost). The issue of changing price levels is discussed further in Chapter 13.

The preceding analysis is directed primarily at fundamental differences between different depreciation methods. Three further aspects of historical cost depreciation deserve mention.

1.   Asset depreciation entirely through use

There exists a small group of assets that depreciate entirely as a result of use, i.e. independently of their age. A good example of such an asset is a freehold mine. For such an asset, a depreciation method that allocates the cost of the asset between the periods of its expected life according to one of the *time-related* procedures discussed so far may be inappropriate, particularly if, as may be quite likely, the quantities mined vary greatly from year to year. It may be better to relate the depreciation charge to the number of units of output produced by the asset during an accounting period. For example, Blue Circle Industries plc provides depreciation on its fixed assets 'by equal amounts over the estimated lives of the assets, except for freehold and leasehold mineral lands, where it is provided on the basis of tonnage extracted' (Annual Report 1992).

Suppose that an organization purchases for £550,000 a mine which is expected to produce a total of 100,000 tons of metal and to have a residual value after so doing of £50,000. A *unit-based* depreciation charge can be calculated from the formula:

$$D_u = \frac{C - S}{N_u}$$

where D_u is the depreciation charge per unit of output, N_u is the total number of units of output expected from the asset, and C and S are as defined previously. The figures above give a depreciation charge *per ton* of metal mined (D_u) as follows:

$$D_u = \frac{550,000 - 50,000}{100,000} = £5$$

The depreciation charge for a particular period will be £5 multiplied by the number of units of output produced during the period.

2.   Repair and maintenance costs

A second important and allied aspect of depreciation concerns the treatment of repair and maintenance costs. If these costs are expected to arise evenly throughout an asset's life it may be sufficient to charge them as expenses in the years in which they are incurred. Typically, however, repair costs for many assets tend to increase as the asset gets older. In addition, major overhauls or maintenance may be required at intervals less frequent than once a year. If in such circumstances the costs are written off as incurred, the total cost of using an asset will be much higher in some years than in others, resulting in a volatile pattern of net income. Such a result may violate the matching principle if the revenue generating potential of the asset is constant from year to year. Suppose, for example, that the asset described previously in Table 6.2 requires a major overhaul, costing £3,000 at the end of the second year of its life. Assuming that straight line depreciation is used, the total cost of using the asset during each year of its life will be as follows:

	Year 1 £	Year 2 £	Year 3 £
Depreciation	4,000	4,000	4,000
Cost of overhaul	—	3,000	—
Total cost	4,000	7,000	4,000

The 'hump' in the second year may be eliminated by spreading the cost of the overhaul over the asset's life, e.g. at the rate of £1,000 each year, giving a total cost per annum of £5,000. Under this method, some part of the cost of major repairs is allocated to years prior to the expenditure being incurred. Consequently, the charges in the years prior to the expenditure are based on an *estimate* of the cost of the overhaul. The accounting entries required to record this treatment are illustrated in the next section.

3. Reassessments of asset life

Finally we consider the adjustments that should be made if original estimates of asset life or residual value are revised. A major factor affecting the expected economic life of an asset is the possibility of obsolescence. An asset is made obsolete when alternative, more efficient assets become available and it is economically worthwhile for the owner of the asset to replace it with a newer model. This is particularly the case with high-technology assets such as computers. The original estimate of an asset's life should include a provision for obsolescence. By its nature, however, this provision may prove to be inaccurate. Similarly it is quite likely that the residual value of an asset, estimated when the asset is acquired, will turn out to be different from the original expectation. If the change in estimated life or residual value is substantial, it may be necessary to revise depreciation calculations to incorporate the new estimates, for example by increasing or decreasing the future annual depreciation charge or by a single adjustment to the written-down book value of the asset. However, it is more common under historical cost accounting for adjustments arising from changed expectations to be dealt with when the asset is disposed of. Thus if, for example, in the case of the asset described in Table 6.2, the actual residual value is £4,000, rather than the estimated £3,000, a surplus or 'profit on sale' of £1,000 will be reported in the year in which the asset is sold. The accounting entries associated with this treatment are described below.

6.4   Accounting entries for depreciation

We now illustrate the accounting entries required to record fixed assets and depreciation, together with the treatment of irregular repair and maintenance costs and profits or losses on disposal of assets. Details of the relevant asset, a machine, are given in Table 6.5. The purchaser of the machine decides to adopt the straight line method of depreciation and to spread the maintenance cost over the life of the asset. Thus the annual depreciation and maintenance charge is as follows:

$$£$$

$$\text{Depreciation} \quad \frac{15,000-3,000}{3} \qquad 4,000$$

$$\text{Maintenance} \quad \frac{3,000}{3} \qquad 1,000$$

$$\underline{5,000}$$

The accounting entries necessary to record the purchase, use and sale of the asset are shown in Table 6.6. The 'accounting equation' format used is the one described in earlier chapters.

For each year of the machine's life net income is reduced by £5,000, the charge for depreciation and maintenance. For presentation purposes, the two components of this charge are shown separately in the income statement. The double entry is completed each year by reducing the asset 'machine' by £4,000 (the annual depreciation charge) and by increasing the 'provision for maintenance' column

Table 6.5 *Details of machine*

Cost (paid in cash)	£15,000
Expected life	3 years
Actual life	3 years
Expected scrap value at end of life	£3,000
Actual scrap value at end of life (received in cash)	£4,000
Expected and actual maintenance cost, paid in cash at the end of the second year of life	£3,000

Table 6.6 *Accounting entries for recording fixed assets, depreciation and planned maintenance*

Transaction		Assets Cash £	+ Machine £	= Provision for maintenance £	+ Revenue £	− Expenses £	
Time 0	Purchase of asset	(15,000)	15,000				
Time 1	Year 1 depreciation and maintenance		(4,000)	1,000		(5,000)	Depreciation and maintenance
Time 1	Book value		11,000	1,000			
Time 2	Year 2 depreciation and maintenance		(4,000)	1,000		(5,000)	Depreciation and maintenance
Time 2	Maintenance payment	(3,000)		(3,000)			
Time 2	Book value		7,000	(1,000)			
Time 3	Year 3 depreciation and maintenance		(4,000)	1,000		(5,000)	Depreciation and maintenance
Time 3	Sale of asset	4,000	(3,000)		1,000		Profit on sale of asset
			0	0			

by £1,000 (the allocated maintenance charge). The 'provision for maintenance' balance may be thought of as an expense incurred but not yet paid (an accrued expense) until the end of year 2 of the asset's life when the payment is made, and thereafter as a payment made for which the benefit has not yet been received (a prepayment). The proceeds from selling the machine are added to the bank balance. The double entry is completed by reducing the machine balance by the amount needed to decrease it to zero (i.e. by £3,000, the *expected* scrap value) and by increasing revenue by the difference between actual and expected sale proceeds (£1,000). Had actual sale proceeds been less than expected, the difference would have been entered as an expense.

As we noted earlier, fixed asset information in the balance sheet is normally presented to show separately the original cost of assets and the attendant accumulated depreciation. In order to facilitate this process, the two components of written-down value are usually recorded in separate columns. To transform the entries for accumulated depreciation from negative to positive figures, the column is switched from the left to the right side of the equation. Extracts of the relevant entries in our example would be as follows:

	... + *Machine* + ... *at cost* £	=	... + *Accumulated* + ... *depreciation* £
Time 0 Cost	15,000		
Time 1 Depreciation			4,000
Time 1 Balances	15,000		4,000
Time 2 Depreciation			4,000
Time 2 Balances	15,000		8,000
Time 3 Depreciation			4,000
Time 3 Balances	15,000		12,000
Time 3 Sale	(15,000)		(12,000)
	0		0

At each point in time, the difference between the totals in the two columns is equal to the net book value shown in Table 6.6.

6.5   Intangible assets

The fixed assets discussed earlier in this chapter fall into a category known as *tangible assets*, i.e. assets that have physical substance and can be 'touched'. There is another category, known as *intangible assets*, which may be defined as expenditure incurred by an organization, in return for which it receives nothing immediately tangible or physical, but which *may* result in the receipt of benefits beyond the accounting period in which the expenditure arises. In other words, apart from their lack of physical substance, intangible assets exhibit very similar characteristics to their tangible counterparts. We now consider briefly the accounting treatment of these intangible assets. They are discussed further in Chapter 17. There are four main types of intangible assets: research and development; goodwill; patents, trademarks and copyrights; and brands.

Research and development

Many organizations incur expenditure on research and development (R&D). Indeed, science- and technology-based companies (for example, those involved in the manufacture of computers and other electronic products, engineering companies and pharmaceutical companies) often spend considerable sums on R&D. In the year to 31 December 1992, Glaxo plc spent £595 million on R&D, which was equivalent to 14.5% of its turnover and approximately 42% of its historical cost pre-tax income. R&D expenditure is usually categorized in a threefold way, as comprising pure research, applied research and development expenditure. Expenditure on pure research is undertaken to advance knowledge with no specific application in mind concerning the results of the research. Applied research involves expenditure to apply the results of pure research to broad areas of an organization's activities. Development expenditure is undertaken to adapt the results of applied research to the improvement of specific processes and products. Although the distinctions between the three categories are often blurred in practice, they are nevertheless relevant because, as we explain shortly, different accounting treatments are sometimes adopted for the different categories. This is especially the case in the UK.

Goodwill

Goodwill may be regarded in broad terms as the difference between the total value of an organization as a single entity, and the sum of the value of its individual net assets (i.e. assets less liabilities) excluding goodwill. It derives from factors such as reputation, expertise and the quality of relationships with customers, suppliers and others with whom the organization transacts. It may be thought of as reflecting the *excess* value of future returns over and above those that would normally be expected from the particular collection of assets owned by the organization. Companies such as Marks and Spencer, Coca Cola, Heinz, Sainsburys and Mercedes-Benz may expect to derive substantial benefits from the reputations they have built up over a number of years. However, in spite of its importance to many organizations goodwill is very difficult to measure. This is largely because the measurement of such attributes as reputation, expertise and prestige is very subjective and not easily quantifiable. For this reason, goodwill is usually recognized in conventional accounting as an asset only when it is purchased (as opposed to when it is generated internally). This occurs most frequently when one organization purchases or 'takes over' another at a price above the sum of the values of the assets of the acquired organization. For example, if one company buys another company for £2 million, and the company being purchased owns net assets valued individually at a total of £1.5 million, goodwill on acquisition is taken as £500,000. Goodwill is discussed further in Chapters 16 and 17.

Patents, trademarks and copyrights

Expenditure on items such as patents, trademarks and copyrights allows an organization the exclusive use of the process or material covered by the patent, trademark or copyright, usually for a predetermined number of years. So long as the process or material concerned is not superseded by another that is more effective or otherwise worthwhile, it has some value to the organization. Once this ceases to be the case, the patent, trademark or copyright has reached the end of its effective life, even if the legal protection it accords has not expired.

Brands

Strictly, brands are a type of trademark, allowing a company the exclusive use of a product name, for example, Kit Kat and Quality Street (Nestlé S.A.), Wispa and Flake (Cadbury Schweppes plc), and *The Sun* and *The Times* (News International plc). Companies owning important brand names may expect to derive substantial benefits from the reputation surrounding the brand, a reputation that may have been built up over many years. Hence product brand names are similar in nature to company goodwill and indeed it is often the presence of brand names that causes one company to purchase another for a price well in excess of its net asset value. The accounting treatment of brands, and the relationship between brands and goodwill is examined in Chapter 17.

6.6   Accounting treatment of intangible assets

The choice of appropriate accounting treatments for intangible assets within the conventional accounting framework produces a classic conflict between the concepts of accruals (or matching) and conservatism (or prudence). On the one hand, intangible assets represent expenditures, the benefits from which are expected to span a number of accounting periods. The matching concept suggests that the expenditures should be matched with the revenues towards which they contribute, implying a treatment similar to that of fixed assets, whereby an item of expenditure should be viewed initially as an asset, and shown as such in the balance sheet, and subsequently be written off to the income statements over the periods during which it produces benefits. Where intangible assets are concerned, amounts written off are normally referred to as *amortization* rather than depreciation. The alternative methods of amortization (depreciation) and their relative characteristics and merits are as described for tangible fixed assets.

On the other hand, there is often a fundamental difference between intangible and tangible assets. With the possible exception of product brands, patents, trademarks and copyrights and certain items of R&D, intangible assets generally have no value if separated from the organization owning them. For example, the goodwill attached to the name of Marks and Spencer could not easily be transferred to another company. This characteristic creates considerable uncertainty about the value of intangible assets relative to the value of tangible assets. For this reason, the concept of prudence suggests that they should be written off at the earliest opportunity. Indeed they are frequently not treated as assets at all but rather as immediate expenses. For example, the current statement of the UK professional accountancy bodies on the treatment of research and development expenditure requires that expenditure on pure and applied research should be written off in the year of expenditure and that the same treatment should be applied to development expenditure unless a stringent set of conditions is satisfied.[5]

Where intangible assets are to be written off over a number of periods, two particular problems arise. The first problem is to identify the cost of the asset. If the asset is bought from a third party, for example the purchase of a patent, the identification of cost poses few problems. Many intangible assets are not acquired in this way, however. Rather they are created within the enterprise (as, for example, is the case with reputation and expertise), and it may be difficult or impossible to identify the particular costs contributing to their creation. This difficulty is so great that only rarely are internally-created intangible assets carried forward in the balance sheet. The second problem is to estimate the time period over which intangible assets are to be amortized. Although this is also a problem with tangible assets, there exist more complications with intangible assets, where the length of time during which an asset will produce net benefits is particularly difficult to identify.[6]

To summarize, in general, expenditure on intangible assets may either be written off in the period in which it is incurred or be dealt with in the same way as

5. Statement of Standard Accounting Practice No. 13, *Accounting for Research and Development*, The Institute of Chartered Accountants in England and Wales, revised January 1989, paragraphs 24 and 25.
6. The difficulties in capitalizing and amortizing intangible assets are examined in Chapter 17.

expenditure on fixed assets, i.e. placed initially in the balance sheet and amortized as an expense over its effective life, subject to any limitations imposed by legislation or by accounting standards.

6.7   Illustration of the accounting treatment of intangible assets

We now provide an illustration and describe the accounting treatment of research and development and of patents. The accounting treatment of purchased goodwill and brands has been the subject of much debate in recent years and is discussed in detail in Chapters 16 and 17.

Research and development

Pittodrie Ltd manufactures a range of chemical products. During year 1, it incurs the following expenditure on research and development:

Development of project Easter. (This has already proved successful. 10,000 units of the associated product were sold in year 1 and future sales are estimated at 30,000 units in year 2, 20,000 units in year 3, and no units thereafter)	£120,000
General research	£50,000
	£170,000

The expenditure of £120,000 incurred on the development of project Easter results in benefits (future sales) that can be identified. Provided that sales are expected to generate surpluses greater than the development costs, an appropriate accounting treatment could be to 'spread' the development expenditure over the life of the product in proportion to the number of product units sold each year. Hence the amount of £120,000 would in the first instance be treated as an asset. It would subsequently be transferred as a cost to the income statement (i.e. matched with revenues) as follows:

		£
Year 1	$\left(\dfrac{10,000}{60,000} \times £120,000 \right)$	20,000
Year 2	$\left(\dfrac{30,000}{60,000} \times £120,000 \right)$	60,000

$$\text{Year 3} \quad \left(\frac{20,000}{60,000} \times £120,000 \right) \qquad\qquad \underline{40,000}$$

$$\underline{\underline{£120,000}}$$

The unallocated cost at the end of each year (£100,000 at the end of year 1 and £40,000 at the end of year 2) would be shown as an intangible asset in the balance sheet of Pittodrie Ltd. (Although such a treatment is currently possible in the UK, the vast majority of organizations write off all their research and development expenditure in the year of its incurrence.)

There is no specific project revenue against which the general research expenditure of £50,000 can be matched. Although it is presumably expected to result at some time in increased net revenues, there is considerable uncertainty attached to both their timing and their amount. In this situation, the concept of prudence would predominate, and the expenditure of £50,000 would be charged as an expense to the income statement in year 1.

Patents, trademarks and copyrights

Suppose that Goldstone Ltd manufactures novelties. It acquires for £150,000 a patent to produce a particular novelty good, the cappielow. When it is acquired by Goldstone Ltd, the patent has a further twelve years to run. Production of cappielows is expected to be profitable during the remaining life of the patent.

On acquisition, the cost of the patent will be treated as an asset. It will then be written off (amortized) over its remaining life of twelve years. The method of amortization chosen may depend on the patterns of benefits expected from production of cappielows. If the benefits are expected to be similar from year to year, the straight line method will probably be used. Under this method, the annual amortization charge will be £12,500 (£150,000 ÷ 12) and the net balance sheet value of the patent will be decreased by £12,500 each year (e.g. it will be £137,500 at the end of the first year). A different pattern of benefits may suggest the use of a different amortization method; for example, the expectation of declining benefits over time may lead to the use of the reducing balance method.

We conclude this section with a general comment on the question as to whether expenditure on intangible assets should be written off immediately or over a number of periods. Most professional accountancy bodies, in the UK and elsewhere, recommend that certain intangible assets, in particular research and development, should be written off immediately. This recommendation is generally based on the difficulty of identifying, and the uncertainty attaching to, future benefits arising from the possession of such assets. Nevertheless, it is presumably the case that organizations undertaking expenditure on intangible assets do so because they expect the expenditure to give rise to future benefits having a present value at least equal to the amount of the expenditure. The immediate amortization of the expenditure, particularly if the amount spent varies considerably over time, may result in wide fluctuations in reported performance from period to period and in the omission from balance sheets of assets having positive values. Such a treatment may be misleading to users of accounting reports who wish to make predictions of an enterprise's likely future performance. The question is particularly relevant with regard to the treatment of purchased goodwill, which may, if included, be the largest single asset on a company's balance sheet. Hence, we shall return to this issue in Chapter 17 when we discuss the accounting treatment of both goodwill and brands.

6.8   The primacy of the income statement or the balance sheet

Throughout this book we have identified the differences and similarities between cash flow accounting and accrual accounting. Many of the differences arise because, under accrual accounting, not all cash outflows are treated as expenses. The purchase and use of fixed assets is a good illustration of this. We have seen in this chapter that if some benefits from the purchase of an asset arise after the accounting period in which the expenditure is incurred, that proportion of the expenditure relating to those future benefits should be treated as an asset. Hence most balance sheets include assets such as buildings, machinery, vehicles and development expenditure. The cost of these assets is allocated between the accounting periods that benefit from their use and in this chapter we have spent some time examining the different methods of depreciation which can be applied to fixed assets. We discovered that there exist significant differences not only between cash flow accounting and accrual accounting but also between different, but equally acceptable, methods of accrual accounting.

Different methods of depreciation generate different depreciation charges in the income statement and different net book values in the balance sheet. This is obvious from a review of the basic accounting equation which we introduced in Chapter 5:

$$\text{Assets} - \text{Liabilities} = \overbrace{\text{Paid-in capital} + \text{Retained income}}^{\text{Ownership interest}}$$

Any item which affects the income statement must also affect the balance sheet, because the income retained for the year is added to previously retained income in the ownership interest section of the balance sheet. Hence, there must be a corresponding impact on one or more of the other *elements* in the accounting equation to maintain the balance. Clearly, the selection by management of a particular method of depreciation will influence both the reported profit figure in the income statement and the reported net asset figure in the balance sheet.

However, we noted earlier that, under the historical cost accrual accounting

Table 6.7 *Details of asset*

Cost 1 January 19X1	£300,000
Estimated useful life	10 years
Residual value	£0
Method of depreciation	straight line
Depreciation for the year	£30,000
Net book value at 31 December 19X1	£270,000

approach, the amount of assets in the balance sheet is represented by costs which have not yet been matched against revenues. This amount does not bear any resemblance to the current value of those assets and the balance sheet, in the words of one critic, is simply 'a dustbin of unallocated costs'. This is the case irrespective of the depreciation method chosen to write off fixed assets.

It would appear, therefore, that under conventional historical cost accounting, the balance sheet is viewed as a less useful, less important statement than is the income statement. However, this conclusion reveals yet another dilemma for regulators seeking a conceptual framework — a coherent set of principles or concepts which can be used as a theoretical basis for determining which events should be accounted for, how they should be measured and how they should be communicated to others (see Chapter 3, Section 3.5). Let us illustrate this with an example.

Table 6.7 presents data for a specific piece of equipment. We know that equally valid alternative figures might be suggested for its estimated useful life and residual value, and that an alternative method of depreciation could have been adopted, but let us accept the data as given. What interests us here is how items in the income statement and the balance sheet are determined.

From the data, depreciation for the year is calculated as £30,000 and is charged to the income statement. The same amount is deducted from the cost of the equipment to produce a net book value of £270,000 in the balance sheet. This £270,000 represents that part of the cost of the machine which has not yet been matched to revenues. This approach to measuring the elements of financial statements is called the *Revenue and Expense view*. In the example above, the depreciation expense is calculated first, and this determines the book value of the asset in the balance sheet. In general, the *Revenue and Expense (income statement)* approach defines income as revenues less expenses, and the income statement is seen as the primary financial statement. The balance sheet is a residual statement — it contains unmatched revenues and expenses.

This is the approach we have adopted so far in this chapter. However, a different approach could be adopted. With reference to the equipment in Table 6.7, suppose an independent valuer valued the machine at £270,000 on 31 December 19X1. An *Asset and Liability* approach would first enter the £270,000 in the balance sheet, and calculate the depreciation for the year as the difference between the cost of the equipment at the beginning of the year and its value at the end of the year. In general, the *Asset and Liability (balance sheet)* approach focuses upon the balance sheet as the primary statement and aims to ensure that all assets and liabilities are properly identified and measured. Income is viewed as the change in net worth where net worth is equal to 'assets minus liabilities'.

In the example above, the depreciation charge for the year as calculated under the revenue and expenses approach, is identical to the change in asset value as calculated under the asset and liability view. In such circumstances, the two approaches will result in the same figures being recorded in the financial statements for expenses and asset values. However the two approaches could give rise to different figures. For example, suppose that the valuer estimated the value of the equipment to be £250,000 at the end of the year. If the income statement approach defines income as *realized* revenues less matched expenses (as in conventional accounting), the depreciation charge would remain £30,000 and the net book value, £270,000. If the balance sheet approach recognizes *unrealized* gains and losses, as well as realized ones, the net book value would be reported as £250,000 and the depreciation charge as £50,000.

The inclusion of unrealized gains and losses in financial statements is not conditional upon a balance sheet approach. However, if regulators considered the balance sheet to be the primary financial statement, it is unlikely that it would continue to be treated as a 'dustbin of unallocated costs'. It is more likely that there would be pressure for it to represent some form of 'net worth' of the organization. This might entail not only the valuation of tangible assets at their current values, but the inclusion of some intangible assets, such as reputation and brand names, which have traditionally been omitted from the balance sheet under the conventional income statement approach. Hence, it is likely that there would be significant, far-reaching consequences if accounting regulators and standard setters were to adopt the balance sheet approach to financial reporting in place of the traditional income statement approach.

Defining the elements of financial statements

The income statement approach which adopts a concept of realized income is essentially the one adopted by conventional accrual accounting and is the approach adopted throughout most of this book. However, most attempts to develop a conceptual framework for accounting have adopted the balance sheet approach (we discuss these attempts in Chapter 15, Section 15.3). Using a balance sheet approach, assets and liabilities are defined first and the other parts of the accounting equation are then derived from these definitions, i.e. ownership interest (or equity) is derived from the measurement of net assets, and income is derived from identifying changes in the balance sheet value of assets and liabilities. Thus, it is crucial that the definitions adopted for assets and liabilities are clear and unambiguous. They determine not only the items reported in the balance sheet, but also those reported in the income statement.

The International Accounting Standards Committee[7] (IASC) has defined an asset as 'a resource controlled by an enterprise as a result of past events and from which future economic benefits are expected to flow', and a liability as 'a present obligation of the enterprise arising from past events, the settlement of which is expected to result in an outflow from the enterprise of resources embodying economic benefits'.

It has also identified the criteria which must be satisfied for an item to be recognized in the accounts. For example, an item meeting the definition of an asset should be recognized if:

(a) it is probable that any future economic benefit associated with the item will flow to or from the enterprise; and
(b) the item has an attribute that can be measured with reliability.

Are these definitions and criteria sufficiently clear and unambiguous to form part of a conceptual framework — to enable the preparers of accounts to determine with confidence what should, and what should not, be included in a balance sheet (and consequently in an income statement also)?

Consider a retailing company which has been established for many years and which has a reputation for selling high quality goods at reasonable prices. All the goods sold in the company's stores are either manufactured by the company or commissioned exclusively for sale in its stores. The goods are identified with the company through the use of a brand name to which the company has a legal title. Is this brand name an asset?

If we apply the IASC definitions and criteria stated above we could argue that the brand name is clearly *controlled* by the company — the company has a legal title to the brand name; it can choose when to use the brand name to endorse items for sale; and no other company may use the name. Furthermore, because the brand name is associated with quality and value for money, it is probable that its use by the company will result in *future economic benefits*. Hence, it would appear that certain brand names not only satisfy the definition of an asset; they also satisfy at least one of the criteria required for them to be recognized in the accounts. However, there remains the problem of the value at which the brand should be included in the accounts. What constitutes an 'attribute that can be measured with reliability'? The cost of purchasing a brand? The cost of building an internally-created brand? The value of the future benefits accruing to a brand? Or the value to a third party which might acquire the brand? Perhaps we can now appreciate the dilemma facing accounting regulators. Their recommendation on the accounting treatment of brands (and many other issues) will have implications for the debates concerning the primacy of historical cost accounting over current value accounting and the primacy of the income statement over the balance sheet.

7. Exposure Draft 32, *Framework for the Preparation and Presentation of Financial Statements,* IASC, May 1988.

Such is the importance of these issues that we shall return to them in Chapter 15, to examine the general problems of defining and recognizing the elements of financial statements, and again in Chapter 17, to examine in depth the problems involved in accounting for intangible assets such as brands and goodwill.

6.9 An illustration from practice — E.H. Booth & Co. Ltd

The complete set of Booths' accounts can be found in Appendix 1.

We begin by identifying the fixed assets figure on the balance sheet of Booths (page 11). There are no intangible assets, but 'Tangible assets' amount to £26,798,485 (1991 £27,737,237). This figure represents the net book value (NBV) of all the tangible fixed assets. In order to break down this amount between the different categories of assets and between cost and accumulated depreciation, we must refer to Note 8 (page 16). As we explained in Section 5.12, the 'Notes to the Accounts' (which begin on page 14) are an integral part of the financial statements. There is simply too much information to be disclosed on the face of the balance sheet, income statement and cash flow statement. Hence companies present a series of sub-totals in the main financial statements and refer the user to a supporting note where appropriate.

Note 8 reveals that:

(a) the net book value of tangible fixed assets (£26,798,485) comprises an original cost of £36,946,468 and accumulated depreciation of £10,147,983;

(b) Land and Buildings comprise approximately 60% (£23 million) of the cost of tangible fixed assets, but almost 80% (£21 million) of their net book value (cost less accumulated depreciation).

It is to be expected that Land and Buildings comprise a larger proportion of the NBV of fixed assets than of their cost. Fixtures, Plant and Vehicles are depreciated more quickly than Land and Buildings. Indeed, as we noted in Section 6.2, freehold land should not be depreciated at all and we should check that this is the case in Booths' accounts. The Statement of Accounting Policies (page 13) reveals that freehold land is not depreciated, although leasehold land is depreciated because it has a finite life — the length of the lease. Freehold buildings are written off on a straight line basis over 50 years.

The Statement of Accounting Policies also reveals that Booths has adopted a mixture of methods to depreciate its fixtures, plant and vehicles. Some assets are being depreciated on a straight line basis, others on a reducing balance basis. All are being written off more quickly than are freehold buildings. As a result, Note 8 reveals that the depreciation charge for the year for Land and Buildings (£332,261) is only 1.4% of the cost of those assets at the beginning of the year.

The depreciation charge for Fixtures, Plant and Vehicles (£995,194) is 7.3% of the historical cost of those assets at the beginning of the year.

The movements (additions, disposals and depreciation charge for the year) on the tangible fixed assets account (Note 8) represent one side of a double entry in the bookkeeping system of Booths. We should be able to identify the corresponding double entry for each movement.

(a) *Additions*. During the year, Booths purchased £404,168 of fixed assets, comprising mainly fixtures, plant and vehicles. The entry in Note 8 refers to the Additions to fixed assets — the corresponding entry should be a decrease in cash or an increase in creditors. The Cash Flow Statement (page 12) includes an item 'Payments to Acquire Tangible Fixed Assets (404,168)' in the section headed 'Investing Activities'. It would appear that all the additions have been paid for by the year end, and the effect of the double entry has been to increase fixed assets and decrease cash by the same amount.

(b) *Disposals*. Booths disposed of assets which had originally cost £53,353 (Note 8, Disposals). These assets had been depreciated over the years and the 'Depreciation' account in Note 8 reveals that the accumulated depreciation on these disposals was £37,888. Thus, Booths disposed of fixed assets with a net book value of £15,465 (£53,353 − £37,888). To ascertain how much Booths received for these assets, we should look again at the Cash Flow Statement (page 12). The amount, 'Receipts from Sale of Tangible Fixed Assets − £15,465', is identical to the NBV of the assets sold, and hence no profit or loss was made on the sales. The effect of the double entry has been to decrease fixed assets and increase cash by the same amount.

(c) *Depreciation*. The total depreciation charge for the year is £1,327,455 (Note 8). The net book value of the fixed assets is reduced by this amount, and one would expect to find the corresponding entry as an expense in the Profit and Loss Account (page 10). In fact, in common with the vast majority of limited companies, Booths discloses very few individual categories of expense on the face of its profit and loss account. It is normal practice to report a figure for 'Operating profit' in the profit and loss account and to refer readers to a note which will disclose various operating expenses which have been deducted in calculating operating profit.

In Booths' Profit and Loss Account, we are referred to Note 2 (page 14) for further explanation of the 'Operating profit' sub-total. There we discover that depreciation of £1,327,455 was charged to the profit and loss account during the year. The effect of the double entry has been to decrease fixed assets and reduce income by the same amount.

We have now satisfied ourselves as to the composition of the 'Fixed Assets — Tangible assets' figure in the balance sheet. Starting with last year's NBV of £27,737,237, the company purchased new assets for cash, disposed of some old assets for cash, and depreciated all the remaining assets excluding freehold land. Because, in 1992, the depreciation charge is greater than the net capital expenditure, the result is a fall in the NBV of Tangible fixed assets to £26,798,485.

We noted earlier that it is Booths' accounting policy to depreciate leasehold land and buildings over the term of the lease, freehold buildings on a straight line basis over 50 years, and freehold land not at all. It is of interest to users of the accounts to know what proportion of land and buildings is freehold, what proportion is leasehold, and whether some of the leases are due for renewal in the near future. Note 8 discloses that Booths owns freehold properties with a net book value of £10,290,460 and leasehold properties with a net book value of £10,864,541. All of the leasehold properties are held on long leases with at least fifty years unexpired. The information in Note 8 referring to 'Interest on loans to finance the development of Land and Buildings' will be explained and analysed in Chapter 11.

Finally, we should note that Booths prepares its accounts under the historical cost convention (Statement of Accounting Policies, page 13). However, several of its stores occupy prime sites which were acquired, in some instances, several decades ago. It would be of interest to both shareholders and management to know what is the market value of the land and buildings. Indeed, the Companies Act requires the difference between the market value of property assets and the balance sheet amount to be disclosed in the directors' report if, in the opinion of the directors, it is significant. Booths' Report of the Directors (page 7) discloses that the market value of the company's land and buildings was in excess of £34 million in 1991. This is approximately £13 million (or 60%) higher than the historical cost net book value of land and buildings reported in the 1992 accounts (£21,155,001, Note 8).

Discussion topics

1. Outline the main methods of calculating depreciation, and discuss their basic differences.

2. What does the term 'depreciation' mean when used by accountants? Explain other possible meanings of the term and discuss why these meanings may not be acceptable to accountants.

3. What do the terms 'use' and 'time' depreciation mean? Can you think of any assets which depreciate purely through time, or purely because of use?

4. What is the difference between depreciation and maintenance cost? What justification is there for including them together?

5. What are the principal types of intangible assets?

6. What distinguishes intangible assets from other fixed assets?

7. Why do you suppose that most professional accountancy bodies recommend that research and development be written off immediately to the income statement? Why is goodwill not treated in the same way?

8. On 1 November 1967, AEI Ltd forecast that its profit for the year to 31 December 1967 would amount to £10 million. The company was taken over by GEC Ltd which later announced that AEI Ltd had incurred a loss of £4.5 million in 1967. Two firms of auditors (one of which had reviewed the original forecast) issued a joint statement which included the following sentence:

> Broadly speaking, of the difference of £14.5 million, we would attribute £5 million to adverse differences which are matters substantially of fact rather than of judgement, and the balance of £9.5 million to adjustments which remain substantially matters of judgement.

Discuss the matters of accounting judgement which might have produced a difference of £9.5 million in the profit figures.

9. Distinguish between the *Revenue and Expenses view* and the *Asset and Liability view* to measuring assets in financial statements.

10. Explain how the revaluation of Booths' land and buildings, referred to in the Report of the Directors (page 7), should be accounted for if Booths adopted a balance sheet approach which recognized unrealized gains and losses when preparing its financial statements.

11. Discuss why it is important to users of accounts that clear and unambiguous definitions of assets and liabilities are adopted in financial statements.

Exercises

6.1 Figaro purchases a machine for £6,000. He estimates that the machine will last eight years and its scrap value will then be £1,000.

- (a) Prepare the accounting equation entries for the first three years of the machine's life and show the balance sheet extract at the end of each year, charging depreciation using the straight line method.
- (b) What would be the net book value of the machine at the end of the third year if depreciation was charged at 20% p.a. using the reducing balance method?

6.2 Ms Carlos, a manufacturer, purchases a motor van on 1 January 19X3 for £10,000. She intends to keep the motor van for four years, at the end of which time she expects to be able to sell it for £4,000. Ms Carlos expects to spend £2,000 on a major overhaul during 19X5 and wishes to spread the cost of the overhaul *equally* over the asset's life.

■ (a) For each of the years 19X3, 19X4, 19X5 and 19X6, calculate the expected total annual cost (depreciation plus overhaul) of the motor van and its expected written-down book value at the end of the year, based on the following methods of depreciation:

   (i) straight line
   (ii) reducing balance
   (iii) sum-of-the-years-digits.

(b) Explain the accounting entries which will be needed to record the cost of the overhaul.

6.3 Zerlina Ltd commenced business on 1 September 19X0. It purchased and sold plant and machinery during the three years ended 31 August 19X3, as follows:

1 September 19X0	Purchased Mk I Blender	for	£10,000
	Purchased Mk I Mixer	for	£12,000
1 September 19X1	Purchased Mk II Blender	for	£11,000
1 September 19X2	Purchased Mk II Mixer	for	£14,000
	Sold Mk I Mixer	for	£6,000
31 August 19X3	Purchased Mk III Blender and received £5,000 trade-in allowance against the Mk I Blender	for	£13,000

■ Show the accounting entries for Zerlina Ltd, necessary to record the above transactions, if depreciation is to be provided:

(a) using the straight line method at an annual rate of 20%.
(b) using the reducing balance method at an annual rate of 30%.

6.4 On 1 July 19X2, Mr Alfredo buys a computer for £4,000. He expects that its economic life will be 5 years, and that it will have a resale value of £500 at the end of that time. He decides to use the straight line method for providing depreciation on the computer.

On 30 June 19X4, Mr Alfredo realizes that his estimate of the computer's economic life was optimistic and that it is unlikely to last beyond 30 June 19X6. He also believes that it will have no scrap or resale value at that time. In consequence, he decides to amend *future* annual depreciation charges so as to write off its entire cost by 30 June 19X6. He does not wish to adjust the written-down book value of the asset at 30 June 19X4.

On 30 June 19X6, Mr Alfredo disposes of the computer by selling it to a scrap metal dealer for £100.

■ Show the accounting entries relating to the computer for the period from 1 July 19X2 to 30 June 19X6, under the following assumptions:

(a) That Mr Alfredo prepares accounts annually to 30 June.
(b) That Mr Alfredo prepares accounts annually to 31 December.

6.5 The following series of *independent* events relate to divisions of the Pango Co. for the year to 31 March 19X9.

(a) Division A bought a machine for £20,000 on 1 January 19X4. The machine was expected to have a useful life of nine years and be sold for scrap for £2,000. The machine was in fact sold on 28 February 19X9 for £12,000. Division A uses straight-line depreciation, and takes no depreciation in the year of purchase.

■ Calculate the gain or loss on the sale of the machine, assuming one full year's depreciation in the year of sale.

(b) Division B owns various items of machinery which, at 1 April 19X8, have attracted total depreciation of £280,000. The balance on the accumulated depreciation account at 31 March 19X9, prior to any adjusting entries, is £300,000. During the year to 31 March 19X9 one machine which cost £94,000 was sold for £70,000. This resulted in a loss of £3,000. No other assets were disposed of during the year.

■ Calculate the depreciation expense for the year.

6.6 Inez Ltd bought a machine for £500,000 on 1 January 19X3 and sold it for £100,000 on 1 January 19X6. The machine was replaced immediately by an identical new model costing £700,000. The market values of the machine at the end of 19X3, 19X4 and 19X5 were estimated as follows:

31 December 19X3   £300,000
31 December 19X4   £150,000
31 December 19X5   £100,000

Inez Ltd prepares accounts annually to 31 December.

■ (a) Prepare a statement showing the amounts to be entered in the company's profit and loss accounts and balance sheets for 19X3, 19X4, 19X5 and 19X6 in respect of the machine bought on 1 January 19X3, for annual depreciation charges, profit or loss on sale of the machine and written-down value at the end of each year, under each of the following assumptions:

  (i)   that depreciation is calculated by the straight line method, at an annual rate of 25%;
  (ii) that depreciation is calculated by the reducing balance method, at an annual rate of 50%;
  (iii) that depreciation is calculated each year as the fall in the market value of the machine during the year.

(b) Using the figures you have calculated in (a), discuss the relative merits of the above three methods of providing for depreciation.

Further reading

Baxter, W.T., *Depreciation*, Sweet and Maxwell, 1971.
Buckley, E., 'Depreciation — a conceptual problem', *Accountancy*, May 1992.
Egginton, D., 'Towards some principles for intangible asset accounting', *Accounting and Business Research*, Summer 1990.
Goodacre, A., 'R & D expenditure and the analysts' view', *Accountancy*, April 1991.
Hendriksen, E.S., *Accounting Theory*, Irwin, 1982.

Holgate, P., 'Time to get off the beaten track', *Accountancy*, July 1987.
Lee, T.A., 'Goodwill: an example of will-o'-the-wisp accounting', *Accounting and Business Research*, Autumn 1971.
Sherwood, K., 'Depreciation, residual values and revaluations', *Accountancy*, February 1983.

CHAPTER 7

Stocks

In this chapter we explain the different possible accounting treatments of stock, or as the asset is sometimes termed 'inventory'. Our explanations of the alternative treatments available for valuing stock will be conducted within the historical cost framework.

As with fixed assets, the accounting entries associated with stock are, in principle, straightforward. The original cost of the stock is treated initially as an asset and subsequently the cost is transferred to the income statement as the asset is used up. Thus, the income statement for a period includes the cost of stock sold during the period, usually termed *cost of sales* or *cost of goods sold*, and the balance sheet at the end of the period shows the cost of stock unsold at the balance sheet date. The accounting entries are illustrated later in the chapter.

Stock is a tangible asset which is used up in order to generate revenue. Many enterprises, for example retail stores such as Marks and Spencer plc and Sainsburys plc, sell stock in the form in which it is purchased, without undertaking any productive or manufacturing operations. For such enterprises all stock is in a similar form — available immediately for resale. Other organizations, for example manufacturing companies such as the Ford Motor Co., buy raw materials and convert them in some way before reselling them. As we saw in Chapter 4, the conversion (or transformation) process involves the use of such factors as labour, machines, power and factory space. In consequence, manufacturing companies hold stock in three different forms:

1. *Raw materials* — representing stock that has been purchased but which has not yet entered the transformation process.
2. *Work in progress* — representing raw materials on which some transformation work has taken place, but which have not yet been converted into a final resaleable form.

3. *Finished goods* – representing items which have been fully transformed and are in a form suitable for resale.

The process whereby raw material stock is converted to finished goods is shown diagrammatically in Figure 7.1. Each of the three upper boxes represents one of the different forms of stock described above. At any time, a manufacturing organization will probably hold stock in each of the three forms (see, for example, Figure 7.2). Broadly speaking, the cost of raw materials is the amount paid for those raw materials which have not yet entered the transformation process; the cost of work in progress is the cost of raw materials on which some conversion work has been undertaken (but which are not yet in a final resaleable form) plus the cost of other inputs, such as labour, machinery and production overheads, which have been incurred in (partially) converting the raw materials; and the cost of finished goods is the raw materials cost plus all costs to convert the stock into

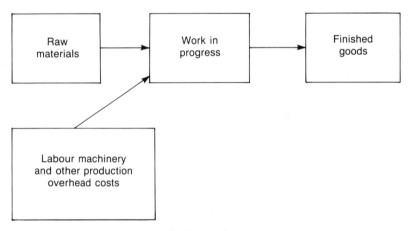

Figure 7.1 *Stock transformation process*

Lonrho Plc and Subsidiaries

NOTES TO THE ACCOUNTS

15 Stocks	1991	1990
	£m	£m
Raw materials and consumables	67	76
Work in progress	36	38
Finished goods and goods for resale	409	459
	512	573

Figure 7.2 *Extract from the Annual Report of Lonrho plc 1991*

a form suitable for resale. In this chapter we devote our attention primarily to the treatment of stocks of raw materials and finished goods and shall examine also the particular problems involved in determining the cost of long-term work in progress.

Having stated earlier that the cost of stock, in whatever form, is treated initially as an asset, and is subsequently transferred as an expense to the income statement, the major problem faced by the organization lies in deciding what is meant by the 'cost' of stock. Much of the chapter is concerned with this problem. Two particular problems arise in identifying the historical cost of stock: the choice of *costing method* and the *stock flow assumption* to be used. We examine both of these issues in the following sections.

7.1   Stock costing methods

The problem of choosing a costing method arises only where an organization undertakes a manufacturing or production process. The problem is to determine whether work in progress and finished goods should be valued at *direct cost* or *full cost*. The aim of the costing method is to reflect how *traceable* are costs to units of finished product. Certain costs such as direct labour and raw material, which are usually combined in a particular proportion into the finished product, are termed *directly traceable*, or simply *direct costs*. The 'directness' suggests that there is a causal link between costs incurred and output produced. The aggregation of direct labour and raw material cost is often termed the *prime cost of production*.

Other costs, although incurred in producing the finished good, are not directly traceable to individual units of production or, if traceable, may possess a very tenuous relationship. These costs comprise both variable and fixed manufacturing overheads. Because of their indirect traceability to production, these costs are commonly termed *indirect costs*. Examples of indirect costs are rent payable, insurance, depreciation and supervisors' salaries. Indirect costs often form the most substantial element of product costs.

The make-up of the cost of a particular product using the criterion of traceability might be as follows:

		£
Direct costs:	Direct labour (2 hours at £5 per hour)	10
	Raw materials (4 kg at £1.50 per kg)	6
	Prime cost	16
Indirect costs:	Total manufacturing overheads, allocated	
	on the basis of ... (see Section 7.2)	18
	Full cost = Total product cost	£34

7.2   The allocation of manufacturing overhead costs

The above illustration of a total product cost shows an element of total manufacturing overheads, allocated on some, as yet unspecified, basis. The allocation of total manufacturing overhead, i.e. both variable and fixed overhead, to units of product is termed *full* or *absorption costing*. The word 'allocation' implies the dividing-up of a single whole into individual parts, and so entails the use of a dividing mechanism — or an allocation or absorption rate. Full costing, therefore, involves the choice of an appropriate mechanism or rate to allocate the total overheads to products. The rate is determined usually by dividing the period's overheads by some measure of the organization's level of productive activity.

Typically, a single rate is not used to allocate all the organization's manufacturing overheads. Overheads are more usually split into their fixed and variable components, and a different allocation rate is applied to each type of overhead. The calculation of the variable overhead per unit is the easier task; variable overhead is normally related to the number of labour hours (or, in capital intensive processes, the number of machine hours) taken to produce one unit. The calculation of the amount of fixed overhead to be allocated to each production unit is much less simple.

At its most basic level, the fixed overhead allocation rate is expressed in the following form:

$$\text{Fixed overhead rate} = \frac{\text{Budgeted fixed overhead for the period}}{\text{Measure of productive activity (estimate)}}$$

For example:

$$\text{Fixed overhead rate} = \frac{£2,500,000}{500,000 \text{ units produced}}$$

$$= £5 \text{ per unit produced}$$

The resultant rate is an *average rate*, based on the assumption that units produced in one period of the year will take up a similar proportion of fixed overhead costs as units produced in other periods. The rate itself depends on two factors: a numerator representing the expected money amount to be incurred for overheads for the period, and a denominator representing the level of productive activity expected during the period which may be expressed in money terms, in hours, or in production units. Because of these different possible methods of measuring productive activity, fixed overhead rates may be expressed as percentages, or as £s per hour, or as £s per unit of production.

Two fundamental problems are thus presented by the choice of a fixed overhead allocation rate. First, how should the organization select the measure of productive activity to be used as the denominator, i.e. as the basis for allocating overheads;

and, following sequentially, how should it interpret any differences arising if the actual number of hours, or units of production, or money amounts comprising the denominator are different from expectations? We now look in turn at each of these two problems.

1. The basis for fixed overhead allocation

Many different bases are used to allocate fixed overheads to products. If the organization produces only one product, the allocation is most often determined simply by dividing fixed overheads by the number of units produced. If, however, the organization produces many different products, one single multipurpose allocation rate may be inappropriate, and different rates (and bases) of allocation may be used for each of the different products. All of this can make for great difficulties in the interpretation of the results of fixed overhead allocation and thus of stock valuation. The following example illustrates some of the issues which can arise when fixed overheads are allocated to production on the basis of different activity measures.

Example
Priestfield Ltd produces two products. Budgeted data for the year are as follows:

	Product A £		Product B £
Direct costs per unit:			
Material (5 kg × £5)	25.00	(3 kg × £7.50)	22.50
Labour (2 hr × £3.75)	7.50	(3 hr × £5)	15.00
Machine cost ($\frac{1}{2}$ hr × £15)	7.50	(1$\frac{1}{2}$ hr × £20)	30.00
Total direct cost per unit	40.00		67.50
Budgeted output (units)	25,000		20,000
Total budgeted overheads (all fixed)		£1,000,000	

The following bases for allocation will be used to illustrate the procedures involved in assigning the total amount for overheads (£1,000,000) to products A and B.

1. Direct labour hours
2. Direct labour cost
3. Machine hours
4. Machine cost
5. Total direct cost
6. Budgeted output

Applying the six different methods gives overhead allocations as shown in Table 7.1. The application of the six different bases of overhead allocation gives six different solutions. In five of the six cases, product B bears the greater proportion

Table 7.1 Priestfield Ltd — different methods of fixed overhead allocation

		Product A	Product B
		£	£
Labour hours:	Total A (2 × 25,000)	50,000	
	B (3 × 20,000)	60,000	
		110,000 hr	
Allocation rate	$\dfrac{£1,000,000}{110,000 \text{ hr}}$ = £9.0909 per labour hour	454,550	545,450
Labour cost:	Total A (£7.50 × 25,000)	£187,500	
	B (£15.00 × 20,000)	£300,000	
		£487,500	
Allocation rate	$\dfrac{£1,000,000}{£487,500}$ = 205% of labour costs	384,600	615,400
Machine hours:	Total A ($\frac{1}{2}$ × 25,000)	12,500	
	B ($1\frac{1}{2}$ × 20,000)	30,000	
		42,500 hr	
Allocation rate	$\dfrac{£1,000,000}{42,500 \text{ hr}}$ = £23.529 per machine hour	294,120	705,880

	Product A	Product B
	£	£

Machine cost:

Total A (£7.50 × 25,000)   £187,500
B (£30.00 × 20,000)   £600,000
£787,500

Allocation rate $\dfrac{£1,000,000}{£787,000}$ = 127% of machine cost

	Product A	Product B
	238,100	761,900

Total direct cost:

Total A (£40.00 × 25,000)   £1,000,000
B (£67.50 × 20,000)   £1,350,000
£2,350,000

Allocation rate $\dfrac{£1,000,000}{£2,350,000}$ = 42.55% of total direct cost

	Product A	Product B
	425,500	574,500

Budgeted output:

Total A   25,000
B   20,000
45,000 units

Allocation rate $\dfrac{£1,000,000}{45,000 \text{ units}}$ = £22.222 per unit

	Product A	Product B
	555,560	444,440

of fixed overheads (ranging between 54% and 76%), whereas if budgeted output is used as the allocation basis, product A, because of its greater output, bears the greater proportion. Which of the methods should be chosen? It is a difficult question to answer. All the methods give answers which, it can be argued, are equally right and, by the same token, are equally wrong — because all the methods are equally *arbitrary*. And in one sense each of the answers produced by these bookkeeping adjustments is acceptable for stock costing purposes as long as it is understood that the results are purely a function of the arbitrary bases used, and as long as the chosen method is applied consistently.

We might argue that it may be more sensible to relate such allocations to the *nature* of the individual product, and thus to the nature of the overhead costs to be allocated. For example, if the product in question is produced by the use of capital intensive methods, so that the bulk of fixed overhead costs reflects this situation, then machine hours might represent the most suitable allocation basis. In our example, this would entail the use of method 3, under which the greater proportion of overhead costs would be allocated to product B, each unit of which uses three times as much machine time as does product A.

If, however, the production process is more dependent on the use of labour, and thus the attendant fixed overhead costs are more likely to be a function of labour intensiveness, it seems more appropriate to use either labour costs or labour hours as the allocation base. In practice, labour hours are more widely used as an allocation basis than labour costs. In our example, method 1 would be used.

Some companies, for example IBM, Hewlett Packard, Philips and Rank Xerox, have taken this approach a stage further and have adopted a system of product costing called *activity based costing* (ABC). ABC seeks to identify the activities which give rise to the overhead costs. The costs are then allocated to products on the basis of the level of activity caused by each product. For example, production scheduling costs and machine set-up costs may be generated by the number of production runs each product generates. A product which is produced in small batches entailing many short production runs would be allocated a higher proportion of production scheduling costs and machine set-up costs than would a product produced in large batches over a small number of production runs.

Such a method of allocating overheads is very useful to management who wish to identify the profitability, and hence the cost, of individual products, and many organizations are introducing ABC into their management accounting systems. However, in financial accounting we are less concerned with individual product costs. We are concerned more with the division of costs between the *total cost of goods sold* and the *total closing inventory*. Hence, a method of allocation less sophisticated than ABC is usually acceptable.

2.   Changes during the period in the basis of overhead allocation

In the previous example we have used predetermined (determined before the time of incurrence) rates to allocate overheads to products. The use of predetermined rates to cost products is necessary, as it is obviously not advisable to wait until the end of an accounting period before preparing stock valuations. For example, large quoted companies must produce interim reports which necessitate interim stock valuations. But the use of estimated overhead rates presents certain interpretational difficulties if the *actual* level of activity (labour hours, production units, etc.) differs from the estimated level used to determine the rate. We can best explain this situation by way of an example.

Suppose that the expected (budgeted) fixed overhead for the forthcoming period is £15,000 and suppose that the firm expects to produce 15,000 units. Production units are to be taken as the basis for overhead allocation. The overhead allocation rate is thus:

$$\text{Allocation rate} = \frac{\text{Budgeted overhead}}{\text{Level of activity}} = \frac{£15,000}{15,000 \text{ units}} = £1 \text{ per unit}$$

This situation is illustrated graphically in Figure 7.3.

Now, suppose that the actual level of activity for the period falls short of the expected level by 5,000 units, so that actual production is only 10,000 units. Figure 7.4 shows the impact of this decrease in volume. Because of the decline in volume from 15,000 units to 10,000 units of production there is a difference between the level of costs expected to be allocated to production (the budgeted figure of £15,000) and the costs actually allocated (10,000 units at £1 per unit equals £10,000). This difference of £5,000 is termed a *volume variance*, because its cause is a change in the volume of production. Volume variances may be favourable or unfavourable. If, as in this example, budgeted fixed overheads (£15,000) are greater than the total of fixed overheads allocated to production (£10,000), then obviously some fixed overheads (£5,000) remain unallocated for the period. These unallocated fixed overheads represent an *unfavourable* volume variance and *in the period's income statement this unfavourable variance is usually treated as an adjustment (i.e. added) to the cost of goods sold.* Conversely, if the volume of production had exceeded expectations and therefore the firm had allocated all its fixed costs (and more) to production, the resultant difference would be termed a *favourable* volume variance and would usually be deducted from the cost of goods sold. Similar variances will arise if actual overhead costs differ from budgeted costs.

7.3 Full costing versus direct costing

We can now illustrate the differences between the two main methods of stock costing, initially by means of a diagram and then by means of a numerical example. Figure 7.5 shows the flows of costs associated with each method. It is the treatment of fixed manufacturing overhead costs which differentiates the two systems. Under full costing, fixed manufacturing overhead costs are allocated to work in progress, and subsequently to finished goods, and are included as an element of cost of

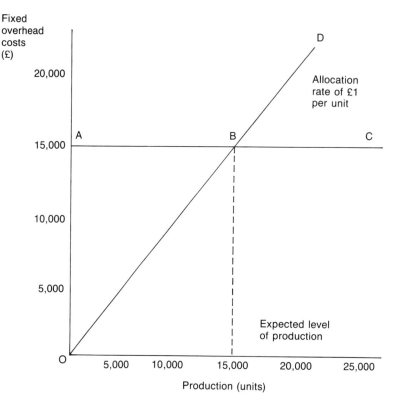

Figure 7.3 *Graphical representation of overhead allocation (1)*

AC   represents the budgeted fixed overhead line, which is constant (£15,000) at all
     levels of production
OD   represents the overhead allocation line on the basis of an allocation rate of £1 per unit
B   represents the point at which the overhead allocation line is expected to intersect
     the budgeted overhead line (i.e. the level of production at which the expected
     overhead of £15,000 is fully allocated to production units)

goods sold in the income statement when the finished goods are sold. Under direct costing, fixed manufacturing overhead costs are treated as an expense of the period rather than as an expense of the product and are written off to the income statement in the period in which they are incurred. The significance of the differences revealed by applying both full and direct costing methods to the same set of data is now explained via the example of Roker Ltd below.

The following data relate to Roker Ltd's level of activity for the years 19X0, 19X1 and 19X2.

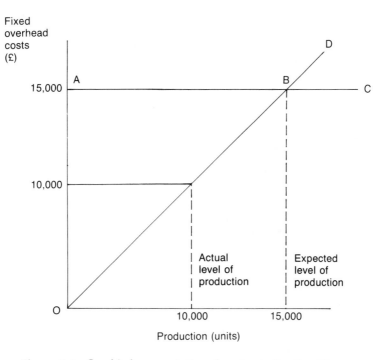

Figure 7.4 *Graphical representation of overhead allocation (2)*

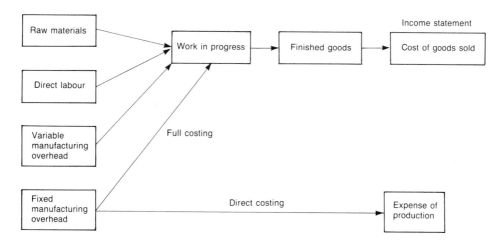

Figure 7.5 *Flow of costs in a manufacturing firm*

		19X0	19X1	19X2
(a)	Sales (in units)	10,000	12,000	2,000
(b)	Selling price (per unit)	£11	£11	£11
(c)	Production (in units)	12,000	12,000	—
(d)	Production costs			
	Direct (per unit)	£3	£3	—
	Fixed (per period)	£24,000	£24,000	—
(e)	Selling and administrative costs			
	Direct (per unit)	£1	£1	£1
	Fixed (per period)	£30,000	£30,000	—
(f)	Opening stock (in units)	0	2,000	2,000

Some comments on the above data are necessary before we begin our analysis. First, for illustrative purposes only, selling price per unit, direct costs per unit, and fixed costs per period are assumed to be constant over the three year period. Second, no production takes place in 19X2 and no fixed costs are incurred in that year. Finally, the full and direct costs per unit of stock are calculated on the basis of production costs only (i.e. all selling and administrative costs are excluded from the stock cost calculation).

Our analysis initially takes the form of income statements prepared for each of the three years under both costing methods. To prepare an income statement under full costing we need first to calculate the full cost per unit of stock. This is done as follows, using production units as the allocation base:

$$\text{Full cost per unit} = \text{Direct cost per unit} + \frac{\text{Total fixed costs}}{\text{Production units}}$$

$$= £3 + \frac{£24,000}{12,000 \text{ units}}$$

$$= £5$$

The cost per unit of stock under direct costing is represented by the direct production cost per unit of £3.

Table 7.2 shows income statements for 19X0, 19X1 and 19X2 prepared under full costing. The format of the full costing income statement reflects Roker Ltd's particular functional activities; thus costs are classified in terms of the functions of production and selling, rather than in terms of their behaviour with respect to the firm's activities. Direct and fixed costs of production are grouped together to determine the total cost of goods sold, and direct and fixed costs of selling are grouped together to determine the total selling costs.

Table 7.3 shows income statements for 19X0, 19X1 and 19X2 prepared under

Table 7.2 Roker Ltd — income statement under full costing

	19X0		19X1		19X2	
	£	£	£	£	£	£
Sales revenue		(10,000 × £11) 110,000		(12,000 × £11) 132,000		(2,000 × £11) 22,000
less: Cost of goods sold						
Opening stock		0		10,000		10,000
add: Cost of production						
Direct	36,000		36,000		0	
Fixed	24,000		24,000		0	
	(12,000 × £5) 60,000		(14,000 × £5) 70,000		(2,000 × £5) 10,000	
less: Closing stock	(2,000 × £5) 10,000	50,000	(2,000 × £5) 10,000	60,000	0	10,000
Gross profit		60,000		72,000		12,000
less: Selling costs						
Direct	(10,000 × £1) 10,000		(12,000 × £1) 12,000		(2,000 × £1) 2,000	
Fixed	30,000	40,000	30,000	42,000	0	2,000
Net income		£20,000		£30,000		£10,000

Table 7.3 *Roker Ltd – income statements under direct costing*

	19X0	£	19X1	£	19X2	£
Sales revenue	(10,000 × £11)	110,000	(12,000 × £11)	132,000	(2,000 × £11)	22,000
less: Direct costs						
Cost of goods sold						
Opening stock		0	(2,000 × £3)	6,000	(2,000 × £3)	6,000
Production costs	(12,000 × £3)	36,000	(12,000 × £3)	36,000		0
		36,000		42,000		6,000
less: Closing stock	(2,000 × £3)	6,000	(2,000 × £3)	6,000		0
		30,000		36,000		6,000
Selling costs	(10,000 × £1)	10,000	(12,000 × £1)	12,000	(2,000 × £1)	2,000
		40,000		48,000		8,000
Contribution margin (£7 per unit)		70,000		84,000		14,000
less: Fixed costs for the period						
Production		24,000		24,000		0
Selling		30,000		30,000		0
		54,000		54,000		0
Net income		£16,000		£30,000		£14,000

Table 7.4 *Roker Ltd — treatment of total production costs for 19X0*

	Full costing £	Direct costing £
Production costs incurred		
Direct	36,000	36,000
Fixed	24,000	24,000
Total	£60,000	£60,000
Split as to:		
Costs assigned to closing stock		
2,000 units × £5 per unit	£10,000	
2,000 units × £3 per unit		£6,000
Costs expensed to income statement	£50,000	£54,000

direct costing. Here the format is very different. It reflects the way costs behave with respect to Roker Ltd's production and sales activities, i.e whether costs are variable (direct) or fixed. Thus, all direct costs are grouped together and deducted from sales revenue to show the *contribution margin*. The contribution margin per unit is £7, being the difference between the sales revenue per unit of £11 and the direct production, selling and administrative cost per unit of £4. Fixed production and selling costs are then deducted from the contribution margin to determine the firm's net income.

The likely differences arising from the application of each costing method should now be clear. Full costing carries forward some of the firm's fixed production costs into closing stock, via a higher cost per unit. (Note that fixed *selling* costs do not affect stock valuation. Closing stock should comprise only those costs which have been incurred in bringing the product to its present location and condition. As closing stock has not yet been sold neither selling costs nor distribution costs can be allocated to it.) Thus, if we examine the net income for 19X0 under each method we see that the full costing income is £4,000 higher than the income under direct costing. This is explained by the treatment of the fixed production costs as shown in Table 7.4. The total production costs for 19X0 (fixed and direct) are £60,000 and are the same for each method. However, under full costing £10,000 of these costs (£6,000 direct costs and £4,000 fixed costs) are included in closing stock and are carried forward to the following period. Hence, this year's reported income is increased by the amount of costs carried forward. Under the direct costing approach only £6,000 of direct costs are carried forward, and all fixed costs are written off immediately as expenses. The difference of £4,000 represents the difference in income for the year as between the two methods.

In 19X1, the net income of £30,000 is identical for each method. Why is this? After all, Roker Ltd is still using a full costing method which costs stock at £5 per unit, which is £2 per unit higher than the direct cost method. The reason is that in 19X1, unlike 19X0, production and sales are equal at 12,000 units, and in consequence, opening and closing stock must be the same (i.e. at the start and end of 19X1, Roker Ltd had 2,000 units in stock). Because opening and closing stocks are the same in terms of units, and there is no difference in the cost per unit, *there cannot be any difference in the income arising from the different methods of stock valuation.*

Finally, in 19X2, when the opening stock of the year is sold and no further production takes place, the direct costing method shows the higher income figure by £4,000. We would expect this to happen as the direct costing approach charges £4,000 *less* against revenue in 19X2 than the full costing approach, because the opening stock under direct cost is lower by £4,000. In 19X2 the previous 'advantages' of using full costing, in terms of showing higher income, have been eliminated.

The disposition of accounting net income over the three years is as follows:

	Full costing £	Direct costing £
19X0 Income	20,000	16,000
19X1 Income	30,000	30,000
19X2 Income	10,000	14,000
Total Income	£60,000	£60,000

Some comments and conclusions from the above analysis follow:

1. In 19X0 the full costing method generates the higher income figure. This occurs because the production level of 12,000 units is greater than the level of sales of 10,000 units. Thus, some production overheads (£4,000) are not written off to the income statement but are carried forward to 19X1. We can therefore state as a general rule that — *if stock levels are rising, full costing will generate the higher income.*
2. In 19X1 the two methods produce the same income figures. We can therefore state that — *if production and sales are equal, and there are no changes in the method of stock valuation, full and direct costing will produce similar figures.*
3. In 19X2, when the opening stock of 2,000 units is sold, and no further production takes place, the variable costing method shows the higher income figure. We can therefore state that — *if stock levels are falling, direct costing will show the higher income.*

7.4 Stock flow assumptions

In many organizations it is not possible to identify which particular items of stock have in fact been sold. For example, a retail tobacconist may buy and sell substantial quantities of a particular brand of pipe tobacco. Suppose he has in stock 200 tins purchased at different times in the past. If he sells 10 tins during a period, he is unlikely to be able to identify from which batch or batches of purchases the tins have come. This would not matter if each tin in stock had cost the same amount. But suppose that the 200 tins had been bought at different prices — the question for the accountant is to decide which prices should be transferred to the income statement as the cost of the 10 tins sold. This problem is resolved by making an *assumption* about the physical flow of stock in a business. Various assumptions are possible, of which the three most common are *first in first out* (FIFO), *last in first out* (LIFO) and *weighted average*.

Under FIFO, it is assumed that when an item of stock is sold or used, that item is the oldest one of its kind held (i.e. the one which first came into stock). Hence, under FIFO the charge for cost of goods sold represents the cost of the first available purchases, and the balance sheet amount of stock still held is assumed to represent the cost of those items purchased most recently. Under LIFO, the opposite assumption is made, i.e. that when a stock item is sold or used, that item is the one of its kind most recently purchased. Hence, under LIFO the charge for cost of goods sold represents the last of the available purchases and the balance sheet value of stock is assumed to be the cost of the earliest purchases. Under the weighted average method, stock sold or used is assumed to be drawn proportionately from the units held at the time of sale or use. Hence stock on hand at any time is assumed to represent a weighted average of stock available during the preceding period.

Each of the above stock flow assumptions may be applied in one of two ways. The first involves the calculation of the cost of stock sold and the consequent stock balance each time a sale is made. This is known as the *perpetual* method, and is used in the main illustration in the following section. The alternative, but less exact procedure, involves a single calculation of the cost of goods sold and value of each type of stock at the end of each period — the *periodic* method. This method is also illustrated in the next section.

The stock flow assumptions described above are made in order to allocate the total cost of stock during a period between the income statement and the balance sheet. *They need not necessarily represent the actual physical movement of stock.* Indeed the need for a stock flow assumption arises because the actual movement of stock cannot be precisely identified. Nevertheless, it may be that one assumption seems more likely than others to reflect actual stock movements. In a later section of this chapter we consider the importance of this characteristic in the selection of a stock flow assumption.

7.5 An illustration of alternative methods

A manufacturing company, Hampden Ltd, produces and sells glebes as shown in Table 7.5. The company has no stock of either glebes or raw materials at the

Table 7.5   *Hampden Ltd — details of glebe production and sales*

			£
1 January }	Costs of raw materials	1,000 units at £3 =	3,000
1 May }	and other direct expenses	500 units at £4 =	2,000
1 October }		500 units at £5 =	2,500
Total units produced during year		2,000	7,500
31 March }	Sales of finished goods	700 units at £10 =	7,000
31 October }		900 units at £10 =	9,000
Total sales during year		1,600	16,000

Notes: 1. All raw materials are converted to finished goods during the year.
2. Production overhead costs amount to £5,000 for the year.

start of the year. The direct costs per unit (of £3, £4 and £5) include the costs of raw materials and of all other direct expenses. In addition, Hampden Ltd incurs fixed production overhead costs of £5,000 during the year. All 2,000 units of raw material are fully converted to finished goods by the end of the year. Thus the company incurs total costs of £12,500 during the year, consisting of £7,500 direct costs and £5,000 fixed overhead costs. The basic problem, using the historical cost framework, is to decide how much of these total costs should be charged as expenses to the income statement and how much should be carried forward as the cost of stock held at the end of the period.

Table 7.6 shows six alternative methods of calculating cost of goods sold (the amount to be charged to the income statement as the cost of stock used) and the balance sheet value of stock (the cost of stock held at the end of the period). Each method is a combination of one of the two costing methods (direct or full costing) and one of the three stock flow assumptions (FIFO, LIFO and weighted average cost) described previously. For each of the three full cost methods, fixed overheads are allocated by dividing the total cost of £5,000 by the number of units converted to finished goods (2,000), giving a cost of £2.50 per unit. This is only one of a number of methods available for allocating fixed overhead costs, as we saw in Section 7.2. Each 'full cost' figure in Table 7.6 is thus equal to the equivalent 'direct cost' figure plus an allocated overhead cost of £2.50 per stock unit.

The figures relating to alternative stock flow assumptions are calculated as follows. Using FIFO, the cost of goods sold is calculated each time sales are made on the assumption that the units sold are those which have been longest in stock. Thus, in relation to the sale of 900 units on 31 October, the units sold are assumed to be the 300 remaining from the batch produced on 1 January at £3 per unit (the other 700 having been sold on 31 March), the 500 produced on 1 May at £4 per unit, and the remainder, 100 units, from the production of 500 units at £5 on 1 October. The closing stock of 400 units is assumed to be drawn from the batch

Table 7.6 *Hampden Ltd — cost of goods sold and balance sheet value calculations for glebe stock: perpetual basis*

Costing method:	Direct cost			Full cost		
Stock flow assumption:	FIFO	LIFO	Weighted average cost	FIFO	LIFO	Weighted average cost
	£	£	£	£	£	£
Cost of goods sold (COGS)						
31 March 700 at £3	2,100	2,100	2,100			
700 at £(3+2.50)				3,850	3,850	3,850
31 October 900 units:						
FIFO: 300 at £3						
500 at £4						
(Balance) 100 at £5	3,400					
LIFO: 500 at £5						
(Balance) 400 at £4		4,100				
WAC: 900 at £4.154*			3,739			
Full Cost: 900 at direct cost						
plus £2.50 per unit				5,650	6,350	5,989
Cost of goods sold	5,500	6,200	5,839	9,500	10,200	9,839
Balance sheet values						
31 December 400 units:						
FIFO: 400 at £5	2,000					
LIFO: 300 at £3						
100 at £4		1,300				
WAC: 400 at £4.154			1,661			
Full cost: 400 at direct cost						
plus £2.50 per unit				3,000	2,300	2,661
Total cost						
(COGS + Balance sheet value)	7,500	7,500	7,500	12,500	12,500	12,500

*[(300 × £3)+(500 × £4)+(500 × £5)] ÷ 1,300 = £4.154

produced most recently (on 1 October) at £5 per unit.

Under LIFO, each batch of glebes sold is assumed to be drawn from the most recently produced units in stock at the date of sale. Hence the units sold on 31 October are assumed to consist of the 500 units produced on 1 October at £5 per unit plus the balance (400 units) from those produced on 1 May at £4 per unit. The units held in stock at the end of the year are assumed to be represented by the 300 units at £3 from the batch produced on 1 January and the 100 units at £4 from the batch produced on 1 May.

Using the weighted average method of costing stock we assume that stock sold is drawn proportionately from the units held at the time of sale. Thus before the sale on 31 October, Hampden Ltd had in stock:

		£
300 units at £3 (the balance of the 1 January production)	=	900
500 units at £4 (produced on 1 May)	=	2,000
500 units at £5 (produced on 1 October)	=	2,500
1,300 units costing a total of		£5,400

The weighted average cost per unit is £4.154 (£5,400 ÷ 1,300 units), and this figure is applied both to the stock sold on 31 October and to the stock remaining at that date which is retained until the end of the year.

Whichever stock flow assumption and costing method are chosen, the following equation (a variant of those introduced in Chapter 5) holds:

$$\text{Opening stock} + \text{Cost of production} = \text{Cost of goods sold} + \text{Closing stock}$$

This may be demonstrated by using the figures in Table 7.6, as follows:

Costing method	Stock flow assumption	Opening stock	+ Cost of production	= Cost of goods sold	+ Closing stock
Direct cost	FIFO	0	+ 7,500	= 5,500	+ 2,000
Direct cost	LIFO	0	+ 7,500	= 6,200	+ 1,300
Direct cost	Weighted average	0	+ 7,500	= 5,839	+ 1,661
Full cost	FIFO	0	+ 12,500	= 9,500	+ 3,000
Full cost	LIFO	0	+ 12,500	= 10,200	+ 2,300
Full cost	Weighted average	0	+ 12,500	= 9,839	+ 2,661

In the case of Hampden Ltd, the 'total cost' of glebes (i.e. the cost of goods sold plus the cost of closing stock) is the same whichever stock flow assumption is adopted, provided that the same costing method is used. This is so because the cost of opening stock is the same in each case (zero). Had opening stocks been costed on different bases, the totals would differ, although the equation would still hold for each method. The equation demonstrates clearly that the problem is one of allocation; specifically of allocating the total cost of stock available between the income statement and the balance sheet.

The figures calculated in Table 7.6 may be used to help calculate Hampden Ltd's net income and to determine its balance sheet for the year. For simplicity, we assume that the glebe is the only product manufactured by the company; that all costs and sales are on a *cash* basis; that the company owns no assets other than stock and cash; and that the company started business on 1 January. Summarized income statements and balance sheets are given in Table 7.7. The

Table 7.7 *Hampden Ltd — Summarized income statements and balance sheets*

Costing method:	Direct cost			Full cost		
Stock flow assumption:	FIFO	LIFO	Weighted average cost	FIFO	LIFO	Weighted average cost
	£	£	£	£	£	£
Income statement						
Sales	16,000	16,000	16,000	16,000	16,000	16,000
less: Cost of goods sold	5,500	6,200	5,839	9,500	10,200	9,839
	10,500	9,800	10,161	6,500	5,800	6,161
less: Overheads	5,000	5,000	5,000	0	0	0
Net income	5,500	4,800	5,161	6,500	5,800	6,161
Balance sheet						
Ownership interest*	5,500	4,800	5,161	6,500	5,800	6,161
Stock of finished goods	2,000	1,300	1,661	3,000	2,300	2,661
Cash**	3,500	3,500	3,500	3,500	3,500	3,500
	5,500	4,800	5,161	6,500	5,800	6,161

* Equal to net income for the year as the balance at the start of the year is assumed to be zero.
** Sales revenue (£16,000) minus direct cost of stock produced (£7,500) and cost of overheads (£5,000) equals £3,500.

differences between the net income figures derive solely from the different costing methods and the different stock flow assumptions. Consequently, for a particular costing method, the income under each stock flow assumption differs solely because of the different cost of goods sold figure. For a particular stock flow assumption, the income figures differ between direct cost and full cost by £1,000 in each case. This is because under the full cost method overhead costs of £1,000 (400 units at £2.50 each) are carried forward as part of the cost of closing stock. Hence, the direct cost and full cost closing stock figures in the balance sheet differ by £1,000 also.

The figures in Table 7.7 illustrate general differences between alternative stock flow assumptions and costing methods. Other things being equal, if *stock costs* increase during an accounting period, cost of goods sold is generally smallest (and income consequently greatest) when FIFO is used. LIFO generally leads to the highest cost of goods sold and the lowest income figure, and the weighted average cost method produces figures between those given by FIFO and LIFO. As we have seen in the previous section, for any given stock flow assumption, the full cost method generally produces higher income figures when *stock levels* are rising (as in the case of Hampden Ltd). This is because part of fixed overhead costs is effectively deferred until a subsequent period. If stock levels fall, however, the 'benefit' from such deferral disappears.

Table 7.8 *Hampden Ltd — alternative calculations of cost of goods sold*

Costing method:	Direct cost			Full cost		
Stock flow assumption:	FIFO	LIFO	Weighted average cost	FIFO	LIFO	Weighted average cost
	£	£	£	£	£	£
Opening stock	0	0	0	0	0	0
Cost of stock produced (including overheads if appropriate)	7,500	7,500	7,500	12,500	12,500	12,500
	7,500	7,500	7,500	12,500	12,500	12,500
less: Closing stock (Table 7.6)	2,000	1,300	1,661	3,000	2,300	2,661
Cost of goods sold	5,500	6,200	5,839	9,500	10,200	9,839

We now turn to the *periodic* basis of stock calculation. This method is widely used in practice. Its basis can be most clearly seen from the equation introduced above. Rearranging that equation enables us to define cost of goods sold as follows:

$$\text{Cost of goods sold} = \text{Opening stock} + \text{Cost of production} - \text{Closing stock}$$

In other words, stock used during a period equals stock held at the start of the period plus stock produced during the period, minus stock held at the end of the period. Hence, cost of goods sold may be calculated by estimating closing stock directly (rather than as a by-product of the cost of goods sold calculation) and subtracting this figure from the sum total of opening stock and cost of production. The relevant figures for Hampden Ltd are shown in Table 7.8.

The periodic basis may produce different answers from those given by the perpetual basis. Consider the case of Hampden Ltd. For each combination of costing method and stock flow assumption a single calculation of cost of goods sold and closing balance sheet value is undertaken at the end of the year. Details are given in Table 7.9. The main difference between the figures in this table and those in Table 7.6 is the omission from the analysis of the different dates of sale and of the particular stock available at each such date. This can lead to some peculiar assumptions, particularly when using LIFO. For example, under LIFO the 1,600 glebes sold during the period are assumed to comprise the 500 units produced on 1 October, the 500 units produced on 1 May and 600 units (the balance) of those produced on 1 January. This clearly ignores the fact that none of the 500 units produced on 1 May was available for sale on 31 March — indeed it implies that at least 100 of those units were sold on 31 March as no more than 900 of the 1,000 units produced on 1 May and 1 October could have been sold on 31 October. Despite this obvious 'inaccuracy', the method does enjoy the

Table 7.9 *Hampden Ltd — cost of goods sold and balance sheet value calculations:
periodic basis*

Costing method:	Direct cost			Full cost		
Stock flow assumption:	FIFO	LIFO	Weighted average cost	FIFO	LIFO	Weighted average cost
	£	£	£	£	£	£
Cost of goods sold — 1,600 glebes						
FIFO: 1,000 at £3						
500 at £4						
(Balance) 100 at £5						
1,600	5,500					
LIFO: 500 at £5						
500 at £4						
(Balance) 600 at £3						
1,600		6,300				
WAC: 1,600 at £3.75*			6,000			
Full cost: 1,600 at direct cost plus £2.50 per unit				9,500	10,300	10,000
Cost of goods sold	5,500	6,300	6,000	9,500	10,300	10,000
Balance sheet values — 400 glebes						
400 at £5	2,000					
400 at £3		1,200				
400 at £3.75			1,500			
400 at direct cost plus						
£2.50 per unit				3,000	2,200	2,500
Total cost (COGS + Balance sheet value)	7,500	7,500	7,500	12,500	12,500	12,500

* $[(1,000 \times £3) + (500 \times £4) + (500 \times £5)] \div 2,000 = £3.75$

advantage that it avoids the cost of maintaining detailed cost records. Use of the
method depends on the relationship between the costs associated with this
'inaccuracy' and the costs of keeping perpetual stock records.

7.6 The choice of a stock flow assumption

Having described the main stock flow assumptions, we now consider their relative
merits and the rationale for choice between them. In times of changing prices

FIFO gives the most outdated figure for cost of goods sold in the income statement but produces the most up-to-date balance sheet figures for closing stock. LIFO gives the opposite results, i.e. it provides an up-to-date figure for cost of goods sold but an outdated figure for closing stock. Weighted average cost gives intermediate results. The choice of stock flow assumptions ultimately should depend on the information required by users and, in particular, on their preference for up-to-date information in either the income statement (LIFO) or the balance sheet (FIFO).

It might also be argued that the method chosen should help a business to make decisions which provide funds for the replacement of stock. Suppose that Ms Parade, a retailer, commences business on 1 January by paying £1,000 into a business bank account. During the following year she buys 50 units of stock at £8 per unit (on 1 February) and 50 units at £12 per unit (on 1 June) and sells 50 units at £15 per unit on 31 December, at which time the current buying price of the stock is £13 per unit. On 31 December she withdraws for personal purposes an amount equal to the business income for the year. She incurs no other expenses and receives no other revenues. Ms Parade's income statement and balance sheet, using alternative stock flow assumptions, are given in Table 7.10. Cash balances at 31 December are comprised of cash paid in (£1,000) plus sales receipts (£750) less cost of stock purchased (£400 + £600 = £1,000) less the amount withdrawn (equal to the income according to the particular stock flow assumption adopted). If Ms Parade wishes to replace the 50 units of stock sold on 31 December, it will cost her £650 (50 × £13). All of the stock flow assumptions show that there is insufficient cash left in the business to make the replacement. LIFO enables the most units to be replaced, FIFO the least.

Both the UK Companies Acts and the EC 4th Directive permit the use of FIFO, LIFO and average cost. However, the UK accounting standard on stocks and long term contracts (SSAP9) questions whether LIFO can give a true and fair view as it can result in a valuation in the balance sheet which bears 'little relationship to recent costs'. FIFO is the most common stock flow assumption adopted by companies in the UK and throughout most of Europe. However, LIFO is popular in Italy and the USA because in these two countries it is allowable for tax purposes and, as we have seen, LIFO produces the lowest income figure when prices are rising.

We conclude this section by reiterating that in most manufacturing organizations stock forms a large percentage of the assets existing at the balance sheet date. For example, stock (in its three forms) represented 18% of ICI plc's *total* assets, and 37% of its *current* assets in its 1992 balance sheet. Examination of ICI's 1992 income statement shows that the charge for cost of goods sold (use of stock during the year) represents 60% of ICI's total expenses and 1,200% (!) of its pre-tax income for the year. Thus a knowledge of the available methods of stock valuation and their respective characteristics is critical to an understanding of their significance in determining both an organization's net income and the level of its current assets. An examination of ICI's accounting policies (Figure 7.6) reveals that it uses full costing and a combination of the FIFO and average cost stock flow assumptions.

Table 7.10 *Ms Parade — income statements and balance sheets using alternative stock flow assumptions*

	FIFO	LIFO	Weighted average cost
Income statements	£	£	£
Sales (50 units at £15)	750	750	750
less: Cost of goods sold			
(50 units at £8)	400		
(50 units at £12)		600	
(50 units at £10)			500
Net income	£350	£150	£250
Balance sheets			
Ownership interest:			
Cash paid in	1,000	1,000	1,000
add: Net income	350	150	250
	£1,350	£1,150	£1,250
less: Amount withdrawn	350	150	250
	£1,000	£1,000	£1,000
Stock:			
(50 units at £12)	600		
(50 units at £8)		400	
(50 units at £10)			500
Cash	400	600	500
	£1,000	£1,000	£1,000

Stock Valuation
Finished goods are stated at the lower of cost or net realizable value, raw materials and other stocks at the lower of cost or replacement price; the first in, first out or an average method of valuation is used. In determining cost for stock valuation purposes, depreciation is included but selling expenses and certain overhead expenses are excluded.

Figure 7.6 *Extract from Annual Report of ICI plc 1992*

7.7   Accounting entries

In this section we illustrate the accounting entries necessary to record the acquisition, conversion and sale of stock. We use the example of Hampden Ltd and make the FIFO perpetual stock flow assumption. Details are as shown in the first and fourth columns of Tables 7.6 and 7.7. We assume that production

Table 7.11 Hampden Ltd — accounting entries for recording stock using FIFO and direct cost

Transaction		Assets		=	Ownership interest + Liabilities + Income	
		Stock	Cash		Income	(transferred to ownership interest)
		£	£		£	
1 January	Production of 1,000 units	3,000	(3,000)			
31 March	Production overheads		(1,250)		(1,250)	(Production overheads)
	Sales of 700 units		7,000		7,000	(Sales)
		(2,100)			(2,100)	(Cost of goods sold)
1 May	Production of 500 units	2,000	(2,000)			
30 June	Production overheads		(1,250)		(1,250)	(Production overheads)
30 September	Production overheads		(1,250)		(1,250)	(Production overheads)
1 October	Production of 500 units	2,500	(2,500)			
31 October	Sales of 900 units		9,000		9,000	(Sales)
		(3,400)			(3,400)	(Cost of goods sold)
31 December	Production overheads		(1,250)		(1,250)	(Production overheads)
31 December	Balances	2,000	3,500	=	5,500	

Table 7.12 *Hampden Ltd — accounting entries for recording stock using FIFO and full cost*

		Assets	+		=	Ownership interest + Liabilities + Income	
		Stock		Cash		Income	(transferred to ownership interest)
		£		£		£	
Transaction							
1 January	Production of 1,000 units	3,000		(3,000)			
31 March	Production overheads	1,250		(1,250)			
	Sales of 700 units			7,000		7,000	(Sales)
		(3,850)				(3,850)	(Cost of goods sold)
1 May	Production of 500 units	2,000		(2,000)			
30 June	Production overheads	1,250		(1,250)			
30 September	Production overheads	1,250		(1,250)			
1 October	Production of 500 units	2,500		(2,500)			
31 October	Sales of 900 units			9,000		9,000	(Sales)
		(5,650)				(5,650)	(Cost of goods sold)
31 December	Production overheads	1,250		(1,250)			
31 December	Balances	3,000	+	3,500	=	6,500	

overheads are paid quarterly, i.e. that £1,250 is paid on 31 March, 30 June, 30 September and 31 December. The accounting equation entries using direct cost are given in Table 7.11, and those using full cost in Table 7.12. In both cases the costs of stock (including production overheads under full costing) are added initially to the asset 'stock' and, on sale, are transferred to the income column (which here represents a condensation of the revenue and the expense columns). The only difference between the two tables relates to the treatment of production overheads. These are deducted directly from revenue where direct costing is used, and indirectly, via cost of goods sold, where full costing is adopted. In the latter case, some of the production overheads are carried forward to the next period as part of the closing stock value.

7.8   The lower of cost and net realizable value rule

We have discussed earlier how conventional accounting practice is heavily influenced by certain accounting concepts including the accruals (or matching) and prudence concepts. The matching concept has determined the treatment of stock described so far in this chapter. The prudence concept is also relevant, however. According to conventional practice, once the 'cost' of each item of closing stock has been determined it must be compared with the net realizable value of closing stock. The net realizable value is the estimated sale proceeds of the stock less any costs still to be incurred in converting the stock to a suitable form for sale and in actually selling it. If the net realizable value of closing stock is lower than its cost (i.e. it will be sold at a loss), then the value of closing stock must be written down from cost to net realizable value. This treatment satisfies both the prudence concept (it recognizes foreseeable 'losses') and the matching concept (if net realizable value is less than cost, there will be insufficient future revenues against which cost can be 'matched').

The accounting entry required to implement the lower of cost and net realizable value rule on an item-by-item basis is as follows:

> If the net realizable value of closing stock is less than its cost, reduce the asset 'stock' by the difference between cost and net realizable value, and increase cost of goods sold by the same figure.

The effect of this entry is that, for balance sheet purposes, stock is valued at the lower of cost and net realizable value.

7.9   Long-term contracts

Two important rules govern the treatment of stock in an organization's financial statements. First, revenue is recognized at the date of sale, and not at the date of production or the date of the receipt of cash. Secondly, in the balance sheet, stock is valued at the lower of cost and net realizable value. However, there are certain *specific* instances in which these rules may be broken. The most common of these instances relates to particular 'one-off' projects undertaken by organizations at the request of individual customers. For example, major long-term engineering and construction projects (the building of an oil rig, a factory or a sports stadium) will probably take place over a long period of time and be the subject of an agreed advance price between constructor and customer. Such long-term contracts are of particular significance to organizations which contract with the government for the supply of military, electronic and defence equipment.

As an extreme example, consider the case of a builder whose only business is the construction of one factory every three years. Application of the conventional historical cost accounting rules of valuing stock at the lower of cost and net realizable value would value work in progress at *cost* at the end of two years in every three, thus showing zero income in each of those two years. The entire surplus from building each factory would be recognized in the third year of each contract. Such a treatment might result in volatile reported annual income figures, and may be misleading to users. For this reason, it is sometimes regarded as acceptable to abate the prudence concept in favour of the matching concept and to recognize a part of the profit on long-term contracts in advance of their completion.

However, adoption of the matching principle does not by itself determine how the profit should be calculated. We suggested earlier that it may be misleading to wait until the date of sale (i.e. the completion and 'delivery' to the customer of, say, a factory) before recognizing any revenue. We now need some guidelines to assist in determining at what stages during the contract revenue should be recognized, and how much revenue should be recognized at each stage.

In most long-term contracts revenue is recognized in stages as the contract proceeds, rather than as a lump sum at the termination of the project. The most usual method of recognizing revenue in stages is via the *percentage of completion* method, under which a proportion of the contract price, determined by the degree of completeness of the project, is recognized as revenue in each period of the project's life. This method is not as arbitrary as it might initially appear. The degree to which a contract is complete will usually be assessed by an independent party, for example an architect or surveyor, and in the later stages of a contract it is normal for an organization to be able to predict with some degree of accuracy the levels of future costs to be incurred. The following example of Brunton Ltd shows how revenue might be recognized under a long-term contract.

Illustration

Brunton Ltd is engaged in a long-term contract to build a bridge. The following information relates to the contract:

	£
Total contract price	4,000,000
Work certified (by architect) to 31 December 19X1	2,500,000
Costs incurred on the contract to 31 December 19X1	2,050,000
Estimated further costs to completion	1,150,000

Assuming that no profit has been taken on the contract in previous years, we can estimate the proportion of the (likely) total profit on the contract for the year to 31 December 19X1. The calculation of the applicable profit is as follows:

(a) *Estimated total profit on the contract*

	£
Contract price	4,000,000
less: Estimated total costs	
(2,050,000 + 1,150,000)	3,200,000
Estimated total profit	£800,000

(b) *Proportion applicable to the period to 31 December 19X1*

$$\frac{\text{Work certified to 31 December 19X1}}{\text{Total contract price}} \times \text{Estimated total profit}$$

$$= \frac{2,500,000}{4,000,000} \times 800,000 = £500,000$$

The profit of £500,000 attributable to the contract is credited to the income statement and debited to the work-in-progress account in the balance sheet at 31 December 19X1. This account would therefore comprise:

	£
Work-in-progress at cost	2,050,000
plus Profit taken to date	500,000
	2,550,000

If by 31 December 19X1 the customer had paid £1,000,000 in 'stage payments' to Brunton Ltd, this amount would be recorded as an increase in Brunton Ltd's cash balance and a reduction in the 'value' of its work-in-progress. Thus the receipt of a stage payment does not affect the income statement, but rather substitutes one asset (cash) for another (work-in-progress). Brunton Ltd's work-in-progress would be reported as follows:

	£
Work-in-progress at cost	
plus Profit taken to date	2,550,000
less Cash received from customer	1,000,000
	1,550,000

Figure 7.2 reveals that Lonrho plc reports its work-in-progress as a net figure. It includes a separate note disclosing the amount of progress payments received.

In practice the applicable profit of £500,000 may be reduced by some further percentage, perhaps to allow for the eventuality that the estimated further costs may increase, or that the customer may not be willing to pay the full price due to poor workmanship. In this case the profit of £500,000 might be reduced by, say, one-quarter, to give a profit for the year of £500,000 × 0.75 = £375,000. This final reduction, in this case 25%, is an arbitrary adjustment. It is an example of the accountant's concept of prudence. Many companies in the UK calculate the profit earned on long-term contracts in a manner similar to that illustrated above. These include GEC, Plessey, Tarmac, and Taylor Woodrow.

7.10   An illustration from practice — E.H. Booth & Co. Ltd

The complete set of Booths' accounts can be found in Appendix 1.

As a retail supermarket, Booths sells stock in the form in which it is purchased, without undertaking any production or manufacturing operations. The figure for stocks in the balance sheet (page 11) is £5,259,191. Note 10 (page 17) confirms that all of these stocks are 'Goods for resale'. There are no raw materials or work in progress.

The Statement of Accounting Policies (page 13) reveals that stocks are valued at the lower of cost and net realizable value. It does not, however, disclose the company's stock flow assumption. This is unusual. Both the market leaders disclose this information (Sainsbury plc uses average cost, and Tesco plc first-in-first-out), although it is perhaps less important in the food retailing industry where stocks are turned over on average every two or three weeks. Because a relatively small amount of stock is held in relation to the annual sales figure, the FIFO and average cost stock flow assumptions produce very similar results even when prices are rising quite rapidly. The adoption of LIFO could lead to an unrealistically low stock figure in the balance sheet, but as we explained in Section 7.6, the use of LIFO is discouraged in the UK, and Booths would most certainly have to disclose the fact had it adopted the LIFO stock flow assumption.

The stock sold during the year is reported in the Profit and Loss Account (page 10) as 'Cost of sales — £67,567,546'. Despite an increase in both Turnover and Cost of sales in 1992 , the stocks figure in the balance sheet is lower in 1992 than in 1991, i.e. Booths requires a lower level of stocks to support a higher volume of sales. This suggests that Booths, along with many other food retailers, continues to improve the efficiency of its operations and distribution network. We shall examine this further in Chapters 10 and 11 when we shall analyse Booths' accounts in an attempt to evaluate the company's operating and financial performance.

Discussion topics

1. Describe the stock conversion process that takes place in a manufacturing enterprise and explain the differences between raw materials, work in progress and finished goods.

2. Explain what you understand by the choice of a 'costing method'. Outline the main alternative methods and discuss their relative merits.

3. Explain what you understand by the choice of a 'stock flow assumption'. Outline the main alternative assumptions and evaluate them.

4. What is the 'lower of cost and net realizable value' rule? Why is it applied?

5. Analyse the relationship between opening stock, closing stock, cost of production and cost of goods sold.

6. Explain, with illustrations, the extent to which historical cost based stock treatments result in the provision of sufficient funds to replace stock as it is used up.

7. Distinguish between the 'perpetual' and 'periodic' bases of stock calculation.

8. How might cost of goods sold be estimated by an enterprise that does not keep detailed stock records?

9. What particular problems of stock treatment are associated with long-term contracts?

Exercises

7.1 Ruiz Ltd buys and sells sarastros. The company prepares accounts annually to 31 October. On 1 November 19X5 Ruiz Ltd had no stock of sarastros.
   On 1 December 19X5 the company purchased 10,000 sarastros at 15p each, and on 1 January 19X6 it purchased a further 5,000 at 18p each. 5,000 sarastros were sold on 1 March 19X6 at a price of 30p each. On 1 May 19X6, 10,000 sarastros were purchased at 20p each and on 1 September 19X6 the company sold 4,000 sarastros at a price of 35p each.

   - (a) Calculate the gross profit made on the sale of sarastros during the year ended 31 October 19X6 and the value of stock of sarastros held at 31 October 19X6, under each of the following stock flow assumptions:
     - (i) last in, first out (LIFO)
     - (ii) first in, first out (FIFO)
     - (iii) weighted average cost.
   - (b) Comment on the relative merits of the above three assumptions for costing stock.

7.2 Mr Aida commences business as a manufacturer of anninas on 1 January 19X1. On that date he pays £200,000 into the business bank account from his personal resources. Each annina requires 2 kg of raw material. Mr Aida purchases the following quantities of raw materials during the two years to 31 December 19X2:

1 January 19X1	10,000 kg at £2.00 per kg	= £20,000
30 June 19X1	10,000 kg at £2.50 per kg	= £25,000
30 September 19X1	5,000 kg at £2.75 per kg	= £13,750
31 January 19X2	10,000 kg at £3.00 per kg	= £30,000
31 July 19X2	8,000 kg at £3.30 per kg	= £26,400
	43,000 kg	

During 19X1, 24,000 kg of raw material are converted to 12,000 anninas. The remaining 1,000 kg held at 31 December 19X1 are in stock at that date. During 19X2 these units, together with the 18,000 kg purchased during 19X2 are converted to 9,500 anninas. Throughout the two-year period, each annina manufactured requires 3 hours of direct labour time. Each hour of direct labour costs £4 during 19X1 and £5 during 19X2. In addition, conversion of raw materials to anninas requires the use of a machine which Mr Aida purchases for £60,000 on 1 January 19X1. The machine has a two-year life and no residual value at the end of that time. Mr Aida wishes to depreciate the machine using the straight line method of depreciation. Manufacturing overheads (excluding machine depreciation, direct labour costs and raw material costs) amount to £30,000 in 19X1 and £27,000 in 19X2. Other expenses are £28,000 for 19X1 and £32,000 for 19X2.

Sales of anninas are as follows:

31 July 19X1	4,000 units at £24.00 per unit	=	£96,000
31 October 19X1	3,000 units at £25.00 per unit	=	£75,000
31 December 19X1	2,000 units at £27.00 per unit	=	£54,000
31 March 19X2	4,000 units at £27.00 per unit	=	£108,000
30 September 19X2	5,000 units at £30.00 per unit	=	£150,000
31 December 19X2	3,500 units at £32.00 per unit	=	£112,000
	21,500 units		

All revenues and payments are made in cash during the year in which they arise. Mr Aida wishes to adopt the FIFO stock flow assumption.

- (a) Prepare Mr Aida's income statements for 19X1 and 19X2, and his balance sheets at 31 December 19X1 and 31 December 19X2, under each of the following costing methods:
  (i) direct cost
  (ii) full cost (allocating appropriate overhead costs on the basis of the number of units produced).
- (b) Show Mr Aida's accounting equation entries for 19X1 and 19X2, assuming that the direct costing method is adopted.
- (c) Comment on the figures revealed by your answer to (a) above.

7.3 Ms Hermann is a shopkeeper who specializes in the purchase and sale of four product lines — riccardos, mantuas, lunas and leonoras. She does not maintain continual stock records, but provides the following information regarding her most recent year's trading:

	Riccardos £	Mantuas £	Lunas £	Leonoras £
Stock at start of year	2,000	6,500	3,200	8,700
Purchase of stock during year	47,800	35,100	63,900	98,200
Estimated cost of stock held at end of year	3,100	12,300	3,300	6,900
Estimated net realizable value of stock held at end of year	3,500	11,600	4,400	8,200

- Calculate the cost of goods sold for Ms Hermann's business for her most recent year's trading. Explain and justify your calculations.

7.4 Mr Giorgio commences business as a retailer of violettas on 1 January. During his first year of trading he buys and sells violettas as follows:

1 January	buys 500 at £75 each
28 February	buys 500 at £80 each
31 March	sells 700 at £100 each
31 May	buys 500 at £70 each
30 June	sells 400 at £95 each
31 August	sells 200 at £85 each
1 September	buys 800 at £65 each
30 November	sells 600 at £105 each

- (a) Calculate Mr Giorgio's gross profit from selling violettas during the year and the balance sheet value of violettas at the end of the year under the FIFO, LIFO and weighted average cost stock flow assumptions, assuming that the calculations are based on:
    (i) the *perpetual* basis
    (ii) the *periodic* basis
  (b) How would your answers to (a) above change if the net realizable value of violettas at 31 December was £68 each?

7.5 Vitellia Ltd was incorporated on 1 January 19X6, with a paid up capital of £8,000,000, to design, develop and manufacture a revolutionary sports motor cycle. During 19X6 the company built up its organization, leased premises, purchased plant and recruited a development team. An amount of £3,000,000 was spent on plant and machinery, whilst the cost of materials, labour and overhead expenses (including depreciation) recorded in the books amounted to £500,000 during the year.

In 19X7, development work on a prototype continued, while the company prepared production facilities against the day when development would be complete. Expenditure of £1,000,000 on tooling costs was incurred, a further £500,000 was spent on an advertising campaign, and the cost of materials used, labour and overhead expenses amounted to £1,000,000. When the company was incorporated, the directors discussed depreciation of fixed assets and settled on a rate of 5% on cost during the development years, and 10% on cost thereafter.

At 31 December 19X7, stocks of raw materials were valued at £200,000. There was no income of any sort during 19X6 and 19X7, and the directors decided to treat development costs as intangible assets in the balance sheet at 31 December 19X7.

On 1 January 19X8, development of the prototype was satisfactorily completed and it was decided to retain the vehicle as a demonstration model. At this time the factory was prepared to produce motor cycles at the rate of 400 per year to be sold direct to the consumer for cash at £2,500 each. However, teething troubles at the factory reduced production for the year to 80 vehicles, of which only 40 were sold. Rigorous economy in the face of this situation reduced labour costs to £50,000 for the year, whilst materials purchased cost £45,000. Advertising and other overhead costs amounted to £450,000. The stock of raw materials on 31 December 19X8 was £95,000, there was no stock of work-in-progress, and closing stocks of finished goods were valued at direct cost. The directors decided to treat the loss for 19X8 as deferred expenditure (i.e. as an intangible asset).

During 19X9, 320 motor cycles were produced, and 200 sold. Direct costs were reduced to £2,000 per vehicle, whilst advertising and overhead expenses were held at £450,000 for the year. Stocks of raw material remained at the same level throughout the year, and stocks of finished goods were accounted for on the FIFO basis. The directors proposed once more to treat the loss as deferred expenditure, arguing that whilst prototype development was completed in 19X7, their market had developed at a slower rate than anticipated. They hope that expanding sales in the future will make it possible to set off development expenditure against revenue in later years when the project has matured.

- (a) Prepare draft balance sheets for Vitellia Ltd as at 31 December 19X7, 19X8 and 19X9, in accordance with the directors' decisions.
- (b) Comment on the manner in which the circumstances outlined above have been treated in the accounts for the last three years, and suggest a course of future actions.

7.6 Ms Ilia and Ms Electra both started business as retailers on 1 January 19X7. During the year to 31 December 19X7, the two women undertook identical business transactions as follows:

- (i) Purchased equipment on 1 January 19X7 for £100,000. The equipment has an estimated life of 5 years, at which time it will be worth £10,000.
- (ii) Paid research and development expenditure of £50,000.
- (iii) Purchased stock as follows:
  1 January 19X7   2,000 units at £50 each
  1 May 19X7   2,000 units at £100 each
- (iv) Sold stock as follows:
  30 September 19X7   2,000 units of £150 each
- (v) Incurred other expenses of £50,000

The two retailers use different accounting conventions for the purpose of calculating profit, as follows:

Depreciation: Ms Ilia uses straight line depreciation. Ms Electra uses the reducing balance method.

Research and development: Ms Ilia writes off R&D expenditure over a 10-year period, using the straight line method. Ms Electra writes off the expenditure in the year in which it is incurred.

Stock: Ms Ilia uses the FIFO method for valuing stock. Ms Electra uses LIFO.

- (a)   Prepare income statements for Ms Ilia and Ms Electra for the year ended 31 December 19X7.
- (b)   Discuss the implications of the income figures in the accounts you have prepared.

7.7 The following independent situations relate to the transactions and events of the Amadeus Co. Ltd.

Situations:

1.   The inventory items on shelf 15-D were counted twice during the 19X1 year-end physical stock-take.
2.   An invoice for goods received in 19X1 (and included in the physical count at the year-end) was not received and recorded until 19X2.
3.   An invoice received in 19X1 was recorded as a purchase in 19X1. The goods were not received until 19X2 and were not included in the 19X1 inventory.
4.   As in situation 3 above, except that the cost of the goods was added to the 19X1 inventory figure.
5.   The items in inventory in Area 6 were not counted during the 19X1 year-end physical stock-take.
6.   Goods received on 31 December in 19X1 were placed in the receiving area and were not included in the year-end physical inventory. The purchase was not recorded in the books until 19X2.
7.   Due to clerical errors, the cost of the 31 December 19X1 inventory was overstated.

   - For each of the seven independent situations above, determine the effect of the error(s) on net income, closing assets, closing liabilities and closing owners' equity for both 19X1 and 19X2. Give your answers in a table with headings as shown below. Use a + sign to indicate an overstatement, a — sign to indicate an understatement and a 0 to indicate no effect. In each case, the comparison should be with a situation in which there are no errors. You may assume that the periodic inventory (stock) method is used to determine quantities at the year-end (i.e. stock is physically counted).

	19X1				19X2			
Situation	Net Income	Assets	Liabilities	Owners Equity	Net Income	Assets	Liabilities	Owners Equity
1								
2								
3								
4								
5								
6								
7								

7.8 While three sisters, Amy, Brenda and Carol were on holiday in France, they obtained the distribution rights for the UK market of a ready-mix flour which was packed in 1 kilo bags for sale to consumers to use to bake a French bread.

On 1 January 19X7 the sisters put £10,000 from their savings into a bank account under the name of the ABC Sisters' Partnership which they had formed for the purpose of distributing the flour. Initially they commenced operations from the rambling old house in which they lived and in discussion concluded not to charge overheads, nor to pay themselves a salary, but rather to share any profits that the partnership might make equally between them on a six-monthly basis.

Once their capital was in the bank they immediately made a purchase of 10,000 bags of the mix which exactly exhausted their initial capital. Although they understood from the supplier that the price they would have to pay for the flour was likely to fluctuate considerably, as they wanted to be able to offer their own customers a stable price on a six-monthly basis, they set their sales price at £1.50 per bag for their launch period.

During the first six months of the Partnership's trading the following transactions took place:

January	Sold	5,000 bags
February	Bought	5,000 bags at £1.20
	Sold	5,000 bags
March	Bought	10,000 bags at £1.00
April	Sold	10,000 bags
May	Bought	5,000 bags at £1.10
	Sold	5,000 bags
June	Bought	5,000 bags at £1.25
	Sold	5,000 bags

Early in July 19X7 each of the sisters independently prepared their own version of the partnership's first half-year performance. On 10 July 19X7 the sisters held a meeting to decide upon the amount to be distributed as their first profit shares.

Amy was more than happy about the situation, saying that each would get more than she originally hoped, and with her share of £4,500 she would take a trip to North America. Brenda said that Amy must have made some mistakes in her calculations because she would only get £4,083 as her third share. Carol could not hold back her growing exasperation over her view of the ineptitude of her sisters calculating profit, and jumped in to say that neither of the other sisters would ever make accountants — because according to her the correct distribution would be £4,214.

An argument started about who was right. When the sisters compared their statements they also found that as well as their income calculations being different, the valuation they had obtained for closing stock on 30 June 19X7 also varied in each case.

- (a) Showing the calculations to support your answers, provide information of which methods each of the sisters had probably used to price out inventories in their various assessments of the partnership's performance. Present your results in tabular form to show the total income for the partnership and the value of the closing stock for each of the methods.

(b) Discuss the major conceptual difficulties associated with pricing out stock as far as the measurement of income and value is concerned. Refer to the sisters' calculations where appropriate.

Further reading

Hendriksen, E.S., *Accounting Theory*, Irwin, 1982.

CHAPTER

8

Sources of Finance

In the previous two chapters we have looked at the accounting treatment of the major classes of assets, and examined some possible ways in which depreciation and cost of goods sold might be calculated. We now turn our attention to the other side of the balance sheet — to the ways in which organizations raise finance — and look at how the receipt of finance, and the payment of rewards to the providers of finance, are dealt with in accounting statements.

Finance includes both ownership interest (sums provided by the owners of an enterprise) and liabilities (sums provided by other parties). The finance raised by an organization is frequently described as its *capital*. We shall henceforth use the terms 'finance' and 'capital' interchangeably. In this chapter we identify the main sources of finance, describe their chief characteristics and explain why it is important to distinguish between them. The three most significant forms of private sector organization — individuals, partnerships and limited liability companies — are differentiated throughout the chapter.

8.1 Long-term and short-term financing

Organizations raise capital to finance the acquisition of assets. As we have seen in previous chapters, assets are acquired for different purposes. Broadly speaking, fixed assets represent the productive long-term capacity of the organization; current assets are held for early resale, or for early conversion into cash in some other way. In consequence, the type of capital required to finance assets varies with the nature of the particular assets. In general, assets that are to be held for a long period should be financed by a stable, long-term source of finance, whereas assets with short or unpredictable lives should be financed by a more flexible, short-term source. For example, an organization would be unwise to raise a 20-year loan to finance an asset to be held for only six months; interest charges will have to be paid for $19\frac{1}{2}$ years after the end of the asset's life. Similarly, it would be risky to finance a long-term investment (e.g. the purchase of plant and machinery) by a bank overdraft that might have to be repaid at short notice.

For many organizations, a substantial part of current assets (stocks and debtors) is financed by current liabilities (primarily trade creditors and bank overdrafts). This is usually a convenient and sensible arrangement, as fluctuations in the level of both current assets and current liabilities tend to be influenced by the level of an organization's activity. The intention in this chapter is to concentrate on long-term capital, which is needed primarily to finance the acquisition of fixed assets and any *permanent* surplus of current assets over current liabilities, i.e. permanent *working capital*, and short-term capital in the form of bank loans and overdrafts. We have discussed the treatment of other sources of short-term finance, e.g. trade creditors and accruals, in Chapter 5 and we shall discuss the *management of working capital* in Chapter 11.

8.2 Sources of long-term capital: individuals

A business run by an individual raises its long-term capital from two main sources:

1. *Long-term loans*, which comprise loans from banks and other organizations and individuals and which are not repayable in the near future.[1]
2. *Ownership interest*, which includes both funds paid into the business by the owner from personal resources, and net income of the business which has not been distributed to the owner (i.e. retained income or retained profits).

Other sources are also used, for example the owner may lease assets, or raise funds via business expansion schemes.

There are three distinguishing characteristics of the two main sources of long-term capital:

(a) the returns they offer,
(b) the provisions relating to the repayment of capital,
(c) their relative degrees of security.

We shall look at each of these in turn.

---

1. The distinction between a long-term and a short-term loan is not clear cut. As a rough rule of thumb, a short-term loan might be regarded as one repayable within two or three years of the granting of the loan and a long-term loan as one payable after a longer period of time.

Returns

The returns payable on long-term loans are usually fixed by contract at the time the loan is advanced. Loan contracts normally demand a periodic payment of a fixed amount (termed *interest*), often once or twice each year. In most cases interest is payable whether or not the organization makes a profit. Thus a contract to loan £100,000 at 10% per annum over 10 years, interest being due at half-yearly intervals, would entail semi-annual interest payments to the lender of £5,000.

The periodic returns to the individual owner are represented by the organization's net income for the period, calculated after the deduction of fixed interest and other expenses. Thus returns to the owner may fluctuate from year to year and indeed may be negative in some years if the business makes a loss. In many cases, the amounts actually withdrawn from the business by its owner (called *drawings*) will not equal the income available. The amount of drawings depends on the availability of cash and on the extent to which funds are needed by the business to purchase new or replacement assets. As we illustrate later, drawings are not treated as an expense under conventional accounting practice, but rather as a deduction from ownership interest.

The above descriptions suggest that the returns on ownership interest are likely to be much more volatile than those on long-term loans; the former will fluctuate with the level of the organization's income whereas the latter are fixed by contract. Volatility is often regarded as a measure of the risk borne by the providers of long-term capital; other things being equal, a risk-averse provider of capital will prefer less volatile to more volatile returns. Thus the owner of a business bears more risk (in relation to returns) than do the providers of long-term capital, although returns over time to the owner may be higher.

Repayment of capital

When a long-term loan is made to an individual it is usual for a date (or series of dates) to be fixed for repayment of the loan. The amount to be paid at each repayment date is also normally agreed in advance.

Ownership interest is, however, not usually repaid until the activities of the business cease, although there is no legal restriction to stop the individual withdrawing some, or even all, of her capital at any time. The amount of capital to be repaid to the owner when the business ceases depends entirely on the position of the business at that time. It is equal to the proceeds from selling assets less the amounts needed to pay all liabilities, including the repayment of long-term loan capital. The amount is unlikely to be equal to the amount represented by ownership interest on the balance sheet, because the assets on the balance sheet are included at their historical cost rather than their realizable value and may exclude certain intangible assets such as goodwill.

Security

Long-term loans are often secured by a *charge* (in favour of the lender) on particular assets of the business. Thus if the interest is not paid, or capital is not repaid on the due date, the lender may take possession of the charged assets and dispose of them. He may retain from the disposal proceeds sufficient to pay outstanding interest and repay the amount of the loan. The balance is returned to the owner of the business. If the loan is not secured, or if the proceeds from selling charged assets are insufficient to pay the amounts due to the lender, he may take action against the owner personally to recover sums owing to him. Thus the liability of an individual for the enterprise's financial obligation is *unlimited*. On the cessation of the business, long-term lenders have a prior claim over the owner on the funds available, in respect of both the payment of interest and the repayment of capital due to them.

The individual is thus the ultimate risk bearer. In respect of both returns and capital repayment she has no security — she must ensure that the business continues to generate surpluses. Her rewards from owning the business comprise the residue after all other claims have been satisfied.

8.3 Sources of long-term capital: partnerships

Partnerships are business structures that are owned, and often managed, by a group of individuals called partners. They range from small, two-partner firms to large multinational organizations. Many large professional organizations, for example firms of accountants, solicitors, doctors and dentists, are partnerships. In 1992, Coopers and Lybrand, the international firm of accountants had over 700 partners in the UK alone, and reported UK fee income in excess of £570 million. Partnerships raise their long-term capital from the same types of sources as individuals, and have very similar rights and obligations. These rights and obligations are determined largely by the requirements of the Partnership Act, 1890. Partners differ from individuals in two main respects. First, if the partnership's resources are insufficient to pay its liabilities, the individual partners are jointly and severally liable for them. In other words, any party or parties to whom the partnership owes money has the right to take action against some or all of the partners in respect of amounts owing to them. For example, if all but one of the partners are without personal resources, the remaining partner is liable in full for all liabilities of the partnership. This can be a heavy burden.

Partnerships also differ from individuals in respect of the partners' joint ownership of the enterprise. It is necessary to divide between the partners both the net income of the partnership and any surplus remaining on its cessation. The division is normally made in accordance with a *partnership agreement* which defines the entitlement of each partner to his or her share in income and capital surpluses. As with individuals, each partner's share of income is not usually treated as an expense. Instead it is added directly to their share of ownership interest, specifically to their capital account. The arrangement for allocating net income between partners may be quite complex and may include provision for payment of 'salary', 'interest on capital', and 'share of residual income'. The total amount due to each partner as the allocation of income, however determined, is added to the capital account. Withdrawals by partners are called drawings and are deducted directly from the capital account of the partner. These accounting treatments are illustrated later in the chapter.

8.4 Sources of long-term capital: limited companies

Ownership interest

We explained in Chapter 1 that limited liability companies were created in response to the need for organizations to raise very large amounts of finance. Thus in order to persuade investors to accept some of the risks associated with an organization's activities, without at the same time expecting them to jeopardize their entire personal fortunes, the right to create limited companies was granted. As the name suggests, the important distinction between *limited liability companies* and other types of organization relates to the potential liability of the owners. The liability of the owners of limited companies for company debts is limited to the amount of capital they have provided or agreed to provide to the company. The owners cannot generally be compelled to find further capital from their private resources if the company has insufficient funds to meet its obligations. Individuals and partners, on the other hand, have unlimited liability for the debts contracted by their business. It is, however, often the case that the owners of *small* limited companies are required by lenders to provide personal guarantees as security for debts. In these cases the practical differences between small companies and partnerships are lessened considerably.

A second major difference between limited companies and other organizations is that the former have a legal identity separate from the identities of their owners. Like individuals and partnerships, limited companies raise long-term finance from two main sources — ownership interest and long-term loans. Ownership interest is created by limited companies selling *shares* in themselves to individuals and organizations. These shares are known as *ordinary* or *equity* shares. The total capital raised in this way is called ordinary share capital or equity capital. Each share has a *nominal* or *par* value of, for example, 5p (Tesco plc), 25p (Sainsbury plc) or £1 (ICI plc). This value has little significance other than as a means of describing

	1992 £'000	1991 £'000
Capital and reserves		
Called up share capital	15,408	15,384
Share premium account	12,629	11,988
Profit and loss account	266,441	216,882
	294,478	244,254

Figure 8.1 *Kwik Save plc — capital and reserves*

the share — *it does not necessarily correspond either with the value of the share (e.g. as determined by the assets of the organization) or even with the price at which it is issued (sold) by the company.* Shares, like many other goods, are usually sold (issued) at the highest price the market will bear. This price is invariably greater than the nominal value and the resultant surplus is called a *share premium*, and is recorded separately in the company's accounts.

The ownership interest, or 'Capital and reserves', section of the balance sheet of Kwik Save Group plc is reproduced in Figure 8.1. Kwik Save has issued 154,080,579 shares with a nominal value of 10p each, amounting to £15,408,000. Many of the shares were issued at a price in excess of 10p and the balance on the share premium account is £12,629,000. Both the nominal value of shares and the share premium are treated as part of a company's ownership interest, i.e. both belong to the owners. The share premium account is often termed a 'capital reserve' and, like the share capital account, cannot be distributed to the owners except on liquidation or in other very limited circumstances.

The other component of ownership interest is the balance on the profit and loss account. This balance represents profits that have not been distributed to the owners, but have been retained in the business. In Figure 8.1, the 'retained profits' of Kwik Save plc amounted to £266,441,000 on 29 August 1992, an increase of £49,559,000 over the previous year. The balance on the profit and loss account is a 'revenue reserve'. The distinction between capital and revenue reserves is important. As stated previously, capital reserves are not normally distributable, whereas revenue reserves represent *undistributed* profits, i.e. profits which have been earned in previous years but have not been distributed to the shareholders. However, although these revenue reserves may, *legally*, be distributed, they do not necessarily represent funds *available* for distribution. It cannot automatically be assumed that if the organization wished to distribute its retained profits sufficient cash would be available for this purpose. It is quite possible for an organization to show both a high level of reserves and a low (or non-existent) level of cash because profits have been reinvested in non-cash assets, such as new machinery or a higher level of stock.

Distributions made by a company to its shareholders (owners), equivalent to the 'drawings' of individuals and partners, are called *dividends*. Unlike the drawings of individuals and partners, dividends are not deducted directly from ownership interest, but rather are treated as an appropriation of the company's net income (i.e. they are deducted from net income). The balance of net income is then added to retained profits.

If a company ceases to trade (i.e. in the event of its liquidation), ordinary shareholders are in much the same position as individuals or partners. They are entitled to share in the distribution of any funds remaining after all other claims have been satisfied. Ordinary shareholders are in fact entitled to the residue of both annual income and amounts available on liquidation, and are thus the ultimate risk bearers, except in so far as their risk is restricted by their limited liability. This explains why equity capital is often termed 'risk capital'.

Except in special circumstances, ordinary share capital that has been paid to a company cannot be repaid until the company is liquidated. However, this does not mean that the owners of the share capital cannot disinvest before the liquidation of the company: shareholders may sell their shares to other individuals or organizations. Being able to buy and sell shares freely and thus invest in different companies at different times is one of the major attractions to investing shareholders. The price at which shares are traded at any point in time is known as their *market value* at the time, and should not be confused with their nominal value, or indeed with any other figure relating to the shares in the financial statements. It is vital to understand that the sale of shares from one shareholder to another does not affect in any way the accounting transactions of the company. It is a private sale between two parties external to the company, and simply represents a change of ownership. The company 'owes' the same amount to the owners, *whoever they may be*. Subject to certain restrictions, a company may purchase its own shares, thereby reducing the company's share capital and cash balance. This action may change both the asset value per share and the earnings per share of the remaining shares.

The shares of many companies, particularly large companies, are traded in a specialized market, called the Stock Exchange.[2] This is primarily a market for 'second hand' shares and securities, although a company wishing to issue additional shares will have regard to the price at which its existing shares are being traded, when deciding on a price for the additional issue. A company that wishes to have its shares traded on the Stock Exchange must apply for its shares to be 'listed' (or 'quoted'). Companies that have applied successfully for a listing are known as *listed companies* (or *quoted companies*) and there were around 2,000 such companies in the UK in 1994. Special accounting requirements apply to listed companies, for example the need to produce semi-annual interim reports. Other companies, which constitute the vast majority of companies in the UK, are called unlisted (or unquoted) companies. Shares in unquoted companies are not so readily marketable, and ownership interest is not spread among so many shareholders. Thus the 120,000 or so shareholders in Tesco plc (a listed company)

2. It is outside the scope of this book to provide a detailed discussion of the role and workings of the Stock Exchange. A good description is contained in Cobham, D., (ed.), *Markets & Deals: The Economics of the London Financial Markets*, Longman, London, 1992.

can buy and sell shares freely at the price determined by the stock market and published widely. However, the 180 shareholders of E.H. Booth and Co. Ltd (an unlisted company) can divest themselves of their shares only by offering them to the directors of the company at a price fixed at the previous annual general meeting.

Loan capital

The basic characteristics of long-term loan capital, in terms of returns, repayment of capital and security, are similar for all types of business structure. There are, however, two main differences in this respect between limited companies and other organizations. The first relates to the terminology used to describe such capital. Long-term loans to limited companies are known variously as *bonds, debentures, loan stock* and *debt capital*, all of which mean essentially the same thing. The second difference is that long-term loans to limited companies may be either *redeemable* or *irredeemable*. Redeemable loans are those under which a date is fixed for repayment of the capital at the time the loan is given. Almost all long-term loans to organizations other than limited companies are of this kind. Irredeemable loans are those where no date is fixed for repayment. The lender may require repayment only if the company defaults on the payment of interest or on some other condition of the loan. The company may usually choose to repay an irredeemable loan when it wishes. Figure 8.2 shows the long-term loan capital of Tesco plc at 29 February 1992. All the loans are redeemable between 1996 and 2015, and the finance lease payments are due between 1993 and 1996.

Preference capital

A third source of long-term capital is available to limited companies — *preference shares*. These are a hybrid of equity and debt capital. Legally, they are part of the ownership interest of a company. In many other respects, however, they resemble long-term loan capital more closely than equity capital. For example, like loan interest, the return on preference shares (the preference dividend) is usually stated at a fixed rate (or more accurately a maximum rate).

The term 'preference' refers to the rights of preference shareholders in relation to ordinary shareholders. First, although the directors can omit to declare a preference dividend, they cannot then declare a dividend on the ordinary shares in the same accounting period. Secondly, in the event of the liquidation of the company, the preference shareholders are repaid up to the limit of their nominal value before the ordinary shareholders recover any sum. Furthermore, if the dividend on a *cumulative* preference share is not paid, that dividend is classified as 'in arrears', and all such arrears must be paid before any dividends can be paid to the ordinary shareholders.

	1992 £m	1991 £m
Amounts falling due after more than one year		
4% unsecured deep discount loan stock 2006 (a)	**68.9**	67.2
4% convertible bonds 2002 (b)	—	0.1
Finance leases (Note 16)	**55.4**	53.8
$10\frac{1}{2}$% bonds 2015 (c)	**0.1**	5.6
Multi-option facility 1992	—	17.8
Other loans 1992	—	19.0
$10\frac{3}{8}$% bonds 2002 (d)	**200.0**	—
$\frac{1}{8}$% deep discount bond 2012 (e)	**50.0**	—
E.C.S.C. loan 1996 (f)	**73.8**	—
	448.2	163.5
Amounts owed to group undertakings	—	—
	448.2	163.5
Convertible capital bond (Note 14)	**200.0**	200.0
	648.2	363.5

Figure 8.2 *Tesco plc — long-term loan capital*

To summarize, the sources of long-term capital available to limited liability companies are, in essence, very similar to those available to other organizations. However, their accounting treatment tends to be more complex because of the greater formality that is attached to their issue, returns and redemption.

8.5 Capital structure

An organization's *capital structure* is the relationship between its various sources of capital. The definition is usually restricted to long-term sources of finance. It is beyond the scope of this book to evaluate the relative merits of alternative sources of finance;[3] the present chapter is concerned rather with the ways in which such alternatives are recorded and reported. Nevertheless, one particular aspect of capital structure is of great interest to those who use accounting reports — the level of the organization's financial *gearing*.

Gearing (or *leverage* as it is termed in the USA) is the relationship between the

3. For an excellent discussion of this topic see for example Brealey, R. and Myers, S. *Principles of Corporate Finance*, McGraw-Hill, 4th edn, 1991, Chapter 18.

Table 8.1 *Grosvenor plc and Brandywell plc — long-term capital details*

	Grosvenor plc £	Brandywell plc £
Ordinary shares:		
2,000,000, each having a nominal value of £1	2,000,000	
10,000,000, each having a nominal value of 25p		2,500,000
Retained profits:	600,000	3,200,000
Long-term loans:		
£3,000,000 10% debentures, redeemable in 2009	3,000,000	
£1,000,000 irredeemable 8% loan stock		1,000,000
Market value per ordinary share	£1.50	75p
Market value per £100 debenture/loan stock	£125	£98

loan capital and equity capital of an enterprise. It may be defined in a number of ways,[4] of which the most common is:

$$\text{Gearing ratio} = \frac{\text{Value of fixed interest capital}}{\text{Total value of the organization}}$$

The total value of the organization is defined as the value of ownership interest plus the value of loan capital. (Note that for the purpose of the gearing definition, preference shares are often treated as loan capital because the preference dividend is usually payable at a fixed or maximum rate.) An organization's gearing is higher, the greater is the proportion of loan capital in its capital structure. To calculate the gearing ratio, 'value' may be taken to refer to either market value or book value. In general, the former is the better measure of the current position of the organization, and is to be preferred.

For example, consider the case of two quoted companies, Grosvenor plc and Brandywell plc. Details of the long-term capital of each company are given in Table 8.1. The gearing ratios of each company, based on market values, are:

$$\text{Grosvenor plc} = \frac{3,000,000(1.25)}{2,000,000(1.50) + 3,000,000(1.25)} = 0.556 \text{ or } 55.6\%$$

$$\text{Brandywell plc} = \frac{1,000,000(0.98)}{10,000,000(0.75) + 1,000,000(0.98)} = 0.116 \text{ or } 11.6\%$$

Gearing ratios based on book values are:

$$\text{Grosvenor plc} = \frac{3,000,000}{(2,000,000 + 600,000) + 3,000,000} = 0.536 \text{ or } 53.6\%$$

4. Other definitions of the gearing ratio are discussed in Section 8.6.

$$\text{Brandywell plc} = \frac{1,000,000}{(2,500,000 + 3,200,000) + 1,000,000} = 0.149 \text{ or } 14.9\%$$

Whether the gearing ratio is based on market or book values, Grosvenor is the more highly geared of the two companies.

The importance of the gearing ratio is that it provides information about one aspect of an organization's risk, its *financial risk*. If an organization increases its gearing, the average return expected by its owners should increase, as a result of the acquisition of 'cheaper' loan financing. In other words, the prior right to income and capital enjoyed by preference shareholders and the lenders of loan capital determines that their required return is generally less than that required by equity owners. On the other hand, the financial risk of owners is increased with higher gearing because of:

(a) the increased risk of loss of control and (possibly) liquidation, if fixed interest payments cannot be met in any year, and
(b) the increased variability of returns to owners.

As an example of the second point, consider the case of two companies, Broomfield Ltd and Cliftonhill Ltd, each of which pays an ordinary dividend each year equal to its income after interest. Broomfield Ltd has no loan capital. Cliftonhill Ltd makes fixed interest payments of £1,000 each year. Annual income before interest and dividends is presently £1,000 for Broomfield Ltd and £2,000 for Cliftonhill Ltd. The figures in Table 8.2 show the effects on the ordinary dividends of each company if income (i) increases by 10%, and (ii) decreases by 10%. The ordinary dividend of Cliftonhill Ltd (the geared company) is more sensitive to changes in pre-interest income than is the ordinary dividend of Broomfield Ltd.

Table 8.2 *Broomfield Ltd and Cliftonhill Ltd — effects on ordinary dividends of changes in income*

	Broomfield Ltd			Cliftonhill Ltd		
	Present income £	*+10%* £	*−10%* £	*Present income* £	*+10%* £	*−10%* £
Income before interest and dividends	1,000	1,100	900	2,000	2,200	1,800
Fixed interest payments	0	0	0	1,000	1,000	1,000
Ordinary dividend	1,000	1,100	900	1,000	1,200	800
Percentage change in ordinary dividend	—	+10%	−10%	—	+20%	−20%

8.6   Short-term bank loans and overdrafts

In this chapter we have focused on long-term sources of capital. However, we have stated above that the financial risk of owners is increased with higher gearing because of the requirement to meet fixed interest payments each year, and the increased volatility of returns to owners. The risk is no less if the loans are short-term. Hence, when assessing the financial risk of owners it may be advisable to compute two gearing ratios — one as illustrated earlier in this section, and another which calculates the ratio of short-term and long-term borrowings and preference shares, to the total sources of finance utilized by the company (i.e. short-term and long-term borrowings, preference shares and equity capital).

In published financial statements, short-term borrowing comprises debt which is to be repaid within one year and is classified as a current liability. Short-term borrowing includes both bank overdrafts and bank loans. A bank overdraft arises when a company (or individual) is overdrawn on its current account. A bank will normally grant permission for a company to utilize an overdraft facility up to some specified maximum amount. The figure in the balance sheet represents the amount overdrawn at the balance sheet date — it may have been much higher or lower at other times during the year. Although many companies appear to have almost permanent overdrafts, the overdraft is classified as a current liability because, legally, it is repayable on demand.

Bank loans differ from overdrafts in that the full amount provided by the bank is normally taken by the company immediately. Bank loans to be repaid within one year comprise at least three types: a short-term loan borrowed for less than one year; a longer-term loan which is repayable in annual instalments — the next instalment is classified as a current liability, the remainder as long-term borrowing; and a long-term loan taken out some years previously and repayable in one lump sum within the next year.

For example, Blue Circle Industries plc reported total borrowings of £571 million at 31 December 1991, of which £88.9m was due to be repaid within one year (Figure 8.3). The company also disclosed preference share capital of £107.3 million and equity capital and reserves of £825.0 million. Hence its gearing ratio based on book values and excluding short-term debt is:

$$\frac{482.1 + 107.3}{482.1 + 107.3 + 825.0} = \frac{589.4}{1414.4} = 41.7\%$$

Using total debt it is:

$$\frac{589.4 + 88.9}{1414.4 + 88.9} = \frac{678.3}{1503.3} = 45.1\%$$

In the case of Blue Circle Industries plc the difference between the two gearing ratios is not material. In other cases, however, the imminent repayment of a large loan, taken out say 10 years previously, could lead to a dramatic difference between the results of the two ratios as the loan is reclassified as a current liability.

Borrowing

	1991 £m	1990 £m
Amounts falling due within one year:		
Debentures and other loans — secured	0.5	0.5
— unsecured	24.8	5.7
Bank loans and overdrafts — secured	2.5	3.2
— unsecured	61.1	84.3
	88.9	93.7
Amounts falling due after more than one year:		
Debentures and other loans — secured	11.0	11.0
— unsecured	252.9	194.6
Bank loans and overdrafts — secured	6.0	7.3
— unsecured	212.2	256.2
	482.1	469.1
Total borrowings	571.0	562.8
Borrowings are repayable over the following periods:		
Within one year	88.9	93.7
Between one and two years	11.6	27.6
Between two and five years	210.1	237.1
Over five years:		
Repayable by instalments	89.5	0.3
Other	170.9	204.1
	571.0	562.8

Figure 8.3 *Blue Circle Industries plc — borrowings*

8.7 Accounting treatment of long-term sources of capital

We now illustrate the recording and presentation of transactions relating to long-term capital for individuals, partnerships and limited companies.

Individuals

Mr Gayfield commences business on 1 January 19X0 by paying £8,000 from his personal resources into a business account. On the same day he receives a loan from Ms Somerset of £3,000 which he also pays into the bank. Interest at 15% is payable on the loan annually in arrears (i.e. the interest is payable at the *end* of each year). The loan is repayable after five years. During the year to 31 December 19X0 Mr Gayfield's business makes sales of £21,260 and incurs expenses, excluding interest, of £14,380. Sales are all for cash and are paid into the bank account. All expenses are paid from the bank account. On 31 December the interest due on the loan, amounting to £450, is paid. During the year, Mr Gayfield withdraws £5,200 from the business bank account for his personal use. This amount includes transfers to Mr Gayfield's personal bank account and invoices paid by the business that relate to Mr Gayfield's personal affairs.

The accounting equation entries necessary to reflect the above transactions are shown in Table 8.3. This information is presented in the form of an income statement and balance sheet in Table 8.4. Note the different treatments accorded to interest paid on the long-term loan (which is regarded as an expense) and payments made to, or on behalf of, the owner (the drawings charged directly to ownership interest). Note also that net income for the year, after interest, is added to ownership interest, and represents Mr Gayfield's return for the year. The treatment adopted in Tables 8.3 and 8.4 would be the same whether or not the owner worked in the business himself. In other words, net income represents both the return on capital paid in *and* the reward paid to Mr Gayfield for his labour.

Partnerships

Ms Sealand and Ms Meadow commence business in partnership on 1 January 19X1. On that date they pay into the business bank account capital from their personal resources as follows: Ms Sealand £12,000, Ms Meadow £9,000. They also receive a loan of £5,000 from Mr Dean which is paid into the bank. The loan is repayable after 10 years, and carries interest at the rate of 10% per annum, payable in arrears. During the following year they receive sales revenue of £32,900 and pay expenses, excluding interest, of £17,600. These amounts are paid into or from the bank account as appropriate. They also withdraw from the partnership bank account the following personal drawings: Ms Sealand £7,300, Ms Meadow £5,800. On 31 December they pay Mr Dean the interest due of £500. Their partnership agreement provides for each partner to be credited at the end of each year with 5% interest on her capital balance at the start of the year. In addition, each partner is to receive an annual salary of £5,000. Any balance of income is to be shared in a 2-to-1 ratio, Ms Sealand to Ms Meadow.

Accounting equation entries to record the above transactions are shown in Table 8.5. The information is presented in the form of accounting statements in Table 8.6. Two elements of the statements in Table 8.6 differ from those given in Table 8.4 and deserve closer attention. The first is that a separate *appropriation statement* is provided, showing how income for the year is divided between Ms Sealand and Ms Meadow in accordance with the details of the partnership agreement. Thus the appropriation statement shows how available income is shared between the owners. Such a statement is not needed for an individual because all income belongs to the (sole) owner. Each partner's share of income is added to their ownership interest. The second differentiating element is that partners' ownership interests are described as capital accounts. (This terminology may also be used for individuals.) In practice, a partner's ownership interest is sometimes

Table 8.3 *Mr Gayfield – accounting entries*

| Transaction | Assets | = | Ownership interest | + | Liabilities | + | Net income | |
	Cash at bank £		Ownership interest £		Loan from Ms Somerset £		Net income £	
Capital paid in	8,000		8,000					
Loan from Ms Somerset	3,000				3,000			
Sales	21,260						21,260	(Sales)
Expenses excluding interest	(14,380)						(14,380)	(Expenses)
Interest to Ms Somerset	(450)						(450)	(Interest)
Drawings	(5,200)		(5,200)					
							6,430	(Net income)
Transfer of net income to ownership interest			6,430				(6,430)	
Balances at end of year	12,230	=	9,230	+	3,000	+	0	

Table 8.4 *Mr Gayfield — accounting statements*

Income statement for the year ended 31 December 19X0

	£	£
Sales		21,260
less: Expenses	14,380	
Interest paid	450	14,830
		£6,430

Balance sheet at 31 December 19X0

Assets		
Cash at bank		£12,230
Ownership interest		
Capital paid in	8,000	
add: Net income for the year	6,430	
	14,430	
less: Drawings	5,200	9,230
Liabilities		
Loan from Ms Somerset		3,000
		£12,230

---

subdivided into a *capital account* (the amount of which is usually unchanged from year to year, and represents the 'permanent' long-term capital provided by the partner) and a *current account* (in which all other transactions, including share of income and drawings, are shown).

Limited companies

Plainmoor Ltd is incorporated (i.e. created) on 1 January 19X2 with *authorized share capital* as follows:[5]

> 1,000,000 50p ordinary shares
> 200,000 £1 irredeemable 12% preference shares

On 1 January, the following capital is *issued* for cash:[6]

> 500,000 50p ordinary shares at a price of £1.50 each
> 100,000 £1 irredeemable preference shares at par (i.e. at the
> nominal value of £1 each)
> £200,000 Irredeemable 10% debentures at par

5. Authorized share capital is the *maximum* amount of share capital a particular company may issue, as agreed by the original promoters of the company. The amount of authorized capital may subsequently be changed if the shareholders so agree.
6. Issued share capital is that part of its authorized share capital issued by a company.

Table 8.5 *Ms Sealand and Ms Meadow — partnership accounting entries*

	Assets		Ownership interest	+ Liabilities	+ Net income	
	Cash at bank £	= Ownership interest Ms Sealand £	+ Ownership interest Ms Meadow £	+ Loan from Mr Dean £	+ Net income £	
Transaction						
Capital paid in	21,000	12,000	9,000			
Loan from Mr Dean	5,000			5,000		
Sales	32,900				32,900	(Sales)
Expenses excluding interest	(17,600)				(17,600)	(Expenses)
Interest to Mr Dean	(500)				(500)	(Interest)
Drawings	(13,100)	(7,300)	(5,800)			
					14,800	(Income)
Transfer of net income to ownership interest (see Table 8.6 for details)		8,100	6,700		(14,800)	
Balances at end of year	27,700 =	12,800	+ 9,900	+ 5,000	+ 0	

Table 8.6   *Ms Sealand and Ms Meadow — accounting statements*

Income statement for the year ended 31 December 19X1

	£	£
Sales		32,900
less: Expenses	17,600	
Interest paid	500	18,100
		£14,800

Appropriation statement for the year ended 31 December 19X1

	Ms Sealand £	Ms Meadow £	Total £
Interest on capital (at 5%)	600	450	1,050
Salaries	5,000	5,000	10,000
Balance (shared 2:1)	2,500	1,250	3,750
	8,100	6,700	14,800

Balance sheet at 31st December 19X1

	£	£	£
Assets			
Cash at bank			£27,700
Capital accounts	Ms Sealand	Ms Meadow	
Capital paid in	12,000	9,000	
add: Share of net income for the year	8,100	6,700	
	20,100	15,700	
less: Drawings	7,300	5,800	
	12,800	9,900	22,700
Liabilities			
Loan from Mr Dean			5,000
			£27,700

During the following year, Plainmoor Ltd makes sales of £175,000 and incurs expenses, excluding interest, of £75,000. Sales revenue and expenses are paid into or out of the company bank account as appropriate. On 31 December, the company pays debenture interest (of £20,000), the preference dividend (of £12,000) and an ordinary dividend of 10p per share (£50,000).[7]

Accounting equation entries for the above transactions are given in Table 8.7.

7. In this case, the amount of dividends is described as an amount per share. This is the usual method of showing dividends. They are sometimes described as percentages, for example as a dividend of 10% or 20%. In such cases, the percentage relates to the *nominal* value of *issued* capital. Thus for Plainmoor Ltd, the ordinary dividend could be described as a dividend of 20%, i.e. 20% of the nominal value of the ordinary shares issued, £250,000 (500,000 × 50p), which equals £50,000.

Table 8.7 Plainmoor Ltd — accounting entries

| | Assets | | Ownership interest + Liabilities + Net income | | | | | |
	Cash at Bank £	=	Ordinary share capital £	+ Preference share capital £	+ Share premium £	+ Reserves £	+ Debentures £	+ Net income £
Transaction								
Ordinary shares issued	750,000		250,000		500,000			
Preference shares issued	100,000			100,000				
Debentures issued	200,000						200,000	
Sales	175,000							175,000 (Sales)
Expenses excluding interest	(75,000)							(75,000) (Expenses)
Debenture interest	(20,000)							(20,000) (Interest)
								80,000 (Income)
Preference dividend	(12,000)							(12,000) (Preference dividend)
Ordinary dividend	(50,000)							(50,000) (Ordinary dividend)
								18,000 (Retained net income)
Transfer of retained net income to reserves						18,000		(18,000)
Balances at end	1,068,000	=	250,000	+ 100,000	+ 500,000	+ 18,000	+ 200,000	+ 0

Table 8.8 *Plainmoor Ltd — accounting statements*

	£	£
Income statement for the year ended 31 December 19X2		
Sales		175,000
less: Expenses excluding interest	75,000	
Debenture interest	20,000	95,000
Income for the year		80,000
less: Appropriations:		
Dividends — preference	12,000	
ordinary	50,000	62,000
Retained income, added to reserves		£18,000
Balance sheet as at 31 December 19X2		
Assets		
Cash at bank		£1,068,000
Capital and reserves		
Authorized 1,000,000 50p Ordinary shares	500,000	
200,000 £1 irredeemable 12%		
preference shares	200,000	
	700,000	
Issued 500,000 50p Ordinary shares	250,000	
100,000 £1 irredeemable 12%		
preference shares	100,000	350,000
Share premium		500,000
Reserves		18,000
Total capital and reserves		868,000
Long-term loans		
Irredeemable 10% debentures		200,000
		£1,068,000

Accounting statements for Plainmoor Ltd, reflecting the information in Table 8.7, are shown in Table 8.8. The principles involved in presenting the income statement are similar to those applied in presenting the accounts of individuals and partnerships; interest on long-term loans (debentures) is treated as an expense, whereas payments to owners (dividends to ordinary and preference shareholders) are treated as appropriations of income. Dividends are equivalent to owners' drawings except that, as we noted earlier, they are not deducted directly from ownership interest, but rather subtracted from net income. The balance sheet is also drawn up on similar lines to those adopted for other organizations except that its content (and that of the income statement) is determined largely by legal requirements. Two particular features of long-term capital are specific to limited companies. The first is the inclusion of *authorized* share capital. This inclusion is demanded by company law. It is important to recognize that this figure (£700,000) does not form part of the company's double-entry records — it is a memorandum entry to indicate the maximum share capital the company is empowered to issue. Hence it is not included in the figure for total share capital and reserves. Second, capital paid in by owners (£750,000 from ordinary shareholders and £100,000 from preference shareholders) is subdivided between issued capital (the nominal value of the shares issued) and share premium (the difference between the amount received and the nominal value). In this case, the share premium is £1 per ordinary share (the issue price of £1.50 minus the nominal value of 50p), giving a total of £500,000. As we noted earlier, a share's nominal value is of no particular significance other than as a means of describing and identifying the share.

8.8 An illustration from practice — E.H. Booth & Co. Ltd

The complete set of Booths' accounts can be found in Appendix 1.
Booths' Balance Sheet (page 11) reveals that total assets comprise:

Fixed assets	£26,798,485
Current assets	5,571,137
	£32,369,622

This amount represents the historical cost (less depreciation where appropriate) of Booths' portfolio of assets on 4 April 1992. The balance sheet reveals also the various sources of capital used to finance these assets:

Short-term creditors	£10,980,498
Long-term creditors	9,795,942
Provisions	587,767
Capital and reserves	11,005,415
	£32,369,622

We shall explain each of these sources of finance below.

Capital and reserves

The Balance Sheet discloses that 'Called up share capital' is £1,268,060 and refers the reader to Note 15 (page 18). In Note 15 we see that the Authorized share capital amounts to £1,312,000. As we stated earlier in the chapter, this is the maximum amount of share capital that the company is currently empowered to issue. It is normally written into the Memorandum of Association when a company is formed. The directors cannot issue shares in excess of the authorized limit without the passing of a resolution at a general meeting of shareholders (the exact procedure for each company is included in its Articles of Association).

The share capital comprises two classes of shares — preference shares and ordinary shares. The directors of Booths are authorized to issue 12,000 Preference shares of £1 each and 1,300,000 Ordinary shares of £1 each. At 4 April 1992, they had issued 12,000 Preference shares and 1,256,060 Ordinary shares. These had been 'allotted' to shareholders and had been 'fully paid'. No shares were issued during the year. We shall now examine each class of shares in turn.

3.5% net cumulative Preference shares of £1 each.   The nominal value of each share is £1 and the dividend payable on each share, each year is 3.5 pence, net of (after deducting) income tax at the basic rate. Hence, the dividend payable on £12,000 3.5% net preference shares is £420 p.a. and this is confirmed in Note 7 (page 15). We explained in Section 8.4 that preference shares, as their name suggests, have some sort of priority over ordinary shares. The maximum rate of dividend on Booths' preference shares is fixed at 3.5 pence per £1 share, but the preference dividend must be paid in full before any dividend is paid to ordinary shareholders. If Booths, or any other company, wished to reinvest all of its post-tax profits in expanding the business, it might not pay a dividend of any sort for several years. However, if the preference shares are 'cumulative' preference shares, as is the case in Booths, then upon the resumption of dividend payments, all arrears of preference dividends must be paid before any ordinary dividends can be paid. Should Booths ever be liquidated, the preference shareholders would be repaid, up to the limit of the nominal value of their shares (£12,000), before the ordinary shareholders received anything.

Ordinary shares of £1 each.   As with the preference shares, the nominal value of each ordinary share is £1. There is no fixed rate of dividend. Each year the directors propose a dividend, the size of which depends upon, *inter alia*, the company's recent performance, its future prospects and its present financial position. Note 7 (page 15) reveals that in the year to 4 April 1992, Booths propose to pay a total dividend of 10.5 pence per ordinary share, amounting to £131,886. As can be seen from the Profit and Loss Account (page 10), Booths reported a profit after taxation of £815,394 for the year, more than six times the size of the proposed dividends. However, even if Booths had made only £100,000 profit or even a loss, it would still, legally, be able to pay a dividend of £131,886 as long as there were sufficient retained profits (i.e. profits made in previous years but not distributed) to cover the dividend.

Most companies simply transfer the profit retained after the distribution of a dividend to the 'Profit and Loss Account' in the Ownership Interest, or Capital and Reserves, section of the balance sheet. The accumulated retained profit is represented by the balance on this account. Booths is unusual in that it 'transfers' most of its retained profit to a 'General reserve', leaving only a small amount of retained profit in the Profit and Loss Account (see pages 10 and 11). This transfer is a bookkeeping entry only. It may be a way for the directors to signal to the shareholders that they have no intention of distributing the profits transferred to the General reserve, but it has no legal consequence. If the balance on the General reserve account comprises accumulated realized profits from previous years, then they are available for distribution. Hence, legally, Booth could have paid an ordinary dividend of up to £9,869,241 in 1992 (i.e. the declared dividend plus the balances on the general reserve and the profit and loss account — £131,886 + £9,710,000 + £27,355 = £9,869,241). However, it does not have the cash resources to pay such a dividend, nor would it be prudent in the circumstances to do so. Perhaps a more important consequence of this legal rule is that a company which discloses accumulated losses in its balance sheet (i.e. a negative balance on the profit and loss account) must subsequently make sufficient profits to eliminate those losses before it can pay a dividend.

Dividends are proposed by the directors, but must be approved by the shareholders, usually at the annual general meeting (AGM). However, as one of the duties of the shareholders at the AGM is to approve the accounts for the year, the meeting normally takes place some time after the year end in order to allow the auditors sufficient time to carry out the audit. Perhaps as a goodwill gesture to the shareholders, or as a statement of confidence about the current year's performance, most companies now pay the dividend in two instalments. An interim dividend can be declared by the directors during the year without seeking the shareholders' approval. By convention this dividend is normally less than half the anticipated total dividend for the year. The directors will ask the shareholders to confirm the interim dividend and to approve their recommended final dividend at the AGM. The shareholders of Booths are invited to approve the accounts and the dividends at the 1992 AGM some five months after the year end (Notice of Meeting, page 5).

Although the interim dividend is paid in the year in which it is declared, the final dividend is accrued as a current liability and paid in the following year. Hence, for most companies the amount of dividends reported in the profit and loss account will not be identical to the amount of dividends paid in the cash flow statement. However, for Booths the two figures are identical because the company has not increased its dividend payment in 1992 (see Table 8.9).

Nevertheless, it is important to note that for most companies the ordinary dividend increases over time and that normally the amount of 'Dividends Paid' disclosed in the cash flow statement will be lower than the amount of 'Dividends' (paid and payable) disclosed in the profit and loss account.

The final dividend for 1992 has been proposed but not paid at the year end. Hence, we would expect to find an amount equal to the final dividend in the

Table 8.9

	Profit and Loss Account 1992 £	Cash Flow Statement 1992 £
1991 Final dividend paid September 1991	—	106,765
1992 Interim dividend paid March 1992	25,121	25,121
1992 Final dividend proposed	106,765	—
	131,886	131,886
1992 Preference dividend paid March 1992	420	420
	132,306	132,306
	(page 10)	(page 12)

current liabilities of Booths. The balance sheet discloses that Creditors: Amounts falling due within one year amount to £10,980,498 and Note 12 (page 17) reveals that one of those liabilities is the proposed dividend of £106,765.

Long-term creditors

The balance sheet reveals that Creditors: Amounts falling due after more than one year amount to £9,795,942 and Note 13 (page 17) satisfies the statutory requirement that this amount should be split into loans wholly repayable within five years, and loans wholly or partly repayable more than five years after the balance sheet date. As we explained earlier in the chapter, as time passes loans due after five years become loans due within five years, and eventually loans due within one year. It is likely therefore that the figure for Bank loans — £1,033,000 in Creditors: Amounts falling due within one year (Note 12, page 17) — represents the 'current maturity' portion of long-term debt. Hence, the total amount of Booths' long-term debt, including that amount due for repayment within the next year, is:

	1992 £	1991 £
Bank loans due <1 year	1,033,000	954,022
Bank loans due >1 year and <5 years	3,873,692	4,505,087
Bank loans due >5 years	5,922,250	6,339,083
	10,828,942	11,798,192

Booths has reduced its long-term borrowing by £969,250 during the year (£11,798,192 − £10,828,942). This could be a net figure, i.e. Booths might have repaid some existing loans and taken out some new ones. However, Note 20 (page 19) reveals that no new loans were taken out in 1992 and that the company has repaid loans of £969,250.

Short-term creditors

From Booths' balance sheet (page 11) we can see that the total for 'Creditors: Amounts falling due within one year' is £10,980,498. Note 12 provides a breakdown of this figure. We have dealt with Trade creditors, Taxation and Accruals in Chapter 5, and with Bank loans and Proposed dividends earlier in this section. We now turn our attention to the Bank overdraft.

A bank overdraft is an indication that a company has overdrawn on its current account. Normally a bank will agree an overdraft limit at the beginning of the year and allow the company complete freedom to draw upon this facility within the limit set. We suggested in Section 8.1 that the type of capital required to finance assets varies with the nature of the particular assets. The overdraft has traditionally been used to cover the fluctuations in a company's cash balance caused by the inevitable leads and lags in production and sales. In other words it has been used to finance the (fluctuating) excess of stocks and trade debtors over trade creditors — the net working capital of a business.

However, Booths' overdraft (£3,742,656) is far greater than that required to finance net working capital. Referring again to Booths' total sources of funds and total uses of funds, it would appear that a significant amount of short term funding is being used to finance fixed assets.

	£		£
		Long term creditors	9,795,942
		Provisions	587,767
		Capital and reserves	11,005,415
Fixed assets	26,798,485		21,389,124
Current assets	5,571,137	Short term creditors	10,980,498
	£32,369,622		£32,369,622

The company might be using part of its overdraft to finance its new buildings and fixtures. We shall examine this situation further in Chapter 11 when we analyse the operating performance and financial position of Booths.

Provisions

Provisions fall into two categories. The first comprises any amount written off by way of providing for depreciation or diminution in the value of assets. We have seen examples of this in previous chapters, for example a provision for the depreciation of fixed assets, and a provision for doubtful debts. Normally these provisions are deducted from the relevant asset rather than being shown separately. The second type comprises any amount retained to provide for any liability or loss which is *either* likely to be incurred, *or* certain to be incurred but uncertain as to the amount or as to the date on which it will arise. It is this second type that appears on the balance sheet of Booths under the heading 'Provision for Liabilities and Charges: Deferred taxation'.

We have stated previously that it is beyond the scope of this introductory textbook to explain the complexities of the corporation tax system in the UK. However, a brief explanation of part of that system is appropriate here. In 1992 the rate of corporation tax was 33%. Booths' 'Profit on ordinary activities before taxation' in that year was £1,404,333 (Profit and Loss Account, page 10). However, the tax charge was not £463,430 (i.e. 33% of the pre-tax profit), but £588,939 (almost 42%). The previous year it had been only 23% of pre-tax profit. Clearly, the corporation tax charge is not determined simply by applying a rate of 33% to the pre-tax profit figure in the profit and loss account. In fact it depends upon an assessment made by the Inland Revenue. The Inland Revenue uses the profit and loss account as a basis for its assessment, but there are some important differences. One such difference is the treatment of depreciation.

We saw in Chapter 6 that companies have considerable flexibility in depreciating fixed tangible assets. Assets can be depreciated over a range of lives using a range of depreciation methods. The Inland Revenue, however, disallows a company's own depreciation charge in calculating taxable profit, and substitutes a more standardized *capital allowance*. For many classes of assets, for example plant and machinery, fixtures and fittings, the *writing down allowance* writes off the cost of an asset more quickly than the company's depreciation charge. For example, in 1992, the writing down allowance applied to plant and machinery, fixtures and fittings was 25% on the reducing balance and has been as high as 100% in the past. This compares with Booths' depreciation rates on fixtures, plant and vehicles of between 10% on cost and 20% on written down value.

Clearly, the total figures for depreciation and capital allowances must be identical over the life of the asset — one cannot depreciate more than the original cost of the asset. Just as we saw when comparing different methods of depreciation in Chapter 6, it is the pattern of the write-off which differs. So, if a company benefits from accelerated capital allowances at the beginning of an asset's life, its taxable profit assessed by the Inland Revenue will be lower than its pre-tax profit reported in the profit and loss account. However, later in the asset's life the difference will reverse and the taxable profit will be higher than the pre-tax profit in the profit and loss account. In effect, the company is postponing, or *deferring*, its tax liability for a number of years — the Inland Revenue is a source of finance!

Nevertheless, the tax will have to be paid one day, so the company recognizes the liability as a 'provision' on the balance sheet. Booths' liability is £587,767.

To the extent that timing differences, such as those caused by different methods of depreciation, are expected to reverse in the future, the tax charge in the profit and loss account is based on the reported profit, the difference between the reported tax expense and the actual charge being described as deferred tax (an amount of £26,887 for Booths, see Note 6, page 15). Any remaining difference for 1992 is caused by differences between reported and taxable profits which will not be reversed because certain expenses shown in the profit and loss account are not allowable deductions for tax purposes, for example some entertainment expenses in the UK. Such differences are permanent and are not added to the deferred taxation provision.

This chapter completes our review and explanation of the constituent elements of the balance sheet, income statement and cash flow statement prepared under historical cost accounting. You should now be in a position to understand the nature, purpose and the limitations of these financial statements, and, in particular, you should be able to comprehend the way in which the double-entry bookkeeping system serves as the basis for the compilation of all entries appearing in all three statements. The following chapter brings together, by way of two detailed bookkeeping examples, most aspects of an organization's transactions, and draws on the ideas and examples used in this and previous chapters.

Discussion topics

1. Outline and explain the relationships you might expect to observe on an enterprise's balance sheet between fixed and current assets on the one hand, and long-term and short-term sources of finance on the other.

2. Describe the main respects in which the financial characteristics of individuals, partnerships and limited companies differ.

3. Discuss the major differences between ownership interest (or equity capital) and long-term loans (or loan capital).

4. Distinguish between 'drawings' and 'dividends'. To what extent does either measure the returns to an organization's owners?

5. What do you understand by a company's 'gearing ratio'? Why is it important?

6. Distinguish between 'appropriations' and 'expenses'.

7. Each of the following terms might be found in a set of accounts. In respect of each, state where it would be found, what it means and which accounting entries it reflects.
   (a) Capital account
   (b) Ordinary share dividends

(c) Loan interest paid
(d) Authorized share capital
(e) Share premium
(f) Current account
(g) 20,000 £1 redeemable 7% preference shares
(h) Reserves
(i) Debenture interest paid
(j) Retained income
(k) Drawings
(l) Preference share dividends
(m) Long-term loan
(n) Balance of partnership profit (share 2:1:1)
(o) 10 million 25p ordinary shares
(p) Irredeemable 13% debentures.

8. Identify the various sources of capital used to finance Booths' portfolio of assets. Contrast these sources of capital with those you would expect to find being used to finance a local corner grocery shop.

Exercises

8.1 Mr Ramphis, a grocer, has prepared the following accounts for his first year's trading from 1 January 19X7.

Profit and loss account for the year ended 31 December 19X7

	£		£
Sales	40,950		
Purchases	24,860		
Gross profit	16,090		
Wages	14,040		
Sundry shop expenses	7,690		
Van expenses	1,770		
Net loss for the year	(7,410)		

Balance sheet on 31 December 19X7

Capital:			
Cash paid in	10,000	Van	5,000
less: Net loss for the year	7,410	Cash at bank	90
	2,590		5,090

Mr Ramphis is perturbed that the accounts do not balance and asks for your assistance. He gives you the following information:

(i) Mr Ramphis has taken groceries to the value of £30 per week for his personal consumption for which no adjustment has been made.

(ii) Included in the purchases figures of £24,860 are goods to the value of £3,500 which were held in stock at 31 December 19X7.

(iii) All sales and purchases were for cash. On 31 December 19X7, Mr Ramphis made sales amounting to £2,500 to a local restaurant. He received payment for these sales on that date, and paid the amount received into the bank account. As yet, no other entry has been made in the records in respect of these sales.

(iv) There was no cash in hand at the end of the year.

(v) The figure for wages is made up as follows:

	£
Mr Ramphis, £150 per week	7,800
Employees' wages, £120 per week	6,240
	14,040

(vi) Sundry shop expenses include £2,000 which was paid on 1 January 19X7, for the purchase of equipment to be used in the shop. Mr Ramphis estimates the life of this equipment at 10 years, and its scrap value at the end of that period at zero.

(vii) The van was purchased on 1 January 19X7. Mr Ramphis estimates that he will keep it until 31 December 19X9, when its value will be about £1,700.

(viii) Depreciation is to be provided on fixed assets using the straight line method of calculation.

■ (a) Prepare a statement with brief explanatory notes showing any adjustments which you think are necessary to the accounts prepared by Mr Ramphis.

(b) Prepare a revised profit and loss account for the year ended 31 December 19X7 and balance sheet as at that date.

8.2 Amonasro and Radames formed a partnership on 1 September 19X2, to buy and sell annas. The terms of the partnership were as follows:

(i) Profits were to be shared $\frac{1}{3}$ to Amonasro and $\frac{2}{3}$ to Radames.

(ii) In addition, Radames was to receive a salary of £2,000 p.a.

(iii) On 31 August in each year, interest was to be credited at the rate of 10% on the balance of each partner's capital account on the previous 1 September.

The balances shown below appeared in the books of the partnership on 31 August 19X3. Amonasro and Radames maintain separate accounts for each item of revenue and expense contributing to income.

	Debit *Assets and* *expenses* £	Credit *Ownership interest,* *liabilities and revenues* £
Capital accounts (capital *introduced on 1 September* *19X2):*		
Amonasro		40,000
Radames		20,000
Drawings:		
Amonasro	12,000	
Radames (including salary)	10,800	
Lease on premises at cost	24,000	
Motor vehicles at cost	7,200	
Office furniture and equipment at cost	2,400	
Cash at bank	20,660	
Sales		133,600
Purchases	87,000	
Discounts allowed to customers	1,940	
Discounts received from suppliers		3,520
Office salaries	11,160	
Rent and rates	7,600	
Insurance	960	
Repairs	660	
Lighting and heating	1,740	
Motor vehicle expenses (excluding depreciation)	3,480	
Carriage and postage	3,620	
General expenses	1,900	
	197,120	197,120

The following additional information is available:

(i)   Straight line depreciation is to be provided at the following rates on cost:
    Motor vehicles   25%
    Office furniture and equipment   10%

(ii)   The value of stock at 31 August 19X3 is estimated at £11,200.

(iii)   A provision of £3,000 for amortization of the lease is to be made.

(iv)   No interest is to be charged on partners' drawings.

- Prepare the partnership profit and loss account for the year ended 31 August 19X3, and balance sheet as at that date.

8.3   Giovanni plc is a long-established public limited company. In the year ended 31 December 19X1 it issued 10,000 shares of £1 nominal value at a premium of £1. Cash was received on 30 December 19X1 and banked on 31 December 19X1. The allotment of shares was made on 31 December 19X1. No entries for either of these transactions have been made in the trial balance which appears below:

	£000's	
	Debit	*Credit*
	£	£
Sales		2,500
Sales returns	100	
Purchases	1,800	
Trade creditors		150
Trade debtors	250	
Bad debts provision at 1 January 19X1		50
Share capital		650
Revenue reserves at 1 January 19X1		400
Fixed assets	300	
Accumulated depreciation 31 December 19X1		150
Depreciation charge for the year	50	
Stock at 1 January 19X1	1,300	
Expenses	100	
	3,900	3,900

Stock at 31 December 19X1 was valued at £1,100,000. The bad debts provision is to be adjusted to £25,000.

■   Prepare the profit and loss account of Giovanni plc for the year ended 31 December 19X1 and the balance sheet as at that date.

8.4   Amneris Ltd was incorporated on 1 May 19X0 with authorized share capital as follows:

5,000,000   50p ordinary shares
1,000,000   £1 irredeemable 14% preference shares

On 1 May 19X0, the following capital was issued for cash:

3,000,000   50p ordinary shares at a price of £1.25 each
700,000   £1 irredeemable preference shares at a price of £1.10 each
£1,000,000   12% debentures at par, redeemable on 30 April 19X9 at par

During the year ended 30 April 19X1, Amneris Ltd acquired fixed assets at a cost of £4,500,000, made sales of £3,200,000 and incurred expenses of £2,400,000 (excluding interest but including £900,000 depreciation on fixed assets). Sales revenue, the cost of fixed assets and expenses (excluding depreciation) were paid into or out of the company bank account, as appropriate. On 30 April 19X1, Amneris Ltd paid one year's interest on the debentures, an annual preference dividend of 14% and an ordinary dividend of 10p per share.

■   (a) Prepare Amneris Ltd's profit and loss account for the year ended 30 April 19X1 and its balance sheet on that date, in a form suitable for publication.

(b) Outline the main characteristics of the various types of capital issued by Amneris Ltd.

Further reading

Brealey, R. and Myers, S. *Principles of Corporate Finance*, McGraw-Hill, 4th edn, 1991.
Cobham, D. (ed.) *Markets and Deals: The Economics of the London Financial Markets*, Longman, London, 1992.
Peasnell, K.V. and Ward, C.W.R., *British Financial Markets and Institutions*, Prentice-Hall International, 1985.
Thomas, W.A., *The Securities Market*, Philip Allan, 1989.

9

Double-entry

Bookkeeping

9.1 Conventional double-entry bookkeeping and the accounting equation

Up to now we have used the expanded accounting equation to record accounting transactions and to reflect their dual nature. We believe that this is the clearest way of demonstrating the structure of transactions-based recording systems. In practice, this particular method of double-entry recording is rarely used. The problem with the accounting equation approach, as we have used it, is simply that it is too cumbersome as a means of maintaining all the accounting records of actual organizations. Our examples have been simplified — a real organization may have many different assets, liabilities and expenses, necessitating, strictly, a very large number of columns in any accounting equation.

We now turn our attention to the method of double-entry recording used almost universally; for convenience we refer to this method as 'conventional' double-entry recording.[1] It is widely known as the 'T' Account approach, for reasons which will become evident as we progress. We also reconcile this method with the accounting equation approach. It should be stressed that identical principles underlie the two methods, and that both lead to the same figures in income statements and balance sheets.

Main differences between the conventional and accounting equation approaches

The differences between the conventional and accounting equation approaches are no more than differences in the method of recording the same information.

1. The principles are identical if the organization has implemented a computerized accounting system. The ledger will comprise a file rather than a book, etc.

Table 9.1 *Illustration of (simplified) trial balance*

	£	£
Land and buildings	XX	
Plant and machinery	XX	
Stock	XX	
Debtors	XX	
Cash	XX	
Share capital ⎫ Ownership interest		XX
Retained profits ⎬		XX
Creditors		XX
Sales		XX
Cost of goods sold	XX	
Expenses	XX	
	XX	XX

They may be summarized as follows:

1. Under the accounting equation approach each asset, liability, etc. has its own column. Under the conventional approach, the accounting equation is replaced by a book (traditionally called a *ledger*) and each accounting equation column is replaced by a page in this ledger. Each page is called an *account*, so, for example, the ledger will include a Cash at bank account, a Machine account, a Stock account, a Capital account, a Long-term loan account, an Income account, and so on.

2. Each column of the accounting equation may include both positive and negative amounts, as for example we showed in our treatment of fixed assets and depreciation in Chapter 6. In a ledger account, 'positive' amounts are shown on one side of the page and 'negative' amounts on the other. At the end of a period, each side of the account is summed, and the difference between the two sides is the *balance* on the account.

3. Under the conventional approach a list of the balances on each account is prepared at the end of each period. This is known as a *trial balance*. An illustrative trial balance is given in Table 9.1. Each balance is equivalent to the balance at the foot of an accounting equation column. The balances in the trial balance are listed vertically (compared with the horizontal presentation of the accounting equation) in two columns. The first column contains the balances on accounts where the sum of the entries on the left-hand side exceeds the sum of those on the right; the other column contains the balances on accounts where the sum of the entries on the right-hand side exceeds the sum of those on the left. The two columns should have equal totals, like the two sides of the accounting equation. The trial balance provides an arithmetic check that two aspects of each transaction have been recorded. It does not, however, indicate whether they have been entered in the correct accounts.

Reconciliation of the conventional and accounting equation approaches

We shall now show that, in spite of their different procedures, the conventional and accounting equation approaches are in fact based on identical principles and lead to identical measures of income and position. Recall the accounting equation which has formed the basis of our double-entry recording:

Assets = Liabilities + Ownership interest + Revenues − Expenses

Rearranging the equation to remove 'negative' columns gives:

Assets + Expenses = Liabilities + Ownership interest + Revenues

Entries on the left of the rearranged accounting equation relate to either assets or expenses, and those on the right to liabilities, ownership interest or revenues. *Balances* on the left of the accounting equation are *uses* of funds, either assets or expenses, and those on the right are *sources* of funds, i.e. liabilities, ownership interest or revenues.

Similar rules apply to the conventional method. For example, amounts that would be added to the left of the rearranged accounting equation or subtracted from the right (remembering that 'negative' entries are not made under the conventional method) are placed on the left-hand side of the account, and amounts that would be added to the right-hand side of the accounting equation (or subtracted from the left-hand side) are put on the right-hand side of the account.

The conventional method avoids the terms left- and right-hand side in favour of the terms *'debit'* and *'credit'*, often abbreviated to *Dr* and *Cr*. As we noted in Chapter 5, a debit entry is one made on the left of an account, and a credit entry is made on the right. These are the *only* meanings which accounting attaches to the terms 'debit' and 'credit'.

Accounting entries should therefore be made as follows:

Entries for	Left-hand side Debit (Dr)	Right-hand side Credit (Cr)
Assets	Increase	Decrease
Expenses	Increase	Decrease
Liabilities	Decrease	Increase
Ownership interest	Decrease	Increase
Revenues	Decrease	Increase

As far as *balances* on accounts at the end of a period are concerned, the following rules hold:

1. If the sum of the entries on the left-hand side of the account is greater than the sum of the entries on the right, the difference is a *debit balance*, and is either an asset or an expense.
2. If the sum of the entries on the right-hand side is greater than the sum

of the entries on the left, the difference is a *credit balance,* and is represented by a liability, ownership interest or revenue.

In the following section we shall work through the recording of a short series of transactions using both the accounting equation and conventional approaches. We provide a more detailed bookkeeping example in Section 9.3. Readers wishing to practice the conventional approach further may use it to rework the accounting illustrations we have given in previous chapters.

9.2   Double-entry bookkeeping: a simple example

Mr Stamford owns and manages a retail business. His balance sheet on 1 January 19X0 is given in Table 9.2. During the year to 31 December 19X0 he undertakes the following transactions:

1. Obtains an additional long-term loan of £4,000 at 10% p.a. interest.
2. Purchases on credit 3,200 units of stock at £20 per unit.
3. Sells on credit 3,000 units of stock at £30 per unit.
4. Receives £85,000 from debtors.
5. Pays £56,000 to creditors.

Table 9.2   *Mr Stamford — balance sheet at 1 January 19X0*

	£	£	£
Fixed assets at cost		27,000	
less: Accumulated depreciation		10,000	17,000
Current assets			
Stock (500 units at £16 per unit)	8,000		
Debtors	6,000		
Cash at bank	2,000	16,000	
less: Current liabilities			
Creditors	5,000		
Accrued expenses	1,000	6,000	
Net current assets			10,000
Total assets less current liabilities			£27,000
Represented by:			
Ownership interest			16,000
Long-term loan at 10% p.a.			11,000
Long-term funds employed			£27,000

Table 9.3 Mr Stamford — accounting equation entries

	Fixed assets £	+ Stock £	+ Debtors £	+ Cash at bank £	= Owners interest £	+ Loans £	+ Creditors £	+ Accrued expenses £	+ Revenues £	− Expenses £	
Balance at 1 January 19X0	27,000 (10,000)	8,000	6,000	2,000	16,000	11,000	5,000	1,000			
Transactions during the year:											
(1)				4,000		4,000					
(2)		64,000					64,000				
(3)		(58,000)*	90,000						90,000	(58,000)	Sales / Cost of goods sold
(4)			(85,000)	85,000							
(5)				(56,000)			(56,000)				
(6)				(9,000)				(1,000)		(8,000)	Expenses
(7)								2,000		(2,000)	Expenses
(8)	(5,000)									(5,000)	Depreciation
(9)				(1,500)						(1,500)	Interest
(10)				(8,000)	(8,000)						
					$\overline{8,000}$				$\overline{90,000}$	$\overline{(74,500)}$	
Transfer of net income to ownership interest					15,500					(15,500)	
	$\overline{12,000}$ +	$\overline{14,000}$ +	$\overline{11,000}$ +	$\overline{16,500}$ =	$\overline{23,500}$ +	$\overline{15,000}$ +	$\overline{13,000}$ +	$\overline{2,000}$ +	$\overline{90,000}$ −	$\overline{90,000}$	

* (500 × £16) + (2,500 × £20) = £58,000 using the assumption that the materials bought first are used first

Table 9.4 *Mr Stamford — 'T' accounts*

Fixed assets (net)				Stock			
Bal. 1 January	17,000	(8)	5,000	Bal. 1 January	8,000	(3)	58,000
		Bal. c/d	12,000	(2)	64,000	Bal. c/d	14,000
	17,000		17,000		72,000		72,000
Bal. 31 December	12,000			Bal. 31 December	14,000		

Debtors				Cash at bank			
Bal. 1 January	6,000	(4)	85,000	Bal. 1 January	2,000	(5)	56,000
(3)	90,000	Bal. c/d	11,000	(1)	4,000	(6)	9,000
	96,000		96,000	(4)	85,000	(9)	1,500
Bal. 31 December	11,000					(10)	8,000
						Bal. c/d	16,500
					91,000		91,000
				Bal. 31 December	16,500		

Ownership interest				Long-term loans			
(10)	8,000	Bal. 1 January	16,000	Bal. c/d	15,000	Bal. 1 January	11,000
Bal. c/d	8,000					(1)	4,000
	16,000		16,000		15,000		15,000
		Bal. 31 December	8,000			Bal. 31 December	15,000

Creditors				Accrued expenses			
(5)	56,000	Bal. 1 January	5,000	(6)	1,000	Bal. 1 January	1,000
Bal. c/d	13,000	(2)	64,000	Bal. c/d	2,000	(7)	2,000
	69,000		69,000		3,000		3,000
		Bal. 31 December	13,000			Bal. 31 December	2,000

Sales				Cost of goods sold			
		(3)	90,000	(3)	58,000		

Expenses				Depreciation expense			
(6)	8,000			(8)	5,000		
(7)	2,000						

Interest							
(9)	1,500						

6. Pays other expenses (excluding depreciation and loan interest) of £9,000, including accrued expenses owing on 1 January 19X0.
7. Accrued expenses at the end of the year amount to £2,000.
8. Charges depreciation of £5,000 on fixed assets.
9. Pays one year's interest on the long-term loans, amounting to £1,500.
10. Withdraws £8,000 from the business bank account for his personal use.

Accounting equation approach

Mr Stamford's accounting equation entries and balances are shown in Table 9.3. The treatment of transactions undertaken during the year has been dealt with fully in previous chapters and we do not need to discuss it further here. The first row of figures in the accounting equation deserves some comment, however. The figures are taken from the balance sheet in Table 9.2 and represent the bottom line of Mr Stamford's accounting equation for the last year. Similarly, the last' line of the accounting equation in Table 9.3 forms the basis of the balance sheet at the end of the current year, and will form the first row of next year's accounting equation.

Conventional accounting approach

Use of 'T' accounts.   The first stage in the conventional approach is to enter each of the transactions in individual accounts. To illustrate the entries we use 'T' accounts, so called because of their design, each one of which represents a page or account in the organization's books of accounts. Each 'T' account is equivalent to an accounting equation column, and the balance on the account at the end of the period is the same as for the equivalent accounting equation column. There is, however, an expansion beyond the accounting equation approach as we have used it so far. Instead of simply having two columns for revenues and expenses, a separate account is kept for *each* item of revenue and expense. The balances on these accounts are transferred to the income statement, usually described in the books as the 'profit and loss account', at the end of the period.

   The 'T' accounts for Mr Stamford are shown in Table 9.4. Note that the positive and negative items which were entered in the same accounting equation column are placed on opposite sides of the 'T' accounts. Transactions are referred to by their numbers and the rules outlined earlier in this chapter are followed to determine on which side of the 'T' account a particular item is entered. We have used abbreviations in our examples ('Bal.' for Balance, 'c/d' for carried down, and so on) whereas in the actual books of account, each account would contain fuller descriptions. For example, the Creditors account might appear as follows on 31 December 19X0 immediately prior to preparing the accounts:

Creditors

		£			£
31 December 19X0	Cash paid	56,000	1 January 19X0	Balance brought down	5,000
			31 December 19X0	Purchases	64,000

Both sides of the account are summed, and the higher figure (£69,000) is entered as the total on *both* sides. Clearly, the excess of the sum of the entries on the right-hand side over that on the left-hand side (£13,000) represents the amount of creditors outstanding at the year-end and must be recorded in the books as such. The technique is to enter this figure twice in accordance with the rules of double-entry. First, it is added to the left-hand side to 'balance' the account at £69,000, and then this balance is 'carried down' to the next year, being entered on the right-hand side as the 'Balance brought down'. The completed Creditors account would appear as follows:

Creditors

		£			£
31 December 19X0	Cash paid	56,000	1 January 19X0	Balance brought down	5,000
31 December 19X0	Balance carried down	13,000	31 December 19X0	Purchases	64,000
		£69,000			£69,000
			1 January 19X1	Balance brought down	13,000

The technique of entering balances 'carried down' and 'brought down' is simply a matter of style, used conventionally to determine and record the balance on each account at the end of a period. Note that the balance on each account in Table 9.4 corresponds to the equivalent figure in the accounting equation in Table 9.3 before net income is transferred to ownership interest.

One further point illustrated by the entries appearing on the creditors' account deserves mention. It is unlikely that the amounts for cash paid and for purchases will represent single transactions. It is more likely that cash will have been paid to a number of different creditors at various times during the year for purchases

Table 9.5 *Mr Stamford — trial balance at 31 December 19X0*

	Dr £	Cr £
Fixed assets (cost £27,000 less accumulated depreciation £15,000)	12,000	
Stock	14,000	
Debtors	11,000	
Cash at bank	16,500	
Ownership interest		8,000
Long-term loans		15,000
Creditors		13,000
Accrued expenses		2,000
Sales		90,000
Cost of goods sold	58,000	
Expenses	10,000	
Depreciation expense	5,000	
Interest	1,500	
	£128,000	£128,000

made at different times. Hence the figures for cash paid and purchases in the creditors' account represent the *total* payments and purchases during the year. If Mr Stamford's transactions had been recorded periodically (e.g. monthly) throughout the year, the creditors' account would include twelve entries each for 'cash paid' and for 'purchases'. The balance on the account will still be £13,000 of course. Similar considerations apply to the other accounts.

Preparation of trial balance.   The next stage in the conventional approach is to check the arithmetical accuracy of the entries. This procedure is equivalent to checking that the two sides of the bottom line of the accounting equation have equal totals. The check is made by preparing a trial balance, which is a listing of the balances on individual accounts, with debit (Dr) balances in the left column and credit (Cr) balances in the right. The sums of the debit and credit balances should be equal. If the totals do not agree, the trial balance will not balance, and the causes of the difference must be traced. Mr Stamford's trial balance is shown in Table 9.5. The balances represented by the first eight items (i.e. down to, and including, accrued expenses) are placed directly in the balance sheet, because they represent assets, liabilities or ownership interest. The remaining five items comprise income statement entries. The balance of these five entries, representing net income for the period, is transferred to ownership interest.

Preparation of the final accounts.   The income statement, or profit and loss account, is another 'T' account, and forms part of the organization's double-entry records. The next stage in the preparation of final accounts using the conventional method is to transfer the balances on the various 'expense' and 'revenue' accounts to

Table 9.6 *Mr Stamford — 'transferring' entries*

Sales		Cost of goods sold	
Profit and 90,000	(3) 90,000	(3) 58,000	Profit and loss account 58,000

Expenses		Depreciation expense	
(6) 10,000	Profit and loss account 10,000	(7) 5,000	Profit and loss account 5,000

Interest			
(8) 1,5000	Profit and loss account 1,500		

Profit and loss account

Cost of goods sold	58,000	Sales	90,000
Expenses	10,000		
Depreciation expense	5,000		
Interest	1,500		
Balance	c/d 15,500		
	90,000		90,000
		Balance	b/d 15,500

the profit and loss account. The last five 'T' accounts are affected, and the 'transferring' entries are shown in Table 9.6.

The closing balance on the profit and loss account of £15,500 represents net income for the year, and is transferred to ownership interest as follows:

Profit and loss account

Ownership interest	15,500	Balance b/d	15,500

Ownership interest

		Balance b/d	8,000
		Profit and	
Balance c/d	23,500	loss account	15,500
	23,500		23,500
		Balance b/d	23,500

Table 9.7 *Mr Stamford — income statement for the year ended 31 December 19X0*

	£	£
Sales		90,000
less: Cost of goods sold		58,000
		32,000
Gross profit		
less: Expenses	10,000	
Depreciation	5,000	
Interest	1,500	
		16,500
Net income for the year		£15,500

Table 9.8 *Mr Stamford — balance sheet at 31 December 19X0*

	£	£	£
Fixed assets at cost		27,000	
less: Accumulated depreciation		15,000	12,000
Current assets			
Stock	14,000		
Debtors	11,000		
Cash	16,500	41,500	
less: Current liabilities			
Creditors	13,000		
Accrued expenses	2,000	15,000	
Net current assets			26,500
Total assets less current liabilities			£38,500
Represented by:			
Ownership interest			
Balance at 1 January		16,000	
add: Net income for the year		15,500	
		31,500	
less: Drawings		8,000	23,500
Long-term loans at 10% p.a.			15,000
Long-term funds			£38,500

The final accounts may now be prepared. The income statement (Table 9.7) is a summary of the figures contained in the profit and loss account in the organization's books. The balance sheet (Table 9.8) is a summary of the balances remaining in the books after the profit and loss account balance has been transferred to ownership interest. Note that details of changes in ownership interest since the last balance sheet are shown, that the original cost of, and accumulated depreciation on, fixed assets are disclosed separately, and that assets and claims are categorized under the main headings of fixed assets, current assets, ownership interest, long-term loans and current liabilities. The income statement and balance sheet prepared from conventional records are identical to those that would have been obtained using the accounting equation information in Table 9.3.

9.3   Double-entry bookkeeping: transactions and adjustments

Bookkeeping and accounting activities

In the previous five chapters we have examined the procedures necessary to prepare the income statement and the balance sheet. To produce meaningful statements of performance (income statement) and position (balance sheet) the accounting process should record all transactions and events which affect the organization's business activities. Further, as we have explained in Chapters 4 and 5, the accounting process must allocate revenues and expenses to the periods in which they are generated and incurred.

The preparation of meaningful financial statements thus comprises two distinct stages: first the recording and classification of a variety of transactions and events, and secondly the allocation of revenues and expenses to specific time periods. The first stage is purely mathematical — the accountant acts as a bookkeeper. The second stage is less mechanical — it involves adjustments to the accounting records and requires the accountant to exercise judgement. We shall examine each stage in turn.

Stage one: bookkeeping activities

(i) Source documents, journals and ledgers.   Most business transactions are supported by some documentary evidence. Raw material purchases are normally accompanied by suppliers' invoices; the local electricity company sends regular bills for the cost of heating and lighting; when a company sells goods it usually sends a sales invoice to the customer and retains a copy for its own records; cheque payments are evidenced by cheque stubs or cheque copies, and receipts by completed paying-in slips. Such documents are called *source documents* and represent the raw material from which financial statements are produced.

At regular intervals (daily, weekly or monthly depending upon the volume of transactions and the managers' efficiency) the financial data contained in the source documents are entered into the accounting records.[2] In the illustration

2. In most larger organizations these accounting records are maintained on a computer. However, as we stated earlier, the principles discussed in this chapter are effectively the same whether records are kept manually or on a computer.

which follows (The Camera Shop Ltd) the data are entered directly into the company's ledger accounts. We have previously referred to these ledger accounts as 'T' accounts. In large organizations the volume of transactions is too great to allow for individual recording in the ledger accounts. Instead the individual transactions are recorded in *journals*, or *day books*, and only the monthly or quarterly totals are entered into the ledger accounts.

The number of separate journals kept by the organization will depend upon the nature of its business, but large organizations normally maintain a sales journal, a purchases journal, a cash receipts journal and a cash payments journal. It is worth emphasising that these journals do *not* form part of the double-entry bookkeeping system — they simply store the data to be transferred or 'posted' later, in aggregate, to the ledger accounts. For example, individual credit sales might be recorded in a sales journal. At the end of the month the credit sales would be totalled and this total would be debited to the Debtors Account and credited to the Sales Revenue Account.

However, the management of a business requires much more information about debtors and creditors than the aggregate total of credit sales and purchases made during an accounting period. Specifically, management should know the exact amount owed to the business by each *individual* customer; know when a *specific* customer has reached his or her limit of credit; and for *control* purposes, have a general history of the purchase and payment patterns of each customer. In addition, managers need to know the exact amounts owing to individual suppliers, so that purchases can be controlled and payments made on time. Details extracted from purchase invoices, copies of sales invoices, cheque stubs and paying-in slips can be used to maintain an updated 'balance outstanding' for each customer and supplier. These records, called *subsidiary ledgers*, are also outside the double-entry bookkeeping system.

In the example which follows, the number of transactions is insufficient to warrant the use of either journals or subsidiary ledgers. Instead, information is recorded directly in the organization's *general ledger* which contains a 'T' account for each classification of asset, equity, liability, revenue and expense. Whether or not journals are maintained, the financial data become part of the double-entry bookkeeping system only when they are entered into the accounts of the general ledger.

(ii) Trial balance.   Each business transaction gives rise to a debit entry and an equivalent credit entry. Hence, the sum of all debit balances must equal the sum of all credit balances at any given time. This can be checked by extracting the balances and listing them in a trial balance. We discussed the nature and usefulness of the trial balance in Section 9.1. However, the fact that the sum of the debit balances equals the sum of the credit balances is not proof that the bookkeeping procedures have been free from error. For example, although the matching of equal debit and credit entries will result in a trial balance which balances, the composition of the trial balance will be incorrect if an item has been

posted incorrectly to the debit of, say, the cash account instead of, say, the depreciation expense account.

Stage two: *from trial balance to financial statements*

(i) Accounting adjustments.   Even in the absence of bookkeeping errors the financial statements cannot normally be prepared directly from the trial balance. We have seen in previous chapters that the accountant must make a series of adjustments in order to match revenues and expenses of particular periods. Matching normally involves the recognition of prepayments, accruals, depreciation and closing stock. These adjustments must be recorded in the relevant general ledger accounts.

The final adjustment prior to the preparation of the financial statements is to transfer the balances on the various 'expense' and 'revenue' accounts to the profit and loss account. The profit and loss account is a 'T' account in the general ledger like the other 'T' accounts referred to above. This transfer of balances means that, apart from the balance on the profit and loss account, no balance remains on any expense or revenue account — there are no balances on these accounts to be carried forward to the next accounting period.

(ii) Income statement and balance sheet.   The final accounts may now be prepared. The income statement is a summary of the figures contained in the profit and loss account in the general ledger. The balance sheet is a summary of the balances remaining (i.e. a sheet of balances) in the ledger after the profit and loss account balance has been transferred to ownership interest.

In the following section we illustrate these procedures by means of a comprehensive review example.

9.4   The Camera Shop Ltd: a detailed illustration

The Camera Shop Ltd sells camera equipment, films and processing chemicals to professional photographers. Its balance sheet at 31 July 19X4 is presented in Table 9.9.

All sales and purchases are on credit. The company's fixed assets consist of shop fittings and office equipment, all of which are depreciated on a straight line basis at an annual rate of 10% on cost. The bank loan was taken out three years ago. Interest is charged at a rate of 15% p.a. payable on 31 March and 30 September; no capital repayments are due until 19X7. The shop is rented at an annual cost of £7,200 and the rent is paid quarterly in advance on 1 March, June, September and December. A stock count and valuation is undertaken at the end of each month so that monthly accounting statements can be prepared. At the

Table 9.9 *The Camera Shop Ltd — balance sheet at 31 July 19X4*

	£	£	£
Assets employed			
Fixed assets			
Shop and office equipment at cost			26,400
less: Accumulated depreciation			12,600
			13,800
Current assets			
Stock		43,670	
Debtors	34,000		
less: Provision for bad debts	1,700	32,300	
Prepaid rent		600	
Cash at bank		1,550	
		78,120	
Current liabilities			
Trade creditors		24,070	
Interest accrued		1,200	
Miscellaneous accruals		740	
		26,010	
Net current assets			52,110
Total assets less current liabilities			65,910
Creditors due after more than one year			
Bank loan			24,000
			£41,910
Capital and reserves			
Share capital			25,000
Retained profit			16,910
			£41,910

end of each month the provision for bad debts is adjusted to an amount equal to 5% of the debtor's balance.

The following is a record of the transactions and events which took place in August 19X4:

Transaction or event	Date	
1	2/8	Received a cheque for £7,000 from Edgbaston Studios in respect of goods sold in July.
2	3/8	Took delivery of film and chemicals costing £1,800

		from Headingley Film and Equipment Company; details are recorded on their invoice no. H42.
3	3/8	Paid £2,500 to Trafford Camera Equipment Ltd on cheque no. 6210.
4	5/8	Sold cameras and darkroom equipment to Trent Photographers for £6,600 on invoice no. 801.
5	9/8	Wrote cheque no. 6211 for £280 to pay an electricity bill accrued at the end of July.
6	11/8	Bought a new word-processor for £850 on cheque no. 6212.
7	12/8	Received supplies of cameras costing £3,600 from Oval Photographic Equipment Ltd; details are recorded on their invoice no. 081.
8	16/8	Sold darkroom equipment, cameras and film to Ms Lord for £5,850 on invoice no. 802.
9	17/8	Cashed cheque no. 6213 to pay wages of £1,230.
10	18/8	Paid £4,000 to Oval Photographic Equipment Ltd on cheque no. 6214.
11	19/8	Paid transport costs of £460, accrued in July, on cheque no. 6215.
12	24/8	Paid dividend of £800 on cheque no. 6216.
13	25/8	Received a cheque for £4,750 from Ms Lord.
14	31/8	Estimated that the cost of electricity used during August was £390.
15	31/8	Owed wages of £1,120 at the end of the month.
16	31/8	A stock count established that the cost of the stock on hand was £44,100.

Our task is to prepare an income statement for the month of August and a balance sheet at 31 August 19X4. We shall adopt the following framework:

Section (a)	Check that the opening balances on the accounts in the general ledger are consistent with those on the balance sheet at 31 July.
Section (b)	Using the double-entry system of bookkeeping, record all transactions for August in the relevant accounts in the general ledger.
Section (c)	Extract a trial balance from the accounts in the general ledger.
Section (d)	Make any necessary adjustments to the figures in order to match correctly the period's revenues and expenses.
Section (e)	Close off the accounts in the general ledger ready for next month's transactions and prepare an income statement and balance sheet.

(a) The opening balances

At the end of July the Camera Shop prepared an income statement for the period 1 July to 31 July (not shown here) and a balance sheet at 31 July (Table 9.9). The figures included in those two financial statements are represented by the balances extracted from the general ledger accounts. The balances on the various revenue and expense accounts have been transferred to the profit and loss account; thus the only balances remaining in the general ledger should be those appearing in the balance sheet at 31 July. We must check that this is so.

The accounts appear in the general ledger sequenced by account number (Table 9.10). The numerical ordering, for ease of understanding, is as follows:

(a) all assets in the order they appear in the balance sheet;
(b) all liabilities in the order they appear in the balance sheet;
(c) all ownership interest accounts;
(d) all revenues;
(e) all expenses and appropriations in the order they appear in the income statement.

Table 9.10 *The Camera Shop Ltd — chart of general ledger accounts*

Account name	Account number
Shop and office equipment — cost	100
— accumulated depreciation	101
Stock	110
Debtors	115
Provision for bad debts	116
Prepaid rent	120
Cash at bank	130
Trade creditors	200
Interest accrued	220
Miscellaneous accruals	230
Bank loan	240
Share capital	300
Retained profit	310
Sales revenue	400
Purchases	420
Cost of goods sold	425
Rent expense	430
Wages expense	431
Heat and light expense	432
Bad debts expense	440
Depreciation expense	450
Interest expense	460
Dividends	500
Profit and loss	600

The accounts are not numbered consecutively because other accounts may be added later and these will require new numbers. This system of ordering is only one of many available (for example, an alternative system is to order the accounts alphabetically).

The ledger accounts presented on pages 276–283 are as they would appear at 31 August and not 31 July (i.e. they comprise part of the solution to this review problem). To see how they would have appeared at 31 July we must ignore all items which have an August date. For example, the accounts numbered 100, 101, 120 and 431 would have appeared at 31 July as follows:

Shop and office equipment: cost	No. 100		*Shop and office equipment:* accumulated depreciation	No. 101
31 July Balance 26,400			31 July Balance 12,600	

Prepaid rent	No. 120		*Wages expense*	No. 431
31 July Balance 600				

(Check all the accounts to satisfy yourself that each balance sheet figure, and no other, has been 'brought forward' correctly in the general ledger.)

(b) Recording the transactions in the general ledger

The Camera Shop does not maintain journals. Instead all transactions are entered directly into the general ledger. In this section we shall explain the bookkeeping entries which are necessary to record the August transactions in the general ledger.

Transaction 1

> 2 August. Received a cheque for £7,000 from Edgbaston Studios in respect of goods sold in July.

The receipt of a cheque for £7,000 increases the cash balance of the Camera Shop and we record this by debiting the Cash at Bank account (Account number 130, hereinafter referred to as AC130). This cash receipt is the result of a sales transaction which occurred at an earlier date. We are informed that the Camera Shop sold goods to Edgbaston Studios for £7,000 in July. No cash changed hands at the time of the transaction and this *credit sale* was recorded in the general ledger by crediting Sales Revenue (AC400) and debiting Debtors (AC115) with £7,000 each. As Edgbaston Studios had not settled their account by 31 July, the £7,000 posted to the Debtors account was included in the balance of £34,000 on that account at 31 July. On 2 August Edgbaston Studios settled its account and its debt is extinguished by making a credit entry of £7,000 in the Debtors account.

Accounting entry:			£	£
2 August	Cash (130)	Debit	7,000	
	Debtors (115)	Credit		7,000

Transaction 2

> 3 August. Took delivery of film and chemicals costing £1,800 from Headingley Film and Equipment Company; details are recorded on their invoice no. H42.

The Camera Shop has received a consignment of film and chemicals from a supplier. The shop has not paid cash on delivery (COD) but has purchased the goods on credit and will pay the supplier at a later date. Although no cash has been paid, the legal title to the goods has passed to the Camera Shop and the transaction must be recorded in the account. As the goods are items of stock which are to be resold at a future date, £1,800 is debited to the Purchases account (AC420). The supplier is now a creditor of the business, and this is recognized by crediting the Trade creditors account (AC200) with £1,800.

Accounting entry:			£	£
3 August	Purchases (420)	Debit	1,800	
	Trade creditors (200)	Credit		1,800

Transaction 3

> 3 August. Paid £2,500 to Trafford Camera Equipment Ltd on cheque no. 6210.

At an earlier date the Camera Shop purchased goods on credit from Trafford Camera Equipment Ltd. At the time of that transaction the purchase value was debited to the Purchases account and credited to the Trade creditors account (as in Transaction 2 above). The Camera Shop is now eliminating its liability to a trade creditor by settling its account. Hence both the balance of Trade creditors (AC200) outstanding and the balance of Cash at bank (AC130) are reduced by £2,500.

Accounting entry:			£	£
3 August	Trade creditors (200)	Debit	2,500	
	Cash at bank (130)	Credit		2,500

Transaction 4

> 5 August. Sold cameras and darkroom equipment to Trent Photographers for £6,600 on invoice no. 801.

No cash was received at the date of sale. However, the goods became the property of Trent Photographers at that date and the sale must be recorded in the accounts of the Camera Shop. Sales revenue (AC400) is credited with £6,600 and as Trent Photographers owes money to the shop we recognize this by debiting the Debtors' account (AC115) with £6,600.

Accounting entry:			£	£
5 August	Debtors (115)	Debit	6,600	
	Sales revenue (400)	Credit		6,600

Transaction 5

> 9 August. Wrote cheque no. 6211 for £280 to pay an electricity bill accrued at the end of July.

An electricity bill for £280 was received on 5 August. The bill referred to the cost of electricity used by the Camera Shop up to 31 July. At 31 July the Camera Shop recognized that it had used, but not paid for, electricity during the month. It estimated (accurately) that the cost was £280 and this amount was debited to Heat and light expense (AC432) and credited to Miscellaneous accruals (AC230). The transaction on 9 August refers to the settlement of the account. Cash (AC130) is credited with £280 and the liability is extinguished by debiting Miscellaneous accruals (AC230) with £280.

Accounting entry:			£	£
9 August	Misc. accruals (230)	Debit	280	
	Cash (130)	Credit		280

Transaction 6

> 11 August. Bought a new word-processor for £850 on cheque no. 6212.

This is a cash transaction — cash was paid at the time of purchase. The word-processor has not been purchased with the intention of resale. It is not, therefore, part of the Camera Shop's stock-in-trade and the cost is *not* entered in the Purchases account. Rather the word processor is a fixed asset which will last, and provide benefits, for several years. It is categorized as Shop and office equipment, and will be depreciated over its useful life.

Accounting entry:			£	£
11 August	Shop and office equipment:			
	cost (100)	Debit	850	
	Cash (130)	Credit		850

Transaction 7

> 12 August. Received supplies of cameras costing £3,600 from Oval Photographic Equipment Ltd; details are recorded on their invoice no. 081.

The transaction is similar to that described as Transaction 2 above. It is a purchase of stock on credit.

Accounting entry: £   £

12 August   Purchases (420)   Debit   3,600
             Trade creditors (200)   Credit   3,600

Transaction 8

16 August. Sold darkroom equipment, cameras and film to Ms Lord for £5,850 on invoice no. 802.

The transaction is similar to that described as Transaction 4 above. It is a sale of goods on credit.

Accounting entry: £   £

16 August   Debtors (115)   Debit   5,850
             Sales revenue (400)   Credit   5,850

Transaction 9

17 August. Cashed cheque no. 6213 to pay wages of £1,230.

The Camera Shop pays staff wages twice a month. Strictly, the wages have been accruing daily over the first 17 days, but as both the expense and the cash settlement occur within the same accounting period the transaction can be recorded as a straightforward cash transaction.

Accounting entry: £   £

17 August   Wages expense (431)   Debit   1,230
             Cash (130)   Credit   1,230

Transaction 10

18 August. Paid £4,000 to Oval Photographic Equipment Ltd on cheque no. 6214.

The transaction is similar to that described as Transaction 3 above. It is the cash settlement of a supplier's account. As the amount paid (£4,000) is greater than the amount purchased from Oval Ltd in August (£3,600, Transaction 7) it is likely that this payment is in respect of goods purchased in July.

Accounting entry: £   £

18 August   Trade creditors (200)   Debit   4,000
             Cash at bank (130)   Credit   4,000

Transaction 11

19 August. Paid transport costs of £460, accrued in July, on cheque no. 6215.

The transaction is similar to that described as Transaction 5 above. It is the cash settlement of a bill which refers to an expense incurred in a previous period.

Accounting entry:		£	£
19 August Misc. accruals (230)	Debit	460	
Cash (130)	Credit		460

Transaction 12

24 August. Paid dividend of £800 on cheque no. 6216.

This transaction involves a cash payment and consequently £800 is credited to the Cash at bank account (AC130). The debit is posted to the Dividends account (AC500) which will be shown as a deduction in the income statement. However, there is an important distinction between the payment of dividends and, say, the payment of wages (see Transaction 9 above). Wages are an *expense* of running the business. They are deducted as part of the calculation of net profit for the period. Dividends are a *distribution* or appropriation of the profit for the period and appear in the income statement *after* net profit has been calculated.

Accounting entry:		£	£
24 August Dividends (500)	Debit	800	
Cash (130)	Credit		800

Transaction 13

25 August. Received a cheque for £4,750 from Ms Lord.

This transaction is similar to that described as Transaction 1.

Accounting entry:		£	£
25 August Cash (130)	Debit	4,750	
Debtors (115)	Credit		4,750

Events 14, 15 and 16

31 August. Estimated that the cost of electricity used during August was £390.

Owed wages of £1,120 at the end of the month.

A stock count established that the cost of the stock on hand was £44,100.

These three items of information do not refer to transactions. They are, however, important in the calculation of accrued expenses at the end of the month and of cost of goods sold for the month and as such will be taken into account in Section (d).

(c) The trial balance

The trial balance is a list of all the accounts used by the business and the balance on each account at a specific date. The fact that the sum of all debit balances equals the sum of all credit balances does not ensure the bookkeeping process has been error-free (see Section 9.3 above). However, a lack of balance does indicate the existence of one or more errors. These errors should be identified before proceeding further.

The trial balance of the accounts of the Camera Shop at 31 August is presented in the first two columns of Table 9.11. *The figures in the trial balance represent the balances in the accounts in the general ledger after recording Transactions 1–13 but before making any end of period adjustments.* The sum of all the debit balances amounts to £116,830 and is equal to the sum of all the credit balances.

(d) Accounting adjustments and worksheets

Table 9.11 is an illustration of an end-of-period accounting worksheet. The major advantage of a worksheet is its comprehensiveness. All 'post trial balance' adjustments can be entered on, and 'draft' financial statements prepared from, the worksheet. Given the chaos that often exists in the accounting departments of business organizations after the financial year end and prior to the completion of the financial statements, accounting adjustments are not usually entered in the general ledger until the financial statements have been agreed. We shall adopt this approach also by completing the accounting process on the worksheet before entering the adjustments in the general ledger. The sequence of steps is as follows:

(a) record the accounting adjustments in the 'Adjustments' columns on the worksheet;
(b) refer to the original trial balance and to the adjustments to produce an 'Adjusted trial balance'; and
(c) produce a draft income statement and balance sheet in the final four columns of the worksheet.

If we are satisfied with the correctness of the draft financial statements, we can record the accounting adjustments in the general ledger and close off each account in readiness for the next accounting period.

The adjustments to be made at 31 August can be ascertained from the information provided earlier in this section. The numbers assigned to the adjustments below can be used to identify the entries made on the worksheet.

> *Adjustment 1.* The Camera Shop depreciates its fixed assets on a straight line basis at an annual rate of 10% on cost. At 31 August the cost of shop and office equipment was £27,250 and thus one month's depreciation amounts to £27,250 × (0.1) ÷ 12 = £227.

Accounting entry:		£	£
31 August	Deprec'n expense (450)	Debit 227	
	Shop and office equipment– accum. deprec'n (101)	Credit	227

Table 9.11 The Camera Shop Ltd — worksheet for the month ended 31 August 19X4

Account No.	Account title	Trial Balance Debit	Trial Balance Credit	Adjustments Debit	Adjustments Credit	Adjusted trial balance Debit	Adjusted trial balance Credit	Income statement Debit	Income statement Credit	Balance sheet Debit	Balance sheet Credit
100	Shop and office equipment – cost	27,250				27,250				27,250	
101	Shop and office equipment – accumulated depreciation		12,600		(1) 227		12,827				12,827
110	Stock	43,670		(7c) 44,100	(7a) 43,670	44,100				44,100	
115	Debtors	34,700				34,700				34,700	
116	Provision for bad debts		1,700		(4) 35		1,735				1,735
120	Prepaid rent	600			(3) 600						
130	Cash at bank	3,180				3,180				3,180	
200	Trade creditors		22,970				22,970				22,970
220	Interest accrued		1,200		(2) 300		1,500				1,500
230	Miscellaneous accruals				(5) 390 (6) 1,120		1,510				1,510

Code	Account										
240	Bank loan		24,000				24,000				24,000
300	Share capital		25,000				25,000				25,000
310	Retained profit		16,910				16,910				16,910
400	Sales revenue		12,450				12,450		12,450		
420	Purchases	5,400			(7b) 5,400						
425	Cost of goods sold			(7a) 43,670 (7b) 5,400	(7c) 44,100	4,970		4,970			
430	Rent expense			(3) 600		600		600			
431	Wages expense	1,230		(6) 1,120		2,350		2,350			
432	Heat and light expense			(5) 390		390		390			
440	Bad debts expense			(4) 35		35		35			
450	Depreciation expense			(1) 227		227		227			
460	Interest expense			(2) 300		300		300			
500	Dividends	800				800		800			
	Subtotals	116,830	116,830	95,842	95,842	118,902	118,902	9,672	12,450		
	Transfer retained profit to ownership interest							2,778			2,778
	Totals	116,830	116,830	95,842	95,842	118,902	118,902	12,450	12,450	109,230	109,230

Adjustment 2.   Interest on the bank loan is charged at a rate of 15% p.a., payable on 31 March and 30 September. No interest need be *paid* in August but we should *accrue* for one month's interest, i.e. £24,000 × 0.15 ÷ 12 = £300.

Accounting entry:			£	£
31 August	Interest expense (460)	Debit	300	
	Interest accrued (220)	Credit		300

Adjustment 3.   The shop is rented at an annual cost of £7,200 and the rent is paid quarterly in advance on 1 March, June, September and December. The rent for the month of August was thus prepaid on 1 June.

We must now recognize as an expense that part of the rental payment which relates to August (£7,200 ÷ 12 = £600).

Accounting entry:			£	£
31 August	Rent expense (430)	Debit	600	
	Prepaid rent (120)	Credit		600

Adjustment 4.   At the end of each month the provision for bad debts is adjusted to an amount equal to 5% of the debtors' balance. At 31 August the balance on the Debtors' account is £34,700, which requires a provision for bad debts of £34,700 × 0.05 = £1,735. As the provision at the beginning of the month was £1,700, a further £35 must be provided against possible bad debts.

Accounting entry:			£	£
31 August	Bad debts expense (440)	Debit	35	
	Prov'n for bad debts (116)	Credit		35

Adjustment 5.   On 31 August the Camera Shop estimated that the cost of electricity used in August was £390. We must record this expense in August and recognize that the Camera Shop owes £390 for electricity at the end of the month.

Accounting entry:			£	£
31 August	Heat and light expense (432)	Debit	390	
	Misc. accruals (230)	Credit		390

Adjustment 6.   The Camera Shop owed wages of £1,120 at the end of the month. The accruals principle applies here in the same way as in Adjustment 5.

Accounting entry:			£	£
31 August	Wages expense (431)	Debit	1,120	
	Misc. accruals (230)	Credit		1,120

Adjustment 7.   A stock count established that the cost of the stock on hand at the end of the month was £44,100.

The Camera Shop has adopted a periodic stock costing system. Under this system an *individual* cost of goods sold figure is not calculated for each transaction. Instead a *total* cost of goods sold figure is calculated at the end of the period. This figure forms the basis of the adjusting entries relating to stock. We explained in Chapter 7 that the cost of goods sold figure is calculated as follows:

$$
\begin{array}{ll}
 & \text{opening stock} \\
+ & \text{purchases for the period} \\
= & \text{cost of goods available for sale in the period} \\
- & \text{closing stock} \\
= & \text{cost of goods sold for the period}
\end{array}
$$

These calculations affect both the Cost of goods sold account (AC425) in the general ledger and the worksheet as follows:

Adjustment 7a. The opening stock figure is transferred from the Stock account (AC110) to the Cost of goods sold account (AC425).

Accounting entry:		£	£
31 August Cost of goods sold (425)	Debit	43,670	
Stock (110)	Credit		43,670

Adjustment 7b. The purchases figure is transferred from the Purchases account (AC420) to the Cost of goods sold account (AC425).

Accounting entry:		£	£
31 August Cost of goods sold (425)	Debit	5,400	
Purchases (420)	Credit		5,400

Adjustment 7c. At this stage there is no closing stock figure in the accounting records. However, the stock at 31 August has been counted and its cost determined at £44,100. This amount must be deducted from the figure for the cost of goods available for sale, i.e. the Cost of goods sold account (AC425) is credited with £44,100. In addition, as the stock on hand at 31 August appears in the balance sheet at that date, £44,100 should be debited to the Stock account (AC110). (Note that the opening stock figure of £43,670 has already been transferred out of the account as part of Adjustment 7a.)

Accounting entry:		£	£
31 August Stock (110)	Debit	44,100	
Cost of goods sold (425)	Credit		44,100

The net effect of these three adjustments is to produce a cost of goods sold figure of £4,970 and a closing stock figure of £44,100.

We can now check the arithmetical accuracy of our bookkeeping. The total of these debit adjustments should equal the total of the credit adjustments. As both columns sum to £95,842, we can now produce an 'Adjusted trial balance' on the worksheet by adding (or subtracting) the various adjustments to (or from) the balances on the original trial balance. Again the sum total of the adjusted debit balances (of £118,902) is equal to the sum total of the adjusted credit balances.

Each of the above adjustments should also be entered in the general ledger. The entries can be identified by reference to the 'Accounting entries' described above and to the 'Adjustments' column on the worksheet.

(e) Closing off the accounts and preparing the financial statements

The balances shown in the 'Adjusted trial balance' on the worksheet are now entered in the columns headed 'Income statement' and 'Balance sheet'. The balances from accounts numbered 100 to 310 are balance sheet items because they represent either assets, liabilities or ownership interest. Those balances from accounts numbered 400 to 500 consist of income statement items. The balance of revenues over expenses and appropriations, representing 'retained profit for the period', is transferred from the income statement to ownership interest in the balance sheet.

Once again these worksheet entries are reflected by corresponding entries in the general ledger accounts. The balances on the various revenue, expense and appropriation accounts (AC400–500) are transferred to the Profit and Loss account (AC600). The balance on the Profit and Loss account is then transferred to the Retained Profit account (AC310). Having 'closed off' all revenue, expense and

Table 9.12 *The Camera Shop Ltd — income statement for the month ended 31 August 19X4*

	£	£
Sales revenue		12,450
Cost of goods sold		4,970
		7,480
Gross profit		
Rent	600	
Wages	2,350	
Heat and light	390	
Bad debts	35	
Depreciation	227	
Interest	300	
		3,902
Net profit		3,578
Dividends		800
Profit for the year, retained		£2,778

Table 9.13 *The Camera Shop Ltd — balance sheet at 31 August 19X4*

	£	£	£
Assets employed			
Fixed assets			
Shop and office equipment at cost			27,250
less: Accumulated depreciation			12,827
			14,423
Current assets			
Stock		44,100	
Debtors	34,700		
less: Provision for bad debts	1,735	32,965	
Cash at bank		3,180	
		80,245	
Current liabilities			
Trade creditors		22,970	
Interest accrued		1,500	
Miscellaneous accruals		1,510	
		25,980	
Net current assets			54,265
Total assets less current liabilities			68,688
Creditors due after more than one year			
Bank loan			24,000
			£44,688
Capital and reserves			
Share capital			25,000
Retained profit			19,688
			£44,688

appropriation accounts in this way, only the 'balance sheet' accounts (AC100–310) show outstanding balances. These balances are carried forward to form the opening balances for the September transactions.

The financial statements can be prepared from the worksheet or the general ledger. If the figures are taken from the ledger, the *balances carried forward* are used to prepare the balance sheet at 31 August, the entries in the *Profit and Loss account* (AC600) are used to prepare the income statement and the entries in the *Cash at bank account* (AC130) are used to prepare the cash flow statement. The completed financial statements are presented in Tables 9.12, 9.13 and 9.14.

Table 9.14   *The Camera Shop Ltd — cash flow statement for the month ended 31 August 19X4*

	£	£
Operating Activities		
Cash received from customers	11,750	
Cash payments to suppliers	(7,240)	
Cash paid to employees	(1,230)	
Net cash inflow from operating activities		3,280
Dividends paid		(800)
Purchase of fixed assets		(850)
Increase in cash		1,630
Cash balance at 31 July		1,550
Increase in cash		1,630
Cash balance at 31 August		3,180

Appendix 9A   The Camera Shop Ltd

Shop and office equipment - cost   No.100

DATE		REF	DEBIT	DATE		REF	CREDIT
31 July	Balance		26,400				
11 Aug	Cash	130	850				
				31 Aug	Balance		27,250
			27,250				27,250
31 Aug	Balance		27,250				

Shop and office equipment - accumulated depreciation   No.101

DATE		REF	DEBIT	DATE		REF	CREDIT
				31 July	Balance		12,600
				31 Aug	Depreciation expense	450	227
31 Aug	Balance		12,827				
			12,827				12,827
				31 Aug	Balance		12,827

Stock   No.110

DATE		REF	DEBIT	DATE		REF	CREDIT
31 July	Balance		43,670	31 Aug	Cost of goods sold	425	43,670
31 Aug	Cost of goods sold	425	44,100				
				31 Aug	Balance		44,100
			87,770				87,770
31 Aug	Balance		44,100				

Debtors   No.115

DATE		REF	DEBIT	DATE		REF	CREDIT
31 July	Balance		34,000	2 Aug	Cash	130	7,000
3 Aug	Sales revenue	400	6,600	25 Aug	Cash	130	4,750
16 Aug	Sales revenue	400	5,850				
				31 Aug	Balance		34,700
			46,450				46,450
31 Aug	Balance		34,700				

Provision for bad debts   No.116

DATE		REF	DEBIT	DATE		REF	CREDIT
				31 July	Balance		1,700
				31 Aug	Bad debts expense	440	35
31 Aug	Balance		1,735				
			<u>1,735</u>				<u>1,735</u>
				31 Aug	Balance		1,735

Prepaid rent   No. 120

DATE		REF	DEBIT	DATE		REF	CREDIT
31 July	Balance		600	31 Aug	Rent expense	430	600
			<u>600</u>				<u>600</u>

Cash at bank   No. 130

DATE		REF	DEBIT	DATE		REF	CREDIT
31 July	Balance		1,550	3 Aug	Trade creditors	200	2,500
2 Aug	Debtors	115	7,000	9 Aug	Misc. accruals	230	280
25 Aug	Debtors	115	4,750	11 Aug	Equipment-cost	100	850
				17 Aug	Wages expense	431	1,230
				18 Aug	Trade creditors	200	4,000
				19 Aug	Misc. accruals	230	460
				24 Aug	Dividends	500	800
				31 Aug	Balance		3,180
			<u>13,300</u>				<u>13,300</u>
31 Aug	Balance		3,180				

Trade creditors No. 200

DATE		REF	DEBIT	DATE		REF	CREDIT
3 Aug	Cash	130	2,500	31 July	Balance		24,070
18 Aug	Cash	130	4,000	3 Aug	Purchases	420	1,800
				12 Aug	Purchases	420	3,600
31 Aug	Balance		22,970				
			29,470				29,470
				31 Aug	Balance		22,970

Interest accrued No.220

DATE		REF	DEBIT	DATE		REF	CREDIT
				31 July	Balance		1,200
				31 Aug	Interest exp.	460	300
31 Aug	Balance		1,500				
			1,500				1,500
				31 Aug	Balance		1,500

Miscellaneous accruals No. 230

DATE		REF	DEBIT	DATE		REF	CREDIT
9 Aug	Cash	130	280	31 July	Balance		740
19 Aug	Cash	130	460	31 Aug	Heat & Light expense	432	390
				31 Aug	Wages expense	431	1,120
31 Aug	Balance		1,510				
			2,250				2,250
				31 Aug	Balance		1,510

Bank loan   No. 240

DATE		REF	DEBIT	DATE		REF	CREDIT
				31 July	Balance		24,000
31 Aug	Balance		24,000				
			24,000				24,000
				31 Aug	Balance		24,000

Share capital   No. 300

DATE		REF	DEBIT	DATE		REF	CREDIT
				31 July	Balance		25,000
31 Aug	Balance		25,000				
			25,000				25,000
				31 Aug	Balance		25,000

Retained profit   No. 310

DATE		REF	DEBIT	DATE		REF	CREDIT
				31 July	Balance		16,910
				31 Aug	Profit & loss	600	2,778
31 Aug	Balance		19,688				
			19,688				19,688
				31 Aug	Balance		19,688

Sales revenue   No. 400

DATE		REF	DEBIT	DATE		REF	CREDIT
				3 Aug	Debtors	115	6,600
				16 Aug	Debtors	115	5,850
31 Aug	Profit & loss	600	12,450				
			12,450				12,450

Purchases   No. 420

DATE		REF	DEBIT	DATE		REF	CREDIT
3 Aug	Trade creditors	200	1,800	31 Aug	Cost of goods sold	425	5,400
12 Aug	Trade creditors	200	3,600				
			<u>5,400</u>				<u>5,400</u>

Cost of goods sold   No. 425

DATE		REF	DEBIT	DATE		REF	CREDIT
31 Aug	Stock	110	43,670	31 Aug	Stock	110	44,100
31 Aug	Purchases	420	5,400				
				31 Aug	Profit & loss	600	4,970
			<u>49,070</u>				<u>49,070</u>

Rent expense   No. 430

DATE		REF	DEBIT	DATE		REF	CREDIT
31 Aug	Prepaid rent	120	600				
				31 Aug	Profit & loss	600	600
			<u>600</u>				<u>600</u>

Wages expense   No. 431

DATE		REF	DEBIT	DATE		REF	CREDIT
17 Aug	Cash	130	1,230				
31 Aug	Misc. accruals	230	1,120				
				31 Aug	Profit & loss	600	2,350
			<u>2,350</u>				<u>2,350</u>

Heat and light expenses   No. 432

DATE		REF	DEBIT	DATE		REF	CREDIT
31 Aug	Misc. accruals	230	390				
				31 Aug	Profit & loss	600	390
			<u>390</u>				<u>390</u>

Bad debts expenses   No. 440

DATE		REF	DEBIT	DATE		REF	CREDIT
31 Aug	Provision for bad debits	116	35				
				31 Aug	Profit & loss	600	35
			35				35

Depreciation expense   No. 450

DATE		REF	DEBIT	DATE		REF	CREDIT
31 Aug	Shop & office equipment– accumulated depreciation	101	227				
				31 Aug	Profit & loss	600	227
			227				227

Interest expense   No. 460

DATE		REF	DEBIT	DATE		REF	CREDIT
31 Aug	Interest accrued	220	300				
				31 Aug	Profit & loss	600	300
			300				300

Dividends   No. 500

DATE		REF	DEBIT	DATE		REF	CREDIT
24 Aug	Cash	130	800				
				31 Aug	Profit & loss	600	800
			800				800

Profit and loss   **No. 600**

DATE		REF	DEBIT	DATE		REF	CREDIT
31 Aug	Cost of goods sold	425	4,970	31 Aug	Sales revenue	400	12,450
	Rent expense	430	600				
	Wages expense	431	2,350				
	Heat & light expense	432	390				
	Bad debts expense	440	35				
	Depreciation expense	450	227				
	Interest expense	460	300				
	Dividends	500	800				
31 Aug	Balance to retained profit	310	2,778				
			__12,450__				__12,450__

Discussion topics

1. Describe the main features of, and differences between, the accounting equation and the 'T' account approaches to recording transactions. Why is the latter more popular in practice?

2. Explain the purpose and usefulness of the trial balance.

3. Explain via equations the relationships which exist between cash payments and expense charges appearing in the income statement.

4. What items would you expect to see appearing on the debit side of the trial balance? On the credit side? What determines the nature of these balances?

5. Explain (in terms of 'debit' and 'credit' entries) how the following items would be recorded using conventional double-entry bookkeeping:
    (a) Purchase of stock on credit.
    (b) Purchase of productive machinery for cash.
    (c) Receipts from customers in respect of credit sales.

(d) Repayment of a loan.
(e) Payment in respect of research and development expenditure.
(f) Sale of goods on credit.
(g) Payments to suppliers in respect of credit purchases.
(h) Payment of wages to clerical assistants.
(i) Payment of wages to labour involved in production.
(j) Amounts received in respect of ordinary shares issued at a premium.
(k) Payment of loan interest.
(l) Provision of an annual depreciation charge on shop fittings and fixtures.
(m) Payment of an electricity bill.
(n) Withdrawal of cash from a business by the owner.
(o) Payment of cash into a business by the owner.

Exercises

9.1 The following information relates to various transactions of Yamadori Ltd for the year ended 31 December 19X8.

1. *Lighting and heating*
Amount owing for electricity at 1 January, £750; payments for electricity during the year, £3,700; payments for gas during the year, £4,900; amount owing for electricity at 31 December, £920; amount owing for gas at 31 December, £630.

2. *Rent and rates*
Rent owing at 1 January, £1,000; rates paid in advance at 1 January, £1,700; payments for rent during the year, £11,000; payments for rates during the year, £7,200; rent owing at 31 December, £2,000; rates paid in advance at 31 December, £1,800.

3. *Trade creditors*
Amount owing to creditors at 1 January, £28,600; purchases during the year, £186,200; cash paid during the year, £171,900; discounts received during the year, £7,400.

4. *Trade debtors*
Amount owing by debtors at 1 January, £39,100; sales during the year, £302,800; cash received during the year, £288,700; discounts allowed during the year, £14,500; bad debts written off during the year, £3,500; goods returned by customers during the year, £1,800.

■ Prepare the ledger accounts ('T' accounts) of Yamadori Ltd for the year ended 31 December 19X8 in respect of:

(1) Lighting and heating
(2) Rent and rates
(3) Trade creditors
(4) Trade debtors

Show the balances brought down at 1 January 19X9.

9.2 On 1 July 19X1, Count Almaviva paid £2,000 into his business as capital. The following transactions then took place:

3 July	Purchased motor van for £800
6 July	Purchased goods on credit from Cherubino, £700
8 July	Paid rent, £40
14 July	Purchased goods on credit from Antonio, £300
16 July	Sold goods for cash, £200
18 July	Sold goods on credit to Marcellina, £400
21 July	Paid for petrol and oil, £20
23 July	Sold goods on credit to Barbarina, £600
25 July	Paid Cherubino £680 in full settlement
30 July	Received £350 from Marcellina but was informed that it would not be possible to collect any more of the debt
31 July	Paid salaries, £100
	Goods, invoice price £80, were returned by Barbarina
	Provided for depreciation on the motor van, £20.

- Write up the necessary entries in the ledger accounts of Count Almaviva and prepare a trial balance at 31 July 19X1.

9.3 Ms Brunnhilde runs a management consultancy business. Her trial balance at 30 April 19X7 is as follows:

	Dr £	Cr £
Bank overdraft		16,100
Debtors	17,400	
Fees earned		118,900
Freehold property at cost	80,000	
Interest paid	4,500	
Long term loan		50,000
Office expenses paid	16,200	
Ownership interest at 1 May 19X6		22,800
Salaries paid	73,600	
Withdrawals by Ms Brunnhilde during the year	16,100	
	£207,800	£207,800

The following additional information is available:

(a) Ms Brunnhilde owes a further £500 interest at 30 April 19X7.
(b) Office expenses include a payment for rates of £2,400 covering the period from 1 April 19X7 to 30 September 19X7.
(c) Office expenses amounting to £1,500 have been incurred but not entered in the books at 30 April 19X7.

- Prepare Ms Brunnhilde's income statement for the year ended 30 April 19X7 and her balance sheet as at that date.

9.4   You are given the following information relating to the year ended 31 December 19X1 for Fenena, who commenced business on 1 January 19X1:

	£
Creditors	6,400
Debtors	5,060
Purchases	16,100
Sales	28,400
Motor van	1,700
Drawings	5,100
Insurance	174
General expenses	1,596
Rent and rates	2,130
Salaries	4,162
Stock at 31 December 19X1	2,050
Sale returns	200
Cash at bank	2,628
Cash in hand	50
Capital introduced	4,100

■ Prepare Fenena's income statement for the year ended 31 December 19X1 and her balance sheet as at that date.

9.5   The 'T' accounts below show the transactions of Abigaille during the month of April:

	Cash					Trade creditors				Stock		
(d)	22,500	(a)	8,200		(g)	19,300	(b)	20,000	(b)	20,000	(j)	500
(i)	40,000	(e)	1,200		(j)	500	(f)	4,400				
(k)	5,200	(g)	19,300									

	Salaries and wages				Debtors				Sales	
(a)	8,200			(c)	27,500	(d)	22,500		(c)	27,500
(l)	400								(k)	5,200

	Furniture and fixtures				Accrued wages			Rent expenses	
(f)	4,400	(h)	100			(l)	400	(m)	200	

	Depreciation			Bank loan			Prepaid rent		
(h)	100				(i)	40,000	(e)	1,200	(m)	200

■ For each of the above entries (a) to (m) describe the nature of the underlying economic event. Be as specific as possible.

9.6 Below is the rough draft of the final accounts of Manon Wholesalers Ltd:

Profit and loss account as at 31 December 19X1

Sales			184,910
less: Opening stock	22,000		
Purchases	91,060		
	113,060		
Closing stock	23,520	136,580	
Warehouse expenses		25,390	
Rent	4,500		
less: Paid in advance	750	3,750	
Wages		7,690	
Bad debts		820	
Directors' fees		4,000	
General expenses		19,000	
Debenture interest		7,500	
Depreciation on van		800	
Dividends received		(3,250)	
Retained profits b/f		(18,140)	184,140
Retained profits c/f			770

Balance sheet for year ended 31 December 19X1

250,000 Ordinary shares		250,000	Cash at bank		530
£200,000 5% Debentures		200,000	Debtors (less bad £820)	55,210	
Creditors:			Gov'ment securities (cost)	16,930	
Trade creditors	39,050		Goodwill	25,000	
Rent	750	39,800			97,140
			Van (cost)		2,600
Reserves:			Stocks (cost)		23,520
General	10,000		Premises (cost)		426,000
Van depreciation	800				
Bad debt provision					
at 1 Jan. 19X1	2,880	13,680			
Profit		770			
		504,250			548,790

These accounts have been drafted by a clerk who has little knowledge of either bookkeeping or presentation of accounts. You may assume that the accounting balances have been copied accurately, and that the errors that prevent the accounts from balancing can be discovered by inspection and arithmetical check etc.

- (a) Prepare a simple calculation ('reconciliation statement') to explain the difference between the two sides of the balance sheet. (If you cannot find all the errors, put in a balancing figure as a 'suspense account balance'. This same amount would then also be a necessary addition to the balance sheet in (b).)

(b) Redraft the accounts in good form, giving effect to the following:
  (i) Allowance has to be made for a final dividend of £12,500.
  (ii) Debenture interest accrued at 31 December 19X1 was £2,500.

9.7 Ms Leporello commenced business as a retail chemist on 1 February 19X7, with an initial capital of £30,000, which she paid into her business bank account. She appointed Mr Masetto shop manager on 1 February 19X7, at an annual salary of £2,000. In addition, Mr Masetto is to receive commission of 20% of the net profit of the business, before charging commission.

During the year ended 31 January 19X8, Ms Leporello did not maintain proper books of account, but after an examination of the available records you ascertain the following:

1. An analysis of the bank statement for the year ended 31 January 19X8 is:

Receipts	£	Payments	£
Capital introduced	30,000	Lease	20,000
Takings banked	123,720	Shop fittings and equipment	8,800
Bank loan	20,000	Motor van	2,740
		Payments to suppliers	112,360
		Interest on bank loan	1,000
		General overhead expenses	8,335
		Rent	3,750
		Balance at 31 Jan. 19X8	16,735
	173,720		173,720

2. All sales were for cash and takings are banked daily, subject to the retention of a cash float of £100. The following payments were made out of cash takings:

	£
Salary — Mr Masetto	1,980
Drawings — Ms Leporello	4,000
Payments to suppliers	1,390
General overhead expenses	840

3. The premises are rented on a long lease, at an annual rental of £5,000.
4. At 31 January 19X8 cheques sent to suppliers, amounting to £2,500, have not been presented to the bank for payment.
5. Invoices from suppliers, amounting to £8,600, have not been paid.
6. Stock at 31 January 19X8 is valued at £36,500.
7. Depreciation is to be provided on the van at the rate of 25% on cost, and on the shop fittings and equipment at 10% on cost.
8. During the year Ms Leporello took goods which had cost £100 for her personal consumption.

■ Prepare a profit and loss account for Ms Leporello for the year ended 31 January 19X8 and a balance sheet as at that date.

9.8 Susanna carries on the business of a self-employed ice cream vendor. The business is seasonal and all the sales are made from a van. Susanna has her accounts of the business prepared each year to 31 December. She has a contract with Gilda Ice Cream Limited whereby she buys all her goods for resale from them at selling price less $33\frac{1}{3}$% and less $2\frac{1}{2}$% for monthly settlement. Susanna always takes the $2\frac{1}{2}$%. She also receives, at the end of the season, a rebate of 1% of the cost of her purchases before cash discount, if her sales for the season which runs from 1 April to 31 October exceed £50,000. In the year under review, she received £600.

The balances on Susanna's books at 31 December 19X0 were:

	£	£
Capital account		16,540
Van at cost	16,000	
Depreciation of van		8,000
Equipment at cost	3,500	
Depreciation of equipment		2,800
Garage rates in advance	90	
Accountancy		600
Balance at bank	8,400	
Garage rent due		50
	27,990	27,990

You obtain the following information concerning Susanna's transactions for the year to 31 December 19X1:

1. From cheque books, paying-in books and bank statements:

	£
Gilda Ice Cream Ltd — goods for sale	53,500
Wages	2,800
Van expenses	3,000
Laundry	1,040
Garage rent (52 weeks)	520
Garage rates (two half-years)	400
Accountancy	600
Rebate from Gilda Ice Cream Ltd	600
New van	11,000
Sundry business expenses	2,780
Private payments	3,200
Cash banked ex takings	75,740
Balance at bank 31 December 19X1	5,900

2. There is no record of takings and some goods for resale have apparently been paid for out of takings. The only cash payments recorded were:

	£
Petrol and oil	270
Casual wages	1,300
Sundry expenses	190

Any cash not accounted for is to be treated as drawings.

3. The old van was traded in for £7,000; it was used as a deposit on a new van costing £18,000.
4. Due to a power supply failure, stock with a resale value of £300 was damaged and had to be destroyed.
5. Depreciation is to be provided on a straight line basis at 25% on the van and 10% on the equipment, the new van to be depreciated as if in use on 1 January 19X1.
6. £640 is to be provided for accountancy.
7. At the year end the amounts for accrued rent and prepaid rates were £60 and £140 respectively.

- Prepare Susanna's income statement for the year ended 31 December 19X1 and her balance sheet as at that date.

9.9 You are provided with the following trial balance of Rigoletto as at 31 December 19X1:

	£	£
Capital account at 1 January 19X1		22,607
Purchases	194,100	
Sales		261,450
Office wages and salaries	16,720	
Rent and rates	4,930	
Debtors	36,150	
Sundry expenses	2,071	
Bad debts written off	942	
Drawings	4,751	
Provision for doubtful debts		1,851
Cash at bank	1,408	
Creditors		17,154
Cash in hand	167	
Stock	41,062	
Motor car — cost	3,600	
— depreciation		1,050
(at 31 Dec. 19X0)		
Discounts received		974
Carriage inwards	436	
Commissions received		1,251
	306,337	306,337

You are provided with the following additional information for the purposes of preparing the final accounts:

1. Closing stock has been valued at £49,678.
2. The rent of the premises is £3,200 p.a. payable half-yearly in advance on 31 March and 30 September.
3. Rates for the year ending 31 March 19X2 amounting to £744 were paid on 11 April 19X1.
4. Depreciation on the car is to be provided using the straight line method at a rate of 20% p.a.

5. The provision for doubtful debts (£1,851) was the general provision which appeared in last year's accounts. During the current year, bad debts of £942 were written off against the accounts of specific customers. It has now been agreed that further debts amounting to £710 are to be written off against specific customers, and the closing provision is to be adjusted to 5% of the revised debtors figure.
6. Wages and salaries to be accrued amount to £1,506.

■ Prepare the profit and loss account of Rigoletto for the year ended 31 December 19X1 and his balance sheet as at that date.

9.10 The following trial balance was extracted from the books of Ernani as at 31 December 19X1:

Trial balance

	£	£
Capital as at 1 Jan. 19X1		82,430
Freehold properties, at cost	59,000	
Motor vans:		
Balance, 1 Jan. 19X1 at cost	15,000	
Additions less sales in year	650	
Accumulated depreciation, 1 Jan. 19X1		6,750
Stock in trade, 1 Jan. 19X1	13,930	
Balance at bank	6,615	
Bad debts	1,075	
Provision for bad debts, 1 Jan. 19X1		275
Trade debtors and creditors	11,320	11,380
Drawings	4,000	
Wages and salaries	13,127	
Motor and delivery expenses	3,258	
Rates	700	
Purchases	108,440	
Sales		142,770
Legal expenses	644	
General expenses	5,846	
	243,605	243,605

Additional information:

1. Stock in trade at 31 December 19X1 was valued at £14,600.
2. Rates paid in advance as at 31 December 19X1 were £140.
3. The provision for bad debts is to be increased to £350.
4. On 1 January 19X1 a motor van which had cost £680 was sold for £125. Depreciation provided for this van up to 1 January 19X1 was £475.
5. Depreciation of motor vans (including additions) is to be provided at 20% of cost.
6. The balance on legal expenses account includes £380 in connection with the purchase of one of the freehold properties.

7. The manager is entitled to a commission of 5% of the net profit, *after* charging the commission.

- Prepare a profit and loss account for Ernani for the year ended 31 December 19X1 and a balance sheet as at that date.

9.11 Abdallo Ltd prepares accounts each year to 31 March, using conventional historical cost accounting methods. The following balances have been extracted from the books of Abdallo for the year ended 31 March 19X8:

	£'000
Issued shared capital	1,000
Reserves	286
Freehold property, at cost	560
Plant and equipment, at cost	724
Plant and equipment — accumulated depreciation at 1 April 19X7	324
Stock in hand at 1 April 19X7	735
Trade creditors	147
Trade debtors	345
Bank overdraft	182
Sales	1,971
Purchases of stock	1,256
Operating expenses (excluding depreciation)	290

The following additional information is available:

1. Stock in hand at 31 March 19X8 has been estimated at £775,000.
2. Depreciation is to be provided on plant and equipment at a rate of 30% using the reducing balance method.
3. It is proposed to pay an ordinary dividend of £150,000 as soon as possible, in respect of the year ended 31 March 19X8.
4. Accrued operating expenses amounting to £8,000 have not yet been entered in the books.

- (a) Prepare the trial balance of Abdallo Ltd at 31 March 19X8, *before* taking account of information in 1 to 4 above.
- (b) Prepare the profit and loss account of Abdallo Ltd for the year ended 31 March 19X8, and balance sheet at that date, *after* taking account of the information in 1 to 4 above.
- (c) Comment briefly on the likely usefulness to shareholders of the accounts you have prepared.

9.12 The accountant of Ottavio Ltd has prepared a trial balance as at 31 December 19X7. From this she has already prepared a draft profit and loss account for 19X7 which reveals a profit for the year of £60,000. This and the remaining balances are listed below:

Profit for the year £60,000; Bank overdraft £70,000;
General reserve £40,000; Land and buildings £200,000;
Trade creditors £210,000; Stock at 31 December 19X7 £110,000;
Share capital £170,000;

Plant and equipment, at cost, £200,000;
Rent, paid in advance, £20,000; Share premium £80,000;
Debtors £250,000; Accrued expenses £25,000;
Accumulated depreciation on plant and equipment £125,000.

However, the following points are brought to your attention:

1. No depreciation has been charged for 19X7. You discover that depreciation is calculated on a straight line basis and that all the plant and equipment was bought on 1 January 19X2.
2. The stock figure was taken directly from the company's records. A physical stock count has since taken place and has shown the stock at 31 December to be worth only £103,000.
3. The last electricity bill received by the company was for the three months up to 31 October 19X7. The next bill is not due until 31 January 19X8. You estimate that this next bill will amount to £3,000.
4. As a result of the company's performance in 19X7, the directors have announced that the company will pay a dividend of £20,000 to its shareholders.

■   (a) Prepare the trial balance from the list of balances provided.
    (b) Taking account of all the information provided prepare a balance sheet for Ottavio Ltd as at 31 December 19X7.
    (c) Comment on the results revealed by the balance sheet.

9.13 Mr Zaccaria buys and sells ismaeles. His draft balance sheet on 31 March 19X0 was as follows:

	£		£
Capital account	134,500	Fixed assets at cost	160,000
		less: Depreciation	65,000
			95,000
Trade creditors	48,000	Stock of ismaeles	31,000
		Debtors	42,000
		Cash at bank	14,500
	182,500		182,500

Mr Zaccaria's transactions during the year ended 31 March 19X1 may be described as follows:

1. Sales amounted to £240,000.
2. The gross profit percentage was 20% of sales.
3. General expenses (excluding depreciation and the cost of ismaeles) amounted to £18,500, and were all paid in cash.
4. No fixed assets were bought or sold. Depreciation on fixed assets amounted to £16,000.
5. Mr Zaccaria withdrew £10,000 from the business for personal expenditure.
6. Debtors at the end of the year were equal to 3 months' sales.
7. Creditors at the end of the year were equal to 2 months' purchases.
8. Stock of ismaeles at the end of the year was sufficient to meet sales requirements for 4 months, assuming sales at the rate of £240,000 p.a.

- (a) Prepare Mr Zaccaria's income statement for the year ended 31 March 19X1 and his balance sheet on that date.
- (b) Mr Zaccaria has little knowledge of accounting. Write a report, explaining to him in simple terms why his income for the year is not equal to the change in his cash balance.

9.14 Victor and Joanna Leser set up in partnership on 1 April 19X1 as Leser & Leser Chartered Accountants and each contributed £10,000 in capital on that date. They employ two people: Ken who is an unqualified bookkeeper and Bob who undertakes general secretarial work. In addition to helping Victor and Joanna with some of the simple accounting tasks for clients, Ken has been given the responsibility for maintaining the firm's accounting records during the year and preparing the annual accounts.

Ken has extracted the following incomplete list of balances at 31 March 19X2:

	£
Fee Income	101,000
Rental paid	8,000
Sundry office expenses	5,750
Office equipment purchased 1.4.X1	1,600
Victor's salary	19,000
Joanna's salary	22,500
Car purchased 1.4.X1	15,500
Heat, light and power	12,400
Debtors ledger balance	16,800
Creditors ledger balance	4,400
Motor expenses	760
Wages — Bob	7,000
— Ken	8,500

There are a number of outstanding matters which Ken has identified as requiring adjustments in the accounts. These are as follows:

Outstanding matters
 (i) A depreciation policy needs to be agreed for the car (which is for business use by Joanna) and the office equipment.
 (ii) Ken has identified a number of debtor accounts which he suspects may not be paid. These include a debt of £1,855 due from Kelco Ltd which has gone into receivership. Ken expects that part of the debt will eventually be recovered.
 (iii) When Ken accepted the appointment with Leser & Leser, it was on the understanding that he would be paid an annual bonus. The amount has yet to be agreed.
 (iv) Due to Bob being sick for two days, two invoices totalling £6,500, authorized by Joanna on 30 March 19X2, had not been typed and processed until 1 April 19X2. They had not been included in fee income.

This being his first year in the job, Ken has decided to ask Joanna's and Victor's advice on the accounting treatment of all the above matters before completing the accounts. They instructed him as follows:

(i) The car and the office equipment were to be depreciated using the reducing balance method at the rates of 30% and 15% respectively.

(ii) The outstanding debt from Kelco Ltd was to be written off. A general provision for bad debts, equal to 9% of the debtor balances, was to be made.

(iii) Ken was to be paid a bonus equal to 1% of net profit (after taking into account the bonus).

(iv) The two invoices were to be included in the fee income of the following year.

- (a) Prepare the trial balance of Leser & Leser *before* taking account of the outstanding matters. You may assume that the information given in the question is complete and that the balancing figure in the trial balance is the cash balance.

  (b) Prepare the profit and loss account for Leser & Leser for the year ending 31 March 19X2, *after* taking into account the outstanding matters and the instructions on their treatment received from Victor and Joanna.

  (c) If Victor and Joanna had allowed Ken to decide on the accounting treatment of all the outstanding matters (except the basis of payment of his bonus), suggest if, how and why his choice of accounting treatment might have differed from theirs. State any assumptions you might make.

9.15 Lescaut plc is a listed company whose major activity is retailing. The company prepares accounts annually to 31 March. The following is a summary of the balances extracted from the books of Lescaut plc for the year ended 31 March 19X6:

	£ millions
Bank overdraft	38.1
Reserves	110.0
Creditors	76.7
Debentures (10% — repayable 19Y5)	800.0
Debtors	8.1
Depreciation: Accumulated provisions at 1 April 19X5:	
Fittings and equipment	372.8
Freehold land and buildings	263.5
Directors' remuneration	0.8
Fittings and equipment, at cost	780.0
Freehold land and buildings, at cost	1,486.0
Goodwill	112.6
Interest payable	82.4
Interim dividend paid (5%)	25.0
Investment income	10.3
Issued share capital	500.0
Overhead expenses	85.5
Profit and loss account	
(credit balance at 1 April 19X5)	275.0
Purchases	432.8
Sales	920.5
Stock (balance at 1 April 19X5)	227.3
Investments in shares	126.4

The following information is also available:

(i) The authorized share capital of Lescaut plc is £700 million.
(ii) Stock at 31 March 19X6 is estimated at £282.9 million.
(iii) Depreciation is to be provided, using the straight line method, at the following rates:

Fittings and equipment	25%
Freehold land and buildings	5%

(iv) No provision has yet been made for audit charges for the year, which are estimated at £500,000.
(v) The directors wish to provide for a final dividend of 10% of the issued share capital, in addition to the interim dividend already paid.
(vi) Interest payable includes debenture interest (£60 million) and bank overdraft interest (£22.4 million). Debenture interest is payable on 30 June and 31 December each year.

■ (a) Prepare the trial balance of Lescaut plc at 31 March 19X6, *before* taking account of points (i) to (vi) above.

(b) Prepare the profit and loss account of Lescaut plc for the year ended 31 March 19X6 and its balance sheet as at that date.

Further reading

Hendriksen, E.S., *Accounting Theory*, Irwin, 1982, Chapters 4–6.
Mace, J.R., 'Accounting as a basis for taxation', in Carsberg, B. and Hope, A. (eds), *Current Issues in Accounting*, Philip Allan, 1984.
Nobes, C., *Introduction to Financial Accounting*, 3rd edn, Routledge, 1992.

CHAPTER

10

Interpretation of Accounts: Ratio Analysis

In Chapter 2, we suggested that users of financial statements require future-oriented information to make rational economic decisions. This future-oriented information includes management's estimates of the amount of, and risk attached to, the entity's future cash flows. We concluded, however, that direct forecasts and forecast-based approaches to the measurement of income and value are unlikely to be included in published financial statements in the foreseeable future, and have thus focused our attention on the income statements, balance sheets and cash flow statements produced by transactions-based, historical cost accounting. This leads us to repeat the question asked in Section 2.5.

> **How should users of financial statements analyse and interpret the (historical) data provided in order to obtain the (predictive) information required?**

In this chapter and the next we shall attempt to answer this question. In particular we shall consider how we might interpret the data provided in the financial statements in order to estimate an entity's future cash flows and their associated risk. In this chapter we analyse the figures included in the balance sheet and profit and loss account. In Chapter 11 we analyse the data provided in the cash flow statements.

10.1 The role of ratio analysis

A popular means of interpreting published financial data involves the calculation of a variety of key ratios. The term *ratio analysis* describes such an exercise. Ratio analysis is based on the notion that the analysis of absolute figures may not be the best means available of assessing an organization's performance and prospects. For example, an annual profit of £20,000 may represent a good level of performance for a local grocer with one shop but a poor achievement for a large company owning a chain of grocery stores. One reason for this is that the two businesses may use very different amounts of capital. Thus the local grocer may be using capital of £50,000, whereas the large company may have capital employed of £50 million. A more meaningful way of measuring profitability would be to relate the profit figure to the capital employed as a ratio or a percentage. Hence the local grocer's return is 40% (£20,000 divided by £50,000 and multiplied by 100 to express the answer as a percentage) and the large company's is 0.04% (£20,000 ÷ £50,000,000 × 100). These ratios better indicate the success of the two businesses in their use of capital, and the above example demonstrates one way in which ratio analysis might be used to measure profitability.

One of the most important purposes of ratio analysis is to help users to appraise an organization's past performance and, from that appraisal, to make judgements about its likely future performance. For example, suppose that a firm has regularly increased its capital employed and has managed to sustain a ratio of profit to capital employed of between 20% and 25% p.a. Those interested in predicting the firm's future performance might use the information together with estimates of the firm's future capital employed, as part of a process to predict its future surplus. Of course, the prediction process is likely to include other variables relating, for example, to environmental conditions, including the rate of inflation, and to a variety of ratios that measure organizational performance. Indeed, profitability is not the only aspect of performance which can be measured by the use of ratios. Ratio analysis may also be used to measure liquidity and solvency. The aim is to develop a set of key ratios each of which should throw some light on at least one aspect of the firm's activities and, as such, should be of some value.

For example, in order to facilitate the prediction of an organization's future performance and its associated risk, we might wish to calculate and evaluate ratios under three general headings: profitability, liquidity and longer-term solvency.

(a) *Profitability* is concerned with how effectively an organization has used its available resources. As we suggested above, an examination of a company's past profitability ratios might be useful in predicting its likely future performance.

(b) *Liquidity* is concerned with the organization's current financial position, and in particular with its capacity to pay its debts as they arise in the short term. If an organization has a liquidity problem, there is an increased risk of its failing to generate *any* future cash flows.

(c) *Longer-term solvency* is concerned with the organization's ability to meet its longer-term financial commitments. It is often related to the composition of its capital structure. For example, a company financed predominantly by loan capital must meet its (high) interest payments as they fall due. The potential consequences of failing to meet these payments increases the risk attached to estimates of the company's future performance.

We shall discuss the usefulness of particular ratios under these three headings in later sections of this chapter.

10.2   Limitations of ratio analysis

Before we begin our examination of particular ratios, we offer some words of warning. Although ratio analysis may be a useful way of interpreting certain types of financial information, its powers should not be overestimated. Its usefulness is restricted in at least two important respects. First, if ratios are calculated from the figures in conventional (i.e. historical cost) accounts, they may not reflect the current (replacement) values of assets or the current costs of operations. This will be a problem if users wish to predict an organization's future performance *and* if they find current values and current costs more helpful for this purpose than historical figures. We argue in Chapter 14 that *both* of these conditions are likely to exist.

Secondly, we must be careful in interpreting particular ratios in isolation. For example, is a ratio of profit to capital employed of 15% p.a. good or bad? The answer depends on the individual circumstances. In an environment where inflation is running at 5% p.a., a 15% return is probably satisfactory, whereas it is almost certainly unsatisfactory if the annual rate of inflation is 100%. Similarly, an annual return of 15% may be acceptable for an organization which operates a low risk line of business but unacceptable for one operating in a highly uncertain and risky environment. In other words, different values of the same ratios (for example, the profitability ratio) may be *expected* for different types of organization, different points or periods in time and different environmental conditions. This complicates the setting of 'target' ratios for an organization. A typical response to this problem is to *compare* the ratios of the organization with the ratios of organizations in a similar line of business, operating in a similar environment during the same period of time,[1] and with the ratios of the same organization for previous (and possibly, via budgets, future) periods. Unfortunately, neither of these solutions is completely satisfactory. First, comparisons with other firms may be invalid if the other firms use different accounting conventions (for example, concerning fixed asset and stock valuation). In consequence similar underlying performances may reveal quite dissimilar ratios and vice versa. Secondly, comparisons of an organization's current performance with its previous

1. See, for example, *Industrial Performance Analysis*, ICC Information Group Ltd, London. The financial statements of 12,000 companies are analysed and aggregated into twenty-five major industrial groupings. Eighteen key ratios covering liquidity, solvency and profitability are produced for each grouping.

performance may be misleading if the environment in which the organization operates changes (for example, if the rate of inflation changes or if its line of business becomes more or less competitive), or if the organization changes its mix of products.

These limitations do not mean that ratio analysis should be discarded as a means of interpretation. Such a course of action would be appropriate only if ratio analysis provided decision makers with information (*additional* to that which they already have) which has a value less than the costs of undertaking the analysis. Rather the limitations mean that ratios should be interpreted with care, and that other factors should be considered in evaluating an organization's performance.

10.3   Illustration of the calculation and usefulness of ratios

We now illustrate the calculation of a number of financial ratios, and discuss their particular limitations and usefulness. We do not attempt to consider every ratio that might be calculated from a set of financial statements. Almost any pair of figures from an income statement and balance sheet could be combined to provide a ratio and clearly some combinations are likely to be more helpful than others. We attempt to identify the more important ratios that should form a part of any evaluation of organizational performance. Other ratios may be appropriate for other situations and analyses.

Two general points relating to the calculation of ratios deserve mention. First, some ratios compare a figure from the income statement (which covers a *period* of time) with a figure from the closing balance sheet (which relates to a *point* in time). An example is the ratio of profit to capital employed. This procedure is acceptable provided that no substantial changes have occurred to the relevant balance sheet figures during the period covered by the income statement. Otherwise, it may be necessary to use an average of opening and closing balance sheet figures to provide a proper and consistent basis for ratio calculation. Consider the case of an organization that gradually increases its capital employed from £200,000 to £400,000 during an accounting period. During the same period, its profit is £40,000. Profit as a percentage of capital at the end of the period is 10% (£40,000 divided by £400,000 × 100). But the capital employed was less than £400,000 for most of the period, and was as low as £200,000 at the start of the period. In such situations, ratios might be better calculated by taking the average balance sheet value of capital employed, rather than the end-period figure. Thus capital employed may be taken as £300,000 [(£200,000 + £400,000) ÷ 2], giving a profit percentage of $13\frac{1}{3}$% (£40,000 ÷ £300,000 × 100).

The second point relates to the way in which ratios are expressed. Some ratios are expressed in their 'raw' form (i.e. as ratios), some as percentages and some as periods of time. This variety of expression is employed to help users to better

Table 10.1 *Maine Ltd — income statements and balance sheets*

	Year 2 £	Year 1 £
Income statements		
Sales	1,200,000	900,000
Cost of goods sold (all variable)	900,000	720,000
Gross profit	300,000	180,000
Overhead expenses, excluding interest	170,000	130,000
Operating profit	130,000	50,000
Interest payable	36,000	0
Net profit, added to reserves	94,000	50,000
Balance sheets as at 31 December		
Land and buildings at written-down value	325,000	150,000
Plant and machinery at written-down value	200,000	60,000
Stocks (at original cost)	75,000	53,000
Trade debtors	140,000	100,000
Cash	24,000	27,000
	764,000	390,000
Trade creditors	(100,000)	(60,000)
Total assets less current liabilities	664,000	330,000
15% bonds (repayable 31 December, Year 16)	240,000	0
	424,000	330,000
Capital and reserves		
Issued ordinary share capital	150,000	150,000
Reserves	274,000	180,000
Owners' capital employed	424,000	330,000

understand the resultant figures; all results could be expressed as ratios but some would be less meaningful in this form. The various forms of presentation, and their usefulness, will be apparent in the example to which we now turn.

The summarized historical cost income statements and balance sheets of Maine Ltd for years 1 and 2 are shown in Table 10.1. The company's performance for the two years may be analysed under the general headings of profitability, liquidity and longer-term solvency.

Profitability

In Chapter 4 we described the activities of a business organization in terms of a *transformation process*, i.e. the process by which the raw factors of production are converted or transformed into the finished goods sold by the organization. Thus an assessment of an organization's profitability is an attempt to evaluate how efficiently the management has carried out the transformation process. By evaluating the management's past performance we may discover information which can be used as a basis for predicting future performance. Profitability ratios indicate how efficiently organizations have used their available resources. Such ratios are normally presented as percentages and, in general, the higher the profitability percentage, the better is the aspect of the organization's performance to which the ratio relates.

Earlier in this chapter we suggested that absolute profit figures may not be the best means available of assessing performance, and that the assessment of profit relative to the capital employed might produce a more useful indication of performance, i.e. one would be less happy with a profit of £20,000 on an investment of £50 million, than with a profit of £19,000 on an investment of £50,000. Consequently, we require some indicator of profitability which measures the profit earned relative to the economic resources available. One such measure, perhaps the most widely quoted of all ratios, is the *return on investment* series of ratios.

Return on investment is not a single ratio. There are many different levels of return — gross profit, operating profit, profit available to shareholders etc. — and many definitions of the investment in (capital employed by) the organization — shareholders' funds, all long-term capital, long-term and short-term capital, etc. These various definitions can produce a series of useful ratios (rates of return) but it is important that the construction of each ratio entails consistency of numerator and denominator, i.e. that the definition of profit is consistent with the definition of capital employed. For example, the appropriate return on shareholders' funds is the profit available to shareholders, and the appropriate return on long-term capital employed is the profit available to all providers of long-term capital, i.e. the profit before interest payable on long-term loans. We begin by examining the return on long-term capital employed.

Return on long-term capital employed may be calculated from the following expression:

$$\text{Return on long-term capital} = \frac{\text{Operating profit (before interest payable)}}{\text{Total long-term capital employed}} \times 100$$

The ratio is consistent in so far that capital employed is based on total long-term funds used by the entity and profit is measured before deducting *any* returns, interest or dividends, to the providers of long-term capital. The figures for Maine Ltd are:

	Year 2	Year 1
Return on long-term capital	$\frac{130,000}{664,000} \times 100 = 19.6\%$	$\frac{50,000}{330,000} \times 100 = 15.2\%$

From Table 10.1 we can see that the amount of capital employed is matched by a corresponding amount of assets in which the capital has been invested. At the end of year 2, owners' capital employed of £424,000 is matched by total assets less total liabilities of £424,000. Long-term capital employed of £664,000 (owners' capital employed plus long-term liabilities) is matched by total assets less current liabilities. Finally, total capital employed of £764,000 (owners' capital employed plus long-term liabilities plus current liabilities) is matched by total assets of £764,000 (fixed assets plus current assets). We saw in Chapter 5 that the technique of double-entry bookkeeping ensures that the *sources* of a company's funds equal the *uses* of those funds, and that the total of ownership interest and all liabilities equals the total assets of the company. Consequently, any ratio expressed as a 'return on capital employed' can also be expressed in the form of a 'return on assets'. For example, the return on long-term capital employed computed above (130,000 ÷ 664,000 × 100 = 19.6%) is identical to the return on total assets less current liabilities.

The return on long-term capital ratio measures the return achieved on the total long-term capital available to managers, i.e. for every £1 of long-term capital invested in the company, the managers of Maine Ltd generated 15.2p in operating profit before interest payable in year 1 and 19.6p in year 2. This ratio is sometimes used as an indicator of the overall effectiveness of a business — the numerator encompasses most items in the income statement (sales less all production, selling and administrative costs) and the denominator encompasses all items in the balance sheet (i.e. total long-term capital, or total assets less current liabilities). However, this very generality limits the usefulness of the ratio as a means of evaluating an organization's performance. For example, we can see that Maine's return increased in year 2, but we do not know *why* it increased, or *whether* the increased return is a good indicator of the return likely to be achieved in the future. We thus need to disaggregate the ratio into its component parts.

The transformation process described in Chapter 4 provides a clue as to how the ratio may be analysed. Entities transform raw materials into finished goods and sell them to customers. To generate a profit the entity must sell its goods and services at a price sufficient to cover its costs. Hence, the success of an enterprise in generating a profit depends upon its ability to:

(a) generate sales from the available economic resources; and
(b) produce income from the sales generated.

The rate of return on long-term capital employed can thus be broken down into two component parts. The first measures how intensively the management has utilized the available resources to generate sales, and is called the 'utilization' or 'asset turnover' ratio. The second measures the proportion of sales which is converted into profit, i.e. the profit as a percentage of sales. This method of separating the rate of return ratio into its component parts was developed by the American company E.I. Dupont de Nemours. The Dupont formula for the return on long-term capital can be expressed as follows:

Return on   = Utilization ratio × Operating profit percentage
long-term capital

which can be expressed as:

$$\frac{\text{Operating profit before interest}}{\text{Long-term capital}}$$

$$= \frac{\text{Sales}}{\text{Long-term capital}} \times \frac{\text{Operating profit before interest}}{\text{Sales}} \times 100$$

We now examine each part in turn.

(a) *Utilization, or asset turnover, ratio.* This ratio measures how efficiently the available resources are used to produce sales. The 'available resources' may be described either as the long-term capital made available to the organization, or as the total assets less current liabilities under the organization's control. The ratio may be calculated from the following expression:

$$\text{Utilization ratio} = \frac{\text{Sales}}{\text{Long-term capital or total assets less current liabilities}}$$

The ratio shows how much in sales revenue is generated from each £1 of long-term capital invested in assets. The higher the ratio the more intensive is the use of assets. The figures for Maine Ltd are:

	Year 2	*Year 1*
Utilization ratio	$\frac{1,200,000}{664,000} = 1.81$	$\frac{900,000}{330,000} = 2.73$

Thus for every £1 of long-term capital invested, Maine generated £2.73 of sales revenue in year 1 and £1.81 of sales revenue in year 2. The ratio provides some information as to how intensively resources have been utilized. For example, if two companies in the same industry own identical assets and set the same selling price for their product, the company utilizing the assets more intensively will generate the higher sales revenue.

One limitation of the utilization ratio is its use of a figure (for long-term capital) from the balance sheet which may be untypical of the capital employed throughout the rest of the year. We noted earlier that one way of reducing this problem is to use an average of the opening and closing balances. In this example we would require information from the balance sheet of Maine Ltd at Year 0 in order to be able to calculate the ratio for Year 1.

(b) *Operating profit percentage.* This measure may also be termed the 'operating profit margin' or 'trading profit margin'. The operating profit percentage is calculated from the following expression:

$$\text{Operating profit} \atop \text{percentage} = \frac{\text{Operating profit before interest}}{\text{Sales revenue}} \times 100$$

The ratio measures the percentage of sales revenue generated as profit for the providers of all long-term capital after deducting the cost of goods sold and other operating costs. The figures for Maine Ltd are:

	Year 2	*Year 1*
Net profit percentage	$\frac{130,000}{1,200,000} \times 100 = 10.8\%$	$\frac{50,000}{900,000} \times 100 = 5.6\%$

For each £1 of sales revenue generated, Maine earned 5.6p of operating profit in year 1 and 10.8p of operating profit in year 2.

Separation of the ratio into the two elements permits further analysis of the causes of the increase in the percentage of return on long-term capital employed, as follows:

	Utilization ratio	×	*Operating profit percentage*	=	*Return on long-term capital*
Year 1	2.73	×	5.6%	=	15.2%
Year 2	1.81	×	10.8%	=	19.6%

These figures indicate that, in year 2, Maine Ltd generated fewer sales per £1 invested, but that on average each £1 of sales produced a higher operating profit. This increase in the operating profit margin more than compensated for the fall in the utilization ratio, with the result that the return on long-term capital increased from 15.2% to 19.6%.

We noted in Section 10.2 that different values of the same ratio may be expected for different types of organization. The profitability ratios for two very different UK companies are shown in Table 10.2. Glaxo plc develops, manufactures and markets high margin, often patent-protected pharmaceuticals. It may take several years of research, development and testing before a particular drug can be released onto the market. A stated philosophy of the supermarket chain Kwik Save plc is to 'stack 'em high, sell 'em cheap', implying a high turnover of goods with relatively low margins. As can be seen from Table 10.2, both companies were extremely successful in 1991 in terms of their return on long-term capital

Table 10.2 *Glaxo plc and Kwik Save plc — measures of profitability, 1991*

	Utilization ratio	×	*Operating profit percentage*	=	*Return on long-term capital*
Glaxo	0.94	×	35.0%	=	33%
Kwik Save	7.73	×	5.2%	=	40%

employed. The utilization ratios and the operating profit percentages confirm the different business strategies of the two companies.

A Dupont style analysis encourages a further disaggregation of these profitability ratios. For example, a change in the operating profit percentage of Maine Ltd may be due to changes in the variable operating costs per unit, to changes in fixed operating costs, or to changes in the gross profit percentage. We shall examine one of these possible reasons, a change in the gross profit percentage.

Gross profit percentage. The gross profit percentage or 'gross profit margin' is calculated from the following expression:

$$\text{Gross profit percentage} = \frac{\text{Gross profit}}{\text{Sales revenue}} \times 100$$

This ratio measures how much each £1 of sales revenue earns as gross profit. The figures for Maine Ltd are:

	Year 2	*Year 1*
Gross profit percentage	$\frac{300,000}{1,200,000} \times 100 = 25\%$	$\frac{180,000}{900,000} \times 100 = 20.0\%$

Thus, for each £1 of sales revenue generated, Maine Ltd earned 20p gross profit in year 1 and 25p gross profit in year 2.

Changes in the gross profit percentage may be due to:

- Changes in the selling prices of products. For example, Maine may have increased its selling price whilst managing to hold down the cost of goods sold.
- Changes in the cost of goods sold per unit of output. Such changes may result from changes in input prices or changes in the efficiency with which inputs are used. For example, suppose Maine held constant its selling price over the two-year period. The increase in sales revenue from £900,000 to £1,200,000 would represent an increase of one-third in the *physical* volume of sales (300,000/900,000). If the costs of goods sold are all variable, changes in the physical volume of sales would not of themselves affect the gross profit percentage (because both sales revenue and cost of goods sold would rise proportionately) although they would of course affect the *absolute* gross profit figure. A one-third increase in the volume of goods sold should result in an increase in the cost of goods sold figure for Maine Ltd to £960,000 (£720,000 x $1\frac{1}{3}$). As the cost of goods sold figure in year 2 was only £900,000, Maine Ltd might have reduced unit input costs and/or improved the efficiency of production.
- Changes in the mix of products sold. For example products with higher gross profit percentages may be substituted for products with lower margins. Even if sales prices, input prices and efficiency of production were unchanged

throughout the two years, Maine's gross profit could have been increased by switching into products yielding a higher margin, e.g. if the whole of Maine's increase in sales (£300,000) was due to the launch of a new product with a gross profit margin of 40%, the total gross profit would increase by £120,000 to £300,000 and the average gross profit percentage would increase from 20% to 25%.

It is beyond the scope of this book to consider any further disaggregation of the return on long-term capital ratio, but even so we have identified some potentially useful information. The increase in the return on long-term capital was achieved by increasing the operating profit margin. This more than compensated for the fall in asset, or capital, utilization. The increase in the operating profit margin was in turn the result of an increase in the gross profit margin. We cannot identify the particular reason(s) for the increase in the gross profit margin from the financial statements themselves, but that information may be available elsewhere in the company's annual report (for example, in the supplementary notes and other statements), or from other sources.

The return on long-term capital employed is an 'entity' ratio. It shows the return to all providers of long-term capital and is therefore unaffected by changes in a company's capital structure, i.e. its mix of equity and debt capital. The derivation of the return on long-term capital is the same whatever the proportion of total capital supplied by loan creditors. However, as we shall see in the section dealing with 'solvency' ratios, the introduction of debt finance can have a significant effect upon the returns to shareholders and their associated risk. This suggests a need to consider also a 'proprietary' ratio which focuses upon the owners of the company.

Return on owners' capital employed. This measure is also called the 'return on equity', the 'return to ordinary shareholders' or the 'return to ordinary shareholders' funds'. The return may be calculated from the following expression:

$$\text{Return on owners'} \atop \text{capital employed} = \frac{\text{Profit after interest}}{\text{Owners' capital employed}} \times 100$$

Note that in order to ensure consistency between the numerator and the denominator, the former is measured as the profit available for owners (i.e. after interest payable) and the latter as owners' capital (i.e. excluding other sources of capital such as long-term loans).[2] The figures for Maine Ltd are:

	Year 2	Year 1
Return on owners' capital employed	$\frac{94,000}{424,000} \times 100 = 22.2\%$	$\frac{50,000}{330,000} \times 100 = 15.2\%$

2. If we were to introduce taxation into this example, the 'profit available for owners' would be represented by 'profit after interest payable and taxation'.

In year 1 the return on owners' capital employed (15.2%) is identical to the return on long-term capital employed because the owners' capital represents the only long-term capital employed. In year 2, the company borrows £240,000 by issuing bonds. The owners' return increases to 22.2% and the overall return on long-term capital increases to 19.6% (as we calculated earlier).

The increased capital raised during year 2 has apparently been used efficiently. The *marginal* return on the new capital is 24.0% $((130,000-50,000) \div (664,000-330,000) \times 100)$. Of the new capital raised (£334,000), £94,000 is from equity in the form of retained profits and £240,000 from the issue of new 15% bonds. Because the new bonds, which represent most of the new capital raised, require a lower return (15% p.a.) than is being earned on the new capital (24.0%), the owners' return increases by more than the total return. Thus the increase in owners' return is due partly to increased profitability and partly to the introduction of 'cheap' debt financing. On the other hand, the owners' return is now subject to increased financial risk as a result of the change in capital structure. Maine Ltd now has an obligation to pay debt interest of £36,000, whatever its net income.

Liquidity

Liquidity ratios provide some indication of an organization's financial position. Financial statement users will probably be interested in liquidity ratios because a weak liquidity position entails an increased challenge to the achievements of long-term objectives (including the generation of future cash flows). This might lead the user to reassess the estimate of a company's future performance, and/or to discount the future cash flows at a higher discount rate. Taken in conjunction with cash flow statements (which we discuss in Chapter 11), liquidity ratios provide information about the organization's ability to generate *cash* and may suggest, by highlighting inefficiencies, ways in which the cash position could be improved. Liquidity ratios are normally presented either as ratios or as time periods and in this section we consider five main liquidity ratios: working capital ratio, liquid ratio, debtor payment period, creditor payment period, and stock holding period.

(a) *Working capital ratio*. The working capital ratio, or 'current ratio', is calculated as follows:

$$\text{Working capital ratio} = \frac{\text{Current assets}}{\text{Current liabilities}}$$

This ratio indicates the firm's ability to meet its short-term cash obligations (current liabilities) out of its current assets without having to raise finance by borrowing, issuing more shares, or selling fixed assets, all of which might adversely affect the firm's ability to generate future net cash flows for the existing participants.

The figures for Maine Ltd are:

	Year 2	*Year 1*
Working capital ratio	$\dfrac{(75,000 + 140,000 + 24,000)}{100,000}$	$\dfrac{(53,000 + 100,000 + 27,000)}{60,000}$
	$= 2.4:1$	$= 3.0:1$

If this ratio provides some indication of an entity's current financial position, one might expect that the higher the ratio the better it is. However, a very high ratio can cause almost as much concern as a very low ratio. A very low ratio might indicate that the company will be unable to meet its short-term obligations as they fall due. A very high ratio might cause the user to query why so much capital has been invested in current assets.

For example, a high ratio arising because the organization holds an abnormally high level of stock at the year end might imply that the firm is experiencing difficulties in selling its products; an abnormally high level of debtors might imply that the firm is experiencing difficulties in collecting cash from its credit customers or that it has extended the credit period to maintain sales in the face of falling demand; a high cash balance might imply the lack of any current worthwhile projects in which to invest.

To determine whether Maine's working capital ratio is within acceptable bounds we could calculate the working capital ratios of other companies in the same industry. There is no general optimal value for the working capital ratio. Indeed there is no general optimal value for most liquidity ratios. The best ratio for a particular organization depends on various factors, including the nature of its business and the environment in which it operates. A ratio value that is ideal for one firm may indicate disaster for another.

For example, businesses which carry very little stock, e.g. airlines, or do not normally extend credit to customers, e.g. food retailers, will have a low working capital ratio. Some relevant working capital ratios for 1992 are British Airways plc 0.68; Sainsbury plc 0.57; Tesco plc 0.60 (Table 10.3). Businesses which carry higher levels of stock and which allow debtors to pay over a longer period, e.g. those in the motor industry, will have a higher working capital ratio (for example, that of Ford Motor Company is 1.82; of Lucas Industries plc 1.70). Whether the working capital ratio for Maine Ltd is satisfactory depends upon the norm for other firms in the same industry. If we discover that similar firms continue to operate successfully with working capital ratios within the range of 1.7:1 to 2.7:1 then the decline in Maine's ratio from 3.0:1 to 2.4:1 suggests a movement towards the norm. The crucial question, however, is whether the decline from 3.0:1 to 2.4:1 is a permanent change or the first stage in a longer-term trend. In the former case, the change may indicate efficient working capital management; the company is tying up less capital in net current assets. In the latter case, a continuation of the trend may eventually result in impending liquidity problems for the company.

The working capital ratio suffers two particular limitations. First, the stock component of current assets is included in our example at its historical cost. However, a principal aim of the ratio is to indicate whether the firm can meet its short-term liabilities out of current assets. The cash and debtors figures (subject to an estimate of those debtors who may default) represent a realistic estimate of the cash available to the company in the near future. The historical cost (and even the replacement cost) of stock is not such a realistic estimate. The *current selling price* of the stock, less any costs still to be incurred prior to sale, would be a better measure of its potential contribution to the firm's liquidity.

Second, the ratio depends on the definitions adopted for the classification of fixed and current assets. As we noted in Chapter 5, different asset classifications may be used which may in turn lead to different working capital definitions. In this respect, the speed at which raw materials are converted into finished goods and sold to customers is important. For example, should raw materials and work in progress be included in the working capital ratio as current assets, if they are not to be converted into finished goods and sold for many months?

In its 1992 Annual Report, Sainsbury plc reported that the cost of the stocks in its stores and warehouses on 14 March 1992 was £362.2 million (Table 10.3). These goods would be sold at a higher value, and converted into cash, in less than three weeks. On 31 July 1992, the stocks of Lucas Industries plc amounted to £437.7 million (Table 10.4). However, it could take up to six months for the raw materials and consumables, and the work in progress, to be converted into cash.

(b) *Liquid ratio.*   One simple, if crude, way of avoiding such problems is to exclude stock from the working capital ratio. The liquid ratio or, as it is sometimes

Table 10.3   *Tesco plc and Sainsbury plc — balance sheets on 29 February 1992 and 14 March 1992, respectively*

	Tesco plc £ million	Sainsbury plc £ million
Current assets:		
Stocks	221.7	362.2
Debtors	39.6	80.8
ACT recoverable	—	37.3
Short-term investments	300.7	189.6
Cash at bank and in hand	38.3	173.9
	600.3	843.8
Current liabilities	1,003.5	1,468.2
Working capital ratio	0.60	0.57
Liquid ratio	0.38	0.33

Table 10.4 *Lucas Industries plc — annual report and accounts 1992*

Note 11: Stocks	1992 £ million
Raw materials and consumables	69.6
Work in progress	211.2
Finished goods	175.3
Payments on account	(18.4)
	437.7

described, the 'quick' or 'acid test' ratio, is calculated from the following expression:

$$\text{Liquid ratio} = \frac{\text{Liquid assets (i.e. current assets excluding stock)}}{\text{Current liabilities}}$$

This ratio represents a more stringent test of an organization's ability to pay its debts as they fall due. This is particularly true in a time of crisis. Stock is excluded for the reasons given above. The resultant figures for Maine Ltd are:

$$\text{Liquid ratio} \quad \frac{(140{,}000+24{,}000)}{100{,}000}=1.6{:}1 \qquad \frac{(100{,}000+27{,}000)}{60{,}000}=2.1{:}1$$

Once again, there is no general optimal value for the liquid ratio. To the extent that it measures an organization's ability to pay its debts in a crisis one might expect that it should not normally fall below 1:1. In 1992 the liquid ratio for Lucas Industries plc was 1.1:1 and for ICI was 1.0:1. However, even this rule of thumb is inappropriate in some cases. Most companies do not experience continuous crises and users might consider managers to be excessively conservative if they always carry extra liquid assets as insurance against the occurrence of an unlikely event. As with the working capital ratio, there exists for each industry a range within which the liquid ratio is deemed satisfactory.

In certain industries the manner in which trade is conducted dictates that the 'normal' liquid ratio is less than 1:1. A large supermarket chain which buys all its stock on credit but sells its products for cash would carry few debtors. It is unlikely that such a business would need a cash balance equal to its liabilities (implying a liquid ratio of 1:1 as debtors are negligible). This situation is confirmed by a glance at the liquidity position of two national supermarket chains, Tesco plc and Sainsbury plc, as reflected in their balance sheets on 29 February 1992 and 14 March 1992 respectively (Table 10.3). Both of these companies operate successfully with a liquid ratio below 0.40:1.

In most circumstances these companies can rely on regular cash receipts from customers to pay creditors as they fall due. As far as Maine Ltd is concerned, its immediate liquidity position seems secure, although it is necessary to determine whether the fall in the liquid ratio between years 1 and 2 is permanent or indicative of a longer-term trend.

The liquid ratio does not provide a complete picture of an organization's ability to survive a liquidity crisis. A strong liquid ratio might suggest that the organization is having difficulty in collecting its debts, whereas a low figure for current liabilities might suggest that creditors are insisting upon speedy payment. In this instance, the ratio may overstate the company's ability to survive a liquidity crisis.[3] On the other hand, the ratio ignores other means available to the organization for raising cash to settle its short-term liabilities. For a highly respected company, a ratio of less than 1:1 might be acceptable because the company's bankers are willing to provide bridging finance in the event of a temporary liquidity crisis.

(c) *Debtor payment period.* An increase in either the liquid or the working capital ratio may be the result of an increase in the debtors figure — perhaps because more goods have been sold on credit, or debtors have been allowed more time to pay, or a combination of the two. The debtor payment period measures the average length of time taken by debtors to pay amounts due to the organization. It is an important aspect of the assessment of management's ability to control working capital and is calculated as follows:

$$\text{Debtor payment period} = \frac{\text{Debtors}}{\text{Credit sales}} \times 365$$

Multiplying the ratio of debtors to credit sales by 365 expresses the payment period in days. Weeks or months could equally well be used. Assuming that all sales are on credit, the figures for Maine Ltd are:

	Year 2	Year 1
Debtor payment period	$\dfrac{140,000}{1,200,000} \times 365 = 43$ days	$\dfrac{100,000}{900,000} \times 365 = 41$ days

A long debtor payment period may have disadvantages. For example, the organization may incur high interest costs on the working capital needed to finance debtors, and also run the risk of incurring bad debts. An increase in the payment period may indicate that the organization is attracting less creditworthy customers, from whom it is more difficult and costly to extract due payments, and/or that there are inefficiencies in credit control management. Thus the increase in the debtor payment period of Maine Ltd might be viewed with some concern, particularly if it is consistent with a recent trend. On the other hand, a longer

---

3. Earlier in this section we suggested that ratios might be interpreted in conjunction with cash flow statements to provide information about the company's ability to generate cash. We shall examine cash flow statements in Chapter 11.

period may mean that fewer customers are taking advantage of any discounts offered, with a consequent reduction in that expense.

(d) *Creditor payment period.* The creditor payment period may also be expressed in months, weeks or days. Expressed in days, it is calculated as follows:

$$\text{Creditor payment period} = \frac{\text{Creditors}}{\text{Credit purchases}} \times 365$$

The creditor payment period represents the average length of time taken by an organization in paying amounts due to its creditors, and is another indicator of the success of management's working capital policies. A difficulty encountered when calculating this ratio in practice is that few companies disclose the figure for purchases (credit or cash) in their accounts. One must estimate the figure from the information which is provided.

In Chapter 7 we defined cost of goods sold as:

$$\text{Cost of goods sold} = \text{Opening stock} + \text{Cost of production} - \text{Closing stock}$$

This expression can be rearranged to define cost of production as:

$$\text{Cost of production} = \text{Cost of goods sold} + \text{Closing stock} - \text{Opening stock}$$

For an organization which undertakes no production (for example a supermarket chain), 'cost of production' is equal to purchases of stock, and the amount of purchases can be calculated by substituting 'purchases' for 'cost of production' in the above expression.

In the case of manufacturing and other companies for which 'cost of production' includes costs which are not incurred on credit (for example, production wages and machine depreciation), it is necessary to estimate what proportion of the total 'cost of production' is in respect of credit purchases. With respect to Maine Ltd, let us assume that:

(a) the company purchases all of its goods on credit;
(b) cost of production is a good approximation for 'purchases';
(c) stocks on hand at the beginning of Year 1 amounted to £45,000.

The calculation of the purchases figures for Maine Ltd is as follows:

	Cost of goods sold	+ Closing stock	− Opening stock	= Purchases
Year 1	720	+ 53	− 45	= 728
Year 2	900	+ 75	− 53	= 922

The figures for the creditor payment period are:

	Year 2	Year 1

Creditor payment period $\dfrac{100{,}000}{922{,}000} \times 365 = 40$ days $\dfrac{60{,}000}{728{,}000} \times 365 = 30$ days[4]

Maine Ltd has increased the average time taken to pay creditors, perhaps because of cash flow difficulties. An undesirable consequence of this increase may be the loss of discounts received for early payment. On the other hand, the company has obtained more credit from its suppliers, thus reducing the need to raise finance from other sources. An important question is whether the increased credit is available permanently. If not, Maine Ltd will have to make arrangements to replace it with other sources.

(e) *Stock holding period.*   The stock holding period (or 'stock turnover period') may also be expressed in any time dimension. Expressed in days it is calculated as follows:

$$\text{Stock holding period} = \frac{\text{Stock}}{\text{Cost of goods sold}} \times 365$$

This ratio measures the average length of time during which an organization holds its stock. For manufacturing firms separate calculations are strictly necessary for raw materials, work in progress and finished goods. The figures for Maine Ltd are:

	Year 2	Year 1

Stock holding period $\dfrac{75{,}000}{900{,}000} \times 365 = 30$ days $\dfrac{53{,}000}{720{,}000} \times 365 = 27$ days

The stock holding period is an important aspect of the evaluation of an organization's working capital management. A long holding period, implying high stock levels relative to the amount of goods sold, has some advantages — for example, it reduces the risk of stock levels falling to zero (stockouts) and the resultant inability to satisfy demand, and it provides more scope for bulk buying and large-scale production runs which may produce quantity discounts and other economies of scale. Alternatively it might indicate the existence of 'slow-moving' or obsolete stock. On the other hand, a short period, implying low stock levels, also has advantages. In particular it leads to lower storage, interest and other costs of holding stock. As with the other working capital ratios, it is hard to say whether Maine's stock holding period is optimal. A period of less than one month seems at first sight to be rather low, but this would not necessarily be the case

4. When the difference between the figures for opening and closing stock is small compared to the cost of goods sold figure, an acceptable approximation to the creditor payment period can be obtained by calculating the expression Creditors/Cost of goods sold × 365. The figures for Maine Ltd produced by this calculation are 41 days and 30 days.

for an organization dealing in perishable goods (for example in 1992 the stock holding period of Tesco plc was 13 days). It would be very low, however, for a business engaged in the manufacture of chemicals and pharmaceuticals or in construction (for example, the stock holding periods in 1991 of ICI plc and Taylor Woodrow plc were 99 days and 97 days respectively).

In this section we have already mentioned two reasons why the various liquidity ratios should be interpreted with care — first, that different industries have different norms, and second, that a high ratio may give a misleading impression of financial strength whilst disguising an inefficient use of funds. A third reason (alluded to earlier in this chapter) concerns the danger in selecting any single figure from an entity's balance sheet, i.e. a single balance sheet figure may be unrepresentative of the year's balance on any particular element of working capital. Managers have been known to manipulate individual working capital figures at the year-end in order to produce apparently healthy ratios. This practice is known as 'window dressing'.

One form of window dressing involves the raising of a short-term loan towards the end of the financial year and repaying the loan soon after the balance sheet date. For example, suppose a company which prepares its accounts to 31 December has the following liquid ratio on 27 December 19X0:

$$\frac{\text{Liquid assets}}{\text{Current liabilities}} = \frac{900,000}{1,200,000} = 0.75\text{:}1$$

The ratio for the company at the end of the previous year was 0.85:1 and the norm for the industry is within the range 0.8:1 to 1:1. The management could increase the liquid ratio to a figure comparable with that of last year and to within the industry's acceptable range by borrowing, say, £600,000 as a short-term loan. The effect of this transaction would be to increase *both* liquid assets (cash) *and* current liabilities (short-term loan) by £600,000. The new liquid ratio would be calculated as:

$$\frac{\text{Liquid assets}}{\text{Current liabilities}} = \frac{1,500,000}{1,800,000} = 0.83\text{:}1$$

The practice of window dressing is referred to in an accounting standard — *SSAP17: Accounting for post balance sheet events* (issued August 1980). However, the standard does not require that artificial transactions designed to alter the appearance of the balance sheet should be reversed in the accounts. Rather, it requires that the effect of such transactions should be disclosed and the standard is generally regarded as rather ineffectual with respect to window dressing.

Readers of published accounts are less likely to be misled by attempts to improve liquidity in the balance sheet by window dressing if they analyse the balance sheet ratios in conjunction with the cash flow statement. In the following chapter we shall examine how changes in the level of working capital (stock, debtors and creditors) have a direct impact upon a company's operating cash flow.

Longer-term solvency

Long-run solvency is concerned with the ability of a company to survive over many years. Declining liquidity and profitability ratios can provide an indication of long-run difficulties. In addition, survival may also be affected by the organization's long-term financial commitments. These commitments are often closely related to the manner in which the organization finances its operations.

We discussed capital structure in Chapter 8. In Section 8.5 we explained the importance of an organization's gearing ratio and suggested that several forms of the ratio can be calculated. Basically, the gearing ratio measures the amount of fixed interest capital raised by an organization as a proportion of the total capital raised. Often, an analyst interested in an organization's long-run solvency will calculate the ratio from the following expression, which relies on balance sheet data:

$$\text{Gearing ratio} = \frac{\text{Long-term fixed interest capital}}{\text{Total long-term capital employed}}$$

where the numerator comprises long-term loans and preference share capital, and the denominator comprises long-term loans, preference share capital, ordinary share capital and reserves.

An alternative gearing ratio is the ratio of long-term fixed interest capital to equity capital (ordinary share capital and reserves), commonly known as the debt:equity ratio. Both measures indicate the relationship between the organization's loan and equity capital. The figures for Maine Ltd, using the first ratio described above,[5] are:

	Year 2	*Year 1*
Gearing ratio	$\frac{240{,}000}{664{,}000} = 0.361$ or 36.1%	$\frac{0}{330{,}000} = 0$

Maine Ltd has increased its gearing from zero to over 36%. This increase should be of interest to any user who wishes to estimate the future cash flows accruing to the shareholders of Maine Ltd, and the risk attached to those cash flows. Its impact can be seen more clearly in the income statement. In Year 2 Maine Ltd pays bond interest of £36,000. This payment must be made whether or not the

5. The figures for Maine Ltd, using the second ratio described in the text are:

	Year 2	*Year 1*
Gearing ratio	$\frac{240{,}000}{424{,}000} = 0.566$ or 56.6%	$\frac{0}{330{,}000} = 0$

It is imperative that the reader of accounts is consistent in the use of *one* of the two ratios described when comparing the gearing ratios of different companies or of the same company over time.

company generates a profit, and we saw in Chapter 8 (see Table 8.2) that the profit available for the shareholders of a geared company is more sensitive to changes in pre-interest profit than is the profit available to the shareholders of a purely equity financed company, which was Maine Ltd's position in year 1.

However, as we explained in Section 8.5, the increased financial risk of the owners (as a result of the requirement to meet fixed interest payments each year and the volatility of their own returns) is no less if the loans are short-term. In recent years many companies have used revolving short-term loans and overdrafts rather than long-term loans to finance longer-lived assets. In addition, we noted previously that long-term loans are transformed into current liabilities on the balance sheet in the year prior to repayment. A gearing ratio based upon *long-term* fixed interest capital only, could be misleading and hence we, and many analysts, prefer to calculate the gearing ratio as follows:

$$\text{Gearing ratio} = \frac{\text{Total fixed interest capital}}{\text{Total fixed interest capital plus equity capital}}$$

where the numerator comprises long-term loans, short-term loans, overdrafts and preference share capital, and the denominator comprises all these elements plus ordinary share capital and reserves. As Maine Ltd has no short-term loans or overdrafts outstanding, the gearing ratio calculated in this way is identical to the ratio calculated above.

The issue of new loan capital often has both benefits and costs for the owners of a company. We saw earlier, in the section dealing with 'profitability' ratios, that one effect of issuing bonds is to increase the return to the owners of Maine Ltd (as the new loan capital has a cost below the return which Maine Ltd earns on its total capital). At the same time, the increased gearing ratio has resulted in an increase in the financial risk of the owners. Both of these effects are reflected in the income statement and this has led to the emergence of an income statement ratio which measures the impact of gearing. The 'times interest covered' ratio calculates the number of times the interest payment is 'covered' by the operating profit before interest. The figures for Maine Ltd using this ratio are:

	Year 2	*Year 1*
Times interest covered	$\dfrac{130,000}{36,000} = 3.6$ times	$\dfrac{50,000}{0} = \infty$

One advantage of the income statement ratio is that it focuses upon the *impact* of the change in capital structure. It provides information which might be used as direct input into a decision model assessing the longer-term solvency of the business, i.e. in estimating future cash flows and their associated risk. In addition, gearing ratios calculated from balance sheet figures are of limited use if they are based on the book values of loan and equity capital. The use of market values provides a better measure of the long-term capital position of the organization.

10.4   Limitations of historical cost ratios

We have mentioned previously that the numerator and the denominator of a given ratio should be consistent, i.e. profit available to shareholders should be related to shareholders' capital employed; profit before interest should be related to all long-term capital employed, etc. In addition, the numerator and denominator should be expressed in measurement scales which are comparable and which thus provide a meaningful result. For example, the ratio of liquid assets (in £) to current liabilities (also in £) produces a meaningful result (i.e. the proportionate excess, or shortfall, of liquid assets over current liabilities), whereas a ratio of sales (in £) to the average age of fixed assets (in years) does not.

On the face of it, the ratios we have examined in this chapter appear to produce meaningful results — the measurement scales appear to be in harmony. For each ratio both the numerator and denominator are expressed in pounds (£). For example, the utilization ratio, expressed as

$$\frac{\text{Sales in } £}{\text{Long-term capital in } £}$$

produces a ratio for Maine Ltd in year 2 of

$$\frac{£1,200,000}{£664,000} = 1.81$$

Similarly the utilization ratio for ICI plc for the year ended 31 December 1991 calculated from its published historical cost financial statements is

$$\frac{£12,488 \text{ million}}{£7,605 \text{ million}} = 1.64$$

We have interpreted this ratio as the amount of sales revenue generated for each £1 of long-term capital invested in the company. But consider what is the aim of producing this (or any other) ratio. We are interpreting historical data in order to obtain predictive information. We are interested in the current year's amount of sales revenue generated per £1 of capital invested largely as a basis for predicting future years' sales revenues (and, eventually, cash flows). Would an extra £1 invested in ICI at the beginning of 1992 generate an additional £1.64 of sales revenue? It is unlikely because the numerator and the denominator of the utilization ratio are not in fact consistent with each other. It is not sufficient that they are both expressed in £s. The sales figure is expressed in £s reflecting current (1991) prices, but the long-term capital figure comprises amounts invested over a period of many years. If we describe the denominator as 'total assets less current liabilities' (TA – CL) the problem is clearer. The denominator includes assets at their historical costs, which reflect some prices which existed in 1975 (property) and in 1980 (plant and machinery).

The utilization ratio for ICI plc, as calculated above, should, strictly, be described as follows:

$$\text{Utilization ratio} = \frac{\text{Sales (1991 prices)}}{\text{TA} - \text{CL (1975–1991 prices)}} = 1.64$$

In other words, if ICI could obtain another £1 of capital in 1991 *and invest it in assets at prices reigning in the period 1975–1991* the ratio of 1.64 may represent a good indicator of future utilization ratios. However, ICI must purchase assets at their current prices, and hence a better indicator of future asset utilization would be represented by a ratio calculated as follows:

$$\text{Utilization ratio} = \frac{\text{Sales (1991 prices)}}{\text{TA} - \text{CL (1991 prices)}}$$

This ratio requires all assets in the balance sheet to be restated at their current costs and would generate a figure which would be significantly lower than the historical cost ratio of 1.64.

A similar problem affects the ratio for the operating profit percentage, which was expressed previously as:

$$\text{Operating profit percentage} = \frac{\text{Operating profit before interest in £s}}{\text{Sales in £s}}$$

The operating profit percentage calculated from the historical cost financial statements of ICI is

$$\frac{£1{,}033 \text{ million}}{£12{,}488 \text{ million}} \times 100 = 8.3\%$$

However, although sales are expressed in current (1991) prices, operating profit is not. Many components of operating profit are expressed in 1991 prices (sales, wages, rent, rates, heating, etc.) but depreciation, in particular, is based upon prices which existed at the time of purchase of the relevant assets. As we have already noted these assets may have been bought as long ago as 1975. Similar problems can occur if older items of stock are included in cost of goods sold. Both problems can be avoided by the use of current costs in the income statement, an area we shall discuss further in Chapters 13 and 14.

We explained earlier that if the asset utilization and operating profit percentage ratios are multiplied, they produce a return on investment ratio as follows:

$$\frac{\text{Sales}}{\text{TA} - \text{CL}} \times \frac{\text{Operating profit before interest}}{\text{Sales}}$$

$$= \frac{\text{Operating profit before interest}}{\text{Total assets less current liabilities}}$$
$$\text{(or long-term capital employed)}$$

Closer examination of the component parts of the ratio reveals that the 'sales' figures cancel out and what remains is a ratio which comprises, for ICI, a profit figure calculated using a mixture of historical prices from 1975–1991, and an asset figure calculated using a (different) mixture of historical prices from 1975–1991. The resulting figure is likely to be of limited usefulness to decision makers.

The potential usefulness of a return on investment figure, both as an indicator of overall performance and as a guide to future performance, would appear to demand that the constituent elements of the income statement and the balance sheet be expressed in comparable current prices. Had Maine Ltd used some form of 'current' cost accounting, the return on investment ratio would have provided a much better indication of management's efficiency in using resources. For example, if asset values and operating costs had been based on current replacement costs, the ratio would have provided an indicator of management's ability to generate sufficient funds to replace assets as they are used, and hence to ensure the long-run survival of the company.

The usefulness of other profitability ratios is similarly limited if costs are measured on an historical rather than a current cost basis. For example, an organization exhibiting a satisfactory gross profit percentage, i.e a surplus of sales revenue over the historical cost of stock used, may not be generating sufficient funds either to replace the stock at current prices or to meet its operating costs. We examine in further detail the differences between historical cost and replacement cost accounting in Chapter 13.

Similar criticisms can be levelled at the ratio expressing the return on owners' capital employed. The figure for owners' capital employed is based on the historical value of capital provided, both in the form of capital paid in and in the form of retained profits (reserves). As far as shareholders are concerned, the real cost of their investment in the company (the 'opportunity cost' of their investment) is represented by the amount sacrificed by not selling their shares, i.e. the *market value* of their shares. The same is true for potential buyers of shares who have to pay the market value rather than the book value to acquire shareholdings. This problem would still exist if the company used some form of current cost accounting, although the differences between the 'book' figures used in the ratio and the 'relevant' return and income figures described above may be smaller. The return to ordinary shareholders depends on the dividends they receive and expect to receive and on the market value of their shares. Neither of these is included in the calculation of return on owners' capital based on the company's income statement and balance sheet.

In addition, profit after interest may have little relationship to cash paid to, or available for, the owners of Maine Ltd. As we shall argue in Chapter 13, the owners' return depends both on the cash distributed by the business during the period and on the value of the business at the end of the period, which in turn depends on the cash expected to be distributed in future periods.

10.5 Summary of the analysis

The financial ratios we have calculated for Maine Ltd for years 1 and 2 are summarized in Table 10.5. In spite of the limitations we have discussed, the ratios, together with the financial statements shown in Table 10.1, do provide a picture of the change in Maine's performance and position between the two years, and may be used as *part* of a process to predict its likely future performance. Maine Ltd has increased its capital during year 2 by £334,000, comprising £94,000 retained profits and £240,000 new long-term debt. The new capital has been used primarily to purchase additional land and buildings and plant and machinery; much of the increase in stocks and debtors is financed by an increase in creditors.

The expansion appears to have been successful. Although fewer sales were generated per pound invested in net assets, sales increased during year 2 by $33\frac{1}{3}$% while the cost of goods sold increased by only 25%. This resulted in an increase in gross profit from 20% to 25%, and although overhead expenses increased by 30%, the operating profit percentage increased from 5.6% to 10.8%. This increase in margin outweighed the fall in the utilization ratio and the company was able to increase its return on total capital employed from 15.2% to 19.6%. Because of the increase in gearing (from zero to over 36%) return on owners' capital increased from 15.2% to 22.2%, benefitting from both the introduction of 'cheaper' debt financing and the increase in total return. The liquidity ratios appear satisfactory for both years. Decreases in the working capital ratios between years

Table 10.5 *Maine Ltd — summary of financial ratios*

	Year 2	Year 1
Profitability		
Return on total long-term capital	19.6%	15.2%
Utilization ratio	1.81%	2.73%
Operating profit percentage	10.8%	5.6%
Gross profit percentage	25.0%	20.0%
Return on owners' capital	22.2%	15.2%
Liquidity		
Working capital ratio	2.4:1	3.0:1
Liquid ratio	1.6:1	2.1:1
Debtor payment period	43 days	41 days
Creditor payment period	40 days	30 days
Stock holding period	30 days	27 days
Capital structure		
Gearing ratio	36.1%	0
Times interest covered	3.6	∞

1 and 2 may be cause for concern if they indicate the start of a longer-term trend. On the other hand, if the changes are permanent they may indicate increased efficiency in the management of working capital. Further analysis of working capital reveals that Maine Ltd is holding its stock for longer and is granting a longer period of credit to its customers. However, it has also increased significantly the average time taken to pay its creditors. It is important to ascertain whether this increased credit is available permanently. Although the increase in gearing has resulted in an increased equity return, it has also increased the financial risk borne by ordinary shareholders. As we noted earlier, a more reliable indicator of the success of the expansion for equity holders would include consideration of its impact on the market value of their shares.

In this chapter we have discussed the usefulness and limitations of a number of important financial ratios concerned with profitability, liquidity and solvency. Many ratios are limited by the fact that they are based on historical cost accounting measures. We have argued that, despite this limitation, they are of some use in appraising an organization's past performance, and in making judgements about its likely future performance. Nevertheless, there are at least two weaknesses in using historical cost accounting measures as a basis for ratio analysis. The first is that the data are historical. We cannot stress too strongly that ratio analysis is not a substitute for forecasts of future sales, costs and cash flows, but rather that it is part of the process for generating and corroborating such forecasts. Hence, a key question concerning the success of the expansion of Maine Ltd, discussed in this chapter, is: 'To what extent will the improved performance resulting from the expansion be sustained in the future?' It is forecasts, not measures of past performance, that are of importance to the decision models of users of financial reports.

The second weakness relates to the use of figures derived from the conventional accounting model. All the ratios calculated in this chapter comprise figures extracted from the income statement and/or the balance sheet. These statements are part of the conventional system of accrual accounting and hence many of the figures extracted from them are subject to the preferences, judgements and objectives of the managers and accountants of Maine Ltd. This weakness may be (partially) overcome by analysing the more objective cash flow statement. An analysis of the cash flow statement is essential also for an assessment of an organization's liquidity and solvency situation and prospects. We stated earlier in this chapter that information about an organization's ability to generate cash could be provided by ratio analysis in conjunction with an analysis of the cash flow statement. We shall analyse the cash flow statement in the next chapter.

Discussion topics

1. You have been approached by a bank manager who has asked your advice on whether to make a loan to a client. The client, who is a retailer, has provided

copies of her profit and loss accounts and balance sheets for the past three years. Describe how you would assess the client's current liquidity position and her liquidity prospects.

2. Discuss the main roles and limitations of ratio analysis, and explain the extent to which ratio analysis alone can be used to appraise an organization's performance.

3. For each of the following ratios, explain briefly how the ratio is calculated, describe the aspects of an organization's activities about which it provides information, and discuss the ratio's particular limitations:

    (a) Working capital ratio
    (b) Liquid ratio
    (c) Creditor payment period
    (d) Stock holding period
    (e) Debtor payment period
    (f) Gearing ratio
    (g) Return on total capital
    (h) Return on owners' capital
    (i) Gross profit percentage
    (j) Operating profit percentage

4. Discuss the problem of establishing 'benchmarks', with which a particular firm's ratios may be compared.

5. Explain how you would use ratio analysis to analyse the performance and position of E.H. Booth and Co. Ltd.

Exercises

10.1 The following are summaries of the published accounts of Siegmund Ltd for the past two years:

Balance sheets as at:	31 October 19X6		31 October 19X7	
	£'000	£'000	£'000	£'000
Ordinary share capital		1,200		1,200
Retained profits		270		290
		1,470		1,490
10% loan stock		800		800
		2,270		2,290

Fixed assets:				
Land and buildings, at cost	520		550	
less: Accumulated depreciation	80	440	90	460
Machinery and vehicles, at cost	1,120		1,340	
less: Accumulated depreciation	580	540	750	590
		980		1,050
Current assets:				
Stock, at lower of cost or market value	830		980	
Debtors, less provision for doubtful debts	650		570	
Cash	120		40	
	1,600		1,590	
less: Current liabilities (creditors)	310	1,290	350	1,240
		2,270		2,290

Profit and loss accounts year ended	*31 October 19X6*		*31 October 19X7*	
	£'000	*£'000*	*£'000*	*£'000*
Sales revenue		2,200		3,200
less: Cost of sales		1,610		2,590
Gross profit		590		610
less: General expenses	210		230	
Depreciation	160	370	180	410
Operating profit		220		200
less: Loan interest		80		80
Net profit for the year		140		120
add: Retained profits at beginning of year		300		270
Available for distribution		440		390
less: Dividends paid		170		100
Retained profits at end of year		270		290

No fixed assets were sold during either year. All dividends due had been paid by 31 October 19X7.

- Interpret the above accounts for a shareholder in Siegmund Ltd who is not familiar with accounting practices. Calculate any ratios that you think may be helpful to the shareholder in appraising the company's performance, and comment on the limitations of such ratios for financial analysis.

10.2 Hagen is considering whether or not to invest a substantial portion of his private capital in Siegfried Ltd. He asks for your advice. Your main source of information about Siegfried Ltd is the balance sheet and profit and loss account for the year to 31 December 19X4:

Balance sheet as at 31 December 19X4			£
Fixed assets			
Land and building (at cost)			200,000
Plant and machinery (at cost less depreciation)			800,000
			1,000,000
Trade investments (at cost)			50,000
Current assets			
Stocks		450,000	
Debtors		1,050,000	
Cash		50,000	
		1,550,000	
less: Current liabilities			
Creditors	400,000		
Taxation	150,000	550,000	1,000,000
			2,050,000
Represented by:			
Share capital and reserves			
Ordinary shares of £1 each			1,500,000
Retained profits			550,000
			2,050,000

Profit and loss account for the year ended 31 December 19X4

	£	£
Sales		3,000,000
less: Cost of sales		1,990,000
Gross profit		1,010,000
less: Operating expenses	410,000	
Bad debts	150,000	
Depreciation	110,000	670,000
Net profit before taxation		340,000
Taxation based on profit above		150,000
Net profit after taxation		190,000
Dividend at 10% on ordinary shares		150,000
Profit retained		40,000
Retained profits, brought forward		510,000
Retained profits in balance sheet		550,000

You also ascertain that Siegfried Ltd has been in business for five years and produces plastic toys. The current market value of its ordinary shares is 125p each.

- (a) Advise Hagen as to his proposed investment on the basis of the available information.
- (b) Advise Hagen what additional information he should seek about the financial affairs of Siegfried Ltd before making a final decision.

10.3 Sharpless Ltd is an old-established firm which manufactures machine parts for the textile industry. For some time now the company's profits have been declining and this year as you prepare to audit the accounts you determine to examine the situation thoroughly.

You have in your possession the most recent statistics published by the Centre for InterFirm Comparison which state that in this particular industry the average company:

1. sells 90p of sales for every £1 invested in assets;
2. earns a gross profit of 15% on each sale;
3. returns a net profit, before interest, of 10% on total assets employed, and provides shareholders with an earnings return of 12% on their capital employed;
4. has on average a stock turnover period, a debtors' credit period and creditors' credit period of 9 weeks, 8 weeks and 7 weeks respectively.

On arrival at the company, you are presented with the 'draft accounts' for 19X8 prepared by the unqualified bookkeeper who heads the accounts department. These draft accounts are shown below. During your visit, the directors announce their intention of paying a dividend of 4p per share.

Profit and loss account

	£
Depreciation — plant and machinery	15,000
Cost of goods sold	415,000
Debenture interest	12,000
Taxation	6,000
Depreciation — motor vehicles	10,000
General expenses	52,000
	510,000
Sales	530,000
Net profit	20,000

Balances after completing profit and loss account

	£'000
Plant and machinery — cost	300
Motor vehicles — cost	90
Accrued expenses	10
Stock on 31 December 19X8	220
Taxation liability	20
Trade creditors	60

Land and buildings — cost	330
Share capital (£1 shares)	270
Reserves at 1 January 19X8	322
Profit for the year	20
Debtors	105
Cash	117
8% debentures	150
Accumulated depreciation:	
Plant and machinery	240
Motor vehicles	70

- (a) Prepare a profit and loss account for Sharpless Ltd for the year ended 31 December 19X8, and a balance sheet as at that date.
- (b) Draft a report to the chairperson of Sharpless Ltd giving reasons for your concern about the company's position, and suggesting possible future action to be taken by the company.

10.4 Below are percentages, etc., for samples of companies in the following industries:

Brewing	Building materials' manufacturers
Cotton (spinning and weaving)	Entertainment and sport
Building and construction	Retail distribution

- Try to identify each industry in the table by comparing it with 'all companies' bearing in mind the obvious facts about each, and also the information given. The order of the columns (A, B, C, etc.) is not necessarily that of the above list.

	All companies	Industry					
		A	B	C	D	E	F
Assets as % of net assets (i.e. total assets minus total current liabilities)							
Fixed assets	52	39	61	84	45	58	94
Stocks	39	46	20	14	63	33	11
Debtors	24	15	22	8	52	28	7
Cash and securities	20	21	24	14	22	25	14
Total assets	135	121	127	120	182	144	126
Bank overdraft	4	2	2	1	11	2	7
Dividends, tax due and other provisions	12	10	11	8	15	19	8
Trade and other creditors	19	9	14	11	56	23	11
Total current liabilities	35	21	27	20	82	44	26
*Gearing ratio** — range in which median company is found		0–10	0–10	11–20	0–10	11–20	11–20

*Percentage of fixed interest and fixed (preference) dividends to total income.

Brewing: Stocks deteriorate fast. Little credit is given or received.

Cotton (spinning and weaving):   Raw materials are bought on 10 days' credit, and sales are on 14 days' credit. Spinners can buy at cheaper prices and get a better range of choice just after the harvest. In the above sample most of the companies prepared their accounts soon after the harvest. The problems facing the industry make borrowing difficult.

Building: The workload is variable. Contracts take a long time to finish. Some big jobs are overseas. Much of the work is done by subcontractors. Costing is slow, and 'retention money' is often held by the customer until the work proves satisfactory. Because of the dangers of taking credit too soon for profit on contracts, debts are often valued at cost and included with stock (which may also include some land and plant).

Building materials' manufacturers: Trade creditors are rather low because of vertical integration. Production may be continuous, and investment in plant high per worker. Trade is poor in winter, and so (if the firm's year ends then) liquidity must be ample yet debtors may be low compared with 'all companies'.

Entertainment and sport: This includes cinemas, stadiums, etc.

Retailing: Although some firms sell for cash only, others give extended credit (e.g. hire purchase). Wholesalers may provide much of the finance.

10.5 Jane Pinkerton's accounts for 19X6 were as follows:

Profit and loss account, year ended 31 December 19X6

	£	£
Sales		40,000
less: Cost of goods sold		32,000
Gross profit		8,000
less: General expenses	2,000	
Depreciation	3,000	5,000
Net profit		3,000

Balance sheet as at 31 December 19X6

	£		£	£
Capital account	30,000	Fixed assets		
		at cost	45,000	
		less: Depreciation	15,000	30,000
Creditors				
(for goods)	4,000	Current assets:		
		Stock	4,500	
Bank overdraft	5,500	Debtors	5,000	9,500
	39,500			39,500

The following information describes Jane Pinkerton's transactions during the year ended 31 December 19X7:

1. Sales increased by 10%.
2. The gross profit rate was 25% of sales.
3. General expenses (all paid in cash) were £2,500.
4. Depreciation of fixed assets was £3,000.
5. The average period of credit allowed to debtors was 3 months.
6. The average period of credit allowed by creditors was 2 months.
7. The stock turnover was 8 times per year.

The average period of credit allowed to debtors and by creditors, and the stock turnover rate are calculated using the *average* of the balances at 1 January 19X7 and 31 December 19X7, for debtors, creditors and stock respectively. All purchases and sales of goods were on credit.

- Prepare Jane Pinkerton's profit and loss account for the year ended 31 December 19X7, and her balance sheet as at that date.

10.6 The following balances have been extracted from the books of Isolde Ltd as at 30 September 19X1:

	£
Creditors	18,900
Sales	240,000
Land at cost	54,000
Buildings at cost	114,000
Furniture and fittings at cost	66,000
Bank overdraft	18,000
Depreciation — buildings	18,000
— furniture and fittings	30,000
Discounts received	5,292
Unappropriated profit at 1 October 19X0	6,000
Provision for doubtful debts	2,448
Goodwill	49,200
Cash in hand	696
Stock at 1 October 19X0	42,744
Interim dividend on preference shares	1,800
Rates	6,372
Wages and salaries	24,000
Insurance	5,688
Returns inwards	1,116
General expenses	1,308
Debtors	37,920
Purchases	131,568
Debenture interest	1,200
Bad debts	2,028
5% debentures	48,000
6% £1 preference shares	60,000
£1 ordinary shares	60,000

General reserve	30,000
Share premium	3,000

Additional information:

1. Stock on hand at 30 September 19X1 was £46,638.
2. Insurance paid in advance was £300.
3. Wages owing were £840.
4. Depreciation is to be provided at 10% on the cost of buildings and at 20% on the written down value of furniture and fittings.
5. Provision for doubtful debts is to be reduced to 5% of debtors.
6. Debenture interest outstanding is £1,200.
7. The directors propose to pay a 5% ordinary dividend and the final preference dividend and to transfer £24,000 to general reserve.

- (a) Prepare the profit and loss account of Isolde Ltd for the year ended 30 September 19X1 and a balance sheet as at that date.
  (b) Examine the accounts you have prepared in (a) above and then answer the questions below:

    (i) How did the share premium account arise?
    (ii) How could the goodwill account have arisen?
    (iii) What is the rate of return on net capital employed and what is the significance of this figure?
    (iv) Which of the reserves are capital reserves and which are revenue reserves, and what, in principle, is the difference between the two?
    (v) The company is relatively highly geared; what does this mean?

10.7 The Cleek Finance Company is attempting to evaluate an applicant (Roak Ltd) for a short-term loan. The following table presents some information concerning the 'average' company in the industry in which Roak Ltd operates, and the corresponding information for Roak Ltd.

	Roak Ltd 31.12.19X0 £	Industry Average 31.12.19X0 £
Cash	2,000	6,000
Short-term investments	2,500	4,000
Accounts receivable (debtors)	29,000	36,000
Prepayments	4,500	7,000
Closing stock	36,000	48,000
Opening stock	32,000	46,000
Accounts payable (creditors)	18,000	25,000
Other current liabilities	11,000	15,000
Sales (all credit)	210,000	330,000
Cost of goods sold	160,000	250,000

- (a) Compute the following ratios for both Roak Ltd and the 'average' company in the industry.
    (i) current ratio

       (ii) quick ratio
      (iii) average number of days to collect accounts receivable
      (iv) average number of days inventory held in stock
      (v) average number of days taken to pay accounts payable.

  (b) In the light of the information provided and your calculations in part (a), prepare a report for Cleek's loan officer outlining those factors which might be useful to her in making her decision.

  (c) What limitations do you see in your analysis and what additional information might be helpful to the loan officer in making her decision?

10.8 Sophie and Jack are planning to set up in business together as Sojie Systems Ltd, selling computer systems and advice. Although they are confident that they have the necessary technical know-how and understanding of the computer business (they both currently work for large computing firms) they are unsure of the financial implications of their plans and have written to you for some advice. You ascertain the following information from their letter.

The company will issue 200,000 £1 ordinary shares which Sophie and Jack will purchase equally at par value for cash. They hope to raise a further £60,000 by way of taking out a loan from the bank at an annual interest rate of 12%. In addition, Jack's mother has agreed to lend the business £20,000 at an interest rate of 10% p.a. Both loans will be repayable after five years.

They have undertaken a market survey of the likely future demand for their services and consequently expect to make average sales of £20,000 per month for the first 8 months. Thereafter they anticipate average monthly sales will increase to £30,000. All sales will be on credit. However, from past experience of the computer business, they anticipate that they will need to employ a debt collection agency to recover about 7% of their total sales. Such agencies normally charge a commission of 10% on all debts recovered. Even after employing a debt collection agency, it is probable that 2% of all debts will be irrecoverable. They expect to make a gross profit margin of 40% of sales.

Sojie Systems Ltd will purchase two cars for £8,000 each which will be required to enable Sophie and Jack to visit clients and make sales. The cars will be replaced every three years at which time the cars will be traded-in at approximately 25% of their original cost. The cars will be used more intensively in the early years of the business, as the client base is built up, and hence depreciation is to be charged using the sum-of-the-years-digits method. The business will be operated from an office building which is to be rented at £500 per quarter, payable in advance. Office equipment costing £25,000 is expected to last for ten years and is to be depreciated on a straight line basis. Overhead expenses are estimated to be 20% of the cost of sales.

Sophie and Jack believe that the venture will be financially viable if the company makes a return of at least 25% on capital employed in the first year of business.

■ (a) Calculate the projected profit for Sojie Systems Ltd for the first year of business.

    (b) Draft a letter to Sophie and Jack explaining whether, on the information they have provided, they will achieve their required rate of return on capital employed and pointing out the problems and limitations of using the forecast rate of return as an indicator of future performance.

Further reading

Holmes, G. and Sugden, D., *Interpreting Company Reports and Accounts*, Woodhead-Faulkner, 1990.

Lev, B., *Financial Statement Analysis: A New Approach*, Prentice-Hall International, 1974.

Parker, R.H., *Understanding Company Financial Statements*, Penguin, 1988.

Reid, W. and Myddleton, D., *The Meaning of Company Accounts*, Gower, 1988.

Tarmari, M., *Financial Ratios: Analysis and Prediction*, Paul Elek, 1978.

Whittington, G., 'The usefulness of accounting data in measuring the economic performance of firms', *Journal of Accounting and Public Policy*, Winter 1988.

CHAPTER

11

Interpretation of

Accounts: Cash

Flow Statements

Most business organizations engage in financing, investing and operating activities in order to generate a profit. In the previous chapter we analysed two major financial statements which provide information on an organization's business activities. The balance sheet describes the organization's financial position at a point in time. In the balance sheet, the results of investment activities are represented by assets and the results of financing activities are represented by liabilities and owners' equity. The income statement describes what happened to the organization during the period between two balance sheets. However, the income statement reflects only *operating* activities. It focuses upon the matching of revenues and costs. It does not reflect the consequences of the *financing* and *investment* decisions taken between two balance sheet dates. A financing decision might involve an issue of shares, or the taking out of a long-term loan. An investment decision might involve the purchase of fixed assets, or the repayment of a long-term loan. Further, by focusing upon the *matching* of operating revenues and costs, the income statement fails to identify the often erratic movements in operating cash flows caused by, for example, the build up of stocks or the slow payment of invoices by debtors.

Thus neither the balance sheet nor the income statement can provide the answers to such important questions as:

(a) How much cash was generated by the company's operating activities and how was it spent?
(b) In which new financing and investment activities did the organization engage during the year?
(c) How much of the new investment was financed by the organization's operating activities and how much was provided by increased borrowing or increased share capital?

333

(d) Why did the mix of assets change during the year?
(e) Where did the organization raise cash in order to redeem its long-standing debt?

Yet the answers to these questions are essential for an assessment of an organization's future prospects because the financing and investment decisions taken in one year affect an organization's profitability, liquidity and solvency for many years in the future.

There is therefore a need for a financial statement which explains the changes between two balance sheets; which discloses where management invested existing funds (i.e. employed the organization's capital) in order to satisfy the interests of participants; and which discloses the sources from which management obtained additional funds to take advantage of new opportunities and satisfy the unfulfilled needs of the participants. Such a statement exists. The results of these 'financial management' decisions are disclosed in the *cash flow statement*.

The cash flow statement discloses the sources and uses of cash during the accounting period. By showing where management committed available cash (uses), acquired additional cash (sources), reduced existing investments (sources), and reduced outstanding claims against the organization (uses), the cash flow statement should assist an external user in an evaluation of the effect of financial management decisions taken during the year. As we explained in the previous chapter when examining ratio analysis, the user must then decide whether these cash movements are 'normal' (in relation to past movements and comparable industry data) or 'abnormal' and thus require further analysis.

11.1   Sources and uses of cash

A close relationship exists between the cash flow statement and the balance sheet. Because the cash balance is an asset (or a liability) in the balance sheet, the nature of the double-entry bookkeeping process means that any change in the cash balance must be reflected by a change in some other balance sheet item or items. Let us explore this relationship further in order to identify the major sources and uses of cash and to better understand the alternative methods of presenting a cash flow statement.

The basic expanded accounting equation is expressed as:

$$FA + Cash + Other\ CA = CL + LTL + OI + NI \tag{11.1}$$

where FA is fixed assets, Other CA is current assets other than cash, CL is current liabilities, LTL is long-term liabilities, OI is ownership interest, and NI is net income (revenue − expenses). We can rearrange this expression to focus upon the cash position:

$$Cash = (CL - Other\ CA) + LTL + OI + NI - FA \tag{11.2}$$

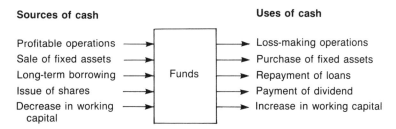

Figure 11.1 *Common sources and uses of cash*

Using the symbol Δ to mean 'change in' we can see that any *changes* in cash must be balanced by one or more changes in the accounts on the right-hand side of the equation:

$$\Delta Cash = \Delta(CL - Other\ CA) + \Delta LTL + \Delta OI + \Delta NI - \Delta FA \qquad (11.3)$$

No matter how complex a company's cash flow statement might appear, or how many items appear on the statement, equation 11.3 shows that there are only five basic sources, and four basic uses, of cash which can explain a change in the cash balance from one period to the next. Thus, an *increase* in the cash balance must be financed from one or more of the five sources of cash represented on the right-hand side of equation 11.3, i.e. a *decrease* in working capital (e.g. a reduction in stock levels or an increase in the amount owing to suppliers), an *increase* in long-term liabilities (e.g. new borrowing), an *increase* in ownership interest (e.g. a new share issue), an *increase* in net income (e.g. income from operations), and/or a *decrease* in fixed assets (e.g. the disposal of plant).

Conversely, a *decrease* in the cash balance means that cash has been used elsewhere. Again this will be reflected in the accounts on the right-hand side of equation 11.3, i.e. as an *increase* in working capital (e.g. an increase in stock levels or the period of credit given to trade debtors, or a decrease in the amount owing to suppliers), as a *decrease* in long-term liabilities (e.g. repayment of a loan), a *decrease* in ownership interest (e.g. payment of a dividend), a *decrease* in net income (e.g. a loss), and/or an *increase* in fixed assets (e.g. purchase of machinery). The common sources and uses of cash are summarized in Figure 11.1.

The above analysis of the sources and uses of cash provides a useful starting point for the preparation of a cash flow statement, to which we now turn.

11.2   Illustration of the preparation of a cash flow statement

The balance sheets of Wembley Ltd, at 31 December 19X0 and 31 December 19X1, are shown in Table 11.1. No fixed assets were sold during 19X1 (i.e. the increase

Table 11.1 *Wembley Ltd — balance sheets and income statement*

Balance sheet as at 31 December	19X1 £'000	19X1 £'000	19X0 £'000	19X0 £'000
Fixed assets at cost	310		195	
less: Accumulated depreciation	95	215	70	125
Current assets:				
Stock	80		40	
Debtors	45		25	
Cash	—		30	
	125		95	
less: Current liabilities				
Bank overdraft	12		—	
Creditors	80		60	
	92		60	
Net current assets		33		35
Total assets less current liabilities		248		160
Loan		15		—
		233		160
Issued share capital		120		100
Profit and loss account		113		60
		233		160
Income statement 19X1				
Sales		400		
Cost of sales		320		
		80		
Depreciation	25			
Interest payable	2			
		27		
Profit retained		53		

in the cost of fixed assets represents the purchase of new assets). The directors of Wembley Ltd have expressed their concern over two matters. First, although they are aware that the company has expanded significantly during 19X1, it is not clear how this expansion has been financed, and in particular whether the funds raised are available on a long-term basis. Secondly, they cannot understand why the company's cash balance has fallen by £42,000 during 19X1 despite the retention of profits of £53,000 for that year. A cash flow statement should help to explain the situation.

A cash flow statement describes the changes in assets, liabilities and owners' equity (uses and sources of cash) between two balance sheet dates. A very crude statement could therefore be prepared by simply recording the change in balance sheet figures. Details are given in Table 11.2. Even from this crude statement we

Table 11.2 *Wembley Ltd — changes in financial position, 19X1*

| | Balance at end of: | | Changes in balance during 19X1 |
	19X1 £'000	19X0 £'000	£'000
Fixed assets at cost	310	195	$+ \Delta 115$
Accumulated depreciation	(95)	(70)	$+ \Delta (25)$
	215	125	$+ \Delta 90$
Stock	80	40	$+ \Delta 40$
Debtors	45	25	$+ \Delta 20$
Cash	(12)	30	$- \Delta 42$
Current liabilities	(80)	(60)	$+ \Delta (20)$
Loan	(15)	0	$+ \Delta (15)$
	233	160	$+ \Delta 73$
Issued share capital	120	100	$+ \Delta 20$
Reserves	113	60	$+ \Delta 53$
	233	160	$+ \Delta 73$

can identify which account balances have changed most significantly and therefore which have provided or used more cash. For example, Wembley Ltd has generated cash by earning a profit from its regular operations and by taking out a long-term loan, and it has invested a considerable sum in fixed assets and stock. However, a more informative presentation would *explain* the changes which have occurred. In this section we shall prepare statements which explain the changes in Wembley's cash balance.

A cash flow statement — the direct method

There are two main methods of presenting a cash flow statement — the direct method and the indirect method. In this section we shall examine the direct method. As its name implies, the direct method is straightforward. Effectively, it presents the cash flows as they would appear in the cash account after aggregating those entries which relate to the same class of activity, e.g. receipts from customers, payments to suppliers and purchases of fixed assets.

We begin by examining the nature of the transactions which gave rise to Wembley's financial position at 31 December 19X1. Table 11.3 presents the accounting records of Wembley Ltd for 19X1. The transactions are self-explanatory. The 'Balances brought forward' and the 'Balances at end of 19X1' have been rearranged and presented as the company's balance sheets in Table 11.1. The entries in the column headed 'Income' have been rearranged and presented as the company's income statement in Table 11.1. Similarly, we can rearrange the entries in the column headed 'Cash' and present them as a cash flow statement for Wembley Ltd for 19X1 (Table 11.4).

Table 11.3 Wembley Ltd — accounting equation entries, year to 31 December 19X1

	Fixed assets £'000	+ Stock £'000	+ Debtors £'000	+ Cash £'000	= Creditors £'000	+ Loan £'000	+ Share capital £'000	+ Income £'000
Balances brought forward	125	40	25	30	60	0	100	60
Transactions:								
1. Purchase of stock on credit		360			360			
2. Cash payment to suppliers				(340)	(340)			
3. } Sale of stock on credit		(320)						(320)
4. }			400					400
5. Cash receipts from customers			(380)	380				
6. Issues of shares				20			20	
7. Receipt of loan				15		15		
8. Purchase of fixed assets	115			(115)				
9. Depreciation charge	(25)							(25)
10. Interest payment				(2)				(2)
Balances at end of 19X1	215	80	45	(12)	80	15	120	113

Table 11.4 *Wembley Ltd — cash flow statement for the year ended 31 December 19X1*

Direct method	£'000	£'000
Operating Activities:		
Cash received from customers	380	
Cash payments to suppliers	(340)	
Interest paid	(2)	
Cash flow from operating activities		38
Investing Activities:		
Purchase of fixed assets	(115)	
Cash flow from investing activities		(115)
Financing Activities:		
Issue of shares	20	
Increase in long-term borrowing	15	
Cash flow from financing activities		35
Net decrease in cash		(42)
Cash at 1 January 19X1		30
Cash at 31 December 19X1		(12)

The reasons for the difference between the *increase* in retained profit (£53,000) and the *decrease* in the cash balance (£42,000) are apparent from a study of the 'Cash' and 'Income' columns in Table 11.3, and hence from a study of the income statement (Table 11.1) and the cash flow statement (Table 11.4) of Wembley Ltd. Cash received from customers is less than sales, cash paid to suppliers is greater than the cost of goods sold, and capital expenditure is far in excess of the depreciation charge. The shortfall in cash caused by these differences has been met by issuing shares, taking out a loan and utilizing the overdraft facility.

However, despite the simplicity of the 'direct' cash flow statement, some users have argued that it does not draw attention to the fundamental differences between profits and cash flows. Rather than require the reader to make comparisons between the cash flow statement and the income statement, the cash flow statement itself should disclose clearly the differences between sales and cash receipts from customers, between cost of goods sold and cash payments to suppliers, and between depreciation and capital expenditure. In other words it should reconcile the profit figure with the change in the cash balance. A cash flow statement prepared according to the indirect method satisfies this requirement.

A cash flow statement — the indirect method

Figure 11.1 and the accompanying analysis provide the rationale for the *indirect method* of presenting a cash flow statement. We shall demonstrate the indirect method by adopting it to present the cash flow statement of Wembley Ltd.

Table 11.5 *Wembley Ltd — cash flow statement for the year*
ended 31 December 19X1

Indirect method	£'000	£'000
Operating Activities:		
Net profit	53	
Depreciation charge	25	
Increase in debtors	(20)	
Increase in stocks	(40)	
Increase in creditors	20	
Cash flow from operating activities		38
Investing Activities:		
Purchase of fixed assets	(115)	
Cash flow from investing activities		(115)
Financing Activities:		
Issue of shares	20	
Increase in long-term borrowing	15	
Cash flow from financing activities		35
Net decrease in cash		(42)
Cash at 1 January 19X1		30
Cash at 31 December 19X1		(12)

One source of cash is the profit earned by a business ('profitable operations' in Figure 11.1), and the indirect method cash flow statement begins with that figure, £53,000 (Table 11.5). However, we know now that several items which appear in an income statement are not reflected by identical cash flows. Hence, we must make some adjustments to the profit figure in order to reconcile it with the cash flow. The depreciation charge is a bookkeeping entry which reduces Wembley's income and the book value of its fixed assets, but has no effect upon the cash balance. The cash flows relating to fixed assets are represented by the amount spent on purchasing (and received on selling) fixed assets during the year. Therefore, in order to identify the cash generated by Wembley's operating activities, we must add back to profit the depreciation charged in the income statement (Table 11.5).

This adjustment has occasionally misled users into believing that depreciation is a source of cash, because it is added to profit. We hope that the explanation above has avoided this confusion. The depreciation charge is a book entry which does not involve any movement of cash. Charging more or less depreciation has no effect whatsoever on the cash generated from operations. For example, if the depreciation charge in 19X1 for Wembley Ltd was £35,000 (i.e £10,000 higher), the net profit would fall to £43,000 (i.e. £10,000 lower) and in the cash flow statement, *the cash flow from operating activities would remain unchanged* at £38,000. Because the depreciation charge has been *deducted* to calculate net profit it must be *added* back to calculate the cash generated from operations.

We noted earlier that the cash received from customers is lower than the sales revenue generated during the year (Table 11.3). The difference (£400,000 − £380,000 = £20,000) must be reflected in an increase in debtors over the period (£45,000 − £25,000 = £20,000, Table 11.3). Hence, in calculating the cash generated from Wembley's operating activities we must deduct from profit any increase in the debtors' balance, i.e. the amount of sales for which, as yet, no cash has been received (Table 11.5). A *decrease* in debtors would, of course, be *added* to the profit figure.

The same principle applies in reconciling the difference between the cost of goods sold figure in the income statement (£320,000), and the cash payment to suppliers (£340,000). The reconciliation is achieved in two stages and can be explained by following the double-entry trail in Table 11.3.

First, although Wembley sold stock costing £320,000 during the year, it purchased stock costing £360,000 (Table 11.3, 'Stock' column). The difference of £40,000 is reflected in the increase in the level of stock over the year, from £40,000 to £80,000. Secondly, Wembley did not purchase stock for cash. Rather, it purchased £360,000 of stock on credit and paid £340,000 cash to its suppliers (Table 11.3, 'Creditors' column). The difference of £20,000 is reflected in the increase over the year in the balance owed to creditors, from £60,000 to £80,000.

Thus, the difference between the cost of goods sold figure in the income statement, £320,000, and the cash payment to suppliers figure in the cash flow statement, £340,000 (i.e. £20,000) can be explained as follows:

Increase in stock purchased	(£40,000)	Use of cash
Increase in creditors outstanding	£20,000	Source of cash
Net effect	(£20,000)	Use of cash

We can now complete and explain the 'Operating Activities' section of the indirect method cash flow statement. Wembley Ltd generated a profit of £53,000 during 19X1. By adding back the depreciation charge of £25,000, we can see that *ceteris paribus* Wembley should have generated cash of £78,000 from its operations. However, the increase in both debtors and stocks reveals that £60,000 of cash has been invested (used) in a higher level of working capital. Wembley has financed part of this investment by increasing the amount it owes to its suppliers (a source of cash). The net effect is an increase in net working capital of £40,000 (£20,000 + £40,000 − £20,000). As illustrated in Figure 11.1, an increase in working capital represents a use of cash and it is the reason why Wembley generated less cash than profit from its operations.

We stated above that the principal advantage of the indirect method over the direct method is that it highlights the differences between operating profit and net cash flow from operating activities and reconciles the two figures. The Accounting Standards Board considers this information to be so important that in FRS 1 — *Cash Flow Statements* (issued 1991), it requires companies to publish a note reconciling the net cash flow from operating activities with the operating profit, whether they report using the direct or the indirect method.

11.3   Interpretation of the cash flow statement

The method by which the 'Cash flow from operating activities' is derived is the only difference between the direct and the indirect cash flow statements. The resultant figure, £38,000 for Wembley Ltd, is identical under both methods, as are all the items included in the 'Investing Activities' and 'Financing Activities' sections of the statements.

Both statements reveal that Wembley made a major investment in fixed assets during the year. Capital expenditure of £115,000 was financed partly by operating cash flows (£38,000), partly by raising long-term finance, both debt and equity (£35,000), and partly by using the company's cash balances (£30,000). The shortfall of £12,000 was met by utilizing an overdraft facility.

By disclosing the sources and uses of cash, the cash flow statement should help an external user to evaluate the effect of financial management decisions taken during the year. As we mentioned earlier, the user must then decide whether these movements are 'normal' (in relation to past movements and comparable industry data) or 'abnormal' and thus require further analysis.

The management of working capital

Over time one would expect any company to generate positive cash flows from operating activities. It would be unlikely to survive otherwise. In fact a company must generate sufficient cash from its operations to reward the various participants or stakeholders in the business. Hence one would expect to see a positive cash flow from operations after paying interest, taxes and dividends. Wembley Ltd generated £38,000 cash flow from operations after paying interest of £2,000. No dividend was paid, and tax is ignored in this example. In the short term, however, an expanding company might experience a negative operating cash flow as it builds up the level of its stock and debtors in line with the increased turnover. An increase in working capital without a corresponding increase in turnover might be evidence of operational inefficiencies. Suppose Wembley had not experienced an increase in sales and was not expecting an increase next year. Reducing its working capital to the level of 19X0 would 'release' £40,000 of cash which could be used to clear the current overdraft and provide funds for more productive investments.

The cash flow statement helps the user to identify the impact of the company's performance in managing working capital. The impact of increases in working capital on operating cash flow can be analysed in conjunction with working capital ratios such as the stock holding period, the debtors' payment period and the creditors' payment period (see Chapter 10). In addition, a useful ratio to monitor a company's investment in working capital over time and against other companies, is that of working capital/sales (Table 11.6). This ratio shows how much capital

Table 11.6 *The management of working capital*

Investment in working capital per £ of sales

	Wembley 19X1 £000	ICI 1992 £m	Tesco 1992 £m
Stock	80	2,273	222
Trade Debtors	45	2,092	0
	125	4,365	222
Trade Creditors	(80)	(1,080)	(500)
Net Working Capital	45	3,285	(278)
Sales	400	12,061	7,097
Net Working Capital per £1 of sales	11.25p	27.2p	(3.9)p
Stockholding period (days)	91	113	13
Debtors payment period (days)	41	63	0
Creditors payment period (days)	91	54	28

is required to finance operations *in addition to* the capital required to finance fixed assets.

Table 11.6 shows that Wembley required 11.25p of working capital for every £1 of sales in 19X1. As with other ratios, the norm will depend upon the type of industry in which the company operates. Thus ICI plc with a stockholding period of over 110 days and a debtors payment period of approximately 63 days, invests 27.2p of working capital per £1 of sales. Tesco plc however holds stock, on average, for only 13 days and does not give any credit to its customers. It does not have a working capital requirement. In effect, Tesco plc purchases goods from its suppliers on 28 days credit, but sells them for cash within 13 days. It retains the cash for a further 15 days, investing it in the business as it pleases.

This highlights the importance of good working capital management in maintaining positive cash flows. Other things being equal this ratio, expressed in pence, gives an indication of the additional cash required for every £1 increase in sales. Thus, if Wembley were to increase sales by 8%, or £50,000, it would require £5,625 (£50,000 × £0.1125) to finance the expected increase in working capital. This is in addition to any investment in fixed assets. If ICI plc's sales increased by £1,000 million (8%), it would need to finance an additional £272 million (!) of working capital. On the other hand if Tesco plc's sales increased by £568m (8%), its suppliers would finance all the increased investment in stock *and* provide an additional £22 million cash for Tesco to invest in other assets.

The above analysis demonstrates that, irrespective of the industry norm, there are cash flow advantages to managing working capital efficiently. We can appreciate why so many 'successful' companies are forced into liquidation because they expand too quickly and have insufficient capital to finance their rapidly increasing working capital requirements. From Table 11.6 it is clear that a reduction in the stockholding period or the period of credit allowed to debtors would reduce the net working capital requirement and so release cash for an investment in fixed assets or to pay off an interest-bearing loan. An increase in the creditor payment period would have the same effect. However, as with many other ratios, changes in these ratios must be analysed carefully. A reduction in stock levels may leave the company vulnerable to stock-outs, and an increase in the creditor payment period may lead to a loss of discounts and less favourable delivery terms. A controlled decrease in the ratio of net working capital per £1 of sales might be evidence of more efficient working capital management. On the other hand, a falling ratio might indicate over-trading. The user must look to further information to explain the change.

Investing and financing activities

We said earlier that we would expect a company to report a positive cash flow from operating activities. We would also expect that, in a steady state, the operating cash flow should be more than sufficient to replace fixed assets as they wear out. From Table 11.5, we can see that Wembley purchased fixed assets costing £115,000, some £77,000 more than the cash generated from operations. However, there are indications to suggest that Wembley is expanding and that these purchases include some new assets in addition to replacement assets.

One indication of expansion is the size of the fixed asset investment (£115,000) compared with the depreciation charge (£25,000). In a steady state, in which a company simply replaces its assets as they wear out, and in which price levels are stable, one might expect the fixed asset investment to be identical to the depreciation charge. Of course, price levels are rarely stable, and historical cost depreciation may be a very poor indicator of the likely cost of replacing fixed assets, especially if they have a useful life of over ten years. The accounts might be of more use to the user if the depreciation charge was based upon the current (replacement) cost of the fixed assets. This would give a rough indication of the amount that Wembley would need to invest in fixed assets each year simply to replace assets that had worn out.

An important ratio, particularly for capital-intensive manufacturers, is that of *cash flow from operating activities to capital expenditure*. For Wembley Ltd this ratio is:

$$\frac{\text{Cash flow from operating activities } less \text{ interest, taxation and dividends}}{\text{Capital expenditure}} = \frac{£38,000}{£115,000} = 33\%$$

In general, the higher this ratio, the greater is the financial flexibility of the organization, i.e. there is less need to raise finance externally. However, as always, one must be cautious in interpreting this ratio. For many companies, capital expenditure is cyclical. Capacity may be increased by the construction of a large-scale plant over a two- to three-year period. Upon its completion, capital expenditure falls for several years until demand catches up with the new capacity. The ratio will fall during the spending phase and rise during the consolidation phase. One must examine the trend over a series of years, and use the ratio to corroborate information gleaned from elsewhere.

A rising ratio may be a cause for concern if it results from the company having cut back its capital expenditure programme. Such a reduction in capital expenditure might affect the company's long-term profitability and solvency either by sacrificing market share through insufficient capacity or by causing the company to fall behind its competitors in the adoption of new technology.

We can see from Table 11.5 that Wembley financed only 33% of its capital expenditure from its operating cash flows (£38,000/£115,000). The remainder came from new equity, long-term loans, cash balances and an overdraft. The layout of the cash flow statement enables the user to identify these sources clearly. The 'Financing Activities' section discloses how much cash was raised from shareholders and how much from creditors. We noted in the previous chapter that the ratio of debt to equity, the gearing ratio, provides information about an organization's financial risk. A study of the 'Financing Activities' section of the cash flow statement over a period of years will reveal a company's recent strategy towards the raising of debt and equity finance.

The final part of Wembley's cash flow statement discloses that the company financed some of its capital expenditure from its own cash balances. The remainder was financed by using an overdraft facility. We mentioned in Chapter 8 that in general, assets that are to be held for a long period should be financed by a stable, long-term source of finance, whereas assets with short or unpredictable lives should be financed by a more flexible, short-term source. This might suggest that, unless Wembley is able to generate operating cash flows in excess of its capital expenditure, it should consider replacing its overdraft with longer-term debt in the near future.

So far in this section we have analysed ratios and sub-totals extracted from the cash flow statement only. Now we introduce a ratio which combines figures from the cash flow statement and the balance sheet:

Wembley Ltd

$$\frac{\text{Total debt}}{\text{Operating cash flow}} = \frac{\text{Short-term debt + current maturity +}}{\text{long-term debt}}$$
$$= \frac{\text{Short-term debt + current maturity + long-term debt}}{\text{Operating cash flow } less \text{ interest, taxation and dividends}}$$

$$= \frac{£27,000}{£38,000} = 0.71$$

This ratio illustrates that Wembley has the ability to liquidate all of its debt within nine months (i.e. 0.71 of a year) if it applies all of its cash flow from operating activities to that purpose. Although a company is most unlikely to apply all of its operating cash flow to debt retirement, the ratio does provide a measure of financial flexibility. For example, a company with the same operating cash flow as Wembley but with a total debt of £266,000 would take seven years to pay off that debt. If much of the debt is due to mature within, say, five years then the ratio highlights the company's need to refinance and alerts the user to the increased risk if credit restrictions should tighten.

Ratios which use cash flows from the cash flow statement and cash or loan balances from the balance sheet possess some advantages over traditional income statement and balance sheet ratios. The traditional ratios comprise figures which are extracted from the historical cost accrual accounting system. Thus, for example, the gearing ratio of total debt:total capital employed (which can also be expressed as total debt:total assets) is affected by the manner in which fixed assets have been depreciated and stocks valued. Similarly, the numerator in the interest-cover ratio (operating profit before interest payable:interest payable) suffers from the same weakness. However, operating cash flow and total debt are two objective, cash-based, easily verifiable figures. When they are combined they produce a ratio which is also relevant to user needs.

11.4　Cash flows and net income

Given the requirement of FRS 1 — *Cash Flow Statements* that companies should provide a note reconciling the net cash flow from operating activities with the operating profit, it is of little significance whether UK companies publish a cash flow statement prepared according to the direct method or the indirect method. What is important is that the statement provides the external user with sufficient disaggregated information to identify and evaluate the results of management's investment and financing decisions. The importance of this disaggregation can be assessed in the context of the evaluation of cash-based and income-based measures of business performance introduced in the earlier chapters. In Chapter 2 we noted that most external users of financial statements would benefit from the publication of a statement of an organization's actual cash flows because cash is essential for the survival of an organization; it is well understood by all external users; it is an objective method of reporting business performance; and it provides useful control information against which to compare previous estimates of performance.

However, we pointed out that, traditionally, historical cash flows were thought to be potentially misleading for two reasons. First, the pattern of an organization's cash surpluses or deficits through time may be erratic — for example, fixed assets may be bought more intensively in some years than in others, even though they may be used on a regular and steady basis. Such erratic cash flow patterns may be misleading to users who wish to make predictions of the organization's *long-term performance*, particularly if those predictions are based on changes in the organization's cash resources over only a small number of years. It is sometimes argued that 'smoothed' income figures may give a better indication of an organization's ability *in the longer term* to generate surpluses to pay dividends, settle debts, pay wages, pay taxes and so on. Secondly, cash flows are sometimes criticized for reporting on the *financial activity* of the receipt and payment of cash rather than the *economic activity* of buying and selling goods and services. Together these two criticisms may imply that cash flow statements do not provide a reliable measure of past economic performance, nor a sound basis for predicting future cash flows.

However, cash flow statements as illustrated in this chapter appear to go some way to answering these criticisms. First, the various sources and uses of cash are disclosed separately, i.e. the cash flow from operating activities is not distorted by large, irregular capital expenditures. Secondly, operating figures based on accrual accounting and operating figures based on cash flows are both disclosed and reconciled in the statement. This enables users to assess the results of both 'economic' and 'financial' activities during the year.

It may still be the case that a time series of income figures gives a better indication of the organization's ability in the long term to generate surpluses. However, we observed in Chapter 10 that some organizations may never attain the 'long term' because of liquidity problems in the short or medium term. It might be argued that 'erratic' cash flows provide the users of financial statements with valuable information about the *riskiness* of the organization's activities. In the *short to medium* term an organization may report positive income figures and yet have no cash to pay its liabilities as they fall due. There are many reasons why an organization's cash flows may be significantly lower than its income figures (e.g. the incurrence of capital expenditure which is continually in excess of the annual depreciation charge; a steady build-up of stock which is not reflected in the cost of goods sold; the recognition of revenues prior to the receipt of cash), all of which should be made clear to external users.

The analysis in this section, in this chapter, and in many previous chapters, suggests that no one method of accounting can evaluate satisfactorily all aspects of an organization's performance and prospects. At the very least, one must examine an organization's profitability, liquidity and solvency and this can be achieved only by a careful analysis of the figures provided in the balance sheet, the income statement *and* the cash flow statement. It is not, and never has been, a question of choosing between accrual accounting and cash flow accounting — both are necessary for an external user to evaluate an organization's past performance and to estimate its future performance.

Finally, we must stress again that even a comprehensive analysis of the balance sheet, income statement and cash flow statement is not a substitute for forecasts of future sales, expenses, capital expenditure and other cash flows. Such an analysis is simply part of the process for generating and corroborating such forecasts. It is the forecasts themselves which are of prime importance to users of financial statements.

11.5 An illustration from practice — E.H. Booth & Co. Ltd

In this section we shall use our knowledge of the way in which accounts are prepared and the key ratios we have introduced in this and the previous chapter to interpret and evaluate Booths' operating and financial performance from its published accounts. There are people who do this professionally. Financial analysts write regular reports for their clients, concluding with a recommendation to buy, hold or sell the shares of the company under scrutiny. Individual analysts normally concentrate on one or two market sectors, producing reports on all the major companies in that sector. Thus the Food Retailing sector team at Barclays de Zoete Wedd Research Limited (BZW) produce regular reports on the performance of Tesco, Sainsbury, Asda and the other large supermarket chains. Large companies might also employ their own analysts to monitor the performance of their competitors and potential takeover targets.

The BZW analysts are unlikely to discover much from an analysis of Tesco's published accounts that they did not already know or, at least, suspect. They will have predicted this year's results after a thorough analysis of last year's accounts, and refined those predictions regularly throughout the year as new information became available. New information includes not only Tesco's interim accounts, press releases, and directors' briefings, but also information about the performance of other companies in the same sector and information about the economy generally, for example changes in interest rates and the level of consumer spending. Consequently, the published accounts often merely confirm the analysts' expectations about this year's results but, perhaps more importantly, they provide them with more detailed information which can be used in predicting future performance.

An analyst's report will include an analysis of past performance, present position and, most importantly, future prospects. As we stated in Chapter 10, the primary aim of financial statements analysis is to interpret the historical data provided in the accounts in order to obtain the predictive information required by users. In this section we shall analyse the performance and financial position of Booths. In particular, we shall assess its profitability, liquidity and longer-term solvency using many of the ratios introduced in this and the previous chapter. However, we shall not simply produce a series of ratios in isolation, but, like the professional analysts, we shall interpret them in the context of our knowledge of the company, the sector and the economy.

Chairman's statement

This is a useful starting point for an analysis of the accounts. It is an opportunity for the chairman to comment on the activities of the company during the previous year, and to give some indication of what the company intends to do in the future.

It is not, however, audited and it is not unusual for some chairmen or chairwomen to be very selective in their comments following a mediocre performance. In the annual report of many plcs, the chairman's statement will address the performance and prospects of the company (or group) as a whole, and a separate 'Financial Review' will examine the performance of individual divisions. The chairman's statement, financial review and company review of Tesco plc amounts to 26 pages of the Annual Report 1992, compared with 20 pages devoted to the financial statements and accompanying notes. Much of the information included in the chairman's statement and the reviews provides useful background information with which to interpret the financial statements.

Booths is not a plc. There are only 180 shareholders and the shares are not traded openly. It should be easy for a shareholder of Booths to obtain information from the directors at the annual general meeting and hence there is less need for the chairman to provide a lengthy statement in the annual report. Booths' chairman's statement is less than one half-page (page 6). Nevertheless it contains some interesting information. It reveals that reported profits represent 'a small increase over the previous year'. As part of our analysis we will examine whether this is an increase in 'real' terms (i.e. after inflation), and whether the previous year's profits had been satisfactory — a 'small increase' over a particularly bad year might be a cause for concern.

The statement claims that, 'Trading at our stores remains good, but we do have large bank loans to service'. This implies that although sales turnover is satisfactory, interest payable is a significant expense and that the company might be highly geared. We shall analyse the company's capital structure and comment on both its liquidity and longer-term solvency.

A reference to the opening of a Sainsbury Superstore close to an older Booths' store warns the reader of the increased competition facing the company in the near future. Information gleaned from the accounts of Tesco and Sainsbury reveals that each of these two companies opens over twenty new stores every year. If indeed Booths 'lost only a very few customers' to the Sainsbury Superstore, we might query whether Sainsbury is in direct competition with Booths. Is Booths perhaps at the lower end of the market, facing competition from supermarket chains such as Kwik Save plc and the other discounters?

The chairman reports that the directors and managers have 'taken many detailed steps to improve our performance within our stores, and are now providing our warehouse with a computerized stock control system'. One presumes that the 'detailed steps' include cost efficiencies such as the installation throughout all stores of electronic check-outs capable of reading bar codes. This enables the prices of goods to be displayed once only, on the shelf, rather than on every tin, packet or bottle. This can lead to a considerable saving, especially when prices are changing frequently as a result of inflation, special discounts and store promotions. A computerized stock control system will involve some capital expenditure now, but lower operating costs in the future as the company benefits from labour savings and a speedier replenishment of goods in the stores. This in turn should lead to less stock being held to service a given volume of sales. (The larger supermarket chains have installed Sales Based Ordering systems, by which stock is automatically reordered from a regional warehouse as it passes over the scanner at the store check-out. The replacement goods are delivered within 48 hours.) We shall examine Booths' capital expenditure and operating costs in our analysis below.

Booths is preparing to build 'a new store on a site we have owned for some time in a good suburban area'. Although it does not need to purchase any land, the cost of building a new store in 1992 is likely to be between five and ten million pounds, depending on its size. The company will need to raise additional finance for this capital expenditure. We shall examine the implications of this for Booths' capital structure and its ability to pay any additional interest charges.

Even at this stage, having read the chairman's statement only, we have some idea of what to expect in the accounts, both this year and in the future. Sales and operating profits have increased satisfactorily, but high interest charges have led to a much smaller increase in net profits. Competition is increasing and Booths' response is to cut operating costs and improve customer service by investing in information technology. High interest charges suggest a high level of borrowing and, given the small number of shareholders, it is likely that any further store expansion will have to be financed by further borrowing. Now that we have a 'feel' for this company and its current situation, let us seek to confirm or reject our expectations by undertaking a thorough analysis of the financial statements.

Turnover

The Profit and Loss Account (page 10) reveals that turnover increased by 8.3% in 1992 (from £68,420,596 to £74,132,518) — but is this good, bad or indifferent? It seems a healthy enough increase especially in the context of the recession in the UK in the early 1990s, but we must satisfy ourselves that we are comparing 'like with like', i.e. we might be less impressed if we discovered that the rate of inflation had been 10% during the year; or that Booths had opened several new stores during 1992; or that the rate of increase over the past few years had been a consistent 12% per annum.

The '5 Yearly Financial Review' (page 20) provides some key financial figures over the past five years. From these we can calculate the annual increase in turnover each year since 1989:

	1988	1989	1990	1991	1992
Turnover (£000)	54,559	57,835	62,826	68,421	74,133
Annual increase %		6.0	8.6	8.9	8.3

It would appear that the increase in turnover has been consistently above 8% since 1990, although this year's increase is slightly lower than either of the two previous years'. However, these figures include an inflationary element. In times of rising prices (inflation), sales revenue will increase even though a company sells the same volume of goods as it did the previous year. In order to calculate the 'real' increase in turnover, we must strip out the inflationary element.

In the UK, inflation is most commonly measured by the increase in the Retail Price Index (RPI) which consists of a weighted average of the changes in the prices of a variety of consumer goods and services. Although Booths' turnover comprises sales of consumer goods in the form of food and associated products, the RPI encompasses a much broader range of consumer goods and services comprising not only food and associated products, but gas and electricity charges, motoring costs and mortgage payments. Nevertheless, it is a useful proxy index to apply to the turnover of a supermarket. (The RPI is discussed further in Chapter 13.)

In April 1991 the RPI was 133.1 and in April 1992 it was 138.8. Hence, we can restate the turnover of 1991 in '1992 prices' by applying a 'conversion factor':

$$\text{1991 turnover} \times \frac{\text{RPI April 1992}}{\text{RPI April 1991}} = \text{1991 turnover in 1992 prices}$$

$$£68,420,596 \times \frac{138.8}{133.1} = £71,350,701 \text{ in 1992 prices}$$

We can convert the turnover of each of the previous years in the same way, using the RPI in April of the relevant year as the denominator in the conversion factor:

	1988	1989	1990	1991	1992
Turnover (£000)	54,559	57,835	62,826	68,421	74,133
RPI adjustment	$\dfrac{138.8}{105.8}$	$\dfrac{138.8}{114.3}$	$\dfrac{138.8}{125.1}$	$\dfrac{138.8}{133.1}$	$\dfrac{138.8}{138.8}$
Turnover in 1992 prices (£000)	71,576	70,231	69,706	71,351	74,133
Annual increase %		(1.9)	(0.7)	2.4	3.9

The annual increase in turnover in 'real terms' shows a different trend from the unadjusted figures. Turnover in 1991 was no higher than it had been in 1988. Inflation, which had been approximately 9.4% in 1990, fell to 6.4% in 1991 and to 4.3% in 1992. Booths' turnover fell in real terms in 1989 and 1990, but has since risen, at an increasing rate. This reflects the oft-stated view of food retailers that it is more difficult to raise the price of food than it is to raise the price of industrial goods. Hence, we might predict (expect) that *ceteris paribus* Booths (and other supermarket chains) will grow more quickly in real terms if the rate of inflation is low.

We have shown that Booths' turnover increased in real terms in 1992. It is possible of course that this was the result of the company opening new stores during the year. More stores would be expected to generate a higher level of turnover. The larger supermarket chains, e.g. Sainsbury and Tesco, provide information on new store openings, and the total sales area (in thousands of square feet), enabling the user to calculate the amount of sales per square foot — a key statistic in the retail trade. This information is not included in the accounts of Booths and we must rely on a more general analysis of the type introduced in Chapter 10.

Profitability

We stated in Section 10.3 that it is preferable, when comparing a figure from the income statement with a figure from the balance sheet, to use an average of the opening and closing balance sheet figures to provide a consistent basis for ratio calculation. Booths' accounts disclose figures for both 1991 and 1992, so it is possible to calculate average balances for the 1992 ratios. However, as part of our analysis we wish to compare the ratios for 1992 with those for 1991, and without access to the balance sheet of 1990 we cannot calculate the average balances for 1991. We shall therefore use end-of-year balances and comment where appropriate upon the limitations of this practice. A summary of the financial ratios used in this analysis is presented in Table 11.7, and the derivation of those ratios is shown in Table 11.8.

During 1992, Booths' return on capital employed increased from 12.7% to 14.9%, and the component elements of this ratio reveal that both the profit margin increased, from 4.0% to 4.3%, and the utilization ratio increased, from 3.15× to 3.47×. Booths is generating more sales revenue from each £1 of long-term capital invested, and is generating more profit from each £1 of sales, than it did in 1991. How might we interpret these ratios?

We shall examine the profit margin first. As we can see, the margin is quite low, less than 4p profit (before interest) on every £1 of sales. In fact, the whole sector is characterized by large sales volumes with relatively low margins (see Table 10.2 for a comparison of companies in the food retailing and pharmaceutical industries). However, because of the high sales volumes, any small increase in margins can result in a significant improvement in the 'bottom line'. We know Booths is cutting costs by computerizing its stock control system, and by introducing efficiencies into its stores. A more efficient stock control and distribution system should also facilitate the selling of more fresh produce with its attendant higher prices and margins. And if Booths has sufficient capacity in place to expand its sales further without additional major capital expenditure, any increase in turnover will reap the benefits of economies of scale, as many costs (property, systems, administration) are predominantly fixed. Indeed, administrative expenses increased by only 4.6% in 1992, compared with an increase of 8.3% in turnover.

Booths' gross margin increased slightly from 8.80% to 8.86%. This compares favourably with the gross margins achieved by the market leaders — Tesco, for

Table 11.7 *E.H. Booth & Co. Ltd — summary of financial ratios*

	1992	1991
Profitability		
Return on long-term capital employed	14.9%	12.7%
Operating profit margin	4.3%	4.0%
Utilization ratio	3.47×	3.15×
Gross profit margin	8.86%	8.80%
Return on equity	7.4%	10.2%
Liquidity		
Current ratio	0.5	0.5
Quick or liquid ratio	0.03	0.04
Stock holding period	28 days	31 days
Debtor payment period	0 days	0 days
Creditor payment period	24 days	26 days
Capital Structure		
Gearing ratio (1)	133%	157%
Gearing ratio (2)	57%	61%
Times interest covered	1.8×	1.4×
Financial flexibility	7.5 years	7.5 years
Working capital management		
Inventory	5,259	5,303
Trade debtors	5	6
	5,264	5,309
Trade creditors	(4,467)	(4,406)
Net working capital	797	903
Sales	74,133	68,421
Net working capital per £1 of sales	1.08p	1.32p

example, reported a 9% gross margin in 1992 — and is significantly higher than the 5.5% reported by Kwik Save, the leading discount retailer. Although Booths' turnover is only about 1% of that of Tesco, the gross margins of the two companies suggest that they offer a similar range of high quality, high margin products — Booths is clearly not a 'discounter'. It has achieved an increase in turnover without reducing its gross margin. However, because of its size, Booths cannot achieve the economies of scale enjoyed by the largest companies. Its administration expenses amount to 5% of turnover, whereas Tesco's amount to only 2.2%. Kwik Save's 'no frills' approach is reflected in a charge for administration expenses equal to only 1.3% of turnover. The high costs of being a small, but full range, high quality supermarket chain are the primary reason for Booths' lower operating profit margin (4.3%) compared with those of Tesco (6.8%) and Kwik Save (4.9%).

The utilization, or asset turnover, ratio measures how efficiently the available resources are used to produce sales. From Table 11.7 we can see that Booths' utilization ratio increased from 3.15 to 3.47 during the year. Not only did turnover

Table 11.8 *E.H. Booth & Co. Ltd — Ratio calculations*

	1992	1991

Profitability
Return on long-term capital:

$$\frac{\text{Operating profit}}{\text{Long term capital employed or Total assets less current liabilities}}$$ $\dfrac{3,178}{21,389} = 14.9\%$ $\dfrac{2,770}{21,727} = 12.7\%$

Utilization ratio:

$$\frac{\text{Sales}}{\text{Long term capital employed or Total assets less current liabilities}}$$ $\dfrac{74,133}{21,389} = 3.47\times$ $\dfrac{68,421}{21,727} = 3.15\times$

Operating profit margin:

$$\frac{\text{Operating profit}}{\text{Sales}}$$ $\dfrac{3,178}{74,133} = 4.3\%$ $\dfrac{2,770}{68,421} = 4.0\%$

Gross profit margin:

$$\frac{\text{Gross profit}}{\text{Sales}}$$ $\dfrac{6,565}{74,133} = 8.86\%$ $\dfrac{6,023}{68,421} = 8.80\%$

Return on equity:

$$\frac{\text{Profit after taxation less preference dividend}}{\text{Ordinary share capital and reserves}}$$ $\dfrac{815}{10,993} = 7.4\%$ $\dfrac{1,053}{10,310} = 10.2\%$

Liquidity
Current ratio:

$$\frac{\text{Current assets}}{\text{Current liabilities}}$$ $\dfrac{5,571}{10,980} = 0.5$ $\dfrac{5,735}{11,744} = 0.5$

Quick ratio:

$$\frac{\text{Current assets less stocks}}{\text{Current liabilities}}$$ $\dfrac{312}{10,980} = 0.03$ $\dfrac{432}{11,744} = 0.04$

Stock holding period:

$$\frac{\text{Inventory}}{\text{Cost of sales}} \times 365$$ $\dfrac{5,259}{67,568} = 28 \text{ days}$ $\dfrac{5,303}{62,398} = 31 \text{ days}$

Debtor payment period:

$$\frac{\text{Trade debtors}}{\text{Sales}} \times 365$$ $\dfrac{5}{74,133} = 0 \text{ days}$ $\dfrac{6}{68,421} = 0 \text{ days}$

Creditor payment period:

$$\frac{\text{Trade creditors}}{\text{Cost of sales}} \times 365$$ $\dfrac{4,467}{67,568} = 24 \text{ days}$ $\dfrac{4,406}{62,398} = 26 \text{ days}$

	1992	1991
Capital Structure		
Gearing ratio (1):		
$\dfrac{\text{Total debt plus preference share capital}}{\text{Ordinary share capital plus reserves}}$	$\dfrac{14,584}{10,993} = 133\%$	$\dfrac{16,136}{10,310} = 157\%$
Gearing ratio (2):		
$\dfrac{\text{Total debt plus preference share capital}}{\text{Total debt plus total share capital and reserves}}$	$\dfrac{14,585}{25,577} = 57\%$	$\dfrac{16,136}{26,446} = 61\%$
Interest cover:		
$\dfrac{\text{Profit before interest payable}}{\text{Interest payable}}$	$\dfrac{3,178}{1,774} = 1.8 \times$	$\dfrac{2,770}{2,041} = 1.4 \times$
Financial flexibility:		
$\dfrac{\text{Total debt}}{\text{Operating cash flow less interest, dividends and tax}}$	$\dfrac{14,572}{1,941} = 7.5 \text{ years}$	$\dfrac{16,124}{2,139} = 7.5 \text{ years}$
Working Capital Management		
Working capital per £ of sales:		
Inventory	5,259	5,303
Trade debtors	5	6
	5,264	5,309
Trade creditors	(4,467)	(4,406)
Net working capital	797	903
Sales	74,133	68,421
Net working capital per £ of sales	1.08 pence	1.32 pence

increase, but total assets less current liabilities decreased, i.e. more sales were generated from a lower asset base. An alternative utilization ratio compares sales turnover to tangible fixed assets (the 'productive' assets). The figures are lower but the trend is the same (an increase from 2.47 to 2.77), and so is the explanation. Booths did not build any new stores in 1992. Note 8 reveals that most of the additions to fixed assets were fixtures, plant and vehicles. The total capital expenditure of £404,168 is very small compared with the £15 million spent on fixed assets in 1990 and 1991 (see the change in Tangible fixed assets in the 5 Yearly Financial Review, page 20).

Whenever a new store is built (at current prices), the company's fixed asset figure increases significantly and suddenly, causing the utilization ratio to fall just as quickly. As the new store begins to generate revenue and its cost is depreciated, so the utilization ratio rises gradually. In 1992 the depreciation charge (£1,327,455) far outweighed the capital expenditure resulting in a fall in the net book value of fixed assets and a rise in the utilization ratio. Given the chairman's statement that a new store is at the planning stage, we would expect capital expenditure to rise significantly in the future and the utilization ratio to fall again.

Although we can comment on the change in the utilization ratio, we are less confident in commenting on the actual figure for the ratio. As is the case for most companies, Booths' assets are reported in the balance sheet at their historical cost — some of those assets, in particular property, may have been purchased several decades ago. The Report of the Directors (page 7) discloses that the market value of the land and buildings was 'in excess of £34 million' in 1991. Only if such information were made available on a regular basis by all companies would we be confident of comparing and interpreting the utilization ratios of one company over time and of different companies.

Booths' solid performance at the operating level is not reflected in its ability to generate improved returns to shareholders. Although the Return on Capital Employed increased from 12.7% to 14.9%, the Return on Owners' Capital Employed fell from 10.2% to 7.4%. The Profit and Loss Account reveals that whereas Operating profit increased by 14.8% to £3,178,359, the profit available for shareholders fell by 22.5% to £815,394. The reason is clear: the increase in the operating profit is more than absorbed by a much higher level of interest payments and a higher tax charge. This is the situation to which the chairman alluded in his statement (page 6). Booths has improved its operating performance, but most of the financial gains have been made by the loan creditors. The profit available to shareholders has fallen and the dividend payment has been held at £132,306 for the fourth successive year.

In summary, Booths has increased its return on capital employed in 1992. In part this is the result of a fall in capital expenditure during the year. However, more positively, it is the result also of an increase in sales from new stores opened in recent years, of an increase in the gross margin of goods sold and of economies of scale, particularly in administrative expenses. The introduction of new technology and the continued increase in turnover should lead to further cost efficiencies, margin improvements and economies of scale. Unfortunately, the high cost of borrowing has meant that the increased profitability at the operating level has not, as yet, been reflected in increased returns to the shareholders. In the immediate future, the company's profitability may be threatened by a further increase in interest payments as additional finance is required to build new stores, and by competition from the market leaders. Such competition might lead to a fall in sales volume and/or a reduction in prices, and hence margins.

Liquidity

In this section we shall examine the liquidity position of Booths. A weak liquidity position means it is more difficult for a company to achieve its long-term objectives including the generation of cash flows. Booths' working capital, or current, ratio is approximately 0.5:1 in both 1991 and 1992, and its quick ratio is a positively minute 0.03 and 0.04 for the two years. Although these ratios are supposed to indicate a firm's ability to meet its short-term cash obligations (current liabilities) out of its current and liquid assets, we noted in Chapter 10 that different norms operate in different industries. Food retailers do not normally extend credit to customers and hence have few, if any, trade debtors. Booths' current ratio of 0.5:1 is similar to those of Sainsbury, 0.57, and Tesco, 0.60 (Table 10.3).

However, Booths' quick ratio of 0.03 is significantly lower than those of Sainsbury, 0.38, and Tesco, 0.33 (Table 10.3). This ratio requires further analysis. If a company has very few debtors, the quick ratio will depend to a large extent upon whether the company has a positive cash balance or a bank overdraft. Sainsbury and Tesco each had a significant amount of cash at bank and short term investments in 1992 (Table 10.3). Booths has no cash and a bank overdraft in excess of £3.7 million (Note 12). This overdraft, together with other 'current' bank loans of over £1 million (Note 12) and long-term loans in excess of £9.7 million (Note 13), has given rise to interest payments which amounted to more than 50% of the operating profit in 1992.

The rate of interest on a bank overdraft fluctuates in line with the Bank of England base rate as determined by the government. Note 13 reveals that the long-term loans also bear interest at a fluctuating rate linked to base rate. Hence, Booths' results are vulnerable to changes in UK interest rates. Interest payable of £1,774,026 in 1992 represents a rate of 11.6% on the average balance of loans and overdraft outstanding of £15,347,794. For each increase or decrease of 1% in the rate of interest, Booths' profit before tax will decrease or increase by approximately £153,478. Between 1991 and 1993 the base rate fluctuated between a maximum of 14% and a minimum of 6%.

In summary, Booths' current ratio is similar to those of the two market leaders but its component elements differ significantly. Both Sainsbury and Tesco hold significant amounts of cash and short-term investments, whereas Booths has a large overdraft. Booths is vulnerable to interest rate changes, and we must now look carefully at the company's longer-term solvency position.

Longer-term solvency

The profit and loss account has revealed a high level of interest payable to lenders (£1,774,026) compared not only with operating profit (£3,178,359), but also with dividends paid to shareholders (£132,306). This suggests a high gearing ratio and we turn to the balance sheet to confirm this.

Booths' fixed interest capital comprises a bank overdraft, long-term debt, including an amount due for repayment within the next year, and preference shares:

	1992 £	1991 £
Bank overdraft	3,742,656	4,325,798
Bank loans due <1 year	1,033,000	954,022
Bank loans due >1 year and <5 years	3,873,692	4,505,087
Bank loans due >5 years	5,922,250	6,339,083
Preference shares	12,000	12,000
	14,583,598	16,135,990

The company's equity capital is represented by

Ordinary share capital	1,256,060	1,256,060
General reserve	9,710,000	9,009,747
Profit and loss account	27,355	44,520
	10,993,415	10,310,327

Booths' gearing ratio (whichever variant is chosen) fell during 1992 (Table 11.7), but it still appears to be very high. The industry average for the two ratios is approximately 35% and 25% respectively. Such a variation from the average deserves further analysis. The average for the industry is dominated by the larger companies, most of which are plcs. In seeking to finance the massive store expansion of recent years these companies have raised large sums of cash from a variety of sources — internal operations, new share issues, bank loans, bonds, etc. — and so have maintained a balance between debt and equity over a period of years. Booths, however, is a family-run company. There is a limit to how much additional cash could be injected by existing shareholders, and the issue of a large number of shares to outsiders would transfer control away from existing shareholders. Currently, 46% of the ordinary share capital and 38% of the preference shares are held by the directors, either in their own right or as trustees (Report of the Directors, page 8). Consequently, internal operations and borrowing are the only feasible sources of finance for Booths' store expansion. The level of gearing and the associated interest cover provide an indication of the limits of Booths' expansionary plans.

The 1992 accounts do not reveal that the company opened a new store in the financial year 1990 and its first superstore in 1991. Unlike a professional analyst, we do not have access to previous accounts to ascertain the cost of these stores and the method of finance chosen. However, the '5 Yearly Financial Review' (page 20) provides some relevant, albeit incomplete, information. The net book value of tangible fixed assets increased from £12,636,450 in 1989 to £21,089,492 in 1990 and to £27,737,237 in 1991 — an increase of £15,100,787 (120%) in two years. Over the same period shareholders' interest increased by only £2,167,017 (£10,322,327 − £8,155,310). Therefore we can assume that most of the increase in fixed assets over the past three years has been financed by borrowing.

This massive increase in the tangible fixed assets and the attendant increase in borrowing gives an indication of the enormous change which has occurred in Booths' financial position in recent years. Major supermarket chains currently open approximately twenty stores a year, resulting in an increase in their net book value of tangible assets of 20−25% p.a. Generally, the finance is raised in the form of debt and equity to maintain a steady gearing ratio over a number of years. Booths has opened two new stores in two years, the net book value of tangible fixed assets has increased by 120%, and most of the finance has been in the form of debt. Booths' gearing ratios of 45% and 31% in 1989[1] (which were normal for a small company in this industry) increased to 157% and 61% in 1991. The decrease in these gearing ratios in 1992 is a step in the right direction, but the decrease must be analysed in the light of the increases of the previous two years — and we know from the Chairman's Statement that the company is planning another new store.

Our brief analysis of the 5 Yearly Financial Review has thrown considerable light upon the financial position of Booths. The company has made a strategic decision to build a small number of new, larger stores. The high cost of construction has been, and will continue to be, financed by borrowing. As with any such investment the new stores must generate sufficient cash flows to pay the high interest payments on the loans, to repay the loans as they mature, and to provide a return for the shareholders. We now turn to an analysis of the cash flow statement in order to ascertain whether sufficient cash flows have been generated and will be generated in the future.

Cash flow statement

Booths' Cash Flow Statement (page 12) tells the story of the company's financial activities during 1992. Booths generated a cash inflow of £4,252,948 from its operating activities, an increase of 3.2% over 1991. Although dividends were held at the same level as in 1991, interest payments increased by 43% to £1,844,325 which represents 43% of the operating cash flow. This is the consequence of a combination of a high level of borrowing and high rates of interest. Corporation tax paid was relatively low, reflecting the benefit of capital allowances on the fixtures and plant purchased for the new superstore in 1991.

The cash flow from operations which remains after paying interest, dividends

---

1. These ratios were calculated from data included in Booths' Annual Report and Accounts 1989 which is not reproduced here.

and taxation amounts to £1,941,095 (£4,252,948 − £1,976,631 − £335,222). This is the sum available for investment in new stores, the refurbishment of existing stores, new information and control systems, and the repayment of existing loans. It is clearly insufficient to finance the construction of a new store. Net capital expenditure in 1991 was £3,183,784 and, as we noted above, over £15 million has been spent on fixed assets since 1989. However, in the period between major store construction it would appear to be sufficient to finance refurbishment, replacements, new stock systems, etc. After net capital expenditure of £388,703 in 1992, the net cash inflow amounted to £1,552,392. This was used to repay long-term loans (£969,250) and reduce the overdraft (£583,142).

It is unlikely that, even without further store expansion, future capital expenditure will be as low as £388,000. Over time, a 'steady-state' company, one that is neither expanding nor contracting, will replace assets as they wear out or are consumed. For such a company, capital expenditure over a number of years should approximate the depreciation charge based upon the current (replacement) cost of those assets. Hence, in times of rising prices and over a number of years, one would expect the capital expenditure of a steady-state company to exceed the historical cost depreciation charge.

Booths' historical cost depreciation charge was £1,327,455 in 1992. The analysis in the previous paragraph suggests that on average over the next few years, Booths' capital expenditure (in 1992 prices) will be at least this amount, even without further major expansion. Given that the maximum cash flow available for fixed asset investment was £1,941,095 in 1992, this implies that, *ceteris paribus*, only about £600,000 p.a. will be available to repay long-term loans and reduce the overdraft.

The financial flexibility ratio of total debt to operating cash flow *less* interest, dividends and taxation (Table 11.7) reveals that Booths has the ability to liquidate all of its debt within seven and a half years if it applies all its operating cash flow to that purpose. (This emphasizes the heavy debt burden of Booths. The corresponding period for Tesco is less than two years, and for Kwik Save less than four months.) Assuming a net cash inflow of £600,000 after steady-state capital expenditure, it would take Booths approximately 24 years to liquidate its debt. We know from Notes 12 and 13 that Booths must repay loans of £1,033,000 in 1993, another £3,873,692 within five years and a further £5,922,250 within nine years. Thus Booths must repay loans in excess of £1 million each year and may be committed also to reducing its bank overdraft from its current level of £3.7 million. It would appear that Booths will need to negotiate new loans in order to retire existing loans and reduce the overdraft. Additional loans will be required to finance any new stores.

Given the apparent strategy of gradual store expansion, Booths is now committed to a relatively high level of gearing for the foreseeable future. Of course, the directors hope that the new stores should generate cash flows in excess of current levels and that these cash flows will be used to reduce the debt more quickly. A reduced level of debt, especially if combined with lower interest rates, would mean lower interest charges and higher net cash inflows. We can now appreciate the uncertainties in generating predictions from an analysis of historical cost financial statements, i.e. if the new stores generate a higher level of operating cash flows, if the major supermarkets do not lure customers away, if costs can be controlled, if interest rates fall, then Booths should generate a good level of profits and cash flows in its next two or three years and reduce its level of gearing. As new information about any of these variables becomes available, so the analysts will refine their forecasts about Booths' future performance. Some of these variables are controllable by Booths' management team, others are not. We conclude our analysis of Booths' financial statements with a variable that is controllable by management and which can have a big impact upon the generation of operating cash flows — the management of working capital.

Working capital management

In 1992, Booths' cash flow from operating activities increased by 3.2% to £4,252,948. Its operating profit increased by 14.7% to £3,178,359. In the following paragraphs we shall explain why the operating cash flow is so much greater than the operating profit and why the *increase* in the operating cash flow is so much lower than the increase in the operating profit.

Booths has adopted the indirect method in presenting its cash flow statement. The statement begins with the 'Net Cash Inflow from Operating Activities' and Note 18 reconciles this figure with the Operating profit in the profit and loss account. For most companies, the operating cash flow is greater than the operating profit. This is because, in calculating the cash flow from operations, depreciation is added back to the operating profit, but the corresponding cash outflow (the purchase of fixed assets) is not deducted. Rather it is disclosed later as an element of the net cash outflow from investing activities. Booths adds back depreciation of £1,327,455 to an operating profit of £3,178,359.

The remaining adjustments to operating profit may be positive or negative. The key adjustments for most companies (and the only adjustments in Booths' reconciliation) are those relating to changes in working capital. We explained earlier in the chapter that an increase in the amount of stock held, or in the amount of debtors outstanding, represents a use of cash, whereas an increase in the amount of creditors outstanding represents a source of cash. Thus in reconciling the accruals-based operating profit figure to the operating cash flow figure we must adjust for changes in the level of stocks, debtors and creditors.

Note 18 reveals that in 1992 Booths 'released' cash by reducing (the amount invested in) stocks and debtors, but 'used' cash resources by reducing (paying off) creditors. Because the reduction in creditors is greater than the reduction in stocks and debtors, the net effect is to reduce the cash available for other purposes. In 1991, the increase in stocks was almost completely offset (financed) by the increase in creditors. Hence, the reduction in debtors in 1991 provided a useful increase in cash available for other purposes.

The changes in the components of Booths' working capital for 1991 and 1992 were as follows (Note 18):

	1992 £	1991 £
Stocks	43,643	(238,576)
Debtors	119,831	191,967
Creditors	(416,340)	232,964
Change in net working capital:		
Increase/(Decrease) in cash available	(252,866)	186,355

The importance of changes in working capital for the operating cash flows of Booths (and indeed any company) is illustrated below:

	1992 £	1991 £
Operating Profit	3,178,359	2,769,745
Add back Depreciation	1,327,455	1,164,215
	4,505,814	3,933,960
Change in net working capital available	(252,866)	186,355
Cash inflow from operating activities	4,252,948	4,120,315

Had there been no change in working capital in either year, the operating cash flow in 1992 (£4,505,814) would have represented an increase of 14.5% over the corresponding figure in 1991 (£3,933,960). However, the reduction in working capital in 1991 and the increase in working capital in 1992 conspire to reduce the increase in operating cash flow (£4,252,948 − £4,120,315) to 3.2%. We shall now attempt to ascertain the reasons for the movements in working capital and, in particular, discover whether it is likely that working capital will continue to increase, and thereby absorb cash resources, in the future. First, however, we must identify which accounts comprise the elements of net working capital in Booths' cash flow statement.

Components of working capital

The decreases in stocks and debtors are verifiable from an examination of the balance sheet:

	Stocks £	Debtors £
1991	5,302,834	431,777
1992	5,259,191	311,946
	43,643	119,831

However the verification of the decrease in creditors (£416,340) requires further investigation. The total short-term creditors figure is disclosed in Note 12 — Creditors: Amounts falling due within one year, and the decrease in 1992 is £763,974 (£10,980,498 − £11,744,472). However, many of the movements in the individual components of this figure are dealt with elsewhere in the cash flow statement. We explained earlier that the movement on the Bank overdraft (£583,142) is identified at the end of the cash flow statement — it is the residual balance. Similarly the movement on Bank loans is included in the Loan repayments figure in the Financing activities section of the statement. We can therefore exclude the movements in both the Bank overdraft and the Bank loans from the movement in creditors.

Remember, we are trying to reconcile the operating profit figure with that of the operating cash flow by adjusting for purchases and expenses which may have been charged in the profit and loss account but for which no cash has yet been paid, i.e. we are looking for movements on certain creditor and accruals accounts. The operating profit in the profit and loss account is struck *before* the tax charge and the dividend appropriation. Hence there is no need to adjust the operating figure for movements in the balances for accruals of 'Current corporation tax', 'Advanced corporation tax' or 'Proposed dividends'. The figures representing the actual Corporation tax paid and Dividends paid are disclosed separately in the cash flow statement.

The same argument applies to accrued interest. Unfortunately, unlike taxation and dividends, there is no accrued interest disclosed separately in Note 12. In fact it is included in the item 'Accruals' along with other accrued expenses such as gas and electricity. The decrease in Accruals is £606,860. However, we wish to adjust operating profit for movements in accruals other than interest payable. Therefore we need to identify the movement in accrued interest and eliminate it from our calculation. Fortunately, this is easy:

	£
Interest payable (Profit and Loss Account)	1,774,026
Interest paid (Cash Flow Statement)	1,844,325
Decrease in accrued interest	70,299

and the decrease in 'Accruals' other than accrued interest is £536,561 (i.e. £606,860 − £70,299).

We can now verify that the decrease in Creditors of £416,340 (Note 18) comprises movements in the following accounts included in 'Creditors: Amounts falling due within one year' (Note 12):

	£
Trade creditors	60,736
Other taxes and social security costs	59,485
Accruals excluding accrued interest	(536,561)
	(416,340)

Movements on the remaining accounts disclosed in Note 12 are all dealt with elsewhere in the cash flow statement.

Analysis of working capital management

The analysis of Booths' cash flow statement has, *inter alia*, identified the importance of good working capital management. This is particularly true when a business is expanding. *Ceteris paribus,* as sales increase so do the levels of stocks, trade debtors and trade creditors, and for most companies this means finding additional cash to finance the additional working capital.

Table 11.7 shows that Booths requires 1.08p of working capital (here defined as the excess of stocks and *trade* debtors over *trade* creditors) for every £1 of sales in 1992. This compares rather unfavourably with the figure of minus 3.9p for Tesco plc. The working capital ratios reveal that whereas the debtors and creditors payment periods are similar for both companies, Booths' average stockholding period is more than double that of Tesco's. In effect, Tesco purchases goods from its suppliers on 28 days' credit, and sells them for cash within 13 days. It retains the cash for a further 15 days investing it in the business as it wishes. Booths purchases goods from its suppliers on 24 days' credit, but sells them for cash on average 28 days later. Booths must find cash to finance its working capital requirements over this four day period. It has working capital requirements of £5,264,012 of which £4,466,846 is financed by its suppliers. The remainder (£797,166) must be financed from other sources, for example the bank or shareholders.

Clearly, one aim of working capital management is to reduce the stockholding period and debtor payment period whilst increasing the creditor payment period, without adversely affecting supplier and customer goodwill. It would appear from Table 11.7 that Booths could make the most impact on reducing working capital by reducing its stockholding period. Tesco derives enormous advantages from its size. It has central distribution warehouses, an integrated sales-based ordering and distribution system and considerable influence over its suppliers. Booths cannot match these advantages and is unlikely to be able to reduce its stock levels to 13 days in the foreseeable future. Nevertheless, the stockholding period has been reduced from 31 days in 1991 to 28 days in 1992, and the chairman's announcement that the company is currently introducing a computerized stock control system suggests that the stockholding period will fall still further in the next few years. This is of great importance. The planned construction of a new store suggests that Booths' turnover will continue to rise in the future. Currently, Booths requires 1.08p of working capital for every £1 of sales, i.e. for every additional £5 million of sales, the company must finance an additional £54,000 of net working capital. However, if the stockholding period was reduced to, say, 19.8 days, Booths would show a 'negative capital requirement' of 1.08p per £1 of sales:

	£000
Stocks (£67,568,000 × 19.8/365)	3,665
Trade debtors	5
	3,670
Trade creditors	(4,467)
Net working capital	(797)
Sales	74,133
Net working capital per £1 of sales	(1.08) pence

In this case, trade creditors (suppliers) would not only be financing the whole of the working capital requirement, but would also be providing an additional £797,000 for Booths to invest elsewhere in the business, or reduce the interest-bearing overdraft. Furthermore, for every £5 million increase in turnover, the suppliers would finance the additional stock requirements and would provide an additional £54,000 to be invested elsewhere.

Summary and conclusion

Booths' performance in 1992 was satisfactory in many respects. Turnover increased in real terms and both the gross margin and operating margin increased, reflecting the cost efficiencies achieved in stock control, distribution and administration. However, the company is paying a high price for the recent rapid expansion of the business. New stores have been financed predominantly by borrowing. The high level of debt, combined with high interest rates during the year, resulted in a sharp increase in interest charges. Thus, despite a good operating performance, Booths' return on equity fell and dividends were held constant for the third successive year.

The company is unfortunate in that its period of expansion has coincided with a period of high interest rates. A fall in interest rates would result in higher net cash inflows and an opportunity to reduce the level of debt. This in turn would reduce the level of interest payments, which would increase the net cash inflow, and so on. However, as the company is committed to building another new store, the level of borrowing is likely to remain high. Nevertheless, significant benefits will flow to the shareholders if interest rates fall, and profit margins are maintained as sales volume continues to increase. There are opportunities also for management to improve margins by continuing to introduce new technology into the company's stock control and distribution systems.

Improved stock control should aid the operating cash flows of the business by reducing the average stockholding period, thereby reducing the amount of capital invested in stocks. If the length of the stockholding period can be reduced below that of the creditors' payment period, then further increases in turnover will actually generate additional finance from suppliers.

However, important though these cost efficiencies are, the most important factors which will determine the future performance of Booths are the pace of expansion and the impact of competition. The major supermarket chains each operate around 400 stores, and each opens approximately 20 stores every year. Finance is generated internally from operations and raised externally through bank loans, the issue of bonds and debentures and the issue of shares. To counter the threat of superstore competition, Booths has adopted a strategy of closing some of the older, smaller high-street stores and opening larger stores on new sites.

However, the building of just one new superstore is capable of changing dramatically the balance sheet of Booths. It is not possible to raise large sums of money from the existing shareholders, and an issue of shares to a wider public would transfer control out of the hands of the (family) directors. The new strategy has forced the company to borrow heavily and the situation is likely to persist for some time. The threat to Booths' future profitability is clear. The company must borrow to finance the new stores and new systems required to compete in the market place. The high cost of borrowing means that Booths must generate a high level of operating cash flows. This cannot be guaranteed if the market becomes saturated with new stores and/or more powerful competitors begin to compete on price.

Discussion topics

1. Explain why an examination of an organization's cash resources may be a crucial part of an evaluation of its performance and prospects.

2. 'Cash flow is the life-blood of any organization. Thus cash flow statements, and not income statements, should be included in financial reports.' Discuss.

3. Outline the main sources and uses of an organization's cash.

4. Distinguish between operating, investing and financing decisions. Why is it important to understand their nature?

5. Explain the difference between the direct and indirect method of presenting the cash flow statement. Which method provides the user with the most useful information?

6. Why is depreciation *added back* to operating profit when constructing a cash flow statement using the indirect method? Can you think of any other income statement expenses which would be treated in the same way as depreciation under the indirect method?

7. How does the cash flow statement help users to identify whether or not a company is managing its working capital efficiently?

8. Suggest reasons why, despite a good operating performance in 1992, the directors of E.H. Booth and Co. Ltd decided not to increase the dividend paid to shareholders.

Exercises

11.1 Biterolf Ltd is a retailing company with numerous stores throughout the UK. It is proposing to open a new store on 1 January 19X6. Initially, the store will be opened for a trial period of six months. Biterolf Ltd will provide any funds required by the new store during the trial period. Biterolf's finance director provides you with the following estimates relating to the new store:

1. Freehold property will be purchased on 1 January 19X6, for £1,000,000 due when the property is purchased.
2. Fittings and equipment costing £300,000 will be purchased and paid for on 1 January 19X6. They will have an estimated life of 10 years.
3. Sales:

January 19X6	£100,000
February 19X6	£150,000
March 19X6 and subsequent months	£200,000 per month

4. Purchases:

January 19X6	£1,200,000
February 19X6 and subsequent months	£150,000 per month

5. One half of all sales will be for cash. The remainder will be on credit, and payment for these sales is expected two months after the sale is made.
6. All purchases will be on credit. One month's credit will be taken.
7. Other expenses are expected to amount to £25,000 per month, payable as they are incurred.

- (a) Prepare a cash budget for the new store covering the trial period from 1 January to 30 June 19X6, showing the funds that will be required from Biterolf Ltd month by month.
- (b) On the basis of the estimated figures, advise the directors of Biterolf Ltd whether the new store is likely to be profitable.

11.2 The following are the balance sheets of Kurwenal Manufacturing Ltd as at 31 December 19X6 and 19X7:

	19X6 £	19X6 £	19X7 £	19X7 £
Fixed assets, at cost	28,200		36,900	
less: Accumulated depreciation	9,300		14,400	
		18,900		22,500
Current assets:				
Stock	15,300		17,700	
Debtors	7,500		7,800	
Cash	1,500		300	
	24,300		25,800	
less: Current liabilities	5,700		3,900	
		18,600		21,900
		37,500		44,400
Issued share capital		24,000		24,000
Retained profits		13,500		20,400
		37,500		44,400

Your client, Ms Kurwenal, owns most of the shares in the company. She writes to you as follows: 'I always thought I was in business to make profits. Now I am not so sure. In 19X7 I made a profit of £6,900 and did not draw any dividend from the company. Despite this, the company had even less cash at the end of the year than at the beginning. Perhaps I should try to make a loss in 19X8'.

- (a) Draft a reply to Ms Kurwenal, explaining to her in non-technical terms the relationship between profits and changes in cash balances. Include in your reply a cash flow statement for the company for 19X7. (No fixed assets were sold or scrapped during 19X7.)
- (b) Discuss briefly the importance of both profits and changes in cash balances to a business enterprise.

11.3   The balance sheets of Flosshilde Ltd for the past two years are shown below. No property or fittings were sold during the year ended 30 September 19X6. However, some plant was sold on 1 October 19X6 for £8,000. This plant had cost £34,000 and had been written down to £16,000 by the date of sale. The loss on sale of £8,000 had been deducted from profit for the year ended 30 September 19X6. No dividends were paid or proposed for the year to 30 September 19X6.

- (a) Prepare a cash flow statement for Flosshilde Ltd for the year ended 30 September 19X6.
- (b) Describe briefly the usefulness of such a statement in assessing the performance of Flosshilde Ltd.

Balance sheets at 30 September	19X5		19X6	
	£'000	*£'000*	*£'000*	*£'000*
Fixed assets				
Freehold property at cost		232		232
Plant and machines at cost	354		420	
less: Depreciation	128		152	
		226		268
Fittings at cost	104		120	
less: Depreciation	34		40	
		70		80
		528		580
Current assets				
Stock	52		108	
Debtors	30		24	
Cash	108		80	
	190		212	
Current liabilities	38		26	
		152		186
		680		766

Capital

Issued share capital	400	400
Profit and loss account	280	286
14% debentures (irredeemable)	—	80
	680	766

11.4   Marcello Manufacturing Co. Ltd makes a single product for which the demand has now stabilized at a sales level of approximately £500,000 p.a. The business was started on 1 November 19X5 and accounts have been prepared for the first two years by the company's unqualified bookkeeper.

Balance Sheets

	31 October 19X6 £	31 October 19X7 £
Cash	64,500	43,000
Debtors	42,000	69,000
Stock	28,500	37,500
Plant	78,000	132,500
	213,000	282,000
Capital (90,000 shares of £1 each)	90,000	90,000
Retained profits	27,000	34,050
Creditors	66,000	37,500
Reserves:		
Tax	18,000	40,500
General	—	45,000
Depreciation	7,800	19,050
Contingency	4,200	6,900
Dividend	—	9,000
	213,000	282,000

Profit and loss accounts

Year ended	31 October 19X6 £	31 October 19X7 £
Materials used	108,000	126,000
Factory wages	153,000	157,500
Factory rent and other expenses	69,000	73,500
Depreciation reserve	7,800	11,250
Office expenses	34,500	39,000
Contingency reserve	4,200	2,700
General reserve	—	45,000
Tax reserve	18,000	40,500
Dividend reserve	—	9,000
Net profit for the year	27,000	7,050
Total sales	421,500	511,500

No plant was sold during the year ended 31 October 19X7. No dividend was paid for 19X6. The managing director proposes that a dividend of 10p per share should be paid in respect of the year ended 31 October 19X7 and has instructed that a reserve be established for this in the above accounts. The other directors are concerned about the proposed payment; they argue that the accounts reveal falling profits and a declining cash balance and that in the circumstances no dividend should be paid.

- Prepare a brief report to the directors advising them on the position. If you think it helpful, include in the report a revised presentation of the profit and loss accounts and balance sheets for the two years and a cash flow statement for the year ended 31 October 19X7. (*Note*: On inquiry you discover that the 'contingency reserve' is for doubtful debts, and is fully justified by the delays in payment of the debtors in question.)

11.5   Professor Parpignol (ex-Professor of Accounting) had been out of a job for 12 months but he still liked to visit the university campus now and again to relive past triumphs. As he sank his eighth pint of beer in a corner of a local public house, he was approached by a former colleague from the Medical School, Dr Goro. As always happened on these occasions, Dr Goro wanted to discuss her latest financial problem whereas Professor Parpignol wanted advice on his latest squash injury.

At the cost of two extra pints Dr Goro got her way. Her problem concerned a company in which she had invested in the hope of receiving regular dividends and a capital growth. She produced the latest set of accounts which she had received that morning. The Chairman's Report stated that the company had recently invested in new capital equipment which would increase profits in the future, but that the consequent cash shortage meant that no dividend could be paid this year. A Cash Flow Statement was included to explain the position.

Dr Goro was confused. In the Statement depreciation was added back to net profit as a 'source'. 'If depreciation is a source of cash then the more capital equipment the company has, the greater is the depreciation figure and so the greater the source of cash. So where *is* the cash? And if there isn't enough cash at present why not depreciate some more?'

Professor Parpignol sent his friend away to replenish the glasses and turned to the Notes to the Accounts. Under the note on fixed asset he saw the following:

	19X1 £	19X2 £
Plant and equipment	576,000	735,000
less: Accumulated depreciation	315,000	265,000
	261,000	470,000

Glancing through the rest of the accounts he noted that the new capital equipment bought during the year had cost £512,000, that old plant had been sold at a loss of £107,000, and that the year's depreciation charge had been £143,000.

When Dr Goro returned, Professor Parpignol passed her a beermat on which he had made a few jottings. These consisted of a reconstruction of the plant and equipment information to show how the figures had been arrived at, and an indication of which figures would appear in the Cash Flow Statement.

Dr Goro was astounded. It all began to make sense now. She turned to thank the Professor — but too late. He was already sliding beneath the table.

- ■ (a) What were the jottings that had so astounded Dr Goro? Reconstruct the year's changes in fixed assets and the Cash Flow Statement entries which Professor Parpignol had produced.
  - (b) Is Dr Goro right in her belief that depreciation is a source of cash?
  - (c) In a wider context discuss the wisdom of a company policy that leads it to undertake expansionary investments to the exclusion of the current dividend.

11.6 Rodolfo forms a company to start a new business on 1 January 19X4. He plans to provide the necessary capital in the form of a subscription for £1 ordinary shares. The following estimates are made about the first six months' business:

	£000
Equipment bought for cash, January	3,000
Stock of goods bought on credit, January	5,500
Sales per month, January to March	2,800
Sales per month, April to June	7,600
Rent per annum, payable quarterly in advance	800
General expenses, per month, cash outlay	350
The estimated gross profit percentage is 25% on sales value	
Stock is to be maintained always at £5,500,000	
Creditors will allow one month's credit. Customers are to	
be allowed two months' credit	
An interim dividend of £1,000,000 is, if profit allows, to be	
paid at the end of June.	

Assume all payments will be made at the end of the month in which they fall due. Depreciation on equipment for the half-year is to be £150,000.

- ■ (a) Calculate the capital Rodolfo should raise if the maximum financial need in the first six months is to be met, but no more.
  - (b) Draft the final accounts for the half-year (profit and loss account and balance sheet), on the assumption that Rodolfo pays in the necessary capital, as calculated in (a), on 1 January.

11.7 Klingsor Clothing Ltd was recently formed by Hilary Parsifal to manufacture a new type of waterproof clothing. In its first month of operations, the firm was involved in the following transactions:

May 1 (i) Hilary Parsifal invested £10,000 cash into the business.
(ii) Waterproof material was bought on credit for £1,700. This amount was paid to the supplier on 15 June.
(iii) Two part-time employees were hired to assemble the waterproof clothing. They were each to be paid £200 per month on the last day of the month.
May 2 Cutting and sewing machinery was purchased. Hilary Parsifal paid £7,200 in cash for this equipment.

May 5   Hilary Parsifal signed an agreement with a local outdoor pursuits retailer to supply waterproof garments in May and June (half the order being delivered in each month). The total order price was £3,600, £1,000 of which was paid to Klingsor Clothing at the time the order was agreed. The remainder would be paid at the end of June.

May 30   The employees were paid. Hilary Parsifal counted her stock and found that £700 of material had not been used. One-half of the waterproof clothing order was delivered as per the agreement.

Hilary Parsifal tells you that the equipment has a three year life with zero scrap value, that no additional waterproof material was purchased in May and that she had no finished items of waterproof clothing nor any work in progress at the end of May.

- ■ (a) Prepare a statement of the operating cash flows occurring in the month of May.
  (b) Prepare a conventional profit and loss account (income statement) for the month of May.
  (c) Compare the two statements and explain which one appears to give the better measure of performance.
  (d) Consider why company financial accounts are published every year. Would longer (e.g. every two years) or shorter (e.g. every 6 months) time periods be better for external users of the company's accounting information?

11.8   The following information relates to the accounts of Astral Ltd.

Profit and Loss Account – Year to 31.12.X2

	£000's	£000's
Sales		3000
Less: Cost of Goods Sold	1800	
Depreciation	120	
Other expenses	600	
		2520
		480

Balance Sheets as at

	1.1.X1 £000's	1.1.X1 £000's	1.1.X2 £000's	1.1.X2 £000's
Fixed assets				
– cost		1200		1560
– depreciation		(420)		(540)
		780		1020
Current Assets:				
Stock	360		530	
Debtors	480		670	
Cash	240		70	
	1080		1270	
Trade Creditors	(300)		(130)	
		780		1140
		1560		2160

Represented by:

Share Capital	660		780	
Retained Profits	900	1560	1380	2160
		1560		2160

'Other expenses' include £400,000 paid for wages. All payments in this category were made in cash.

- (a) Calculate the following:
  — cash received from customers
  — total cost of goods purchased
  — amount of cash paid to suppliers
- (b) Calculate the net cash provided from operating activities using *both* the indirect *and* the direct method.
- (c) Discuss the usefulness of a cash flow statement and explain why it complements the information provided in the profit and loss account and balance sheet.

11.9 The following is the balance sheet of Zinnan Ltd as at 31 December 19X8.

	£		£
Share capital*	100,000	Land	52,000
Retained profit	32,500	Machinery**	65,000
Long-term loan	20,500	Investments	25,000
Debentures	35,000	Stock	34,000
Creditors	20,000	Debtors	20,000
		Cash	12,000
	208,000		208,000

* Share capital comprises 100,000 £1 shares
** Machinery is stated net of depreciation

During 19X9 the following events occurred:

- (i) Net income for 19X9 was £42,000 after charging £15,500 depreciation on machinery but before taking account of any amortization on the patent (see (v) below).
- (ii) Zinnan sold an investment for £12,600 which resulted in a gain of £1,100. The gain has been included in net income.
- (iii) Land was purchased for £27,500 and Machinery was purchased for £19,500. Both purchases were made in cash.
- (iv) The long-term loan was paid off in full and debentures of £15,000 were paid off at par value and a new issue of debentures of £10,000 was made.
- (v) Zinnan purchased a patent to produce Cuddlers for £33,000. The patent had a further six years to run and the production of Cuddlers is expected to be profitable during the remaining life of the patent.
- (vi) At 31 December 19X9, creditors were £20,000, debtors were £44,000 and stock was £60,000.
- (vii) 50,000 £1 shares were issued at £1.50 each.
- (viii) The directors declared a dividend of 20p per share which has not yet been paid and which has not been taken into account in arriving at net income.

- (a) Prepare a balance sheet for Zinnan Ltd as at 31 December 19X9.
  (b) Prepare a cash flow statement for the year to 31 December 19X9.

11.10 Triaz Ltd buys and sells computing equipment. Its summarized accounts for the past two years are as follows:

Profit and loss accounts, year ended 31 March

	19X5 £000	19X5 £000	19X6 £000	19X6 £000
Sales		685		832
Less Cost of sales		428		501
Gross profit		257		331
Add Profit on sale of equipment		—		12
		257		343
Less Operating expenses:				
Rent, rates, lighting, heating, etc.	67		75	
Salaries	47		52	
Depreciation of equipment	82		108	
Other expenses	12	208	18	253
Net profit		49		90
Dividend paid		30		50
Retained profit		19		40

Balance sheets at 31 March

	19X5 £000	19X5 £000	19X6 £000	19X6 £000
Fixed assets:				
Equipment at cost		410		540
Less Accumulated depreciation		230		298
		180		242
Current assets:				
Stock	143		249	
Trade debtors	76		138	
Cash at bank	231		111	
	450		498	
Less Current liabilities	43	407	63	435
		587		677
Share capital and reserves:				
Issued share capital		400		400
Retained profits		87		127
		487		527
Long-term loan		100		150
		587		677

No equipment was purchased or sold during the year ended 31 March 19X5. Equipment sold during the year ended 31 March 19X6 had cost £50,000 and accumulated depreciation of £40,000 had been provided by the date of sale.

- (a) Prepare a cash flow statement for Triaz Ltd for the year ended 31 March 19X6 to explain the change in the company's cash position during the year.
- (b) Discuss the usefulness of the cash flow statement to the management of Triaz Ltd.

Further reading

Accounting Standards Board, *FRS 1: Cash Flow Statements*, ASB Ltd, 1991.

Board, J. and Day, J.F.S., 'The information content of cash flow figures', *Accounting and Business Research*, Winter 1989.

Crichton, J., 'Cash flow statements — what are the choices?', *Accountancy*, October 1990.

Egginton, D.A., 'In defence of profit measurement: Some limitations of cash flow and value added as performance measures for external reporting', *Accounting and Business Research*, Spring 1984.

Lee, T.A., 'A case for cash flow reporting', *Journal of Business Finance*, Summer 1972.

Lee, T.A., 'The cash flow accounting alternative for corporate financial reporting', in van Dam, C. (ed.), *Trends in Managerial and Financial Accounting*, Martinus Nijhoff, 1978.

Lee, T.A., 'Cash flow accounting and reporting', in Lee, T.A. (ed.), *Developments in Financial Reporting*, Philip Allan, 1981.

Lee, T.A., 'Cash flow accounting and the allocation problem', *Journal of Business Finance and Accounting*, Autumn 1982.

Wearing, R.T., 'Cash flow and the Eurotunnel', *Accounting and Business Research*, Winter 1989.

PART

3

Limitations of the Conventional Model

12 *Problems with the Conventional Accounting Model*

Historical cost accounting has been used for some five hundred years, and we have spent the last eight chapters explaining the principles underlying the preparation of historical cost financial statements within the conventional accounting framework. Does that mean that we (and others) consider the conventional historical cost accounting framework to be the best method available for the determination of net income and financial position?

From the beginning of this book we have defined the primary purpose of accounting as the identification, measurement and communication of useful information to decision makers. Because there is a variety of ways of carrying out this process, we introduced a set of evaluative criteria for alternative accounting methods. These criteria were categorized as relating either to the *usefulness* or to the *feasibility* of the various methods. In Chapter 2 we noted that management forecasts of future cash flows are potentially very relevant to users' decisions but that such forecasts are subjective, difficult to verify and may involve the disclosure of confidential information. Consequently, we concluded that it is most unlikely that cash forecasts will form the basis of published statements in the foreseeable future.

In Chapter 2 we also noted that historical cash flows satisfy the criteria of objectivity and verifiability but could, in certain circumstances, produce misleading figures, for example when entities trade extensively on credit, and/or incur large amounts of capital expenditure. Accrual accounting tries to avoid this problem by recognizing transactions at the time of sale and purchase rather than at the time of cash receipt and cash payment, and by spreading the cost of long-lived assets over their useful lives. Further, we noted that in times of stable prices, historical cost accounting generates an income figure which is both a good measure of past performance and a good indicator of future performance. In so far as (historical) cash flow statements are of value, they should be regarded as supplementary to income statements and balance sheets prepared on an accruals basis as we argued in Chapter 11.

It may therefore seem that conventional historical cost accounting satisfies both the usefulness and feasibility criteria. However, our earlier evaluation of the usefulness of historical cost figures assumed stable prices. But prices are rarely stable and over the past two or three decades there have been frequent movements in price levels in most Western countries. Inflation, more than any other event, has caused accountants to question the suitability of historical cost accounting as a method of reporting business performance and to give serious consideration to other accounting methods. And changing prices are not the only source of problem for the conventional accounting model. In this chapter we provide an overview of the major areas of difficulty and in the following chapter we examine in more detail alternative accounting treatments to reflect the impact of changing prices.

12.1   Limitations of the conventional model

In order to illustrate some of the limitations of the conventional model, consider the case of Edgeley Ltd, whose accounts for 199X are summarized in Table 12.1.

Edgeley Ltd is a retailing company with premises in Scotland. The company was established twenty years ago, at which time it purchased its existing premises for £500,000. The premises are being depreciated over a fifty-year period using the straight line method. The directors of Edgeley estimate that the premises are now worth some £5 million. Equipment and fittings are also depreciated by the straight line method, using an annual rate of 15%. Closing stock is included at cost, using the first in, first out (FIFO) stock flow assumption.

Since Edgeley's incorporation, its directors have pursued a policy of providing a high quality of service and seiling high quality products. This policy has proved successful and the company has a well trained and loyal workforce and enjoys a high degree of customer loyalty. Its name, image and customer base are the envy of local competitors.

In the following sections we explore the extent to which the company's current position and prospects are reflected in its financial statements.

12.2   Outdated historical costs

The conventional historical cost accounting model reports measures of performance and position which are based largely on the original or historical costs of the resources used by the reporting entity. For example, Edgeley owns

Table 12.1 *Edgeley Ltd*

Income statement for the year ended 31 December 199X

	£000	£000
Sales		1,010
Cost of goods sold		595
Gross profit		415
Light, heat, wages etc.	140	
Depreciation	55	
		195
Net profit		220
Dividends		50
Retained profit		170

Balance sheet at 31 December 199X

	£000	£000
Fixed assets		
Premises at cost	500	
less Accumulated depreciation	200	300
Equipment and fittings at cost	300	
less Accumulated depreciation	185	115
		415
Current assets		
Stock	140	
Debtors	35	
Cash at bank	85	
	260	
Current liabilities		
Creditors	105	
Net current assets		155
Total assets less current liabilities		570
Capital and reserves		
Share capital		250
Retained profit		320
		570

premises which it bought twenty years ago for £500,000 — the figure (less accumulated depreciation) which is reported on the balance sheet. Furthermore, it is the original cost which forms the basis of the annual depreciation charge in the income statement. How useful are the income statement and balance sheet numbers, which relate to the premises, to a user of Edgeley's accounts wishing to form a view of the company's current position and of its prospects?

The depreciation charge is £10,000 (£500,000 ÷ 50) per annum. Yet, the current value of the premises is estimated at £5 million. And, if they have a remaining life of only thirty years, the annual straight line depreciation charge should be some £167,000 (£5 million ÷ 30). Inclusion of this figure in place of the historical cost depreciation charge of £10,000 would reduce reported net profit from £220,000 to £63,000. On the other hand, there has been an appreciation in the value of the premises. Should some recognition of this gain, amounting to £4.5 million in the twenty years since the premises were purchased, not be included in the financial statements? This is an issue to which we return in the next chapter. Suffice to say at this stage that the £10,000 historical cost depreciation charge in the income statement does not appear to tell the whole story of the changes in wealth resulting from ownership and use of the premises during 199X.

What of the balance sheet position? The premises are shown at a figure of £300,000, an amount which bears little resemblance to their current value of £5 million. This may mislead users in at least two respects. First, they will have an understated impression of the value of the company's assets. This may be important, for example, to a lender who is asked to advance a loan to the company and who wishes to form a view as to the security underlying the loan if the company fails to make interest payments or capital repayments on the due dates. Secondly, understating the asset base overstates the return which the company appears to be earning. We discussed ratio analysis in Chapter 10. The accounts in Table 12.1 suggest that Edgeley is earning a return on net assets employed (here defined as total assets less current liabilities) of 38.6% (220,000 ÷ 570,000 × 100). Suppose that the premises were included at their current value. Net assets would become £5,270,000 (570,000 − 300,000 + 5,000,000) and the return on net assets employed, ignoring any possible changes to the depreciation charge to reflect the increase in the value of the premises during the year, would be 4.2% (220,000 ÷ 5,270,000 × 100).

Another way of looking at this problem is to ask what would have been the position had the company purchased the *identical* premises during the current year instead of twenty years ago. In that case, the balance sheet would show a cost of some £5 million and the income statement would bear a charge of some £167,000, leading to a return on net assets far lower than is shown in the accounts in Table 12.1, for a business which in all physical respects is identical to that described for Edgeley Ltd. If one purpose of accounting reports is to treat identical items equivalently, the conventional model fails.

Similar arguments, albeit on a more modest scale, apply to stock. Stock is charged to the income statement when it is sold, as part of cost of goods sold, at its original cost. This may be a poor representation of what it would have cost to buy the stock at the date of sale and of what it will cost to replace it — which may be of relevance to a user who wishes to estimate the likely future profitability of the business. Similarly, the balance sheet figure for stock may not be a good indication of its current value. The extent of the understatement (or possibly the overstatement in times of falling prices) of the income statement charge and the balance sheet value will depend on the rate at which stock is 'turned over' (i.e., the period between its purchase and sale) and on the rate at which its price increases or decreases.

To summarize, the conventional accounting model takes little account of the current costs or values of the resources used in a business, which are likely to be more relevant than are historical costs in the measurement of efficiency and in the prediction of future performance.

12.3   Holes in the balance sheet

While some assets and liabilities are included in conventional balance sheets at figures which bear little resemblance to their current values, others are not included at all! Consider the case of Edgeley Ltd. We are told that it has a well-trained and loyal workforce and enjoys a high degree of customer loyalty and that the company's name, image and customer base are the envy of local competitors. These attributes result from past expenditures, for example on advertising and staff training, and seem likely to provide future benefits in terms of increased sales levels, the ability to charge higher prices and so on. Yet they appear as assets only rarely in accounts prepared using the conventional model. Why?

In order to be included as an asset on the balance sheet under the conventional method, an item must satisfy two main tests:

(1) It must satisfy the definition of an asset. In Chapter 6, we introduced the International Accounting Standards Committee (IASC) definition of an asset as 'a resource controlled by an enterprise as a result of past events and from which future economic benefits are expected to flow.'

(2) Its amount must be capable of being measured with reasonable certainty.

Many of the items relevant for Edgeley satisfy the first condition. For example, the company's reputation, well-trained staff and loyal customer base are likely to produce benefits in the future. Other items, which are often excluded from balance sheets, also pass the first test, for example brand names, research and development expenditure, distribution networks and monopolistic market positions. The exclusion of such items, which are often intangible assets, under historical cost accounting, is more often the result of their failure to clear the second hurdle — their original costs cannot be identified with reasonable certainty. For example, a well-trained and cooperative workforce may be the result of many small items of expenditure over a number of years on training courses, bonus schemes and so on, some of the benefits of which arise during the period in which they are incurred. Similarly, a valuable brand name might be the result of many years of advertising and other promotional expenditure, part of which stimulated demand immediately. Tracing those costs, and differentiating those which provide an immediate benefit from those which provide long term benefits, may not be feasible. It may, of course, be easier to measure the current value of such assets than their original cost. We return to the treatment of intangibles in Chapter 17.

Assets are not alone in being excluded from conventional balance sheets. Liabilities sometimes suffer the same fate. For example, organizations sometimes lease assets rather than buying them. A lease involves one party (the lessee) who wishes to enjoy the use of an asset agreeing to make a number of payments to the owner of the asset (the lessor), in return for which the lessee is entitled to exclusive use of the asset for a specified period, which may vary from a few days to the entire life of the asset. The legal ownership of the asset remains with the lessor and the conventional treatment in the accounts of the lessee will sometimes be to recognize only the lease payments as costs as they fall due, with no recognition on the balance sheet of either the asset or the obligation to make future lease payments. And yet, in terms of economic substance, what is the difference between borrowing money to purchase an asset and signing a lease which allows exclusive use of the asset, possibly for most or all of its useful life, in return for an agreement to make regular lease payments? The lease payments involve cash outflows little different from the interest payments and capital repayments associated with a loan. It is important to note here that standard setting bodies in many countries have now recognized this particular conflict between legal form and economic substance and have introduced accounting standards which require certain leased assets to be accounted for as though they had been purchased with the proceeds of a loan. Such leases are called *finance leases*. Even in those countries, however, certain other leases, called *operating leases*, are still recognized only by charges in the income statement, even where they involve an irrevocable obligation to make future payments, i.e. they involve a liability. Other schemes exist whereby financial obligations are kept off the balance sheet and the reasons for their existence are discussed further in Section 12.5.

12.4   Too many choices

The well-known tale of the client who asks her accountant 'what was my profit for last year?', only to receive the reply 'what figure did you have in mind madam?' is not entirely without foundation! The range of income statement and balance sheet figures which may, in accordance with accepted accounting conventions, be generated from a set of transactions is remarkably large.

Consider the case of Edgeley Ltd. Its closing stock figure of £140,000 is the result of applying the FIFO stock flow assumption. As we have already seen (Chapter 7), other assumptions are possible. For example, Edgeley might have chosen instead to use the *weighted average* assumption which, in times of rising prices, would have resulted in a lower closing stock figure and a different income figure. Whether the income figure would have been higher or lower will depend on the size and age of opening stock and on the rate at which stock prices have changed. For a manufacturing company, the balance sheet amount of stock and the income statement figure will also depend on the extent to which, and the method by which, overhead costs have been included in stock valuation.

Choice is also available in calculating the annual depreciation charge, as we saw in Chapter 6. Edgeley Ltd might have chosen a method different from straight line, or assumed a different life. For example, had the directors assumed a life for the premises of one hundred instead of fifty years, the annual depreciation charge would have been halved. Use of the reducing balance method of depreciation for equipment and fittings would result in a higher depreciation charge in the early years of the asset's life and a lower charge in the later years.

Stock and depreciation are only two of a large number of areas in which accounting policy choices are available. In Chapters 16 and 17 we will discuss the various treatments which might be used in accounting for the acquisition of one company by another, each of which might lead to a very different income and value number. Other less dramatic examples include: the treatment of development expenditure which, in certain circumstances, may be either written off immediately against profits or capitalized and amortized over its useful life; the treatment of interest costs incurred in financing the construction of assets such as buildings, which may be either treated as part of the capital cost or written off as expenses against income; and the choice of currency exchange rate to be used when the income statement of a foreign subsidiary company is to be translated to the currency unit of the home country of the parent company.

12.5 Creative accounting

The preceding sections have demonstrated the almost infinitely large scope which exists for arriving at numerous different measures of income and value from any one set of transactions. This opportunity may sometimes be used by the managers of organizations to further their own self-interest. In order to understand the reasons for this it is necessary to understand something of the role of regulation and of the capital market in financial reporting. (This is an issue which we introduced in Chapter 3 and shall return to in more detail in Chapter 15.)

While most writers agree that the purpose of accounts is to provide useful information to shareholders, lenders and other users and to facilitate the enforcement of contracts, the terms of which include reference to accounting information, there is less agreement about the need for accounting information to be subject to regulation, either by legislation or by accounting standards. Some argue that in the absence of market inefficiencies, market forces will result in managers publishing accounting information if they wish to raise equity capital from outside shareholders and debt capital from lenders. Managers not doing so would have to pay returns on capital well above the market average or, in the extreme, would not be able to raise funds at all. Hence market forces would result in appropriate financial reporting by organizations at least in so far as the relationship between managers and fund providers is concerned.

The opposite view is that because of inefficiencies in the markets for capital, information and managerial labour, there is a need for regulation if managers are not to be in a position to exploit their informational advantage to the detriment of users. A related argument concerns the informational efficiency of the capital market specifically. There is evidence to support the view that the capital market responds rapidly and in an unbiased manner to all publicly available information and that it can distinguish between accounting information that signals a 'real' change in an organization's position or performance and information that is 'cosmetic' and has no implications for the 'real' position of the organization (this is called the semi-strong form of the Efficient Markets Hypothesis). One implication of this form of efficiency is that disclosure is important whereas the choice of accounting treatment is not. However, some recent evidence casts doubt on the literature supporting the semi-strong form of the EMH.

Moreover, the use of security market efficiency as a criterion ignores the wider set of users whose information needs are not reflected in capital markets. Even if market efficiency is adopted as a criterion, it should be recognized that it is concerned solely with the efficiency of the market in processing information quickly and without bias but says nothing about the optimal allocation of resources or the distribution of wealth.

There are, however, reasons to believe that, even if the capital market is semi-strong efficient, the choice of accounting treatment may be as important as disclosure. Consider, in particular, the interests of managers. They might increase their own welfare in three ways:

(1) If their remuneration is linked directly to accounting profits, for example in their contracts of employment, they might adopt accounting treatments which increase reported profit. For example, managers' contracts of employment may provide for part of their annual remuneration to be paid in the form of a bonus, calculated as a percentage of annual reported profit.

(2) If they receive share options (i.e. options to buy shares in the future at current prices or less), they might increase share price by adopting treatments which increase future cash flows and — eventually — future profits (for example by relieving debt constraints, reducing taxable profit, avoiding price controls, and maximizing return on government contracts where price or return is linked to accounting profits). Note that this second category may involve *increases or decreases* in reported profit or a change in some other aspect of the accounts such as gearing, depending on the particular company and the particular effect which its managers wish to achieve. If share price is increased, other shareholders may also gain, albeit at the expense of others such as lenders and other taxpayers.

(3) They might increase their value in the managerial labour market by being seen to be involved in running apparently 'profitable' companies. While

there is quite strong evidence that the stock market is efficient in the semi-strong form, similar evidence is not available in respect of the managerial labour market. This opportunity to increase a manager's 'market value' probably applies only to a few senior managers in each company — but they may be the ones who influence the accounting treatment adopted by the company.

Even if the capital market is efficient, managers may not believe that it is. Hence they may adopt accounting treatments which show financial performance and position in the best possible light in the expectation that this will result in the highest possible share price. Their actions will be identical to those adopted by managers operating in capital markets which are not efficient.

Regulation may be necessary to restrict organizations' choice of accounting treatments if the above real consequences are regarded as undesirable. It may also be necessary to increase comparability between the reports of different organizations. Most users of financial reports, such as shareholders, analysts, lenders and employees, make decisions which depend on a comparison of the performance, position and prospects of different organizations. If the relevant measures are based on different accounting treatments, apparent differences may be the result either of the application of different accounting procedures or of differences in real performance or position. Users may be unable to identify which differences are cosmetic and which are real, with the result that meaningful comparisons are impossible.

The preceding analysis suggests that accounting standards or other forms of regulation are necessary to limit the ability of the preparers of accounts to increase their own welfare at the expense of users and other groups. The problem is one of market failure, a situation in which intervention and regulation are often thought desirable. It also suggests that standards are needed to increase comparability between the financial reports of different organizations which should assist the efficient allocation of capital and other resources. Whether seeking comparability is worthwhile in all cases depends on the costs involved in relation to the benefits.

A further problem is the relationship between external financial reporting and internal decision making. If the capital market is inefficient, or if managers believe it to be so, the need for managers to recognize the impact of decisions on performance *reported* in external financial statements may distort internal decision-making procedures. A simple example will serve to demonstrate the problems created for managers by the need to comply with conventional external reporting procedures which do not always articulate well with decision-making techniques which take a long-term view.

Suppose that a company is considering whether to invest £20 million in a substantial advertising campaign. The cost would be incurred in the coming year and would result in additional net cash inflows and profits of £5 million in the year after the campaign and in each subsequent year indefinitely. The company's required rate of return on this type of investment is 15% per annum. The use of discounted cash flow techniques shows the advertising campaign to be very attractive. It has an internal rate of return of 25% (well above the company's required return), and a net present value of +£13.3 million. However, in its external financial statements the company will report income in the coming year, when the expenditure is incurred, lower than it would otherwise have been, assuming that the entire cost of the advertising is written off as incurred (the normal treatment under current practice). It is true that the reported income of subsequent years will be higher, but some investors may decide to sell their shares at the end of the coming year on the basis of that year's reported results. Unless the stock market has full information concerning the future benefits expected from the advertising campaign, and impounds it correctly into the company's share price, the lower reported income could lead to a share price temporarily lower than it should be. This would lead to a loss for investors who sell.

Managers may decide not to undertake the advertising because they believe, rightly or wrongly, that the market is inefficient. In other words, management decisions may be severely constrained by external reporting requirements. This provides a further incentive for managers to engage in creative accounting.

12.6   Conclusions

In this chapter we have described and illustrated some of the major problems currently faced by the conventional accounting model — in particular, its use of outdated historical costs, its failure to recognize on the balance sheet certain types of assets and liabilities, and the availability of too much choice in identifying appropriate accounting treatments, particularly in an environment where so much emphasis seems to be placed on one earnings number. As we have seen, those responsible for the preparation of financial statements have incentives to exploit these problems to further their own ends by engaging in creative accounting. Not only does this involve the expenditure of valuable resources, not least of which is the time of accountants and other financial experts, but it also undermines the credibility of financial statements and of the profession which is responsible for their production.

In the next chapter we consider the extent to which the use of accounting models which make use of current, rather than historical, costs and values might eliminate some of the problems we have discussed.

Discussion topics

1. 'Historical cost accounting has been used satisfactorily for centuries. Why change now?' Discuss this assertion critically and answer the question posed.

2. Explain and discuss why some types of assets and liabilities rarely appear on balance sheets.

3. Is the wide choice of accounting treatments available to the preparers of accounts a good thing? Why (or why not)?

4. Explain and discuss the view that there is no place for regulation in accounting.

5. 'Every company in the country is fiddling its profits. Every set of published accounts is based on books which have been gently cooked or completely roasted .... It is the biggest con trick since the Trojan horse .... In fact this deception is all in perfectly good taste. It is totally legitimate. It is creative accounting.' (Ian Griffiths, *Creative Accounting*, 1986).

   Explain why company managers might be willing to expend resources on creative accounting and why they might resist attempts by regulators to reduce the degree of flexibility available to the preparers of accounting statements.

Further reading

Arnold, J., Boyle, P., Carey, A., Cooper, M. and Wild, K., *The Future Shape of Financial Reports*, ICAEW/ICAS, 1991.

Barrett, M.J., Beaver, W.H., Cooper, W.W., Milburn, J.A., Solomons, D. and Tweedie, D., 'American Accounting Association Committee on Accounting and Auditing Measurement, 1989–90', *Accounting Horizons*, September 1991.

Griffiths, I., *Creative Accounting*, Firethorn Press, 1986.

Hines, R., 'Financial accounting: in communicating reality, we construct reality' *Accounting, Organisations and Society*, Vol. 13, No. 3, 1988.

Revsine, L., 'The selective financial misrepresentation hypothesis', *Accounting Horizons*, December 1991.

Smith, T., *Accounting for Growth*, Century Business, 1992.

Tweedie, D. and Whittington, G., 'Financial reporting: current problems and their implications for systematic reform', *Accounting and Business Research*, Winter 1990.

Whittington, G., 'Accounting standard setting in the UK after 20 years: a critique of the Dearing and Solomons Reports', *Accounting and Business Research*, Summer 1989.

13 Accounting for Changing Prices

We explained in Chapter 12 that one of the major problems with the conventional accounting model is that it reports measures of performance and position which are based largely on the (outdated) historical costs of resources used. In this chapter we describe and evaluate several alternative methods of accounting for changing prices.

13.1 Changing price levels

In 1984 a professor at the University of Manchester purchased a house for £30,000. In 1993 she spent a sabbatical year in the USA and rented out the house for a sum that provided her with £6,000 after all expenses. She was delighted with the '20% return' on her investment. But was her return really so high? In 1993 houses similar to the professor's were being bought and sold for £100,000. Presumably the professor (we hasten to add that she was not a professor of accounting) could have sold her house for £100,000 prior to her departure to the USA. If so, perhaps her return from renting was only 6% — £6,000 on £100,000.

To the professor it did not matter which rate of return figure she used — it was important only that she received the highest rent possible. But the decisions of a business manager might be influenced by the reported rate of return. If one division of the business is showing a return of 20%, the manager of the business may be tempted to authorize the investment of more money in that particular division. If the division shows a return of only 6% he may be better advised to recommend closing it down and investing the money in a bank account. Inflation is important to accountants because it can distort the accounting figures upon which such decisions might be based. In particular, in inflationary times the historical costs of certain assets will be significantly below their current values, and the historical costs of assets 'consumed' will be lower than their current costs. As a result, the organization's net assets figure may be understated and its net income figure overstated in historical cost accounts. For example, suppose the data relating to the house above referred to an industrial building with an estimated useful life of 50 years. Should the asset be disclosed in the balance sheet at £30,000 (historical cost) or £100,000 (current value) and should the depreciation charge in the income statement be £600 (based on historical cost) or £2,000 (based on current value)?

The existence of changing price levels has prompted accountants to reconsider two fundamental principles upon which conventional accounting is based — the use of historical cost as the method of asset valuation and the use of money as the unit of measurement. We have shown above and in the previous chapter how historical costs can become outdated, but to appreciate the attention which has been given to the appropriateness of the unit of measurement we must clarify what we mean by 'changing price levels'.

It would not have been unusual in some recent years to read that, over a twelve-month period, the price of calculators had fallen by 25%, the price of a new car had risen by 15%, and the rate of inflation was 10%. The variety of figures may be confusing, and part of the confusion arises because two types of price changes are involved. Changes in *specific price levels* reflect the price changes of specific items such as calculators and cars. Changes in *general price levels* reflect the price changes of a group, or basket, of goods and services. Changes in specific price levels, which may vary widely, contribute to the overall price change as reflected in the general price level. *Inflation* refers strictly to a change in the general price level and, in the UK, inflation is most commonly measured by the increase in the retail price index (RPI) which consists of a weighted average of the changes in the prices of a variety of consumer goods and services.

The RPI is not a perfect consumer index because it does not take into account all items on which people spend money, nor does it cover spending by the whole community. Rather it is intended to measure a representative national basket of goods and services. The RPI is constructed monthly and is based on the prices of a large number of different goods and services. Each item in the index is given a 'weight' according to its comparative importance, and a weighted index is constructed. The base date for the current RPI is January 1987 and a selection of RPI numbers is provided in Table 13.1. The percentage change from year to year is calculated as follows:

$$\frac{\text{Change in index}}{\text{Previous year's index}} \times 100 = \text{Yearly percentage change}$$

which for 1988, for example, is

$$\frac{(110.3-103.3)}{103.3} \times 100 = 6.8\%$$

Table 13.1 *UK Index of Retail Prices: January 1987 = 100*

	Retail Price Index	Annual percentage increase in retail prices
December 1960	12.7	
December 1965	15.1	
December 1970	19.2	
December 1975	37.0	
December 1980	69.9	
December 1981	78.3	12.0
December 1982	82.5	5.4
December 1983	86.9	5.3
December 1984	90.9	4.6
December 1985	96.0	5.6
December 1986	99.6	3.7
December 1987	103.3	3.7
December 1988	110.3	6.8
December 1989	118.8	7.7
December 1990	129.9	9.3
December 1991	135.7	4.5
December 1992	139.2	2.6

When the general price level increases it takes more UK pounds to buy the same basket of goods and services than previously. As a result, the *purchasing power* of the pound declines, i.e. as the general price level changes, so the amount of goods and services that can be purchased with a pound also changes. This suggests that in terms of its ability to buy goods and services the pound is an unstable unit of measurement. The implication for accounting should now be obvious. In periods of significant changes in the general price level the pounds disclosed in financial statements represent past acquisition costs only. As different acquisitions take place at different times, these (different) pounds are not, strictly speaking, additive.

We stated earlier that, in times of rising prices, the income figure reported in historical cost accounts might be 'overstated'. This is not meant to imply that there is some 'correct' income figure which should be disclosed. There is no such thing! Income can be defined in several ways and, given the role which accounting plays in providing information to interested groups, we should not be surprised to learn that different users may wish to use different income figures for different decisions. Much of this chapter is concerned not with determining which is the correct way to calculate income, but with identifying which methods of accounting produce income figures and asset values which are useful for decisions.

13.2 Income determination

We begin our analysis of changing prices by illustrating the artificial nature of income figures. Suppose that Mr Blundell commences trading on 1 January with

Table 13.2 *Mr Blundell — Conventional financial statements*

Income statement for the year	£
Sales	25
Cost of goods sold	10
Income	15

Balance sheet at 31 December	Prior to withdrawal of cash £	After withdrawal of cash £
Assets:		
Cash	25	10
Ownership interest:		
Initial capital	10	10
Income for the year	15	—
	25	10

£10 in cash. On that date he purchases one item of stock for £10. He holds the stock until 31 December, on which date he sells it for £25 cash. During the year the RPI increases by 20% and the replacement cost of the stock increases by 50% to £15. Table 13.2 illustrates the financial statements which Mr Blundell would prepare by applying conventional historical cost accounting. The historical cost of the goods sold, £10, is matched against the sales revenue of £25 to produce an income of £15. At the year end the balance sheet reveals an asset, cash, of £25, and ownership interest of £25, comprising opening capital of £10 and income for the year of £15. Given a reported income figure of £15 it might not be unreasonable for Mr Blundell to assume that he could withdraw £15 from the business and spend it. If he does withdraw £15 for his personal use, the ownership interest will be reduced by £15, and the cash balance of £25 will be reduced by £15 to £10. At the end of the year the business appears to be in exactly the same position as it was at the beginning of the year — it possesses assets of £10 in cash, this amount having been supplied by the owner.

However, as he contemplates another year's trading Mr Blundell may not be totally convinced that the business is in the same position at the end of the year as it was at the beginning, and he may question the wisdom of withdrawing, and spending, all the first year's income. Part of the problem is that in determining the amount to be withdrawn from the business he has relied upon one income figure (that measured by historical cost), which is only one of several which could have been calculated. Let us consider how it is possible for several different income figures to be calculated from this simple set of transactions.

The *economic concept of income* has been defined by Hicks[1] as 'the amount which a man can consume during a period and still remain as well off at the end of the period as he was at the beginning', and this definition has been used by some as a basis for defining accounting profit. For example, a company's profit can

1. Hicks, J.R., *Value and Capital*, 2nd edn, Oxford University Press, 1946.

be defined as the amount it can distribute to its shareholders and be as well off at the end of the year as it was at the beginning.[2] Neither of these definitions views income as the result of matching costs and revenues. Rather the process involves the valuation of assets at the end of a period and the setting aside of a sufficient amount to ensure that the organization is as 'well off' at the end of the period as it was at the beginning, i.e. maintaining its capital. The surplus, if any, is income.

If no distributions have been made during the period this process can be expressed as follows:

$$I_{0 \to 1} = V_1 - V_0$$

where $I_{0 \to 1}$ is the income for the period from time 0 to time 1, and V_0, V_1 are the capital values at time 0 and time 1 respectively.

However, this approach raises two questions. First, how to value assets at the beginning and at the end of the year, and second, how to measure 'well-offness'. The value of assets at the beginning of a period cannot be compared realistically with the value of assets at the end of a period because, by definition, they exist at different times. To compensate for this disparity one of the values must be adjusted to the time scale of the other. Accountants have, in general, preferred to adjust the opening valuation to make it comparable with the value at the end of the period.

It should now be clear that the calculation of income figures depends upon (at least) two factors:

(a) *Asset valuation*: How should the entity's assets be valued at the beginning and the end of a period?
(b) *Capital maintenance*: What adjustment (if any) should be made to the opening capital (ownership interest) valuation to make it comparable with the closing valuation?

Initially we will examine these two distinct stages of income determination independently of each other. In the following section we begin by considering the rationale for three different concepts of capital maintenance.

13.3   Capital maintenance concepts

The situation described in Table 13.2 enables us to examine the impact of different concepts of capital maintenance upon reported income figures independently of the choice of an asset valuation method. In this particular example there is no

2. Alexander, S.S., 'Income measurement in a dynamic economy' (revised by D. Solomons), in Baxter, W.T. and Davidson, S. (eds), *Studies in Accounting Theory*, Sweet and Maxwell, 1962.

need to choose a method of valuing assets because the business holds only cash at both the beginning and the end of the year. On 1 January the net assets of the business comprise £10 cash; on 31 December, prior to the decision to withdraw money from the business, they comprise £25 cash. The final income figure will therefore depend upon the capital maintenance concept adopted, i.e. how the value of net assets held at the beginning of the period is restated to make it comparable with the value of net assets at the end of the period.

The rationale for the capital maintenance concept adopted in Table 13.2 is simple. If the business possesses £25 on 31 December (the end of the period), and £10 on 1 January (the beginning of the period) then Mr Blundell must set aside only £10 to be as well off at the end of the period as at the beginning. Consequently, £15 can be 'consumed' as income. Under this concept of capital maintenance, Mr Blundell is deemed to be as well off *in money terms* on 31 December as he was on 1 January. The *money capital* (of £10) has been maintained and there is an implicit assumption that £10 at the beginning of the year can be compared with £10 at the end of the year.

It could be argued, however, that Mr Blundell is not as well off in terms of 'general purchasing power' at the end of the year as he was at the beginning. Holding cash of £10 on 31 December would not enable him to buy as many goods and services as holding £10 on 1 January. Given the rise of 20% in the RPI he would need £12 (£10 × 1.20) to buy the same basket of consumer goods at the end of the year that he could have bought with £10 at the beginning of the year. Thus, if he wishes to maintain the *general purchasing power* of his capital he must retain £12 in the business. The procedure is reflected in column (ii) of Table 13.3 where a *capital maintenance adjustment* of £2 is made, and income is calculated as the residual figure of £13.

Table 13.3 *Mr Blundell — Effect on income of different concepts of capital maintenance*

Balance sheets at 31 December (prior to withdrawal of cash)

Capital maintained in terms of:	money	general purchasing power	operating capacity
	(i)	(ii)	(iii)
	£	£	£
Assets:			
Cash	25	25	25
Ownership interest:			
Initial capital	10	10	10
Capital maintenance adjustment	—	2	5
Income for the year	15	13	10
	25	25	25

The general purchasing power concept of capital maintenance uses an index which approximates the (general) spending habits of the owner. The owner is termed a 'proprietor', and this concept of capital maintenance is often termed a 'proprietary' concept. An alternative approach is to consider 'well-offness' from the point of view of the business entity. We noted in Chapter 3 that financial statements are prepared on the assumption that the entity is a going concern and in this example one would expect Mr Blundell to continue to buy and sell items of stock in the following year. Well-offness at the year-end could be defined in terms of the entity's ability to operate at the same level of activity in the following year. Consequently, rather than seeking to maintain the purchasing power of the owner, we could select a capital maintenance concept which maintains the *operating capacity* of the business by setting aside sufficient funds to maintain the *physical* size of the entity. This approach to capital maintenance is often termed an 'entity' approach, to distinguish it from the proprietary approach explained earlier. At the beginning of the year the business had sufficient funds to buy one item of stock. In order to purchase one item of stock at the end of the year, i.e., in order to maintain the entity's operating capacity, £15 (the current cost of the stock) must be retained in the business. This procedure is reflected in column (iii) of Table 13.3 where a capital maintenance adjustment of £5 is made and income is calculated as the residual figure of £10. Note that although three different income figures are produced by the three methods, the asset amount (£25 in cash) is the same under each method.

13.4   Methods of asset valuation

We noted in Section 13.2 that methods of measuring income and position (which we call 'accounting methods') may be classified according to two main characteristics — an asset valuation method and a capital maintenance concept. The chosen asset valuation method determines the value of assets in the balance sheet and the operating costs in the income statement. The choice of capital maintenance concept determines how much income is set aside to maintain the value of opening capital.

The example set out in Table 13.3 was concerned primarily with showing the impact of different capital maintenance concepts on the net income figure. Because the example looked at assets held only at the beginning and end of the year (when the only asset possessed was *cash*), it ignored the problems presented when fixed assets or stock are held, either during the year (as is the case in the example itself) or at the end of the year. In other words, the example was kept deliberately simple. In practice any business which owns fixed assets or stock *at any time during the year* possesses assets to which alternative valuation methods could be applied.

One method of asset valuation is *historical cost*, the method which we have described so far in this book, and which forms the primary basis of asset valuation in many countries, including the UK. If this method is adopted, assets are 'valued' at their original purchase price (less any applicable depreciation). Thus land purchased on 1 January 1974 for £100,000 would be assigned a figure of £100,000 in the historical cost accounts prepared on 31 December 1994 (and on any other date also).

A fundamental weakness of the historical cost method during times of rising prices can be explained by reference to Table 13.4. Figures can be added together, or subtracted from one another, only if they are expressed in a common measurement unit. For example, an international businessman who decides to count the cash in his wallet whilst flying between Frankfurt and New York might discover 120 dollars, 200 Deutschmarks and 100 pounds. Presumably he would not simply mutter that he was down to his 'last 420' and order another gin and tonic. He cannot meaningfully add together dollars, Deutschmarks and pounds because they represent different units of measurement. In particular they represent a different general purchasing power (e.g. one pound can currently — in 1993 — purchase approximately 2.5 times as many goods as can one Deutschmark) and one would expect the businessman to convert his cash into one currency, representing one common measure of purchasing power, before adding together the three amounts. In Table 13.4 all the costs are expressed in pounds sterling, and yet it can be argued that the addition of 100,000 '1982 pounds' to 380,000 '1991 pounds' is as meaningless as adding pounds to dollars, and for the same reason — they represent a different general purchasing power. The Retail Price Index stood at 82.5 in December 1982 and 135.6 in November 1991. £1 in December 1982 could have purchased 1.64 times as many goods and services as £1 in November 1991.

One way of eliminating this problem is to convert the costs of all assets into pounds of *current purchasing power*, i.e. to express the costs of all assets in pounds possessing the same general purchasing power. This can be achieved by using the RPI. As the RPI stood at 82.5 in December 1982 and at 135.7 in December 1991, we could express the asset, land, in December 1991 pounds by converting

Table 13.4 *Extract from a balance sheet using the historical cost method of asset valuation*

	£
Balance sheet at 31 December 1991	
Fixed assets:	
Land (purchased December 1982)	100,000
Buildings, net (purchased December 1984)	420,000
Plant and machinery, net (purchased June 1989)	650,000
	1,170,000
Current assets:	
Stock (purchased November 1991)	380,000
Cash	80,000
	£1,630,000

the £100,000 from pounds of December 1982 to pounds of December 1991 as follows:

$$£100,000 \times \frac{135.7}{82.5} = £164,485$$

In general the conversion, or restatement, can be expressed as follows:

$$\text{Asset cost} \times \frac{\text{Index adjusting to}}{\text{Index adjusting from}}$$

i.e.

$$\frac{\text{Index at balance sheet date}}{\text{Index at date item first recorded in books of account}}$$

The restated costs of the assets of the company, all of which are presumed to have been bought at different times, are illustrated in Table 13.5. The *extent* of the difference between the figures presented in Table 13.4 and those in Table 13.5 is immediately apparent. Remember also that these different figures relate to exactly the same assets.

By applying a general price index to the cost of assets, the current purchasing power method of accounting takes no account of the *specific* price changes affecting an entity's resources and consequently, as a means of updating asset values, it is unlikely to provide more than a rough approximation to the current values or costs of those resources. Methods of asset valuation which take account of the changes in cost or value of specific assets are called *current cost*, or *current value*, methods of asset valuation. These methods may be based upon replacement costs (i.e. current buying prices), on realizable values (i.e. current selling prices), or on a mixture of both.

Replacement costs might be obtained from several sources including suppliers' price lists, professional valuers or the entity's own costs of production. Table 13.6 illustrates how different sources might be used for different assets in order to produce a replacement cost balance sheet.

Table 13.5 *Extract from a balance sheet using the 'pounds of purchasing power' method of asset valuation*

Balance sheet at 31 December 1991	£CPP
Fixed assets:	
Land (100,000 × 135.7/82.5)	164,485
Buildings, net (420,000 × 135.7/90.9)	626,997
Plant and machinery, net (650,000 × 135.7/115.4)	764,341
	1,555,823
Current assets:	
Stock (380,000 × 135.7/135.6)	380,280
Cash	80,000
	£2,016,103

Table 13.6 *Extract from a balance sheet using the replacement cost method of asset valuation*

	£
Balance sheet at 31 December 1991	
Fixed assets:	
Land (valued by a professional valuer)	300,000
Buildings, net (valued by a professional valuer)	1,000,000
Plant and machinery, net (from manufacturers' price lists)	850,000
	2,150,000
Current assets:	
Stock (from up-to-date internal costings)	385,000
Cash	80,000
	£2,615,000

13.5   Classification of reporting methods

We stated above that methods of measuring net income and financial position could be classified according to two main characteristics — an asset valuation method and a capital maintenance concept. The asset valuation method determines the value of assets in the balance sheet and the operating costs shown in the income statement. The choice of capital maintenance concept determines how much income (however measured) is set aside to maintain the value of opening capital. We have introduced briefly three methods of asset valuation (historical cost, current purchasing power and current cost) and three methods of maintaining capital (in terms of money, purchasing power and operating capacity). The alternative reporting methods classified in accordance with these two characteristics are shown in Table 13.7.

Table 13.7 *Alternative methods of accounting*

Capital maintenance	Asset valuation	Historical cost	Historical cost × general price index	Current cost (e.g. replacement cost, realizable value)
Money capital		√(A)	X	√(C)
Money capital × General price index (i.e. owners' general purchasing power)		X	√(B)	√(D)
Operating capacity		X	X	√(E)

√ = Possible combination
X = Unlikely combination
(A)...(E) = Classification of available method

Of the nine possible combinations of asset valuation and capital maintenance, five represent theoretical and practical possibilities and have been described for convenience by a letter. These letters have no significance other than as descriptive devices within this text. Method A describes conventional accounting practice which has been considered extensively in this book. Under method B the historical costs of assets are restated at the end of the accounting period by means of a general price index to express them in terms of pounds of current purchasing power. In addition, the money capital is restated by means of a general price index to maintain its general purchasing power. Methods C, D and E use current costs or current values to value assets and differ only as to how much of the reported income should be set aside to maintain the value of capital.

13.6   The inflation accounting debate in the UK

During the past twenty years or so, attempts have been made in the UK and elsewhere to introduce variants of methods B, C, D and E in supplementary accounts, but with little success. We shall look briefly at the history of the inflation accounting debate in the UK and at why the preparers of accounting statements were so reluctant to accept the recommendations of the Accounting Standards Committee (ASC). Indeed it is a widely-held view that the failure of the ASC to successfully implement its recommendations for accounting for changing prices was a major factor in its demise in 1990.

In January 1973, the ASC issued its first Exposure Draft on inflation accounting (ED8) which was converted to a *provisional* standard (PSSAP7) in May 1974. Both recommended the use of supplementary CPP accounting, i.e. method B. It is interesting to note that PSSAP7 was the only provisional standard issued by the ASC during its existence — possibly an early sign that even the standard setters were not confident about their recommendation! The government of the day, concerned about rising inflation and not wishing to 'institutionalize' it in an accounting treatment based so closely on changes in the RPI, then set up a committee (the Sandilands Committee, named after its chairman) to recommend an alternative treatment. The Sandilands Report was issued in September 1975 and recommended the use of current cost accounting with operating capacity capital maintenance — method E. The ASC was asked to develop the detailed rules.

In November 1976, the ASC issued ED18, which at over 100 pages was the longest ever exposure draft and which attempted to rewrite almost the whole of accounting in accordance with the broad framework of the Sandilands Report. The reaction was a 'back-benchers' revolt' in the accountancy profession and compulsory CCA was rejected by the members of the Institute of Chartered Accountants in England and Wales at a special meeting in July 1977. This event was followed in November 1977 by the issue of a brief set of guidelines (the Hyde Guidelines) intended primarily for companies listed on the Stock Exchange and proposing an interim and very brief supplementary current cost accounting system, and by the withdrawal in January 1978 of PSSAP7.

In April 1979, ED24 was issued; this document was more extensive than the Hyde Guidelines but less so than ED18. It recommended the reporting of *supplementary* CCA profit and balance sheet numbers and, with relatively little modification, became SSAP16, which was issued in March 1980 — the first full UK standard on accounting for changing prices. Although compliance with the standard was initially high, the preparers of accounting statements soon became disillusioned. In an attempt to secure compliance, the ASC issued ED35 in July 1984. This exposure draft involved no major changes to the principles of SSAP16 but it was less onerous; both the disclosure requirements and the number of companies to which it related were fewer than under SSAP16. But it was too late! By mid-1985, less than 20% of companies were complying with the requirements of SSAP16. ED35 was withdrawn in March 1985 to be followed eventually by the withdrawal of SSAP16 itself in April 1988.

Why did the ASC fail? Almost all the pressure to drop SSAP16 came from the preparers of accounts. There was little adverse comment from users, and the government during the 1980s was publicly expressing concern at the ASC's failure to obtain agreement on a method of accounting for changing prices. Why were preparers so concerned as to be willing to challenge the authority of the ASC? The reasons which were claimed included the following. First, it was argued that the cost of preparing the information was excessive, although research undertaken at the time suggested that the cost was very small as a percentage of the total accounting costs of most organizations. Second, it was claimed that the supplementary current cost information was confusing to users although, again, there was little evidence to support this claim. Indeed, what evidence there is suggests that the capital market at least, is quite sophisticated in dealing with and interpreting this sort of information. Third, it was argued that the information was of little significance when inflation was low — and by the mid-1980s inflation had fallen to about 5% per annum (see Table 13.1), compared to rates of 15%–20% in the mid-1970s. This argument suffers from a number of flaws. Many companies still owned assets which had been purchased ten years or more previously, and in the decade to 1985 the RPI increased by over 150% or $2\frac{1}{2}$ times. Even with inflation at only 5% per annum, prices increase by over 60% every ten years. And finally, as we have seen, relatively low rates of general inflation may mask much larger changes in the specific prices of some assets.

So were there other reasons for preparer resistance? For most companies, CCA under method E results in profit figures which are lower than those produced by historical cost accounting, primarily because some operating costs (in particular, depreciation and cost of goods sold) are based on current rather than historical values and capital has to be maintained in terms of operating capacity. In Chapter 12 we explained why many managers prefer to report higher, rather than lower, profits. It is possible that the reluctance of managers to disclose CCA profit numbers was simply because they were too low.

The inflation accounting saga in the UK highlights some interesting messages. It underlines the fragility of a standard setting process with only weak enforcement powers, one of the items we discussed in Chapter 3 and to which we shall return in Chapter 15. It demonstrates the reluctance of many preparers of accounts to adopt accounting treatments which lower their reported profits. And it does seem to have clarified the choice between CPP and CCA; very few commentators disagreed that if some form of accounting for changing prices is needed, it should be based on CCA rather than CPP. For that reason, and in the expectation that at some time in the future inflation rates will rise sufficiently to revive the inflation accounting debate, in the next section we shall discuss in more detail replacement cost accounting.

13.7   Replacement cost accounting

In this section we examine replacement cost accounting which, as its title suggests, produces income statements and balance sheets calculated on the basis of the (hypothetical) cost to the organization of replacing its assets. In other words the system presumes the organization will continue into the future (i.e. it will be a going concern) by replacing its existing assets as and when necessary. Replacement cost accounting is a widely advocated variant of current cost or current value accounting. Like historical cost accounting it incorporates the buying prices of assets, but it differs from historical cost accounting in one important respect: historical cost accounting deals with *past* purchase prices, whereas replacement cost accounting deals with *current* purchase prices. Like historical cost accounting, replacement cost accounting matches costs with revenues: however the integral difference is that replacement cost accounting matches the *current* replacement cost of resources used, rather than the *past* costs of such resources. Thus a replacement cost income statement will show figures for depreciation and cost of goods sold which differ from those in an historical cost statement if the asset prices to which these expenses relate have increased (or decreased) during the period.

Let us consider first why replacement cost accounting might provide the users of accounting statements with information not available from historical cost accounts. Figure 13.1 shows the after-tax net income of UK companies for the ten-year period, 1970 to 1979. It is based on historical cost calculations and shows an encouraging picture of steadily increasing net income throughout the decade — and yet many UK companies experienced severe difficulties during the 1970s. Some were forced into liquidation when they failed to generate sufficient *cash* resources to pay for more highly priced labour, materials and capital equipment; investment in fixed assets by manufacturing industry in 1979 was lower in real (i.e. inflation-adjusted) terms than it had been in 1970; and unemployment continued to rise into the 1980s. So what happened to the encouraging income trend illustrated in Figure 13.1?

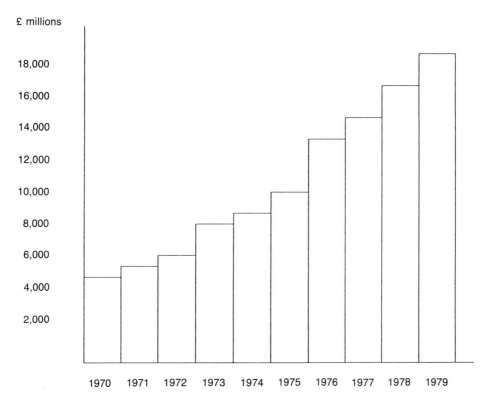

Figure 13.1 *UK industrial and commercial companies' income before interest but after tax,
1970–79*

The answer is that much of the historical cost income was required to maintain
and *replace* existing fixed assets and stocks. Figure 13.2 reveals the extent to which
the historical cost income of UK industrial and commercial companies was pre-
empted by this requirement. The shaded area represents the expenditure required
to *maintain* and *replace* the *current* investment in buildings, plant and stocks, i.e.
the expenditure on 'real', or 'growth', investment has not been included. The
graph which emerges (i.e. below the shaded area) highlights the difficulties faced
by UK companies in 1974 and 1975 in particular, and is consistent with the liquidity
crises experienced by many companies during those two years. Figure 13.2 also
indicates the percentage of the reported historical cost income which was available
after the maintenance and replacement of existing physical assets. Less than 30%
was available for other purposes in 1974, and the figure did not rise above 55%
for the remainder of the decade.

The government and the accountancy profession became increasingly concerned
that users of accounting reports might be misled into making incorrect and costly
decisions. For instance, investors may make poor decisions about buying or selling
shares on the basis of reported historical cost income; creditors may not recognize

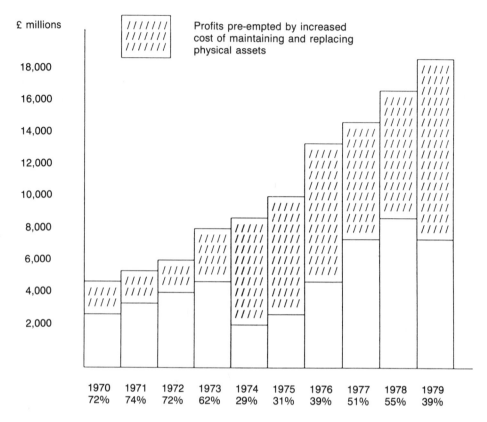

£ millions

Profits pre-empted by increased cost of maintaining and replacing physical assets

	1970	1971	1972	1973	1974	1975	1976	1977	1978	1979
	72%	74%	72%	62%	29%	31%	39%	51%	55%	39%

Proportion of HC income available after maintenance and replacement of physical assets (%)

Figure 13.2 *UK industrial and commercial companies' income before interest but after tax, 1970–79*

that a company is physically contracting, as the historical cost statements could give an incorrect impression of growth and reinvestment; and employees' negotiators may be encouraged by reported historical cost income to pursue excessive wage claims, without realizing that the full settlement of such claims could affect the survival of the company, and hence the job security of its workforce. It would appear desirable that the underlying economic situation is clearly disclosed to all users of financial statements. One way of achieving this objective is to report an income figure based upon the procedures illustrated in Figure 13.2 instead of, or in addition to, the historical cost income as reflected in Figure 13.1.

The above issues illustrate potential problems caused by the effect of rising prices on historical cost income at the aggregate level in the UK in the 1970s. Let us now turn to the example of Ms Shielfield, to examine the effect of rising prices on historical cost income for an *individual* business, and to identify the relationship between historical cost and replacement cost income.

Suppose Ms Shielfield buys and sells an electronic space-war game called 'Ledger Attack'. By buying the games for £5 each and selling for £12, she expects to show a profit of £7 on each game sold. For an individual game (i.e. an item of stock) her historical cost income is as shown in Figure 13.3. (This is, of course, a very simple example. A manufacturer would incur expenses to transform input factors into finished goods ready for sale.)

Suppose Ms Shielfield purchases her first electronic game on 1 January, for £5. On 31 March her supplier announces a price increase of £3, to £8. Under historical cost accounting this price increase would not be recorded by Ms Shielfield. Replacement cost accounting, however, requires that the replacement costs of assets are matched against current revenues, and thus Ms Shielfield would update the cost of all her existing stock to £8 (Figure 13.4). This corresponding unit increase of £3 is usually termed a *holding gain* or a *revaluation surplus*. Holding gains arise as a result of holding, rather than using, assets. Strictly, they represent the gain, or cost saving, accruing to an organization as a result of acquiring an asset at the time it was purchased rather than at the later time it is used or sold. As the game is still held by Ms Shielfield on 31 March the holding gain is, as yet, *unrealized*. We will presume at this stage that Ms Shielfield's capital is maintained in *money* terms (i.e. the amount of her balance sheet figure for capital is not adjusted to reflect price changes). *Under this method all holding gains are treated as additions to income, rather than as additions to capital. This is an important assumption and should be continually borne in mind when interpreting the figures.*

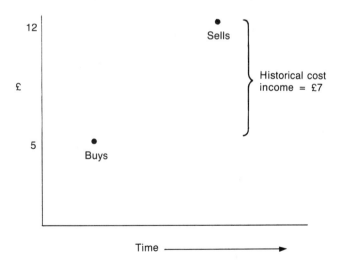

Figure 13.3 *Historical cost income*

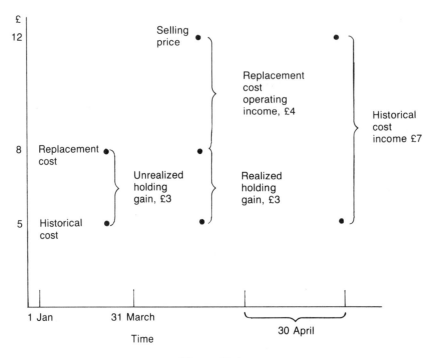

Figure 13.4

On 30 April Ms Shielfield sells the game for £12. The historical cost profit is £7, but this can now be divided into two components — replacement cost operating profit of £4 and a *realized* holding gain of £3. The dichotomy between operating profit and holding gains is an important characteristic of replacement cost income; the recognition of two distinct components of income should give users additional information. The historical cost approach blurs the distinction between holding and operating activities; results of the two types of activity are not reported separately and increases in asset values are recognized only when the asset is sold or otherwise disposed of. For example, if Ms Shielfield makes up her accounts to 30 April, the historical cost income of £7 will equal the replacement cost income of £7 (both income figures comprising replacement cost operating income of £4, and a realized holding gain of £3). If, however, Ms Shielfield's financial year ends on 31 March her historical cost income will be reported as zero in that year, and £7 in the following year when the stock is sold. The replacement cost income will be reported as £3 in the first year (an unrealized holding gain), and £4 in the second year (operating profit).

Thus, although historical cost income comprises both replacement cost operating income and realized holding gains, the holding gains may already have been recognized (as unrealized gains) in the replacement cost accounts of a previous period.

13.8 Main differences between replacement cost and historical cost accounting

Both historical cost and replacement cost methods of accounting are transactions-based approaches to reporting business performance. However, we have identified some important differences of principle between the two methods, and in this section we make use of a simple example to illustrate and explain these differences. Let us look more closely at the totality of Ms Shielfield's operations.

Suppose Ms Shielfield commences business on 1 January 19X0. On that date she pays £100 from her own resources into the business bank account and uses the money to buy 20 units of stock at a cost of £5 each. On 31 December 19X0 she sells 10 units of stock for £12 per unit and buys a further 10 units at a cost of £8 each. On 31 December 19X1 she sells 10 units of stock for £15 per unit and buys a further 14 units at a cost of £10 each. All purchases and sales are for cash. For simplicity, we assume that Ms Shielfield undertakes no transactions other than those described above during the two-year period.

Ms Shielfield's historical cost accounts for the two years, assuming use of the FIFO stock flow assumption (see Chapter 7), are shown in Table 13.8. In Table 13.9 we show the accounting equation entries required to record Ms Shielfield's transactions using the replacement cost method. Ms Shielfield's replacement cost accounts for the two years are shown in Table 13.10. Assuming that capital is maintained in *money* terms, the replacement cost accounts differ from the historical cost accounts in two main respects:

1. *Net income*: Under the historical cost approach, net income is defined as revenues less the historical costs of the resources used in earning them.

Table 13.8 *Ms Shielfield — Historical cost income statements and balance sheets*

		19X0 £		19X1 £
Income statements				
Sales	(10 × £12)	120	(10 × £15)	150
less: Historical cost of stock sold	(10 × £5)	50	(10 × £5)	50
Historical cost income		70		100
Balance sheets				
Ownership interest:				
Opening balance		100		170
add: Income for the year		70		100
		170		270
Stock	(10 × £5 + 10 × £8)	130	(10 × £8 + 14 × £10)	220
Bank balance	(100 − 100 + 120 − 80)	40	(40 + 150 − 140)	50
		170		270

Table 13.9 *Ms Shielfield — Accounting equation entries: replacement cost*

	Stock + £	Cash at bank £	= Ownership interest £	+ Operating income £	+ Holding gains £
19X0					
1 January:					
Owner pays in capital		100	100		
Purchases stock (20 units)	100	(100)			
31 December					
Increase in replacement cost of stock (£3)	60				60
Sells stock (10 units)		120		120	
	(80)			(80)	
Purchases stock (10 units)	80	(80)		40	60
Transfer income			100	(40)	(60)
Balances	160	40	200		
19X1					
31 December:					
Increase in replacement cost of stock (£2)	40				40
Sells stock (10 units)		150		150	
	(100)			(100)	
Purchases stock (14 units)	140	(140)			
				50	40
Transfer income			90	(50)	(40)
Balances	240	50	290		

Under the replacement cost approach, income is split into two components — operating income and holding gains. *Operating income* is defined as revenues (as under historical cost) less the replacement costs of the resources used. *Holding gains* are increases in the monetary value of assets held during the period covered by the income statement. Thus Ms Shielfield's *operating income* for 19X0 is £40 (10 units sold at £12 per unit less the current replacement cost of the units at the date of sale, i.e. less 10 units at £8). Similarly, her operating income for 19X1 is £50 (10 units sold at £15 per unit less the current replacement cost of the units sold, 10 units at £10). Ms Shielfield's *holding gains* for 19X0 are £60 (an increase from £5 to £8 during the year in the replacement cost of each of the 20 units held during that period). Her holding gains for 19X1 are £40 (an increase from £8 to £10 in the replacement cost of each of the 20 units held during the year).

The holding gains of a period may be either *realized* (if the asset has been sold or used during the period) or *unrealized* (if the asset is held at the end of the period). So, for example, Ms Shielfield's holding gains of £60 for 19X0 comprise £30 realized gains (£3 per unit on the 10 units sold) plus £30 unrealized gains (£3 per unit on the 10 units held at the end of the year which were bought at the start of the year). Similarly, the holding gains of £40 for 19X1 comprise realized gains of £20 (£2 per unit on the 10 units sold) and unrealized gains

Table 13.10 *Ms Shielfield — Replacement cost income statements and balance sheets*

	19X0	£	£	19X1	£	£
Income statements						
Sales	(10 × £12)		120	(10 × £15)		150
less: Replacement cost of stock sold	(10 × £8)		80	(10 × £10)		100
Replacement cost operating income			40			50
Holding gains:						
Realized	(10 × £3)	30		(10 × £2)	20	
Unrealized	(10 × £3)	30		(10 × £2)	20	
			60			40
Total replacement cost income			100			90
Balance sheets						
Ownership interest:						
Opening balance			100			200
add: Income for the year			100			90
			200			290
Stock	(20 × £8)		160	(24 × £10)		240
Bank balance			40			50
			200			290

of £20 (£2 per unit on the 10 units held at the end of the year which were in stock at the beginning of the year). The categorization of holding gains as either realized or unrealized is helpful in reconciling historical cost and replacement cost income figures as we explain shortly.

2. *Asset value*: Under the historical cost approach, we have seen that assets are generally valued for balance sheet purposes at their original costs less accumulated depreciation. Under the replacement cost approach assets are included in the balance sheet at their current values (i.e. net replacement cost) at the balance sheet date. Thus Ms Shielfield's stock at the end of 19X0 is included in her balance sheet as £160 (20 units at a replacement cost value at the end of 19X0 of £8 per unit). Similarly, stock at the end of 19X1 is valued for balance sheet purposes at £240 (24 units at £10 per unit, the replacement cost at the balance sheet date). Broadly speaking, replacement cost means the cost of replacing an asset of similar age and condition or, more specifically, the cost of replacing the *services* given by a similar asset. For fixed assets, this value may sometimes be difficult to determine directly, particularly where no efficient second-hand market for the asset exists. For example, it is relatively

easy to determine the net replacement cost of a six-year-old Ford Escort car, but not of a six-year-old grinding machine. In such cases, net replacement cost is often approximated by including the replacement cost of an equivalent *new* asset (i.e. taking account of technological change) and deducting from it an appropriate amount for accumulated depreciation (based, of course, on the replacement cost rather than the historical cost of the asset).

Ms Shielfield's accounts, prepared on the replacement cost basis described above, are shown in Table 13.10. We now use the figures for 19X1 from Tables 13.8 and 13.10 to summarize broadly the relationships between replacement cost and historical cost measures of income and position.

- *Replacement cost income* and historical cost income for a period differ in their treatment of holding gains. Total replacement cost income comprises replacement cost operating income plus all holding gains which *arise* during the period. Historical cost income comprises replacement cost operating income plus all holding gains which are *realized* during the period. Hence, for the second year of Ms Shielfield's business, the replacement cost income (operating income plus holding gains, £90) equals historical cost income (£100) plus unrealized holding gains *arising during the period* (£20) minus holding gains realized during the period but which *arose during previous periods* (£30, being the gain made during 19X0 on the 10 units purchased at the start of that year which were sold in 19X1 — this gain is included in the historical cost income for 19X1 but has already been included in the replacement cost income for 19X0 as an unrealized gain).
- *The replacement cost of assets* at the end of a period is comprised of the historical cost value plus any holding gains relevant to the assets. The replacement cost value of Ms Shielfield's stock at the end of the second year (£240), equals the historical cost value (£220) plus the sum of all holding gains that have arisen during the current and previous periods and that have not been realized by the end of the period (i.e. £20 is the unrealized gain on the 10 units of stock purchased at the end of 19X0 which are still held at the end of 19X1).

The effect of the above relationships is that, in order to convert historical cost records and accounts to a replacement cost basis, three main adjustments are required:

(a) *Asset values* are increased (or decreased) each period to reflect changes in their replacement costs. Only assets whose values are not fixed in money terms (i.e. non-monetary assets) are affected, e.g. fixed assets and stock. The monetary values of other (i.e. monetary) assets, e.g. cash and debtors, whose values are fixed in money terms, require no adjustment.
(b) *Unrealized holding gains* on non-monetary assets are calculated for each period as they arise, and are included in total replacement cost income for the period in which they arise.

(c) *Operating costs* for each period are changed, where necessary, to convert them from historical to replacement costs. Strictly speaking, the current costs of *all* resources should be matched against revenues at the date of sale. In general, adjustments are required only to depreciation charges on fixed assets and to the cost of using stock, both of which are based on the balance sheet values of assets which are changed under the replacement cost approach. The costs of other resources, for example, wages, lighting, heating, rent, vehicle maintenance and fuel, and so on, tend to be paid at approximately the same time as the resources are used and, in consequence, their actual (original) cost is equal to their replacement cost at the date of use.

At the simplest level, the procedure for converting historical cost accounts to replacement cost accounts is straightforward. The values of non-monetary assets are regularly (at least at the end of each accounting period) updated to their replacement costs. The double entry is completed by increasing net income by the same amount — the holding gains on the assets. When assets are used or sold, the cost of using or selling them is based on their (updated) replacement costs.

We noted in the previous section that interest in replacement cost accounting in the UK was stimulated by the belief that historical cost accounting 'overstated' the reported income figure during a period of rising prices. And yet, despite rising prices, the replacement cost income of Ms Shielfield in 19X0 is greater than the corresponding historical cost income. The explanation of this apparent contradiction is straightforward. The move from a historical cost *valuation of assets* to a replacement cost valuation results in an increase in reported net income for Ms Shielfield because unrealized holding gains are included in the total replacement cost income figure. However, how much of that income is set aside to maintain the value of capital depends upon the *capital maintenance concept* adopted. Figure 13.2 illustrated the current cost income figure for UK companies after capital had been maintained in terms of operating capacity, i.e., *no holding gains* were included in the income figure. In the replacement cost financial statements of Ms Shielfield money capital only is maintained and *all holding gains* are included in the income figure. As we noted earlier in this chapter, the reported income figure depends upon both the asset valuation method and the capital maintenance concept adopted. In the next section we shall examine further the effect on replacement cost income of adopting different methods of capital maintenance.

13.9 Current costs and alternative capital maintenance concepts

In this section we consider the effect of adopting different capital maintenance concepts in conjunction with the replacement cost method of asset valuation. The example of Ms Shielfield valued assets by reference to replacement costs, and maintained capital *in money terms*. The main difference between financial statements prepared under different capital maintenance concepts lies in the way in which holding gains on non-monetary assets are reported in the income statement. If operating capacity is maintained, holding gains are reported as part of capital maintenance. If owners' purchasing power is maintained, part of the holding gains are reported in the income statement and the remainder as part of capital maintenance.

Table 13.11 shows the effect of the three different concepts of capital maintenance on the financial statements of Ms Shielfield for 19X1 and assumes an increase of 5% in the RPI during the year. Only extracts from the financial statements are presented because the balance sheet values for assets and liabilities, and the income statement entries for current revenues and replacement costs, *are identical under all three methods*. If the business maintains its capital in terms of operating capacity no holding gains are included in the income statement. By implication such gains are not available for distribution and total income is equal to operating income. In such cases, replacement cost income may be considerably lower than historical cost income if asset prices are rising. As assets sold or used during the year are charged to the income statement at their replacement cost,

Table 13.11 *Ms Shielfield — Alternative concepts of capital maintenance*

| | \(\)19X1 Capital maintenance concept | | | | | |
| | Money | | Owners' purchasing power | | Operating capacity | |
	£	£	£	£	£	£
Income statement						
Operating income		50		50		50
Holding gains	40		40		40	
Less: Capital maintenance adjustment	—	40	10	30	40	—
Total replacement cost income		90		80		50
Balance sheet						
Ownership interest:						
Opening balance		200		200		200
Capital maintenance adjustment		—		10		40
		200		210		240
Total income for the year		90		80		50
		290		290		290

the operating income figure represents the surplus after charging sufficient to ensure that the company can maintain its fixed assets and stocks at their present level. The replacement cost/operating capacity method of accounting emphasizes the entity's ability to continue its operations at the same level of activity in the future.

This method can be categorized as adopting an entity view of accounting in that it maintains the 'well-offness' of the entity as a whole rather than the well-offness of any individual participant group. To that extent it can be argued that the adoption of the current cost/operating capacity method of accounting represents a shift away from the traditional emphasis on shareholders as the focus of financial statements. By emphasizing the entity's viability as a going concern it provides information of wider interest to those interested in its future.

A proprietary view of an organization is, as we noted earlier, one which sees the organization as an extension of the owners' personal property, i.e. the organization is a legal structure by which means the owners' assets are managed. According to this view, financial statements should consist primarily of reports to the owners. The current cost/money capital, and current cost/owners' purchasing power methods of accounting are consistent with this approach. As Table 13.11 shows, all or part of the holding gains which have arisen during the year are added to replacement cost operating income to arrive at total replacement cost income. If the *total* replacement cost income of Ms Shielfield's business was distributed to her, i.e. if the distribution was greater than the replacement cost operating income, Ms Shielfield might be realizing the benefits of the holding gains whilst at the same time running down the level of her future operations.

Of course, the decision to make a distribution to owners depends upon other factors in addition to the current year's income figure. It cannot automatically be assumed that if an organization wished to distribute its profits, sufficient cash would be available for this purpose. Nevertheless, it is clear from Table 13.11 that if Ms Shielfield was hoping to pay herself a handsome amount at the end of the year, she would draw more encouragement from the income figures generated by the two proprietary methods of accounting than from the income figure produced by the replacement cost/operating capacity method.

It is worth noting that the capital maintenance adjustment required to maintain the owners' purchasing power is calculated by applying the increase in the Retail Price Index to the ownership interest balance at the beginning of the year (£200 × 5% = £10 in the case of Ms Shielfield). If the increase in the RPI is greater than the increase in the prices of the entity's own assets, as reflected in the figure for holding gains, the capital maintenance adjustment required to maintain the owners' purchasing power will be greater than the holding gains included in the income statement. In this instance, total replacement cost income under the replacement cost/owners' purchasing power method would be lower than replacement cost operating profit.

Discussion topics

1. Explain what is meant by 'capital maintenance' and outline the effect of capital maintenance adjustments on an organization's income.

2. Distinguish between the maintenance of operating capacity and the maintenance of the general purchasing power of owners' equity. What views of the organization do the two methods of capital maintenance imply?

3. Why does the instability of the monetary unit present so many problems to accountants? What types of organization are likely to be most affected by such instability?

4. 'CPP accounting adds nothing to historical cost accounting which is useful to users'. Discuss this comment.

5. Explain how accounting methods of measuring income and value may be categorized according to the asset valuation method and the capital maintenance concept they adopt.

6. Distinguish between 'replacement cost operating income' and 'holding gains', and discuss the possible importance of the distinction.

7. Explain the difference between 'realized' and 'unrealized' holding gains.

8. Describe the main respects in which replacement cost measures of income and value differ from their historical cost counterparts.

9. Outline the main adjustments which are necessary to convert historical cost to replacement cost accounts.

Exercises

13.1 On 1 January 19X8 Titus started a business selling home-brewing kits. On that date he paid into the bank £100,000 of which £70,000 was used to buy premises on a new industrial estate.

On 30 June 19X8 he bought 20,000 units of stock for £80,000 on credit. On 31 December, when the replacement cost of stock was £5 per unit, he sold 10,000 units for cash at £7.50 per unit and paid the amount of £80,000 due to his suppliers. At the end of the year an identical building, recently completed on the estate, was purchased by another firm for £80,000, although a valuer valued Titus' building at only £72,000 on 31 December. Titus depreciates fixed assets on a straight line basis over 10 years, assuming zero residual value. The Retail Price Index moved as follows:

1 January 19X8	100
30 June 19X8	110
31 December 19X8	120

- (a) Prepare for Titus a balance sheet at 31 December 19X8, and an income statement for the year ended 31 December 19X8, in terms of:

(i)   historical cost accounting;
(ii) current purchasing power accounting.

(b)   Comment on the usefulness of the accounts you have prepared in (a) (i)
and (ii) above.

13.2 Manrico Ltd is a small limited company which rents its property to tenants. Its balance
sheet at 1 January 19X7 is as follows:

	£	£
Fixed assets		
Freehold property (original cost		
and current value at 1 Jan. 19X7)		6,000
Current assets		
Rent due from tenants	500	
Cash	1,000	1,500
		7,500
less: Current liabilities		
Expenses owed by Manrico Ltd		300
		7,200
Represented by:		
Share capital		
5,000 Ordinary shares of £1 each		5,000
Retained profits		2,200
		7,200

Manrico Ltd's transactions for the year to 31 December 19X7 are as follows:

1. Borrows £15,000 from Fiordiligi Finance Ltd.
2. Buys additional property for cash of £20,000.
3. Receives rent from tenants of £8,500, representing the amount due at 1 January
19X7, and all rent due in respect of 19X7.
4. Pays expenses of £4,300 being expenses owing at 1 January 19X7, and all expenses
due in respect of 19X7.
5. Buys 2,000 £1 shares in Pamina Ltd for £2,000.

You are told:

(i)   The total market value of the freehold property at 31 December 19X7 is £50,000.
(ii) The market value of a £1 share in Pamina Ltd at 31 December 19X7 is £1.50.

■ (a)   Prepare for Manrico Ltd a balance sheet at 31 December 19X7 and an income
statement for the year ended 31 December 19X7 using historical cost
accounting.
(b)   Prepare for Manrico Ltd a balance sheet at 31 December 19X7 and an income
statement for the year ended 31 December 19X7 using replacement cost
accounting, maintaining capital at its money level.
(c)   Comment on your results.

(*Note*: Ignore depreciation and changes in the *general* level of prices.)

13.3   Mr Publius commenced business on 1 July 19X7. On that date he paid £20,000 into the business bank account from his personal savings. On the same date he purchased a machine for £13,000 and 10,000 units of stock at 50p per unit. He estimated that the machine would last for 8 years, at the end of which time it would have a scrap value of £1,000. Mr Publius wishes to use the straight line method of providing depreciation on the machine.

On 30 June 19X8 Mr Publius sold 8,000 units of stock for £11,000 and paid operating expenses amounting to £4,500. He also purchased a further 9,000 units of stock at 55p per unit. At 30 June 19X8 the cost of machines like the one owned by Mr Publius was 15% higher than at 1 July 19X7.

- ■   (a)   Prepare Mr Publius' income statement for the year ended 30 June 19X8 and balance sheet as at that date using *each* of the following methods:
    - (i)   historical cost accounting;
    - (ii)   replacement cost accounting, maintaining capital at its money level.
  - (b)   Discuss the relative usefulness of the figures you have calculated.

13.4   Mr Cavaradossi commences business as a manufacturer of scarpias on 1 June 19X7. On that date, he pays £6,000 into a business bank account from his personal bank account, and buys 200 units of raw material at £20 per unit.

During the year ended 31 May 19X8, 150 units of raw material are converted to 150 scarpias. The remaining 50 units of raw material are still in stock at 31 May 19X8.

On 31 May 19X8, Mr Cavaradossi pays from the business bank account production workers' wages of £7,000 and other expenses amounting to £4,000. On the same date he sells 150 scarpias at £100 each, and pays the proceeds into the business bank account. He also replaces the 150 units of raw material used, at the current market price of £30 per unit.

During the year ended 31 May 19X8, the general price index increased from 200 to 220.

- ■   (a)   Prepare Mr Cavaradossi's income statement for the year ended 31 May 19X8 and his balance sheet as at that date using each of the following methods:
    - (i)   historical cost accounting;
    - (ii)   replacement cost accounting, maintaining capital in terms of operating capacity;
    - (iii)   replacement cost accounting, maintaining capital in terms of general purchasing power.
  - (b)   Comment on the relative usefulness of the figures you have calculated.

13.5   Ms Tosca starts up her business on 1 January 19X7, with £300 cash and £2,000 stock. The stock comprises two identical items which were acquired immediately prior to the start of the period (i.e. the current value at the start of the period was £1,000 for each item).

During the year to 31 December 19X7, work is performed on one stock item only, the wages for which are paid on 31 December and amount to £500. On 31 December, the worked stock item is sold for £2,200, and replaced by an unworked item costing £1,500. The increase in the general price index for the year is 20%.

■ (a) Prepare Ms Tosca's balance sheet at 31 December 19X7 and her income statement for the year ended on that date, using each of the following methods:

  (i) historical cost accounting;
  (ii) replacement cost accounting — maintaining capital by a general price index;
  (iii) replacement cost accounting — maintaining the operating capacity of the business;
  (iv) current purchasing power accounting.

(b) Comment on the relative merits of the alternative capital maintenance concepts used in (a) above.

13.6 Tamino Ltd buys and sells papagenos. The company prepares its accounts annually to 31 December. During the year ended 31 December 19X9, it undertook the following transactions in papagenos:

		Units	Price per unit £
1 January	Stock on hand	0	—
2 January	Purchases	4,000	6.00
30 June	Purchases	6,000	8.00
31 December	Sales	8,000	10.00

The purchase price of papagenos at 31 December was £9.00 per unit.

■ (a) Calculate the gross profit made on the sale of papagenos during the year ended 31 December 19X9 *and* the balance sheet value of the stock of papagenos held at 31 December under each of the following methods:

  (i) historical cost accounting, using the first in, first out (FIFO) stock flow assumption;
  (ii) historical cost accounting, using the last in, first out (LIFO) stock flow assumption;
  (iii) historical cost accounting, using the weighted average stock flow assumption;
  (iv) replacement cost accounting.

(b) Discuss the relative merits of the above four methods for calculating cost of goods sold and the balance sheet value of stock.

Further reading

Baxter, W.T., *Inflation Accounting*, Philip Allan, 1984, Chapters 4, 7, 8, 9, 10.
Edwards, E.O. and Bell, P.W., *The Theory and Measurement of Business Income*, University of California Press, 1961.
Hope, A., 'Accounting and changing prices', in Carsberg, B. and Hope, A., *Current Issues in Accounting*, 2nd edn, Philip Allan, 1984.

Scapens, R.W., *Accounting in an Inflationary Environment*, 2nd edn, Macmillan, 1981.

Tweedie, D. and Whittington, G., 'Inflation accounting — the right choice?' *Accountancy*, October 1985.

Tweedie, D. and Whittington, G., 'Inflation accounting: the first of the choices', *Accountancy*, November 1985.

Tweedie, D. and Whittington, G.,'Towards a system of inflation accounting', *Accountancy*, December 1985.

Whittington, G., *Inflation Accounting: An Introduction to the Debate*, Cambridge University Press, 1983, Chapters 3–5.

14 *Evaluation of Alternative Accounting Methods*

In Chapter 2 we suggested that most users of financial statements have two main, interdependent information requirements:

(a) forecasts of some aspects of the future performance of the reporting entity, and

(b) regular reports explaining both differences between forecast and actual performance, and changes in forecasts if expectations have changed.

While the need for, and requirements of, forecasts may differ from user to user, we suggested that most users are interested in the cash flows of the entity. However, what appears beneficial to the interests of one, or more, groups of participants may be detrimental to the interests of others. Management, who may have most to lose by the disclosure of forecasted information, comprise a powerful lobby opposing such disclosures. As a result some participants are deprived of a basic input for their decision models, i.e. forecasts of future cash flows.

The information currently disclosed in financial statements is concerned with *past* performance and *current* position. External users must analyse and interpret this historical information in order to estimate an entity's *future* business performance and financial position. This leads us once more to the following fundamental question:

> **How should users of financial statements analyse and interpret the (historical) data provided in order to obtain the (predictive) information required?**

In previous chapters we have discussed some means for choosing between alternative reporting methods (Chapter 3), described historical cost, current purchasing power and replacement cost approaches to the measurement of income and value (Chapters 4–9 and Chapter 13), and explained how financial statements might be interpreted to analyse organizational performance (Chapters 10 and 11). In those chapters we discussed and made a preliminary evaluation of the alternative accounting treatments available for particular items. However, a full assessment of the usefulness of particular accounting treatments involves a consideration of broader issues, such as the choice of a basis of valuation. For example, in Chapter 6 we compared and contrasted different historical cost based depreciation methods but pointed out that a more fundamental question concerns whether depreciation should be based on historical cost, current cost, or some other measure. The purpose of this chapter is to take a wider view of some of the issues raised in previous chapters, and to evaluate the alternative accounting methods described previously.

We first review the possible criteria for selecting between alternative accounting methods and describe the general characteristics by which such accounting methods may be classified. We then apply the criteria to a broad evaluation of the alternative accounting methods. Our conclusions are tentative, reflecting the differences of opinion and lack of empirical (i.e. real-world) evidence that presently exist in the area of financial reporting.

14.1   Criteria for choice of accounting method

In Chapter 3 we discussed various criteria for choice of accounting method. We here review and, to a limited extent, expand those arguments. The problem of deciding what financial information ought to be reported is complicated by the existence of different users of accounting reports, and thus of possible conflicts in preferences for information.

Broadly, the problem of choice can be tackled in one of two ways. The first approach might be termed the *user decision orientated* approach. This entails an identification of the main groups of users and an assessment of the ability of alternative accounting methods to satisfy their information requirements. The assessment is often based on an examination of users' decision models. User decision orientated approaches were discussed in Chapter 2. We include in this section a summary of those discussions. The second approach is more limited and concerns the choice of accounting methods for quoted (listed) companies only. It might be termed the *efficient capital market* approach. This approach involves an examination of the efficiency of the capital market (i.e. the Stock Exchange) in incorporating accounting (and other) information in share prices, and is thus concerned mainly with the allocation of investors' resources.

User decision orientated approach

The user decision orientated approach considers the ability of alternative accounting methods to provide information useful to users' decision models.

Initially, the information requirements of each user group (e.g. shareholders, employees, creditors, etc.) are considered separately. When (and if) the best reporting method is agreed for each group, the further question arises as to whether the various methods can be combined into one general purpose report, or whether the best methods for each group differ so much that a special report must be provided for each group. The five steps involved in applying a user decision orientated approach are:

1. Identify groups of users and determine the information requirements of each group.
2. Specify alternative reporting methods.
3. Specify a testing procedure which relates the available courses of action (alternative accounting methods) to the information requirements of each group.
4. Use the testing procedure to select the best reporting method for each group, after taking account of the cost of implementing each reporting method.
5. Assess the extent to which the various preferred reporting methods might be combined in a general purpose report.

The results of the above procedure are unlikely to remain stable through time. For example, users' understanding of accounting information may change and thus their responses to alternative reporting methods may alter. It is therefore important that the procedure should be repeated regularly.

In Chapter 2 we identified the following external user groups for consideration: employees and trades unions; government; creditors and lenders; customers; shareholders and investment analysts. We considered their decisions and suggested the sort of accounting information which might be of help to them. Although we did not attempt to develop detailed decision models for each group, our analysis suggested that for major decisions, information relating to some aspects of an entity's future performance was relevant. This led us to the conclusion that competing accounting methods should be (at least partially) assessed against two interdependent criteria: their *predictive value* (i.e. their usefulness in enabling users to estimate future relevant events) and their *control* properties (i.e. their usefulness in assisting users to monitor an organization's performance through time).

The analysis was based primarily on our assumptions about the sort of decisions taken by different users. This type of *a priori* analysis, based on assumptions and opinions, suffers the weakness that it is not supported by *empirical* evidence (i.e. it is not supported by observations of real-world behaviour). Ultimately, the only way of resolving disputes concerning the usefulness of alternative accounting methods is by gathering empirical evidence about the extent to which, and the ways in which, the alternative methods are used. At least three variants of this approach are available:

(1) ask a sample of users what sort of information they require, using questionnaire and interview techniques;

(2) conduct controlled experiments, by providing a sample of users with alternative forms of accounting information and asking them to make hypothetical decisions on the basis of that information;
(3) observe and analyse the actual decisions taken by users in response to available information.

None of these variants is free from problems. For example, variant (1) involves the selection of a representative (unbiased) sample of users and the design of a questionnaire that does not influence their replies. Variant (2) relies on the responses of users to hypothetical decisions in the same way as they would react to real-world problems. Variant (3) requires the researcher to distinguish between users' actions which are motivated by the information provided, and those that result from other factors, such as changes in environmental conditions. In addition, all three variants suffer the disadvantage that users' responses may be conditioned by the sort of information they are receiving at present and have been accustomed to receive in the past. A reliable empirical experiment would involve the provision of a variety of information for a long period of time, before we could test users' preferences for particular information. In respect of alternative asset valuation methods this procedure has been facilitated by accounting standards in the UK, USA, and elsewhere, which required certain organizations to provide both current cost and historical cost information. (See Chapter 13, Section 13.6 for a summary of the recent history of current cost accounting in the UK.)

Efficient capital market approach

Efficient capital market tests are a form of the third empirical approach discussed above. Such tests involve an analysis of decisions taken by users in response to available information. In particular they are concerned with the speed with which, and the extent to which, accounting and other information is reflected in current share prices. For example, studies have been undertaken which examine the reaction of share prices to the announcement of accounting numbers (e.g. annual earnings numbers) and to changes in accounting methods (e.g. methods of calculating depreciation and of valuing stock or fixed assets). The capital market is said to be efficient if it responds rapidly and without bias to new information. However, the efficient capital market approach is concerned only with the allocation of investors' resources and is thus of little help in assessing the usefulness of accounting reports to other participants.

In addition to its limited scope, the efficient capital market approach is concerned primarily with the efficiency of the market in processing available information, i.e. it is (self-evidently) not concerned with alternative, but as yet unprovided, accounting information. Thus capital market efficiency cannot, by itself, be used to assess the *desirability* of alternative accounting methods, although it may be of some use in assessing their *effects*.

One important test of capital market efficiency asks the following question. Can the market (e.g. the Stock Exchange) distinguish between accounting information that signals a 'real' change in an organization's position or performance (for example, information about increased turnover that might lead to an increase in distributable cash flows in the future) and information that is 'cosmetic' and has no implications for the 'real' position of an organization (for example, information about increased earnings resulting purely from a change in depreciation method)? In practice, there may be few changes to accounting methods that are entirely 'cosmetic'. A change in an organization's depreciation method may seem at first sight to have no 'real' information value in the sense that it signals no 'real' change in the organization's performance (i.e. it does not change its cash flows). On further investigation, though, it might be found to influence the timing of the organization's cash receipts (if, for example, the organization is involved in government contracts under which payments are related to accounting costs such as depreciation) or its taxation liability (for example, in countries such as the USA where the accounting charge for depreciation forms the basis for the tax allowance for depreciation). If the capital market *is* able to distinguish between 'real' and 'cosmetic' changes ('real' changes thus having an effect on share prices, 'cosmetic' changes having no such effect) then at least organizations need not spend time (and incur costs) in choosing between accounting methods, the differences between which are purely 'cosmetic'. In such cases, any one method contains the same amount of information as any other.

Interpersonal utility comparisons

In our discussion of both user decision orientated and efficient capital market approaches we have noted the problem caused by the existence of potential conflicts between and within groups concerning the provision of relevant information. *Intergroup* conflicts arise when the provision of certain information is beneficial to one group and harmful to another (for example, increased information to employees may enable them to negotiate higher wages, one result of which may be an increase in the selling price which is passed on to customers). *Intragroup* conflicts arise when information benefits certain members of a particular user group but is disadvantageous to other members of the same group. For example, a company operating two separate plants might pay the same wage rate to employees in both locations based upon the joint output of the two plants. Disaggregated information which showed one plant to be more productive might prove to be helpful to one group of employees in subsequent wage negotiations, but detrimental to the interests of the other group. Intergroup and intragroup conflicts are inevitable in such situations. The resolution of such conflicts requires some form of social value judgement, i.e. a judgement as to whether the benefits to one group or subgroup arising from a change in accounting method outweigh the costs to others in *social* terms. Social value judgements may have to be made ultimately by government, or by another body (such as the accounting profession) with the implicit or explicit approval of government.

Other criteria

Our approach thus far has suggested that *in our opinion* relevance to user decisions (i.e. predictive value and control) should, in most cases, be regarded as the most important criterion for evaluating accounting methods. In Chapter 3 we categorized the main criteria for choice as relating to either the *usefulness* or the *feasibility* of alternative accounting methods. Within the category of usefulness we included *predictive value and control* (discussed above) and also *timeliness*, *comparability*, *objectivity* and *understandability*. The criterion of timeliness suggests that the usefulness of accounting information is greater, the shorter the time period between the outcome and the report of an event. Comparability (often termed 'consistency') means that accounting information should be prepared on comparable bases both through time and between organizations. Objectivity is concerned primarily with the extent to which accounting information is free from bias. Understandability means the extent to which those who use accounting information understand the basis upon which it has been prepared.

The set of criteria relating to the feasibility of accounting methods encompasses *verifiability* and *measurability*. Verifiability relates to the extent to and ease with which the information contained in an accounting report can be checked. The criterion of measurability suggests that an accounting system which enables more factors to be measured (with some degree of certainty) is to be preferred.

In the next section we describe the nature of economic (forecast-based) measures of income and value and suggest that they might provide a benchmark against which various (transactions-based) accounting approaches could be evaluated. This role for economic measures is based on the *a priori* argument that they have high predictive value and control properties. Thus an accounting method that is consistently a good estimator of economic measures should be ranked highly.

The criteria developed thus far are concerned primarily with the benefits associated with different accounting methods. We should not forget that the choice of accounting method depends also on its associated costs. The best accounting method is the one with the greatest surplus of benefits over costs. For this purpose, costs include not only the costs of producing and analysing the information, but also the costs suffered by particular participants if information is disclosed which is detrimental to their interests.

The identification of an optimal accounting method would be straightforward if one method were superior to all others in terms of its ability to satisfy *all* criteria, including that of cost. As we shall see, this is not the case — different criteria are probably best satisfied by different accounting methods. Furthermore, there is no easy way of expressing benefits in a common unit of measurement. In consequence we believe that an unambiguous cost–benefit analysis of alternative methods is not possible at present. We shall attempt to identify strengths and weaknesses of particular accounting methods and use the results to make a preliminary assessment of their relative merits. Our inability to draw firm conclusions about the superiority of some methods over others simply reflects the present state of accounting as a developing discipline.

14.2 Economic measures of income and value

Each of the accounting methods described in Chapter 13 derives net income and financial position on the basis of *actual transactions*. An alternative method of income determination may be derived from the concepts of economics. This method is based on the discounted cash flow approach described in the appendix to Chapter 2, and relies on the use of forecasts (of future cash flows) rather than on past transactions. In this section and the next we explain this method briefly and discuss the role and usefulness of economic measures generally. First, however, a word of caution. Because of their dependence on forecasts, and their consequent high degree of subjectivity, economic measures have found little favour amongst accounting practitioners who seek to measure and report an organization's past performance. Nevertheless, such measures may provide a *benchmark* against which various transactions-based approaches can be evaluated. It is for this reason that we consider them here.

The economic value of an organization at any point in time is usually defined as the discounted present value of all net cash distributions the organization expects to make in the future. The economic income of the organization for a particular period is described as the increase in its capital value during that period, after making suitable adjustments for dividends paid and capital introduced. Under conditions of certainty both the future cash distributions and the future discount rates are known in advance, i.e. estimates of both future cash distributions and appropriate discount rates will not vary depending on the time at which estimates are made. In consequence, the following expression may be used to calculate economic value and economic income if certainty is presumed:[1]

$$\text{Economic value } EV_t = \sum_{j=t+1}^{n} \frac{D_j}{(1+i)^{j-t}} \tag{14.1}$$

where EV_t is the economic value at time t, D_j is the cash distribution to be made at time j, i is the appropriate discount rate (assumed to be constant from period to period), and n is the last time at which a cash distribution is expected.

$$\text{Economic income } EI_{t-1 \to t} = EV_t - EV_{t-1} + D_t - CI_t \tag{14.2}$$

where $EI_{t-1 \to t}$ is the economic income for the period from time $t-1$ to time t, EV_t, EV_{t-1} are the economic values at time t and time $t-1$ respectively, D_t is the cash distribution made at time t, and CI_t is the capital introduced at time t.

In order to simplify the analysis, we shall treat capital introduced as a negative dividend payment. In consequence, the term CI_t disappears from expression (14.2). The following illustration explains the application of this method.

Ashton Ltd has been trading for many years. It is the company's policy to

---

1. See the appendix to Chapter 2 for an explanation of discounting methods and of the sigma (Σ) notation.

distribute all net cash inflows as dividends as they arise. The company's cost of capital is 20% p.a. The directors intend to pay dividends of £50,000 after one year (i.e. at time 1) and £60,000 at the end of all future years.

Using expression (14.1) we may calculate the present economic value of Ashton Ltd (EV_0) and its expected economic value at all subsequent points in time, as follows:[2]

$$EV_0 = \sum_{j=1}^{\infty} \frac{D_j}{(1.2)^j}$$

$$= \frac{50,000}{(1.2)} + \frac{60,000}{(1.2)^2} + \frac{60,000}{(1.2)^3} + \ldots$$

$$= \frac{50,000}{(1.2)} + \left[\frac{60,000}{0.2} \times \frac{1}{1.2} \right]$$

$$= 41,667 + 250,000$$

$$EV_0 = \underline{£291,667}$$

$$EV_1 = \sum_{j=2}^{\infty} \frac{D_j}{(1.2)^{j-1}}$$

$$= \frac{60,000}{(1.2)} + \frac{60,000}{(1.2)^2} + \frac{60,000}{(1.2)^3} + \ldots$$

$$= \frac{60,000}{0.2}$$

$$EV_1 = \underline{£300,000}$$

The economic value at time 2 and all subsequent times will also be £300,000 because at any (annual) point in time after time 2 the company expects to receive £60,000 p.a. indefinitely. Thus the economic value at any point in time after time 1 is the discounted present value, at 20% interest, of a perpetuity of £60,000, i.e. £300,000.

The economic income of Ashton Ltd for each future period may be calculated from expression (14.2), as follows:

$$EI_{0 \to 1} = EV_1 - EV_0 + D_1$$
$$= 300,000 - 291,667 + 50,000$$

$$EI_{0 \to 1} = \underline{£58,333}$$

$$EI_{1 \to 2} = EV_2 - EV_1 + D_2$$
$$= 300,000 - 300,000 + 60,000$$

$$EI_{1 \to 2} = \underline{£60,000}$$

2. The symbol ∞ means infinity.

The economic income for all subsequent periods will also be £60,000 as economic value does not change after time 2 and the constant annual distribution is £60,000. Under conditions of *certainty* the economic income of a period is equal to the economic value at the start of the period multiplied by the discount rate (i.e. $EI_{t-1 \to t} = i \times EV_{t-1}$). Thus, in the case of Ashton Ltd, economic income for the period from time 0 to time 1 (£58,333) may, alternatively, be calculated as 20% of the value at time 0, i.e. as 20% of £291,667, and for each subsequent period as 20% of £300,000.

Let us now analyse the effect of the above on an individual shareholder in the company. This may lead to a clearer understanding of the principles underlying the economic value approach. Suppose that Mr Home owns 10% of Ashton Ltd. His share of the company's value at time 0 (t_0) and time 1 (t_1) and of the dividend paid by the company during the period from time 0 to time 1 is as follows:

	Ashton Ltd £	Mr Home (10%) £
Economic value, t_0	291,667	29,167
Economic value, t_1	300,000	30,000
Dividend paid by company, $t_0 \to t_1$	50,000	5,000

How much better off is Mr Home at the end of the period (t_1) than he was at the beginning (t_0), as a result of owning 10% of the company?

	£	£
At t_0 his share of the company was worth		29,167
At t_1 his share of the company is worth	30,000	
and he has cash from the dividend of	5,000	35,000
His 'gain' during the period is		5,833

We can now interpret the gain of £5,833 in capital maintenance terms as representing the maximum amount Mr Home could spend during the period from his share in Ashton Ltd, and still be as well off (in terms of money capital) at the end of the period as he was at the beginning. If he sold £833 of his share in the company and spent the proceeds, together with the cash distribution of £5,000, he would be left with a share in the company worth £29,167 — the same as at the start of the period. As a result of his ownership of 10% of Ashton Ltd, Mr Home has gained £5,833 in the period from time 0 to time 1. Under the forecast-based approach to income and value measurement, this amount is called his income from the company.

The above illustration uses the simplifying assumption of certainty. In reality, organizations operate under conditions of uncertainty. In consequence, the estimated values of future cash distributions will normally depend on the information available at the time at which the estimate is made, i.e. expectations may change as time passes. In addition, different discount rates may be appropriate for different periods, and estimates of the appropriate discount rates may change over time. A detailed consideration of economic measures of income and value under uncertainty is outside the scope of this text. However, it is important to recognize that, because expectations will change as time passes, calculations of economic values will vary depending on when the calculation is undertaken. In consequence, economic income, which is based on changes in economic value (expression (14.2)), will also be affected by changes in expectations. Such changes to economic income are often referred to as *windfall gains*.

14.3   The role and usefulness of economic measures

We argued in Chapter 2, and reiterated at the start of this chapter, that, in general, most users of accounting reports have two main, interdependent information requirements:

(a) forecasts of some aspects of the future performance of the reporting entity, and
(b) regular reports explaining both differences between forecasted and actual performance, and changes in forecasts if expectations have changed.

We argued further that although the aspects of an organization's performance for which forecasts are required may differ from user to user, most users are interested in its cash flows. Hence, it would seem sensible for organizations to provide two types of financial statement:

(a) a statement of forecasts of the entity's expected future cash flows, and
(b) a statement of the entity's actual cash flows together with an explanation of the differences between the forecasted and the actual cash flows.

It would also seem to be appropriate for some estimate of the uncertainty associated with the expected future cash flows to be disclosed, to help the user select an appropriate discount rate.

How far would a method of reporting, based on economic measures of income and value, go towards satisfying the assumed information needs of an organization's owners? The most powerful argument supporting economic income and value measures is that they are based on the discounting of expected cash flows, using a discount rate which is appropriate to the risk of the cash flows. These data are essentially the same as those required by owners; estimated future cash flows, a discount rate based on the risk of the estimated cash flows, and actual cash flows of the period under consideration together with changes in expectations during that period.

Suppose that for each period an organization reported its estimated economic income for the period, subdivided into expected income and windfall gains.

Expected income would indicate to the owner the management's estimate of the amount of cash flows which *could* be distributed in each future period, without reducing the organization's capital in money terms. Economic value would indicate management's estimate of the discounted present value of expected future cash distributions.

The owner also requires an indication of how effective are the organization's managers in setting estimates and achieving estimated performance. In a reporting system based on economic measures, this indication would be provided primarily by reported windfall gains, which reflect changes in expectations about cash flows or discount rates. An organization which regularly reports relatively high windfall gains or losses may be operating in particularly volatile markets, or may be employing managers who have poor estimating ability, or who are deliberately distorting reported income and value figures. If reported windfall gains or losses are consistently in the same direction and of similar size, an owner may conclude that management's current estimates are likely to be optimistic (if windfall losses are regularly reported) or pessimistic (if windfall gains are regularly reported). If over a number of periods a mixture of windfall gains and losses is reported, and if their size is significant, an owner will need to weigh the possible causes and modify his or her opinion of the managers' estimates accordingly.

The above analysis suggests that a reporting system based on economic measures of income and value should not necessarily be regarded as ideal. However, such a system would help owners to estimate the efficiency of an organization's managers in making predictions and in achieving predicted performance. Consequently, it may provide owners with information for their decision models at least as useful as would be provided by any alternative (transactions-based) method which involves reporting past performance and current position.

However, the very relationship between economic value and future cash flows which makes relevant the reporting of economic value and income contains its own potential downfall, i.e. an accounting method based upon economic value will be subject to criticisms similar to those levelled at financial statements incorporating cash forecasts. Economic measures are based on estimates of future cash flows and discount rates which are not objective and cannot be verified; and changes in economic values, as a result of changes in expectations, may provide information which could be advantageous to competitors. In addition, the resulting pattern of income places undue emphasis on the recognition of the opportunities of realizing gains rather than on the production or sale involved in their realization.

For our present purposes, however, it does not matter that a reporting method based on economic measures of income and value is impractical. Even if it is, economic income and value provide *benchmarks* against which alternative, more practical accounting methods may be assessed. Let us explain the rationale of this argument.

We have noted a relevant method of reporting to be one which represents a good basis for predicting the expected value of, and the risk attached to, the organization's future cash distributions. As part of the prediction process, the reporting method should also enable owners to explain both differences between estimated and actual distributions and changes in expectations regarding future distributions. For various reasons it is unlikely that the forecasted information will be provided directly, and hence published financial statements will continue to be based predominantly on transactions-based accounting methods. What we need is a way of assessing whether the information provided by practical, feasible accounting methods (based upon historical cost, adjusted historical cost or current cost methods of asset valuation) can be interpreted to provide the predictive and control information required by users.

Economic measures of income and value could help to provide the way. Economic value is based upon estimates of future cash flows and the risk associated with them. This is the sort of information required by users. In addition, economic values are reported in a format which allows easy comparison with values, or costs, generated by more practical methods of asset valuation. If a particular accounting method consistently enables good estimates of economic measures to be achieved, then that method is as useful as a method based on economic measures, subject to the costs of making the estimates and their degree of accuracy. Economic measures of income and value can therefore be used as a benchmark, or intermediate criterion, against which other (transactions-based) measures may be evaluated.

14.4   Alternative accounting methods for external reporting

Accounting reporting methods may be classified according to two characteristics — their valuation method and their capital maintenance concept (see Chapter 13). The asset valuation method determines the value of assets in the balance sheet and the operating costs in the income statement. The capital maintenance concept determines how much of income is set aside to maintain the value of the invested capital.

Assets may be valued, and costs determined, using one of the following five transactions-based methods:

1. Historical cost,
2. Historical cost adjusted by a general price index,
3. Current cost/value: (a) Replacement cost,
                              (b) Realizable value,
                              (c) 'Value to the firm'.

We have examined and discussed in previous chapters the nature of historical cost, adjusted historical cost and replacement cost asset valuations. The realizable value of an asset is the price at which the asset could be sold in a normal business transaction. 'Value to the firm' involves the comparison of various asset valuation methods. It is defined as the *lower* of replacement cost and value in use, where value in use is the *higher* of realizable value and the discounted present value of the net future benefits expected from use of the asset. If this seems difficult to understand at the moment, we shall explain more fully its calculation, and that of realizable value, later in this chapter.

Capital may be maintained using:

1. Maintenance of money capital.
2. Maintenance of the general purchasing power of owners' equity.
3. Maintenance of operating capacity (i.e. maintenance of the physical capability of the enterprise).

We have not included economic measures of income and value in the above categorizations because we do not see them as feasible methods of reporting business performance; their importance is as benchmarks against which alternative transactions-based methods can be assessed. Our purpose in this chapter is to evaluate existing methods and others that we believe might replace (or supplement) them. In the next two sections we evaluate the alternative capital maintenance concepts and asset valuation methods described above.

14.5   Evaluation of capital maintenance concepts

In Chapter 13 we compared and reached some conclusions as to the relative merits of alternative capital maintenance concepts. We now summarize those conclusions. The justification for making capital maintenance adjustments (i.e. those based on maintaining the firm's operating capacity or the general purchasing power of owners' funds) is that they avoid the distribution of the organization's 'real' capital. This justification places a substantial emphasis on the measurement of income, in terms both of amounts currently available for distribution and of the prediction of future performance.

However, one might argue that it may not be in the interests of those associated with an organization to maintain its real capital. It might be better in certain cases to increase current distributions (to owners, employees and so on) and reduce the scale of future activities if parts of the organization's activities are unprofitable or are located in a contracting sector of the economy. For example, an organization which manufactures calculators may be acting in the best interests of its participants if it decides to reduce its production of battery-powered calculators, particularly if it decides instead to make solar-powered calculators. Distribution decisions should be based on investment and financing opportunities available and expected to become available and on the consumption preferences of the participants, rather than on accounting measurements of past performance.

The criteria discussed earlier in this chapter are similarly not affected significantly by the choice of a capital maintenance concept. The main difference between financial statements prepared using different capital maintenance concepts lies in the way in which holding gains on non-monetary assets (primarily stock and fixed assets) are reported. We discussed this at some length in Chapter 13. If capital is maintained in money terms, holding gains are reported in the income statement. If operating capacity is maintained, holding gains are reported as part of ownership interest in the balance sheet. If owners' purchasing power is maintained, part of the holding gains are reported in the income statement and the remainder as part of ownership interest. Thus although the choice of capital maintenance concepts affects directly an organization's net income (see Table 13.3), full disclosure of holding gains should ensure that, for all but the most naive user, each capital maintenance concept conveys the same information.

14.6   Evaluation of asset valuation methods

Historical cost

From the inception of double-entry recording until some twenty years ago, historical cost was almost universally accepted as the most appropriate means of measuring costs and assets in external accounting reports. Hence one argument often advanced in its favour is that it has stood the test of time, i.e. it has provided numbers which have been *used* (and presumably deemed to be *useful*). It does not, however, follow that numbers prepared on some other basis could not also have been used, or that a method that was useful in the past will continue to be useful in the future. It is also argued that historical cost numbers are objective because they represent the prices at which actual transactions have taken place and, in consequence, there should be little dispute about whether or not the numbers are 'correct'. The validity of this argument is weakened by the need to match costs with revenues. Matching involves subjectivity. For example, the calculation of the amount of annual depreciation of a fixed asset depends directly on subjective estimates of its remaining useful life and residual value. Similar considerations apply to stock and debtors. Another argument in favour of historical cost relates to the cost of its application. It is frequently argued that it is cheaper to implement than alternative methods, primarily because change would involve additional costs. We discuss the relative cost of other methods below.

Various arguments have been advanced against the use of historical cost, particularly during periods of inflation. Such arguments usually relate to its inadequacy as a means of controlling and assessing the efficiency of resource use. A historical cost balance sheet is not a statement of the current value of assets, and performance measured against the (outdated) historical cost of resources gives little indication of how well managers have performed in the past or of how well they are likely to perform in the future. These limitations severely restrict the comparability of financial statements prepared on a historical cost basis. It is possible for two organizations to own assets with identical current values and yet report different historical costs in the balance sheet and charge different historical costs in the income statements. As the financial statements of the two organizations lack comparability, so do many of the attendant performance ratios.

Other disadvantages might be cited. For example, historical costs rarely measure the relevant (opportunity) costs of using resources; and as a consequence of adopting the 'fundamental concept' of prudence, there is widespread use of conservatism in the preparation of financial statements, at the possible expense of such other qualities as relevance. Finally, it is difficult to make a case supporting the predictive value of historical cost numbers; or to establish a relationship between historical cost income and economic income. Economic values are forward-looking and based upon estimates of future cash flows. Historical costs are backward-looking and based upon past transactions. Only in those cases where there have been few, or no, environmental changes, e.g. changes in price levels, technology and customer preferences over a period of many years, would these two methods be closely related. These conditions rarely, if ever, exist. We saw in Chapter 10 how historical cost profitability ratios can give a misleading indication of future performance if both the income and balance sheet figures include costs and assets at prices which are out of date.

Historical cost adjusted by a general price index

This method 'values' assets in pounds of current purchasing power (CPP). The advantages and disadvantages claimed of CPP figures have much in common with those claimed for unadjusted historical costs. By applying a widely used general index (the Retail Price Index) to the historical cost of past transactions, CPP figures are easily verifiable, and the cost of preparing CPP accounts is not excessive. In addition, by separating operating profit from any gains or losses on holding monetary items, the method highlights two separate aspects of managerial performance — operating efficiency and financial management.

However, the close association of CPP and historical cost methods of asset valuation implies that many of the disadvantages of historical cost apply equally to the CPP method. Objectivity is reduced by the need to make judgements in respect of particular attributes of fixed assets, stock and debtors and although operating profit is separated from gains or losses on holding monetary items, that profit may not itself be a good indicator of managerial performance in the past or in the future. In particular, the values of assets and the cost of using them do *not* reflect current replacement costs or realizable values, unless such costs and values have increased at exactly the same rate as the general price index since the assets were purchased. Furthermore, some users may be misled into believing that the adjusted figures do represent current replacement costs or realizable values, and may consequently make incorrect decisions. If this is so, the CPP method fails to satisfy the criterion of understandability.

It also fails to satisfy the criteria of consistency and comparability. We noted in Chapter 13 that it is possible for two assets with identical current values to be measured differently under CPP accounting. It is also the case that assets with identical costs at the time of purchase will be reported as having identical CPP (and historical) costs thereafter, even though their current values might diverge. Not only do CPP asset values and income figures lack comparability, but as a result so do any ratios based upon those figures.

Finally, the CPP approach to asset valuation is backward-looking. It is based upon the historical cost of past transactions, and the figures derived from this approach are unlikely to have any relationship with forecast-based figures which determine economic income and value.

Current cost or current value

The terms 'current cost' and 'current value' are used to describe those accounting methods which value assets by reference to current prices. There are a number of asset valuation methods which may be included within this definition. For example, an asset's value may be determined by its current replacement cost as we saw in Chapter 13, or by current selling price, or by its value 'in use', i.e. a value based upon its contribution to the organization's business. We deal in turn with each of the three variants of current cost.

(i) **Replacement cost** We have seen that an important characteristic of replacement cost accounting is its recognition of different aspects of managerial activity via the separate treatment of operating income and holding gains. Operating income is calculated by matching revenues with the current replacement costs of operating resources. Holding gains are increases in the replacement costs of assets occurring during the accounting period. The split is significant because, as we suggested in Chapter 13, it may help satisfy the criteria of predictive value and control.

An operating surplus suggests that the organization has generated sufficient revenue to cover the current replacement costs of the resources used. This *may* suggest that it will be able to continue doing so in the future, although a fuller judgement depends on forecasts of how future economic conditions will be likely to affect the organization. Nevertheless, the information provided is more current than that revealed by historical cost income statements, and it tackles a fundamental problem facing most organizations, i.e. their ability to replace resources as they are used.

Holding gains suggest changes in the cash-generating potential of assets. A positive holding gain (increase in an asset's value) usually results from an increase in the future benefits the asset is expected to provide; this implies that a present holding gain indicates an increase in future operating income.[3] Thus holding gains (or losses) provide some indication of possible changes in the trend of operating income. The dichotomy between operating income and holding gains may also be useful in assessing the efficiency of managers. It may aid decisions (by shareholders) as to whether to retain or replace the management and/or whether to increase its remuneration. It emphasizes two different aspects of management activity: the success of managers in purchasing assets in advance of a price rise (measured by holding gains), and the efficiency of managers in operating assets (measured by operating income).

It is also argued that replacement cost asset values provide information useful in predicting future performance. The current replacement cost of an asset reflects, to some extent, the future benefits likely to be derived from its use. This suggests a possible link between replacement cost and economic value. For example, few organizations would replace assets unless the future discounted benefits (economic value) exceed the purchase price (replacement cost). The extent to which likely future benefits are reflected in current replacement cost depends on the nature and efficiency of the market in which the asset is traded.

The final advantage claimed for replacement cost is that, relative to historical cost, it increases the degree of comparability between the reports of different organizations. The values of assets and operating costs are measured in terms of current prices, so that similar organizations reporting on the same date should disclose costs and values computed on comparable bases, even if the age structure of their assets is different. The same cannot be said of historical cost accounts. As we saw in Chapter 10, it is essential that assets and operating costs are measured in terms of current prices in order to produce meaningful ratios which evaluate an organization's past performance, compare that performance with other similar organizations, and estimate the organization's likely future performance.

Various criticisms have been levelled against the use of replacement costs in financial statements, for example that replacement cost figures are expensive to calculate. During the 1980s many large organizations in the UK and USA were required to prepare and publish replacement cost information. Most organizations chose to continue to record transactions at historical cost and to make periodic revisions to incorporate changes in replacement cost. These revisions were usually made once a year, at the year-end, although some companies made quarterly or, occasionally, monthly revisions. Although this sort of procedure involves additional clerical costs, there is evidence to suggest that the extra cost of annual

---

3. An increase in an asset's value does not always imply an increase in future operating income. For example, an asset's value may increase if it is used in an industry whose members enjoy some degree of monopoly protection. If the monopoly protection is removed, new firms may enter the industry to take advantage of the 'monopoly' profits, thus bidding up the price of the asset but also reducing the expected profits of each existing member of the industry because total industry profits now have to be shared between more firms.

revisions is slight, particularly in relation to the cost of maintaining the basic historical cost records.[4]

A second argument frequently advanced against replacement cost accounting is that it lacks objectivity; the adjustments required to the basic historical cost records may be based on indices of specific price changes published by the Central Statistical Office, on manufacturers' price lists or on information gleaned from the internal records of the organization. In other words, there may be several different 'replacement costs' for the same asset, unless it is traded in a very efficient market. For example, the cost of a two-year-old Vauxhall Cavalier may vary depending upon its condition and upon the source from which it is acquired. However, although there may not be a unique replacement cost for a two-year-old Cavalier (or for many other assets), it may still be that net replacement cost is more 'objective' as a valuation basis than written-down historical cost. We noted above that subjective estimates of remaining life and residual value are required to calculate historical cost. The calculation also depends on the chosen method of depreciation. It is possible (even probable) that if a number of accountants were asked to estimate the replacement cost and written-down historical cost of a two-year-old Cavalier and were given no further guidance as to which valuation conventions to use, their estimates of replacement cost would be less widely dispersed than those of historical cost. Thus, insofar as a consensus view may be taken as a measure of objectivity, replacement cost figures may well be more objective than historical costs, particularly in relation to assets which have an active second-hand market.

A final problem concerns the definition of replacement costs when technology is changing. An organization may own an asset (Mark I) which has been superseded by a more efficient one (Mark II). Is the appropriate replacement cost of the Mark I asset the cost of buying another Mark I asset of similar age and condition, or is it the cost of acquiring the same production potential from a Mark II asset? The latter seems more likely, as it appears more likely that the organization would buy a Mark II asset if it had to replace its asset. However, it may be difficult (and hence costly) to calculate the cost of obtaining, from the Mark II asset, services identical to those available from the Mark I. For example, suppose the Mark I model has a production capacity of 200,000 units p.a., and the Mark II has a production capacity of 300,000 units p.a. Under these conditions the replacement cost of the *services* provided by the Mark I asset would appear to be two-thirds of the appropriate written-down cost of a Mark II asset. However, the Mark II model might process a different mix of raw materials, use more, or less, labour

---

4. See, for example, Scapens, R.W., Southworth, A.J. and Stacy, G.H., *Case Studies in Current Cost Accounting*, Institute of Chartered Accountants in England and Wales, 1983; Hope, A. *Accounting for Price-level Changes — A Practical Survey of Six Methods*, Institute of Chartered Accountants in England and Wales Research Committee Occasional Paper No. 4, 1974; Dockweiler, R.C., 'The practicability of developing multiple financial statements: a case study', *The Accounting Review*, October 1969.

and power, have a different maintenance contract etc. — all of which affect the cost of replacing the services provided by the Mark I model.

(ii) **Realizable value** The realizable value of an asset is the price at which the asset could be sold in a normal business transaction. This may be very different from the amount that would be raised in a forced liquidation. For example, a second-hand car dealer, forced to dispose of his entire stock of second-hand cars within a few days, may have to accept much lower prices than he could obtain by selling them in the normal course of his business over a period of three or four months.

Perhaps the most popular argument in favour of realizable value as a measure of the current value of an asset is that it is the most appropriate indication of the *sacrifice* involved in using the asset, i.e. by using the asset the organization is foregoing the opportunity to sell it. It is sometimes argued that avoidance of the cost of replacing an asset is not an alternative available to an organization once the asset has been purchased. For example, suppose a company purchases a machine for £20,000 in 19X0. In 19X2 the replacement cost of a two-year-old machine is £17,000 and the realizable value is £11,000. It is argued that the sacrifice involved in using the asset in 19X2 is the £11,000 foregone — the £17,000 does not measure any form of sacrifice made by the company.

This line of argument has led some proponents of the realizable value method to claim that the realizable value of an asset is relevant to *all* decisions concerning its use, i.e. sale of the asset should always be considered as one possible course of action. These lines of argument have their roots in the concept of relevant costs for management decisions concerning the use of assets,[5] but seem basically to be flawed for the purpose of selecting a valuation method for external reports. First, they are not consistent even with the logic of determining relevant costs for decisions. The replacement cost of an asset is very often the relevant (opportunity) cost of using it; if the asset is to be replaced eventually, the relevant cost of its use is the amount the organization must pay to acquire a replacement. (This point is clarified further in the later discussion of 'value to the firm'.) Second, there seem to be no obvious reasons to assume that a cost which is relevant to managers, who must make decisions about the optimal use of assets, is also relevant to external users, who generally have no control over such decisions.

There is, however, a more persuasive argument for using realizable values in external reports. The basis of this view is that they provide an indication of an organization's ability to adapt to changing environmental and economic conditions, particularly in the short run. An organization that is unable to adapt in the short run may not survive to the long run. One aspect of an organization's adaptability is its ability to raise cash to undertake new investment. To some extent, this depends on its ability to generate funds to repay long-term capital

5. See, for example, Arnold, J. and Hope, A., *Accounting for Management Decisions*, 2nd edn, Prentice-Hall International, 1990, Chapter 5.

and to pay interest. It also depends on the ability to raise capital quickly to exploit short-term opportunities. The realizable values of the organization's assets are an important contributory factor to this ability. They indicate the amounts that could be raised quickly to finance new investments, both by selling the assets themselves and by pledging them as security for loans from banks and other lenders. In Chapter 10 we suggested that an analysis of an organization's liquidity position would be more meaningful if non-monetary assets such as stock and work in progress were always valued at their realizable values.

In discussing the merits of replacement costs we argued that they provide a yardstick against which to assess management's ability to generate sufficient funds to replace assets as they are used. Realizable values provide a different yardstick: one that indicates management's ability to generate a better return than could be achieved by selling the organization's assets and investing the proceeds elsewhere. This yardstick indicates one ambivalent characteristic of realizable value systems — they concentrate heavily on the short-run performance of an organization and on its potential liquidation rather than on its performance as a going concern. This emphasis may be inappropriate for an organization operating in a healthy economic environment, although it could provide important information about an organization struggling to survive in a weak or declining economy.

This concentration upon short-run performance suggests that, *a priori*, realizable values are unlikely to be good indicators of future performance. A going concern, by definition, is expected to continue to operate into the foreseeable future and hence replace its assets as they wear out. Even if the going-concern assumption is relaxed, realizable values will be accurate predictors of future cash flows only if the assets are sold off individually.

The idea that an organization's assets might be sold and the proceeds invested elsewhere implies a *proprietary* view of the firm, i.e. the realizable value method views the organization as a collection of assets which can be (broken up and) sold by the managers or the owners at any time. This view conflicts with the more generally accepted *entity* view of the firm, as a collection of individuals or groups (participants) whose collective participation is essential for the continued existence of the organization.

Additional arguments have been advanced against the use of realizable values. As with replacement costs, they may involve additional preparation costs. A further difficulty lies in the treatment of highly specialized assets, for example oil rigs and specialized manufacturing plant. Such assets may cost many millions of pounds but, because of their highly specialized nature, may have very low realizable values almost immediately after acquisition. Realizable value accounting may therefore result in the whole cost of an asset being written off early in its life. Whether or not this is a desirable consequence depends on the uses of the information. It is a very conservative treatment, resulting in extremely low income figures during the first year or so of an asset's life, and relatively high income figures (via low or non-existent depreciation charges) thereafter. In some respects, a realizable value income statement would approximate a statement of past cash flows. Again, this suggests that realizable values do not provide a sound basis for forecasting an organization's likely future performance. Indeed the case for using realizable values is rarely, if ever, argued in terms of their predictive value. This final criticism may be the most pertinent. If, as we have argued, predictive value is a crucial attribute of any reporting method, the fact that little (successful) attempt has been made to show that realizable value numbers possess this attribute suggests that they may not represent a useful basis of asset valuation.

(iii)   **Value to the firm**   Value to the firm (or 'deprival value') has its roots in economics, and is related closely to the concept of opportunity cost. It is the current cost asset valuation method which was recommended by the UK professional accountancy bodies.[6] The means of determining the value to the firm of an asset is depicted in Figure 14.1, and illustrated in Table 14.1.

The term 'deprival value' provides a clue as to the rationale behind this method of asset valuation. In essence the method asks the following question. 'What would be the cost incurred by the firm if it was deprived of a particular asset?' Would management replace it with another, similar asset (in which case the cost to the firm would be the replacement cost)? Or would management decide the asset was not worth replacing (in which case the cost to the firm would be the revenue foregone from being unable to sell the asset or to use it in the business)? Thus the deprival value, or value to the firm, depends upon the relationship between the replacement cost, realizable value and economic value (discounted present value) of an asset.

We should begin our analysis of the concept of 'value to the firm' by asking two questions. First, should the asset be kept for use or sold immediately? The answer depends on the relationship between economic value and realizable value. If the economic value of the asset is greater than its realizable value it should be kept. If the realizable value is greater than the economic value it should be sold. One would therefore expect most fixed assets to have an economic value greater than their realizable value (otherwise the assets would already have been sold). Most items of stock will, however, have a realizable value higher than their economic value. The higher of these two values is often called the 'value in use'. Hence the value in use for items of stock is generally their realizable value.

Second, we should ask, 'What action should the firm take if it is deprived of the asset?' The answer depends on the relationship between its replacement cost and its value in use. If replacement cost is less than value in use, it is worthwhile replacing the asset, and the sacrifice suffered by the firm as a result of deprival is the replacement cost of the asset. If replacement cost is greater than value in use, it is not worthwhile replacing the asset, and the loss suffered by the firm is the asset's value in use. The rules for determining value to the firm should

---

6. See Statement of Standard Accounting Practice No. 16 *Current Cost Accounting*, The Accounting Standards Committee, March 1980, particularly paragraphs 42 and 43.

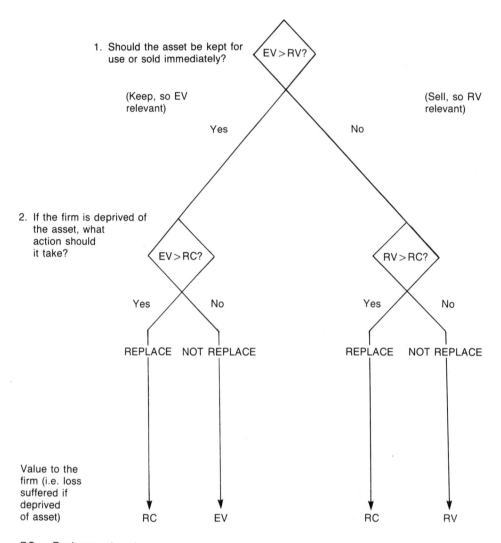

1. Should the asset be kept for use or sold immediately?

EV > RV?

(Keep, so EV relevant)

(Sell, so RV relevant)

Yes

No

2. If the firm is deprived of the asset, what action should it take?

EV > RC?

RV > RC?

Yes   No

Yes   No

REPLACE   NOT REPLACE

REPLACE   NOT REPLACE

Value to the firm (i.e. loss suffered if deprived of asset)

RC   EV

RC   RV

RC = Replacement cost
EV = Economic value (discounted present value of future net benefits from asset)
RV = Realizable value

Figure 14.1 *The determination of the 'value to the firm' of an asset it owns*

become clearer if we apply them to particular types of asset. We thus consider each of four asset types illustrated in Figure 14.1 and Table 14.1. The first branch of Figure 14.1 corresponds to Asset A in Table 14.1. These figures could describe a profitable fixed asset. It has an economic value greater than its realizable value, so the organization would continue to use the asset, and as the replacement cost

Table 14.1 *Illustration of 'value to the firm' calculations*

	Asset A £	Asset B £	Asset C £	Asset D £
Replacement cost	200,000	180,000	18,000	63,000
Realizable value	100,000	15,000	30,000	6,000
Economic value	250,000	60,000	500	1,000
Stage 1 Calculate 'value in use' (equal to the *greater* of realizable value and economic value)	250,000	60,000	30,000	6,000
Stage 2 Calculate 'value to the firm' (i.e. the loss the firm suffers if deprived of the asset, given by the *lower* of replacement cost and value in use)	200,000	60,000	18,000	6,000
Value to the firm	Replacement cost	Economic value	Replacement cost	Realizable value

is lower than the economic value, the organization would replace the asset in the event of deprival. Replacement cost (£200,000) is thus the relevant value to the firm.

The second branch of Figure 14.1 corresponds to Asset B in Table 14.1. Asset B best describes an old item of plant with little, or no scrap value. The company still finds it worthwhile to operate the machine (rather than sell it) but could not generate sufficient revenue to warrant replacing it. Consequently, if deprived of the asset the company would not replace it and would incur a cost equal to the net revenue foregone (the economic value of £60,000).

The third branch corresponding to Asset C might represent a profitable line of stock. The company itself cannot use the items but their realizable value is high. Clearly the company would wish to continue selling this product and if deprived of its present stock it would replace it. The value to the firm is the replacement cost of £18,000.

Finally, the fourth branch corresponding to Asset D might describe a line of obsolete stock which could be sold only at a heavily discounted price, or an obsolete fixed asset awaiting disposal. The company would aim to sell the asset rather than keep it, but would not replace the asset if deprived of it. The value to the firm is the realizable value of £6,000.

The examples and analysis above result in the following concise definition of value to the firm: *the lower of replacement cost and value in use, where value in use is the higher of realizable value and economic value.*

The main argument for 'value to the firm' as the appropriate basis of valuation is that the value to a firm of an asset it owns is the difference between the value of the firm with the asset and its value if it was deprived of the asset. The arguments are analogous to those used to determine the relevant cost (opportunity cost) of using particular items of stock or particular machine services. As a measure of the cost of using particular assets, there seems little doubt that value to the firm is useful to *management* in making resource allocation decisions. However, our concern is with the usefulness of asset valuation methods to users *other than* managers and there is no reason to assume that what is useful to managers (who have control over particular resources) is also useful to other users (who generally have not). The usefulness of value to the firm to non-management groups must be argued using other criteria.

Figure 14.1 and Table 14.1 show that for most fixed assets and items of stock, value to the firm is represented by replacement cost. Realizable values and economic values are relevant only where changing technological factors and demand conditions result in the unprofitability of replacement when the asset reaches the end of its useful life. Insofar as replacement cost is the appropriate measure, the arguments we outlined earlier for and against its use also apply here. Arguments for and against the use of economic value were discussed in Section 14.3. For both replacement cost and economic value we have presented *a priori* arguments in their favour on grounds of their predictive value. It seems likely that asset values based on value to the firm, which entails the calculation of both replacement cost and economic value, are also likely to provide information that has predictive value. Indeed, provided that the values *and bases of valuation* of individual assets or groups of assets are reported, it may be that value to the firm has more predictive value than replacement cost alone, as it does not involve reporting the replacement cost of assets that will not be replaced.

If individual values and bases of valuation are not disclosed for individual assets or groups of assets, value to the firm may be less useful. Users attempting to interpret such figures will be faced with values for a variety of assets, and will not know which are replacement costs, which are economic values, which (possibly) are realizable values and which are a mixture of the three. If, as is likely, prediction models require different treatments for different valuation bases, users will be unable to make full use of the information in the report.

A major disadvantage of value to the firm as a method of asset valuation is that of cost. In particular, the need to calculate the economic values of *all* assets (in order to determine the value in use) imposes a substantial cost on preparers.

14.7   Conclusions

Having discussed possible criteria to evaluate alternative accounting methods and having applied those criteria to the various capital maintenance concepts and asset valuation/cost determination methods, we may now make some tentative observations. Remember that we categorized criteria under the three main headings of *usefulness*, *feasibility* and *cost*. First we suggest that the choice of a capital maintenance concept is not of great importance. Different concepts involve little more than either the alternative positioning of holding gains, or the inclusion of general price change information that is already available from other sources. These concepts are not concerned with more fundamental problems of disclosure. No one capital maintenance concept seems to provide more information to users than any other.

The same is not true of alternative asset valuation methods. Fundamental differences exist between methods based on historical costs and those based on current costs. Our *a priori* analysis suggested that current cost-based methods are likely to be more useful to external users than those based on historical costs. In particular, the role of current cost methods as inputs to prediction models (their predictive value and control properties) seems to be more obvious. In addition, the measurement of current costs seems, in most cases, to be no less feasible than the measurement of historical costs when the latter involve subjective allocations (for depreciation, cost of stock used and so on). Though current cost systems are more costly to operate, we would argue that, on balance, the additional cost is more than justified by their extra usefulness.

The choice between alternative current cost systems is more difficult. Our analysis suggested that there is little to choose between them on grounds of either feasibility or cost. However, replacement cost methods seem to be superior in terms of their usefulness. The *a priori* arguments in favour of their predictive value and control properties are much stronger than those for realizable value systems; primarily because replacement cost measures focus on the long-term prospects of an organization, whereas realizable value measures place heavy emphasis on the short term. In order to provide maximum information, it may be that *both* replacement cost and realizable value measures should be reported. The use of deprival values as estimates of current costs, involving measures based on a mixture of replacement values and economic values, may increase the usefulness of a system based only on replacement costs or realizable values. On the other hand, the determination of deprival values requires the calculation of three separate values for each asset and thus is likely to be more costly than the consistent use of only one valuation method.

We should point out that there is evidence to suggest that our preference for current cost-based systems is not universally shared. For example, the vehemence of the debate concerning SSAP16 (see Chapter 13, Section 13.6), which required the disclosure of detailed current cost information by large organizations, suggests that many practising accountants, both in industry and within the profession, disagree strongly with the need for companies to produce current cost information. It may well be that the bases of their arguments are somewhat different from those put forward in this and earlier chapters, i.e. they may not regard predictive value and control information as paramount. Indeed, a frequently advanced argument against current cost accounting, which we find a little difficult to accept, is that the cost of producing such information is prohibitive, and in many cases is greater than the attendant benefits. Other possible reasons were given in Chapter 12 and relate to managers' reluctance to adopt any accounting treatment which results in a reduction in reported profit.

Discussion topics

1. Discuss why the distinction between 'expected income' and 'windfall gains' may be important to users of the measurements, particularly insofar as the users wish to make predictions.

2. Do you think that a study of economic measures of income and value is helpful to an accounting student? Why (or why not)?

3. 'The "opportunity values" (or "deprival values") of assets are clearly relevant to managers who have to make decisions about the utilization of the assets. But why should they be of any interest to those, like employees and investors, who generally have no control over the uses to which individual assets are put?' Explain and discuss.

4. Discuss the view that conflicts between and within groups of users of accounting statements cannot be resolved analytically and that, in consequence, it is impossible to define optimal accounting procedures.

5. Describe and evaluate the main arguments advanced for and against the use of each of the following methods of asset valuation in accounting reports:
    (a) Replacement cost
    (b) Realizable value
    (c) Historical cost
    (d) Value to the firm.

6. 'The point at issue, of course, is not *whether* to value by current entry or exit prices, but *when* to shift from entry to exit values.' (E.O. Edwards, 1975.) (Note that entry and exit prices mean replacement costs and realizable values respectively.) Explain and discuss this statement, and consider the *relative* merits of replacement cost and realizable values as means of attributing current values to assets and costs in accounts.

7. Explain and illustrate what you understand by 'user decision orientated' approaches to the choice of accounting method.

8. Discuss the view that 'the correct measurement of income is the *only* important feature of external accounting reports'.

9. Discuss whether historical cost accounting measures are more objective than those based on the use of current values.

10. Explain and illustrate how to calculate the 'value to the firm' of an asset it owns.

Exercises

14.1 You are the auditor of two manufacturing companies, Musetta Ltd and Mimi Ltd, both of which were incorporated on 1 January 19X8. Each company issued 300,000 shares of 25p each on that date. During the year to 31 December 19X8 both companies undertook the *same* basic economic events and in January 19X9 they each present you with their draft accounts for auditing.

The first thing you notice is that the profit and loss accounts and the balance sheets are not at all similar, and a telephone conversation with the accountants at the two companies reveals that the accountant at Musetta was under instruction to produce accounts which would impress the shareholders with the company's first year of trading, whilst the accountant at Mimi was instructed to avoid giving the employees any ammunition for their impending wage claim.

The economic events for 19X8 for both companies were as follows:

1. Both companies bought raw materials on credit during the year as follows:

1 January	50,000 units	at 25p each
1 March	40,000 units	at 40p each
1 April	40,000 units	at 50p each

   Each unit of sales consumed one unit of raw material. At the end of the year, Musetta and Mimi each owed £25,000 for materials.
2. Production began on 1 May, and sales amounted to 100,000 units at £1 each. By 31 December, the companies had each received £75,000.
3. Plant was bought for £60,000 at the start of the year by both companies. From your experience of other companies, you ascertain that the plant will last between 5 and 10 years, and that the scrap value can vary from zero to £6,000.
4. For both companies, productive wages were £13,000; indirect costs (factory power, light, heat, etc.) £7,800, and administrative salaries £17,200.
5. Both companies incurred general overheads of £15,000 during the year, of which £10,000 was spent on the development of a revised product to be marketed in 19X9, and £2,000 was spent on an advertising campaign to be run over the next three years.

- (a) Reproduce the profit and loss accounts for both companies for the year ended 31 December 19X8, and the balance sheets at that date, bearing in mind that both accountants were aware of the basic accounting conventions.
- (b) Calculate the following ratios: asset utilization, profitability and return on capital employed. Are the differences material?
- (c) Does it matter that companies have considerable discretion over the methods they can use for preparing accounts? Would it be 'better' if all companies used the same methods?

14.2 Your client, Mr Colline, is considering purchasing the consultancy practice of Ms Benoit. Ms Benoit's latest balance sheet is as follows:

Balance sheet at 31 October 19X7

Capital account		£	Fixed assets	£	£
Balance at 1 November 19X6		31,000	Freehold premises, at cost		25,000
add: Net profit for the year		8,600	Office equipment, at cost	3,200	
			less: Depreciation	800	2,400
		39,600			
less: Drawings		9,500	Motor vehicle, at cost	3,800	
			less: Depreciation	1,900	1,900
		30,100			29,300
Current liabilities			Current assets		
Accrued expenses	400		Debtors		3,800
Bank overdraft	2,600	3,000			
		33,100			33,100

Mr Colline estimates that the current values of Ms Benoit's fixed assets are:

	Replacement value £	Realizable value £
Freehold premises	40,000	38,000
Office equipment	3,800	1,000
Motor vehicle	2,300	1,500

In addition to the fixed assets, Mr Colline would take over the current assets and liabilities. He believes that £500 of the debtors are irrecoverable.

Ms Benoit's net profits for the past five years (calculated on the conventional historical cost basis) have been as follows:

		£
Year ended 31 October	19X3	7,000
	19X4	7,400
	19X5	8,800
	19X6	8,200
	19X7	8,600

Mr Colline has recently inherited £200,000 which is at present earning an annual rate of interest of 10%. If he buys Ms Benoit's business he will pay for it out of this inheritance. Mr Colline is presently employed at an annual salary of £4,000, and would relinquish his employment in order to run the business.

- Draft a report to Mr Colline advising him, on the basis of the above information, how much he should offer for Ms Benoit's business. Include in your report a note of any additional information that you think would be useful before a final decision is made.

Further reading

Alexander, S., 'Income measurement in a dynamic economy' (revised by Solomon, D.) in Baxter, W.T. and Davidson, S. (eds), *Studies in Accounting*, Institute of Chartered Accountants in England and Wales, 1977.

Arnold, J., 'Capital market efficiency and financial reporting', in Carsberg, B.V. and Dev, S. (eds), *External Financial Reporting*, Prentice-Hall International, 1984.

Arnold, J. and El-Azma, M., *A Study of the Relative Usefulness of Six Accounting Measures of Income*, Institute of Chartered Accountants in England and Wales, Research Committee Occasional Paper No. 13, 1978, Section III.

Barton, A., 'Expectations and achievements in income theory', *The Accounting Review*, October 1974.

Baxter, W.T., *Inflation Accounting*, Philip Allan, 1984, Chapter 12.

Beaver, W.H., *Financial Reporting: An Accounting Revolution*, Prentice-Hall International, 1981.

Carsberg, B., Arnold, J. and Hope, A., 'Predictive value: a criterion for choice of accounting method', in Baxter, W.T. and Davidson, S. (eds), *Studies in Accounting*, Institute of Chartered Accountants in England and Wales, 1977.

Chambers, R.J., *Accounting, Evaluation and Economic Behaviour*, Prentice-Hall International, 1966.

Drake, D. and Dopuch, N., 'On the case for dichotomizing income', *Journal of Accounting Research*, Autumn 1965.

Edey, H.C., 'CCA and HCA: fact and fantasy', *Accountancy*, August 1982.

Hicks, J.R., *Value and Capital*, 2nd edn, Oxford University Press, 1946, Chapter 14.

Inflation Accounting Committee, *Report of the Inflation Accounting Committee*, Cmnd. 6225, HMSO, 1975.

Lee, T.A., 'Reporting cash flows and net realizable values', *Accounting and Business Research*, Spring 1981.

Lee, T.A., *Income and Value Measurement*, 2nd edn, Nelson, 1981.

Parker, R.H. and Harcourt, G.C. (eds), *Readings in the Concept and Measurement of Income*, Cambridge University Press, 1969, Parts I, II and III.

Revsine, L., *Replacement Cost Accounting*, Prentice-Hall International, 1973.

Solomons, D., 'Economic and accounting concepts of income', *The Accounting Review*, July 1961.

Sterling, R.R. (ed.), *Asset Valuation and Income Determination — A Consideration of Alternatives*, Scholars Book Co., 1971.

Tweedie, D. and Whittington, G., 'Inflation accounting — the right choice?', *Accountancy*, October 1985.

Tweedie, D. and Whittington, G., 'Inflation accounting: the first of the choices', *Accountancy*, November 1985.

Tweedie, D. and Whittington, G., 'Towards a system of inflation accounting', *Accountancy*, December 1985.

Whittington, G., *Inflation Accounting: An Introduction to the Debate*, Cambridge University Press, 1983, Chapter 6.

Whittington, G., 'Accounting and economics', in Carsberg, B. and Hope, A. (eds), *Current Issues in Accounting*, 2nd edn, Philip Allan, 1984.

Advanced Issues

15 Conceptual Frameworks

and International

Harmonization

15.1 Introduction

In Chapter 3 we considered the need for some accounting regulations in the UK.[1] We suggested that there are at least two reasons why management should not be given complete freedom to determine what accounting information should be included in the financial statements. The first is that of *information asymmetry*. As managers have access to information about all aspects of the organization's activities, it is possible that they might exploit this situation to further their own goals at the expense of others.

The second reason is that of *comparability*. There are several valid methods of reporting items and transactions of interest to users. However, an external user group might be very confused if companies which undertook identical transactions during the year were able to report anything from a large profit to a large loss. Similarly, user groups are likely to be confused if individual companies were able to report similar transactions differently from year to year.

Consequently, regulators have acted on behalf of shareholders, creditors, employees and others to alleviate the problems of both information asymmetry and the potential lack of comparability — both through time and between entities. More information is now available to external user groups in the UK as a result of legislation and accounting standards which require or recommend the disclosure of certain items and transactions. In addition, accounting standards have increased the comparability of accounts by limiting the choice of financial accounting

1. Much of this chapter develops issues which were introduced in Chapter 3. We therefore recommend that you are familiar with the contents of Chapter 3 before studying this chapter.

treatments and by prescribing, where appropriate, a standardized method of accounting.

We noted in Chapter 3, however, that the move towards an increased level of standardization is fraught with difficulties. The aim of standardization is to ensure as far as possible that different entities apply similar accounting treatments to similar transactions. This aim could be achieved simply by prohibiting the use of all but one accounting treatment of each transaction, issue or event. This would be standardization based on *uniform* accounting practice, and could be achieved with little more than the random choice of one accounting treatment from a range available. Alternatively, standardization could be based on *best* accounting practice, which implies an evaluation of alternative treatments and the choice of that which best satisfies the selected criteria.

We concluded that, other things being equal, standardization based on best accounting practice is preferable to standardization based on uniform accounting practice. We concluded also that, unfortunately, this preferred form of standardization would remain unattainable unless, and until, there is agreement upon what are the objectives of financial statements, who are the users of financial statements and what decisions they take.

The search for agreement on these issues has led accounting regulators and academics alike to seek a *conceptual framework* which would underpin not only the standard setting process, but also financial reporting generally. Since the 1970s regulatory bodies have sought to provide a coherent set of principles or concepts which can be used as a theoretical basis for determining what events should be accounted for, how they should be measured and how they should be communicated to others. This search has taken place at both a national and an international level.

In Chapter 3, we noted that the standard setting body in the UK, the Accounting Standards Board (ASB) has recently begun to develop its own conceptual framework in the form of a Statement of Principles. In the following sections we examine the ASB's Statement of Principles (Section 15.2) and locate it within other attempts to develop a conceptual framework for financial reporting (Section 15.3). In Section 15.4 we identify some of the problems faced by regulators in attempting to develop an *agreed* conceptual framework and note that, despite the enormous difficulties involved and past failures, regulators continue to search for one.

A major motivation behind these attempts has been the desire to improve and increase standardization of accounting practice based on best practice. In Chapter 3 we explained that there are enormous differences between the accounting practices of different countries. In Section 15.5 we consider the increasing pressure to reduce these differences and improve international standardization of accounting practices. In Section 15.6 we consider some of the more important factors which have influenced accounting development in different countries in order to understand the difficulties involved in eliminating such differences. We conclude this chapter with a brief discussion in Section 15.7 of some recent attempts by the International Accounting Standards Committee (IASC) to improve international standardization, including its attempt to establish an international conceptual framework.

15.2 The ASB's Statement of Principles

Many of the difficulties faced by standard setters, which were outlined in Chapter 3, are caused by individual members of the standard setting body each operating from their own set of concepts and each seeking to achieve different objectives. Everyone has their own implicit conceptual framework for financial reporting. If it were possible to arrive at an agreed conceptual framework this would define some common ground for the standard setting committee and would help ensure that new members start from the same basis as existing members. The alternative, which exists in many parts of the world, is that each standard may be developed by a different group of individuals each with their own views and based on a different set of concepts from its predecessor. This describes the situation which existed in the UK until the early 1990s.

One of the ASB's first decisions was to develop a Statement of Principles (hereafter referred to as the Statement) which would seek to achieve the benefits associated with a conceptual framework, outlined in Chapter 3. The purpose of the Statement is explained in its introduction.[2] In general, the purpose is to improve the comparability and understandability of financial statements by establishing a consistent and coherent set of concepts to guide accounting practice.

It is intended that these concepts should be applied by regulators, preparers of accounts and their auditors in determining which events should be accounted for, how they should be measured and how they should be communicated to others. Users of accounts could then understand the basis on which the accounts have been prepared and might be able to interpret more accurately the information contained within them. To this end, when completed, the ASB's Statement will have an introduction, explaining the purpose and scope of the Statement, and seven chapters as follows:

Chapter 1 *The Objective of Financial Statements* — what is the purpose of preparing and presenting financial statements?

Chapter 2 *The Qualitative Characteristics of Financial Information* — what are the attributes of financial information that enable financial statements to fulfil their purpose?

Chapter 3 *Elements of Financial Statements* — how should assets, liabilities, equity, gains and losses, etc. be defined?

2. ASB, 'The objective of financial statements and the qualitative characteristics of financial information', *Accountancy*, September 1991.

Chapter 4   *The Recognition of Items in the Financial Statements* — an element may exist but can we measure it with sufficient reliability to include it in the accounts?

Chapter 5   *Measurement in Financial Statements* — having agreed that an asset, liability, etc., should be recognized in the accounts, at what cost or value should it be shown?

Chapter 6   *Presentation of Financial Information* — in what way should we present the accounting numbers derived from applying the concepts in Chapters 1 to 5, in order to best meet the objective of financial statements?

Chapter 7   *The Reporting Entity* — what principles should govern accounting for a number of companies which are linked together in some way?

There is no simple or unambiguous answer to each of the questions posed by the seven chapters. Nevertheless, at the time of writing, the ASB has formulated, in exposure draft or discussion draft form, its own solutions to the first six of the seven problem issues outlined above, and expects to publish its views on the seventh shortly. Thus it has drafted six of the seven chapters of its Statement. When the final chapter is complete and the ASB has had sufficient time to consider the comments of interested parties, it will issue the Statement in a final form. The Statement will then serve as a guide to the future work of the ASB although it will not have the authority of an accounting standard.

Each of the issues covered in the Statement have already been discussed in previous chapters or will be discussed in the remainder of the book. Table 15.1 identifies where the relevant discussion on each of the issues is to be found within this book.

It is no accident that the issues covered by the ASB's Statement coincide with those covered in this introductory book since they lie at the heart of financial accounting. We have attempted to develop an understanding of financial accounting based on our own particular view of its role and nature. In the

Table 15.1   *Conceptual framework issues covered in this book*

ASB Chapter		This book Chapter(s)
1	Objective of financial statements	1 and 2
2	Qualitative characteristics	3
3	Elements of financial statements	6
4	Recognition of items	6
5	Measurement	13 and 14
6	Presentation	12
7	The reporting entity	16

remainder of this section we shall outline the ASB's view on each of the issues and, where appropriate, we will compare it to the view developed in this book.

(i) The objective of financial statements and the qualitative characteristics of financial information

Chapters 1 and 2 and the introduction to the ASB's Statement are published in its exposure draft — *The Objective of Financial Statements and the Qualitative Characteristics of Financial Information* — which we discussed in Chapter 3, Section 3.7. We recap the salient points here.

The objective of financial statements must be the starting point of any conceptual framework. The ASB view is clearly stated in Chapter 1 of the Statement as:

> to provide information about the performance and financial adaptability of an enterprise that is useful to a wide range of users in making economic decisions (para. 12).

These users are identified as including 'present and potential investors, employees, lenders, suppliers and other trade creditors, customers, governments and their agencies and the public'. This list is very like the one we introduced in Chapter 1. However, whereas our discussion did not give priority to any particular group or groups, the ASB's Statement gives primacy to the investor user group. The significance of giving primacy to investors in terms of developing an agreed international conceptual framework will be discussed in Section 15.5.

Examples of the needs for information are provided for each user group. Thus employees are assumed to be interested in information about the stability and profitability of their employer and in information that enables them to assess the ability of the enterprise to provide remuneration, retirement benefits and employment opportunities.

The primary attributes that make information provided in financial statements useful to users are identified as relevance and reliability. In addition, comparability and understandability are identified as important but secondary characteristics. The components of these four qualitative characteristics and their interrelationship are expressed in Figure 3.3, p. 78.

Chapters 1 and 2 of the Statement form the foundation for the other chapters just as our Chapters 1 to 3 form the basis for the rest of this book. The characteristics which are assumed to make information useful are used, for example, to help determine how an asset is to be defined or whether to include an asset in the financial statements. This point is important since, if the ASB were to adopt a different view of the objective of financial statements and the attributes which enable them to fulfil their purpose, it is very likely that they would have to revise all their other concepts and principles.

(ii)   Elements of financial statements

Whilst to the unsophisticated user of accounts, the definitions of asset and liability may appear obvious, it has become apparent in recent years that the absence of precise definitions has resulted in a variety of different interpretations amongst preparers (and users) of accounts. In our earlier discussion of fixed assets (see Chapter 6), we noted the difficulties of establishing whether expenditure on certain items such as developing or maintaining a brand name should be treated as an asset or written off immediately. This is only one of a myriad of problem areas associated with the lack of a clear definition of the elements of financial statements.

Importantly, this lack of definition has enabled some companies to move assets and liabilities on and off the balance sheet in such a way as to hinder the usefulness of financial statements. Whilst this usually involves companies in a series of complex transactions, we will illustrate the problem with a simple example.

Consider two companies A and B which each make up their accounts to 31 December each year. Each owns a property with a book and market value of £1 million at 1 January 19X1. Both companies wish to raise £1 million finance for an investment opportunity. However, each company engages in a different set of transactions in order to raise the finance.

On 1 January 19X1, company A, using its property as security, raises £1 million by acquiring a 10 year loan from a bank at an interest rate of 10% p.a. Assuming that company A depreciates its property over 100 years, its financial statements for 19X1 will include the following:

Balance sheet	£
Fixed assets	
Property	1,000,000
Less depreciation	(10,000)
	990,000
Long-term liabilities:	
Loan from Bank	1,000,000
Income Statement	
Depreciation of property	10,000
Interest charge	100,000

Company B raises £1 million by selling its property to a bank on 1 January 19X1 for £1 million. At the same time, company B enters into an agreement with the bank to repurchase the property in 10 years time for £1 million. In the meantime the bank rents the property to company B at an annual rental charge which is equal to a 10% per annum interest charge on a £1 million loan. Because company B no longer legally owns the property it removes it from its books and the financial statements for 19X1 include the following:

Balance sheet   £
  Fixed assets
    Property   —

  Long-term liabilities:
    Loan from Bank   —

Income Statement
  Annual rental charge   100,000

By selling the property and agreeing to repurchase it in the future, company B has managed to raise £1 million without showing a liability on its balance sheet. Yet, we could argue that the *economic substance* of the transaction undertaken by company B is no different to that undertaken by company A — both raise £1 million cash, both incur an annual charge of £100,000 (equal to 10% per annum on a £1 million loan) and both continue to enjoy full use of the property.

The problem is that, despite the similarity in the economic effect of the transactions, the financial statements of the two companies give different impressions of current position and future liabilities. This may result in users making different economic decisions depending on how the transactions are accounted for, even though the economic substance of the transactions is the same. The problem arises because company B has adopted a legal definition of an asset and liability whereas a user of accounts may think of assets and liabilities in some other (economic) terms.

The above example illustrates the need to agree on definitions for assets and liabilities but similar examples could be provided for other elements of the financial statements such as gains and losses. Chapter 3 of the ASB's Statement — *The Elements of Financial Statements* — recognizes the need to identify the elements of financial statements and the essential features which each of them must possess to be included in the financial statements. It is an important part of ensuring financial information is useful — relevant, reliable, comparable and understandable — to users.

Seven elements are identified as follows: assets, liabilities, equity, gains, losses, contributions from owners, distributions to owners. Each of these terms is related to the others:

> assets and liabilities are mirror images of each other; equity is the difference between an entity's assets and its liabilities; gains and losses are respectively increases and decreases in equity other than those which relate to transactions with owners (para. 2).

Definitions are provided for each of the seven elements:

> *Assets* are rights or other access to future economic benefits controlled by an entity as a result of past transactions or events.

Liabilities are an entity's obligations to transfer economic benefits as a result of past transactions or events.

Equity is the ownership interest in the entity: it is the residual amount found by deducting all liabilities of the entity from all of the entity's assets.

Gains are increases in equity, other than those relating to contributions from owners. Gains include 'revenue gains' (commonly called revenue) and gains arising from changes in market values (e.g. from a revaluation of property).

Losses are decreases in equity, other than those relating to distributions to owners. Losses include 'revenue losses' (commonly called expenses) and losses arising from changes in market values.

Contributions from owners are increases in equity resulting from investments made by owners in their capacity as owners. The most common form of equity contributions from owners is cash.

Distributions to owners are decreases in equity resulting from transfers made to owners in their capacity as owners. These include the payment of dividends and the return of capital.

These definitions are important for deciding whether an item constitutes an element and, if so, as which element it should be included.

Let us return to our example above and consider the implications of these definitions for the accounting treatment of the transactions of company B. Even though the legal ownership of the property has been transferred to the bank, company B continues to use the property and therefore has 'access to the future economic benefits' which flow from it. If the rental agreement grants company B *control* over the property, e.g. company B can use it itself or re-let it and receive all the benefits, then the property should be accounted for as an asset of company B.

If the property is an asset of company B then there must be an equivalent liability somewhere. By agreeing to repurchase the property in the future, company B has an obligation to transfer economic benefits (£1 million) as a result of past transactions (entering into the sale and repurchase agreement). Thus, the £1 million proceeds of the sale would constitute a liability under the ASB's definition of liabilities. Hence, the financial statements of both company A and company B would show an asset and an equivalent liability. The ASB adopt an economic (rather than legal) definition of an asset because it is considered more relevant for users' decisions. Consequently, following the ASB's definitions of elements is expected to lead to information about the position and performance of company B that is more relevant, comparable and understandable.

Chapter 3 of the Statement is concerned with defining elements in order to determine whether an item falls within one of the definitions. But satisfying the definition of an element does not guarantee that the item will be recognized in the financial statements. For this to be the case, it must *also* meet the recognition criteria discussed in Chapter 4 of the Statement.

(iii) The recognition of items in the financial statements

Recognizing an item in the financial statements involves incorporating the item into the primary financial statements. It is not the same as disclosing information about the item in the notes without including it in the statement totals. Chapter 4 of the Statement — *The Recognition of Items in the Financial Statements* — explains that in order to meet the objective of financial statements, items should be recognized in the financial statements if:

(a) the item meets the definition of an element of financial statements, *and*
(b) there is sufficient evidence that the change in assets or liabilities inherent in the item has occurred (including where appropriate, evidence that a future inflow or outflow of benefit will occur); *and*
(c) the item can be measured as a monetary amount with sufficient reliability.

Let us use a simple example to illustrate how these criteria might be applied. Consider a pharmaceutical company which has spent £10 million during the year on a project to research a new chemical which might be used in developing a new drug for heart disease. Applying criterion (a), the expenditure would appear to satisfy the definition of an asset since the company has the rights to any future economic benefits (profits from the sales of a new drug) which might flow from the expenditure. However in order to be treated as an asset it must also satisfy criteria (b) and (c).

The second criterion is that of 'evidence of occurrence'. Chapter 4 of the Statement explains that 'a transaction, by definition, always involves an obvious change in the composition of the assets and liabilities of the entity' (para. 29). Transactions might be contrasted with contracts where commitments rather than transactions form the basis for any change in assets and liabilities. Since the research expenditure constitutes a transaction, then it would appear to meet criterion (b).

The third criterion is whether the item can be measured at a monetary amount with sufficient reliability (note that reliability is one of the two primary attributes identified in Chapter 2 of the Statement). Chapter 4 of the Statement provides a similar example to ours to illustrate the application of criterion (c). It identifies a wide range of possible outcomes associated with such a project ranging from zero benefit (if unsuccessful), through some benefit (if it results in a product for which there is low demand) to a very high level of benefit (if it results in a unique product for which there is high demand). It is pointed out that, until the research progresses, there may be little evidence of what the outcome will be. Moreover, it is unlikely that there will be a direct market in similar research projects by which to translate these benefits into monetary terms. Thus, the Statement concludes that the monetary amount of this asset is very uncertain and different measurers of the benefits of the project are likely to arrive at amounts that are very different. Consequently, the expenditure on the research project fails to meet the recognition criterion (c) and should not be incorporated within the primary financial statements.

If, however, an item does satisfy the criterion for recognition, subsequent events or transactions may occur that affect the recognized item. These events may either cause the item to require *remeasurement* (e.g. an increase in market values may trigger the revaluation of property) or necessitate the *derecognition* of the item (e.g. the sale of stock). The difference between the initial recognition of an item and any subsequent remeasurement is developed in the next chapter of the statement which deals with measurement.

(iv) Measurement in financial statements

Having established that an item should be recognized in the financial statements it is necessary to indicate how that item should be measured. Currently, balance sheets of UK companies are a mixture of historical costs and assets which have been revalued on an irregular basis. The balance sheet typically includes some items at cost, some at a recent valuation and some at an out-of-date valuation. Because there is no requirement to revalue assets, different companies have adopted different treatments for similar items. The result is inconsistent and confusing financial statements.

We suggested in Chapter 13 that accounting reporting methods may be classified according to two characteristics — their valuation method and their capital maintenance concept. Chapter 5 of the Statement — *Measurement in Financial Statements* — deals with both of these characteristics in attempting to lay down the principles which should guide the measurement of assets and liabilities.

The Statement contrasts the use of historical cost in financial reporting with systems based on current values and suggests that current values are generally more relevant (although arguably more subjective) than historical costs. Thus it concurs, in principle, with our conclusions in Chapter 14 that current cost-based asset valuation methods are likely to be more useful to users than those based on historical cost.

Whilst the fundamental choice of valuation method is seen to be between the use of historical cost and some form of current value, the Statement falls short of recommending either one. Instead it adopts what it describes as 'an evolutionary development of eclectic valuation methods in response to developing user needs'[3] (para. 61). What this amounts to is a modified historical cost system combining elements of both valuation methods. Thus it suggests that when items are first recognized (initial recognition), the measurement method will typically be a cost-based method. However it argues that the 'soundest method of valuing assets at the second (remeasurement) stage of recognition' is a current cost-based one. Similar arguments are applied to the valuation of liabilities.

As we discussed in Chapter 13 there are a number of current cost-based

---

3. Accounting Standards Board, Discussion Draft, *Statement of Principles Chapter 5: Measurement in Financial Statements*, ASB Ltd, March 1993, para. 61.

valuation methods available. The Statement identifies three of these — entry values (which include replacement cost), exit values and value in use. It suggests that whilst each has a potential contribution to make to the economic evaluation of an entity, it would be expensive and confusing to provide information on several alternative bases. As a practical solution to the problem, it recommends adoption of the concept of 'value to the business'. 'Value to the business' or 'value to the firm' as we described it in Chapter 14, involves the comparison of various asset valuation methods. It is defined in the Statement as the *lower* of replacement cost or recoverable amount. Recoverable amount is defined as the *higher* of value in use and net realizable value.

In summary, the Statement concludes that assets and liabilities should be valued initially at cost but should be remeasured using the current cost-based method of 'value to the business'. In Chapter 14 we pointed out that there is much resistance to the comprehensive adoption of current cost for preparing financial statements, not least amongst preparers of accounts. In this light we would suggest that the ASB's decision to adopt a form of modified historical cost system might owe as much to the practical problem of gaining acceptance of its Statement as it does to theoretical principles.

The second characteristic of a reporting method is the capital maintenance concept. The concept of capital maintenance adopted will determine the amount and significance of both the 'total gains and losses' and the narrower 'profit or loss' that are recognized (these terms will be explained in the following discussion of Chapter 6 of the Statement).

Chapter 5 of the Statement argues that all three capital maintenance concepts — nominal money capital, current purchasing power capital maintenance and physical (or operating capacity) capital maintenance — have potential user relevance and none has greater reliability than the valuation measures with which they are associated (see Chapter 13, Table 13.7). It concludes that it is possible to combine different concepts of capital maintenance within a single financial reporting statement and thus leaves the issue of choice of capital maintenance concept somewhat open and unresolved.

(v) Presentation of financial information

Having established which items are to be included in the financial statements and how they are to be measured, there remains the question, in what way should these numbers be presented? In principle, we could simply list the elements to be recognized, appropriately measured, in a random order within a single statement. Such a presentation is, however, unlikely to best meet the objective of financial statements which is to provide information that is useful (relevant, reliable, comparable, understandable etc.) to a wide range of users. Chapter 6 of the Statement — *Presentation of Financial Information* — recognizes the importance of presentation and lays down the principles to be followed in guiding decisions about the arrangement of information in financial reporting.

There are three main ways that accounting information can be presented — as part of a *primary reporting statement* (such as the balance sheet), as *notes* accompanying the reporting statements, or as *supplementary information*. Supplementary information is distinguished from the primary statements and notes in that it is not required to be audited. Notes to financial statements amplify or explain the items included in the primary financial statements and in some cases may provide information not included in the primary statements. To appreciate the different forms of presentation we recommend that you browse through the annual reports of several public limited companies.

As we discussed in Chapter 12, there is a view that capital markets are semi-strong efficient with respect to processing information, which implies that disclosure is important whereas the choice of accounting treatment is not. This view suggests that it does not matter whether items are included in the primary financial statements or in the notes to the accounts, as long as they are fully disclosed. This view is not reflected in the ASB's Statement. Chapter 6 (and Chapter 4) of the Statement emphasize that including items in the notes to the accounts is not the same as incorporating them in the primary reporting statements. Such a view is consistent with the objective of financial statements which is to provide information to a wide set of users, some of whose needs are not reflected in capital markets, irrespective of the belief or otherwise in security market efficiency.

In previous chapters we have identified and discussed three primary reporting statements — the income statement (or profit and loss account), the balance sheet and the cash flow statement. The ASB identify a fourth — the statement of total recognized gains and losses. Whereas we identified one primary statement of financial performance (the income statement), the ASB identifies two (the profit and loss account and the statement of total recognized gains and losses). These two statements disclose the major components of an enterprise's gains and losses in the broad sense in which these terms are defined in Chapter 3 of the Statement (see (ii) above). The statement of total recognized gains and losses is an extra statement which shows *all changes in equity* of the enterprise from activities or events (excluding those deriving from contributions from, or distributions to, owners). It includes, but is not limited to, the profit or loss of a period.

In addition to the profit or loss for the period the statement of total recognized gains and losses is likely to include items such as any gains or losses arising from the revaluation of fixed assets. Currently, any differences arising when assets are revalued are accounted for by increasing or decreasing shareholder reserves. This practice, known as reserve accounting, can make it difficult for users of accounts to identify and appreciate the impact of such changes on the financial performance of the enterprise. Thus, whilst the information entities are required to provide in the fourth statement is not new, it is considered to be more useful when presented in this way.

One widely cited example of the possible consequences of including gains and losses in reserves, rather than in a more transparent statement of gains and losses, is the international trading company Polly Peck, which crashed in 1990. In the three years prior to the crash, Polly Peck's financial statements included the following figures:

	Exchange Losses	*Net Profits*
	£m	*£m*
1987	35.9	86.2
1988	170.3	144.1
1989	44.7	161.4

The exchange losses resulted from the translation of the accounts of foreign subsidiaries, which had been prepared using the currencies of the foreign subsidiaries themselves, into £ sterling. Losses arose because the currencies of the subsidiaries were depreciating relative to the £. Accounting practice at the time was to take such losses (or gains) direct to reserves rather than to the income statement. Thus the net profit figures shown were *before* any allowance was made for the exchange losses. It has been argued that users, including investment analysts, did not take proper account of the losses because of their relatively remote disclosure as a movement on reserves in the notes to the financial statements. Indeed, at least one firm of stockbrokers included Polly Peck as a 'buy' recommendation only days before the company collapsed!

Apart from recommending a fourth primary statement, Chapter 6 of the ASB's Statement lays down a number of principles concerning the presentation of information within these statements. Notably, it argues that within the profit and loss account, information which shows separately the results of continuing and discontinued operations would be useful to users. It also provides guidelines about the level of aggregation which might best provide useful, cost-effective information. For example, it suggests that good presentation involves the separate disclosure of 'items which are unusual in amount or incidence judged by the experience of previous periods'.[4]

(vi)   The reporting entity

The final chapter of the Statement will deal with the principles which should govern accounting for a number of companies which are linked together in some way. It is expected to cover such issues as what is a group (for financial reporting purposes), which entities should be shown as subsidiaries, what is the basis for equity accounting? We introduce the issue of accounting for groups in Chapter 16 and explore some of the problems which the ASB will have to resolve in its Statement. At this stage it is necessary simply to note that the issue is seen to be of sufficient importance to constitute a separate chapter in the ASB's Statement.

4. Accounting Standards Board, *Exposure Draft — Statement of Principles Chapter 6: Presentation of Financial Information*, The Accounting Standards Board Ltd, 1991.

The development of a Statement of Principles has involved the ASB in considerable time and effort. It has taken three years to produce drafts of six chapters and will require further time to draft the seventh and to refine and amend all the chapters once comments have been received from interested parties. Moreover, it has absorbed many of the resources of the ASB (notably the time and effort of the salaried members of the ASB) and limited their ability to deal with more specific accounting problems. Developing the Statement is not therefore a costless exercise. The question then arises as to whether the time, effort and resources expended in its development are likely to produce sufficient benefits in terms of improvements in financial reporting.

Is the statement likely to lead to an improvement in standardization based on best practice? What are the problems it might encounter in fulfilling its purpose? In order to answer these questions it is necessary to appreciate that the ASB are not the first to recognize the potential benefits associated with a conceptual framework and to attempt to develop one. In the following section we consider the ASB's Statement in relation to previous attempts to provide an agreed conceptual framework and we identify some of the problems involved in achieving the benefits associated with it.

15.3   The search for a conceptual framework

Given the potential advantages of a conceptual framework outlined in Chapter 3, Section 3.5, it is not surprising that regulators, the accountancy profession and academics worldwide have been involved in attempts to develop one for many years. The earliest attempts were undertaken by academics, mainly in the US as part of their efforts to develop a theory for accounting. As early as 1940, academic studies were published which attempted to present a framework which could be regarded as a coherent and consistent foundation for the development of accounting standards.[5]

From the 1960s, the accountancy profession in both the UK and the US took a particular interest in developing a conceptual framework. This was largely as a result of problems associated with companies taking advantage of flexibility in permitted accounting practices to present their activities in the best possible light. The profession was criticized for allowing too much flexibility in the choice of accounting treatments and for failing to deal with the deficiencies in accounting practice. Action to increase the standardization of accounting was needed. Two developments followed. The first was the establishment of standard setting bodies in the UK (the Accounting Standards Steering Committee (ASSC) in 1971) and in the US (the Financial Accounting Standards Board (FASB) in 1973). The second

5. Paton, W.A. and Littleton, A.C., *An Introduction to Corporate Accounting Standards*, Monograph No. 3, American Accounting Association, 1940.

was the publication of reports by the accountancy profession, in both the UK and US, aimed at developing a conceptual framework.

The Corporate Report

In the UK in 1975, the ASSC (which became the ASC in 1976) published a discussion paper — *The Corporate Report*. The report was written by a group of academics and professional accountants who had been commissioned by the ASSC. It adopted a view of accounting similar to the one presented in this book and in the ASB's Statement, i.e. that the purpose of accounting statements is to provide information useful to users. It discussed many of the issues covered some years later in the ASB's Statement, including the qualitative characteristics of financial information, measurement methods and presentation of financial statements. However its conclusions were potentially more far reaching than the ASB's Statement. In particular, it recommended that in order to meet the needs of a wide group of users, enterprises should publish not one extra statement, but several, including an employment report and a statement of future prospects. For a variety of reasons, including a hostile reception from preparers of accounts, the report failed to make an impact on the practical work of the accounting standard setters.

Several other reports exploring the possibility of developing a conceptual framework were either commissioned or considered by the ASC during its lifetime. However, none had any significant impact on the practical work of the ASC and accounting standards were developed on an *ad hoc* basis. Consequently, it is probably reasonable to state that UK SSAPs, developed by the ASC, constituted uniform, rather than best, accounting practice.

The FASB conceptual framework

In the US, the FASB began work on the development of a conceptual framework soon after its inception in 1973. Its starting point was a report published by the *Trueblood Committee*, a study group set up by the profession in 1971 to consider the establishment of accounting principles. However, unlike the ASSC, it continued with its project and produced a number of Statements of Financial Accounting Concepts (SFACs) which form the basis of its conceptual framework. The first of these was published in 1978 and the last in 1985. Six SFACs have been issued in all, of which one (SFAC No. 4) deals with the objectives of financial reporting by non-business organizations and another (SFAC No. 3) has been superseded by SFAC No. 6. The four remaining concept statements are as follows:

SFAC No. 1 Objectives of Financial Reporting by Business Enterprises

SFAC No. 2 Qualitative Characteristics of Accounting Information

SFAC No. 6   Elements of Financial Statements

SFAC No. 5   Recognition and Measurement in Financial Statements of Business Enterprises

The issues covered by these four concept statements are the same as those covered in chapters 1 to 5 of the ASB's Statement of Principles. This raises the question of why the ASB bothered to spend so much time developing its own chapters when it might have adopted the FASB's? In part, the answer must lie in the rather disappointing experience of the FASB framework in terms of its ability to achieve the benefits envisaged for it.

The benefits envisaged for the FASB project were similar to those aimed for by any conceptual framework project. Thus it was expected that a conceptual framework would guide standard setters, provide a frame of reference for resolving accounting questions in the absence of a specific standard, determine the bounds for judgement in preparing financial statements, increase users' understanding of, and confidence in, financial statements and enhance comparability.[6]

Critics have suggested that the FASB has failed to apply the conceptual framework when developing accounting standards on specific issues, and have identified inconsistencies between standards and the concept statements. They also point to the fact that, despite the framework, FASB has issued over 100 individual, detailed accounting standards which, they argue, is hardly likely to increase users' understanding of, and confidence in, financial statements. It is doubtful whether the FASB conceptual framework has led to the consistent development of accounting standards on the basis of best practice.

Many of the criticisms of the FASB framework stem from the fact that the framework is seen to be incomplete. No concept statements have been produced on the issues of presentation or the reporting entity and, importantly, it failed to deal with the fundamental issues of recognition and measurement. Rather than providing prescriptive guidance on these issues, SFAC No. 5 goes little further than restating the concepts in SFAC 2 and 6 and providing a description of current practices. Without clear guidance on what constitutes best practice in the recognition and measurement of items, it is difficult to see how the framework can work as a coherent set of principles leading to consistent standards.

This is clearly one of the areas which the ASB needs to improve upon if it wants its Statement of Principles to be a success. It is perhaps also one of the most controversial areas. In our earlier discussion of Chapter 6 of the ASB's Statement — *Measurement in Financial Statements* — we pointed out that the decision to adopt a modified historical cost system appeared to owe as much to pragmatism as to principles. In addition we noted that the chapter appears to have left the issue of capital maintenance somewhat unsettled. Nevertheless, the ASB has gone

---

6. Financial Accounting Standards Board, *Scope and Implications of the Conceptual Framework Project*, FASB, 1976, p.2.

further towards resolving the fundamental issue of measurement than did the FASB.

The search continues

By attempting to develop its own framework, the ASB has signalled its view that the FASB have not developed an *acceptable* conceptual framework even though they are clearly in agreement with some aspects of it. But the FASB are not the only regulators to have attempted to develop a conceptual framework before the ASB, although they were the first. More recently, the IASC has published a 'Framework for the Preparation and Presentation of Financial Statements' which sets out the principles of accounting in an international context. We return to this briefly in Section 15.6 when we discuss international attempts at standardization. In addition to the IASC, The Canadian Institute of Chartered Accountants and the Australian Accounting Research Foundation jointly with the Australian Accounting Standards Review Board have published statements of conceptual frameworks prior to the publication of the ASB's Statement of Principles. However none was considered sufficiently acceptable for wholesale adoption in the UK.

15.4   The problems of developing an agreed conceptual framework

The existence of so many frameworks and the fact that, after more than twenty years, regulators have failed to agree upon a single one, suggests the scale of the problems involved. Two questions in particular have been the subject of much debate. The first is whether a conceptual framework could ever lead to an unambiguous basis for prescribing accounting policy. The second is whether and how accounting standard setters can deal with the politicization of accounting standards caused by conflicting interests of the various groups of users. Thus, even if a conceptual framework could be agreed upon by standard setters, would it be acceptable to the various participants in financial reporting or could it be made enforceable?

The first fundamental problem derives from the issue of *social choice* in accounting standard setting. Different groups may have different views as to the objective of financial reporting, and even as to who has the right to information about an organization. Even if agreement could be reached on these general issues, it is more than likely that there will be conflicting views as to what constitutes relevant or reliable information and about the costs and benefits of providing that information.

These problems have led critics to suggest that it is impossible to develop a set of rules which can be applied to accounting alternatives in a way which will satisfy everybody. They have argued that any conceptual framework will necessarily embody the interests of one user group at the expense of others. Nevertheless, some of these critics perceive that a conceptual framework may still have benefits in terms of providing a direction for standard setters and reducing the influence of personal biases on specific accounting issues, but they would claim that it can never be a universally accepted framework.

The second major problem in establishing an acceptable conceptual framework is related to the first. Suppose a framework was developed which was capable of providing clear guidelines concerning choices between alternative accounting methods — would it be accepted by the various groups interested in financial reporting? For example, if the conceptual framework led to the requirement for companies to publish profit forecasts, would companies comply with the requirement? In Chapter 2 we noted how, despite the potential usefulness to investors and others of such information, companies do not at present provide it. Indeed, management have vigorously rejected any suggestions that they should provide such information.

Managers' acceptance of accounting standards is influenced by their own motivations in preparing financial reports (see, for example, Chapter 12), which may conflict with the objectives laid down in a conceptual framework. If preparers of accounts decide to ignore a particular accounting standard, it may be difficult for regulators to force them to comply. A stark example of this problem is illustrated by the demise of the UK accounting standard SSAP 16 — *Current Cost Accounting*. The standard required companies to publish supplementary current cost information but was very unpopular amongst preparers of accounts. So many companies ignored the requirements of the standard that the standard setters were forced to withdraw it. Thus, whether or not managers would comply with any given standard is likely to depend on whether or not they accepted the basis on which the recommendation was made (i.e. the conceptual framework) and/or on the power of the standard setters to enforce their recommendations.

The demise of SSAP 16 took place under the auspices of the old standard setting body — the ASC. In Chapter 3, we noted that the new standard setting structure includes the Financial Reporting Review Panel which aims to overcome some of the problems of non-compliance associated with the previous structure. As the ASB develops and eventually implements its Statement of Principles, the Review Panel may prove to be crucial in its success. The challenge facing the ASB is therefore twofold. It must ensure that it develops a complete and consistent Statement of Principles (to avoid the criticisms levied at the FASB framework) and it must also ensure that companies comply with any recommendations which flow from it.

However, we commented in Chapter 3 that the regulatory framework and the accounting practices found in the UK are very much a product of its underlying economic, legal, social and other environmental factors. It is likely therefore that different factors will have influenced the development of accounting practice and regulation in different countries. Hence, it is possible that from country to country, the major users of financial statements will differ, the objectives of financial statements will differ and the primary qualitative characteristics of accounting information (the criteria by which alternative methods of accounting are evaluated) will differ. And yet, there is a growing need to develop a (conceptual) framework that has international application in order to obtain the benefits of standardization based on best practice at a global level. Multinational companies raise finance and publish financial statements in a number of countries and individual users of accounts are increasingly becoming involved, and taking an interest, in the activities of foreign entities. In the following section we shall examine the pressures which have led to an increased interest in establishing standardized accounting practice at an international level.

15.5   Pressures for international standardization

The world market for financial and accounting information has undergone a considerable upheaval in response to market forces. The emergence of a 'global' international capital market is a driving force for the standardization of accounting practices throughout the world. For example, Japanese and US institutional investors are making increasing use of the growing number of stock markets in Western Europe, in order to exploit the resources available and to enjoy the benefits of less tightly-regulated regimes. The result of this increase in the use of stock markets is a growing emphasis on the disclosure of financial information and, in particular, consolidated information. Unfortunately, accounting practices are not, as yet, standardized on a global basis. Hence, each company must decide which standards to adopt when presenting its financial statements to the stock markets — national standards (which may be unacceptable elsewhere), US GAAP (with its considerable amount of detail and lack of flexibility), or international standards?

Adopting different sets of standards can lead to very large differences in the reported results and position of companies. For example, in 1991 the accounts of SmithKline Beecham, a multinational pharmaceutical company, showed a net income of £638 million under UK GAAP. However, when the same transactions were reported under US GAAP, net income fell to £474 million — a reduction of 26%. The difference between reported shareholders' equity figures was even greater — £743 million under UK GAAP and £4,113m under US GAAP.

These differences are further illustrated in a study published in 1993 — *International Accounting and Auditing Trends*.[7] The authors of the study, the US-based Centre for International Financial Analysis and Research (CIFAR), restated

7. Centre for International Financial Analysis and Research, *International Accounting and Auditing Trends*, 3rd edn, CIFAR, 1993.

Table 15.2   *Changes to net income: effect of restatement to common standards*

	%
Sweden	+ 60
Germany	+ 44
Japan	+ 12
Italy	+ 11
Belgium	+ 9
France	+ 6
UK	+ 4
Switzerland	− 8

the accounts of companies in a variety of countries using one set of standards which were considered by them to constitute best practice. The changes to net income which resulted are shown in Table 15.2. The reasons for such wide differences arise from the variations in standards applied at a national level. The report identifies two particular areas which give rise to large differences in reported figures as the treatment of tangible fixed assets and goodwill. In addition to variations in reported figures, the presentation of annual reports differs greatly between countries with some, such as Switzerland, providing hardly any disclosure to explain the items reported in the primary reporting statements. Such wide variations in measurement and disclosure practices make it very difficult for users of accounts, such as international investors, to compare the performance of companies whose accounts are drawn up using different standards.

The increase in the use of stock markets has been accompanied by an increase in the number and size of multinational companies. Such companies raise finance, pay taxes and are subject to local audits in a variety of different countries. They, like the international investors referred to above, would benefit from an increased level of standardization of accounting methods. At present however, even within the EU, there exist many difficulties for groups of companies operating across national borders. For example:

(a) An Italian company wishing to prepare consolidated financial statements for its subsidiaries in Spain and Portugal, will not be able to use the local statutory accounts prepared by each subsidiary. It must first spend time, and incur cost, restating each subsidiary's accounts to eliminate the effects of adjustments made to satisfy the requirements of the local tax authorities.

(b) A Belgian company wishing to diversify into Germany and Denmark by making acquisitions will experience difficulties in using the published financial statements to help determine the price it should offer. In addition to variations in the legal structures of its chosen targets, it will find variations in the way published profits are calculated, and the way assets are valued for balance sheet purposes.

(c) A French company wishing to obtain a listing on the London and Frankfurt stock exchanges will not be able to rely only on meeting the requirements of the Paris Bourse. It will need to meet, and understand, the different regulatory requirements of the markets in each country.

The growth of multinational companies and the globalization of capital markets are exerting strong pressures on accounting regulators to develop an international conceptual framework for financial reporting which will lead to the standardization of financial statements on a worldwide basis. Unfortunately for the regulators, there is much diversity in the current range of international accounting practices as we have illustrated above. In the following section we consider why the objectives of financial statements, the users of financial statements, the methods of accounting used, and the regulatory framework, differ from country to country.

15.6   International differences in accounting regulation

If the development of accounting practice is influenced by economic, social and political factors, then it is not surprising to discover that different accounting methods, regulatory frameworks and even objectives of financial statements, exist in different countries. In this section we consider some of the more important factors which have influenced accounting development, including the sources of finance, the nature of the legal system, the influence of taxation and the strength of the accountancy profession. Our identification of these factors draws heavily on the book *Comparative International Accounting* by Christopher Nobes and Robert Parker[8] and we recommend it to readers who wish to explore these factors in more depth.

(i)   Sources of finance

The frameworks for financial reporting as presented by the ASB in the UK, the FASB in the USA and the IASC (see Sections 15.2 and 15.3 above), all agree that the objective of financial statements is to provide information about an organization that is useful to a range of users. The range of users is very wide but the FASB's statement on objectives focuses on the information needs of investors and creditors, and both the IASC and the ASB state that:

> As investors are providers of risk capital to the enterprise, the provision of financial statements that meet their needs will also meet most of the needs of other users that financial statements can satisfy.

8. Nobes, C. and Parker, R., *Comparative International Accounting*, Prentice Hall 1991.

This focus upon investors implies that shareholders are the main source of finance for business organizations, and that they rely upon published information because the organizations are run by professional managers, i.e. that there is a divorce between the ownership (shareholders) and the control (management) of the entity. This is certainly the case in the USA and the UK where, in both countries, more than 2,000 domestic companies have stock exchange listings. However, in continental Europe, finance has traditionally come from other sources.

In Germany, the banks not only provide debt finance, but are often also important shareholders of companies. In France and Italy, many companies are financed by either the banks or the state, and a large number of companies are family businesses. The banks or the state will, in many cases, nominate directors and thus be able to obtain information directly from the company's internal records. Hence, the pressure for the public disclosure of accounting information is likely to be much less in those countries in which the private, individual investor is a less important source of finance.

If the most important providers of finance have access to a company's internal records, and even to management meetings, then there is less need also for an independent audit, where an auditor reports to the 'outsider' owners on the financial statements prepared by 'insider' management. This has implications for the size of the accountancy profession, and its influence in regulating accounting practice. We examine this further below.

(ii) Legal systems

In Chapter 3 we noted that the two primary sources of accounting regulation are the law and the accountancy profession. We have already intimated that the influence of the accountancy profession might differ between countries, but one might expect the law to be a constant factor.

In fact there are two major legal systems in the Western developed world: the English common law system and the Roman legal system. A common law legal system includes only a limited amount of statute law. These statutes are interpreted by the courts, and so a large amount of case law is generated to supplement the statute law. A common law rule provides an answer to a specific case, and although it might provide some guidance through its precedence, it does not necessarily formulate a general rule for the future.

Common law systems are found in the UK, Ireland, USA and Australia amongst others. In these countries, company law does not contain a myriad of detailed accounting rules concerning the presentation and content of financial statements.

The Roman legal system has long been adopted throughout most of continental Europe and is far more dependent upon the formulation of rules by government. It is often described as Codified Roman Law. The consequences for accounting are significant. In 'Roman' countries, there exist company laws, or commercial codes, or even accounting plans which have established detailed rules for the content and presentation of financial statements. Thus, in Germany, company accounting has traditionally been seen as a branch of company law.

Where governments have sought to collect standardized financial data as an aid to controlling the economy, much of the detail of government-controlled rules may be found in accounting plans. The French *plan comptable général* is prepared by a government committee and is enforced by law. Similar plans exist in Belgium and Spain.

(iii) Taxation

Although the tax authorities are important users of financial statements, both the ASB and the FASB have identified investors as the primary users, and neither have afforded the tax authorities more than a cursory glance. This may be because in the UK and the USA, the taxation rules are different from the accounting rules in several respects, and companies will provide the tax authorities with amended, or even completely separate, financial statements.

An example of the difference in the accounting and taxation rules in the UK is that of depreciation. In the published accounts the cost of a fixed asset is allocated as fairly as possible to the income statement over a number of years, generally equal to the asset's economic life. Judgement is required to determine the asset's likely economic life and a 'fair' allocation of the cost over that life. However, the amount of depreciation for tax purposes is determined by tax law — it is standardized and leaves no room for judgement. For tax purposes, companies must substitute the standardized 'capital allowances' for their own asset-specific depreciation. Capital allowances usually represent a form of accelerated depreciation, and can be varied by the Chancellor of the Exchequer in order to provide investment incentives. In the UK the rates have varied from 25% p.a. on a reducing balance basis, to 100% in the first year.

Elsewhere, however, there may exist a requirement that the figures in the tax accounts should be identical to those in the financial statements. This principle is traditional in Germany, France, Belgium, Italy and Spain amongst others. In these countries, the tax regulations lay down specific depreciation rates to be used for particular assets. Where accelerated depreciation allowances are claimed for tax purposes, they must be charged in the published accounts too.

(iv) True or correct?

Both the ASB and the FASB have declared that the objective of financial statements is to provide information about an organization that is useful to a range of users. Both have also agreed that preparers and regulators should recognize investors as the principal user group. This has led both regulatory bodies to construct a framework for financial reporting which draws heavily upon the requirements of investors' decision models. We have seen that the ASB has identified relevance and reliability as the primary characteristics of useful information. Relevant information includes that which has predictive value and that which possesses confirmatory value. Comparability is identified as a secondary characteristic.

This ranking is understandable, given the stated objective of financial statements and the choice of investors as the principal user group. Investors require information to help them evaluate, confirm and correct their past evaluations, and to help in their prediction of future events which will affect the reporting entity. Comparability is desirable in that it enables investors to compare the performance and position of different entities, but it is perhaps more important that the accounting methods chosen by individual companies should produce figures which are relevant to the users' decision models and that they represent faithfully the underlying transactions, i.e. they present a true and fair view.

However, it is not clear that a similar framework or a similar ranking would have emerged from the deliberations of regulators in certain European countries. Where the investor group, comprising banks, the state and family owner-managers, has traditionally had access to the internal records of the company, it is unlikely that this group would be the focus of a framework for 'external' financial reporting. And even if its information requirements were considered, the needs of banks and the state might be different from those of individual shareholders.

We can now begin to appreciate the difficulties in developing an international framework for financial reporting. Where the investor group is less important as an external user group, and tax rules are a strong influence on the accounting rules, the framework may differ significantly from that presented by the ASB.

For example, although tax authorities are interested in the prospects of organizations in order to determine future taxation policies, their needs are, in general, less future-oriented than those of investors. Primarily, they require information about a company's past performance in order to levy a tax charge. In the interests of equity amongst taxpayers, it is important that companies calculate their taxable profit according to the same set of rules. Thus one might expect a framework for tax accounting to include standardization (comparability) as the primary characteristic. Moreover, for most purposes, the tax authorities would be satisfied with standardization based upon *uniform* accounting practice, whether or not it also represented *best* accounting practice. They require only that the financial statements are 'correct', in that they have been produced according to the rules, rather than that they are 'true', in that they fairly represent the underlying economic events.

(v) Accountancy profession

We began this section with a reference to the frameworks for financial reporting which have been developed by the ASB and the FASB. The importance of these two bodies in the regulatory framework reflects strong accountancy professions in both the UK and the USA. In turn, the size and influence of the accountancy profession in a particular country may be the result of the four factors considered above.

For example, where the main providers of finance comprise the state, the banks and owner-managers, there is likely to be less need for independent auditors than where there is a large body of private shareholders and public organizations. Where external financial reporting has developed as a response to a government's desire to control the economy, or to collect taxes, it has been sufficient to prepare published accounts according to a set of standards based on uniform practice. In such cases it is important only that the accounts are correct, not that they represent a true and fair view. This reduces the need for judgement in the preparation and audit of accounts, and hence for the expertise of a large, well-qualified accountancy profession. Similarly, there is less need for the expert judgement of an accountant under codified Roman law, where detailed accounting rules are enshrined in legislation.

We can now appreciate why the accountancy professions in the UK and the USA have been so much more influential in developing accounting standards both nationally and internationally than, say, some of their continental European counterparts. In both the UK and the USA, there is a common law system which does not lay down detailed accounting rules, and the financial statements are generally independent of specific tax regulations; private shareholders, individual and institutional, are a major source of finance and rely heavily upon audited financial statements for their information needs. Each of these factors encourages the development of flexibility, judgement, fairness and experimentation in accounting practice — it is not enough to prepare the accounts 'according to the rules'.

Reconciling the differences

One might feel, after reading this section, that there is little prospect of developing a conceptual framework for financial accounting that would be acceptable internationally. The differences in objectives, users and accounting practices between, say, the 'flexible' UK financial reporting system and the much more 'rigid' German system, are so great that it would be difficult to find much common ground.

However, as we stated earlier, market forces are exerting pressures on companies to standardize their financial reports. The emergence of a global international capital market has been a considerable influence on the harmonization of accounting practice. Large public companies are now able to raise finance with relative ease on stock markets in Europe, Japan and the USA. However, to do so they must satisfy the accounting requirements of the relevant stock exchange. For example, we noted earlier that many companies registered in France and Germany traditionally had raised most of their finance from the banks. Now, some are replacing bank finance with funds raised on national and international stock markets. The price they must pay for this facility is an increased level of disclosure in their financial statements in accordance with recognized international accounting standards.

Even so, market forces may also need the support of legislation to hasten the process of harmonization (or standardization). Until 1990 only a few German companies were required to consolidate the accounts of their subsidiaries, and even then foreign subsidiaries were exempt. (The tax authorities levy tax upon individual companies, not groups of companies.) In an effort to increase the level of standardization in the financial statements of large companies, the EU issued the Seventh Directive which requires that parent companies must produce group accounts in the form of consolidated accounts (we explain the terms 'consolidation' and 'group accounts' in Chapter 16).

In fact, EU Directives have been very influential not only in standardizing the format and content of financial statements, but also in reducing some of the historical differences which exist between European countries. For example, we noted earlier some obvious differences between the historical context of financial reporting in the UK and that in Germany. The common law system in the UK, and the predominance of the investor user group over the banks and the tax authorities, has resulted in a large accountancy profession whose members are called upon to exercise their judgement in interpreting rather flexible accounting standards and a limited amount of legislation. Even the four fundamental concepts upon which UK financial statements were based, adherence to which was presumably necessary to give a true and fair view, were included not in law but in an accounting standard. In Germany, the Roman law system and the influence of the banks and the tax authorities, have resulted in accounting being viewed more as a branch of company law. A major role of accountants is to ensure compliance with the rules.

The consequences of two such different historical contexts emerged in the wording of UK and German audit reports. Traditionally, UK audit reports confirmed that the accounts gave a 'true and fair view' of the company's position and performance, whereas German audit reports stated that the accounts 'conformed to proper accounting principles.'

The EU Fourth Directive began the process of narrowing the gap between these two stances. Its first draft was heavily influenced by German company law, but successive drafts reflected the influence of the UK accountancy profession. In its ultimate form, it represented a compromise which caused both groups to adapt their long held views. German accountants must now recognize the establishment of the 'true and fair view' as a predominant principle in the preparation of financial statements (and its implications for the use of judgement) and the existence of some flexibility in the presentation of accounts. The Directive shifted the emphasis away from the German preference for uniform accounting practices to facilitate the collection of aggregated data, towards the UK preference for providing information about individual companies in a form which is useful to a range of users. For their part, UK accountants must accept some constraints on flexibility in the presentation of accounts and the fact that accounting concepts and issues of asset valuation are now enshrined in law rather than included in some, more flexible, accounting standard.

The EU Directives have gone some way to increasing the harmonization of accounting practices among member countries. But even then, large variations still exist as illustrated in Table 15.2. Moreover, countries such as the USA, Japan and Canada which have large, influential stock exchanges and which are the home base of important multinational companies, are not members of the EU. Thus there is a need to achieve harmonization at a global level as well as at a European level. Arguably the most important body working for international standardization on a worldwide level (rather than the more restricted area of the EU) is the International Accounting Standards Committee (IASC). In the following section we examine the work of the IASC, including its attempt to establish an international conceptual framework and consider whether it is likely to succeed in its aims.

15.7   International harmonization and the IASC

In Chapter 3 we introduced the IASC as a major international influence on UK standards. Its primary aim is to 'formulate and publish in the public interest accounting standards to be observed in the presentation of financial statements and to promote their worldwide acceptance and observance'.[9] Thus it aims to influence the financial reporting practices of every country in the world.

Membership of the IASC comprises some 100 accountancy bodies from about 80 different countries. The IASC board, responsible for publishing standards, consists of up to seventeen members; nine or ten developed countries such as the UK, USA, Japan and Germany, three or four developing countries and up to four other organizations representing user groups (e.g. the International Co-ordinating Committee of Financial Analysts). It adopts a standard setting process similar to that adopted by the ASB (outlined in Chapter 3) and the FASB. Thus it publishes exposure drafts, receives comments from interested parties (including users of accounts) and makes any changes deemed necessary before issuing an accounting standard.

One way of viewing the IASC is to think of it as the international equivalent of the ASB or the FASB in that it is a private sector standard-setting body and any standards it develops are greatly influenced by the accountancy profession. However, the 100 member accountancy bodies of the IASC come from countries

---

9. International Accounting Standards Committee, *Constitution of the International Accounting Standards Committee*, IASC, 1982.

with very different traditions in financial reporting practice. Moreover, unlike the ASB or the FASB, the IASC has no authority and therefore no direct means of enforcing its recommendations and must rely upon the support of governments, accountants and stock exchanges to back its standards.

As the pressures for international harmonization have increased and as various bodies around the world, such as the EU, have become increasingly involved in this process, the IASC has attempted to increase its influence on the international scene. In the late 1980s, as part of its campaign to increase its influence, it began work on two interrelated projects — the development of a conceptual framework, and a comparability project aimed at reducing the options within its standards.

Developing an international conceptual framework

Given that the aim of the IASC is to develop and promote accounting standards on a worldwide basis, its mission might be greatly assisted if it were to establish an international conceptual framework which was acceptable in all countries. Amongst the benefits of establishing such a framework would be increased international comparability of financial statements and increased user understanding and confidence in international financial reporting. Indeed, as noted in Section 15.3 above, the IASC has published a *Framework for the Preparation and Presentation of Financial Statements* which sets out the principles of accounting in an international context. However, publishing a framework is just the first step in establishing it. As we discuss below, the problems faced by the IASC in establishing and gaining acceptance for such a framework are even greater than those faced by national standard setters such as the ASB and FASB (see Section 15.4).

In Section 15.4 we stated that there are at least two major difficulties in establishing an acceptable conceptual framework. The first is concerned with the issue of social choice — that because there are so many user groups with conflicting views and requirements, it is impossible to establish a generally acceptable conceptual framework. We have seen in the previous section that the ASB and the FASB have each implicitly recognized this by basing their frameworks around the requirements of the private investor user group. As investors have long been viewed as the most important users of published financial statements in the UK and the USA, critics have suggested that the two frameworks merely legitimize existing social choices. Consequently, neither framework is likely to transfer easily into different countries and societies where other user groups are considered to be at least as important as investors.

Despite the potential problems involved in transferring a national view of financial reporting into an international context, the IASC has adopted a view of financial reporting which is consistent with the FASB framework. Indeed some critics have argued that the IASC framework is little more than an encapsulation of the FASB's four concept statements (see pp. 465–466) and have suggested that it therefore suffers from the same limitations. This similarity may be the result of the IASC's high regard for the FASB concepts and/or it may reflect the influential position of the US accountancy profession in determining IASC policy. Whatever the reasons, the acceptability of the framework and the social choices which underpin it, will ultimately be tested by the reactions of companies and national standard setters.

This brings us to the second problem which we have identified: whether the various participants involved in financial reporting would accept, or could be forced to accept, a conceptual framework from which all accounting rules and regulations would derive. The problem is one of compliance and enforcement. Unfortunately, as we noted above, the IASC has no authority of its own and must rely heavily on the support of its members who are professional accountancy bodies. In the previous section we explained that the influence of the accountancy profession on accounting regulation varies widely between countries, and in some countries such as Germany and Japan, the profession has little opportunity or no authority to influence accounting rules. Consequently, in order to secure compliance with its framework and any standards which flow from it, the IASC must rely on regulators in different countries *accepting* its recommendations.

Increasing the comparability of financial statements

How likely is it, then, that the IASC framework will improve and increase international harmonization and lead to, amongst other things, increased comparability of financial statements? Since its inception in 1973, the IASC has issued over 30 international accounting standards (IASs) aimed at harmonizing accounting practice worldwide. However, whilst these have resulted in some improvement in financial reporting on a worldwide basis (e.g. some smaller countries have adopted IASs directly), large variations in accounting practices still exist (see, for example, Table 15.2). This has led to criticism that the IASC is failing to achieve its objective of harmonizing international accounting practice.

One of the reasons for the IASC's limited success so far, is that the standards it has issued permit too many options for the accounting treatment of like transactions or events. For example IAS2, which deals with the assignment of cost to inventories, permits three different valuation bases — LIFO, FIFO or base-stock. These options have often been included in order to gain the acceptance of countries with the most powerful accountancy bodies — notably the USA and the UK. Thus it is likely that LIFO was included as a permitted option in valuing stock because it is allowed in the USA. However, as the needs of international users of accounts have increased and the globalization of capital markets has progressed, these variations have become less acceptable.

In the late 1980s, the IASC recognized the need to reduce the number of available options within its accounting standards and published an exposure draft in 1989, *E32 — Comparability of Financial Statements*[10] — proposing an improved set of international standards. This publication coincided with the publication of its framework. The IASC stated that one of the criteria it had used for choosing between alternative accounting treatments in E32 was conformity with its proposed *Framework for the Preparation and Presentation of Financial Statements.* Other criteria included current worldwide practices in national accounting standards, law and GAAP, the views of regulators and their representative organizations and consistency within and amongst IASs.

E32 identifies 29 issues covered in 13 standards where a choice of accounting treatment for like transactions or events is allowed. In many cases it recommends the removal of choice by specifying a single treatment but in a limited number of cases some choice is still allowed although a preferred method is indicated. For example, on the issue of assigning cost to inventories, E32 recommends FIFO or weighted average cost as the preferred treatment, permits LIFO and eliminates base stock as an option. It is unlikely that the decision to continue to permit LIFO was a consequence of applying the criterion of conformity with the IASC's framework. It is more probably a consequence of using the criteria which take account of current worldwide practice (notably US GAAP) and the views of regulators (notably the FASB).

Despite issuing the exposure draft in 1989, this comparability project is not yet complete, though it has made some progress. In part, this is due to the consultation process which the IASC follows before issuing standards. Appreciating and responding to the comments and objections of member accountancy bodies in nearly 80 countries, as well as responding to the views of the international business and finance community, national standard setters and others, is no simple matter. This is especially so when those countries and organizations are likely to hold differing views as to the characteristics, if not the objective, of financial reporting.

However, we might have expected these fundamental problems to have been resolved following the publication of the IASC's conceptual framework. In theory at least, a conceptual framework should provide a coherent and complete set of principles for developing accounting practice and reducing political pressures on standard setters. If so, the IASC should be able to develop and justify any recommended changes to its standards on the basis of its framework and should only consider objections to its proposals based on arguments consistent with its stated concepts.

Unfortunately, the IASC framework is not very detailed and, some argue, is incomplete with respect to certain issues, e.g. like the FASB framework it fails to prescribe a preferred measurement method or methods. (The ASB appear to

---

10. International Accounting Standards Committee, *Exposure Draft 32, Comparability of Financial Statements: Proposed Amendments to International Accounting Standards 2, 5, 8, 9, 11, 16, 17, 18, 19, 21, 22, 23 and 25,* IASC, 1989.

have implicitly recognized these limitations since they drew heavily on the IASC text for chapters 1 and 2 of their own statement but have developed different and more detailed criteria in later chapters.) Moreover, since the IASC has no authority of its own, it can only increase comparability by ensuring that any recommendations it makes are accepted. This was implicitly recognized by the IASC when they identified the criteria to be used in choosing between alternative treatments as including the views of regulators and their representative bodies. Since the options in IASs were put there in the first place in order to gain international agreement, removing them is unlikely to prove very acceptable.

Rationalizing any changes on the basis of 'best practice' as defined by the IASC (and the FASB and ASB), may not be acceptable to the myriad of constituents who have an interest in international reporting and who may have different views as to what constitutes best practice. Consequently, in order to reduce the number of options the IASC may have to select accounting treatments based on their widespread acceptability. Thus, it may only prove successful in its comparability project by developing standards which constitute uniform, rather than best, practice.

15.8   Summary

In theory, the establishment of a conceptual framework for financial reporting to guide the development of accounting standards should provide benefits to regulators. In practice, as we have seen, the difficulties to be overcome before such a framework can be agreed, are substantial. These difficulties are even greater if regulators aim to establish a set of generally agreed principles applicable on an international basis. Despite these problems, both national and international standard setters continue to search.

In this chapter we have described the search for a conceptual framework. The ASB's Statement of Principles was used to illustrate the essential features of a conceptual framework and to identify some of the problems in establishing agreement for some or all of its principles. We then considered other attempts to develop such a framework and discovered that the frameworks presented by the ASB, FASB and IASC have some similarities, notably they all emphasize the primacy of the investor user group. This focus on one group has ensured that, so far, these frameworks are less than comprehensive. Nevertheless, the consistency of the focus upon the investor group does suggest a level of agreement amongst those standard setters who have sought a conceptual framework. It may also imply that standardization of accounting practice throughout the world is likely to continue to increase.

However, the ASB and FASB set standards in countries which have a tradition of investor primacy and are heavily influenced by the accountancy profession. Moreover, accountants from the UK and US are very influential on the IASC.

Consequently, these frameworks may not reflect the view of financial reporting adopted in countries which are neither investor-orientated in their provision of accounting information nor significantly influenced by the accountancy profession when developing accounting regulation. We saw in Section 15.6 that many countries in continental Europe have these characteristics. Nevertheless, as long as the globalization of stock markets and the growth of multinational businesses continue to create a demand for standardized accounting information, the focus upon the investor group may continue.

The need for a more comprehensive international framework, dealing with the needs of other user groups, is likely to gain more support only if, and when, international regulators recognize a need to take full account of international concerns over environmental issues and other users' rights to accounting information. Even then, the likelihood of ever establishing an internationally agreed conceptual framework is limited by the need to reconcile the differences in the economic, social and political environments of different countries. We noted in the introduction that a major motivation behind these attempts has been the desire to improve and increase standardization based on best practice. However, we have suggested that increased standardization on a worldwide basis may only be attainable by developing standards which ultimately constitute uniform, rather than best, practice.

Discussion topics

1. Suggest reasons why the ASB decided to develop a Statement of Principles. Do you think that the time and effort put into the project will be worth it?

2. Identify the issues covered in the ASB's Statement of Principles. How are they different or similar to the issues covered by the FASB's concept statements?

3. How does Chapter 3 of the ASB's Statement of Principles define an asset? What is the difference between the ASB's definition and a legal definition of an asset? Why does it matter which definition companies adopt in their financial statements?

4. Explain the three main ways that accounting information can be presented. Do you think it matters whether items are included in the primary financial statements or disclosed in the notes to the accounts as long as they are included somewhere? Why?

5. Apart from the ASB's Statement of Principles, identify two attempts to develop a conceptual framework. Why do you think the ASB decided to develop its own framework rather than adopt one of these other ones?

6. Explain the two fundamental problems in establishing an agreed conceptual framework.

7. Explain why there is pressure to increase international standardization of accounting practice. Who do you think will be the main beneficiaries of international standardization?

8. Identify four factors which have influenced accounting development in different countries. Which of these factors account for the differences between accounting practice in the UK and Germany?

9. Identify two major bodies working for international standardization of accounting practices. What form of regulation does each adopt in attempting to achieve it?

10. What is the primary aim of the IASC? How might a conceptual framework assist it in achieving this aim? Do you think such a framework could also hinder its aim?

11. Explain the purpose behind the IASC's comparability project. What are the criteria which have been used to choose between alternative accounting treatments? Why do you think these criteria were used?

12. Discuss the main difficulties facing the IASC in completing its comparability project successfully.

Further reading

In addition to the following, the reader is referred to the further reading listed at the end of Chapter 3.

The latest drafts of chapters of the ASB's Statement of Principles are published in the annual publication of the Institute of Chartered Accountants in England and Wales, *Accounting Standards*.

Accounting Standards Committee, 'ASC foreword to IASC E32 — Comparability of financial statements', *Accountancy*, March 1989.

Archer, S. and McLeay, S., 'Financial reporting by interlisted European companies: issues in transnational disclosure', in Hopwood, A.G. (ed.), *International Pressures for Accounting Change*, Prentice-Hall, 1989.

Choi, F.D.S. and Mueller, G.G., *International Accounting*, Prentice-Hall, 1992.

Davies, M., Paterson, R. and Wilson, A., *UK GAAP: Generally Accepted Accounting Practice in the United Kingdom*, 3rd edn, Chapter 2, Macmillan, 1992.

Cairns, D., 'IASC's blueprint for the future', *Accountancy*, December 1989.

IASC, *Framework for the Preparation and Presentation of Financial Statements*, International Accounting Standards Committee, 1988.

IASC, 'Towards the international harmonisation of financial statements', *Accountancy*, March 1989.

Nobes, C. and Parker, R.H., *Comparative International Accounting*, Prentice-Hall, 1991.

Nobes, C., 'The origins of the harmonising provisions of the 1980 and 1981 Companies Acts', *Accounting and Business Research*, Winter 1983.

Page, M., 'The ASB's proposed objective of financial statements: marching in step backwards? A review essay,' *The British Accounting Review*, March 1992.

Parker, R.H., 'Importing and exporting accounting: the British experience', in Hopwood, A.G. (ed.), *International Pressures for Accounting Change*, Prentice-Hall, 1989.

Parker, R.H., 'Questions and answers on the Fourth Directive', *Accountant's Magazine*, September 1978.

Peasnell, K.V., 'The function of a conceptual framework for corporate financial reporting', *Accounting and Business Research*, Autumn 1982.

Purvis, S., Gernon, H. and Diamond, M., 'The IASC and its Comparability project: prerequisites for success', *Accounting Horizons*, June 1991.

Solomons, D., 'The political implications of accounting and accounting standard setting', *Accounting and Business Research*, Spring 1983.

Acquisition and merger accounting is one of the least understood aspects of the recent takeover boom. It is also, as the Bank of England has rightly diagnosed, very important because it has a dramatic impact on corporate behaviour. If acquisitive entrepreneurs are allowed to inflate their earnings through creative accounting, thereby boosting their own share prices, sound companies will end up in the wrong hands and the market in corporate control will be distorted. All the signs are that this has been happening in Britain, most notably in retailing, but also in other sectors of the market.

For this the Accounting Standards Committee must take a fair share of the blame ...

(Financial Times, 1st Leader, 7 July 1987)

The editorial from which the above quotation has been taken was headed 'Fiddling the Bid Figures'. It implies that accounting treatments can have very real effects on economic behaviour (an issue which we discussed in Chapter 12) and that the managers of acquisitive companies were taking advantage of the opportunities available under standard accounting practice to show the results of their takeover activities in the best possible light. In this chapter, we shall provide an introduction to the accounting treatment of groups of companies in sufficient detail to allow an understanding of the broad principles involved and of the controversies surrounding the area, some of which are developed in more detail in the next chapter. The topic is complex and a full explanation and analysis is beyond the scope of this text. References to some of the more advanced literature are given in the further readings at the end of this and the next chapter.

1988 was a year of record takeover activity in the UK and the accounting effects of the acquisitions made will continue up to and beyond the end of this century.

The value of acquisitions and mergers within the UK was some £22 billion. In addition, UK companies spent some $44 billion on the acquisition of foreign companies, of which some 75% was spent on US companies. By comparison, Canadian, French and Japanese companies each spent some $11 billion on foreign acquisition, US and Swiss companies $9 billion each, Australian companies $6 billion and German companies $3 billion. These figures include some very large individual bids, including Grand Metropolitan's $5.8 billion takeover of Pillsbury and Nestlé's $4.9 billion successful bid for Rowntree.[1] The high level of takeover activity in the UK continued during 1989 but fell away dramatically in the early 1990s.

In the next section we explain the rationale for group accounts. We then consider the different categories of relationship which might exist between companies in a group and describe and discuss the accounting treatment generally adopted for each of them. We explain some of the respects in which group accounting offers the opportunity for creative accounting and conclude the chapter with an example which covers a number of the accounting treatments explained earlier.

16.1   Rationale for group accounts

Groups are a number of companies linked together in some way, the most common of which is that one company (normally called the *holding company*) owns some or all of the shares in the others, so as to be able to exercise some control over their behaviour. One company may own a controlling interest in many — often several hundred — others. The essence of group accounts is that an attempt is made to combine together the performance and position of each company within the group to provide a picture of the group's overall performance and position. Why?

Consider the case of Hoell Ltd and Subbord Ltd whose income statements and balance sheets for 19X5 are shown in Table 16.1. Hoell Ltd (the holding company) owns the entire share capital of Subbord Ltd (normally called the *subsidiary company*). Suppose that no attempt is made to prepare group accounts and that each company issues only its own financial statements. (Note that we shall restrict our consideration in this chapter to the income statement and balance sheet. Where group financial statements are issued they will, in practice, also include a group cash flow statement.) The shareholders in Hoell Ltd and others who make use of its accounts, will receive only the accounts of Hoell Ltd as shown in the first column of Table 16.1. How much information will a user get from these accounts, bearing in mind that Hoell owns the entire capital of Subbord and exercises complete control over its resources?

As regards Subbord's *performance*, the users will know only that Subbord paid

1. For further details see *Deal Watch 1989*, KPMG Peat Marwick, 1989.

Table 16.1 *Hoell Ltd and Subbord Ltd — Financial statements for 19X5*

	Hoell Ltd £	Subbord Ltd £
Income statement		
Operating profit	100,000	50,000
Dividend from Subbord to Hoell	10,000	(10,000)
Net income retained	110,000	40,000
Balance sheets		
Net assets	1,100,000	450,000
Investment in Subbord (at cost)	150,000	—
	1,250,000	450,000
Share capital	500,000	100,000
Retained income	750,000	350,000
	1,250,000	450,000

Hoell a dividend of £10,000 during the year. They will not know that Subbord made a profit of £50,000 during the year, which may be an important indicator of the level of dividends it will be able to pay to Hoell in the future. As far as Subbord's *position* is concerned, users will know only that the investment in Subbord cost £150,000. They will not know that its current net assets have a book value of £450,000. The overall performance and position of the group are not fully reflected in the accounts of Hoell alone. If users were in a position to see the accounts of Subbord as well as those of Hoell, they would, with a modest amount of calculation, be able to derive for themselves a picture of the group. But the calculation required would be far from modest if Hoell had several hundred subsidiary companies rather than just one, as is often the case with holding companies!

In order to overcome these problems, the accounts of all companies within the group are combined or *consolidated* to recognize that the group as a whole constitutes one economic entity and not a series of independent companies and to provide information to the ultimate 'owners' of each company within the group. In subsequent sections we consider the variety of ways available for achieving this consolidation.

16.2 Categories of group relationships

Unfortunately (at least for accounting students!), not all relationships between one company and another are as straightforward as that between Hoell Ltd and Subbord Ltd, where one company completely owns and controls the other. The company which owns shares in the other sometimes does not own all of the equity shares and the shares which it does own may not confer rights to control or voting rights, equivalent to other equity shares. The issue of control is at the heart of group relationships and is an area which has caused many problems for accountants. We shall return to the issue of control briefly in a later section (Section 16.6) but at this stage we shall assume that the ownership of equity shares confers rights to control the operations of a company according to the proportion of shares held in that company.

There are broadly three categories of group relationship, depending on the proportion of equity shares held. They are as follows.

1. *Subsidiary companies*. One company is normally a subsidiary company of another where the investing company owns *more than 50%* of the equity share capital of the investee company. In the UK, the definition is extended to include, as an alternative, the situation where the investor company controls the composition of the Board of Directors of the investee company, or where it exerts a *dominant influence* over the investee company, or where the investor and investee company are managed on a unified basis. Where one company is a subsidiary of another, *full consolidation* or *acquisition accounting* is used to prepare the group accounts. (We explain this procedure in the next section.)

2. *Associated companies*. One company is normally an associated company of another where it is not a subsidiary company but where the investing company exercises *significant influence* over the investee company — such influence is often assumed where the investing company owns *at least 20%* of the equity share capital of the investee company. *Partial consolidation* or *equity accounting* is used to account for associated companies in group accounts. (We explain this procedure in Section 16.5.)

3. *Trade investments*. Where one company owns, as a long-term investment, shares in another which is neither a subsidiary nor an associated company, the investment is called a trade investment. A trade investment is accounted for in group accounts as was the investment of Hoell Ltd in Subbord Ltd. Dividends are treated as income in the income statement when they are received and the investment is shown in the balance sheet at the lower of original cost and market value. The market value of the investment should be disclosed in the notes to the accounts if it is materially different from the figure shown in the balance sheet.

16.3   Acquisition accounting

In this section we explain how to account for a subsidiary company in group accounts. We use the example of Missen Ltd and Brace Ltd, details of whose balance sheets are given in Table 16.2. We concentrate at this stage on the preparation of the group (or consolidated) balance sheet because that is where most of the problems lie. The consolidated income statement is little more than the sum of the income statements of the individual companies in the group. We

Table 16.2 *Missen Ltd and Brace Ltd — Accounts information*

Summarized balance sheets for Missen Ltd and Brace Ltd at 31 December 19X5 are as follows:

	Missen £	Brace £
Fixed assets	127,000	54,000
Investment in Brace at cost	83,000	—
Stocks	65,300	35,100
Loan to Brace	38,400	—
Debtors (accounts receivable)	46,600	26,300
Cash at bank	19,900	12,400
	380,200	127,800
Less Loan from Missen	—	(38,400)
Other current liabilities	(78,700)	(16,500)
	301,500	72,900
Represented by:		
Share capital	180,000	40,000
Retained profits	121,500	32,900
	301,500	72,900

Missen owns 60% of the share capital of Brace which it acquired on 1 January 19X3. At that date, the retained profits of Missen were £95,100 and of Brace, £15,000. There have been no changes in the share capital of either company since 19X2.

provide an example later in this chapter. Missen owns 60% of the share capital of Brace, which it acquired three years ago. Broadly speaking, consolidation of the balance sheets involves adding together the assets and liabilities of the two companies in order to show the position of the group as a whole. *Note that this is normally the case even when the holding company owns less than 100% of the subsidiary.* Recognition of the fact that the holding company does not own all the shares of the subsidiary is achieved by including as a liability an amount called *minority interest*, which represents the interest of other shareholders in the assets and liabilities of the subsidiary. The justification for this treatment is that it provides a picture of the resources that are within the control of the group which is clearer than that which would be given if the group balance sheet included only the holding company's proportion of each class of asset and liability. Because Missen Ltd owns a majority of the equity shares in Brace Ltd, it is in a position to exercise control over all of Brace Ltd's net assets and not just 60% of them. In addition to minority interest, there are two other calculations which are peculiar to group accounts and which frequently cause problems to students. They are the calculations of *goodwill* and of *group reserves*. We deal further with each of these below.

The steps involved in the preparation of a consolidated balance sheet are illustrated in the worksheet in Table 16.3. They are as follows.

Table 16.3 *Missen Ltd and Brace Ltd — Preparation of consolidated accounts*

| | Balance sheets | | Consolidation adjustments | | | Final balance sheet |
	Missen Ltd	Brace Ltd	Inter-company loan	Goodwill	Minority interest	
	£	£	£	£	£	£
Fixed assets	127,000	54,000				181,000
Investment in Brace	83,000	–		(83,000)		–
Goodwill	–	–		50,000		50,000
Stocks	65,300	35,100				100,400
Loan to Brace	38,400	–	(38,400)			–
Debtors	46,600	26,300				72,900
Cash at bank	19,900	12,400				32,300
	380,200	127,800				436,600
Loan from Missen	–	(38,400)	38,400			–
Other current liabilities	(78,700)	(16,500)				(95,200)
	301,500	72,900				341,400
Share capital – Missen	180,000	–				180,000
Share capital – Brace	–	40,000		(24,000)	(16,000)	–
Retained profits – Missen	121,500	–				121,500
Retained profits – Brace	–	32,900		(9,000)	(13,160)	10,740
Minority interest	–	–			29,160	29,160
	301,500	72,900				341,400

1. Cancel out common items

In the case of Missen and Brace, the common item is the inter-company loan of £38,400. This is shown as an asset in Missen's balance sheet and a liability in that of Brace. For the group balance sheet, the two items are netted off to reflect the fact that there is no asset or liability for the group as a whole.

2. Revalue the assets and liabilities of the subsidiary at the date of acquisition to their 'fair values'

As we shall see, the calculation of goodwill involves a comparison of what the holding company paid for its investment in the subsidiary and what it acquired in terms of net assets. For this purpose, it is necessary to estimate the value of the net assets at the time of acquisition. We shall discuss the use of fair values more fully in a later section (Section 16.6). In order to keep the present example as simple as possible, we assume at this stage that the fair values of Brace Ltd's net assets on 1 January 19X3 were equal to their book values.

3. Add together the assets and liabilities of the holding and subsidiary companies with the exception of the cost of investment and share capital and reserves

The excluded items are necessary for the calculations of goodwill, minority interest and group reserves. The items which are simply added together are as shown in Table 16.3: fixed assets (£181,000); stocks (£100,400); debtors (£72,900); cash at bank (£32,300); and other current liabilities (£95,200).

4. Calculate goodwill

Goodwill is calculated only once — at the date of acquisition. *It is not re-calculated each year.* It is the difference between what the holding company paid for its investment in the subsidiary and what it acquired in terms of identifiable net assets (valued at their fair values) at the date of acquisition. In so far as it is meaningful to ascribe a description to goodwill it represents the cost of net assets acquired which are not recognized as separately identifiable net assets in the balance sheet of the acquired company, for example, the value of the company's reputation, the quality of its staff, its market position, and so on. We discuss goodwill, and some of the many problems it poses for accountants, in Chapter 17.

In order to explain the calculation of goodwill, consider the acquisition of Brace by Missen. Missen paid £83,000 for its investment in 60% of the share capital of Brace. In return it acquired a right (through its shareholding) to 60% of the net assets of Brace. Remember from the accounting equation that:

Net Assets = Share Capital + Reserves (Retained Profits)

Thus, Brace's net assets at 1 January 19X3 equalled its share capital and retained profits at that date. So we may calculate goodwill in Brace at 1 January 19X3 as:

Amount paid		£83,000
Less Net assets acquired:		
Share capital — 60% × £40,000	£24,000	
Retained profits — 60% × £15,000	9,000	33,000
Goodwill		£50,000

The remaining 40% of share capital and reserves is transferred to minority interest, together with the 40% share of post-acquisition retained profits to which the minority shareholders are entitled.

Once the amount has been calculated, there are at least two possible treatments for goodwill. The first, which is favoured in most countries, is to capitalize it as an asset and amortize it (i.e., write it off) against profits over a period not exceeding its useful economic life. The second, which is allowed in some countries and, at the time of writing, is favoured in the UK, is to write it off immediately against reserves.

5. Calculate minority interest

If the subsidiary is not 100% owned, the minority share of all share capital and reserves at the group balance sheet date (or, put another way given the accounting equation, the minority share of the subsidiary's net assets at the group balance sheet date) is calculated and shown on the group balance sheet as a liability. In the case of Missen and Brace, the minority interest is:

$$40\% \times £72,900 = £29,160$$

This is made up as follows:

	£
40% × share capital (£40,000)	16,000
40% × retained profits at acquisition (£15,000)	6,000
40% × post-acquisition retained profits	
(£32,900 − £15,000 = £17,900)	7,160
Minority interest	29,160

6. Calculate group reserves

Group reserves comprise all the reserves of the holding company plus the holding company's share of the *post-acquisition* reserves of the subsidiary company. Recall that the pre-acquisition reserves of the subsidiary are included as part of the goodwill calculation. The group treats as its retained profits only its share of the retained profits (or other reserves) of the subsidiary which have been earned since the date of acquisition. Group retained profits for Missen and Brace are:

Table 16.4 *Missen Ltd — Group balance sheet*

Missen Ltd Group Balance Sheet at 31 December 19X5		£
Assets	Goodwill	50,000
	less Amortization	7,500
		42,500
	Fixed assets	181,000
	Stocks	100,400
	Debtors	72,900
	Cash at bank	32,300
Total assets		429,100
Ownership, interest	Share capital	180,000
and liabilities	Retained profits	124,740
	Interest of minority shareholders	29,160
	Current liabilities	95,200
Total funds employed		429,100

	£
Missen — 100% × £121,500	121,500
Brace — 60% × post-acquisition retained profits (£32,900 − £15,000 = £17,900)	10,740
Group reserves	132,240

It is apparent from the worksheet in Table 16.3 what has happened to the retained profits of Brace Ltd. 60% of the pre-acquisition retained profits have been transferred to the goodwill calculation (£9,000), 40% of both pre- and post-acquisition retained profits have been transferred to minority interest (£13,160), leaving 60% of post-acquisition retained profits to go to group reserves (£10,740).

Note that the share capital of Missen (£180,000), the holding company, goes directly to the group balance sheet.

The figures to appear in the group balance sheet are shown in the final column of Table 16.3. They are re-presented in the form of a group balance sheet in Table 16.4. For the purposes of this illustration, we assume that Missen has opted to amortize goodwill against profits over a period of 20 years. Thus accumulated amortization at 31 December 19X5 (three years) is three-twentieths of £50,000, which equals £7,500.

16.4 Merger accounting

In general, when two companies join together to form a business combination one of the companies is dominant and effectively takes over the other by purchasing a majority or all of the shares in the other company from its existing shareholders in return for cash, its own shares or loan capital, or some mix of these. In that case, acquisition accounting, as described in the previous section, should be used. But acquisition is not the only way for two companies to combine. With the consent of their shareholders, two companies may agree to merge or to 'pool their interests'. An example was the merger of Habitat/Mothercare with British Home Stores (BHS) in the UK in 1986. The merger was achieved by the creation of a new company, Storehouse plc, in which the shareholders of Habitat/Mothercare and BHS each received shares in return for their existing shares in the two merging companies. An alternative means of effecting a merger is to use one of the existing companies as a 'shell' and to give shares in that company to the shareholders of the other party to the merger.

The perceptive reader will already have spotted a serious problem. How are we to distinguish between a merger which is effected by the shareholders in one company receiving shares in the other and an acquisition in which the acquisition price is satisfied by the shareholders in the acquired company receiving shares in the other company? This problem was sufficiently severe to cause a delay in the UK of over 14 years between the (then) Accounting Standards Steering Committee issuing its first pronouncement on the subject (*Exposure Draft 3, Accounting for acquisitions and mergers*, January 1971) and the Accounting Standards Committee issuing a standard (*SSAP 23, Accounting for acquisitions and mergers*, April 1985). Furthermore SSAP 23, which lays down conditions which must be met if merger accounting is to be used, says that if the conditions are met, merger accounting may (rather than must) be used. The scope for creative accounting is evident and is explored further in Section 16.6 and in Chapter 17. The problems of merger accounting have led to its being prohibited in many countries, the two major exceptions being the UK and the USA, although in the latter its use is obligatory if the conditions to satisfy the definition of a merger are met.

In this section, we shall ignore the problems of defining a merger satisfactorily and concentrate on exploring the differences in accounting treatment between mergers and acquisitions. These are best understood if the fundamental difference between an acquisition and a merger is appreciated. With an acquisition there is a clear cut-off date at which time the acquired company is treated by the acquiring company in its group accounts as a newly-acquired asset. A merger, on the other hand, involves no acquisition but rather a joining together of interests — the group is treated simply as the sum of what the two companies would have reported had they remained independent of each other. This fundamental difference leads to a number of differences in accounting treatment. There are five main differences.

1. *Pre-combination reserves/retained profits.* As we have seen, the pre-combination reserves of a subsidiary company in an acquisition are incorporated within the goodwill calculation (i.e., they are capitalized). Under merger accounting, they remain as part of group reserves.

2. *Profit during the year of combination.* Under acquisition accounting, if an acquisition takes place part way through an accounting period, only the profit earned by the subsidiary *after* the date of acquisition is included in the group income statement for the period. Under merger accounting, the full period's profit of both companies is included in the group income statement, even if the merger takes place on the last day of the accounting period.

3. *Goodwill.* Under merger accounting there is no goodwill because there is no acquisition.

4. *Share premium.* If an acquisition is paid for by the issue of shares at a premium (i.e., at a price above their nominal value — see Chapter 8, p. 220), the premium is recognized in the group balance sheet. Under merger accounting, shares are swopped at their nominal value and no share premium is recognized.

5. *Fair values of assets.* The requirement to revalue separately identifiable assets to their fair values arises under acquisition accounting because the cost of the assets to the acquirer has to be determined. As a merger, by definition, does not involve an acquisition, there is no requirement to ascribe fair values to assets at the date of combination.

We may illustrate the basic principles involved in preparing a group balance sheet using merger accounting and contrast such a balance sheet with the one obtained using acquisition accounting, by considering the example of Expanned plc and Stayd plc. Details of the two companies' summarized balance sheets are given in Table 16.5 and group balance sheets, prepared using both merger and acquisition accounting, are shown in Table 16.6.

It is apparent from Table 16.6 that the group balance sheet, prepared using merger accounting, is simply the summation of the figures in the individual balance sheets of Expanned and Stayd. It differs from the group balance sheet under acquisition accounting in the following respects.

1. There is no figure for goodwill under merger accounting. The goodwill figure using acquisition accounting is calculated as follows:

	£	£
Cost of acquisition (2,000,000 shares at £4 each)		8,000,000
Less Net assets acquired at fair value:		
Fixed assets	1,500,000	
Current assets	6,500,000	
	8,000,000	
Current liabilities	(3,000,000)	5,000,000
Goodwill		3,000,000

2. Both the fixed and current assets of Stayd (but not Expanned) are included

Table 16.5   *Expanned plc and Stayd plc — Accounts information*

Expanned plc, whose ordinary £1 shares are listed on the Stock Exchange at £4 each, has made an offer for the whole of the ordinary share capital of Stayd plc. The offer, on the basis of one share in Expanned in return for one share in Stayd, was accepted and completed on 31 December 19X7.

At that date, the summarized balance sheets of the two companies, before recording the issue of new shares in Expanned, were:

	Expanned plc £	*Stayd plc* £
Fixed assets at net book value	6,000,000	1,000,000
Current assets	6,000,000	6,000,000
	12,000,000	7,000,000
3,000,000 ordinary shares of £1	3,000,000	—
2,000,000 ordinary shares of £1	—	2,000,000
Retained profits	4,000,000	2,000,000
Current liabilities	5,000,000	3,000,000
	12,000,000	7,000,000
Fair values of assets at 31.12.X7:		
Fixed assets	7,000,000	1,500,000
Current assets	6,000,000	6,500,000

Table 16.6   *Expanned plc and Stayd plc — Group balance sheets*

Balance sheets at 31 December 19X7

	Expanned plc £000	*Stayd plc* £000	*Group*	
			Merger basis £000	*Acquisition basis* £000
Goodwill	—	—	—	3,000
Fixed assets	6,000	1,000	7,000	7,500
Current assets	6,000	6,000	12,000	12,500
	12,000	7,000	19,000	23,000
Share capital	3,000	2,000	5,000	5,000
Share premium	—	—	—	6,000
Retained profits	4,000	2,000	6,000	4,000
Current liabilities	5,000	3,000	8,000	8,000
	12,000	7,000	19,000	23,000

at their fair values under acquisition accounting but at their book values under merger accounting.

3. Under acquisition accounting, a share premium is recognized in respect of the shares issued by Expanned to purchase the shares of Stayd. The

premium is £3 per share (the difference between the market value of £4 and the nominal value of £1) multiplied by the number of shares issued (2,000,000), a total of £6,000,000. Under merger accounting, the transaction is treated as a straight share exchange, with no premium being recognized. Note that in both cases the group's issued share capital is £5,000,000 — the new issued share capital of Expanned.

4. Group retained profits under the merger basis are the sum of the retained profits of the two companies. Under acquisition accounting, all of the holding company's retained profits are included (£4,000,000 for Expanned) but none of the subsidiary's because they were all earned prior to the acquisition date.

This simple example illustrates some of the potential benefits resulting from the use of merger accounting, for the managers of companies who wish to improve their reported performance and position. (We discussed why company managers might want to do this in Chapter 12.) Under the merger basis, group retained profits are higher, expanding the pool from which future dividends may be paid. A higher profit can be reported during the year of combination — any profits earned by Stayd during 19X7 would be included in the group income statement for that year, whereas none of the profits would be included if acquisition accounting was used (unless the acquisition had taken place part way through the year, in which case the relevant proportion would have been recognized). Under merger accounting there is no embarrassing goodwill number to get rid of, either by reducing reserves or by amortization against future profits. And finally, future depreciation charges and the costs of using the current assets of Stayd will be based on book values and not on the (higher) fair values included under acquisition accounting. However, as we shall see in Section 16.6, this last argument is reversed if fair values are included at a figure lower than book values. The above advantages may go some way to explaining why a number of companies have constructed acquisitions to satisfy the conditions which must be met if merger accounting is to be used.

16.5 Associated companies

We explained earlier that some investments by one company in another fall short of creating a holding company/subsidiary company relationship but imply a stronger interest than exists with a trade investment. Such investments result in one company exerting a significant influence over the affairs of another (often assumed when at least 20% of the equity shares are owned), in which case the company in which the investment is held is called an associated company. Where such a relationship exists, the investing company will normally show in its group accounts a proportion of both the income and the net assets of the associated company, equal to the proportion of the shares it holds in the associated company. This is called *equity accounting*.

We shall again use a simple example to illustrate the accounting treatment. Relevant accounting information concerning Antelopes plc and Bisons Ltd is given in Table 16.7 and the resulting group accounts of Antelopes plc are shown in Table 16.8.

Consider first the group profit and loss account. The holding company's income statement includes only the dividend of £7,500 received from Bisons. Under equity accounting, group income includes the holding company's share of all the associated company's profit (or loss), i.e. the group profit and loss account of Antelopes includes £45,000 (25% × £180,000). Because the dividend received from Bisons has been paid out of this amount, it is excluded as a separate entry to avoid double-counting. A note is included showing how much of the group retained profit is retained by the holding company and how much by the associated company. £67,500 is retained by Antelopes (as per its own income

Table 16.7 *Antelopes plc and Bisons Ltd — Accounting information*

Antelopes plc owns 25% of the share capital of Bisons Ltd. The 150,000 shares were purchased five years ago for £225,000. At that time, the balance sheet of Bisons Ltd was as follows:

Net assets (at fair value)	£750,000
Represented by:	
Share capital (ordinary £1 shares)	£600,000
Reserves	150,000
	£750,000

The current balance sheets of the two companies are as follows:

	Antelopes plc £	Bisons Ltd £
Net assets	1,000,000	1,500,000
Investment in Antelopes Ltd	225,000	—
	1,225,000	1,500,000
Represented by:		
Share capital (ordinary £1 shares)	900,000	600,000
Reserves	325,000	900,000
	1,225,000	1,500,000

Income statements for the year just ended are as follows:

	Antelopes plc £	Bisons Ltd £
Operating profit	120,000	180,000
Dividend received from Bisons Ltd	7,500	—
	127,500	180,000
Dividend paid	60,000	30,000
Retained profit, added to reserves	67,500	150,000

Table 16.8 *Antelopes plc — Group accounts*

Antelopes plc — Group profit and loss account

	£
Operating profit:	
Antelopes plc	120,000
Share of associated company	45,000
	165,000
Less Dividend paid	60,000
Retained profit for the year	105,000

	£
Retained by Antelopes plc	67,500
Retained by associated company	37,500
	105,000

Antelopes plc — Group balance sheet

	£	£
Net assets		1,000,000
Investment in associated company:		
Share of net assets	375,000	
Premium on acquisition	37,500	412,500
		1,412,500
Represented by:		
Share capital (ordinary £1 shares)		900,000
Reserves		512,500
		1,412,500

statement, and *including* the dividend from Bisons of £7,500) and £37,500 by Bisons (Antelopes' share of Bisons' profit — £45,000 — *less* the dividend payment of £7,500 which represents a transfer of retained profit from Bisons to Antelopes).

The group balance sheet includes Antelopes' share of Bisons' net assets, i.e. £375,000 (25% × £1,500,000), together with the premium paid on acquisition, insofar as it has not been written off. Note that the premium paid on acquisition is equivalent to the goodwill figure calculated under acquisition accounting and it should be dealt with in the same way — either being amortized against group profit over its useful economic life or written off immediately against reserves. The calculation in our illustration is:

	£
Amount paid	225,000
Less share of net assets acquired	
(25% × £750,000)	187,500
Premium on acquisition	37,500

Group reserves include all the reserves of the holding company plus the post-acquisition reserves of the associated company — exactly as was the case under acquisition accounting. The figure for our example is:

		£
Reserves of Antelopes		325,000
Share of reserves of Bisons		
(25% × [900,000 − 150,000])		187,500
Group reserves		512,500

16.6 Creativity in group accounting

A number of aspects of accounting for groups provide the flexibility necessary to allow company managers to choose a treatment which shows their organization's performance and/or position in the best possible light. In Section 16.4 we explained how, by structuring an acquisition so as to allow merger accounting to be used, it is possible to enhance current profit by including the acquired company's full profit for the period during which the combination is effected, even if that is some way through the period; future profits may be increased by avoiding the need to revalue the acquired company's assets to their fair values; future profits may be increased or reserves protected by avoiding the need to recognize and write off goodwill; and reserves may be enhanced by including the pre-acquisition reserves of the acquired company.

It is also sometimes possible to avoid the inclusion of the full results of a subsidiary company where those results imply poor performance (for example where losses have been made) or a weak financial position (for example where the subsidiary has a high level of borrowing). This is sometimes done by arguing that to consolidate would be 'misleading', that the subsidiary's business is 'significantly different' from that of the rest of the group, or that the cost of undertaking the consolidation would be 'unreasonably expensive'. Companies which are, in substance, subsidiaries may on occasion be excluded because they are given a legal form which enables them to be defined legally as non-subsidiaries. This is a complex and controversial area which is outside the scope of this book. The reason for mentioning it is to make the reader aware that very few aspects of accounting are cut and dried, none less so than acquisition accounting!

We turn finally in this section to the use (and misuse) of fair values, which have been introduced earlier in this chapter. The fair value of an asset (or liability) is the amount for which it could be exchanged in an arm's length transaction. Again, this is a complicated area and we restrict ourselves to a simple example to illustrate the scope for creativity. Remember that under both acquisition and equity accounting, the net assets of the acquired company at the date of acquisition should be re-stated to their fair values. The fair values ascribed affect both the goodwill figure and post-acquisition profits. This is significant if goodwill is written off against reserves (rather than against future profits) or if it is written off against future profits over a period longer than that used to write off the assets which have been re-stated at fair values.

Consider a simple example. Suppose that A acquires B, whose only asset is stock, which has a book value of £80,000. The purchase consideration is £100,000. The managers of A are considering whether to set up a provision to write down B's stock by £30,000, i.e. whether to adjust it to a 'fair value' of £50,000. It is important to recognize that in practice managers have considerable scope in this sort of matter, particularly where specialized assets are involved, which have no readily observable market value. Suppose further that A will write off any goodwill on acquisition against reserves. The position at acquisition, with and without the provision, is as follows:

	No provision £	Provision £
Purchase consideration	100,000	100,000
Net assets acquired	80,000	50,000
Goodwill (written off against reserves)	20,000	50,000

Suppose that the stock is sold soon after the acquisition date for £110,000. The impact on group profit will be:

	No provision £	Provision £
Sales	110,000	110,000
Cost of sales	80,000	50,000
Profit (added to reserves)	30,000	60,000

This is the sort of magic of which accounting is sometimes capable! By setting up the provision of £30,000, the managers of A could increase their immediate post-acquisition profit by £30,000. The only cost is that group reserves at the date of acquisition would decline by an extra £30,000 but that amount would be replaced (by additional retained profits) as soon as the stock is sold.

Perhaps the major area of controversy in group accounting relates to the treatment of goodwill — an area which we consider in more detail in the next chapter.

16.7 A further example of group accounting

We conclude this chapter with a further example of accounting for groups. Information concerning three companies in which Paddington plc owns shares is given in Table 16.9.

Consider first the nature of Paddington's relationship with each company. Based on the percentage of shares owned (the only relevant information available concerning the relationships), Mash is a trade investment as less than 20% of its

Table 16.9 *Paddington plc — Group accounts information*

Paddington plc owns part of the share capital of three companies, Mash plc, Trapper Ltd and Deejay Ltd. The following information relates to these three companies.

	Mash plc	Trapper Ltd	Deejay Ltd
Income Statements for the year ended 31 December 19X4			
	£000	£000	£000
Profit before taxation	2,775	738	1,404
Less Taxation	270	170	508
Profit after taxation	2,505	568	896
Dividends	660	400	340
Retained profit, added to reserves	1,845	168	556
Balance sheets at 31 December 19X4			
	£000	£000	£000
Fixed assets	5,735	5,389	1,365
Net current assets	6,117	1,119	5,372
	11,852	6,508	6,737
Less Long-term liabilities	0	685	625
Net assets	11,852	5,823	6,112
Issued share capital	3,000	2,000	1,400
Retained profits	8,852	3,823	4,712
	11,852	5,823	6,112
Percentage of share capital owned by Paddington plc	10%	80%	25%
Dates shares acquired	1.7.X1	1.1.X4	1.1.X0
Acquisition cost	£1,500,000	£5,000,000	£930,000
Retained profits at date of acquisition	£6,149,500	£3,655,000	£2,191,200
Total market value at 31 December 19X4	£29,605,000	Not available	Not available

In the case of each company, when Paddington plc acquired its shareholding, the fair values of the company's net assets were equal to their balance sheet value. None of the companies has issued any further share capital during the period of Paddington's ownership.

shares are owned, Trapper is a subsidiary company because a majority of its shares are owned, and Deejay is an associated company as Paddington owns between 20% and 50% of its shares. Hence the three companies will be treated differently in the consolidated accounts. Let us look at each of them separately.

Mash plc

As a trade investment, the only effect Mash will have on the group accounts will be through the payment of dividends and through the inclusion of the investment on the balance sheet. In the group income statement, the dividend received of £66,000 (10% × £660,000) should be shown. On the group balance sheet, the investment should be shown at its cost of £1,500,000, as this is below market value. Because the market value (10% × £29,605,000 = £2,960,500) is significantly different from cost, the market value should be shown as a note to the balance sheet.

Trapper Ltd

As a subsidiary, the basic treatment for Trapper will be to add all of its individual assets and liabilities (a net amount of £5,823,000) and its profit after taxation to the equivalent figures of the rest of the group, subject to the following adjustments:

		£	£
Goodwill:	Purchase consideration		5,000,000
	Acquired:		
	Share capital (80% × £2,000,000)	1,600,000	
	Retained profits at acquisition		
	(80% × £3,655,000)	2,924,000	4,524,000
	Goodwill		476,000

Goodwill should either be capitalized and amortized over a period no longer than its useful economic life or written off immediately against reserves.

Minority interest:	£
In the group balance sheet (20% × £5,823,000)	1,164,600
In the group income statement (20% × £568,000)	113,600

Note that *all* of Trapper's profit (£738,000), taxation (£170,000) and profit after taxation (£568,000) should be added to the equivalent group figures. The minority share of £113,600 is then deducted from group profit after taxation.

Retained profits:	
Add to group reserves (80% × £168,000)	£134,400

Deejay Ltd

As an associated company, a proportion (25%) of Deejay's income and net assets will be included in the group accounts. In the group balance sheet, the following will be shown:

	£	£
Share of net assets: 25% × £6,112,000		1,528,000

Premium on acquisition:

	£	£
Purchase consideration		930,000
Acquired:		
Share capital (25% × £1,400,000)	350,000	
Retained profits at acquisition		
(25% × £2,191,200)	547,800	897,800
Premium on acquisition		32,200

The premium on acquisition should either be capitalized and amortized over a period no longer than its useful economic life or written off immediately against reserves.

Share of reserves: 25% × (£4,712,000 − £2,191,200)   £630,200

In the group income statement the following should be shown separately: share of profit of associate, £351,000 (25% × £1,404,000); share of taxation of associate, £127,000 (25% × £508,000); and share of profit after taxation of associate, £224,000 (25% × £896,000). There should also be shown by way of note the share of group profit retained by the associated company, amounting to £139,000 (25% × £556,000).

In this chapter we have provided an introduction to group accounting, sufficient to explain the underlying principles and to provide a foundation for our further analysis of intangible assets in the next chapter.

Discussion topics

1. 'The takeover bubble has burst — at least we don't need to worry about group accounting for the time being.' Discuss.

2. Describe the different types of relationships which might exist between companies in a group and explain in words the broad accounting treatment adopted for each.

3. What are the main accounting treatment problems which arise in acquisition accounting? Provide a brief description of each one.

4. Outline the main differences between acquisition and merger accounting and explain why company managers might opt for one treatment rather than the other where they have a choice.

5. When does an associated company relationship arise? Explain how it is accounted for.

Exercises

16.1 The draft balance sheets of Trunk Ltd, Sack Ltd and Pouch Ltd on 31 December 19X6 were as follows:

	Trunk Ltd £	Sack Ltd £	Pouch Ltd £
Fixed assets	233,400	255,600	121,000
Investments: in Sack Ltd	300,000		
in Pouch Ltd	70,000		
Net current assets	94,300	79,700	117,600
	697,700	335,300	238,600
Financed by:			
Issued ordinary shares of £1 each	350,000	250,000	150,000
Revenue reserve	347,700	85,300	88,600
	697,700	335,300	238,600

    (i) Trunk Ltd purchased 200,000 shares in Sack Ltd at £1.50 per share on 31 December 19X3 when Sack's revenue reserve balance was £44,000.

    (ii) Trunk Ltd purchased 37,500 shares in Pouch Ltd for £70,000 on 31 December 19X4 when Pouch's revenue reserve balance was £56,600.

    (iii) None of the companies proposes to pay a final dividend for 19X6. Each paid an interim dividend of 10p per share on 30 June 19X6.

- (a) Prepare the consolidated balance sheet of the Trunk Group as at 31 December 19X6. (*Assume* for this part that the fair values of the net assets of Sack and Pouch were equal to their book values at the dates when Trunk purchased shares in the two companies.)
- (b) Explain how the consolidated profit and loss account and balance sheet of the Trunk Group would be affected if the fair values of the fixed assets of Sack and Pouch had been materially greater than their book values at the relevant acquisition dates.
- (c) Discuss the rationale for including in consolidated accounts the fair values at acquisition of assets in subsidiaries and the historical cost values of assets in the holding company.

16.2 On 1 January 19X7 Garfunkel Ltd purchased 90% of the ordinary shares of Simon

Ltd for £117,000, paid in cash. Garfunkel Ltd has no other subsidiary or associated companies. At that date, the balance sheets of the two companies were as follows:

	Garfunkel Ltd £	Simon Ltd £
Fixed assets at written down value	120,000	40,000
Investment in Simon Ltd	117,000	—
Stock	65,000	50,000
Amounts receivable	23,000	15,000
Cash	60,000	20,000
	385,000	125,000
Less: Amounts payable	44,000	20,000
	341,000	105,000
Issued ordinary shares of £1	200,000	50,000
Retained profits	141,000	55,000
	341,000	105,000

During the year ended 31 December 19X7, Garfunkel Ltd made a net profit of £40,000 and Simon Ltd a net profit of £30,000. Neither company paid or proposed a dividend during the year.

- (a) Assume that the fair values of Simon's net assets at 1 January 19X7 were as shown in its balance sheet at that date and that goodwill was written off against retained profits immediately on acquisition. Ignore taxation. Calculate the following for the Garfunkel group:
  - (i) Earnings per share for 19X7;
  - (ii) Minority interest at 31 December 19X7;
  - (iii) Group retained profit at 31 December 19X7.
- (b) Assume now that the fair value of Simon's stock at 1 January 19X7 (all of which was sold during 19X7) was £30,000. All other conditions are as in (a) above. Calculate the following for the Garfunkel group:
  - (i) Earnings per share for 19X7;
  - (ii) Minority interest at 31 December 19X7;
  - (iii) Group retained profit at 31 December 19X7.
- (c) Comment on the implications of your answers to (a) and (b) above.
- (d) Explain how Garfunkel Ltd might deal with the goodwill arising on its acquisition of Simon Ltd if it does not wish to write it off immediately against retained profits.

16.3 The following are the summarized balance sheets of Supersonics plc and Celtics Ltd at 31 December 19X9:

	Supersonics plc £m	Celtics Ltd £m
Investment in Celtics at cost	15.0	—
Fixed assets	61.5	12.0
Current assets	47.0	28.5
Current liabilities	(21.0)	(13.5)
	102.5	27.0
Share capital	20.0	4.0
Reserves	82.5	23.0
	102.5	27.0

Supersonics acquired 80% of the share capital of Celtics for cash on 31 December 19X6, at which time the reserves of Supersonics were £58.0m and those of Celtics £11.5m. There have been no changes in the issued share capital of either company since 1 January 19X7.

- (a) Calculate the following for the consolidated balance sheet of Supersonics plc and its subsidiary, assuming that the book values of Celtics Ltd's assets and liabilities at the date of acquisition were a good approximation of their fair values:
    - (i) Goodwill arising on acquisition;
    - (ii) Minority interest at 31 December 19X9;
    - (iii) Group reserves at 31 December 19X9, assuming that goodwill is written off immediately against reserves on acquisition.
  - (b) Explain how the consolidated profit and loss account and balance sheet of the Supersonics group would be affected if the fair values of the fixed assets and stock of Celtics Ltd had been materially greater than their book values at 1 January 19X7.

16.4 The following are the draft profit and loss accounts of Hakim plc and Dworkin Ltd for the year ended 31 December 19X0:

	Hakim plc £m	Hakim plc £m	Dworkin Ltd £m	Dworkin Ltd £m
Sales		18.7		6.6
Cost of goods sold		8.8		2.2
Gross profit		9.9		4.4
Less Depreciation	2.4		1.0	
Other expenses	5.1	7.5	2.8	3.8
Net profit		2.4		0.6

Hakim plc acquired the entire share capital of Dworkin Ltd (5 million £1 shares) on 1 July 19X0 in return for 5 million of its own £1 shares, at which time the shares had a market value of £2 each. Dworkin's summarized balance sheet at 1 July 19X0 was as follows:

	£m	£m
Plant and machinery at cost	5.0	
Less accumulated depreciation at 30 June 19X0	2.0	
		3.0
Net current assets		3.2
		6.2
Share capital		5.0
Reserves at 1 January 19X0		0.9
Retained profits to 30 June 19X0		0.3
		6.2

The fair value of Dworkin's plant and machinery at 1 July 19X0 was estimated at £4.5 million and of stock (included in net current assets in the summarized balance sheet at £1 million) at £1.3 million. All stock on hand at 1 July 19X0 was sold by 31 December 19X0. The plant and machinery was estimated to have a remaining life of 3 years from 1 July 19X0 and no residual value at the end of that time. Both Hakim and Dworkin use the straight line method of depreciation.

Hakim's issued share capital at 1 January 19X0 comprised 10 million £1 shares. The only change in its issued share capital during the year was in respect of the 5 million shares issued to the shareholders in Dworkin.

If acquisition accounting is used, Hakim wishes to capitalize goodwill and write it off against profits over its useful economic life estimated at 10 years.

Assume that Dworkin's revenues and expenses shown in its draft profit and loss account all occurred evenly throughout the year.

- (a) Calculate the group earnings per share of Hakim plc for 19X0 assuming:
   (i) that acquisition accounting is used;
   (ii) that merger accounting is used.
   (b) Calculate the earnings per share of Hakim plc for 19X0 had it not acquired Dworkin Ltd.
   (c) Discuss the results of your calculations.

Further reading

Accounting Standards Committee, *SSAP 1: Accounting for Associated Companies*, ASC, April 1982.
Accounting Standards Committee, *SSAP 14: Group Accounts*, ASC, September 1978.
Accounting Standards Committee, *SSAP 22: Accounting for Goodwill*, ASC, July 1989.

Accounting Standards Committee, *SSAP 23: Accounting for Acquisitions and Mergers*, ASC, April 1985.

Crichton, J., 'A new approach to consolidated accounts', *Accountancy*, August 1990.

Munson, R. and Holgate, P., 'ED48 — the demise of the merger', *Accountancy*, May 1990.

Robins, P., 'Spotlight on acquisition', *Accountancy*, November 1989.

Taylor, P.A., *Consolidated Financial Statements*, Harper & Row, 1987, particularly Parts I and II.

1. For further details see *Deal Watch 1989*, KPMG Peat Marwick, 1989.

17

Intangibles Revisited

The accounting treatment of certain types of intangible assets has become a topical and somewhat controversial area in a number of countries during the past decade. A particular problem has been the treatment of goodwill which, as we shall see in this chapter, has implications for other intangibles such as brand names, newspaper and magazine titles and customer lists. In the UK, for example, in the decade to 1987, goodwill as a percentage of bidding companies' net worth increased from 1% to 44%. In consequence, the accounting treatment of goodwill has become a major issue for reporting enterprises and for accounting regulators. There appear to have been two main reasons for the increase. The first was the increasing proportion of companies taken over in the services sectors (where a substantial part of an organization's value may be accounted for by intangible assets, many of which have traditionally been included as part of goodwill) rather than in the manufacturing sector. The second was a rapidly rising stock market which resulted in ever larger differences between the market and book values of organizations and between the price paid for companies and the 'fair values' of their separately identifiable assets.

Our reasons for devoting a chapter to the accounting problems posed by intangibles are not simply the result of their current topicality. It is possible, after all, that the problems will be resolved and replaced by others. They are more that the issues raised illustrate the myriad of conceptual and political problems faced by those responsible for recommending accounting practices and getting their recommendations accepted by those responsible for the preparation of accounting statements. In that context, this chapter will serve as a useful means of revising many of the issues we have discussed earlier and of pulling together some of the threads which run through the book. In particular, this chapter should be read in the light of what we have already said about the role of regulation (Chapter 3), the use of conceptual frameworks (Chapter 15), and the motives of the managers who are responsible for the preparation of accounts (Chapter 12).

The meaning and accounting treatment of intangibles were introduced in Chapter 6. We shall concentrate in this chapter on the problems posed by goodwill and group accounts. In order to understand the nature of these problems, it is important to have mastered the basic accounting treatments introduced in Chapter 16.

We start by reviewing the background to the debate, including a discussion of the purposes of financial statements and of the importance of managerial self-interest in understanding the tensions between preparers and users. After explaining the nature of goodwill and the particular problems it has created in the UK, we review the principles and criteria developed throughout the book and apply them to an evaluation of alternative treatments. Finally we suggest a possible way forward.

17.1   Background

In this section we review some of the issues which provide a background to the debate about the accounting treatment of goodwill and related intangibles, with particular reference to the UK. During the past decade, accounting treatments generally have attracted increasing attention. The reasons for this are diffuse. There has been an increase in capital market activity, in terms of the number of shares available, the wider spread of share ownership and the increasing number and size of takeovers (see Chapter 16). These have resulted partly from the increasing globalization of financial, industrial and commercial markets, partly from the UK government's policy of privatizing public corporations and selling large parts of them to individuals, and partly from an increase in the number of individuals with a direct interest in pension funds and other institutional investors. The effect of this increase in activity and interest has been to throw a spotlight on financial reports and the usefulness of the information contained in them to a wide range of users. The spotlight has highlighted a number of areas in which it might be said at best that the accounting treatments adopted by preparers do not always accord with what the woman or man in the street might expect. Obvious examples, which we have discussed in earlier chapters, include the use of historical costs in balance sheets (Chapter 12) and depreciation figures which do not measure falls in value (Chapter 6).

We might term these differences between what the numbers in financial reports mean and what a large number of users perceive them to mean, the *accounting information perception gap*. This gap has led to spiralling demands for more comprehensible and rational accounting information from preparers and users alike.

In assessing the value of accounting information it must be recognized that it is part of a much wider information set available to users of financial reports. For example, investment analysts will have regard to international, national and industry information as well as to an individual company's accounting statements in formulating their advice. Furthermore, the increasing number of individual investors, pension scheme members and so on, will often have to rely on summary information prepared by experts such as stockbrokers and financial journalists. This summary information is often based on simplified ratios and numbers taken directly from a company's accounts, with little adjustment for the eccentricities found in currently acceptable accounting practices. Even the *Financial Times* is guilty of this simplistic treatment as an examination of its financial pages soon shows. In particular, *earnings per share* numbers are widely used by stockbrokers and financial journalists with little in the way of health warnings! Such a treatment means that many individual investors may have little idea of the underlying performance and position of their companies even if more sophisticated investors are able to see through the haze of current practice. The position is likely to be similar for many other users such as employees, trade creditors and customers, who are unwilling or unable to take advantage of expert professional advice.

Purposes of financial statements

We have argued that financial statements have two main purposes which may be described broadly as to provide information to assist user decisions and to assist in the enforcement of contracts. Consider the first purpose. From a normative perspective, financial statements are intended to

> provide information about the financial position, performance and financial adaptability of an enterprise to a wide range of users in making economic decisions.[1]

In order to make economic decisions, users may need to form predictions about the future and to check the extent to which actual performance corresponds to their forecasts. Thus financial statements should be capable of providing information which has some predictive value and which holds management accountable for the resources entrusted to it. This latter information is an important component of forming subsequent forecasts.

The users of financial statements include a wide array of organizational participants including, for example, 'present and potential investors, employees, lenders, suppliers and other trade creditors, customers, governments and their agencies and the public'.[2] Since the objects of prediction and the basis of accountability may differ between or even within these groups of users, operationalizing the objective of providing useful information is a complex task.

---

1. Accounting Standards Board, *The Objective of Financial Statements and the Qualitative Characteristics of Financial Information*, The Accounting Standards Board Ltd, 1991, para. 12.
2. Accounting Standards Board, *op. cit.*, para. 9.

For example, investors may be interested primarily in predicting the future profitability of an enterprise in order to help them determine whether they should buy, sell or hold shares. The public, on the other hand, may be less interested in profitability and more concerned with predicting the contribution of an enterprise to the local economy in terms of both benefits (e.g. employment opportunities) and costs (e.g. damage to the local environment).

Recognizing the diversity of needs and the variety of information needed to satisfy them, it has to be acknowledged that one set of financial statements cannot be expected to satisfy all these information needs simultaneously. Some writers have argued that, because all users of accounts have some interest in the financial position, performance and adaptability of the reporting entity, the provision of information which will satisfy the needs of investors will also meet most of the needs of other users. The persuasiveness of this argument rests on two assumptions: first, that there is sufficient overlap between the needs of different user groups, and secondly, that there is adequate and accessible information available to users other than investors, from sources other than financial statements.

These assumptions are problematic. The economic decisions of different groups or subgroups of users will not necessarily be based on similar objectives (as we explained in Chapter 2). The first assumption treats much of the financial information needed by non-investors as a subset of the information required by investors and thereby ignores the presence of conflicts and contradictions between the needs of different user groups, and indeed within user groups, which result from differing objectives. Such conflicts and contradictions cannot necessarily be accommodated solely by the provision of additional information to some users but may require the reconstitution of existing financial information in alternative forms. The meaning of financial performance, costs and benefits or even assets and liabilities cannot be assumed to be the same for all users of financial statements concerned with economic decisions.

The second assumption underlying the presumed primacy of investor needs in financial statements rests on a belief that enterprises or others do, or will, provide adequate supplementary information to satisfy the informational needs of users other than (some) investors. Unfortunately it seems unlikely that such an open-book policy is, or is likely to be, adopted by enterprises voluntarily except in circumstances where it is perceived to be in the best interests of managers. Consequently, unless enterprises are required by regulation or some other means to grant such access to information, user needs cannot be assumed to be met through this process.

While these issues are important, this chapter is written within the restrictions of the present situation, i.e. the provision of one set of financial statements to all users and limited user access to further information.

The second purpose of financial statements is to assist in the enforcement of contracts, the terms of which include reference to accounting information. These contracts may be between management and a number of different user groups or between groups of users, and may take a variety of forms. For example, lending contracts may include terms and conditions which are defined by particular accounting ratios and management remuneration may be partially dependent on accounting measures.

Managerial self-interest

In Chapter 12 (Section 12.5) we introduced the notions of regulation and capital market efficiency, notions which were developed in Chapter 15. We also explained in Section 12.5 why managers might wish to choose accounting treatments to maximize their own welfare. Because these ideas are central to the analysis in this chapter, we shall review them briefly here. The argument runs broadly as follows. Managers almost always possess more information about the organizations they manage than do any other organizational participants, e.g. investors, employees, suppliers, customers and so on. In other words, the markets which govern the relationships between managers and other participants (capital markets, labour markets, product markets, etc.) are not efficient because they do not provide equal access to information for all those using them. In consequence, managers have an incentive to make use of their informational advantage to improve their own welfare. As far as accounting treatments are concerned, they might do this by choosing treatments which show their performance and position in the best possible light. This will often involve choosing treatments which maximize reported profit figures and/or show a strong balance sheet, for example by minimizing the reported level of gearing by reducing reported borrowings or increasing owners' equity. In the next section we apply this background framework to explain why there has been such a fuss about the accounting treatment of goodwill.

17.2   The nature of goodwill

Consider first what is meant by the term goodwill. The very term, goodwill, indicates its early roots — it was initially used to mean value created by customer loyalty. Later, this view was broadened to cover other intangibles capable of enabling a firm to generate profits in excess of the normal yield on other identifiable assets. In short, goodwill was taken to mean the capitalized value of 'super profits'.[3] According to the super profits perspective, goodwill is an

---

3. See, for example, Edey, H.C., 'Business valuation, goodwill and the super-profit method', in Baxter, W.T. and Davidson, S. (eds), *Studies in Accounting Theory*, Sweet and Maxwell, 1962.

asset in its own right. Therefore, not only can goodwill arise through purchase (as was explained in Chapter 16), it can also be generated internally. This is an important characteristic, to which we shall return later.

However, the view of goodwill which has been most influential in accounting thought is the one described in Chapter 16; that it constitutes the excess of purchase price over and above the value assigned to the net assets acquired exclusive of goodwill. In accounting terms, it is calculated as the difference between the price paid or payable for a business and the sum of the fair values of its identifiable assets and liabilities.

In these terms, while it may be generated internally, goodwill (by definition) is not recognized until a business is sold/purchased. It then reflects the difference between the going concern value of the acquired business and the value of the collection of individual assets and denotes the advantages or disadvantages enjoyed by a business as a whole which are not attributable to the identifiable assets and liabilities.

Whilst current accounting practice tends to treat goodwill as comprising a single figure, it is possible to conceptualize it as having a number of different components. In addition to the going concern value of a business, calculated goodwill may include a number of identifiable intangible assets whose separability and/or valuation is debatable (though not unthinkable), together with an element of over- or under-payment by management.

The going concern element of goodwill reflects the ability of an established business to earn a rate of return on a collection of assets and liabilities different from that which could be expected if the net assets were acquired separately. Its value will be dependent on factors related to market imperfections. For example, goodwill can be expected to be greater for a business which has the ability to earn monopoly profits and/or where the transactions costs involved in transforming a collection of individual assets into a business are high. Of course acquisitions are motivated in large measure by the hope that the value of the combined company will exceed the sum of the stand-alone values of the buyer and seller, i.e. that there will be synergistic benefits. Thus calculated goodwill will also reflect the expected benefits arising from jointness of activities which are not reflected in identifiable assets. The going concern value of an enterprise can therefore be taken to include the expected benefits arising from both market imperfections and jointness of activities.

Calculated goodwill may also reflect the acquisition of one or more identifiable intangible assets such as brands, distribution networks and customer lists. For example, brand names have generally been included as part of the goodwill figure following an acquisition. It has been argued that such intangibles cannot be separated from other elements of goodwill due to the problems of identifying and valuing them. However, over the last few years, some companies, particularly in the UK, have incurred significant costs in obtaining expert valuations for brands and have managed to establish them as identifiable intangible assets, by including them in their published financial statements and having them validated by the auditors. It is possible that businesses could obtain expert valuations and/or establish property rights for intangible assets where there were previously none. For example, managers may attempt to provide valuations of customer lists or highly-skilled employees through the establishment of contracts (e.g. insurance or employment) or by commissioning expert valuers. If, as in the case of brands, auditors are persuaded of the validity of these valuations, something which previously had been termed 'goodwill' may be validated and accepted as an identifiable asset. Thus identifiable intangible assets are a changing concept, as is that element of goodwill which they comprise for any given enterprise.

If it were feasible to extract accurately the going concern value and the value of intangible assets from calculated goodwill, the remaining figure could be viewed as an over- or under-payment. For example, when making a bid for a company, management may form incorrect predictions of its market position, influence and prospects or produce inaccurate assessments of the value of intangibles. Alternatively, managers may deliberately 'over' or 'under' bid in the belief that the market is inefficient or to further their own personal goals.

In summary, calculated goodwill arising on acquisition may be decomposed into three parts:

(a) the fair value of separately identifiable intangible assets;
(b) the present value of benefits arising (not reflected in (a)) from jointness of activities and market imperfections such as monopoly position and barriers to entry;
(c) under- or over-payment.

This decomposition will form an important part of our later analysis in this chapter.

17.3   The problem of goodwill

For the reasons already explained (Sections 12.5 and 17.1), most companies (including acquisitive companies) tend to prefer higher profits (to make their takeover activities look successful) and lower gearing and/or higher shareholders' funds (to alleviate borrowing restrictions and/or to 'strengthen' their balance sheets to reduce the risk of being taken over or to put them in a stronger position to take over other companies). In consequence, they are unlikely to welcome accounting treatments which force them to write goodwill off against reserves or, in particular, against future profits.

Historical background to the problem in the UK

The Companies Act 1948 (8 Sch 21 (2)), as amended by the Companies Acts 1981 and 1989, requires that where goodwill is treated as an asset (i.e. where it is not written off immediately) it should be amortized systematically over a period chosen by the directors, who must justify the period chosen. Until the early 1980s, most companies chose to leave goodwill on their balance sheets as an asset without amortization, justifying this on the ground that its economic life was indefinite — there was no reduction in reserves and no charge against profits.

In 1984, the Accounting Standards Committee introduced SSAP 22 (*Accounting for Goodwill*), under which goodwill had to be written off immediately against reserves (the preferred treatment) or amortized against future profits over its 'useful economic life'. Because it avoided any charge against post-acquisition profits, the first treatment was adopted almost universally but soon led to some companies running up against borrowing restrictions or Stock Exchange regulations (which required them to seek the approval of shareholders if they wished to acquire another company whose assets exceeded 25% of their own). They were also concerned that their balance sheets were 'weakened', making it less easy for them to take over other companies and easier to be taken over. (Few company managers appear to believe in the Efficient Markets Hypothesis.)

Two illustrations of the accounting problems posed by goodwill are provided by Saatchi and Saatchi and by WPP, both advertising and public relations companies. After acquiring several advertising and marketing agencies including the large US agency, Ted Bates Inc., Saatchi and Saatchi reported goodwill of £177,200,000 on its consolidated balance sheet in 1985 (see Table 17.1, column (i)). The company also published a pro-forma balance sheet which reported the financial position after the writing-off of goodwill to reserves (Table 17.1, column (ii)). The company's reported net assets were reduced by 71% as a result of this bookkeeping entry.

Table 17.1 *Saatchi and Saatchi — Balance sheet as at 30 September 1985*

	(i) £000	(ii) £000
Fixed assets		
Intangible assets	177,200	—
Tangible assets	32,008	32,008
Investments, etc.	8,476	8,476
	217,684	40,484
Net current assets	70,522	70,522
Total assets less current liabilities	288,206	111,006
Creditors: amounts falling due after more than one year	(20,250)	(20,250)
Provisions and minority interests	(18,206)	(18,206)
Net assets	249,750	72,550
Capital and reserves	249,750	72,550

Table 17.2 *WPP Group balance sheets for 1987 and 1988*

	1987 £'000	1988 £'000
Fixed assets		
Intangible assets	—	175,000
Tangible assets	79,184	86,378
Investments	3,464	4,678
	82,648	266,056
Current assets	473,645	407,248
Current liabilities		
Creditors (due within one year)	(454,733)	(437,079)
Creditors (due after one year)	(91,333)	(140,761)
Provisions	(74,719)	(34,603)
Net assets (liabilities)	(64,492)	60,861
Capital and reserves		
Called up share capital	3,670	3,973
Merger reserve	(89,423)	(150,603)
Other reserves	13,233	185,259
Profit and loss account	6,963	21,052
Shareholders' funds	(65,557)	59,681
Minority interests	1,065	1,180
	(64,492)	60,861

Even more dramatic was the writing off of goodwill by another UK advertising agency, WPP, which had acquired the US agency, J. Walter Thompson, and other firms in the late 1980s. The group's 1987 and 1988 balance sheets are shown in Table 17.2. The figure for goodwill was greater than both the reserves and the called-up share capital. Hence, its write-off in 1987 resulted in the capital and reserves of WPP being reported as a negative amount at the end of 1987. Normally this would be taken as evidence that the company is insolvent. In this case it might be taken as evidence of the inappropriateness of applying an accounting standard on goodwill to an acquisitive service company.

During 1988, the group decided to recognize as intangible assets the value of certain corporate brand names, including that of J. Walter Thompson. The effect on its balance sheet is evident from Table 17.2. We discuss the reasons for, and the mechanics of, this sort of treatment in the remainder of this chapter.

The use of 'creative accounting'

As neither of the treatments permitted in SSAP22 was satisfactory, companies turned to creative accounting to avoid the intention of SSAP22. There were two main methods:

1. Structure the acquisition so as to account for it as a merger, thereby avoiding the need to recognize goodwill (as we explained in Chapter 16, Section 16.4).
2. Call the goodwill something else — 'brands' being the most popular choice. Brands, unlike goodwill, were not the subject of an accounting standard and so did not have to be written off. This was the route chosen by WPP.

The ASC recognized that its intentions were being frustrated and responded with three exposure drafts (EDs), all of which were published in 1990: ED 47, *Accounting for Goodwill*, which would, if adopted, prohibit the immediate write-off of goodwill against reserves and require its amortization against profits over a maximum period of 20 years normally; ED 48, *Accounting for Acquisitions and Mergers*, which would, if adopted, impose tough new conditions for the use of merger accounting which would virtually eliminate its use; and ED 52, *Accounting for Intangible Fixed Assets*, which would, if adopted, require brands to be treated as part of, or in the same manner as, goodwill. Other similar intangibles would also have to be written off against profits in the same way as goodwill.

If adopted, these three treatments would have reduced dramatically the scope for companies to choose their own treatments for goodwill and other intangibles. This may explain the cries of outrage which greeted the proposals (mostly from preparers and some of their auditors).

Inconsistent accounting

An important criterion in the selection of financial reporting procedures might be argued to be that accounting treatments should not alter the economic decisions which would have been taken had all parties to the decision been in possession of the same, full information. This is one dimension of the problem of asymmetric information discussed previously, whereby reporting the results of transactions in different ways may result in different actions and ultimately in different distributions of wealth. This may not be an issue if capital and other markets are sufficiently efficient to see through accounting treatments and ignore any distortions they create and if we assume that all parties to economic transactions are fully represented by market relationships (but which 'market', for example, represents the public and government?). In that case it would not matter which treatment was adopted. However, consider the following situations:

1. *Goodwill vs other intangibles.* Suppose that goodwill has to be written off against profits or reserves whereas other intangible assets do not. Assuming, as we have done, that most company managers prefer higher to lower profits and lower to higher levels of gearing, then, other things being equal, they will prefer to invest in other intangibles rather than in goodwill. In addition, they may be willing to incur costs to reclassify part or all of goodwill as other types of intangible.

2. *Purchased vs internally-created goodwill and other intangibles*. A similar potential bias is introduced if purchased goodwill and other intangibles are accounted for differently from internally-created intangibles. Different accounting treatments may result in very large differences in income statement and balance sheet figures if one category of intangibles (internally-created) is written off immediately against profit while the other (purchased) is capitalized on the balance sheet and possibly amortized against profit over a quite long period or written off against reserves. Under such circumstances, managers will prefer to invest in purchased intangibles rather than to create them internally.

3. *Goodwill and other intangibles vs other assets*. If some types of intangible asset do not have to be written off against profit whereas other assets do, via a periodic depreciation charge, managers may prefer to purchase intangible rather than tangible assets, other things being equal.

In each of the above cases it is apparent that company managers will be motivated to buy one type of asset rather than another or to incur costs in reclassifying particular types of asset, for reasons which owe more to accounting treatment than to real economic considerations. One consequence of this may be to distort the competitive position of different companies. For example:

1. *UK vs other (particularly North American) acquiring companies*. It has been argued that UK acquirers have enjoyed an advantage over US and other rivals because the UK acquirers have not had to write goodwill off against profits. If true, that creates international economic distortions. Furthermore, it is not clear that those distortions work in favour of the UK companies. It may be that the effect is that UK companies pay too much for companies they acquire, which is hardly advantageous.

2. *Acquisitive companies vs others in the UK*. Almost all companies spend money to create goodwill (and other intangibles). Acquisitive companies spend it on buying the goodwill, brands, etc. in large chunks from other companies. Companies which grow organically spend the money in smaller, and perhaps more even, chunks on staff training, advertising, marketing and so on. Such companies have to write off that expenditure immediately against profits. If we are to create a *truly* level playing field, either goodwill and other intangibles which are acquired by takeover should be written off immediately *against profits* or internally created goodwill and other intangibles should be capitalized and dealt with in the same way as similar assets acquired by takeover.

The ability of alternative accounting treatments to influence economic behaviour and to have economic consequences is a key factor which standard setters should consider when making their recommendations.

17.4   Conceptual issues and criteria

In Chapters 3 and 15 we introduced a theoretical approach to resolving accounting problems in the form of a conceptual framework. We noted that this approach was being actively pursued by accounting policy makers in different countries, including the ASB in the UK and the IASC internationally. Recall that this approach, rather than focusing upon the *impact* of different accounting treatments, focuses upon the *needs* of users, in determining appropriate accounting treatments. We shall now briefly consider its application to the problem of accounting for goodwill.

Qualitative characteristics

The first conceptual issue to consider is the qualitative characteristics of accounting information. The two qualitative characteristics most directly concerned with goodwill are reliability and comparability. Reliability will be discussed below in relation to the nature of goodwill as an asset. *Comparability* requires consistency both throughout an enterprise and over time for that enterprise, and between different enterprises. Here there are significant issues to be considered: in particular 'internal' vs purchased goodwill, and the 'level playing field' arguments for different enterprises both within the UK and in different countries. These issues were discussed in Section 17.3 above.

The problem of achieving consistency between 'internal' and purchased goodwill would indicate either the elimination of all goodwill from the balance sheet or the capitalization of both types of goodwill. However, applying the consistency argument may result in the rejection of potentially 'useful' information concerning purchased goodwill simply because of the difficulties involved in accounting for internal goodwill. Furthermore, excluding all goodwill from the balance sheet might be at the expense of achieving consistency of treatment with other types of assets.

We could also include a consideration of the comparability of different accounting treatments with international practices. Clearly, applying the criterion of comparability alone does not resolve the goodwill problem.

Is goodwill an asset?

At the heart of the goodwill problem is whether goodwill is an asset to be included in the balance sheet. The definition of an asset introduced in Chapter 6, Section 6.8 was 'a resource controlled by an enterprise as a result of past events and from which future economic benefits are expected to flow'. If we view goodwill as comprising the three constituent parts identified in Section 17.2 above, it would be difficult to argue that (c) — the under- or over-payment — is an asset. But what about components (a) and (b)? It is difficult to be clear whether or not these are 'a resource controlled by an enterprise'. It might be argued that to be controlled, a resource needs to be 'separable', i.e. capable of being sold (or presumably acquired) independently of the other assets in the business. In this case, it is possible to acknowledge that intangible assets such as brands, even if only rarely, may be sold or acquired independently of the remainder of the business. Moreover, since brands and other intangible assets are expected to produce enhanced earnings in the future, component (a) would appear to satisfy the definition of an asset. But what about component (b) — the present value of benefits arising (not reflected in (a)) from jointness of activities and market imperfections such as monopoly position and barriers to entry — does this satisfy the definition of an asset?

It is difficult to see how (b) constitutes a separately identifiable asset. However, it could be argued that the accounting problem arises only because one separately identifiable asset (the investment in the business acquired) has been disaggregated for the purposes of consolidation into underlying 'assets' and 'liabilities'. In other words, the problem is created because of accounting procedures. If the investment in the subsidiary in the parent company's balance sheet is deemed to meet the definition of an asset, then we could argue that the difference on consolidation is also an 'asset'. Thus, it might seem that a logically consistent way of undoing the effect of consolidation is to treat (b) *as though it were an asset*. This kind of analysis would lead to a situation where both components (a) and (b) were viewed as satisfying the definition of an asset.

Should we recognize goodwill as an asset?

Meeting the definition of an asset does not, however, guarantee an item a place in the balance sheet. To be included in the balance sheet, an asset must also satisfy the criteria for recognition. Following the IASC recognition criteria introduced in Chapter 6, an asset should be recognized if it is probable that any future economic benefits associated with the item will flow to the enterprise; and the item has a cost or value that can be measured with reliability. The first criterion would eliminate speculative or highly risky expected cash flows from the balance sheet. The second seeks to establish a reliable (and therefore verifiable) basis of measurement. How does our concept of goodwill satisfy these criteria? We could argue that goodwill should be included in the balance sheet only insofar as there is reasonable certainty that the amount placed on it does not exceed its value to the enterprise.

The perceptive reader will have realized that the application of a conceptual framework approach to resolving accounting problems such as goodwill does not offer a panacea for all accounting's problems. Conflicts between criteria and difficulties in operationalizing concepts make its application a subjective process.

Nevertheless, it does offer a framework for considering the problem of accounting for goodwill in a consistent and coherent manner. However, it does not provide (nor does it aim to provide) any consideration of the impact of different accounting treatments on various groups in society. For example, it fails to take into account the possible reactions of managers in terms of investment decisions. Arguably, an approach which combines *both* an appreciation of the conceptual issues *and* a recognition of the ability of alternative accounting treatments to influence behaviour and to have potential consequences, is more likely to produce accounting recommendations which are both consistently developed and practically feasible than is either approach alone.

17.5   Alternative accounting treatments

In this section, we summarize the advantages and disadvantages of each of the alternative treatments of *purchased* goodwill in terms of the principles and criteria discussed in the previous section. Our analysis recognizes the need to consider the possible reactions of managers to alternative methods when determining accounting policy. In the next section, we shall extend the analysis to consider other intangibles and internally-created goodwill. The main accounting treatments for dealing with purchased goodwill in group accounting are:

- merger accounting
- immediate write-off against profits
- immediate write-off against reserves
- capitalization and amortization
- capitalization and revaluation
- capitalization, revaluation and amortization.

Merger accounting

One way of dealing with goodwill is to find some means by which it is not recognized in the first place. As we saw in Chapter 16 (Section 16.4), under merger accounting goodwill does not arise because an acquisition is not deemed to have occurred, the existing assets of the two merging entities simply being added together. However, where it is used to account for a combination which is in reality an acquisition, merger accounting involves the use of legal structures to distort the reporting of the underlying substance of a transaction.

Immediate write-off against profits

The justification for immediately writing off goodwill against profits is based on concerns about measurability and consistency. The measurability rationale for the immediate expensing of goodwill is that its continuing value cannot be measured with an acceptable degree of accuracy. The consistency argument is that although it might be possible to identify certain separable intangible assets as part of the purchased goodwill figure, such intangibles would not be recognized if they were created internally. Since expenditures on 'home-grown' intangibles would ordinarily be expensed, so too for the sake of consistency should purchased intangibles (see Section 17.3).

Opposition to the immediate expensing of goodwill is likely to be considerable. It is unpopular with preparers for the sorts of reasons that merger accounting is popular. In addition, the argument that purchased intangibles, including goodwill, should be treated in the same way as expenditures on internally-created intangibles is not completely persuasive. The problem with recognizing internally-generated intangibles is that it is often extremely difficult to separate everyday 'maintenance' expenditures from those incurred to create intangibles, and the investment element might be small in relation to the maintenance part. In such cases the recognition problem may well raise doubts as to whether the capitalization of internally-created intangibles is worth the effort and cost involved. The same need not be true for purchased goodwill.

Immediate write-off against reserves

From a theoretical point of view, immediate write-off of goodwill against reserves is hard, if not impossible, to justify. It is simply an expedient way of disposing of an unwanted debit without reducing reported profit. What it does do is break the relation between reported profits and net assets, and thereby weaken the 'policing' mechanism that ensures that (in the long run) aggregate reported profits will be unaffected by the choice of accounting methods. UK practice in this area is out of line with that in the USA and most other European countries, possibly resulting in the reported profits of British companies being viewed in some quarters as of 'lower quality'.

Another unsatisfactory aspect of writing off goodwill against reserves is that it creates a possible bias against real investment in the economy. As noted above, much research and development expenditure has to be immediately charged against profits and investment in plant and equipment has to be depreciated. Charging goodwill to reserves can create the illusion of highly acquisitive companies being more profitable than other businesses, thereby biasing the 'buy-or-make' decision. (See Section 17.3 for a fuller discussion of this topic.)

Capitalization and amortization

In the majority of developed countries goodwill is immediately capitalized and amortized against the profits of future years. (Companies usually have the option of writing off goodwill immediately against profits.) A major criticism of this approach is that the amortization of goodwill is even more arbitrary than other forms of depreciation. It is usually possible for preparers to determine the economic life of depreciating assets, even if they cannot find a non-arbitrary way of allocating cost over that life. With goodwill this is much more difficult, if not impossible.

The main virtues of the capitalize-and-amortize treatment of goodwill are, first, that (in common with certain other treatments) it is simple and cheap to implement. Simplicity and cheapness of method are no small virtues when drawing up the consolidated financial statements of acquisition-hungry businesses with complex group structures and operations in different parts of the world. Second, the treatment is consistent with the treatment for other assets and reduces the scope for manipulating results by manipulating the categorization of assets.

Capitalization and revaluation with or without amortization

An alternative to the systematic amortization of original cost is to revalue goodwill periodically. As with certain other assets (e.g. property) this does not rule out the possibility of amortization. Continuing with the property analogy, it is possible to envisage a system which would require regular revaluation for intangibles or a system which required amortization in combination with periodic revaluation.

Where it is possible to place a fair value on all or part of goodwill at the time of acquisition it should usually also be possible to update such valuations at later dates. In most cases, the assets will have finite lives, so depreciation or amortization charges will have to be made in subsequent periods. Where it is argued that the lives are effectively indefinite, because of the nature of the asset and the commitment to continuous maintenance (e.g. certain brands and trademarks), periodic valuations will be essential.

Conclusion

The treatments of purchased goodwill discussed in this section all have deficiencies. Merger accounting solves the goodwill problem by effectively making sure a difference on consolidation never arises. As such it cannot really be described as an accounting treatment 'solution'. Immediate write-off of goodwill against profit seems unduly conservative whereas capitalization and subsequent amortization appears to be a recognition policy which is markedly less demanding but introduces inter-period allocations of expenses which are even more arbitrary than is usual in accounting. Immediate write-off to reserves would seem to have only one virtue: it makes an embarrassing number go away! A policy which offers the prospect of combining aspects of immediate write-off to profit with capitalization and revaluation/amortization would seem to have some merit, from the perspectives of theory (e.g., consistency with the rest of accounting), informativeness, and preparer acceptance and we discuss it further in the next section.

17.6   The way forward?

In this section, we suggest a package of accounting measurement and disclosure treatments for goodwill and other intangibles which will be useful to users and which will satisfy the requirements of contracting arrangements based on the use of accounting numbers. Our basic proposition, expanded below, is that intangibles (including parts of what is traditionally termed 'goodwill') should be permitted to be treated as assets provided that their existence and amount can be satisfactorily justified; while any writing off should be against profits, not against reserves.

Information content

The key function of accounting reports is to provide information. The history of accounting for goodwill is one of considerable controversy about where to 'place' the item in the financial statements. There are, however, good reasons to doubt whether the informativeness of the accounts is greatly changed by the choice of treatment (rather than by the extent of disclosure), with one major exception. If goodwill is broken down or decomposed into separately identifiable intangibles and a residual, including any under- or over-payment, each identified component is likely to have different information content and thus the disaggregated amounts will have more information content than the present practice of reporting a single number, regardless of where it is located in the accounts. Furthermore, the different elements may require different treatments, particularly where contractual terms include accounting numbers or where there are other economic consequences which vary depending on the treatment adopted.

Thus the decomposition of goodwill may have implications for improving both its disclosure and measurement in financial statements. We discuss below some of the problems of determining appropriate (re)valuation and depreciation methods for identified intangibles. However done, the mere act of labelling should serve to throw a spotlight on the nature of the asset(s) acquired or created.

Possible accounting treatment(s)

It is important to recognize the impossibility at the present time of agreeing a single definitive measurement treatment for goodwill. Until such agreement can be reached — if it ever is — plentiful disclosure will be required to allow users to form their own judgements and to constrain the extent to which the preparers of accounts can be creative in order to further their own self-interest.

As we explained in Section 17.2, goodwill, as the term is presently used, comprises:

(a) the fair value of separately identifiable intangible assets;
(b) the present value of benefits arising (not reflected in (a)) from jointness of activities and market imperfections such as monopoly position and barriers to entry;
(c) under- or over-payment.

As regards purchased goodwill, at the time of acquisition (a) should be treated as an asset and (c) should be transferred to profit and loss (or to reserves if it is regarded as an unrealized gain). Item (b) is more problematic as it is unlikely to be separately identifiable. However as, by definition, it is expected to provide future benefits it possesses one essential characteristic of an asset and may be treated as such provided that it can be measured with reasonable certainty.

The procedure to assign amounts to the three components might be as follows. (We provide a numerical example shortly.) Fair values will be assigned under (a) to as many separately identifiable intangibles as meet the necessary recognition tests. The total fair value of (a) and (b) is then calculated by applying a valuation test to them *jointly* (given the impossibility of valuing (b) separately). The difference between this figure and the sum of the values under (a) is the 'fair value' of (b). The difference between the sum of these fair values (together with the fair value of the tangible net assets) and the total cost of the acquisition is the over- or under-payment referred to as (c). Where over-payment is identified this should be written off immediately to profit and loss account, leaving the fair value of (b) to be capitalized as 'difference on consolidation' along with the fair value of (a) and of the tangible net assets. Where there is under-payment, the amount of the under-payment should be credited as an unrealized gain to reserves, subject to any restrictions imposed by company law (which we discuss further below).

It is appropriate here to note some empirical evidence on acquisitions.[4] The evidence suggests that although acquiring firms lose only marginally on average from their takeover activities, the average disguises wide differences. Some takeovers are very profitable, while others are disastrous. The auditors will need to be satisfied that the combined value of (a) and (b) is justifiable (with the consequential implications for the amount of (c)). Their task will not be easy since, *at the time of acquisition, the managers of acquiring firms are unlikely to be willing to admit (even to themselves) to over-payment.*

Subsequent to acquisition, both (a) and (b) should, like other assets, be amortized *against profit* over their useful economic life. As with other assets, the

4. See, for example, Limmack, R.J., 'Corporate mergers and shareholder wealth effects: 1977–1986', *Accounting and Business Research*, Summer 1991.

amortization charge in a period will need to be increased if the 'systematic' charge results in a written-down value which is above the estimated current value. This further requirement will also effectively capture any over-payment (component (c)) which was not picked up at the time of acquisition.

Consider a simple example to illustrate the above procedures. A acquires B for £20 million. At the date of acquisition, B has net assets, excluding intangibles, with a fair value of £6 million. B also has separately identifiable intangible assets of £9 million (component (a) above). The directors of A estimate the value of B, based on past and projected earnings and risk, etc., at £18 million. Then the value of (b) is £3 million (£18 million less £6 million less £9 million). The remainder of £2 million is over-payment (component (c)) and should be written off immediately against profit. Components (a) and (b), a total of £12 million, will be capitalized and written off against profit over their useful lives. Each year a test will be applied to ensure that the written-down combined value of (a) and (b) is below its current value.

Alternatively, suppose that in the above example the value of B is estimated at £22 million rather than £18 million, but all other data are the same. The allocation of values under the present UK Companies Act rules would be: tangible net assets, £6 million; intangibles (a), £9 million; difference on consolidation (b), £5 million. The total equals the cost of acquisition of £20 million. The theoretical alternative, suggested above, would be to capitalize (b) at £7 million with a credit to reserves for the under-payment of £2 million.

The calculation of any gain or loss on disposal will depend on how 'goodwill' has been treated. To the extent that it has been expensed immediately or capitalized and amortized against profit, as we suggest, then the calculation is as for any tangible asset. The difference between sale proceeds and written down amount should be shown as a gain or loss in the profit and loss account. If there is any goodwill which has, in the past, been written off against reserves it should now be written back and treated as part of the cost of the disposal in calculating the gain or loss.

As discussed in Section 17.3, capitalization of part of purchased 'goodwill' will result in inconsistent accounting and in an 'uneven playing field' if internally-created intangibles are not treated similarly. For that reason, internally-created intangibles may be dealt with in the same way as purchased ones — in which case they should be included as assets and depreciated and should possibly be subject to the same valuation tests. In view of the difficulty which is often experienced in identifying the cost of internally created intangibles, their inclusion should probably be at the discretion of managers, subject always to their satisfying the auditors of the reasonableness of the existence and value of the assets.

Valuation tests

It will be necessary both on acquisition and at the end of each subsequent year for the directors to confirm that the amount at which intangible assets, including components (a) and (b) of the decomposed goodwill figure, are included in the consolidated balance sheet does not exceed their current value. Because (b) will not be capable of independent valuation, the test will have to be applied to (a) and (b) jointly. This will not be simple. It may be necessary, for example, to value the subsidiary as a whole and subtract the value of net assets other than intangibles to estimate the current value of (a) and (b). Unless the subsidiary is a listed company, which will rarely be the case, it may be necessary to estimate future earnings and their uncertainty in order to arrive at a valuation. This is likely to include an analysis of results achieved in the past. If part of the subsidiary's value derives from market imperfections (for example monopoly position), it will be necessary to consider for how long those imperfections will continue to exist, raising questions such as whether they are protected by regulation. No single mechanistic formula exists for this analysis.

Disclosure requirements

Because the value (and sometimes the existence) of intangible assets is often more uncertain and almost always less well understood than that of tangible assets, their inclusion in balance sheets will call for a higher level of disclosure to enable users to form judgements concerning the reasonableness of the values used and the benefits and costs of recognizing the intangibles. If companies choose to treat part of 'goodwill' as assets (bearing in mind that any residual part must be written off immediately against profit) they might be required to disclose the following types of information:

1. The basis upon which the valuation has been made. This will include both financial and non-financial information, for example relating to market share, distribution networks, customer lists, expected future 'super profits' and so on. The intention is to enable users to form their own expectations concerning whether the items included might reasonably be regarded as assets and whether the basis upon which they have been valued is reasonable.
2. *Other factors to enable users to assess the reliability and worthwhileness of the valuations.* These could include the name of the valuer and the cost of undertaking the valuation. Disclosure of the identity of the valuer will assist users in evaluating the degree of expertise underlying the valuation. Disclosure of the cost would allow users to form a judgement as to whether the costs incurred in creating intangible assets are worthwhile.

Of course, in order to include intangibles as assets, managers will also have to persuade the company's auditors that the amount at which they are included is reasonable. Although these disclosure requirements are more severe than those which apply to tangible assets they are probably justifiable in view of the relative novelty of valuing intangibles.

One implication of this approach is that managers will have to choose whether to write off the elements of goodwill and other intangibles immediately against profit and loss, or incur (and disclose) the costs of justifying their recognition as assets in the balance sheet. It may be objected that allowing such choice is inconsistent with requiring a 'true and fair view' that is consistent across all companies in accounting for the 'same' situation. For example, the Financial Accounting Standards Board in the USA increasingly requires, rather than merely permits, capitalization of those assets that it considers pass the definition and recognition tests. However, as the recognition that information is itself costly, and that a cost–benefit test needs to be applied to all disclosure and measurement, is fundamental to the framework of principles adopted by both the International Accounting Standards Committee and the Accounting Standards Board (as well as by the FASB in its *Statement of Financial Accounting Concepts No. 2*), it is consistent to recommend that the choice of whether those costs should be borne should be made by those in the best position to measure them, namely company management. From this perspective, accounting standards complement managerial choice over accounting method and disclosure rather than standing in opposition to them.

Consistency

We have argued that consistency is an important criterion in the selection of accounting treatments. There are several implications for the present debate.

First, there should be consistency through time. Once a company has adopted a policy for a particular intangible or group of intangibles it should stick with it. So, for example, if the value of brands is recognized as an asset, the only way of removing them from the balance sheet subsequently is by write-off to the profit and loss account.

Secondly, in view of the uncertainties involved and of the novelty of the approach we have suggested, we do not think that it would be desirable to require companies to treat all 'goodwill' identically. At this stage it should be left to the judgement of managers, subject to the approval of the auditors, to decide whether to capitalize and amortize intangibles or whether to write their cost off immediately against profit. However, the cost of *all* intangibles, including goodwill, should be charged against profit eventually — we can see no argument for any part of the cost being written off against reserves.

Managerial self-interest

We have argued (Chapter 12, Section 12.5) that the managers of companies have much more information about their companies than do investors and other users. Given that managers are human, then some of them at least will be motivated by self-interest and that self-interest may be best served by concealing some information from other parties. In a free market economy it is the job of government to intervene when self-interest is believed to be causing a market not to operate in the best interests of society. It is to reduce abuse of the informational advantage enjoyed by managers that we have accounting standards and other forms of regulation (see Chapter 3).

The disaggregation of calculated goodwill may be important not only in reflecting the nature of goodwill but in creating it. In particular, if accounting rules were established which distinguished between intangible assets and other elements of goodwill, managers may have incentives to classify as much as possible into one category or the other. This could result in managers incurring costs to employ legal and other experts to create property rights and provide valuations thereby creating markets for assets which previously did not exist. It could be argued that these incentives exist under current accounting rules. Current financial reporting requirements, however, do not hold managers directly accountable for any costs incurred in establishing or creating identifiable intangibles in terms of disclosure. Users are provided with information on the benefits of intangibles such as brands in terms of balance sheet valuations without any corresponding information as to the costs incurred in obtaining that information. The suggestions in this section would level, to some extent, the informational playing field between the preparers and users of accounting statements.

In this chapter, we have discussed at some length the problems posed by accounting for goodwill and other intangibles. The discussion has focused on the UK but the analysis applies for the most part to many other countries. Although the problems are of topical interest in themselves, our main purpose in devoting an entire chapter to the issues was to illustrate how a framework of accounting principles might be used to tackle accounting problems — in the case of goodwill one of the most intractable of accounting problems! Our recommendations are derived from the framework we developed in Part 1. Even so, they are not conclusive and we have identified various aspects of our suggested approach which require further elaboration and research, some of which would only be possible in the light of experience gained after implementation of the recommendations. Furthermore, it will be apparent to the perceptive reader that a number of the recommendations will be unpopular with at least some preparers of accounts. Yet again, it is apparent that accounting problems are rarely susceptible to straightforward solutions!

Discussion topics

1. Why has the accounting treatment of goodwill and related intangibles become so topical during the past decade?

2. Is goodwill an asset? If so, why does it present so many more problems to accountants than do other assets?

3. Explain and discuss the merits of different definitions of goodwill.

4. In what respect is the current accounting treatment of purchased goodwill inconsistent with the treatment of other intangibles, tangible assets and internally-created goodwill? Discuss the possible economic consequences of these inconsistencies.

5. Discuss the extent to which the application of a conceptual framework approach to the accounting treatment of goodwill is likely to be fruitful.

6. Discuss the merits of alternative accounting treatments of purchased goodwill.

7. If goodwill and other intangibles are treated as assets in accounting statements, explain why it may be necessary to require a more detailed disclosure of the treatment adopted than is required for other assets.

Further reading

AAA, American Accounting Association Committee on Accounting and Auditing Measurement, 1989–90, *Accounting Horizons*, September 1991.

Arnold, J., Egginton, D., Kirkham, L., Macve, R. and Peasnell, K., *Goodwill and Other Intangibles*, The Institute of Chartered Accountants in England and Wales, 1992.

ASB, *The Objective of Financial Statements and the Qualitative Characteristics of Financial Information*, The Accounting Standards Board Limited, 1991.

ASC, *Statement of Standard Accounting Practice 22, Accounting for Goodwill*, Accounting Standards Committee, 1984.

ASC, *Statement of Standard Accounting Practice 23, Accounting for Acquisitions and Mergers*, Accounting Standards Committee, 1985.

ASC, *Exposure Draft 47, Accounting for Goodwill*, Accounting Standards Committee, 1990.

ASC, *Exposure Draft 48, Accounting for Acquisitions and Mergers*, Accounting Standards Committee, 1990.

ASC, *Exposure Draft 52, Accounting for Intangible Fixed Assets*, Accounting Standards Committee, 1990.

Barwise, P., Higson, C., Likierman, A. and Marsh, P., *Accounting for Brands*, Institute of Chartered Accountants in England and Wales and London Business School, 1989.

Corfield, K., *Intangible Assets: Their Value and How to Report Them*, Coopers & Lybrand Deloitte, 1990.

Edey, H.C., 'Business valuation, goodwill and the super-profit method', in Baxter, W.T. and Davidson, S. (eds), *Studies in Accounting Theory*, Sweet and Maxwell, 1962.

Egginton, D.A., 'Towards some principles for intangible asset accounting', *Accounting and Business Research*, Summer 1990.

Higson, C., *The Choice of Accounting Method in UK Mergers and Acquisitions*, Institute of Chartered Accountants in England and Wales, 1990.

Hughes, H.P., *Goodwill in Accounting: A History of the Issues and Problems*, Georgia State University, 1980.

IASC, *International Accounting Standard No. 22, Accounting for Business Combinations*, International Accounting Standards Committee, 1983.

Lev, B., 'Observations of the merger phenomenon and a review of the evidence', in Stern, M. and Chew, D.H. (eds), *The Revolution in Corporate Finance*, Blackwell, 1986.

Limmack, R.J., 'Corporate mergers and shareholder wealth effects: 1977–1986', *Accounting and Business Research*, Summer 1991.

Power, M. (ed.), *Brand and Goodwill Accounting Strategies*, Woodhead-Faulkner, 1990.

Power, M., 'The politics of brand accounting in the United Kingdom', *European Accounting Review*, May 1992.

Solomons, D., *Guidelines for Financial Reporting Standards*, Institute of Chartered Accountants in England and Wales, 1989.

Tonkin, D.J. and Robertson, W.R., 'Brands and other intangibles fixed assets', in Tonkin, D.J. and Skerratt, L.C.L. (eds), *Financial Reporting, 1990–1991: A Survey of UK Reporting Practice*, ICAEW, 1991.

Turley, S., 'Rank Hovis McDougall Plc', in Taylor, P. and Turley, S. (eds), *Case Studies in Financial Reporting Practice*, Philip Allan, 1991.

CHAPTER

18

Summary and Review

This book has been concerned with the provision of information by organizations to participants. Its approach reflects our view that the purpose of accounting is to provide information useful for decision-making. This particular emphasis was reflected in Part 1, where we considered the information requirements of the users of financial accounts. In Part 2 we described and explained the concepts and principles which presently underlie the preparation of financial accounts and discussed the interpretation of accounts. In Part 3 we described some limitations of the conventional accounting model and discussed and evaluated several reporting methods which have been suggested as modifications or alternatives to existing practice. In Part 4 we introduced some more advanced financial reporting issues: the development of conceptual frameworks and international harmonization, accounting for groups and the accounting treatment of intangibles.

In this final chapter, we review the objectives of the book and the main principles suggested for the evaluation of financial accounting procedures. We then outline the limitations to the scope of the book, given that it is impossible to cover all aspects of financial accounting in a single text! Finally, we consider the current state of financial accounting and suggest some directions in which it might develop in the future.

18.1 Review of objectives

We summarized our objectives in the Introduction as follows:

1. To provide a framework for the evaluation of alternative methods of financial accounting, based on the assumption that the primary purpose of financial accounting is to provide information which is useful for decisions.

2. To explain the fundamental concepts and principles underlying historical cost accounting, so that the reader of financial reports may understand more clearly the basis upon which such reports are prepared and appreciate both their strengths and their limitations.
3. To describe and evaluate alternative approaches to the measurement of an organization's performance and position.
4. To instil in readers a critical and analytical attitude to financial accounting, which will enable them to understand and evaluate future changes to financial accounting practices.

Each of these objectives can be attained only by the application of certain principles to the evaluation of alternative financial accounting methods. We now turn to a summary of those principles.

18.2   The main principles

Although there is no universally accepted definition of the objective and subject matter of accounting or its role, our view is well reflected in two definitions which we introduced in Chapter 1:

> [Accounting is] the process of identifying, measuring and communicating economic information to permit informed judgements and decisions by the users of the information.[1]

> [The objective of financial statements is to] provide information about the financial position, performance and financial adaptability of an enterprise to a wide range of users in making economic decisions.[2]

Both definitions suggest that, in order to assess the value of accounting information, it is necessary to consider who are the *users* of the information and what are the *decisions* they might take. As decisions are concerned with choices between alternative future courses of action, information useful for decisions generally relates to the future. This is true for virtually all users and decisions although, of course, the precise information required may vary from user to user and from decision to decision. However, the information currently provided in financial accounts is almost always concerned with past performance and present position. Users must analyse and interpret this historical information in order to make their predictions. This difference in time between the period to which

1. American Accounting Association, *A Statement of Basic Accounting Theory*, AAA, 1966, page 1.
2. Accounting Standards Board, *The Objective of Financial Statements and the Qualitative Characteristics of Financial Information*, The ASB Ltd, 1991, para. 12.

the information relates and that for which it is useful led us to ask the following fundamental question in Chapter 2:

How should users of financial statements analyse and interpret the (historical) data provided in order to obtain the (predictive) information required?

The answer to this question provides the key to the evaluation of alternative accounting methods. Perhaps the most important criterion for choosing an accounting method is the extent to which it provides relevant information, i.e. information which helps users in their predictions. Of course, other criteria must also be considered, for example the reliability and cost of alternative methods. We discussed some of these criteria in Chapter 3. Nevertheless, any evaluation of a financial accounting system which ignores its potential relevance to users' decisions is likely to be vacuous.

18.3   Limitations to the scope of the book

It is not possible in a single (introductory) text to consider all the concepts and practices necessary to understand the role and scope of financial accounting. Our main aim throughout has been to provide a conceptual foundation and framework rather than to offer a detailed explanation of current practices. This aim accords with our objective of instilling in readers a critical and analytical attitude to financial accounting, which will enable them to understand and evaluate future changes to financial accounting practices. Hence one limitation to the scope of the book is that we have not covered in detail the very large number of requirements imposed on the preparers of accounts in the UK by accounting standards and company law. We have mentioned these detailed requirements only where necessary and then usually to amplify arguments. In our view an emphasis on detailed requirements would use valuable space and would detract from our main objectives by overwhelming readers with extensive practical details before they had grasped the essential conceptual issues.

Limitations of space have also prevented us from exploring, in as much detail as we would have wished, the financial accounting problems which face both public sector and not-for-profit organizations. Not all participants in these types of organization will have the same aims and thus require the same information as those in the organizations on which we have concentrated. In consequence, it is possible that financial accounting systems relevant to private sector, profit-orientated organizations will not be so for other types of organization. We should stress, however, that the main principles introduced in Part 1 and many of the concepts and procedures described in Parts 2, 3, and 4 are applicable to all reporting organizations.

18.4   The current state of financial accounting

Historical cost accounting has been the basis of accounting practice since the time of its development in the fourteenth and fifteenth centuries. However, during the second half of the twentieth century it has been the subject of increasing criticism, resulting primarily from changes in the environment in which organizations exist. The fact that historical cost accounting has been broadly successful in satisfying demands during the past five centuries says much for its durability and usefulness; it does not mean, however, that it will necessarily continue to meet those demands in a future environment which is likely to be volatile and unpredictable.

In this section we consider five particular respects in which environmental changes have induced or are likely to induce pressures for change in extant financial accounting methods.

Inflation

As we explained in Chapter 12 and subsequently, the existence of inflation complicates considerably the problem of interpreting the meaning of historical cost accounts; historical cost numbers are a disparate batch of figures, based on units of measurement (£s arising at different times in the past) which are not comparable. The *problem* is widely recognized by the accountancy profession throughout the Western world — unfortunately there is little agreement concerning the appropriate *solution*. Accounting for changing prices is an area which is likely to occupy accountancy practitioners and academics for some years to come.

Complexity

Most organizations now operate in environments which are far more complicated than those faced by their predecessors. Advances in transportation and communications during the twentieth century have resulted in the creation and expansion of vast multinational companies such as General Motors, Unilever, ICI, and Ford, as well as in the growth of much smaller organizations which, while still operating within one country, have a much wider geographical and product coverage than previously. A single income statement and balance sheet may be of use to the participants in a centrally-located organization with only a small number of activities, but of how much use are they to the participants of ICI, say, which has divisions active in agriculture, fibres, industrial explosives, oil, organic chemicals, paint and decorative products, petrochemicals and plastics, and which manufactures in over 15 countries around the world? The need for much more disaggregated information than is currently available is apparent, and it seems likely that this is an area for future developments in financial accounting. Furthermore, it is increasingly recognized that the heavy emphasis which has traditionally been accorded to the profit or earnings (per share) number is probably misplaced. In an increasingly complex world it is unlikely that any single number can capture the variety of facets which contribute to the changes in an organization's worth during a period.

Information technology

The advances in information technology which have taken place during the past 30 years, and which are likely to move even faster in the future, may well prove to be the most significant environmental change to influence the content and form of financial accounts. It is now possible to manipulate and access data at a speed which was unimaginable only 15 or 20 years ago. Changes in information technology have already had a major impact on the internal accounting procedures of organizations. They have, as yet, had less influence on the ways in which an organization's performance and position are reported to its external participants. That situation is almost sure to change as national and international communications networks provide the facilities for households, businesses and other organizations to be linked together and to transmit information between themselves at high speed and low cost. For example, it is easy to imagine that by the early part of the next century a company's accounts will no longer be printed and distributed by post to its shareholders but rather each shareholder will enjoy direct access to the company in respect of the particular information which he or she requires (subject, of course, to consideration of such matters as confidentiality). It is impossible to predict all the changes which will occur to financial accounting as a result of new information technology; however, it is probable that they will be extensive and important.

Users

Financial reports have traditionally been addressed to an organization's owners (shareholders) and creditors (including the providers of long-term loan capital). As we noted in Part 1, many other groups and individuals participate in an organization and are affected by its actions. The rights of these other participants to receive information are increasingly being recognized. The present importance of the net income or net profit figure (available for owners) reflects the traditional orientation of financial accounts towards the providers of capital. As the claims of other participants, for example employees, customers, and government (representing society at large) are admitted it is likely that alternative forms of report will be developed to satisfy their information requirements.

Creative accounting

At various points in this book we have explained the scope which still exists for the preparers of accounts to 'choose' the accounting numbers they wish to report. In a nutshell, for most sets of transactions there is a very large number of (different) accounting performance and position numbers which may be calculated using currently acceptable accounting practices. This variety provides a temptation to indulge in 'creative accounting' which some managers have difficulty resisting. Standard setters in the UK and elsewhere are now very well aware of the problem and are beginning to take steps to find solutions. It might be expected that considerable progress will be observed over the next decade. The present situation undermines the credibility of the accountancy profession and utilizes accounting resources which could be applied more productively elsewhere.

The above brief review of the current and likely future state of financial accounting suggests that many changes will be necessary before the end of the twentieth century. We hope that an understanding of the framework, principles and concepts which we have developed in this book will be of some help in an evaluation of those changes.

Discussion topics

1. 'Users of financial accounts need information about the future. The accounts provide information about the past.' Explain and discuss this apparent dilemma.

2. Outline the major changes likely to be seen in financial accounting practices in the next 20 years.

3. Speculate on ways in which advances in information technology might affect the reporting practices of organizations in the future.

4. Discuss the extent to which the information requirements of all groups of users of an organization's accounts are satisfied at present.

5. In what respects might participants in public sector and not-for-profit organizations require different information from that which is useful to participants in private sector, profit-orientated organizations?

Exercise

18.1 Mr Tannhauser started business on 1 January 19X3. The following is an extract from a letter he wrote to you on 1 January 19X4:

> My transactions for 19X3 were as follows. On 1 January, I opened a business bank account and paid £30,000 into it from my savings bank account. I

purchased some office equipment for £1,500. (As you know, I use one room of my private house as an office.) I expect that this equipment will last at least 10 years, although it will be worth very little at the end of that time. Indeed, I would probably not get more than £150 if I were to sell it now, even though the cost of replacing it with similar second-hand equipment would be at least £1,800. I also bought a van on 1 January which cost me £4,500. I expect to sell this at the end of 19X4. When I bought it I thought I would get at least £3,000 for it in December 19X4 but with the current fuel situation that looks like an overestimate. Only yesterday my local garage offered me £2,700 for it, although I saw a similar model advertised for sale today at £3,600.

As to trading activities, I bought 2,000 donners in January for £6,000. I sold 1,500 of these immediately at £6 each and still have the rest. The current selling price of donners is £3.30 but I am keeping those that I have not sold as I am expecting a rise in the price shortly. It could even reach £6 again by the end of 19X4. Maybe I should buy some more! In April I bought 10,000 used loges for £15,000. This turned out to be a bad buy. I did manage to sell 4,000 in September for £4,500 but the best offer I have had for the rest is £3,000 and I do not feel inclined to take such a heavy loss yet. In July I managed to pick up 500 fasolts cheap (only £15 each) and sold them immediately to Ms Fafner for £18,000. She paid me £12,000 in September and still owes me the balance. I am a little worried because I have not seen her at the golf club since September and there is a persistent rumour that she is on the verge of bankruptcy. At least all my other transactions were for cash. My last transaction was in October when I bought 10,000 frohs for £22,500 which I paid in cash. I sold 4,000 of these in November for £12,000 and another 4,000 in December at £3.75 each. The current selling price is £3.90.

Overhead expenses were fairly low. I spent about £60 a month on petrol and maintenance for the van and about the same amount again on other expenses. I transferred £600 each month from the business account to my private account. (My monthly salary before I went 'self-employed' was £600 and I did not see why I should work for myself for less!)

What bothers me is whether I made the right move in setting up on my own. I have given up a safe job and 10% p.a. interest on the money I withdrew from my savings bank account (£30,000 in the business bank account may seem a bit high to you but I think this sort of sum is necessary to clinch unexpected deals). I thought that you, as an accountant, might be able to let me know how much I made during 19X3.

■ Draft a reply to Mr Tannhauser answering, as far as you think possible, the questions in the final paragraph of the above extract. Include in your reply a discussion of the income measurement problems raised by the various transactions undertaken by Mr Tannhauser during 19X3.

E.H. Booth & Co. Ltd

Report &

Accounts 1992

BOOTHS
the good grocers

Report
& Accounts
1992

Financial Highlights

	1992 £000 (52 weeks)	1991 £000 (52 weeks)
Sales	74,133	68,421
Profit before Taxation	1,404	1,373
Dividends	132	132
Retained in Business	683	920
Capital Expenditure	404	7,834
Dividend per £1 Ordinary Share	10.5p	10.5p

Contents

E. H. BOOTH & CO. LTD.

Board of Directors

Chairman	J. G. Booth
	H. M. Booth, MBE, J.P.
	E. Woodhouse
	N. Standing, F.C.A.
	E. J. Booth
	S. K. Booth
	D. G. Booth

Secretary   N. Standing F.C.A.

Registered Office   **4 Fishergate,**
Preston

Bankers   **National Westminster Bank P.L.C.**

Solicitors   **Napthen, Houghton, Craven**
Preston

Auditors   **Moore & Smalley**
Preston

E.H. BOOTH & CO. LTD.

Notice of Meeting

Notice is hereby given that the Annual General Meeting of the Company will be held at Broughton Park Hotel, Preston, on Wednesday, the 16th day of September 1992 at 7.30 o'clock in the evening.

AGENDA

1. To read and approve the minutes of the last Annual General Meeting.

2. To receive and approve the Directors' Report and Accounts for the year ended 4th April, 1992.

3. To confirm the payment of the interim dividend paid on 31st March, 1992.

4. To declare a final dividend.

5. To re-elect the Auditors and authorise the Directors to fix their remuneration.

6. To fix the fair value of the shares for the ensuing year.

7. To transact any other ordinary business.

By Order of the Board,
N. STANDING,
Secretary

21st August, 1992
4 Fishergate,
Preston

Every Member entitled to attend and vote at this meeting may appoint a proxy to attend and vote instead of him, and that proxy need not be a member.

5

E.H. BOOTH & CO. LTD.

Chairman's Statement

The company has produced a commendable performance this year with profits of £1,404,333, a small increase over the previous year. Trading at our stores remains good, but we do have large bank loans to service.

Many of our stores retain a very strong loyalty amongst our customers, and this was shown recently when a Sainsbury Superstore opened not far from our 1978 Supermarket in Fulwood, Preston, and we lost only a very few customers.

We have taken many detailed steps to improve our performance within our stores, and are now providing our warehouse with a computerised stock control system.

We are currently in the process of planning a new store on a site we have owned for some time in a good suburban area, and are constantly receiving letters from people pleading with us to place one of our stores in their town which encourages us to think that we do have a unique formula rather different from our competitors.

John Booth

E. H. BOOTH & CO. LTD.

Report of the Directors

The Directors have pleasure in submitting their ninety fifth annual report, together with the audited accounts for the year ending 4th April, 1992.

RESULTS AND DIVIDENDS

	£	£
Trading Profit for the Year, after taxation		815,394
Retained Profit brought forward		44,520
Total distributable profit		859,914
Dividends paid and proposed	132,306	
Transfer to General Reserve	700,253	832,559
Retained profit carried forward		£27,355

REVIEW OF THE BUSINESS

The company's principal activity during the year was the retailing of food and associated products.

A review of the Company's performance during the year and an indication of future developments, is contained in the Chairman's Statement on page 6.

FIXED ASSETS

The movement of fixed assets is shown in Note 8 on page 16.

A professional revaluation of the Company's interest in land and buildings was last carried out in 1991, and the market value at that time was in excess of £34,000,000. This valuation has not been incorporated in these accounts.

POLITICAL AND CHARITABLE DONATIONS

The Company made no political donations during the year and charitable donations amounted to £1,694 (1991 : £1,422).

EMPLOYMENT POLICIES

The Company promotes the involvement of its employees in the running of its business by operating a profit sharing bonus scheme and encouraging employee share ownership.

Disabled persons seeking employment are considered on the basis of their aptitudes and abilities.

DIRECTORS

The names of the Directors are shown on page 4. With the exception of Mr J. F. Hunter who retired on 18th September, 1991, all served throughout the year.

Mr E. Woodhouse will retire at the Annual General Meeting. The Directors wish to thank him for his loyal and invaluable support over his 22 years membership of the Board.

7

E. H. BOOTH & CO. LTD.

DIRECTORS' INTEREST IN SHARES

The directors have the following interests in the shares of the Company.

	Ordinary Shares of £1 each	
Beneficial:	**4th April '92**	6th April '91
J. G. Booth	131,370	131,370
H. M. Booth	135,717	122,717
E. Woodhouse	12,040	12,040
N. Standing	11,888	11,888
E. J. Booth	12,165	12,165
S. K. Booth	17,208	17,208
D. G. Booth	6,850	6,850
As Trustee:		
J. G. Booth and H. M. Booth	50,180	50,180
J. G. Booth, H. M. Booth and N. Standing	64,892	64,892
J. G. Booth and N. Standing	30,450	30,450

	Preference Shares of £1 each	
Beneficial:	**4th April '92**	6th April '91
J. G. Booth	45	45
H. M. Booth	44	44
As Trustee:		
J. G. Booth and H. M. Booth	1,700	1,700
J. G. Booth, H. M. Booth and N. Standing	2,833	2,833
J. G. Booth and N. Standing	889	889

COMPANY STATUS

The Company is a close company within the provisions of the Income and Corporation Taxes Act 1988.

AUDITORS

A resolution to re-appoint Moore & Smalley as Auditors will be placed before the Annual General Meeting.

By Order of the Board,
N. STANDING
Secretary.

3rd August, 1992
4 Fishergate,
Preston.

8

E. H. BOOTH & CO. LTD.

Report of the Auditors
to the members of
E. H. Booth & Co. Limited

We have audited the financial statements on pages 10 to 19 in accordance with auditing standards.

In our opinion the financial statements give a true and fair view of the state of the Company's affairs at 4th April, 1992 and of the profit and cashflows for the year ended on that date and comply with the Companies Act 1985.

Preston.
3rd August, 1992

MOORE & SMALLEY
Chartered Accountants
Registered Auditors

9

E.H. BOOTH & CO. LTD.

Profit and Loss Account - 4th April 1992

	Note	1992 £	1991 £
Turnover		74,132,518	68,420,596
Cost of sales		67,567,546	62,397,755
Gross profit		6,564,972	6,022,841
Administrative expenses		3,667,799	3,504,953
		2,897,173	2,517,888
Other operating income	1	281,186	251,857
Operating profit	2	3,178,359	2,769,745
Interest payable	3	1,774,026	1,396,853
Profit on ordinary activities before taxation		1,404,333	1,372,892
Tax on profit on ordinary activities	6	588,939	320,300
Profit on ordinary activities after taxation		815,394	1,052,592
Dividends	7	132,306	132,306
		683,088	920,286
Retained profit brought forward		44,520	24,234
		727,608	944,520
Transfer to general reserve	16	700,253	900,000
Retained profit carried forward		£27,355	£44,520

10

E. H. BOOTH & CO. LTD.

Balance Sheet - 4th April 1992

	Note	1992 £	1992 £	1991 £	1991 £
ASSETS EMPLOYED					
FIXED ASSETS					
Tangible assets	8		26,798,485		27,737,237
CURRENT ASSETS					
Stocks	10	5,259,191		5,302,834	
Debtors	11	311,946		431,777	
		5,571,137		5,734,611	
CREDITORS					
Amounts falling due within one year	12	10,980,498		11,744,472	
NET CURRENT LIABILITIES			(5,409,361)		(6,009,861)
TOTAL ASSETS LESS CURRENT LIABILITIES			21,389,124		21,727,376
CREDITORS					
Amounts falling due after more than one year	13		9,795,942		10,844,170
			11,593,182		10,883,206
PROVISION FOR LIABILITIES AND CHARGES					
Deferred taxation	14		587,767		560,879
			£11,005,415		£10,322,327
CAPITAL AND RESERVES					
Called up share capital	15		1,268,060		1,268,060
General reserve	16		9,710,000		9,009,747
Profit and loss account			27,355		44,520
			£11,005,415		£10,322,327

Approved by the Board on 3rd August, 1992.

J. G. BOOTH   } Directors
H. M. BOOTH

11

E. H. BOOTH & CO. LTD.

Cashflow Statement
for the year ended 4th April 1992

	Note	1992 £	1992 £	1991 £	1991 £
Net Cash Inflow from Operating Activities	18		4,252,948		4,120,315
Returns on Investments and Servicing of Finance					
Interest Paid		(1,844,325)		(1,287,707)	
Dividends Paid		(132,306)		(132,306)	
Net Cash Outflow from Returns on Investments and Servicing of Finance			(1,976,631)		(1,420,013)
Taxation					
Corporation Tax Paid (including Advance Corporation Tax)			(335,222)		(561,539)
Investing Activities					
Payments to Acquire Tangible Fixed Assets		(404,168)		(3,205,698)	
Receipts from Sale of Tangible Fixed Assets		15,465		21,914	
Net Cash Outflow from Investing Activities			(388,703)		(3,183,784)
Net Cash Inflow/(Outflow) Before Financing			1,552,392		(1,045,021)
Financing					
Loan Repayments	20		(969,250)		(156,683)
INCREASE/(DECREASE) IN CASH AND CASH EQUIVALENTS	19		£583,142		£(1,201,704)

12

E. H. BOOTH & CO. LTD.

Statement of Accounting Policies - 4th April 1992

BASIS OF ACCOUNTING

The accounts of the Company have been prepared under the historical cost convention and in accordance with the provisions of Schedule 4 Companies Act 1985.

TURNOVER

Turnover represents takings for the year, excluding value added tax, and is based upon a 52 week accounting period (1991 : 52 weeks).

DEPRECIATION

Depreciation is provided on all tangible fixed assets, other than freehold land, at the following rates:-

Freehold buildings	— 2% on cost
Leasehold land and buildings	— evenly over the term of the lease
Fixtures, plant and vehicles	— Over the estimated useful lives of the assets at rates of 10% p.a. on cost and 20% p.a. on written down value

STOCKS

Stocks are valued at the lower of cost and net realisable value.

DEFERRED TAXATION

Provision is made for deferred taxation under the liability method at current rates of corporation tax, unless the potential taxation liability is unlikely to become payable within the foreseeable future.

FIXED ASSETS

Interest on loans to finance new developments is added to the cost of the development during the development period.

13

E.H. BOOTH & CO. LTD.

Notes to the Accounts - 4th April 1992

	1992 £	1991 £
1. OTHER OPERATING INCOME		
Rental income	£281,186	£251,857
2. OPERATING PROFIT		
Operating profit is stated after charging:		
Depreciation	1,327,455	1,164,215
Directors' Remuneration:		
Fees	7,000	2,400
Other emoluments	396,205	383,359
Pension contributions	22,129	25,827
Auditors' remuneration	11,400	10,500
3. INTEREST PAYABLE		
On bank loans and overdrafts wholly repayable within five years	422,800	512,759
On bank loans repayable over more than five years	1,351,226	884,094
	£1,774,026	£1,396,853
4. DIRECTORS' REMUNERATION		
Emoluments, excluding pension contributions:		
Chairman	£73,052	£67,510
Highest paid director	£75,631	£70,236
The emoluments of the other directors, excluding pension contributions were in the following ranges:		
£0 - £5,000	1	–
£5,000 - £10,000	–	1
£20,000 - £25,000	1	–
£35,000 - £40,000	–	1
£45,000 - £50,000	–	3
£50,000 - £55,000	3	–
£65,000 - £70,000	–	1
£70,000 - £75,000	1	–

E.H.BOOTH & CO. LTD.

Notes to the Accounts - 4th April 1992

	1992 £	1991 £
5. EMPLOYEES		
The average weekly number of employees was 1,406 (1991 : 1,443)		
Staff costs during the year amounted to:		
Wages and salaries	7,883,646	7,364,550
Social security costs	532,871	503,891
Other pension costs	266,329	249,114
	£8,682,846	£8,117,555
6. TAXATION		
The charge on the profits of the year consists of:		
U.K. Corporation tax at 33% (1991 : 34%)	546,446	154,845
Deferred taxation	26,887	165,455
	573,333	320,300
Under provision in previous year	15,606	–
	£588,939	£320,300
7. DIVIDENDS		
Preference shares		
Paid at 3.5 pence per share (1991 : 3.5p)	420	420
Ordinary shares		
Interim paid at 2.0 pence per share (1991 : 2.0p)	25,121	25,121
Final proposed at 8.5 pence per share (1991 : 8.5p)	106,765	106,765
	£132,306	£132,306

15

E. H. BOOTH & CO. LTD.

Notes to the Accounts - 4th April 1992

8. TANGIBLE FIXED ASSETS

	Land and Buildings £	Fixtures, Plant and Vehicles £	Total £
Cost			
At 6th April 1991	22,976,414	13,619,239	36,595,653
Additions	38,949	365,219	404,168
Disposals	(1,000)	(52,353)	(53,353)
At 4th April 1992	£23,014,363	£13,932,105	£36,946,468
Depreciation			
At 6th April 1991	1,527,101	7,331,315	8,858,416
Charge for the year	332,261	995,194	1,327,455
On disposals	–	(37,888)	(37,888)
At 4th April 1992	£1,859,362	£8,288,621	£10,147,983
Net book value at 4th April 1992	£21,155,001	£5,643,484	£26,798,485

	1992 £	1991 £
Net book value of land and buildings comprises:		
Freehold	10,290,460	10,451,480
Long leasehold (more than 50 years unexpired)	10,864,541	10,997,833
	£21,155,001	£21,449,313
Interest on loans to finance the development of Land and Buildings added to the cost of that development during the development period	–	£643,820

9. CAPITAL COMMITMENTS

In addition to the liabilities incorporated in the accounts, the company had the following commitments:

Contracted for	140,000	70,000
Authorised but not contracted for	80,000	45,000
	£220,000	£115,000

16

E.H. BOOTH & CO. LTD.

Notes to the Accounts - 4th April 1992

	1992 £	1991 £
10. STOCKS		
Goods for resale	£5,259,191	£5,302,834
11. DEBTORS		
Trade Debtors	4,821	5,717
Prepayments and accrued income	307,125	426,060
	£311,946	£431,777
12. CREDITORS: AMOUNTS FALLING DUE WITHIN ONE YEAR		
Bank overdraft	3,742,656	4,325,798
Bank loans	1,033,000	954,022
Trade creditors	4,466,846	4,406,110
Advance corporation tax	44,032	44,032
Current corporation tax	528,125	301,296
Other taxes and social security costs	299,131	239,646
Accruals	759,943	1,366,803
Proposed dividend	106,765	106,765
	£10,980,498	£11,744,472
13. CREDITORS: AMOUNTS FALLING DUE AFTER MORE THAN ONE YEAR		
Bank loans repayable by instalments over more than five years:-		
Due within 5 years	3,873,692	4,505,087
Due after 5 years	5,922,250	6,339,083
	£9,795,942	£10,844,170

The loans repayable over more than 5 years are repayable
by instalments over 9 years.

These loans bear interest at rates of up to 1¹/:% over National Westminster Bank base rate.
The bank loans of £10,828,942 (1991: £11,798,192), are secured by legal mortgage over certain
freehold properties.

17

E. H. BOOTH & CO. LTD.

Notes to the Accounts - 4th April 1992

	1992 £	1991 £
14. DEFERRED TAXATION		
Corporation tax at 33% (1991 : 34%) deferred by accelerated capital allowances	623,355	596,468
Advance corporation tax recoverable	(35,588)	(35,589)
	£587,767	£560,879

15. SHARE CAPITAL

	Authorised		Allotted and fully paid	
	1992 £	1991 £	1992 £	1991 £
3.5% net cumulative				
Preference shares of £1 each	12,000	12,000	12,000	12,000
Ordinary shares of £1 each	1,300,000	1,300,000	1,256,060	1,256,060
	£1,312,000	£1,312,000	**£1,268,060**	£1,268,060

	1992 £	1991 £
16. GENERAL RESERVE		
At 6th April 1991	9,009,747	8,109,747
Transfer from Profit and loss account	700,253	900,000
	£9,710,000	£9,009,747

17. PENSION COMMITMENTS

The company has a contributory pension scheme designed to provide pension benefits for all eligible employees. The cost of the company's contribution arising from current service is charged against profit as the service arises. The company has no pension commitments to former directors or employees.

18

E. H. BOOTH & CO. LTD.

Notes to the Accounts - 4th April 1992

	1992 £	1991 £
18. RECONCILIATION OF OPERATING PROFIT TO NET CASH INFLOW FROM OPERATING ACTIVITIES		
Operating Profit	3,178,359	2,769,745
Depreciation	1,327,455	1,164,215
Decrease/(Increase) in Stocks	43,643	(238,576)
Decrease in Debtors	119,831	191,967
(Decrease)/Increase in Creditors	(416,340)	232,964
	£4,252,948	£4,120,315

	1992	1991
19. ANALYSIS OF CHANGES IN CASH AND CASH EQUIVALENTS DURING THE YEAR		
Balance Brought Forward	(4,325,798)	(3,124,094)
Net Cash Inflow/(Outflow)	583,142	(1,201,704)
Balance Carried Forward	£(3,742,656)	£(4,325,798)

	1992 £	1991 £
20. ANALYSIS OF CHANGES IN FINANCING DURING THE YEAR		
Loans		
Balance Brought Forward	11,798,192	7,326,699
Repayments	(969,250)	(156,683)
New Agreements	–	4,628,176
Balance Carried Forward	£10,828,942	£11,798,192

19

E.H. BOOTH & CO. LTD.

5 Yearly Financial Review

	1988	1989	1990	1991	1992
Turnover	54,559,295	57,834,816	62,826,266	68,420,596	74,132,518
Profit before taxation	1,309,246	1,969,102	2,138,620	1,372,892	1,404,333
Shareholders interest	7,089,506	8,155,310	9,402,041	10,322,327	11,005,415
Tangible fixed assets	11,318,420	12,636,450	21,089,492	27,737,237	26,798,485
Ordinary dividends paid (Net)	106,765	131,886	131,886	131,886	131,886

20

Index